Quantitative Metnods for Business

Visit the *Quantitative Methods for Business, Fifth Edition* companion website at **www.pearsoned.co.uk/waters** to find valuable student learning material including:

- Reviews of important material
- Data sets for problems, examples and cases in the book
- Spreadsheet templates for calculations
- Additional material to extend the coverage of key topics
- Proofs and derivations of formulae
- Answers to problems
- Additional worked examples and case studies
- A list of useful websites

Quantitative Methods for Business

FIFTH EDITION

Donald Waters

**Financial Times
Prentice Hall
is an imprint of**

Harlow, England • London • New York • Boston • San Francisco • Toronto
Sydney • Tokyo • Singapore • Hong Kong • Seoul • Taipei • New Delhi
Cape Town • Madrid • Mexico City • Amsterdam • Munich • Paris • Milan

Pearson Education Limited

Edinburgh Gate
Harlow
Essex CM20 2JE
England

and Associated Companies throughout the world

Visit us on the World Wide Web at:
www.pearsoned.co.uk

First published 1993
Second edition published under the Addison-Wesley imprint 1997
Third edition 2001
Fourth edition 2008
Fifth edition published 2011

ISBN 978-0-273-73947-0

British Library Cataloguing-in-Publication Data
A catalogue record for this book is available from the British Library

Library of Congress Cataloging-in-Publication Data
Waters, C. D. J. (C. Donald J.), 1949–
   Quantitative methods for business / Donald Waters. — 5th ed.
     p. cm.
   ISBN 978-0-273-73947-0 (pbk.)
   1. Industrial management–Mathematical models. 2. Decision making–
Mathematical models. I. Title.
   HD30.25.W384 2011
   658.4′03–dc21

                                                        2011000148

10 9 8 7 6 5 4 3 2 1
15 14 13 12 11

Typeset in 10/12pt Sabon by 35
Printed by Ashford Colour Press Ltd, Gosport

TO CHARLES

BRIEF CONTENTS

CONTENTS

Supporting resources
Visit **www.pearsoned.co.uk/waters** to find valuable online resources.

Companion website for students:
- Supporting material to help your understanding
- Data sets for problems, examples and cases in the book
- Spreadsheet templates for calculations
- Additional material to extend the coverage of key topics
- Proofs and derivations of formulae
- Answers to problems
- Additional worked examples and case studies
- List of useful websites

For instructors:
- Complete, downloadable instructor's manual
- PowerPoint slides that can be downloaded and used for presentations
- Review of key aims and points of each chapter
- Worked solutions to problems
- Comments on case studies
- Copies of figures and artwork from the book
- Test bank of multiple choice questions
- Additional worked examples and case studies

The companion website also provides these features:

- Search tool to help locate specific items of content
- E-mail results and profile tools to send results of quizzes to instructors
- Online help and support to assist with website use and troubleshooting

For more information please contact your local Pearson Education sales representative or visit **www.pearsoned.co.uk/waters**

PREFACE

Managers are the people who run their organisations. They make decisions in complex circumstances and for this they need many skills, including problem-solving, leadership, communications, analysis, reasoning, experience and judgement. Many of their decisions are based on numerical information. For instance, they have to consider income, profit, production levels, productivity, interest rates, forecast demand, costs and all the other information that is presented as numbers. And this means that managers must have some understanding of quantitative methods, while the ability to work with numbers is one of the basic skills of management. This does not mean that managers have to be professional mathematicians, but they do need to understand quantitative reasoning and be able to interpret numerical results.

If you are a student of management, you will almost certainly do a course in quantitative methods. This course might come in various guises, such as quantitative analysis, decision-making, business modelling, numerical analysis, business statistics and so on. This book covers the key material in these courses. It describes a range of quantitative methods that are widely used in business, and which you will meet somewhere in your courses. Specifically, the book gives a broad introduction to quantitative methods that can be used in the early years of an HND, an undergraduate business course, an MBA or many vocational and professional courses. It is aimed at anyone who wants to know how quantitative ideas are used in business – and it describes methods that you will meet in your courses, and then later in your working life.

Management students come from different backgrounds, so we cannot assume much common knowledge or interests. In this book we start with the assumption that you have no previous knowledge of management or quantitative methods. Then the book works from basic principles and develops ideas in a logical sequence, moving from underlying concepts through to real applications.

One common observation is that management students can find quantitative ideas difficult or intimidating. You are probably not interested in mathematical abstraction, proofs and derivations – but more in results that you can actually use in business. This is why the book has a practical rather than a theoretical approach. We have made a deliberate decision to avoid proofs, derivations and rigorous (often tedious) mathematics. Some formal procedures are included, but these are kept to a minimum. At the same time we emphasise principles, but leave computers to do the routine calculations. In practice, spreadsheets are a particularly useful tool and we illustrate many ideas with Microsoft Excel (but you can get equivalent results from any spreadsheet).

Contents

Managers can use almost any kind of quantitative methods in some circumstances, so there is an almost unlimited amount of material that we could put into the book. To keep it to a reasonable length we have concentrated on the most widely used topics. However, we have still kept a broad view, describing many topics rather than concentrating on the details of a few, and not emphasising some topics at the expense of others. Some useful additional topics are described in the accompanying website at **www.pearsoned.co.uk/waters**.

For convenience the book is divided into five parts that develop the subject in a logical sequence. Many people find probabilistic ideas more difficult than deterministic ones, so we have drawn a clear separation between the two. The first three parts describe deterministic methods, and the last two parts cover problems with uncertainty.

- *Part One* gives an introduction to quantitative methods for managers. These first three chapters lay the foundations for the rest of the book, saying why managers use quantitative methods, and giving a review of essential quantitative tools.
- *Part Two* describes data collection and description. All quantitative methods need reliable data, so these four chapters show how to collect this, summarise it and present it in appropriate forms.
- *Part Three* shows how to use these quantitative ideas for solving different types of problems, including measuring performance, finance, regression, forecasting and linear programming.
- *Part Four* describes some statistical methods focusing on probabilities, probability distributions, sampling and statistical inference.
- *Part Five* shows how to use these statistical ideas for problems involving uncertainty, including decision analysis, quality, inventory and project management, queues and simulation.

The whole book gives a solid foundation for understanding quantitative methods and their use in business.

Format

Each chapter uses a consistent format which includes:

- a list of chapter contents
- an outline of material covered and a list of things you should be able to do after finishing the chapter
- the main material of the chapter divided into coherent sections
- worked examples to illustrate methods
- 'ideas in practice' to show how the methods are actually used
- short review questions throughout the text to make sure you understand the material (with solutions in Appendix A)
- key terms highlighted in the chapter, with a glossary at the end of the book
- a chapter review listing the material that has been covered
- a case study based on material in the chapter
- problems (with solutions given on the companion website at **www.pearsoned.co.uk/waters**)
- research projects, which allow you to look deeper into a topic
- sources of information, including references, suggestions for further reading and useful websites.

To summarise

This is a book on quantitative methods for business and management. The book:

- is an introductory text that assumes no previous knowledge of business, management or quantitative methods
- takes a broad view and is useful for students doing a wide range of courses, or for people studying by themselves
- covers a lot of material, concentrating on the most widely used methods
- develops the contents in a logical order
- presents ideas in a straightforward, reader-friendly style
- avoids abstract discussion, mathematical proofs and derivations
- gives example of real applications from a wide range of organisations
- uses spreadsheets and other software to illustrate calculations
- includes a range of learning features to help you to understand the material.

Companion website

The companion website for the book is **www.pearsoned.co.uk/waters**. This contains valuable teaching and learning information.

For students:
- Study material designed to help your understanding
- Data sets for problems, examples and cases in the book
- Spreadsheet templates for calculations
- Additional material to extend the coverage of key topics
- Proofs and derivations of formulae
- Answers to problems
- Additional worked examples and case studies.

For lecturers adopting the book for courses:
- A secure password-protected site with teaching material
- PowerPoint slides that can be downloaded and used for presentations
- A review of key aims and points for each chapter
- Worked solutions to problems
- Comments on case studies
- Copies of figures and artwork from the book
- Additional worked examples and case studies.

Acknowledgements and trademarks

A lot of software is available to support quantitative methods. The following list includes packages that are mentioned in the book, with their developers (with apologies for any errors or omissions). You can find more information about products from company websites.

Excel, Word, PowerPoint, Microsoft Office, Microsoft Project and Visio are trademarks of Microsoft Corporation; Microsoft Excel screenshots are reprinted with permission from Microsoft Corporation; Amode is a trademark of Mindsystems Pty Ltd; Analyse-it is a trademark of Analyse-it Software Ltd; ConceptDraw, ConceptDraw MindMap and ConceptDraw Project are trademarks of Computer Systems Odessa Corporation; CorelDraw and Quattro Pro are trademarks of Corel Corporation; CPLEX, Freelance Graphics, ILOG and Lotus Symphony are trademarks of IBM Corporation; DrawPlus and Harvard graphics are trademarks of Serif Corporation; Fast Track Schedule is a trademark of AEC Software; Fico Xpress is a trademark of Fair Isaac Corp; GAMS is a trademark of GAMS Development Corporation; GLPX, PSPP and SimPy are supplied by the Free Software Foundation Inc.; Gnumeric and Gnome are part of the Free Software Desktop Project; Google and Google Docs are trademarks of Google Inc.; iMindMap is a trademark of BUZAN Online Ltd; Jmp and SAS are trademarks of SAS Institute, Inc.; Linear Algebra 2 is a trademark of Orlando Mansur; LINDO is a trademarks of Lindo Systems, Inc.; Matrix ActiveX is a trademark of Bluetit Software; MindManager is a trademark of MindJet Corp.; Minitab is a trademark of Minitab, Inc.; NovaMind is a trademark of NMS Global Pty Ltd; Numbers is a trademark of Apple Inc.; OpenOffice Calc is a trademark of OpenOffice.Org; Oracle Projects is a trademark of Oracle Corporation; Primavera Project Planner is a trademark of Primavera Systems, Inc.; Renque is a trademark of RND Technology Consultants; SimEvents is a trademark of MathWorks; Simul8 is a trademark of Simul8 Corp; SIMSCRIPT is a trademark of California Analysis Center Inc.; SmartDraw is a trademark of SmartDraw.com; SPC XL is a trademark of SigmaZone.com; S-plus is a trademark of Mathsoft, Inc.; SPSS is a trademark of SPSS, Inc.; STATISTICA is a trademark of StatSoft; SuperProject is a trademark of Computer Associates International; Systat and Sigmaplot are trademarks of Systat Software Inc.; TurboProject is a trademark of IMSI; UltimaCalc is a trademark of Iconico.

Publisher's acknowledgements

We are grateful to the following for permission to reproduce copyright material:

Figures
Figure 3.19 from *The Visual Display of Quantitative Data*, 2nd ed., Graphics Press (Tufte, E. 2001), reprinted by permission; Figure 5.14 from Glossary of Mathematical Mistakes, http://members.cox.net/mathmistakes/glossary1.htm, Paul Cox.

Screenshots
Microsoft Excel spreadsheets are reprinted with permission from Microsoft Corporation.

In some instances we have been unable to trace the owners of copyright material, and we would appreciate any information that would enable us to do so.

PART ONE

Background

Managers are the people who run their organisations. To do this effectively, they need many skills, with key ones being the ability to analyse and solve problems. In practice, management problems come in many forms, but they share common features. Here we focus on one of these features – the reliance on numerical data.

Almost every problem in business includes some numerical information, and managers routinely use a range of quantitative methods to analyse it. This book describes some of the most common methods. These play an essential role in the decision-making of every organisation, and they form a set of tools that every manager should understand and use effectively.

The book is divided into five parts, each of which covers a different aspect of quantitative methods. This first part describes the underlying concepts of quantitative methods, setting the context for the rest of the book. The second part shows how to collect, summarise and present data, and the third part uses this data to solve some common management problems. The fourth part introduces the ideas of statistics, and the fifth part uses these to solve problems involving uncertainty.

There are three chapters in this first part. Chapter 1 reinforces the idea that managers constantly use numbers, and they must understand a range of quantitative analyses. The rest of the book describes these in more detail. But before we start we have to review some underlying principles, and make sure that you are familiar with some basic quantitative tools. In particular, Chapter 2 describes numerical operations and algebra, and Chapter 3 shows how to draw graphs. You have probably met these before, but this is a good time for some revision.

Chapters in the book follow a logical path through the material, as shown in the following map. You will probably find it best to tackle each chapter in turn, but you can take a more flexible approach if you prefer.

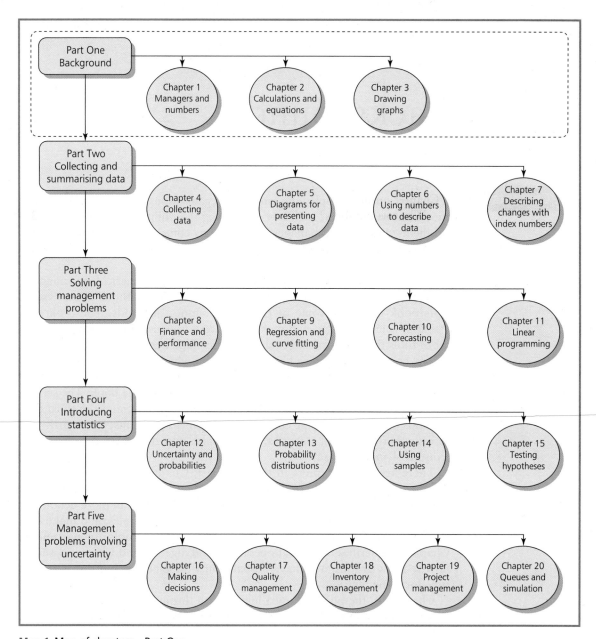

Map 1 Map of chapters – Part One

CHAPTER 1

Managers and numbers

Chapter outline

Managers have many roles, but these can be summarised as analysing and solving problems. These problems come in many forms, but they have common features. In particular, they nearly always include some numerical information. It follows that managers must understand numerical ideas and be familiar with a range of quantitative analyses. This chapter considers the importance of numbers and calculations, the use of numerical information by managers and the way in which quantitative models are used to tackle problems.

After finishing this chapter you should be able to:

- appreciate the importance and benefits of numbers
- say why quantitative methods are particularly useful for managers
- understand the use of models
- describe a general approach to solving problems
- use computers for calculations.

Why use numbers?

On an ordinary day, you might notice that the temperature is 17°C, petrol costs £1.30 a litre, 2.1 million people are unemployed, house prices rose by 8% last year, employees want a pay rise of £1.50 an hour, a football team has won its last seven games, 78% of people want shops to open longer hours, your telephone bill is £95 and a candidate won 32,487 votes in an election. These numbers give essential information. They have the benefit of giving a clear, precise and objective measure. When the temperature is 30 degrees, you know exactly how hot it is; when a bar contains 450 grams of chocolate, you know exactly how big it is; and your bank manager can say exactly how much money is in your account. On the other hand, when you cannot measure something it is much more difficult to describe and understand. When you get a pain in your stomach it is very difficult to describe the kind of pain, how bad it is or how it makes you feel. When you read a book it is difficult to say how good the book is or to describe the pleasure it gave you.

So the first benefit of numbers is that they give a clear measure – and a second benefit is that you can use them in calculations. If you buy three bars of chocolate that cost 30 pence each, you know the total cost is 90 pence; if you pay for these with a £5 note you expect £4.10 in change. If you start a 120 km journey at 12:00 and travel at 60 km an hour, you expect to arrive at 14:00.

- Any reasoning that uses numbers is quantitative.
- Any reasoning that does not use numbers, but is based on judgement and opinions, is qualitative.

WORKED EXAMPLE 1.1

An automatic ticket machine accepts only pound coins. The numbers of tickets it gives are:

£1 – 1 ticket, £2 – 3 tickets, £3 – 4 tickets, £4 – 5 tickets, £5 – 7 tickets.

How can you get the cheapest tickets?

Solution

You can do a simple calculation to find the best value for money. You know that:

- £1 gives 1 ticket, so each ticket costs £1 / 1 = £1
- £2 gives 3 tickets, so each ticket costs £2 / 3 = £0.67
- £3 gives 4 tickets, so each ticket costs £3 / 4 = £0.75
- £4 gives 5 tickets, so each ticket costs £4 / 5 = £0.80
- £5 gives 7 tickets, so each ticket costs £5 / 7 = £0.71

Buying three tickets for £2 clearly gives the lowest cost per ticket.

Numbers increase our understanding of things – and it is impossible to lead a normal life without them. This does not mean that we all have to be mathematical whiz-kids – but it does mean that we have to understand some numerical reasoning and know how to work with numbers. We must know that having €1,000 in the bank is not the same as having €500, nor is it the same as having an overdraft of €1,000.

Usually we use numbers for precise calculations. When you go into a supermarket you know that you will get exactly the right bill, and after paying you should get exactly the right change. But sometimes we are happy with rough estimates. For example, if you have a credit card bill of €1,000 and can repay €100 a month, you know that it will take about a year to clear the account. Similarly, if you read a page a minute you can finish a 55-page report in about an hour; when you see a car for sale, you do not know exactly how much it costs to run, but a rough estimate shows whether you can afford it; when you get a quotation for some work by a builder you can quickly check that it seems reasonable; and before you go into a restaurant you can get an idea of how much a meal will cost.

Numbers and management

Numbers are such an integral part of our lives that it comes as no surprise that managers use quantitative reasoning to aid their decisions. They measure performance in terms of profit, return on investment, turnover and share price; to increase returns they look at growth, costs, profitability and sales; when considering output they measure capacity, productivity and employee numbers; to assess marketing they look at the number of customers, market share and sales; annual accounts give a numerical review of overall performance. In reality, it is difficult to find any aspect of management that does not involve some kind of quantitative analysis. The collection of methods used for these analyses are loosely described as quantitative methods.

> **Quantitative methods** form a broad range of numerical approaches for analysing and solving problems.

You should not be surprised that managers rely on quantitative reasoning because this is a routine part of most jobs. Engineers do calculations when they design bridges; doctors prescribe measured amounts of medicines; mobile phone companies monitor traffic on their networks; accountants give a quantitative view of performance. If you imagine that managers do not use formal analyses but can somehow guess how to make the right decisions using their intuition and judgement, you are very much mistaken. In this book, we want to overcome the strange idea that managers instinctively 'know' the solutions to their problems, and instead we show how they really make decisions. Of course, this does not mean that managers have to do all the analyses themselves; they can get assistance from relevant experts – in the same way that they use experts in communications, information processing, accounting, law and all the other specialised areas. However, managers really do have to be aware of the analyses available, understand the underlying principles, recognise the limitations, have intelligent discussions with experts and interpret the results.

In reality, no problem is entirely quantitative and judgement, intuition, experience and other human skills are important. You can see this in areas such as industrial relations, negotiations, recruitment, setting strategic goals and personal relations. But even here managers should consider all available information before reaching their decisions – and quantitative methods often give valuable insights. Figure 1.1 shows the usual approach to decisions, where managers identify a problem, do quantitative and qualitative analyses, evaluate the results, make their decisions and implement them.

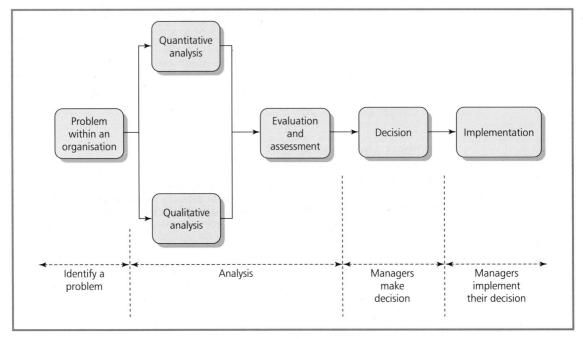

Figure 1.1 Usual approach to making a decision

WORKED EXAMPLE 1.2

The policy of Benchmark Global Consultants is to employ one consultant for every 10 clients on their books. Last month they had 125 clients. How many consultants should they employ?

Solution

A purely quantitative analysis suggests employing 125 / 10 = 12.5 consultants. They could employ part-time staff, but this may not be feasible, particularly if the number of clients keeps changing. Realistically the company could round the number of consultants to either 12 or 13. The best decision depends on a range of qualitative factors – such as competition, economic conditions, expected changes to client numbers, amount of work sent by each client, attitudes of consultants, type of business, planned staff departures, recruitment, training, seasonal trends, long-term contracts and so on. Managers must review all the available information – both quantitative and qualitative – before making their decision.

Review questions (Appendix A at the end of the book gives answers to all the review questions.)

1.1 What are the benefits of quantitative methods?

1.2 Do quantitative analyses make the best decisions?

1.3 Managers must be good mathematicians. Do you think this is true?

1.4 Why has the use of quantitative methods by managers increased in the past 20 years?

IDEAS IN PRACTICE   RPF Global

Patrick Chua is the senior vice-president of RPF Global, a firm of financial consultants with offices in major cities around the Pacific Rim. He outlines his use of quantitative ideas as follows.

'Most of my work is communicating with managers in companies and government offices. I am certainly not a mathematician, and am often confused by figures – but I use quantitative ideas all the time. When I talk to a board of directors, they won't be impressed if I say, "This project is quite good; if all goes well you should make a profit at some point in the future." They want me to spell things out clearly and say, "You can expect a 20% return over the next two years."

My clients look for a competitive advantage in a fast-moving world. They make difficult decisions. Quantitative methods help us to make better decisions – and they help to explain and communicate these decisions. Quantitative methods allow us to:

- look logically and objectively at a problem
- measure key variables and the results in calculations
- analyse a problem and look for practical solutions
- compare alternative solutions and identify the best
- compare performance across different operations, companies and times
- explain the options and alternatives
- support or defend a particular decision
- overcome subjective and biased opinions.

Quantitative methods are an essential part of any business. Without them, we just could not survive!'

Source: Chua P., talk to Eastern Business Forum, Hong Kong, 2010.

Solving problems

Building a model

'Quantitative methods' is a broad subject that includes many different approaches – but they all start with a model of a problem. In this sense, a 'model' is a simplified representation of reality, and we are not talking about toys or games. The main features of a model are:

- it is a representation of reality
- it is simplified, with only relevant details included
- properties in reality are represented by other properties in the model.

There are several types of model, but the most widely used by managers are symbolic models. These have properties in reality represented by some kind of symbol. So, a symbolic model for the amount of value added tax payable is:

$$\text{VAT} = \text{rate} \times \text{sales}$$

where the symbol 'VAT' in the model represents the amount of tax paid in reality, and the symbols 'rate' and 'sales' represent the actual rate of VAT and value of sales.

If a company sells a product for £300 a unit, a model of its income is:

$$\text{income} = \text{number of units sold} \times \text{selling price}$$
$$= \text{number of units sold} \times 300$$

We can extend this model by finding the profit when it costs the company £200 to make each unit:

$$\text{profit} = \text{number of units sold} \times (\text{selling price} - \text{cost})$$

or

$$\text{profit} = \text{number of units sold} \times (300 - 200)$$
$$= \text{number of units sold} \times 100$$

This equation is our model. It has the advantage that we can do experiments with it, perhaps seeing how the profit changes with the selling price or number of units sold. This is an important point – that we can change things in the model to assess their affects. If we did not have the model, our only option would be to experiment with real operations, getting the company to actually change its selling price and then measuring the change in profit. This kind of tinkering with real operations has the obvious disadvantages of being difficult, time-consuming, disruptive and expensive – and it might cause permanent damage. It may also be impossible – for example, a wholesaler cannot find the best location for a new warehouse by experimentally trying all possible locations and keeping the best. Experimenting with real operations is at best expensive and at worst impossible, so the only feasible alternative is to build a model and experiment with this.

Stages in problem-solving

Earlier we said that there are four stages in tackling a problem – identifying the problem, analysing it, making decisions and implementing the results. You can see the central role of models in this process when we add some details to the four stages (as shown in Figure 1.2).

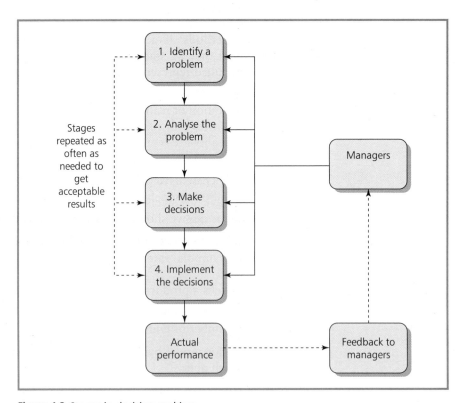

Figure 1.2 Stages in decision-making

Stage 1: Identify a problem. At the end of this stage, managers should have a clear understanding of the problem they are tackling, its context and the requirements of their solution. For this stage they might:

(a) Do an initial investigation – looking at operations, identifying difficulties and recognising that there really is a problem.
(b) Define the problem – adding details to the initial investigation, saying exactly what the problem is (and not just its symptoms), its context, scope, boundaries and any other relevant details.
(c) Set objectives – identifying the decision-makers, their aims, improvements they want, effects on the organisation and measures of success.
(d) Identify variables, possible alternatives and courses of action.
(e) Plan the work – showing how to tackle the problem, schedule activities, design timetables and check resources.

Stage 2: Analyse the problem. At the end of this stage, managers should have a clear understanding of their options and the consequences. For this they might:

(a) Consider different approaches to solving the problem.
(b) Check work done on similar problems and see if they can use the same approach.
(c) Study the problem more closely and refine the details.
(d) Identify the key variables and relationships between them.
(e) Build a model of the problem and test its accuracy.
(f) Collect data needed by the model and analyse it.
(g) Run more tests on the model and data to make sure that they are working properly, are accurate and describe the real conditions.
(h) Experiment with the model to find results in different circumstances and under different conditions.
(i) Analyse the results, making sure that they are accurate and consistent.

Stage 3: Make decisions. This is where managers consider the results from analyses, review all the circumstances and make their decisions. There are three steps:

(a) Compare solutions, looking at all aspects of their performance.
(b) Find solutions that best meet the decision-makers' objectives.
(c) Identify and agree the best overall solution.

Stage 4: Implement the decisions. At this point managers turn ideas into practice, moving from 'we should do this' to actually doing it. For this they:

(a) Check that the proposed solution really works and is an improvement on current performance.
(b) Plan details of the implementation.
(c) Change operations to introduce new ways of doing things.
(d) Monitor actual performance – after implementing their decisions, managers still have to monitor operations using feedback to compare actual performance with plans to make sure that predicted results actually occur. And if things are not going as expected, they have to adjust the operations and plans.

In practice, managers can rarely take these stages in strict sequence because they often hit problems and have to return to an earlier point. For example, when making a decision in stage 3 they might find that they do not have enough information and return to stage 2 for more analysis. So they keep returning to earlier stages as often as needed – or until the time available for making the decision runs out.

People take slightly different views of these stages, such as Finlay and King's[1] description of conceptualisation, verbalisation, symbolisation, manipulation and representation. Waters[2] describes observation, modelling, experimentation and implementation, and a classic work by Ackoff[3] describes six stages of defining a problem, building a model, testing the model, getting a solution to the problem, implementing the solution and controlling the solution. However, the important point is not the names, but that managers actually adopt a formal process for tackling problems, and that there are several stages between identifying the problem and implementing the solution.

In our view, the analysis and modelling is done mainly in stage 2, and this is where you find most quantitative methods. Actually, the quantitative analysis itself can include several stages. For instance, managers might start by identifying the overall approach to tackling a problem, then move through research, modelling, data collection, experimentation and ending with analysis of the results. Figure 1.3 shows a more detailed view of decision-making when these extra elements are added to stage 2. We describe the details of this approach in the rest of the book.

IDEAS IN PRACTICE   BG Group

BG Group is an international energy group with a turnover of around $15 billion a year. Its main business is the supply of natural gas. This is a 'clean' fuel, and because the worldwide demand for energy is growing, sales are expected to rise significantly over the next 10 years. To meet this demand BG has to continually find and develop new reserves.

National governments generally regard gas fields as a vital strategic resource, so they keep tight control over them. To develop a field, governments divide it into blocks and invite energy companies to bid for exploration rights. BG, along with every other energy company, has to decide whether to bid for exploration rights in available blocks, and how much to bid. These are important decisions that are characterised by high costs (typically hundreds of millions of dollars), long lead times (typically five years before a project starts earning money), limited lifetime (there is a finite amount of gas available) and complex tax and contractual arrangements.

BG considers many factors in each decision. Firstly, there are qualitative factors, particularly their rigorous ethical guidelines and business principles. These are important in showing how BG Group does business and what it stands for – and how it deals with issues such as gas finds in sensitive environments, conflict zones or areas where indigenous peoples are contesting land rights. Other qualitative questions concern the availability of alternative projects, structure of the company's long-term portfolio of fields, partnerships, public perception of the company, effect on share value, and so on.

Secondly, there are quantitative factors. These focus on two issues:

- Risks – where geologists look at the chances of finding gas and the likely size of discoveries, engineers look at potential difficulties with production, health and safety look at safety and environmental risks, and economists look at likely demand, prices and commercial risks.
- Return from the project, starting with the basic formula:

    net cash flow = revenue – costs – taxes

Managers review the results from both qualitative and quantitative analyses before making any decision.

Sources: BG Annual Reports and websites www.bg-group.com and www.thetimes100.co.uk

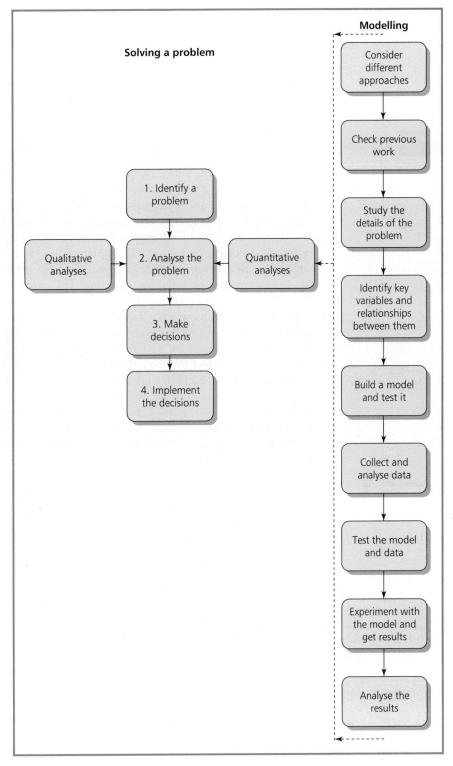

Figure 1.3 The role of modelling in solving a problem

1.5   Why do managers use models?

1.6   What are the stages in solving a problem?

1.7   Where do quantitative models fit into this approach?

1.8   Is there only one correct way to tackle a problem?

Useful software

An obvious problem with calculations is that we can all make mistakes with even the simplest bit of arithmetic. Thankfully, we can use calculators for simple arithmetic and computers for anything more ambitious. Then, you might ask, why you should do any calculations – why not leave everything to the computer? A standard answer is that you have to understand the methods so that you can interpret and implement the results they give. If you are simply handed a numerical result, you have no idea of its accuracy, relevance, assumptions or anything else. And you certainly have no insight into the calculations or 'feel' for the numbers. You need at least some contact with the calculations to say whether the results make sense or are absurd. If your computer says that a company made £140 million profit last year or that a share price rose by 1200% overnight, it might be good news – or you might have some feel for the calculations and realise that there is a mistake. If your computer calculates an answer of 15 km, this may be good – but it was nonsense when a study quoted this as the diameter needed for a sewer pipe in Karachi.[4] So it is always useful to do some calculations – if only to see what is happening and check the results.

There is a huge amount of software available for helping managers with their calculations, and spreadsheets are particularly useful. These consist of a grid of related cells, with the rows numbered 1, 2, 3 etc. and the columns labelled A, B, C etc. Then each cell in the grid has a unique address such as A1, A2, B1, C6 or F92. Each cell contains:

- a simple number – for example, we can set cell B1 to equal 21, and B2 to 12
- or a calculation – so we can set cell B3 to equal the sum of cells B1 and B2
- or a label – so we can set cell A3 to contain the word 'Total'.

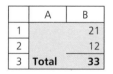

Figure 1.4 Example of a spreadsheet calculation

You can see the result in Figure 1.4. The benefit of this format is that you can change the value of any cell (such as B1 or B2) and the spreadsheet will automatically do the calculations.

The most widely used spreadsheet is Microsoft Excel, but there are several alternatives including IBM Lotus Symphony, Apple's Numbers, OpenOffice Calc, Quattro Pro, Gnumeric and Google Doc's spreadsheet. In this book we illustrate calculations with a generic spreadsheet, which is based on Microsoft Excel. However, you can use any relevant package for calculations – and the only guidance is to use the software that you are happiest with. If you want lessons or revision in the use of spreadsheets, some books are suggested in the sources of information at the end of the chapter.

Spreadsheets are easy to use and have a standard format for doing many calculations – but they have limitations. Sometimes it is easier to use a specialised package that is better at handling data, uses the best method to solve a particular problem, includes special procedures, and gives results in the best format. But specialised software can be more complicated and more expensive, so you have to balance the benefits with the extra effort and cost.

WORKED EXAMPLE 1.3

In Worked example 1.1 we described an automatic ticket machine that accepts only pound coins and gives out:

1 ticket for £1, 3 tickets for £2, 4 tickets for £3, 5 tickets for £4, and 7 tickets for £5.

Use a spreadsheet to find the best value from the machine.

Solution

Figure 1.5(a) shows the calculations for this and Figure 1.5(b) shows the results. If you do not

understand these results, it is worth getting some practice with spreadsheets. The key point is that each cell can contain a number, a calculation or a label. An equals sign shows that it contains a calculation – such as '=A4/B4', where cell C4 contains the result of dividing the value in cell A4 by the value in cell B4. The calculations can include standard functions, such as 'SUM' (adding the values in a range of cells), 'MAX' (finding the maximum value), 'MIN' (finding the minimum value), and the conditional 'IF'.

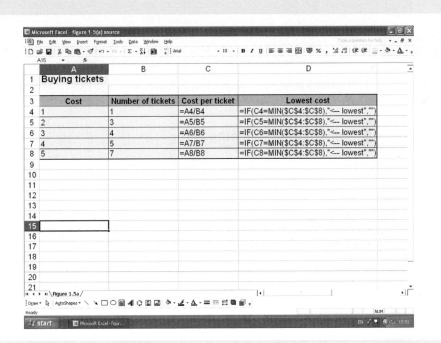

Figure 1.5(a) Spreadsheet calculations for ticket machine

Worked example 1.3 continued

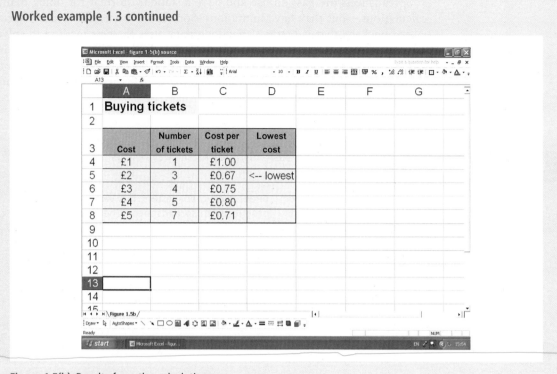

Figure 1.5(b) Results from the calculations

Review questions

1.9   To get a feel for a calculation you should do it by hand first, and then use a computer to check the result. Do you think this is true?

1.10   Why would you use general-purpose software like spreadsheets when there are specialised packages for most problems?

IDEAS IN PRACTICE   **'I'm no good at maths . . .'**

Tom Geoghegan says, 'The British are uniquely happy to admit being bad at maths'. Most people in the world are proud of their education and attainments, and British people would not be happy to admit failings in other areas, such as reading. However, despite many campaigns and noticeably higher earnings for people with mathematical qualifications, people still go around saying, 'I am no good at maths . . .'. Alan Stevans of the Institute for Mathematics and its Applications says, 'I hear the general public saying it, and particularly journalists on television – newsreaders say they've always been rubbish at it – as if they're proud of it'.

Worryingly, this extends to the highest levels. When Randolph Churchill was Chancellor of the Exchequer in the nineteenth century, he said of decimal points, 'I could never make out what those damned dots meant'. A century later his successor Gordon Brown said while visiting a school, 'I did maths at school and for a year at university, but don't think I was ever very good at it'.

Marcus de Sautoy said that, 'It's bizarre why people are prepared to admit that . . . (they) can't think logically' and he sums up his attitude saying, 'I would rather do business with someone who admits they're good at maths'.

Sources: Geoghegan T., How to solve the British maths problem? BBC News Magazine, 4/6/2008 and at www. news.bbc.co.uk: www.manchesterevening news.co.uk.

CHAPTER REVIEW

This chapter introduced the idea of quantitative analysis and the use of numbers in everyday life.

- Numbers have two major advantages. Firstly, they give a clear, concise and objective measure of a feature; secondly, we can use them in calculations.

- Business problems almost invariably have some numerical features. To deal with these, managers need some appreciation of quantitative methods. This does not mean that they have to be expert mathematicians, but they must have a basic understanding of the principles.

- Quantitative methods normally use symbolic models, which represent real features by symbols. In particular, they use equations to describe real problems.

- A general approach to problem-solving has four stages: identifying a problem, analysing it, making decisions and implementing the results. Quantitative methods form a key part of the analysis stage.

- Computers do the routine arithmetic for quantitative methods using standard software, particularly spreadsheets – but you still need some feel for the calculations and results.

CASE STUDY   Hamerson and Partners

Albert Hamerson is Managing Director of his family firm of builders' merchants. He is the third generation to run the company and is keen for his daughter, Georgina, to join him when she leaves university. Georgina is also keen to join the company, but she is not sure what kind of job she wants.

Hamerson and Partners is essentially a wholesaler. They buy 17,000 different products from 1,100 manufacturers and importers, including all the usual materials needed by builders. Their main customers are small building firms, but they have some long-term contracts with bigger organisations, and many one-off and DIY customers. The company works from four sites around Dublin and Cork and employs over 300 people.

Georgina feels that the company is getting behind the times. She assumed that computers would reduce the amount of paperwork, but when she goes into company offices she is surprised at the amount of paper. For instance, she thought that most orders would be collected automatically through the company's website, but she saw that they were also written on scraps of paper, printed forms, faxes and downloaded e-mails. When she walks around the stores, things still seem to be organised in the way they were 20 years ago.

Georgina has several ideas for improvements – many emerging from her university studies in mathematics and business. She wants to develop these ideas, and imagines herself as an 'internal consultant' looking around the company, finding areas for improvement and doing projects to make operations more efficient. One problem is that her father has had little contact with quantitative analyses beyond reading the company accounts. He makes decisions based on experience gained through 35 years of work with the company and discussions with staff. He is not sure that Georgina's mathematical training will be of any practical value.

After some discussion, Georgina agreed to write a report describing the type of problem that she could tackle. She will outline her approach to these problems and the benefits the company could expect. Then she will spend some time in her next vacation looking in more detail at one of these problems.

Question

- **If you were in Georgina's position, what would you put in your report? What benefits do you think that she could bring to the company?**

PROBLEMS

The answers to these problems are given on the companion website: **www.pearsoned.co.uk/waters**

1.1 At last year's Southern Florida Amateur Tennis Championships there were 1,947 entries in the women's singles. This is a standard knockout tournament, so how many matches did the organisers have to arrange?

1.2 European coins have denominations of 1, 2, 5, 10, 20 and 50 cents, and 1 and 2 euros. What is the smallest number of coins needed to pay exactly a bill of €127.87?

1.3 Sally was pleased when a meal at the Golden Orient restaurant appeared to cost $28 for food and $16 for drinks. Unfortunately, her final bill added 15% alcohol duty, 10% service charge, 12% federal tax, 6% state tax and 2% city tax. How much did she pay for extras, and what was her final bill?

1.4 A family of three is having grilled steak for dinner, and they like to grill their steaks for 10 minutes on each side. Unfortunately, the family's grill pan is only big enough to grill one side of two steaks at a time. How long will it take to cook dinner?

1.5 A shopkeeper buys an article for £25 and then sells it to a customer for £35. The customer pays with a £50 note. The shopkeeper does not have enough change, so he goes to a neighbour and changes the £50 note. A week later the neighbour tells him that the £50 note was a forgery, so he immediately repays the £50. How much does the shopkeeper lose in this transaction?

1.6 Devise a scheme for doctors to assess how bad a stomach pain is.

1.7 Design a fair system for electing parliamentary candidates.

RESEARCH PROJECTS

1.1 It might seem an exaggeration to say that every problem that managers tackle has a quantitative aspect. Do a review of the types of decisions made by managers, and see if you can find examples of problems that are purely qualitative.

1.2 You can use computers for any of the arithmetic described in this book, and it would be particularly useful to have a spreadsheet with good graphics. Make sure that you are familiar with the computers and software available, and know how to use them.

1.3 The following table shows the number of units of a product sold each month by a shop, the amount the shop paid for each unit, and the selling price. Use a spreadsheet to find the total values of sales, costs, income and profit. What other analyses can you do?

Month	Year 1			Year 2		
	Units sold	Unit cost to the shop	Selling price	Units sold	Unit cost to the shop	Selling price
January	56	120	135	61	121	161
February	58	122	138	60	121	161
March	55	121	145	49	122	162
April	60	117	145	57	120	155
May	54	110	140	62	115	150
June	62	106	135	66	109	155
July	70	98	130	68	103	156
August	72	110	132	71	105	157
September	43	119	149	48	113	161
October	36	127	155	39	120	161
November	21	133	161	32	126	160
December	22	130	161	25	130	160

Remember that the data sets used in the book are all given in the resources of the companion website **www.pearsoned.co.uk/waters**.

1.4 Many websites give tutorials on the different types of quantitative problems faced by managers. These tutorials are produced by universities, institutions, publishers, training companies, software providers, tutoring services, consultants and so on. Do some searches to find useful sites for your course.

Sources of information

References

1 Finlay P.N. and King M., Examples to help management students to love mathematical modelling, *Teaching Mathematics and its Applications*, Vol. 5(2), pages 78–93, 1986.

2 Waters D., *A Practical Introduction to Management Science*, Addison Wesley Longman, Harlow, 1998.

3 Ackoff R.L., *Scientific Method*, John Wiley, New York, 1962.

4 Mian H.M., personal correspondence, 1986.

Further reading

There are several general books on quantitative methods for business, with the following giving a good starting point:

Curwin J. and Slater R., *Quantitative Methods for Business Decisions* (6th edition), Cebgage Learning, London, 2007.

Morris C., *Quantitative Approaches in Business Studies* (7th edition), FT Prentice Hall, Harlow, 2008.

Oakshot L.A., *Essential Quantitative Methods for Business Management and Finance* (3rd edition), Palgrave, Basingstoke, 2006.

Swift L. and Piff S., *Quantitative Methods for Business, Management and Finance* (3rd edition), Palgrave, Basingstoke, 2010.

Wisniewski M., *Quantitative Methods for Decision Makers* (5th edition), FT Prentice Hall, Harlow, 2009.

Many books describe how to use spreadsheets at different levels:

Albright S., *Management Science Modelling*, South Western College Publishing, Cincinnati, OH, 2008.

Artymiak J., *Beginning Open Office Calc*, Apress, New York, NY, 2010.

Barlow J.F., *Excel Models for Business and Operations Management* (2nd edition), John Wiley, Chichester, 2005.

Harvey G., *Excel for Dummies*, John Wiley, Chichester, 2006.

Jelen M. and Girvin B., *Slaying Excel Dragons*, Holy Macro! Press, Uniontown, OH, 2010.

Moore J.H. and Weatherford L.R., *Decision Modelling with Microsoft Excel* (6th edition), Prentice Hall, Upper Saddle River, NJ, 2001.

Morris S., *Spreadsheets with Excel*, Butterworth-Heinemann, Oxford, 2006.

Ragsdale C., *Spreadsheet Modelling and Decision Analysis* (5th edition), South-Western College Publishing, Cincinnati, OH, 2008.

Rendell I. and Mott J., *Advanced Spreadsheet Projects in Excel*, Hodder Education, London, 2008.

Whigham D., *Business Data Analysis Using Excel*, Oxford University Press, Oxford, 2007.

Winston W., *Microsoft Office Excel 2007*, Microsoft Press, Redmond, WA, 2007.

Winston W. and Albright S.C., *Spreadsheet Modeling and Applications*, Brooks/Cole, Florence, KY, 2004.

Useful websites

The general website accompanying this book is at **www.pearsoned.co.uk/waters**. This contains a lot of useful information, including a list of other useful websites.

You can find details of software from suppliers' sites, such as www.microsoft.com and www.IBM.com. There is a huge amount of information on the Web, and it is best to start with a search engine, like those you can find at www.altavista.com, www.baidu.com, www.bing.com, www.google.com, www.lycos.com, www.webcrawler.com and www.yahoo.com.

Calculations and equations

Chapter outline

The following chapters describe quantitative methods that are widely used by managers. But before looking at these in detail, you have to be happy with some basic tools of arithmetic. This chapter reviews these tools. You have probably met these before, and can move through this chapter fairly quickly. On the other hand, you might find some new material and want to spend more time on it.

It is important that you understand the material in this chapter because it is used throughout the rest of the book. If you have any problems, it is worth spending time sorting them out. You might want more information on some topics and you can find suggestions for further reading at the end of the chapter.

After finishing this chapter you should be able to:

- understand the underlying operations of arithmetic
- work with integers, fractions, decimals and percentages
- round numbers to decimal places and significant figures
- understand the principles of algebra
- solve an equation to find a previously unknown value
- appreciate the use of inequalities
- understand the principles of simultaneous equations
- use algebraic methods to solve simultaneous equations
- work with powers and roots
- describe numbers in scientific notation
- use logarithms.

Working with numbers

This chapter reviews the basic tools of arithmetic. For this review our only assumption is that you are familiar with numbers and can do simple calculations. You can see that:

- If you buy 10 loaves of bread costing 92 pence a loaf, the bill is £9.20.
- If you drive a car at 80 kilometres an hour, it will take 5 hours to travel 400 kilometres.
- If you spend €500 a month on housing, €200 a month on food and entertainment, and €300 a month on other things, your total expenditure is €1,000 a month, which is the same as €12,000 a year or €230.77 a week.
- If a company has a gross income of $2 million a year and costs of $1.6 million a year, it makes a profit of $400,000 a year.

Arithmetic

There are four basic operations in arithmetic: addition, subtraction, multiplication and division. We describe these with the notation:

- $+$ addition   e.g. $2 + 7 = 9$
- $-$ subtraction   e.g. $15 - 7 = 8$
- $\times$ multiplication   e.g. $4 \times 5 = 20$
- $/$ division   e.g. $12 / 4 = 3$

There are variations on this notation, and you will also see:

- division written as $12 \div 4 = 3$ or $12/4 = 3$
- multiplication written as $4.5 = 20$ or $4(5) = 20$.

Calculations are always done in the same order, with multiplication and division done before addition and subtraction. If you see $3 + 4 \times 5$, you do the multiplication first to give $3 + 20 = 23$. Whenever there is any doubt about the order of arithmetic, you can put brackets around the parts of the calculation that are done together. Then:

$$(3 + 4) \times 5 = 7 \times 5$$
$$= 35$$

while

$$3 + (4 \times 5) = 3 + 20$$
$$= 23$$

Calculations in brackets are always done first, so the general order of calculation is:

1 Calculations inside brackets, starting from the inside set and working outwards
2 Raising to powers (which we mention later in the chapter)
3 Multiplication and division in the order they appear
4 Addition and subtraction in the order they appear

So:

$$12 \times 2 + 4 + 2 = 24 + 4 + 2$$
$$= 30$$

And we can use brackets to change the order of calculation, so that:

$$12 \times (2 + 4 + 2) = 12 \times 8$$
$$= 96$$

and

$$12 \times (2 + 4) + 4 = 12 \times 6 + 4 = 72 + 4$$
$$= 76$$

If one set of brackets is not enough, you can 'nest' more sets inside others. Calculations always start with the inside set of brackets and work outwards, so that:

$$((32 / 2) + (6 / 3)) - 1 = (16 + 2) - 1 = 18 - 1$$
$$= 17$$

while

$$(32 / (2 + 6)) / (3 - 1) = (32 / 8) / 2 = 4 / 2$$
$$= 2$$

Calculations with a lot of brackets look messy, but you should have no problems if you always take them in the standard order.

Numbers are either positive when they are above zero, or negative when they are below zero. So +10 is positive (but the positive sign is usually implicit, so we write this as 10), and −10 is negative. You should remember three things about negative numbers. Firstly, adding a negative number is the same as subtracting a positive number, so:

$$8 + (-5) = 8 - (+5) = 8 - 5$$
$$= 3$$

Secondly, when you multiply or divide a positive number by a negative number, the result is negative:

$$4 \times (-2) = -8 \quad \text{and} \quad 15 / (-5) = -3$$

Thirdly, when you multiply or divide two negative numbers, the result is positive:

$$(-4) \times (-2) = 8 \quad \text{and} \quad (-15) / (-5) = 3$$

To summarise this:

positive × positive = positive	positive ÷ positive = positive
positive × negative = negative	positive ÷ negative = negative
negative × negative = positive	negative ÷ negative = positive

---

WORKED EXAMPLE 2.1

What are the values of:

(a) $(10 + 20) - (3 \times 7)$?
(b) $((-2 \times 4) \times (15 - 17)) \times (-3)$?
(c) $(20 - 5) \times (30 / (2 + 1))$?

Solution

(a) $(10 + 20) - (3 \times 7) = 30 - 21$
$= 9$

(b) $((-2 \times 4) \times (15 - 17)) \times (-3) = ((-8) \times (-2)) \times (-3)$
$= 16 \times (-3)$
$= -48$

(c) $(20 - 5) \times (30 / (2 + 1)) = 15 \times (30 / 3) = 15 \times 10$
$= 150$

Fractions and decimals

The numbers in Worked example 2.1 are integers, which means that they are whole numbers, such as 20, 9 and 150. To make long numbers easier to read, we usually divide them into groups of three digits separated by commas, such as 1,234,567. Some people prefer spaces to commas, so you also see 1 234 567.

When we divide integers into smaller parts, we get fractions. For example, when two people share a bar of chocolate they get a half each. We can describe fractions as either:

- common fractions (invariably just described as 'fractions') – such as $\frac{1}{2}$ or $\frac{1}{4}$
- decimal fractions (usually described as 'decimals') – such as 0.5 or 0.25.

You meet decimals more often, as they are the standard format for calculators and computers. But fractions can save a lot of effort with certain problems. The top line of a fraction is the numerator, and the bottom line is the denominator:

$$\text{fraction} = \frac{\text{numerator}}{\text{denominator}}$$

If you multiply or divide both the numerator and the denominator by the same amount, the fraction keeps the same value. So 5/10 is the same as 1/2 (dividing both the numerator and the denominator by 5) or 20/40 (multiplying both by 4).

To change fractions into decimals, you divide the numerator by the denominator, so that $\frac{1}{4}$ is 1 divided by 4, which is 0.25. To change a decimal with one digit to a fraction, you put the number after the decimal point over 10, so 0.6 = 6/10 = 3/5. If there are two digits after the decimal point you put them over 100 $\left(\text{so } 4.59 = 4\dfrac{59}{100}\right)$, if there are three digits you put them over 1000 $\left(\text{so } 12.273 = 12\dfrac{273}{1000}\right)$ and so on.

WORKED EXAMPLE 2.2

Describe as decimal fractions: (a) 5/4, (b) 38/8, (c) −12/16.
Describe as common fractions: (d) 0.4, (e) 3.75, (f) 6.125.

Solution
Using long division (or preferably a calculator) you can see that:

(a) 5/4 = 1.25
(b) 38/8 = 19/4
   = 4.75

(c) −12/16 = −3/4
     = −0.75

Expanding the decimal fraction gives:

(d) 0.4 = 4/10
    = 2/5

(e) $3.75 = 3\dfrac{75}{100}$
    $= 3\dfrac{3}{4}$

(f) $6.125 = 6\dfrac{125}{1,000}$
    $= 6\dfrac{1}{8}$

To multiply fractions together, you multiply all the numerators together to give the new numerator, and you multiply all the denominators together to give the new denominator.

WORKED EXAMPLE 2.3

Find the values of: (a) 1/2 × 1/5, (b) 1/4 × 2/3, (c) −1/4 × 2/3 × 1/2.

Solution
Multiplying the numerators together and the denominators together gives:

(a) 1/2 × 1/5 = (1 × 1) / (2 × 5)
    = 1/10
(b) 1/4 × 2/3 = (1 × 2) / (4 × 3) = 2/12
    = 1/6
(c) −1/4 × 2/3 × 1/2 = (−1 × 2 × 1) / (4 × 3 × 2) = −2/24
    = −1/12

To divide one fraction by another, you invert the fraction that is dividing and then multiply the two together. (This might seem rather strange until you work out what is actually happening.)

WORKED EXAMPLE 2.4

Find the values of: (a) (3/5) ÷ (4/5), (b) 3/6 × 2/5 ÷ 3/7, (c) 2/5 ÷ 16/4.

Solution
Inverting the dividing fraction and then multiplying gives:

(a) (3/5) ÷ (4/5) = 3/5 × 5/4 = (3 × 5) / (5 × 4) = 15/20
    = 3/4
(b) 3/6 × 2/5 ÷ 3/7 = 3/6 × 2/5 × 7/3
    = (3 × 2 × 7) / (6 × 5 × 3) = 42/90
    = 7/15
(c) 2/5 ÷ 16/4 = 2/5 × 4/16 = (2 × 4) / (5 × 16) = 8/80
    = 1/10 .

To add or subtract fractions, you have to adjust the fractions until they all have the same denominator. In other words, you take each fraction in turn and multiply the top and bottom by the number that gives this common denominator – and then you add or subtract the numerators.

WORKED EXAMPLE 2.5

Find the values of: (a) 1/2 + 1/4, (b) 1/2 + 4/5, (c) 3/4 − 1/6.

Solution

(a) We have to get the same denominator for both fractions. The easiest value is 4, and to get this we multiply the top and bottom of the first fraction by 2. Then:

$$1/2 + 1/4 = 2/4 + 1/4 = (2 + 1)/4 = 3/4$$
$$= 0.75$$

(b) This time the easiest denominator for both fractions is 10, which we get by multiplying the top and bottom of the first fraction by 5 and the second fraction by 2. Then:

$$1/2 + 4/5 = 5/10 + 8/10 = 13/10$$
$$= 1.3$$

(c) Here the easiest denominator is 12, which we get by multiplying the top and bottom of the first fraction by 3 and the second fraction by 2, giving:

$$3/4 − 1/6 = 9/12 − 2/12 = 7/12$$
$$= 0.583$$

Calculations with fractions soon becomes very messy, so if you are doing a lot of arithmetic it is easier to work with decimals – and, of course, to use a computer or calculator.

WORKED EXAMPLE 2.6

A Canadian visitor to Britain wants to change $350 into pounds. The exchange rate is $1.94 to the pound and the bank charges a fee of £10 for the conversion. How many pounds does the visitor get?

Solution

$350 is equivalent to 350 / 1.94 = £180.41. Then the bank takes its fee of £10 to give the visitor £170.41.

Percentages give another way of describing fractions. These are fractions where the bottom line is 100, and the '/100' has been replaced by the abbreviation '%'. If you hear that '60% of the electorate voted in the last election', you know that 60/100 or 60 people out of each 100 voted. We can represent this as:

■ a common fraction: 60/100 = 3/5
■ a decimal fraction: 0.6
■ a percentage: 60%.

To describe one figure as a percentage of a second, you divide the first figure by the second and multiply by 100. So to describe 15 as a percentage of 20, you calculate $15 / 20 \times 100 = 0.75 \times 100 = 75\%$: to describe 7 as a percentage of 28, you calculate $7 / 28 \times 100 = 0.25 \times 100 = 25\%$.

To find a given percentage of a number, you multiply the number by the percentage and divide by 100. So to find 25% of 200, you calculate $200 \times 25 / 100 = 50$: to find 45% of 80, you calculate $80 \times 45 / 100 = 36$: to find 100% of 65, you calculate $65 \times 100 / 100 = 65$. The last of these results is useful because it reminds us that 100% of something is all of it – and when you hear that someone 'gives 110% of their effort' you recognise this as nonsense.

On the other hand you can spend 110% of your income in the short term, but it is certainly time to worry about the longer term!

WORKED EXAMPLE 2.7

Find: (a) 17/20 as a percentage, (b) 80% as a fraction, (c) 35% as a decimal, (d) 40% of 120, (e) 36 as a percentage of 80, (f) if the price of a $25 book rises by 10%, what is its new price?

Solution

(a) Multiplying the top and bottom of the fraction by 5 shows that 17/20 = 85/100 = 85%.

(b) 80% = 80/100
      = 4/5
(c) 35% = 35/100
      = 0.35
(d) 40% of 120 = 120 × 40 / 100 = 4800 / 100
                  = 48
(e) 36/80 × 100 = 45%
(f) 10% of $25 = 25 × 10 / 100 = $2.50, so the new price is 25 + 2.50 = $27.50

WORKED EXAMPLE 2.8

If you multiply 20% of 50 by 1/4 of 60 and divide the result by 0.25 of 80, what answer do you get?

Solution

Doing this in stages:

20% of 50 = 50 × 20 / 100 = 10
1/4 of 60 = (1 / 4) × 60 = 15
0.25 of 80 = 0.25 × 80 = 20

Then the calculation is:

(10 × 15) / 20 = 150 / 20 = 7.5

Rounding numbers

If you calculate 4/3 as a decimal, the answer is 1.333333333 . . . where the dots represent an unending row of 3s. For convenience, we round such numbers to one of the following:

- A certain number of decimal places, showing only a reasonable number of digits after the decimal point. Rounding to two decimal places gives 1.33.
- A certain number of significant figures, showing only the most important digits to the left. Rounding to four significant figures gives 1.333.

By convention, when rounding to, say, two decimal places and the digit in the third decimal place is 0, 1, 2, 3 or 4, we round the result *down*; when the digit in the third decimal place is 5, 6, 7, 8 or 9, we round the result *up*. Then 1.64 becomes 1.6 to one decimal place, while 1.65 becomes 1.7; similarly, 12.344 becomes 12.34 to four significant figures, while 12.346 becomes 12.35.

The purpose of rounding is to give enough information to be useful, but not so much as to overwhelm us with detail. There is no rule for choosing the number of decimal places or significant figures, except the rather vague advice to use the number that best suits your purpose. When people ask how tall you are, you probably give an answer to the nearest centimetre or inch;

employers might quote salaries rounded to the nearest thousand pounds; the populations of towns are often rounded to the nearest 10,000; major companies report their profits to the nearest million pounds. So two useful guidelines for rounding are:

■ Give only the number of decimal places or significant figures that is useful. For instance, it never makes sense to quote a figure of £952.347826596 and we generally round this to £952.35 – or £952, £950 or £1,000 depending on circumstances.

■ Results from calculations are only as accurate as the data used to get them. If you multiply a demand of 32.63 units by a unit cost of €17.19, you should quote the total cost to at most two decimal places. So you should not describe the result as 32.63 × 17.19 = €560.9097, but you should describe it as €560.91 (or €561, €560 or €600, again depending on the circumstances).

WORKED EXAMPLE 2.9

What is 1,374.3414812 to (a) four decimal places, (b) two decimal places, (c) four significant figures, (d) two significant figures?

Solution

(a) 1,374.3415 when rounded to four decimal places
(b) 1,374.34 to two decimal places
(c) 1,374 to four significant figures
(d) 1,400 to two significant figures

IDEAS IN PRACTICE T.D. Hughes Ltd

T.D. Hughes Ltd are retailers of high-quality furniture, and they sell a particular dining room table for £8,000. Last summer they had some difficulty with supplies and raised the price of the table by 20%. When supplies returned to normal, they reduced the higher price by 20% and advertised this as part of their January sale.

Some customers were not happy with this deal, saying that the company had only returned the table to its original price. But company managers pointed out that increasing the original price by 20% raised it to 120% of £8,000, which is (120 / 100) × 8,000 = £9,600. Then reducing the higher price by 20% took it down to 80% of £9,600 which is (80 / 100) × 9,600 = £7,680. There was a genuine reduction of £320 or a proportion of 320/8,000 = 4%. If they had wanted to return the table to its original price, they would have reduced it by the proportion 1,600/9,600, which equals 16.67 / 100 or 16.67%.

Source: company promotional material.

Review questions

2.1 Why should you do any calculations by hand, when computers can do them more easily and accurately?

2.2 What is the value of: (a) (–12) / (–3), (b) (24/5) ÷ (3/7), (c) ((2 – 4) × (3 – 6)) / (7 – 5)?

2.3 What is the difference between 75%, 3/4, 15/20 and 0.75? Which is the best format?

2.4 What is 1,745,800.36237 rounded to three decimal places and to three significant figures?

Changing numbers to letters

Suppose you want to see how the cost of running a car depends on the distance you travel. In one month you might find that you drive 6,000 km at a total cost of £2,400. Then you find the cost per kilometre by dividing the cost by the number of kilometres travelled, giving 2,400 / 6,000 = £0.40 per kilometre. In general, this calculation is:

$$\text{cost per kilometre} = \frac{\text{total cost}}{\text{number of kilometres travelled}}$$

Rather than writing the equation in full, you can save time by using some abbreviations. You can abbreviate the total cost to T, which is simple and easy to remember. And you can abbreviate the cost per kilometre to C and the number of kilometres travelled to K. Putting these abbreviations into the general equation gives:

$$C = \frac{T}{K} = T / K$$

Now you have an equation relating the variables in a general, concise and accurate form. The only difference from the original equation is that you have used letters to represent quantities. This is the basis of algebra – which uses symbols to represent variables and to describe the relationships between them.

You can substitute known values into an equation. For example, if you find that over a certain period the total cost (T) is €600 to travel 1,000 km (K) we can say that:

$$C = T / K = 600 / 1,000 = 0.6, \text{ or more fully €0.6 per km}$$

We chose the abbreviations C, T and K to remind us of what they stand for. We could have chosen any other names, perhaps giving:

$c = t / k$
$y = x / z$
COST = TOTAL / KILOM
COSTPERKM = TOTALCOST / KILOMETRES

Provided the meaning is clear, the names are not important. But if you want to save time, it makes sense to use short names, such as a, x and N. However, one thing that you have to be careful about is the assumption in algebra that adjacent variables are multiplied together – so $a \times b$ is written as ab, $4 \times a \times b \times c$ is written as $4abc$, $a \times (b + c)$ is written as $a(b + c)$, and $(a + b) \times (x - y)$ is written as $(a + b)(x - y)$. This causes no problems with single-letter abbreviations but can be misleading with longer names. If you abbreviate the total unit cost to TUC, it makes no sense to write an equation:

TUC = NTUC

when you really mean

TUC = $N \times T \times$ UC

With algebra we only replace specific numbers by general names, so all aspects of the calculations remain the same. In particular, there are still the four basic operations (addition, subtraction, multiplication and division) and they are done in the same order (things inside brackets, raising to powers, multiplication and division, and then addition and subtraction).

We can use the example of the cost of driving a car to illustrate another important point. The cost per kilometre is essentially fixed and a driver cannot change it – so in the equation above C is constant. However, the number of kilometres travelled, K, and the total cost, T, can both vary. So equations describe the relationships between:

- constants – which have fixed values, and
- variables – which can take different values.

WORKED EXAMPLE 2.10

What is the equation for the percentage of people who voted in an election? What is the percentage if 55,000 people were eligible to vote and 23,000 actually voted?

Solution

We have to take the number of people who actually voted, divide this by the number of people who could have voted, and then multiply the result by 100. This is rather long-winded, so we can use some abbreviations, starting by defining:

v = the number of people who actually voted
n = the number of people who could have voted
p = the percentage of people who actually voted

Then the calculation is:

$$p = (v / n) \times 100$$

If we know that $n = 55,000$ and $v = 23,000$, we can substitute these into the equation to give:

$$p = (v / n) \times 100 = (23,000 / 55,000) \times 100$$
$$= 0.418 \times 100$$
$$= 41.8\%$$

WORKED EXAMPLE 2.11

How would you calculate: (a) $10(x + 2)$ when $x = 7$ (b) $w(x + y)$, (c) $p - (s - 2t)$, (d) $(a + b)(c + d)$?

Solution

(a) The equation shows that we multiply 10 by $(x + 2)$ and we know that $x = 7$, so we can say that:

$$10(x + 2) = 10 \times (x + 2) = 10 \times (7 + 2) = 10 \times 9$$
$$= 90$$

(b) Here we have to multiply everything inside the brackets by w, so:

$$w(x + y) = wx + wy$$

You can always check your results by substituting test values, such as $w = 2$, $x = 3$ and $y = 4$. Then:

$$w(x + y) = 2(3 + 4) = 2 \times 7 = 14$$
$$wx + wy = (2 \times 3) + (2 \times 4) = 6 + 8$$
$$= 14$$

(c) The minus sign before the brackets means that we effectively have to multiply everything inside the brackets by -1, giving:

$$p - (s - 2t) = p + (-1) \times (s - 2t) = p - s + 2t$$

(d) Here the two expressions inside brackets are multiplied together, so we have to multiply everything inside the first bracket by everything inside the second bracket. The easiest way to arrange this is:

$$(a + b)(c + d) = (a + b) \times (c + d)$$
$$= a \times (c + d) + b \times (c + d)$$
$$= (ac + ad) + (bc + bd)$$
$$= ac + ad + bc + bd$$

Remember that you can always check the results of algebra by substituting trial values. Here we can take trial values of $a = 1$, $b = 2$, $c = 3$ and $d = 4$. Then the original equation has:

$$(a + b) \times (c + d) = (1 + 2) \times (3 + 4) = 3 \times 7$$
$$= 21$$

And our solution has:

$$ac + ad + bc + bd = 1 \times 3 + 1 \times 4 + 2 \times 3 + 2 \times 4$$
$$= 3 + 4 + 6 + 8$$
$$= 21$$

The two answers are the same, so our algebra is clearly correct.

WORKED EXAMPLE 2.12

A department has an annual budget of $200,000, which it divides between capital expenditure (C), running costs (R) and overheads (O). How can you describe its expenditure?

Solution

Total expenditure is $C + R + O$ and this must be less than or equal to the budget, so:

$$C + R + O \leq 200,000$$

Review questions

2.5   Why do managers use algebra?

2.6   Is the order of doing algebraic calculations always the same?

2.7   What is the difference between a constant and a variable?

2.8   Is it better to write an equation in the form speed = distance / time, SPD = DST / TME or $S = D / T$?

Solving equations

An equation shows the relationship between a set of constants and variables – saying that the value of one expression equals the value of a second expression. We can use an equation to find the value of a previously unknown constant or variable. This is called solving an equation.

You can use an equation to find one unknown value. You do this by re-arranging the equation so that the unknown value is on one side of the equals sign, and all known values are on the other side. To rearrange an equation you have to remember that it remains true when you do the same thing to both sides – so you can add a number to both sides, or multiply both sides by a constant, and so on. Returning to the equation for the cost of running a car, $C = T / K$, we can multiply both sides of the equation by K and get:

$$C \times K = \frac{T}{K} \times K$$

Here the right-hand side has K / K. When you divide anything by itself you get 1, so we can cancel – or delete – the K / K to give $T = C \times K$. Dividing both sides of this new equation by C gives:

$$\frac{T}{C} = C \times \frac{K}{C} \quad \text{or} \quad K = \frac{T}{C}$$

All three forms are simply rearrangements of the first equation, and if you know two values you can use the appropriate form to find the third.

WORKED EXAMPLE 2.13

Suppose that $a + b = c + d$, when $a = 2$, $b = 6$ and $c = 3$. How can you solve the equation?

Solution

You solve the equation to find the unknown value of d, from the other known values. For this you rearrange the equation to get d on one side of the equals sign and all the other variables on the other side. Specifically, you can subtract c from both sides to get:

$$d = a + b - c$$

and then substituting the known values gives:

$$d = 2 + 6 - 3 = 5$$

WORKED EXAMPLE 2.14

Rearrange the following equation to find the value of y when $a = 2$, $b = 3$ and $c = 4$:

$$\frac{(2a - 7)}{6y} = \frac{(3b - 5)}{2c}$$

Solution

The unknown variable is y, so we have to rearrange the equation to put y on one side and all the known values on the other side. We can start by multiplying both sides of the equation by $(6y \times 2c)$ to get everything on one line:

$$\frac{(2a - 7)(6y \times 2c)}{6y} = \frac{(3b - 5)(6y \times 2c)}{2c}$$

Cancelling the $6y$ from the left-hand side and the $2c$ from the right-hand side gives:

$$(2a - 7) \times 2c = (3b - 5) \times 6y$$

or

$$2c(2a - 7) = 6y(3b - 5)$$

Then we can separate out the y by dividing both sides by $6(3b - 5)$:

$$y = \frac{2c(2a - 7)}{6(3b - 5)}$$

Substituting $a = 2$, $b = 3$ and $c = 4$:

$$y = \frac{(2 \times 4)(2 \times 2 - 7)}{6(3 \times 3 - 5)}$$

$$= \frac{8 \times (-3)}{24} = -1$$

Notice that you can find only *one* unknown value from a single equation. So if an equation has two unknowns, say, $x + y = 10$, you cannot find values for both x and y. If you have several unknowns, you need several equations to find all of them (which we discuss in the next section). And remember that an equation works only if the units are consistent, so you have to be careful to use the same units (say hours, tonnes and dollars) in all parts of the equation.

WORKED EXAMPLE 2.15

Last October the Porth Merrion Hotel paid £1,800 for heat and power, with heat costing £300 more than double the cost of power. How much did power cost?

Solution

If we call the cost of power in the month P, then the cost of heat is $2P + 300$. The hotel's total cost is P for power plus $2P + 300$ for heat, and we know that this came to £1,800, so:

$$P + 2P + 300 = 3P + 300 = 1,800$$

Subtracting 300 from both sides gives:

$$3P = 1,500$$

or

$$P = £500$$

Power cost £500 and heat cost $2P + 300 = 2 \times 500 + 300$
$$= £1,300.$$

Worked example 2.15 shows that the steps in solving an equation are as follows:

1 Define the relevant constants and variables.
2 Develop an equation to describe the relationship between them – which builds a model of the problem.
3 Rearrange the equation to separate the unknown value from the known values.
4 Substitute the known values to solve the equation.

WORKED EXAMPLE 2.16

Sempervig Securitas employs 10 people with costs of €500,000 a year. This cost includes fixed overheads of €100,000, and a variable cost for each person employed. What is the variable cost? What is the total cost if Sempervig expands to employ 20 people?

Solution

If we let t = total cost per year, o = annual overheads, v = variable cost per employee, and n = number of people employed, then the total cost is:

total cost = overheads + (variable cost × number employed)

or

$$t = o + vn$$

We know the values for t, o and n, and we want to find v. So we rearrange the equation by subtracting o from both sides to give $t - o = nv$, and then dividing both sides by n:

$$v = \frac{t - o}{n}$$

Substituting the known values:

$$V = \frac{500,000 - 100,000}{10}$$

= €40,000 a year for each employee.

If the company expands, we find the new total cost, t, by substituting known values for v, o and n in the original equation:

$$t = o + vn = 100,000 + 40,000 \times 20$$
$$= €900,000 \text{ a year.}$$

WORKED EXAMPLE 2.17

1,200 parts arrived from a manufacturer in two batches. Each unit of the first batch cost $37, while each unit of the second batch cost $35. If the total cost is $43,600, how many units were in each batch?

Solution

If we let f be the number of units in the first batch, the number of units in the second batch is $(1,200 - f)$ and the total cost is:

$$37f + 35(1,200 - f) = 43,600$$

So

$$37f + 42,000 - 35f = 43,600$$
$$37f - 35f = 43,600 - 42,000$$
$$2f = 1600$$
$$f = 800$$

The first batch had 800 units and the second batch had 1,200 − 800 = 400 units.

Inequalities

Sometimes we do not have enough information to write an equation, but we may still be able to describe some sort of relationship. For example, we might not know the rate of inflation exactly, but we know that it is less than 4%. We can describe this as an inequality. There are five types of inequality:

- $a < b$ means that a is less than b
- $a \leq b$ means that a is less than or equal to b
- $a > b$ means that a is greater than b
- $a \geq b$ means that a is greater than or equal to b
- $a \neq b$ means that a is not equal to b.

Then we can write inflation < 4%; profit > 0 to show that it is always positive; and €1,000 ≤ cost ≤ €2,000 shows that the cost is between €1,000 and €2,000.

As with equations, inequalities remain valid if you do exactly the same thing to both sides. So you can multiply, divide, add and subtract anything, provided you do it to both sides. If you take a basic inequality $x \geq y$, add 20 to both sides, multiply the result by 2, and divide by a, you still get valid inequalities:

$$x + 20 \geq y + 20$$
$$2x + 40 \geq 2y + 40$$
$$(2x + 40) / a \geq (2y + 40) / a$$

However, there is one awkward exception to this rule – when you multiply or divide both sides by a negative number, you have to change the direction of the inequality. We can show why this happens with the obvious statement that $3 > 2$. If you just multiply both sides by -1, you get the false statement that $-3 > -2$, but changing the direction of the inequality gives the correct version of $-3 < -2$.

WORKED EXAMPLE 2.18

What can you say if (a) $6x - 4 \geq 4x + 3$, (b) $y / (-3) > 4$?

Solution

(a) Rearranging this in the usual way gives:

$6x - 4 \geq 4x + 3$ or $6x - 4x \geq 3 + 4$

so

$2x \geq 7$ or $x \geq 3.5$

(b) We have to be a little more careful here. We can multiply both sides by -3, but must remember to change the direction of the sign:

$y / (-3) > 4$ means that $y < 4 \times (-3)$

or

$y < -12$

Review questions

2.9 What is meant by 'solving an equation'?

2.10 Can you solve an equation of the form $y = 4x + 3$, where both x and y are unknown?

2.11 If you know values for p, q and r, how could you solve the following equations?

(a) $4r / (33 - 3x) = q / 2p$
(b) $(q - 4x) / 2q - 7p / r = 0$

2.12 What is an inequality?

Simultaneous equations

You can solve an equation to find the value of one previously unknown variable. But when you want to find values for several unknown variables, you have to use more than one independent equation. Specifically, to find values for n variables, you need n independent equations relating them. For instance, suppose that you have two unknowns, x and y. If you know only that $x + y = 3$, you cannot find values for both x and y. But if you also know that $y - x = 1$, then you have two independent equations relating the variables and can find values for both of them (here $x = 1$ and $y = 2$).

In this sense 'independent' means that the two equations are not simply different ways of saying the same thing. For instance:

$$x + y = 10 \quad \text{and} \quad x - 10 = y$$

are not independent because they are different forms of the same equation. Similarly:

$$x + y = 10 \quad \text{and} \quad 2x + 2y = 20$$

are not independent – again, they are simply different forms of the same equation.

> ■ Independent equations that show the relationship between a set of variables are called simultaneous equations.
> ■ Solving simultaneous equations means that you find values for all the variables.

Solving simultaneous equations

Suppose that you have two unknown variables, x and y, related by two simultaneous equations:

$$x - y = 7 \tag{1}$$

$$x + 2y = 6 \tag{2}$$

You solve these to find the values of x and y. The easiest way of doing this is to put one equation in the form '$x =$ something', and then substitute this value for x into the second equation. Here you can write the first equation as

$$x = y + 7$$

and substituting this in the second equation gives:

$$x + 2y = 6 \quad \text{or} \quad (y + 7) + 2y = 16$$

Then

$$3y + 7 = 16 \quad \text{so} \quad 3y = 9 \quad \text{or} \quad y = 3$$

This gives one variable, and if you substitute $y = 3$ back into the first equation you get:

$$x - y = 7 \quad \text{so} \quad x - 3 = 7 \quad \text{or} \quad x = 10$$

giving the value of the second variable. You can check these values, $x = 10$ and $y = 3$, in the second equation, giving:

$$x + 2y = 10 + 2 \times 3 = 16 \quad ✓$$

which confirms the result.

Unfortunately, this method of substitution becomes very messy with more complicated equations. An alternative approach multiplies one equation by a number that allows the two equations to be added or subtracted to eliminate one of the variables. When one variable is eliminated, we are left with a single equation with one variable – which we can then solve. Then substituting this value into either of the original equations gives the value of the other variable. This sounds rather complicated, but it is easy to follow in an example.

WORKED EXAMPLE 2.19

Two variables, x and y, are related by the equations:

$$3y = 4x + 2 \quad\quad\quad (1)$$

$$y = -x + 10 \quad\quad\quad (2)$$

What are the values of x and y?

Solution

If you multiply equation (2) by 3, you get the revised equations:

$$3y = 4x + 2 \quad \text{as before} \quad\quad (1)$$

$$3y = -3x + 30 \quad\quad\quad (3)$$

Now subtracting equation (3) from equation (1):

$$3y - 3y = (4x + 2) - (-3x + 30)$$
$$= 4x - (-3x) + 2 - 30$$

so

$$0 = 7x - 28$$
$$x = 4$$

This gives one variable, which you substitute in one of the original equations, say (1), to give the value for the other variable:

$$3y = 4x + 2$$

so

$$3y = 4 \times 4 + 2$$
$$y = 6$$

You can check these answers in equation (2):

$$y = -x + 10$$

or

$$6 = -4 + 10 \quad ✓$$

which confirms the solution.

You can always solve sets of proper simultaneous equations, but there are two things that you have to be careful with. We have already mentioned the first of these, which is that the equations must be independent. Suppose that you have two equations:

$$2x + y = 6 \quad\quad\quad\quad\quad\quad\quad\quad\quad\quad\quad (1)$$

$$6x + 9y = 18 \quad\quad\quad\quad\quad\quad\quad\quad\quad\quad (2)$$

Multiplying equation (1) by 3 immediately gives equation (2), so there is really only one equation and you cannot find two unknowns.

The second problem is a contradiction. Suppose you have:

$$x + y = 7 \quad\quad\quad\quad\quad\quad\quad\quad\quad\quad\quad (1)$$

$$2x + 2y = 12 \quad\quad\quad\quad\quad\quad\quad\quad\quad\quad (2)$$

Multiplying equation (1) by 2 gives $2x + 2y = 14$ which contradicts the second equation. Such a contradiction means that there is no feasible solution and you have to assume that there is a mistake in one of the equations.

WORKED EXAMPLE 2.20

What is the solution to the following set of simultaneous equations?

$$x + 2y = 7 \tag{1}$$

$$2x + y = 5 \tag{2}$$

Solution

Multiplying equation (1) by 2 gives the revised equations:

$$2x + 4y = 14 \tag{3}$$

$$2x + y = 5 \text{ as before} \tag{2}$$

Subtracting equation (2) from equation (3) gives:

$$3y = 9 \text{ or } y = 3$$

You can substitute this into one of the original equations, say (1), to get the value for x:

$$x + 2y = 7$$

so

$$x + 6 = 7 \text{ or } x = 1$$

Checking these answers in equation (2):

$$2x + y = 5 \text{ or } 2 + 3 = 5 \ \checkmark$$

which is correct and confirms the solution.

Finding more variables

Simultaneous equations are not limited to two unknown values. You can have any number, but to solve them you must have the same number of simultaneous equations as unknowns. So if you have, say, four variables, you need four simultaneous equations to find all the values. The method of solving these larger sets of equations is essentially the same as for two equations, and you manipulate the equations until you can progressively find values. Again, this sounds complicated, but is easy to see with an example.

WORKED EXAMPLE 2.21

Solve the simultaneous equations:

$$2x + y + 2z = 10 \tag{1}$$

$$x - 2y + 3z = 2 \tag{2}$$

$$-x + y + z = 0 \tag{3}$$

Solution

You can start by using equations (2) and (3) to eliminate the variable x from equation (1):

■ Multiplying equation (2) by 2 gives:

$$2x - 4y + 6z = 4$$

Subtracting this from equation (1) gives:

$$5y - 4z = 6 \tag{4}$$

■ Multiplying equation (3) by 2 gives:

$$-2x + 2y + 2z = 0$$

Adding this to equation (1) gives:

$$3y + 4z = 10 \tag{5}$$

Now you have two equations, (4) and (5), with two unknowns, y and z, and you can solve them as before. Adding equations (4) and (5) gives:

$$8y = 16 \text{ or } y = 2$$

Substituting this value for y in equation (4) gives the value for z:

$$10 - 4z = 6 \text{ or } z = 1$$

And substituting these two values for y and z into equation (1) gives the value for x:

$$2x + 2 + 2 = 10 \text{ or } x = 3$$

Now you have $x = 3$, $y = 2$ and $z = 1$, and can confirm these values by substituting them in equations (2) and (3):

$$3 - 4 + 3 = 2 \ \checkmark \tag{2}$$

$$-3 + 2 + 1 = 0 \ \checkmark \tag{3}$$

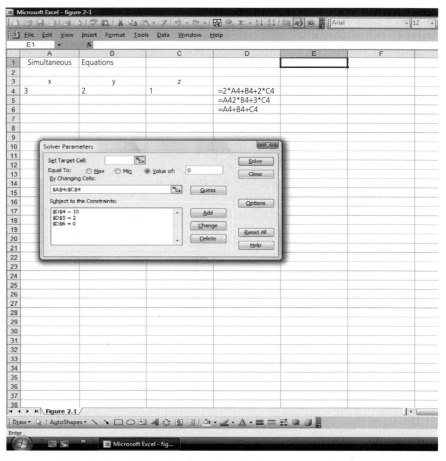

Figure 2.1 Using the Excel 'Solver' tool to solve simultaneous equations

Clearly, this kind of arithmetic manipulation gets messy and it is easier to use a computer. There are several approaches to this. One uses matrix arithmetic, which is described in the additional material given in the website for this book at **www.pearsoned.co.uk/waters**. Another uses standard software specially designed for simultaneous equations (such as UltimaCalc, Matrix ActiveX or Linear Algebra 2). A third option is to use a standard spreadsheet tool, such as 'solver' in Excel. Figure 2.1 illustrates the type of result you get when 'solver' tackles the problem above.

Review questions

2.13 What are simultaneous equations?

2.14 How many simultaneous equations would you need to find six unknown variables?

2.15 If $x + y = 5$ and $2x = 14 - 2y$, can you find values for x and y?

Powers and roots

Sometimes you want to multiply a number by itself several times. For instance, you may hear that the price of an item is doubling every year – and if its price is £1 this year, in future years its price will be £2, £4, £8, £16, £32, £64 and so on. The conventional way of describing such repeated calculations is to use a superscript – or power – to show how many times you have done the multiplication. When you multiply a variable b by itself twice you get b^2, which is described as 'b to the power 2' or 'b squared'. When you multiply b by itself three times you get b^3, which is described as 'b to the power 3' or 'b cubed'. Then:

b to the power $1 = b = b^1$
b squared $= b \times b = b^2$
b cubed $= b \times b \times b = b^3$
b to the fourth $= b \times b \times b \times b = b^4$
and in general,
b to the power $n = b \times b \times b \times \ldots (n \text{ times}) = b^n$

Taking a specific value for b, say 3, we have:

3 to the power $1 = 3^1 = 3$
3 squared $= 3 \times 3 = 3^2 = 9$
3 cubed $= 3 \times 3 \times 3 = 3^3 = 27$
3 to the fourth $= 3 \times 3 \times 3 \times 3 = 3^4 = 81$
and in general,
3 to the power $n = 3 \times 3 \times 3 \times \ldots (n \text{ times}) = 3^n$

Suppose that you want to multiply two powers together, such as $b^2 \times b^3$. You can find the result by writing the calculation in full:

$$b^2 \times b^3 = (b \times b) \times (b \times b \times b) = b \times b \times b \times b \times b = b^5$$

This illustrates the general rule that:

> When multiplying, add the powers:
>
> $b^m \times b^n = b^{m+n}$

For example, $4^2 \times 4^4 = 4^6$, which you can confirm by expanding the calculation to $4^2 \times 4^4 = 16 \times 256 = 4{,}096 = 4^6$. In passing we should mention two common errors, and emphasise that:

- $b^m + b^n$ does ***not*** equal b^{m+n} ✗
- $a^n + b^n$ does ***not*** equal $(a + b)^n$ ✗

You can check these by substituting, say, $a = 4$, $b = 3$, $m = 1$ and $n = 2$. Then:

- $b^m + b^n = 3^1 + 3^2 = 1 + 9 = 10$ which ***does not*** equal $b^{m+n} = 3^{1+2} = 3^3 = 27$
- $a^n + b^n = 4^2 + 3^2 = 16 + 9 = 25$ which ***does not*** equal $(a + b)^n = (4 + 3)^2 = 7^2 = 49$

To do a division, such as b^5 / b^2, you can again find the result by writing the calculation in full:

$$\frac{b^5}{b^2} = \frac{b \times b \times b \times b \times b}{b \times b} = b \times b \times b = b^3$$

This illustrates the general rule that:

When dividing, subtract the powers:

$$\frac{b^m}{b^n} = b^{m-n}$$

For example, $5^4 / 5^3 = 5^{4-3} = 5^1$, which you can confirm by expanding the calculation to $5^4 / 5^3 = 625 / 125 = 5 = 5^1$.

An interesting result comes when $m = n$. For example, when $m = n = 3$, then:

$$\frac{b^3}{b^3} = \frac{b \times b \times b}{b \times b \times b} = 1$$

but:

$$\frac{b^3}{b^3} = b^{3-3} = b^0$$

So $b^0 = 1$. This is a general rule that anything raised to the power 0 equals 1.

WORKED EXAMPLE 2.22

What are the values of (a) $b^4 \times b^2$, (b) $b^6 \div b^2$, (c) $b^6 - b^3$, (d) $2^3 \times 2^2$, (e) $3^4 \div 3^2$, (f) $x(1 + x)$, (g) $(b^m)^n$?

Solution
Using the rules above:

(a) $b^4 \times b^2 = b^{4+2} = b^6$
(b) $b^6 \div b^2 = b^{6-2} = b^4$
(c) Trick question! You cannot simplify $b^6 - b^3$ (and it is *not* b^{6-3}, which would be b^6 / b^3).
(d) $2^3 \times 2^2 = 2^{3+2} = 2^5$
$= 32$

(e) $3^4 \div 3^2 = 3^{4-2} = 3^2$
$= 9$
(f) We have to multiply the first x by everything inside the brackets, giving:

$$x(1 + x) = (x \times 1) + (x \times x)$$
$$= x + x^2$$

(g) To raise b^m to the power n, we multiply b^m by itself n times. But b^m is b multiplied by itself m times, so now we are multiplying b by itself mn times. This gives the general rule that $(b^m)^n = b^{mn}$.

WORKED EXAMPLE 2.23

Expand the expressions (a) $(1 + b)^2$, (b) $(y - 1)(y + 4)$, (c) $(1 + a)(1 - a)$.

Solution
(a) The square applies to the whole bracket, so:

$$(1 + b)^2 = (1 + b) \times (1 + b)$$

which we can expand to give:

$$1(1 + b) + b(1 + b) = (1 + b) + (b + b^2)$$
$$= 1 + 2b + b^2$$

(b) We have to multiply everything inside the first brackets by everything inside the second brackets, giving:

$$(y - 1)(y + 4) = y(y + 4) - 1(y + 4)$$
$$= y^2 + 4y - y - 4$$
$$= y^2 + 3y - 4$$

(c) Again we multiply everything inside the first brackets by everything inside the second brackets:

$$(1 + a)(1 - a) = 1(1 - a) + a(1 - a)$$
$$= 1 - a + a - a^2$$
$$= 1 - a^2$$

Negative and fractional powers

The rule of division says that $b^m / b^n = b^{m-n}$, but what happens when n is bigger than m? If, say, $n = 4$ and $m = 2$, we get $b^m / b^n = b^2 / b^4 = b^{2-4} = b^{-2}$ and we have to interpret a negative power. To do this we can expand the calculation:

$$\frac{b^2}{b^4} = \frac{b \times b}{b \times b \times b \times b} = \frac{1}{b^2}$$

So $b^{-2} = 1/b^2$, which illustrates the general rule:

$$b^{-n} = \frac{1}{b^n}$$

One final point about raising to powers concerns fractional powers, such as $b^{1/2}$. You can see how to interpret this from the work that we have already done. If you square $b^{1/2}$ you get:

$$b^{1/2} \times b^{1/2} = b^{1/2+1/2}$$
$$= b^1$$
$$= b$$

When you multiply $b^{1/2}$ by itself you get b. But by definition, the number that you multiply by itself to give b is the square root of b. So $b^{1/2}$ must be the square root of b, which we write as $\sqrt{b}$. Now we have:

$$b^{0.5} = b^{1/2}$$
$$= \sqrt{b}$$

In the same way we can show that:

- $b^{0.33} = b^{1/3}$ which is the cube root of b (the number that gives b when multiplied by itself three times)
- $b^{0.25} = b^{1/4}$ which is the fourth root of b (the number that gives b when multiplied by itself four times)
- and so on.

We can extend this reasoning to more complex fractional powers. For example:

$$b^{1.5} = b^{3/2} = (b^{1/2})^3$$
$$= (\sqrt{b})^3$$
$$b^{2.5} = b^{5/2} = (b^{1/2})^5$$
$$= (\sqrt{b})^5$$

WORKED EXAMPLE 2.24

What are the values of (a) $1/b^4$, (b) $b^5 \times b^{1/2}$, (c) $25^{1/2}$, (d) $9^{1.5}$, (e) $8^{0.67}$?

Solution

Using the standard rules:

(a) $1/b^4 = b^{-4}$

(b) $b^5 \times b^{1/2} = b^{5+1/2} = b^{5.5} = b^{11/2} = (b^{1/2})^{11}$
$= (\sqrt{b})^{11}$

(c) $25^{1/2} = \sqrt{25}$
$= 5$

(d) $9^{1.5} = 9^{3/2} = (9^{1/2})^3 = (\sqrt{9})^3 = 3^3$
$= 27$

(e) $8^{0.67} = 8^{2/3} = (8^{1/3})^2 = 2^2$
$= 4$

WORKED EXAMPLE 2.25

If you leave £100 in the bank earning 6% interest, at the end of n years you will have £100 $\times$ 1.06^n (we discuss this in Chapter 8). How much will you have at the end of each of the next 10 years?

Solution

We could do these calculations separately:

- at the end of the first year you have 100×1.06^1 = £106
- at the end of the second year you have $100 \times 1.06^2 = 100 \times 1.1236 = £112.36$,
- and so on.

However, it is much easier to use a spreadsheet for this kind of repeated calculation. Figure 2.2(a)

shows the results for this example, while Figure 2.2(b) shows the formulae used in the calculations. Notice that calculations in spreadsheets do not use superscripts, so you have to use the symbol ^ to raise something to a power. Then a^b becomes a^b, 3^2 becomes 3^2, and 5 raised to the power -2 becomes 5^-2. (Alternatively, you can use the standard spreadsheet function POWER(a,b) which finds a^b.)

The calculation in, say, cell B10 finds 1.06^2. For this it takes the interest rate in cell B3, divides it by 100 and adds 1 to get 1.06; raising this to the power in cell A10 gives 1.06^2 and multiplying this by the £100 in cell B5 gives the value at the end of the second year in cell C10.

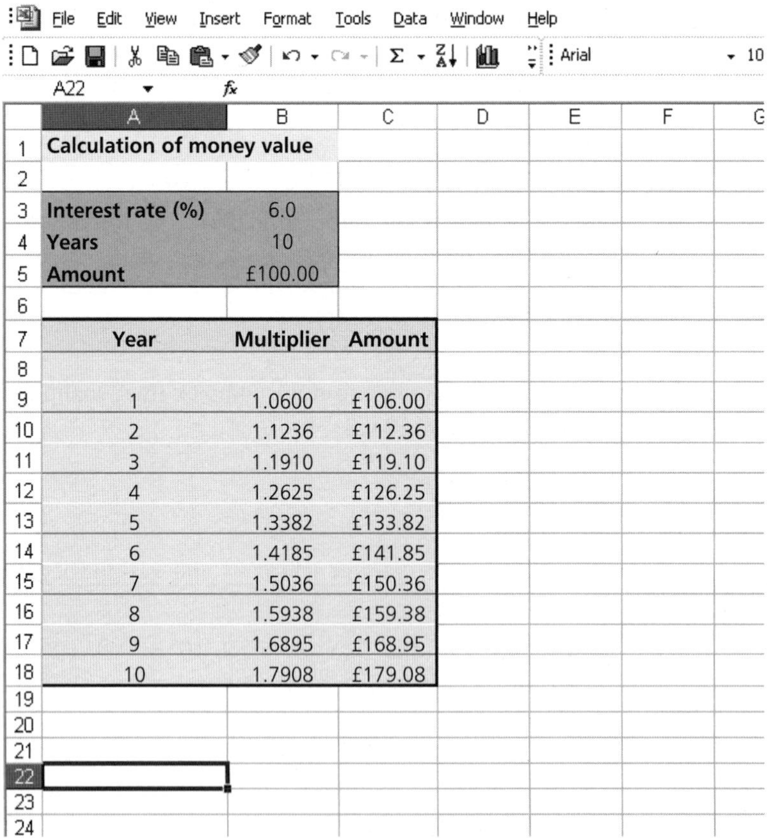

	A	B	C	D	E	F	G
1	**Calculation of money value**						
2							
3	**Interest rate (%)**	6.0					
4	**Years**	10					
5	**Amount**	£100.00					
6							
7	**Year**	**Multiplier**	**Amount**				
8							
9	1	1.0600	£106.00				
10	2	1.1236	£112.36				
11	3	1.1910	£119.10				
12	4	1.2625	£126.25				
13	5	1.3382	£133.82				
14	6	1.4185	£141.85				
15	7	1.5036	£150.36				
16	8	1.5938	£159.38				
17	9	1.6895	£168.95				
18	10	1.7908	£179.08				
19							
20							
21							
22							
23							
24							

Figure 2.2(a) Spreadsheet giving the results for Worked example 2.25

Worked example 2.25 continued

	A	B	C	D
1	**Calculation of money value**			
2				
3	**Interest rate (%)**	6		
4	**Years**	10		
5	**Amount**	100		
6				
7	**Year**	**Multiplier**	**Amount**	
8				
9	1	=(1+(B3)/100)^A9	=B9*B5	
10	2	=(1+(B3)/100)^A10	=B10*B5	
11	3	=(1+(B3)/100)^A11	=B11*B5	
12	4	=(1+(B3)/100)^A12	=B12*B5	
13	5	=(1+(B3)/100)^A13	=B13*B5	
14	6	=(1+(B3)/100)^A14	=B14*B5	
15	7	=(1+(B3)/100)^A15	=B15*B5	
16	8	=(1+(B3)/100)^A16	=B16*B5	
17	9	=(1+(B3)/100)^A17	=B17*B5	
18	10	=(1+(B3)/100)^A18	=B18*B5	

Figure 2.2(b) Formulae for the calculations in Worked example 2.25

Scientific notation

We can use powers to give a convenient notation for very large and very small numbers. This is scientific notation which is used in many calculators, and describes numbers in the format:

$$a \times 10^b$$

where

- a is a number between 1 and 10 (or −1 and −10 for negative numbers)
- b is a power of 10.

This notation uses the fact that $10^1 = 10$, $10^2 = 100$, $10^3 = 1000$, and so on. Then we can describe a number such as 120 by 1.2×100, which is 1.2×10^2. Similarly:

- $12 = 1.2 \times 10$
  $= 1.2 \times 10^1$
- $1{,}200 = 1.2 \times 1{,}000$
  $= 1.2 \times 10^3$
- $12{,}000 = 1.2 \times 10{,}000$
  $= 1.2 \times 10^4$

- 1,380,197.892 is about 1.38×10^6
- The UK's annual exports are about $£3.9 \times 10^{11}$.

You find b, the power of 10, by counting the number of places to the left that the decimal point has to move. For example, with 15,762 the decimal point moves four places to the left, so 10 is raised to the power 4, giving 1.5762×10^4.

We can use the same notation to describe very small numbers, using the fact that $10^{-1} = 0.1$, $10^{-2} = 0.01$, $10^{-3} = 0.001$, and so on. Then we can take a number like 0.0012 and describe it as 1.2×0.001, which is 1.2×10^{-3}. Similarly:

- $0.12 = 1.2 \times 0.1$
    $= 1.2 \times 10^{-1}$
- $0.012 = 1.2 \times 0.01$
    $= 1.2 \times 10^{-2}$
- $0.000012 = 1.2 \times 0.00001$
    $= 1.2 \times 10^{-5}$
- $0.00000429 = 4.29 \times 0.000001$
    $= 4.29 \times 10^{-6}$.

Here you find the power of 10 by counting the number of places to the *right* that the decimal point has to move. For example, with 0.0057 the decimal point moves three places to the right, so the 10 is raised to the power −3, giving 5.7×10^{-3}.

WORKED EXAMPLE 2.26

Use scientific notation for (a) 123,000, (b) two million, (c) 0.05, (d) 0.000123.

Solution
The key thing is to count the number of places the decimal point has to move – if it moves to the left the power is positive; if it moves to the right the power is negative. Then:

(a) $123,000 = 1.23 \times 10^5$
(b) two million $= 2,000,000$
    $= 2 \times 10^6$
(c) $0.05 = 5 \times 10^{-2}$
(d) $0.000123 = 1.23 \times 10^{-4}$

When computers use scientific notation they often use a slightly different convention. In particular, the '×10' is replaced by the letter E, and this is followed by the power that 10 is raised to. So 2×10^4 becomes 2E+04, 1.23×10^5 appears as 1.23E+05, and 4.56×10^{-4} becomes 4.56E–04.

Logarithms and the exponential function

One other format for numbers uses logarithms. Until calculators appeared, these were the easiest way of doing some calculations, and they are still the best way of solving certain types of problem. However, they are now used far less frequently than in the past.

When we write $8 = 2^3$ we are representing one number (8) by a second number (2) raised to a power (3). This is a surprisingly useful format, with the general form:

$$n = b^p$$

The second number, b, is called the base, and the power, p, is called the logarithm (usually abbreviated to 'log'). So the logarithm of a number is the power to which you raise the base to give the number. This is a messy statement, but you can see how it works from these examples.

- $16 = 2^4$, so the logarithm to the base 2 of 16 is 4, which means that you raise the base 2 to the power 4 to give 16. We normally write this as $\log_2 16 = 4$.
- $9 = 3^2$, so the logarithm to the base 3 of 9 is 2, which means that we raise the base 3 to the power 2 to give 9, and we write this as $\log_3 9 = 2$.
- $10^3 = 1,000$, so the logarithm to the base 10 of 1,000 is 3, which we write as $\log_{10} 1,000 = 3$.

When:

$$n = b^p$$

then:

$$p = \log_b n$$

In practice, only two types of logarithm are used much:

- Common logarithms use the base 10, so that:

$$y = \log x \quad \text{means that} \quad x = 10^y$$

If you do not explicitly put in the base of the logarithm, it is assumed to be 10.

- Natural logarithms use the base e, which is the exponential constant. It seems very strange to use this number, which equals 2.7182818 and is calculated from $(1 + 1/n)^n$, where n is a very large number. However, it appears surprisingly often when, for example, you want to describe random events, exponential growth or exponential decline. We meet it several times in later chapters, but for now we will simply say that natural logarithms are written as:

$$y = \ln x \quad \text{meaning that} \quad x = e^y$$

WORKED EXAMPLE 2.27

What are the values of (a) $\log_2 32$, (b) log 1,000, (c) ln 2?

Solution

(a) $\log_2 32$ is the power to which you raise the base 2 to give 32. As $2^5 = 32$, this power is 5 and $\log_2 32 = 5$. You can confirm this using the LOG function in Excel; this has the format LOG(number,base), so LOG(32,2) returns the value 5.

(b) log 1,000 is a common logarithm, and is the power to which you raise 10 to give 1,000. As $10^3 = 1,000$, this is 3 and log 1,000 = 3. You can confirm this using the LOG10 function in Excel; this has the format LOG10(number), so LOG10(1,000) and LOG(1,000,10) both return the value 3.

(c) ln 2 is a natural logarithm, and is the power to which we raise e to give 2. There is no easy way to calculate this, but you can find it from the LN(number) function in Excel; this has the format LN(number), so LN(2) and LOG(2,2.7182818) both return the value 0.6931, meaning that $e^{0.6931} = 2$.

You probably think that the whole notation of logarithms is rather obscure – and it is certainly less relevant now that we use computers. However, they can still simplify some calculations and solve problems where numbers are raised to unknown powers.

WORKED EXAMPLE 2.28

If $2^x = 32$, use logarithms to find the value of x.

Solution

When a number is raised to an unknown power, the only way that you can find the power is to use logarithms. When $n = b^p$, then $p = \log_b n$, so we can rewrite $2^x = 32$ as $x = \log_2 32$. But in Worked example 2.7 we found that $\log_2 32 = 5$, so the result is $x = 5$, which you can check by doing the calculation.

Review questions

2.16 Rank in order of size $4^{1/2}$, 4^{-1}, 4^1, 1^4, $(\frac{1}{2})^{-4}$ and $(\frac{1}{2})^4$.

2.17 What is the value of $x^{1.5} / y^{2.5}$ when $x = 9$ and $y = 4$?

2.18 What is the value of 41.1635^0?

2.19 Write 1,230,000,000 and 0.000000253 in scientific notation.

2.20 What is a logarithm and when would you use one?

IDEAS IN PRACTICE Canada Revenue Agency

Benjamin Franklin said, 'In this world nothing can be said to be certain, except death and taxes'.[1] Governments in most countries use similar calculations to assess income tax, and we can illustrate this with the calculations done in Canada. Every Canadian citizen completes an income tax return for each financial year. In principle, the calculations are fairly straightforward, but most people find them both arduous and traumatic. Canada Revenue Agency describes the steps as follows:

1 Calculate total income for the tax year – which includes most income but with some exceptions such as child tax credit, veterans' disability allowance, lottery winnings and welfare payments.
2 Calculate taxable income – by subtracting payments for pension plans and other allowed expenses from the total income.
3 Find the gross federal tax – which is taxable income × tax rate. There are higher tax rates for higher incomes, so this calculation has to include amounts paid in each tax band.
4 Calculate tax credits – which are individual tax credits that give a personal allowance, and further allowances for children, education fees, medical expenses and other allowed expenses.
5 Find the basic federal tax – by subtracting the tax credits from the gross federal tax and adding any adjustments for foreign earnings.
6 Add federal surtax – when the basic federal tax is above a certain limit, a percentage of the amount over this limit is added as a federal surtax.
7 Add the provincial tax – which is a proportion of the federal tax.
8 Add provincial surtax – when the provincial tax is above a certain limit, a percentage of the amount over this limit is added as a provincial surtax.
9 Subtract tax that has already been paid – usually from pay cheques or advances.
10 This gives the total amount payable or to be refunded.

This is clearly a simplified description, but you can see that – like many aspects of business and life in general – it depends on a lot of calculations. Not surprisingly, there is a thriving business for accountants who help people to fill in their returns.

Sources: Websites at www.cra-arc.gc.ca and www.statcan.ca. Federal and Provincial General Tax Guide and Returns, CRA, Ottawa.

CHAPTER REVIEW

This chapter reviewed some of the basic tools that are needed to understand later chapters.

- All quantitative reasoning is based on numbers. These appear in different forms, including integers, decimals, fractions and percentages.

- Numbers are used in arithmetic, where there are standard rules for raising to powers, multiplication, division, addition and subtraction.

- Algebra is based on the use of abbreviated names for constants and variables.

- These names are used in equations of the form $a = b$ to give precise and general descriptions of relationships. An equation remains true when you do the same thing to both sides.

- You solve an equation by using known values to find a previously unknown value for a constant or variable. To do this, you rearrange the equation until the unknown value is on one side of the equals sign, and all the known values are on the other side.

- Inequalities give less precise descriptions of relationships, typically of the form $a < b$. You handle these in the same way as equations, but have to be careful with the direction of the sign when multiplying or dividing by a negative number.

- You can use a set of simultaneous equations to find the values of several unknown variables. In particular, to find n unknown variables you need n independent, simultaneous equations.

- You can solve simultaneous equations algebraically using either substitution or a process of elimination. For complex problems it is always easier to use computers, either using specialised software or the appropriate tools in a spreadsheet.

- Superscripts show that a value is raised to a particular power – or multiplied by itself this number of times. There are standard rules for manipulating powers.

- Scientific notation describes a number in the format $a \times 10^b$.

- A logarithm is defined as the power to which a base is raised to equal a number. When $n = b^p$, then $p = \log_b n$. Common logarithms use the base 10, while natural logarithms use the base e.

If you want to learn more about any point mentioned in this chapter, you can look at a more detailed book on mathematics. Some of these are listed in the further reading list at the end of the chapter.

CASE STUDY **The Crown and Anchor**

Tina Jones runs the Crown and Anchor pub in Middleton, along with her husband and staff of eight. The riverside pub has a core of local customers, but half of its business depends on tourists and passing trade. In recent years, the pub has expanded its sales of food, and this has become an increasingly important source of income. Now Tina wants to make some improvements to the dining room and hopes that the bank will lend her the money. She is sure that the improvements will increase profits and wants to make a good case to her bank manager.

Tina has kept a record of the average number of meals served each day over the past two years, and the daily income from food (Table below). Now she wants to do some work on these figures and present them in a convincing way. Of course, her sales depend on a number of factors. Some of these are under her control, such as the menu, quantity of food, quality of cooking and serving, etc. Some are outside her control, such as the trends in eating out, national income, and local unemployment. She wants to include all of these factors in a report to the bank manager.

	Year 1			Year 2		
	Dinners	Lunches	Income (£)	Dinners	Lunches	Income (£)
January	25	6	180	32	30	441
February	23	6	178	30	25	405
March	24	8	196	31	24	415
April	26	9	216	32	26	440
May	27	9	230	35	30	463
June	42	32	525	45	35	572
July	48	36	605	51	38	590
August	48	37	603	50	45	638
September	35	34	498	38	41	580
October	31	30	451	35	36	579
November	30	31	464	32	35	508
December	37	38	592	48	54	776

Question

■ **What do you think Tina should put in her report? How can she use the figures that she has collected – or other figures that are publicly available? What other information should she collect?**

PROBLEMS

2.1 What are the values of (a) -12×8, (b) $-35 / (-7)$, (c) $(24 - 8) \times (4 + 5)$, (d) $(18 - 4) / (3 + 9 - 5)$, (e) $(22/11) \times (-18 + 3) / (12/4)$?

2.2 Simplify the common fractions (a) $3/5 + 1/2$, (b) $3/4 \times 1/6$, (c) $3/4 - 1/8$, (d) $-18/5 \div 6/25$, (e) $(3/8 - 1/6) \div 4/7$.

2.3 What are the answers to problem **2.2** as decimal fractions?

2.4 What is (a) 23/40 as a percentage, (b) 65% as a fraction, (c) 17% as a decimal, (d) 12% of 74, (e) 27 as a percentage of 85?

2.5 What is 1,037 / 14 to (a) three decimal places, (b) one decimal place, (c) two significant figures, (d) one significant figure?

2.6 In one exam 64 people passed and 23 failed; in a second exam 163 people passed and 43 failed. How could you compare the pass rates?

2.7 A car travels 240 kilometres in three hours. What is its average speed? What is the equation for the average speed of a car on any journey?

2.8 Shopkeepers buy an item from a wholesaler and sell it to customers. How would you build a model to describe their profit?

2.9 Logan Bay School has £1,515 to spend on footballs. Match balls cost £35 each, and practice balls cost £22 each. The school must buy 60 balls each year, so how many of each type should it buy to exactly match the budget?

2.10 Sanderson Bhp finds that 30% of its costs are direct labour. Each week raw materials cost €2,000 more than twice this amount, and there is an overhead of 20% of direct labour costs. What are the company's weekly costs?

2.11 Lun Ho Stadium sells 2,200 tickets for a concert. It sells a quarter of them at a 20% discount and a further 10% at a 40% discount. How much must it charge for tickets if it wants to generate an income of $40,000?

2.12 Mario bought a round of five beers and three glasses of wine in a bar. He paid with a €20 note and noticed that his change contained at least one euro coin. He thought that each beer costs more than €2, so what can he say about the price of a glass of wine?

2.13 What can you say if (a) $3x + 4 \geq 6x - 3$, (b) $2x + 7 > 13 > 3x - 4$?

2.14 Solve these simultaneous equations:
(a) $a + b = 3$ and $a - b = 5$
(b) $2x + 3y = 27$ and $3x + 2y = 23$
(c) $2x + 2y + 4z = 24$ and $6x + 3y = 15$ and $y + 2z = 11$
(d) $x + y - 2z = -2$ and $2x - y + z = 9$ and $x + 3y + 2z = 4$
(e) $4r - 2s + 3t = 12$ and $r + 2s + t = -1$ and $3r - s - t = -5$

2.15 Sven Hendriksson finds that one of his productivity measures is related to the number of employees, e, and the production, n, by the equations:

$$10n + 3e = 45 \quad \text{and} \quad 2n + 5e = 31$$

What are the current values for e and n?

2.16 What are the values of (a) $x^{1/2} \times x^{1/4}$, (b) $(x^{1/3})^3$, (c) $9^{0.5}$, (d) $4^{2.5}$, (e) $7^{3.2}$, (f) $4^{1.5} \times 6^{3.7} / 6^{1.7}$?

2.17 If $\log a = 0.3010$, $\log b = 0.4771$ and $\log c = 0.6021$, what is the value of $\log (ab/c)$? Can you use this result to find some general rules for arithmetic with logarithms?

2.18 If $3,000 = 1,500 \times 1.1^n$, what is the value of n?

RESEARCH PROJECTS

2.1 Companies' annual reports show a lot of quantitative information. This usually goes beyond basic accounts and includes operational, environmental, social and competitive performance. Examine the report of a major company and describe the quantitative analyses that it contains. (You can find some useful information in company websites.)

2.2 Jefferson Young & Co. is a manufacturer of automotive components. Over the past 14 months, they have collected information about production, income and costs. They keep this information in a simple spreadsheet, with the format shown in Figure 2.3. Describe how this spreadsheet works and what it shows. What else could they do with the data? What other features do you think they should add to the spreadsheet?

2.3 A lot of websites give tutorials on various topics of mathematics that are useful for managers. These are produced by universities, professional institutions, publishers, training companies, software providers, tutoring services, consultants and so on. Do some searches on the Web to find sites that are useful for this book.

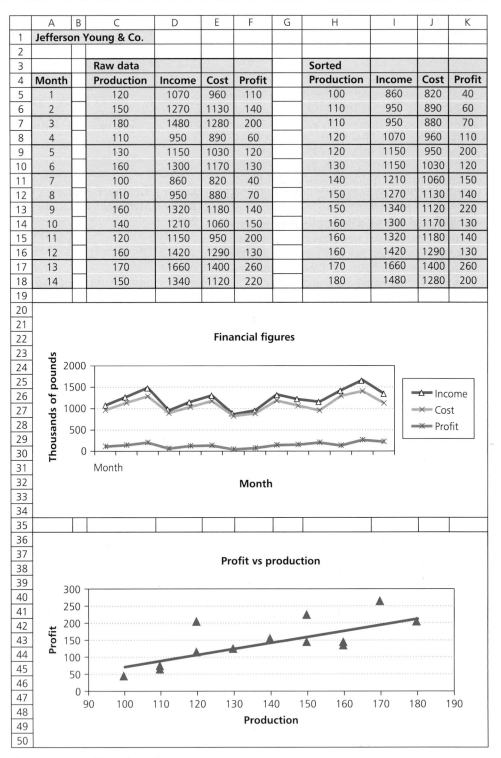

	A	B	C	D	E	F	G	H	I	J	K
1	Jefferson Young & Co.										
2											
3			Raw data					Sorted			
4	Month		Production	Income	Cost	Profit		Production	Income	Cost	Profit
5	1		120	1070	960	110		100	860	820	40
6	2		150	1270	1130	140		110	950	890	60
7	3		180	1480	1280	200		110	950	880	70
8	4		110	950	890	60		120	1070	960	110
9	5		130	1150	1030	120		120	1150	950	200
10	6		160	1300	1170	130		130	1150	1030	120
11	7		100	860	820	40		140	1210	1060	150
12	8		110	950	880	70		150	1270	1130	140
13	9		160	1320	1180	140		150	1340	1120	220
14	10		140	1210	1060	150		160	1300	1170	130
15	11		120	1150	950	200		160	1320	1180	140
16	12		160	1420	1290	130		160	1420	1290	130
17	13		170	1660	1400	260		170	1660	1400	260
18	14		150	1340	1120	220		180	1480	1280	200
19											

Figure 2.3 Spreadsheet for Jefferson Young & Co.

Sources of information

Reference

1 Letter to Jean Baptiste le Roy, 13th November 1789, published in *Works of Benjamin Franklin*, 1817.

Further reading

Many books introduce the ideas of mathematics, ranging from the trivial through to the very difficult. If you want some further information, the following list gives some useful ideas.

Amdahl K. and Loats J., *Algebra Unplugged*, Clearwater Publishing, Broomfield, CO, 1996.

Barlow J., *Excel Models for Business and Operations Management* (2nd edition), John Wiley, Chichester, 2005.

Bradley T. and Patton P., *Essential Mathematics for Economics and Business*, John Wiley, Chichester, 2002.

Eaton G., *Fundamentals of Business Maths*, CIMA Publications, London, 2009.

Economist, Numbers Guide: Essential Business Numeracy, Economist Books, London, 2003.

Francis A., *Business Maths and Statistics*, Thomson Learning, London, 2004.

Gibilisco S., *Algebra Know-It-All*, McGraw Hill, New York, 2008.

Gough L., *The Financial Times Guide to Business Numeracy*, FT Prentice Hall, Basingstoke, 1994.

Jacques I., *Mathematics for Economics and Business* (5th edition), FT Prentice Hall, Basingstoke, 2006.

Lerner J. and Don E., *Schaum's Outline of Basic Business Mathematics*, McGraw-Hill, New York, 2000.

Rowe N., *Refresher in Basic Maths* (2nd edition), Thomson Learning, London, 2001.

Soper J., *Mathematics for Economics and Business* (2nd edition), Blackwell, Oxford, 2004.

Sterling M.J., *Business Math for Dummies*, John Wiley, Chichester, 2008.

Useful websites

www.pearsoned.co.uk/waters – the companion website for this book. This contains a list of useful websites.

Drawing graphs

Chapter outline

Graphs give a lot of information in a simple and effective format. This chapter shows how to draw line graphs on Cartesian coordinates. We start with simple linear graphs, and then move on to more complicated functions, including quadratic equations, higher polynomials and exponential curves. We return to this theme in Chapter 5, when we discuss other types of diagram for presenting information.

After finishing this chapter you should be able to:

- appreciate the benefits of graphs
- use Cartesian coordinates to draw graphs
- draw straight-line graphs and interpret the results
- draw graphs of quadratic equations and calculate the roots
- draw graphs of more complicated curves, including polynomials and exponential curves
- use graphs to solve simultaneous equations.

Graphs on Cartesian coordinates

Chapter 2 showed how to build an algebraic model of a situation. However, when given a set of equations, most people find it difficult to understand what is happening, or to follow the logic. Diagrams are much better at presenting information, and you can look at a well-drawn diagram and quickly see its main features. We develop this theme in Chapter 5, but here we introduce the idea of a graph – sometimes called a line graph – to show the relationship between two variables.

Cartesian axes

The most common type of graph uses two rectangular (or Cartesian) axes. A horizontal axis is traditionally labelled x, and a vertical axis is labelled y (as shown in Figure 3.1). Then x is the independent variable, which is the one that we can set or control, and y is the corresponding dependent variable, whose value is set by x. Then x might be the amount we spend on advertising (which we control) and y the resulting sales (which we cannot control); x might be the interest rate that we charge for lending money, and y the corresponding amount borrowed; x might be the price we charge for a service, and y the resulting demand.

When we talk about dependent and independent variables, we do not assume any cause and effect. There might be a clear relationship between two variables, but this does not necessarily mean that a change in one actually causes a change in the other. For example, a department store might notice that when it reduces the price of overcoats the sales of ice cream rise. There is a clear relationship between the price of overcoats and the sales of ice cream, but one does not *cause* the other – and both are really a result of the prevailing

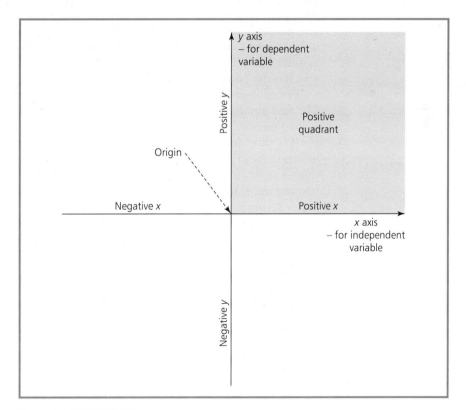

Figure 3.1 Cartesian axes

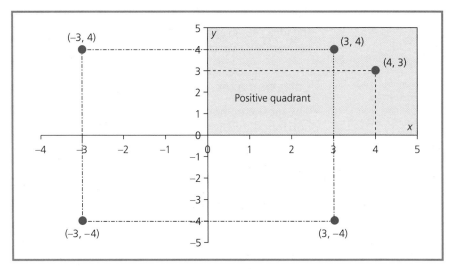

Figure 3.2 Locating points with Cartesian coordinates

weather. Unfortunately, people do not always recognise this, and they imagine ridiculous causes-and-effects (which we discuss in Chapter 9).

The point where the two axes cross is the origin. This is the point where both x and y have the value zero. At any point above the origin y is positive, and at any point below it y is negative; at any point to the right of the origin x is positive, and at any point to the left of it x is negative. Often, we are only interested in positive values of x and y – perhaps with a graph of income against sales. Then we show only the top right-hand corner of the graph, which is the positive quadrant.

We can describe any point on a graph by two numbers called coordinates. The first number gives the distance along the x-axis from the origin, and the second number gives the distance up the y-axis. For example, the point $x = 3$, $y = 4$ is three units along the x-axis and four units up the y-axis. A standard notation describes coordinates as (x, y) – so this is point $(3, 4)$. The only thing you have to be careful about is that $(3, 4)$ is not the same as $(4, 3)$, as you can see in Figure 3.2. And these points are some way from $(-3, 4)$, $(3, -4)$ and $(-3, -4)$.

Points on the x-axis have coordinates $(x, 0)$ and points on the y-axis have coordinates $(0, y)$. The origin is the point where the axes cross; it has co-ordinates $(0, 0)$.

WORKED EXAMPLE 3.1

Plot these points on a graph.

x	2	5	7	10	12	15
y	7	20	22	28	41	48

Solution

As all the numbers are positive, we need draw only the positive quadrant. Then the first point, (2, 7), is 2 units along the x-axis and 7 units up the y-axis, and is shown as point A in Figure 3.3. The

Worked example 3.1 continued

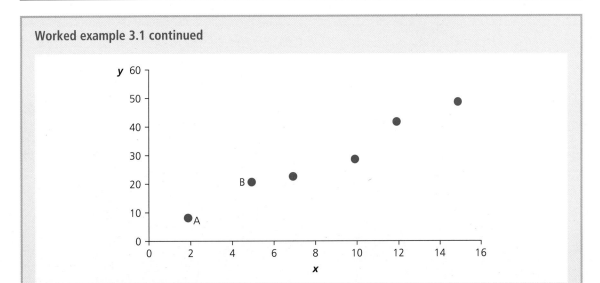

Figure 3.3 Graph of points for Worked example 3.1

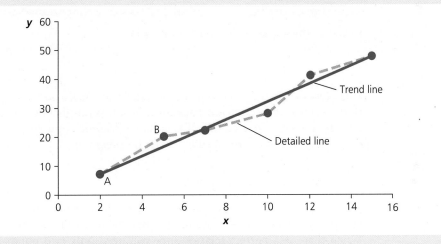

Figure 3.4 Connecting points to emphasise the relationship

second point, (5, 20), is 5 units along the *x*-axis and 20 units up the *y*-axis, and is shown by point B. Adding the other points in the same way gives the result shown in Figure 3.3.

There is a clear relationship between *x* and *y*, and we can emphasise this by drawing a line through the points. We might decide to show all the details by drawing a line connecting each point , or we can draw a straight line through the points to emphasise the general trend (shown in Figure 3.4).

You might like drawing graphs in the traditional way, by hand on graph paper – but it is easier and more reliable to use a specialised graphics packages. Many of these are available, such as ConceptDraw, CorelDRAW, DrawPlus, Freelance Graphics, Harvard Graphics, PowerPoint, Sigmaplot,

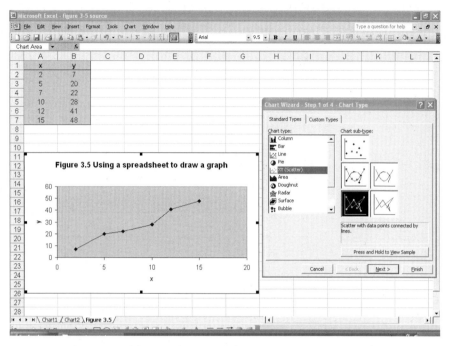

Figure 3.5 Using a spreadsheet to draw a graph

SmartDraw, Visio and so on. Many other packages also have graphics functions, such as presentation packages, desktop publishing packages, design packages and picture editors. Excel has a graphics function, and Figure 3.5 shows an example of the results when you press the 'chart wizard' button.

Drawing straight-line graphs

The simplest type of graph shows a straight line through a set of points – so you plot a series of points (x, y) and then draw a straight line through them. When there is a perfect relationship, you need only two points to draw this kind of graph. We can illustrate this by drawing a graph in which y has a constant value whatever the value of x. For instance, if $y = 10$ for all values of x, then we can take two arbitrary values of x, say 2 and 14, and get the two points (2, 10) and (14, 10). Then drawing a straight line through these points gives a line that is 10 units above the y-axis and parallel to it, as shown in Figure 3.6.

In general, a graph of $y = c$, where c is any constant, is a straight line that is parallel to the x-axis and c units above it. This line divides the area of the graph into three zones:

- at any point *on* the line, y is equal to the constant, so $y = c$
- at any point *above* the line, y is greater than c, so $y > c$
- at any point *below* the line, y is less than c, so $y < c$

We could equally say:

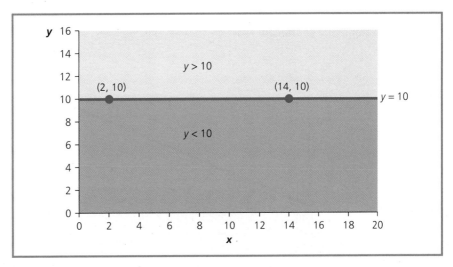

Figure 3.6 Straight-line graph of $y = 10$

- at any point *on or above* the line, y is greater than or equal to c, so $y \geq c$
- at any point *on or below* the line, y is less than or equal to c, so $y \leq c$.

The graph of $y = c$ is a straight line, and any relationship that gives a straight-line graph is called a linear relationship. Most linear graphs are not parallel to the x-axis, but they either slope upwards or downwards. For example, the time needed for a train journey (y) rises with the length of the journey (x), giving a graph that slopes upwards to the right. All linear relationship have the general form:

$y = ax + b$

where:

- x and y are the independent and dependent variables
- a and b are constants.

WORKED EXAMPLE 3.2

Draw a graph of $y = 10x + 50$.

Solution
This is a straight-line graph of the standard form $y = ax + b$, with $a = 10$ and $b = 50$. We need only two points to draw the line and can take any convenient ones. For instance, we can arbitrarily take the points where $x = 0$ and $x = 20$.

- When $x = 0$, $y = 10x + 50 = 10 \times 0 + 50 = 50$, which defines the point (0, 50).
- When $x = 20$, $y = 10x + 50 = 10 \times 20 + 50 = 250$, which defines the point (20, 250).

Plotting these points and drawing a line through them gives the graph shown in Figure 3.7.

Worked example 3.2 continued

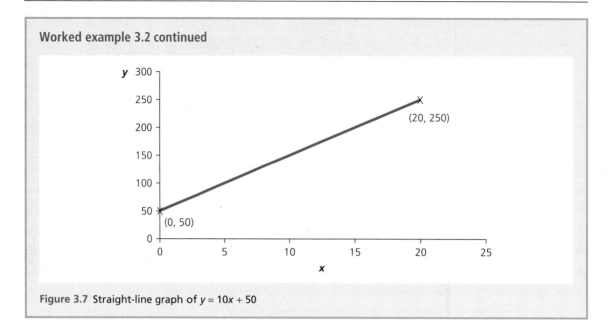

Figure 3.7 Straight-line graph of $y = 10x + 50$

When you look at a straight-line graph, there are two obvious features:

- the intercept, which shows where the line crosses the y-axis
- the gradient, which shows how steep the line is.

When the line crosses the y-axis, x has the value 0. And if you substitute $x = 0$ into the equation $y = ax + b$, you see that $ax = 0$, so $y = b$. In other words, the constant b is the intercept of the line on the y-axis.

The gradient of a line shows how quickly it is rising (or falling), and is defined as the change in y for a unit change in x. The gradient of a straight line is clearly the same at any point, so we can find the increase in y when x increases from, say, n to $n + 1$:

- when $x = n$, $y = ax + b$
$$= an + b$$
- when $x = n + 1$, $y = ax + b = a(n + 1) + b$
$$= an + a + b.$$

The difference between these two is a, and this shows that an increase of 1 in x gives an increase of a in y. So the constant a is the gradient, meaning that the general equation for a straight line is:

$y = \text{gradient} \times x + \text{intercept}$

WORKED EXAMPLE 3.3

Describe the graph of the equation $y = 4x + 20$.

Solution

This is a straight-line graph with intercept of 20 and gradient of 4, as shown in Figure 3.8.

You can also see that:

- for any point actually on the line, $y = 4x + 20$
- for any point above the line, $y > 4x + 20$
- for any point below the line, $y < 4x + 20$.

You can check this by taking any arbitrary points. For example, when $x = 10$ the corresponding value of y on the line is $y = 4 \times 10 + 20 = 60$, giving the point P at (10, 60). The point Q has coordinates (10, 100) and is above the line, and y is clearly greater than $4x + 20 = 60$; the point R has co-ordinates (10, 20) and is below the line, and y is clearly less than $4x + 20$.

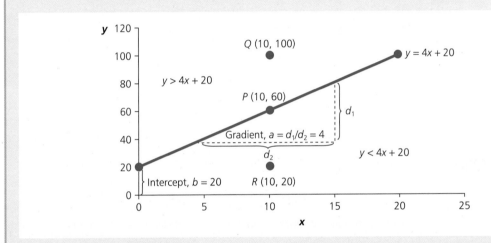

Figure 3.8 Straight-line graph of $y = 4x + 20$

WORKED EXAMPLE 3.4

Anita has noticed that the sales of a product vary with its price, and in particular:

sales = 100 − 5 × price

What are sales when the price is 6?

Solution

Substituting the price, 6, into the equation gives sales of $100 − 5 \times 6 = 70$. But we can find more information from a graph. The relationship is a straight line with the equation $y = ax + b$, where y is the sales, x is the price, a is the gradient of −5, and b is the intercept of 100. The negative gradient shows that y decreases as x increases – and

with every unit increase in price, sales fall by 5. To draw the graph (shown in Figure 3.9) we take two arbitrary points, say $x = 0$ and $x = 10$:

- when $x = 0$, $y = 100 − 5x = 100 − 5 \times 0 = 100$, giving the point (0, 100)
- when $x = 10$, $y = 100 − 5x = 100 − 5 \times 10 = 50$, giving the point (10, 50).

There is an upper limit on sales, given by the intercept – and when the price is reduced to zero the expected sales are limited to 100. Any point above the line shows that sales are higher than expected, while any point below shows that they are lower.

Worked example 3.4 continued

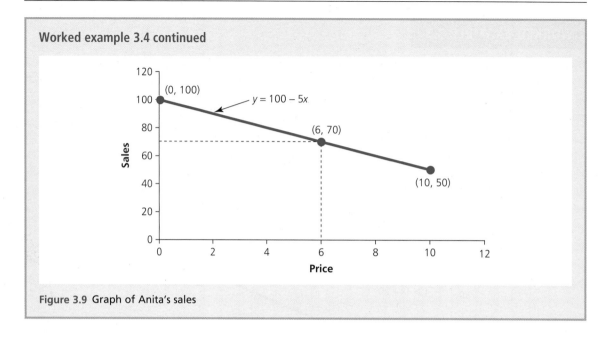

Figure 3.9 Graph of Anita's sales

Review questions   3.1   What is meant by a dependent variable?

3.2   Graphs show the changes in y caused by changes in x. Is this true?

3.3   With Cartesian coordinates, what are the coordinates of the origin?

3.4   Is there a difference between the points (3, −4) and (−3, 4)?

3.5   Describe the graph of the equation $y = -2x - 4$.

3.6   What are the gradients of the lines (a) $y = 10$, (b) $y = x$, (c) $y = 10 - 6x$?

3.7   If $y = 3x + 5$, what can you say about all the points above the graph of this line?

Quadratic equations

Any relationship between variables that is not linear is – not surprisingly – called a non-linear relationship. These have more complicated graphs, but we can draw them using the approach that we used for straight lines, which is to:

- take a series of convenient values for x
- substitute them into the equation to find corresponding values for y
- draw a line through the points.

The only concern is that more complicated relationships need more points to show the exact shape of the curve.

WORKED EXAMPLE 3.5

Draw a graph of the equation $y = 2x^2 + 3x - 3$, between $x = -6$ and $x = 5$.

Continuing with other values for x gives the following table.

x	−6	−5	−4	−3	−2	−1	0	1	2	3	4	5
y	51	32	17	6	−1	−4	−3	2	11	24	41	62

Solution

We have to take a convenient series of values for x between −6 and +5 and substitute them into the equation to find corresponding values for y, so we might start with:

- $x = -6$, and substitution gives $y = 2x^2 + 3x - 3 = 2 \times (-6)^2 + 3 \times (-6) - 3 = 51$
- $x = -5$, and substitution gives $y = 2x^2 + 3x - 3 = 2 \times (-5)^2 + 3 \times (-5) - 3 = 32$

Plotting these points on Cartesian axes and drawing a curved line through them gives the graph in Figure 3.10.

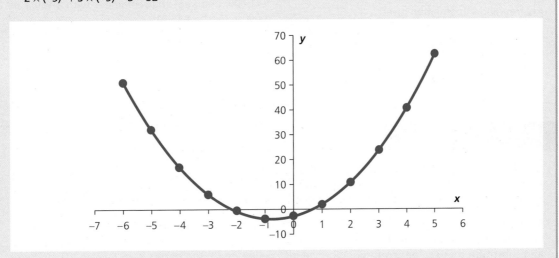

Figure 3.10 Graph of $y = 2x^2 + 3x - 3$

Worked example 3.5 gave an illustration of a quadratic equation, which has the general form $y = ax^2 + bx + c$, where a, b and c are constants. Their graphs are always U-shaped when a is positive – but when a is negative the graph is inverted and looks like a hill rather than a valley. The top of the hill, or bottom of the valley, is called a **turning point** where the graph changes direction and the gradient changes sign.

Quadratic equations are quite common. For instance, suppose economies of scale and other effects mean that the average cost of making a product changes with the number of units made. The basic cost of making one unit might be €200, and this falls by €5 for every unit of weekly production. This means that with a weekly production of x units, the unit cost is $200 - 5x$. If there are fixed overheads of €2,000 a week:

$$\text{total weekly cost} = \text{overheads} + \text{number of units made in the week} \times \text{unit cost}$$
$$= 2,000 + x \times (200 - 5x)$$
$$= 2,000 + 200x - 5x^2$$

WORKED EXAMPLE 3.6

Sonja Thorsen bought shares worth €10,000 in her employer's profit-sharing scheme. When the share price rose by €10, she kept 1,000 shares and sold the rest for €11,000. How can you describe her share purchases?

Solution
If Sonja originally bought x shares, the price of each was €10,000 / x. When this rose to (10,000 / x + 10) she sold (x – 1,000) shares for €11,000. So:

$$11,000 = \text{number of shares sold} \times \text{selling price}$$
$$= (x - 1,000) \times (10,000 / x + 10)$$

Rearranging this equation gives:

$$11,000 = (x - 1,000) \times \left(\frac{10,000}{x} + 10 \right)$$

$$= 10,000 + 10x - \frac{10,000,000}{x} - 10,000$$

or

$$11,000x = 10,000x + 10x^2 - 10,000,000 - 10,000x$$

which means that:

$$10x^2 - 11,000x - 10,000,000 = 0$$

In the next section we show how to solve this equation, and find that Sonja originally bought 1,691 shares. You can check this answer by substitution. If she bought 1,691 shares at 10,000 / 1,691 = €5.91 each, and when the price rose to €15.91, she sold 691 of them for 691 × 15.91 = €11,000, and kept the remainder with a value of 1,000 × 15.91 = €15,910.

WORKED EXAMPLE 3.7

Draw a graph of $y = 15 + 12x - 3x^2$ for values of x between –2 and 6. Where does this curve cross the x-axis?

Solution
We can take a series of convenient values for x and substitute these to get corresponding values for y, as follows.

x	–2	–1	0	1	2	3	4	5	6
y	–21	0	15	24	27	24	15	0	–21

Plotting these points and joining them together gives the results in Figure 3.11. As a has a negative value of –3, the graph is an inverted U, and you can see that it crosses the x-axis at $x = -1$ and $x = 5$.

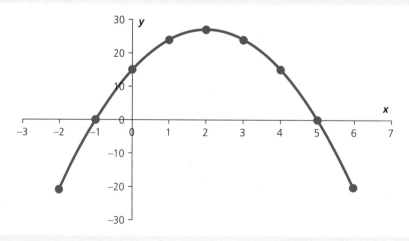

Figure 3.11 Graph of $y = 15 + 12x - 3x^2$

In Worked example 3.7, we found two points where the graph crossed the x-axis. By definition, these are the points where $ax^2 + bx + c = 0$, and they are called the roots of the quadratic. You can estimate these from a graph, but there is a standard calculation for finding them (whose derivation you can find in the companion website **www.pearsoned.co.uk/waters**). This shows that the two points where $y = 0$ correspond to the values of x where:

$$x = \frac{-b + \sqrt{b^2 - 4ac}}{2a} \quad \text{and} \quad x = \frac{-b - \sqrt{b^2 - 4ac}}{2a}$$

In Worked example 3.7, $a = -3$, $b = 12$ and $c = 15$, and substituting these values gives:

$$x = \frac{-12 + \sqrt{12^2 - 4 \times (-3) \times 15}}{2 \times (-3)} \quad \text{and} \quad x = \frac{-12 - \sqrt{12^2 - 4 \times (-3) \times 15}}{2 \times (-3)}$$

$$= \frac{-12 + \sqrt{(144 + 180)}}{-6} \qquad\qquad = \frac{-12 - \sqrt{(144 + 180)}}{-6}$$

$$= \frac{-12 + 18}{-6} \qquad\qquad\qquad = \frac{-12 - 18}{-6}$$

$$= -1 \qquad\qquad\qquad\qquad = 5$$

This confirms the results from the graph, that the curve crosses the x-axis at the points $(-1, 0)$ and $(5, 0)$.

WORKED EXAMPLE 3.8

Find the roots of the equation $2x^2 + 3x - 2 = 0$.

Solution
This is a quadratic with $a = 2$, $b = 3$ and $c = -2$. Substituting these values into the standard equations gives the two roots:

$$x = \frac{-b + \sqrt{b^2 - 4ac}}{2a}$$

$$= \frac{-3 + \sqrt{3^2 - 4 \times 2 \times (-2)}}{2 \times 2}$$

$$= \frac{-3 + \sqrt{25}}{4}$$

$$= 0.5$$

and

$$x = \frac{-b - \sqrt{b^2 - 4ac}}{2a}$$

$$= \frac{-3 - \sqrt{3^2 - 4 \times 2 \times (-2)}}{2 \times 2}$$

$$= \frac{-3 - \sqrt{25}}{4}$$

$$= -2$$

You can check these values by substituting them in the original equation:

$$2 \times 0.5^2 + 3 \times 0.5 - 2 = 0$$

and

$$2 \times (-2)^2 + 3 \times (-2) - 2 = 0$$

The only problem with calculating the roots comes when $4ac$ is greater than b^2. Then $b^2 - 4ac$ is negative, and we have to find the square root of a negative number. This is not defined in real arithmetic, so we conclude that there are no real roots and they are both imaginary.

3.8   Are the graphs of all quadratic equations exactly the same shape?

3.9   What are the roots of a quadratic equation?

3.10 What can you say about the roots of $y = x^2 + 2x + 3$?

3.11 Why is it better to calculate the roots of a quadratic equation than to read them from a graph?

IDEAS IN PRACTICE   Emjit Chandrasaika

In his spare time, Emjit Chandrasaika sells computer software through his website. Because he does this from home, and considers it a mixture of business and pleasure, he does not keep a tight check on his accounts. He thinks that he gets a basic income of £12 for every unit he sells a month, but economies of scale mean that this increases by £2 for every unit. He estimates that the fixed costs of his website, advertising and time is £1,000 a month.

If Emjit's income per unit is $12 + 2x$, where x is the number of units that he sells per month, then:

profit = number of units sold per month
$\quad \times$ unit income − overheads
$\quad = x(12 + 2x) - 1{,}000$
$\quad = 2x^2 + 12x - 1{,}000$

When this equals zero, his income just covers his costs, and this happens when:

$$x = \frac{-b + \sqrt{b^2 - 4ac}}{2a}$$

$$= \frac{-12 + \sqrt{12^2 - 4 \times 2 \times (-1{,}000)}}{2 \times 2}$$

$$= 19.6$$

or

$$x = \frac{-b - \sqrt{b^2 - 4ac}}{2a}$$

$$= \frac{-12 - \sqrt{12^2 - 4 \times 2 \times (-1{,}000)}}{2 \times 2}$$

$$= -25.6$$

Obviously, he cannot sell a negative number of units (like −25.6) so the answer comes from the positive number, 19.6. The conclusion is that Emjit must sell 20 units a month to make a profit. His actual sales are much higher than this, and are rising by 50% a year. This analysis encouraged Emjit to consider a move into full-time web sales.

Drawing other graphs

When we can express one variable, y, in terms of another, x, we say that 'y is a function of x', and write this as $y = f(x)$. With a straight line, y is a linear function of x, which means that $y = f(x)$ and $f(x) = ax + b$; with a quadratic $y = f(x)$, and $f(x) = ax^2 + bx + c$. This is just a convenient shorthand that can save time explaining relationships. You can draw a graph of any relationship where y is a function of x; meaning that $y = f(x)$.

Polynomials

Straight lines (where $y = ax + b$) and quadratic equations (where $y = ax^2 + bx + c$) are two examples of polynomials. This is the general term used to describe equations that contain a variable, x, raised to some power. For straight lines we raised x to the power 1, for quadratics we raised x to the power 2; and for more complicated polynomials we raise x to higher powers. For instance, cubic equations contain x raised to the power 3, with the form $y = ax^3 + bx^2 + cx + d$. Higher polynomials have more complex curves, and to draw their graphs we have to plot enough points to show the details.

WORKED EXAMPLE 3.9

Draw a graph of the function $y = x^3 - 1.5x^2 - 18x$ between $x = -5$ and $x = +6$.

Solution
Figure 3.12 shows a spreadsheet of the results. The top part shows a series of values of y calculated for x between −5 and 6; then the Chart Wizard draws the results. The graph has a trough around $x = 3$ and a peak around $x = -2$. Cubic equations always have this general shape, with two turning points, but they vary in detail; some are the other way around, some have the two turning points merged into one, and so on.

Figure 3.12 Graph of $y = x^3 - 1.5x^2 - 18x$

Exponential curves

In Chapter 2 we mentioned the exponential constant, e, which is equal to 2.7182818 . . . This strange number is useful for describing functions that rise or fall at an accelerating rate. Exponential curves have the general form $y = ne^{mx}$, where n and m are constants. The exact shape depends on the values of n and m, but when m is positive there is an accelerating rise – described as exponential growth – and when m is negative there is a decreasing fall – described as exponential decline.

WORKED EXAMPLE 3.10

Draw graphs of $y = e^x$ and $y = e^{0.9x}$ for values of x between 0 and 10.

Solution

Figure 3.13 shows these results in a spreadsheet. When e is raised to a positive power, the characteristic exponential curves rise very quickly with x.

	A	B	C	D	E	F	G	H	I	J	K	L
1	Graphs of exponential growth											
2												
3	x	0	1	2	3	4	5	6	7	8	9	10
4	$e^{0.9x}$	1	2	6	15	37	90	221	545	1339	3294	8103
5	e^x	1	3	7	20	55	148	403	1097	2981	8103	22026
6												
7												
8												

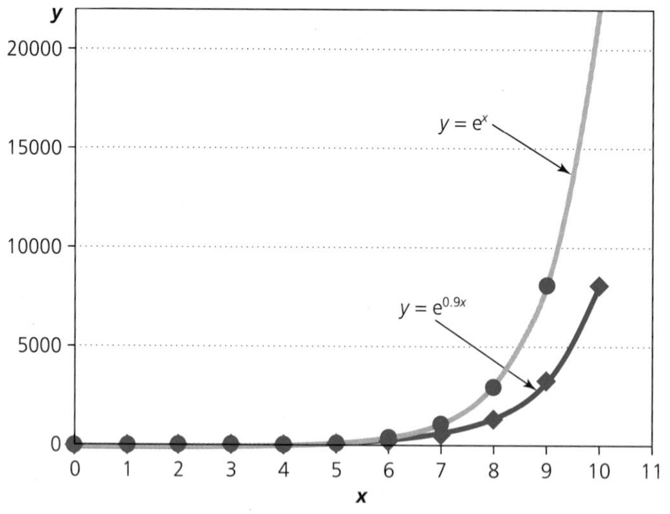

Figure 3.13 Graphs of exponential growth

WORKED EXAMPLE 3.11

Draw the graph of $y = 1000e^{-0.5x}$ between $x = 0$ and $x = 10$.

Solution

Figure 3.14 shows the calculations and graph on a spreadsheet. When e is raised to a negative power, the exponential curve falls quickly towards zero and then flattens out with increasing x.

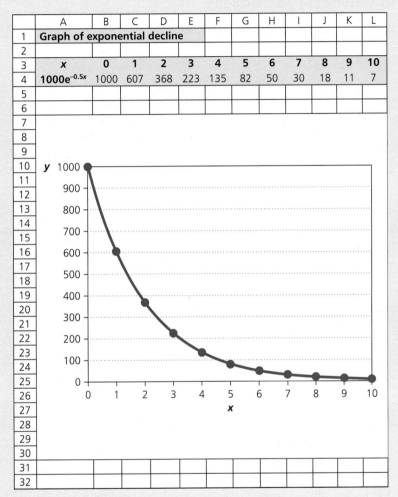

	A	B	C	D	E	F	G	H	I	J	K	L
1	Graph of exponential decline											
2												
3	x	0	1	2	3	4	5	6	7	8	9	10
4	$1000e^{-0.5x}$	1000	607	368	223	135	82	50	30	18	11	7

Figure 3.14 Graph of exponential decline

IDEAS IN PRACTICE   Konrad Schimmer

You can find examples of graphs in almost any newspaper or magazine. Many of these are time series, which show a series of observations taken at regular intervals of time – such as monthly unemployment figures, daily rainfall, weekly demand for a product and annual profit. Financial analysts use many types of graph to give a clear picture of trends and underlying patterns.

Ideas in practice continued

Konrad Schimmer is a financial analyst of the Frankfurt Stock Exchange, and he plots graphs for every aspect of companies' performances. Typically he plots the quarterly profit for the past six years, monthly sales for the past three years and closing share price over the past year. Figure 3.15 shows one of his graphs comparing the closing share prices of two companies at the end of each week for the past year. Konrad studies the details of such graphs looking for trends, unusual patterns, possible causes and how the company is likely to perform in the future. He has used this approach to amass considerable wealth.

Source: Schimmer K., *Using Charts to Identify Stock Market Trends*, Financiers' Roundtable, Frankfurt, 2010.

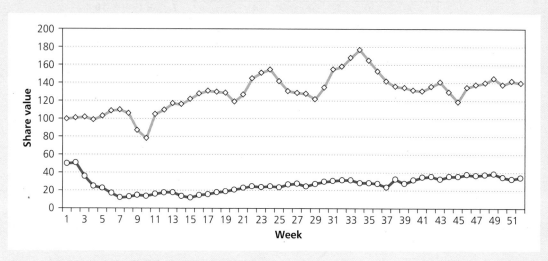

Figure 3.15 Comparison of closing weekly share prices

Graphs of simultaneous equations

In Chapter 2 we discussed simultaneous equations, where several equations apply at the same time. For example, with two variables we might find that

$$3y = 4x + 2 \tag{1}$$

$$y = -x + 10 \tag{2}$$

You can draw a graph with both equations on the same axes. As each equation is a straight line, you get the results shown in Figure 3.16.

The first equation is true at any point on one of the lines, and the second equation is true at any point on the other. It follows that both equations are true at the point where the lines cross. This is near to the point where $x = 4$ and $y = 6$ (confirming a result that we calculated in Worked example 2.19). This means that you can use a graph to solve simultaneous equations when there are two variables. An extension to the basic method replaces linear equations by more complicated ones, and sees where two curves intersect.

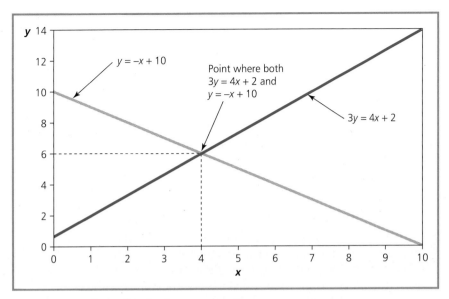

Figure 3.16 Graph to solve simultaneous equations

WORKED EXAMPLE 3.12

Use a graph to solve the simultaneous equations

$$y = 2x + 10 \qquad (1)$$

$$2y = 5 - x \qquad (2)$$

What happens if equation (2) is replaced by the quadratic equation $2x^2 + 3x - 2 = 0$?

Solution

Figure 3.17 shows a graph of these two equations, and you can see that the lines cross at about the point where $x = -3$ and $y = 4$. If you substitute these two values into the equations you get:

$$4 = 2 \times (-3) + 10 \quad \checkmark \qquad (1)$$

$$8 = 5 - (-3) \quad \checkmark \qquad (2)$$

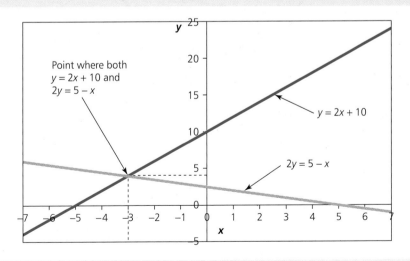

Figure 3.17 Graph of $y = 2x + 10$ and $2y = 5 - x$

Worked example 3.12 continued

Both of these are correct, which confirms the results from the graph.

If the second equation is replaced by the quadratic, you can tackle the problem in exactly the same way. The easiest way to draw the quadratic curve is to take a range of values, say from $x = -5$ to $x = +4$, and substitute them into $2x^2 + 3x - 2 = 0$ to give:

x	−5	−4	−3	−2	−1	0	1	2	3	4
y	33	18	7	0	−3	−2	3	12	25	42

The straight line of $y = 2x + 10$ crosses the quadratic curve at two points, at about (2, 14) and (−3, 5), as shown in Figure 3.18. At these two points, both equations are true. You can calculate the points more accurately by saying both equations are satisfied when:

$$y = 2x^2 + 3x - 2 \text{ and } y = 2x + 10$$

so when both equal y you have:

$$2x^2 + 3x - 2 = 2x + 10$$

and rearranging this gives:

$$2x^2 + x - 12 = 0$$

You can solve this using the standard equation described earlier, and the solutions are $x = 2.21$ and $x = -2.71$. Substituting these two values for x into one of the original equations, say $y = 2x + 10$, gives the corresponding values for y.

- When $x = 2.21$, $y = 2x + 10 = 2 \times 2.21 + 10 = 14.42$, giving the point (2.21, 14.42), which we estimated to be (2, 14).
- When $x = -2.71$, $y = 2x + 10 = 2 \times (-2.71) + 10 = 4.58$, giving the point (−2.71, 4.58), which we estimated to be (−3, 5).

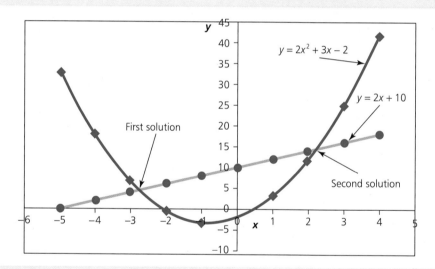

Figure 3.18 Replacing a linear equation by a quadratic

Review questions

3.12 What is a polynomial?

3.13 What is a turning point in a graph?

3.14 How can you draw a graph of exponential growth?

3.15 Can you draw a graph of $y = 12x + 7z$, where both x and z are variables?

3.16 What does it mean when two graphs cross each other?

3.17 Why is it generally better to use algebraic rather than graphical methods to solve simultaneous equations?

IDEAS IN PRACTICE   Misleading graphs

Graphs give a very clear view of information – but this impression can be misleading. Tufte collected many examples of misleading graphs including the classic view of traffic deaths in Connecticut following stricter enforcement of speed limits. Figure 3.19(a) gives the published view, with stricter enforcement having a clear effect on deaths. Figure 3.19(b) shows a different view, which suggests that more investigation is needed.

Graphs can be misleading because the people drawing them make genuine mistakes. But it is more worrying when people deliberately present information in a confusing way, perhaps to support their own opinions or to give a false view of a product. Several common faults in drawing graphs are:

- not putting scales on axes or labelling them properly
- not starting scales at zero
- using inappropriate or discontinuous scales
- not including all the relevant information, or ignoring certain results.

Chapter 5 returns to this theme of presenting information properly in graphs.

Source: Tufte E., *The Visual Display of Quantitative Information* (2nd edition), Graphics Press, Chesire, CT, 2001.

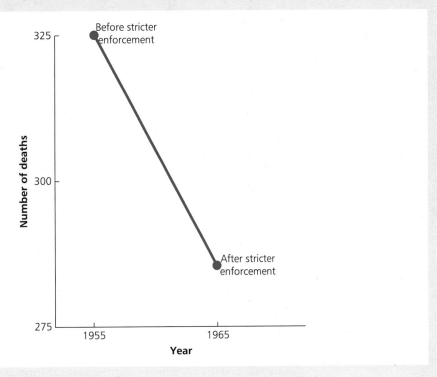

Figure 3.19(a) Initial view of traffic deaths following stricter enforcement of speed limits

Ideas in practice continued

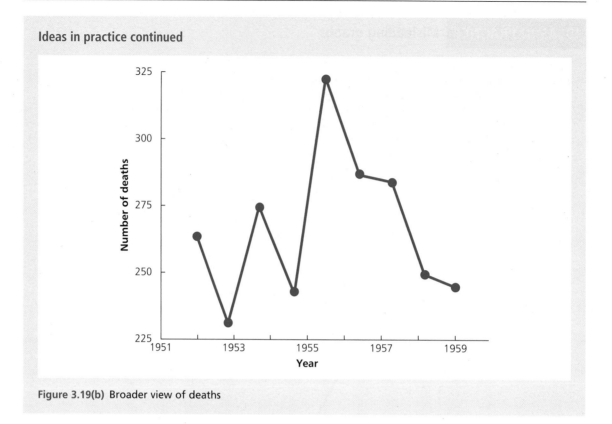

Figure 3.19(b) Broader view of deaths

CHAPTER REVIEW

This chapter showed how to draw different types of graph.

- Diagrams give an easy and efficient way of presenting information, and people can quickly identify the main features and patterns.
- Graphs are one of the most useful types of diagram, and usually use Cartesian coordinates to show a relationship between two variables.
- Straight-line graphs have the form $y = ax + b$, where a is the gradient and b is the intercept on the y-axis. You can draw straight-line graphs by plotting two points and drawing the line through them.
- For more complicated curves, you have to plot a number of points and draw a line through them. We used this method to draw graphs of quadratic equations, which have the general form $y = ax^2 + bx + c$. These graphs are U-shaped – or an inverted U when a is negative.
- The roots of a quadratic equation are the points where the curve crosses the x-axis. There is a standard calculation to identify these points.
- You can use the standard method for drawing graphs for any relationship where y is a function of x – described as $y = f(x)$ – including higher polynomials and exponential curves.
- You can solve simultaneous equations with two variables using graphs, but you have to be careful because the results may not be very accurate.

CASE STUDY   McFarlane & Sons

John McFarlane works for his family company, which has sold traditional clothing from four shops in the east of Scotland since 1886. He wants to compare the performance of each shop, and has collected some detailed information for the past year. Now he wants a convenient format to present this to the company Board of Directors.

John's problem is that he has a huge amount of data. The following table shows the number of units of five products sold each month in each of the shops. John has this kind of information for several hundred products, along with costs, profit margins, advertising expenditure – and many other figures.

Month	Shop	Product A	Product B	Product C	Product D	Product E
January	1	15	87	2	21	65
	2	12	42	0	15	32
	3	8	21	3	33	40
	4	7	9	3	10	22
February	1	16	80	1	22	67
	2	16	43	2	12	34
	3	8	24	5	31	41
	4	8	8	2	9	21
March	1	18	78	6	15	70
	2	16	45	6	8	30
	3	8	21	8	23	44
	4	10	7	2	8	19
April	1	21	83	11	16	71
	2	17	46	13	7	30
	3	11	19	9	25	47
	4	9	8	4	9	21
May	1	24	86	2	25	66
	2	20	49	7	16	32
	3	14	23	3	37	46
	4	10	6	3	13	22
June	1	27	91	3	33	65
	2	23	52	1	17	33
	3	15	20	0	51	47
	4	12	9	2	17	10
July	1	27	88	2	38	65
	2	22	55	0	20	38
	3	16	20	2	58	46
	4	9	8	1	19	20
August	1	20	90	1	37	68
	2	21	57	0	24	35
	3	11	23	1	60	40
	4	10	8	0	20	18
September	1	17	84	7	26	65
	2	17	63	8	17	31
	3	10	21	4	39	46
	4	6	7	9	12	19

▶

Case study continued

Month	Shop	Product A	Product B	Product C	Product D	Product E
October	1	17	85	24	19	70
	2	14	61	23	13	33
	3	11	21	21	30	39
	4	9	7	19	11	21
November	1	15	85	37	11	69
	2	13	55	36	10	33
	3	9	22	28	15	44
	4	9	9	19	5	21
December	1	15	88	81	17	68
	2	12	54	65	14	34
	3	7	18	67	24	40
	4	8	7	53	8	22

Question

■ **How could John McFarlane use graphs to present information to the company Board of Directors?**

PROBLEMS

3.1   Draw a graph of the points (2, 12), (4, 16), (7, 22), (10, 28) and (15, 38). How would you describe this graph?

3.2   Draw a graph of the following points. What can you say about the results?

x	1	3	6	8	9	10	13	14	17	18	21	25	26	29
y	22	24	31	38	41	44	52	55	61	64	69	76	81	83

3.3   The number of people employed in a chain of workshops is related to the size (in consistent units) by the equation:

employees = size / 1,000 + 3

Draw a graph of this equation and use it to find the number of employees in a workshop of size 50,000 units.

3.4   Draw graphs of (a) $y = 10$, (b) $y = x + 10$, (c) $y = x^2 + x + 10$, (d) $y = x^3 + x^2 + x + 10$.

3.5   What are the roots of (a) $x^2 - 6x + 8$, (b) $3x^2 - 2x - 5$, (c) $x^2 + x + 1$?

3.6   Deng Chow Chan found that the basic income generated by his main product is £10 a unit, but this increases by £1 for every unit he makes. If he has to cover fixed costs of £100, how many units must he sell to cover all his costs?

3.7   The output, y, from an assembly line is related to one of the settings, x, by the equation

$$y = -5x^2 + 2,500x - 12,500$$

What is the maximum output from the line, and the corresponding value for x?

3.8   Martha Berryman finds that the unit cost of using production equipment is:

$$cost = 1.5x^2 - 120x + 4,000$$

where x is the number of units produced. Draw a graph to find the lowest unit cost. What production level does this correspond to?

3.9   Compare the graphs of $y = 2^x$ and $y = 3^x$.

3.10   Draw a graph of $y = 1/x$ for values of x between −5 and +5.

3.11 If you leave £100 in the bank earning 6% interest, at the end of n years you will have 100×1.06^n. Draw a graph of this amount over the next 20 years.

3.12 Use graphs to solve these simultaneous equations:

(a) $a + b = 3$ and $a - b = 5$
(b) $2x + 3y = 27$ and $3x + 2y = 23$
(c) $2x + 2y + 4z = 24$ and $6x + 3y = 15$ and $y + 2z = 11$

3.13 Sven Hendriksson finds that one of his productivity measures is related to the number of employees, e, and the production, n, by the equations:

$$10n + 3e = 45 \quad \text{and} \quad 2n + 5e = 31$$

What are the current values for e and n?

3.14 Where does the line $y = 20x + 15$ cross the line $y = 2x^2 - 4x + 1$?

3.15 Where does the line $y = e^{2x}$ cross the line $y = x^2 + 10$?

RESEARCH PROJECTS

3.1 Spreadsheets are a convenient way of drawing graphs, but there are more specialised graphics packages. What additional features do these specialised packages have? Do a small survey of packages, comparing their graphics features. What other features would you like?

3.2 Find some examples of graphs presented in newspapers and magazines. Describe some that are particularly good, and others that are particularly bad. What can the producers of the bad ones learn from those who presented the good ones?

3.3 You can monitor the trends in share prices using various indices, such as the London Stock Exchange FTSE 100 or FTSE 250 indices. Similar indices are calculated for other stock exchanges, such as the Nikkei in Tokyo, Dow-Jones in New York, Hang Seng in Hong Kong, Dax in Frankfurt and CAC in Paris. Collect some figures for a specific company over a period and draw graphs to compare its performance with the broader stock market. Can you find any obvious trends? What do you expect to happen in the future?

Sources of information

Further reading

Most of the books on mathematics mentioned in Chapter 2 include sections on graphs. Some other useful books on graphs include:

Few S., *Show Me the Numbers*, Analytics Press, Oakland, CA, 2004.

Janert P.K., *Gnuplot in Action*, Manning Publications, Greenwich, CT, 2009.

Jelen W., *Charts and Graphs*, Pearson Education, Toronto, 2010.

Robbins N.B., *Creating More Effective Graphs*, John Wiley, Chichester, 2005.

Tufte E., *The Visual Display of Quantitative Information* (2nd edition), Graphics Press, Cheshire, CT, 2001.

Walkenbach J., *Excel 2007 Charts*, John Wiley & Sons, New York, 2007.

Zelazny G., *Say it with Charts* (4th edition), McGraw-Hill, New York, 2006.

PART TWO

Collecting and summarising data

This book is divided into five parts. The first part looked at the background and context for quantitative methods. It showed why managers need numerical skills, and it reviewed the tools they use.

Even the best quantitative methods have no value unless managers can collect the necessary data. There is no point in developing a model for, say, company profits unless managers can gather all the related information about costs and incomes. This second part of the book shows how to collect, summarise and present data. Then the third part looks at ways of using information to solve specific types of problem. The fourth part describes some useful statistics, and the fifth part uses these to solve problems involving uncertainty.

There are four chapters in this part. Chapter 4 discusses the actual collection of data and how it can be organised. The raw data often has too much detail, so it has to be summarised and presented in ways that highlight its important features – Chapter 5 shows how to do this with different types of diagrams. Chapter 6 continues this theme by looking at numerical descriptions of data. Chapter 7 describes index numbers, which monitor changing values over time.

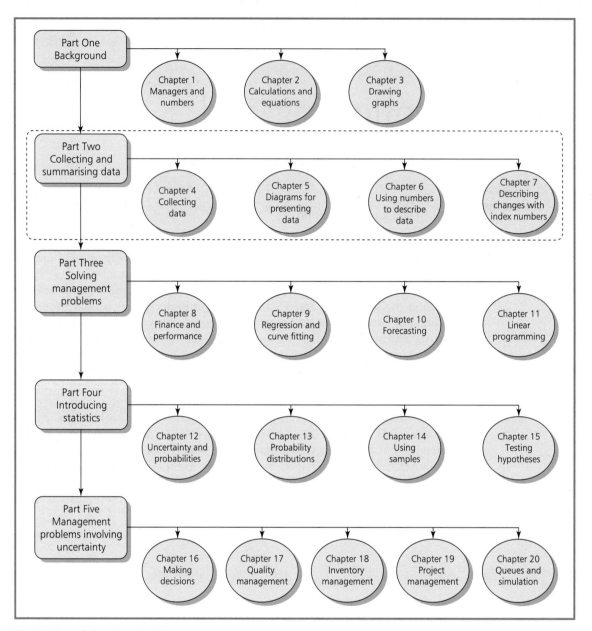

Map 2 Map of chapters – Part Two

Collecting data

Chapter outline

All quantitative analyses need reliable data. To make reasoned decisions, managers have to collect this data from a variety of sources. But there are many types of data, and each can be collected, analysed and presented in different ways. This chapter discusses the most common ways of collecting data. In practice, this usually means sampling, where data is collected from a representative sample of possible sources. Later chapters discuss the analysis and presentation of this data.

After finishing this chapter you should be able to:

- appreciate the importance of data collection
- discuss the amount of data to be collected
- classify data in different ways
- identify sources of data
- understand the concept of populations and samples
- discuss the reasons for using samples
- describe and use different types of sample
- consider different ways of collecting data from samples
- design questionnaires.

Data and information

You often hear the terms 'data' and 'information' used to mean the same thing – some collection of facts. However, there is really a difference between the two.

> **Data** are the raw numbers or facts that we process to give useful **information**.

78, 64, 36, 70 and 52 are data that we process to give the information that the average exam mark of five students is 60%. A government census collects data from individuals, and processes this to give information about the population as a whole. Analysts collect data about businesses and process it to give information about their performance. Researchers use market surveys to collect data and process it to give information about consumer opinions. The principle is always that data consists of raw numbers and facts, while information gives some useful knowledge.

Managers need relevant information for their decisions. To get this, they start with data collection, then process the data to give information, and present the results in the best formats (as shown in Figure 4.1). The implication is that data collection is essential in every organisation, because it starts the process of decision-making – and without proper data collection, managers cannot make informed decisions.

Figure 4.1 shows the three main steps in preparing information:

1 Data collection
2 Processing to give information
3 Presentation.

In this chapter we concentrate on data collection, while the following chapters look at processing and presentation. This seems a sensible approach because it follows the natural timing – but things are not really this simple, and your planned use of data affects the way that you collect it. Suppose you want some data about the city of Malaga. If you are going there on holiday, you might use your phone to get weather forecasts for the next week; if you want information about local companies, you might look at their websites; if you want details of the city's history, you might look in an encyclopaedia; if you want to know the attitude towards business, you might send out a questionnaire; if you want to see how busy the streets are, you might do a survey.

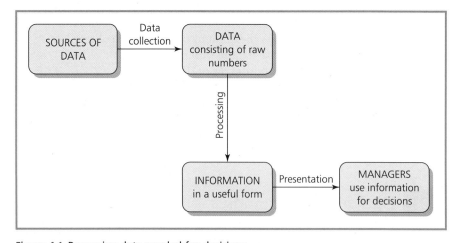

Figure 4.1 Processing data needed for decisions

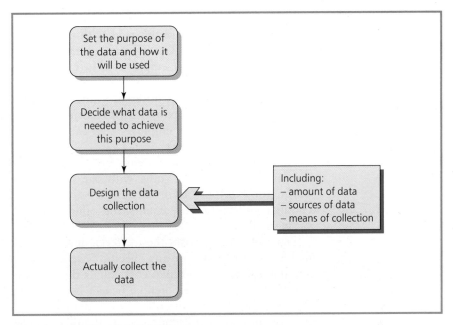

Figure 4.2 Planning data collection

So the first step is really to define the purpose of the data and how it will be used. The second step is to decide which data is needed to achieve this purpose. Then the third step is to design the data collection and actually set about collecting it (as shown in Figure 4.2).

At first, it seems easy to collect data. After all, you can use a search engine on the Web to find a huge amount of data about almost anything. Unfortunately, you soon find that most of this is irrelevant, faulty, and you are swamped by details that are of no interest. If you want data that is relevant for your needs and is accurate and reliable, you have to plan the collection more carefully.

Amount of data

Three important questions for data collection are the amount of data, its source and the means of collection. Starting with the amount of data, managers want enough to enable good decisions to be made, but not so much that they are swamped by irrelevant detail. This balance can be difficult. There is often a huge amount of data they could collect, and which might be useful. But all data collection and analysis costs money, so they must resist the temptation to go on a spree and collect everything available. Imagine that you use a questionnaire to collect a group of people's answers to five questions. As you are sending a questionnaire you might as well add some extra questions to get a few more details. But if you end up with, say, 20 questions, you have the extra costs of collecting and analysing 15 questions that do not say anything useful – and you irritate people who have to spend more time completing the questionnaire.

In principle, we can define a marginal cost as the extra cost of collecting one more bit of data, and this rises with the amount of data collected. You can find some general data about, say, the Burlington Northern Railroad very easily (it runs trains, employs staff etc.); for more detailed data you need a trip to a specialised transport library (perhaps finding what kinds of engines it has, or staff at different grades); for yet more detailed data you need to search the company's own records; for yet more detailed data you need a special survey of employees. At each stage, the more data you want, the more it costs to collect.

On the other hand, the marginal benefit of data – which is the benefit from the last bit collected – falls with the amount collected. The fact that Burlington Northern Railroad runs a rail service is very useful, but as you continue collecting more details, the value of each bit of data gets progressively smaller.

Figure 4.3 summarises these effects, and shows how to identify the optimal amount of data for any specific purpose. In principle, you collect the amount where the marginal cost equals the marginal benefit. If you collect less than this, you lose potential benefit because the cost of collection is less than the benefit; if you collect more data than this, you waste resources because the cost of collection is more than the benefit.

In reality, it is virtually impossible to find convincing values for the marginal cost and benefit, so people simply collect the amount that their experience and judgement suggest is reasonable. An important factor in this decision is the time available. Some methods of data collection are very fast

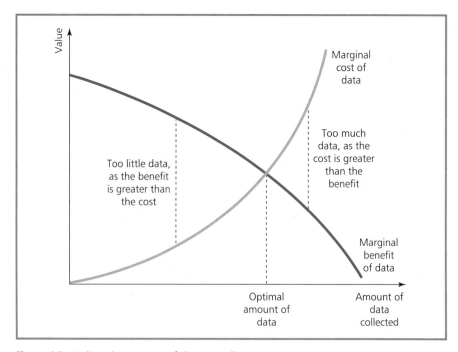

Figure 4.3 Finding the amount of data to collect

(such as searching websites) but other methods need a lot of time (such as running consumer surveys). There is always pressure on managers' time, so they prefer fast methods – arguing that when data collection takes too long, the results become obsolete and irrelevant before they prepared. Unfortunately, when managers do not allow enough time for proper data collection, they encourage shortcuts and assume that any data – even if slightly inaccurate – is better than no data at all. Sometimes this is true. If a company does not have time for a full market survey, it can still get useful information from a limited study; and when you buy a car it is better to get some information from salespeople, even if their replies do not tell the whole story. Often, though, wrong data can be worse than no data at all. A limited market survey might give misleading results that encourage a company to start a hopeless venture, and salespeople might underestimate the running costs of a car so that you get into debt trying to pay them. Inaccurate data can lead to bad decisions – so the clear message is that managers need accurate data, and this needs careful planning.

Review questions

4.1   What is the difference between data and information?

4.2   Why is data collection important to an organisation?

4.3   'It is always best to collect as much data as possible.' Do you think this is true?

IDEAS IN PRACTICE   **Survey into use of quantitative methods**

In 2002 Peder Kristensen sent a questionnaire to 187 managers asking them how much they used standard quantitative analyses. Some of the results were quite disappointing. Peder said, 'Some methods were widely used – such as break-even analyses, basic statistics and inventory control. On the other hand, some common methods – such as linear programming and regression analysis – were used surprisingly little. My survey included small companies that are less likely to use sophisticated methods, but the results were still disappointing.'

Peder soon recognised a fault in his data collection. He explained, 'It was the most basic and embarrassing mistake. I assumed that most managers would be familiar with a range of quantitative methods. I simply asked questions like "Do you use linear programming?" Actually, relatively few of the managers had any formal training in quantitative methods, and were unlikely to use them.'

In 2006 Peder repeated the survey, sponsored by a software company, which was convinced that managers' needs were not being met. This time he asked questions like 'Do you know about linear programming? If the answer is "yes", do you use it in your work?' The following table shows some of his results.

Topic	Percent aware of	Percent of these using
Descriptive statistics	93	98
Discounted cash flow	78	87
Forecasting	74	83
Inventory control	69	65
Regression	67	79
Project planning – CPM	58	76
Project planning – PERT	51	61
Linear programming	47	53
Queuing models	41	38
Integer programming	25	27

Many people believe that managers do not use quantitative methods because they do not trust them, or they believe that the analyses are too difficult or inappropriate. Peder showed that an important factor is that managers often have little formal training and do not use quantitative methods simply because they do not know about them.

Types of data

We can classify data in several ways. One way that we have already used describes data as either quantitative (based on numbers) or qualitative (where there are no numbers). Quantitative data is much easier to collect, analyse and describe, so you should use it whenever possible. You can even transform data that is essentially qualitative into a quantitative form. For example, when people have different opinions about some issue, you cannot measure those opinions but you can ask if they agree with a particular statement. Then you might say, '70% of people agree with the statement that . . .'. Sometimes you can add a notional scale. When doctors want to know how bad a patient's pain is, they ask them to rank it on a scale of 1 to 10 – and questionnaires often ask respondents to rate the strength of their opinion on a scale of, say, 1 to 5.

However, we cannot transform all data into a convincing quantitative form, and when Browning asks, 'How do I love thee? Let me count the ways . . .'[1] we know that this is more for effect than for realism. A useful classification of data checks how easy it is to measure, and then describes it as nominal, ordinal or cardinal.

- Nominal data is the kind that we really cannot quantify with any meaningful units. The facts that a person is an accountant, or a country has a market economy, or a cake has cream in it, or a car is blue are examples of nominal data because there are no real measures for these. The usual analysis for nominal data is to define a number of distinct categories and say how many observations fall into each – which is why it is also called categorical or descriptive data. A survey of companies in a town might give the nominal data that 7 are manufacturers, 16 are service companies and 5 are in primary industries. A key point about nominal data is that the order in which the categories are listed does not matter, as you can see from the example in Figure 4.4.
- Ordinal data is one step more quantitative than nominal data. Here we can rank the categories of observations into some meaningful order. For example, we can describe sweaters as large, medium or small. The order of these categories is important because we know that 'medium' comes between 'large' and 'small' – but this is all we can say. Other examples of ordinal data are the strength of people's opinions on a scale of 1 to 5, socioeconomic descriptions of people as A, B1, B2, C1 etc. and exam results as distinction, pass or fail. The key point is that the order of the categories is important, which is why ordinal data is sometimes described as ordered or ranked.
- Cardinal data has some attribute that can be measured directly. For example, we can weigh a sack of potatoes, measure the time taken to finish a job, find the temperature in an office, and record the time of deliveries. These measures give a precise description, and are clearly the most relevant to quantitative methods.

We can divide cardinal data into two types depending on whether it is discrete or continuous. Data is discrete if it takes only integer values. The number of children in a family is discrete data, as are the numbers of cars

---

(a) Nominal data

Percentage of respondents who would vote for political party X	35%
Percentage of respondents who would vote for political party Y	40%
Percentage of respondents who would vote for political party Z	20%
Percentage of respondents who do not know who they would vote for	5%

(b) Ordinal data

Percentage of people who feel 'very strongly' in favour of a proposal	8%
Percentage of people who feel 'strongly' in favour of a proposal	14%
Percentage of people who feel 'neutral' about a proposal	49%
Percentage of people who feel 'strongly' against a proposal	22%
Percentage of people who feel 'very strongly' against a proposal	7%

(c) Cardinal data

Percentage of people in a club who are less than 20 years old	12%
Percentage of people in a club who are between 20 and 35 years old	18%
Percentage of people in a club who are between 35 and 50 years old	27%
Percentage of people in a club who are between 50 and 65 years old	29%
Percentage of people in a club who are more than 65 years old	14%

Figure 4.4 Typical analyses for nominal, ordinal and cardinal data

owned, machines operated, shops opened and people employed. Continuous data can take any value and is not restricted to integers. The weight of a packet of biscuits is continuous, and can take values like 256.312 grams – as are the time taken to serve a customer, the volume of oil delivered, the area covered in carpet and the length of a pipeline.

Sometimes there is a mismatch in data types. For example, the lengths of people's feet are continuous data, but shoes come in a range of discrete sizes that are good enough for most needs; people's heights are continuous, but most people describe their height to the nearest centimetre or inch. If the units of measurement are small, the distinction between discrete and continuous data begins to disappear. For instance, salaries are discrete as they are multiples of a penny or cent, but the units are so small that it is reasonable to describe them as continuous.

Primary and secondary data

Another important classification of data describes the way it is collected. This is often characterised as 'field research' when you actually go out and collect data yourself (to get primary data), or as 'desk research' when you look for data that someone else has already collected (described as secondary data).

- **Primary data** is new data collected by an organisation itself for a specific purpose.
- **Secondary data** is existing data that was collected by other organisations or for other purposes.

Primary data has the benefits of fitting the needs exactly, being up to date and being reliable. Secondary data might be published by other organisations, available from research studies, published by the government, already available within an organisation and so on. This has the advantages of being much cheaper, faster and easier to collect. It also has the benefit of using sources that are not generally available, as firms are willing to give information to impartial bodies, such as governments, international organisations, universities, industry representatives, trade unions and professional institutions.

If there is reasonable secondary data, you should use it. There is no point in spending time and effort in duplicating data that someone already has. For instance, when you want views on future economic conditions it is better to use figures already prepared by the government rather than starting your own survey. Unfortunately secondary data is often not reliable enough for a particular purpose, is in the wrong form or is out of date. Then you have to balance the benefits of having primary data with the cost and effort of collecting it. For major decisions it is worth collecting primary data, in the way that organisations run market surveys to collect customer reactions before launching new products. Otherwise it is better to use secondary data.

In practice, the best option is often a combination of primary and secondary data – perhaps with secondary data giving the overall picture and primary data adding the details. For example, a UK logistics company might get a broad view of industrial prospects from secondary data collected by the government and the European Union; more details come from secondary data collected by the Road Haulage Association and the Chartered Institute for Transport and Logistics. Then the company can collect specific primary data from its customers.

Review questions	
4.4	Why is it useful to classify data?
4.5	How can you classify data?
4.6	What is the difference between discrete and continuous data?
4.7	Give examples of nominal, ordinal and cardinal data.
4.8	'Primary data is always better than secondary data.' Do you agree?

IDEAS IN PRACTICE   Finding secondary data

There are many sources of secondary data. For example, the UK government's Statistical Service publishes broad reviews in a *Monthly Digest of Statistics*[2] and an *Annual Abstract of Statistics*.[3] Their *Guide to Official Statistics*[4] lists the more specialised figures they publish. Other countries have similar publications, and the results are summarised by international bodies such as the United Nations, the European Union, the World Bank and the International Monetary Fund. Most of this data is available on official websites.

In addition to government information, a huge amount of data is published by individual companies and organisations – as well as information provided by services such as Reuters, CNN, BBC, the *Financial Times*, etc., or survey companies, such as Gallup, Nielsen and Mori. There is a huge amount of information – of widely variable quality – on websites, and it is often best to start looking with a search engine, like those you can find at www.altavista.com, www.baidu.com, www.bing.com, www.google.com, www.lycos.com, www.webcrawler.com and www.yahoo.com.

Using samples to collect data

When there is no appropriate secondary data, you have to collect your own primary data. You do this from the relevant population. Here we are using 'population' in the statistical sense of all people or entities that share some common characteristic. For instance, when Royal Mail wants to see how long it takes to deliver first-class letters, the population is all the letters that are posted first-class; a consumer organisation testing the quality of Whirlpool dishwashers would define the population as all the dishwashers made by Whirlpool; a toy manufacturer getting reactions to a new game might define the population of potential customers as all girls between the ages of 6 and 11.

Obviously, it is important to identify the appropriate population because a mistake here makes all the subsequent data collection and analysis pointless. But this is not as easy as it seems. The population for a survey of student opinion is clearly the students – but does this mean only full-time students, or does it include part-time, day-release, short-course and distance-learning students? What about students who are doing a period of work experience, school students and those studying but not enrolled in courses? If the population is 'imported cars', does this include those where components are imported but assembly is done in this country, or those where almost-finished cars are imported for finishing here or those where components are exported for assembly and the finished car is then brought back? Even when we can identify a population in principle, there can be difficulties translating this into actual sources of data. For instance, it is easy to describe the population of houses with broadband connections, but it is much more difficult to identify them all. Similarly, it would be difficult to identify populations of people who bought an imported television set within the last five years, or people who use a particular supermarket or people who caught a cold last winter. The answer is, generally, to ask a very large number of people and then ignore everyone who does not have the features you want – but this approach raises other problems with bias, efficiency and reliability.

When you can get a complete list of a population, you have a sampling frame. Some common sources of sampling frames include electoral registers, memberships of organisations (such as the Automobile Association), lists of employees, customer loyalty cards, account holders, registered users, website addresses and credit rating agencies. But even when you have a sampling frame your troubles are not over because a common problem concerns the size of the population. The sampling frame of, say, 'households that use electricity in Germany' has over 60 million entries. Then there are two alternatives:

- a census collecting data from every entry in the sampling frame – which is the whole population
- a sample collecting data from only a representative sample of entries in the sampling frame.

What does it really mean when an advertisement says that 'eight out of ten dogs prefer' a particular brand of dog food?

Solution

It probably means that in a particular, relatively small test – and under certain conditions – eight out of ten dog owners who expressed an opinion said that their dog seemed to show some preference for this food over some alternative they were offered.

Types of sample

When a population is small and the results are important, it is worth doing a census and collecting data from every member of the population. A company might run a census of every person working in a department to get their views on a proposed reorganisation, a service might ask all of its users to comment on its quality and a housing association might ask all of its tenants about a proposal.

A census clearly gives the most accurate results – but it is never completely accurate because there are inevitably errors, misunderstandings and omissions. A census of people living in Copenhagen, for example, will always find that some people are ill, on holiday, travelling, or cannot answer or simply refuse to answer. So a census is difficult, time-consuming, expensive – and still not entirely reliable.

Sampling is inherently less accurate – but it is also easier, cheaper and faster. Of course, the main difficulty is identifying a sample that gives a fair representation of the whole population. This difficulty highlights the major weakness of samples, which is the uncertainty about results that can never give an entirely accurate picture of the population. When your breakfast cereal contains 20% fruit, you do not expect every spoonful to contain exactly this amount. However, we can choose samples carefully to make them more reliable. In particular, the samples should be big enough to give a fair representation of the population, but small enough to be practical and cost effective. We return to this problem of sample size in Chapter 14, but here we consider the different ways of choosing a representative sample (illustrated in Figure 4.5).

Cosmetic companies spend a lot of money on research – both scientific research to develop new products and market research to measure customer reactions. You can see the results in many of their advertisements. Historically, these advertisements could make unsupported claims like 'Women prefer our products', but now you see more rigorous statements along the lines of 'In tests 70% of 290 women said that they prefer our products'. When Olay tested their Regenerist 3 Point Treatment Cream, they had Cutest Systems Limited appoint a panel of 160 women to measure the effectiveness. When Boots wanted to test their No. 7 Protect and Perfect Beauty Serum (a treatment to reduce the apparent aging of skin) the University of Manchester tested the effects on a panel of 60 women.

A common problem with such surveys is choosing an appropriate sample. Ideally this should be some kind of random sample – but some surveys have introduced bias by offering respondents free samples, using existing teams of respondents, asking people already browsing their websites, or targeting people who are likely to give a particular response.

Sources: www.lorealparis.com; www.olay.co.uk; Watson R.E.B. et al., A cosmetic 'anti-aging' product improves photo-aged skin, *British Journal of Dermatology*, 161(2), 419–426, 2009.

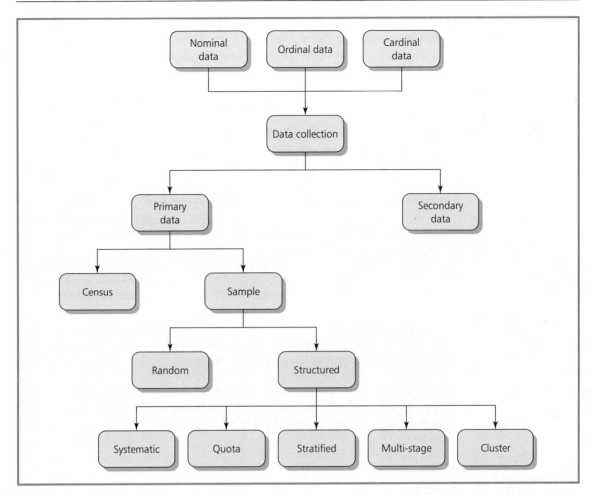

Figure 4.5 Types of samples

Random sample

A random sample is the most common type, and has the essential feature that every member of the population has exactly the same chance of being chosen to supply data. If you randomly choose one member of a football team, it means that all 11 members form the population and each has exactly the same chance of being chosen.

But this does not mean that a random sample is disorganised or haphazard. If you want some data about tinned soup, you could go to a supermarket and buy the first dozen tins of soup you see. This is haphazard – but it is certainly not random becuase tins of soup in every other shop have no chance of being chosen. When a television programme asks people to phone in to give their views, only certain types of people bother to respond, and they form nothing like a random sample of viewers.

With a raffle you can take a genuinely random sample by putting numbers into a hat and choosing one without looking. On a bigger scale, national lotteries usually have some mechanism for selecting numbered balls at random.

In business, a more common approach uses random numbers, which are a stream of random digits – such as 5 8 6 4 5 3 0 1 1 7 2 . . . You can find examples of these using the RAND function in a spreadsheet, which generates a random number between 0 and 1, or RANDBETWEEN (lower, upper) which generates a random integer between 'lower' and 'upper'. (Actually, computers generate 'pseudo-random' numbers but they are good enough for most purposes.)

Suppose that you want to collect data from a random sample of people visiting an office. Using the string of random digits above, you could stand by the door and interview the fifth person to pass, then the eighth person after that, then the sixth after that, then the fourth after that, and so on. The result is a completely random sample, which should give a fair representation of the population. The underlying assumption is that your sample is big enough to give this accurate representation. We describe some calculations for this in Chapter 14.

If a sample does not reflect the population exactly it is said to be biased. If you know that 10% of shops in a town centre opened within the past 2 years, but find that a sample contains 30% of shops opened in this time, then your sample is biased in favour of newer shops. It can be difficult to avoid such bias. If you decide to save time by simply writing down a series of digits that looks random, you will always introduce bias – perhaps reflecting your preferences for even numbers, sequences that are easy to type on a keyboard or numbers that are under stronger fingers on a number pad. Similarly, if you ask interviewers to select people at random they will give a biased sample because they approach people they find attractive, and avoid those they find unattractive, very tall people, people in an obvious hurry, people in groups and so on.

WORKED EXAMPLE 4.2

J.T. Eriksson received 10,000 invoices in the last financial year. Their auditors do not have time to examine all of these, so they take a random sample of 200. How could they organise the sample?

Solution
The auditors could start by forming the sampling frame listing the invoices and numbering them 0000 to 9999. Then they can generate a set of 200 four-digit random numbers, such as 4271, 6845, 2246, 9715, 4415, 0330, 8837 etc. Selecting invoices numbered 4271, 6845, 2246, etc., gives a completely random sample.

Even a well-organised random sample can be affected by a few atypical results. A survey of the amount people spend on transport is biased if one randomly chosen person is a film star who just bought a Boeing 747. We can avoid problems like this by adding some structure to the sample. The results are not entirely random, but they maintain significant random elements – and they aim at giving results of equivalent accuracy, but with a much smaller and more convenient sample.

Systematic sample

One way of organising a non-random sample is to collect data at regular intervals with a systematic sample. For example, you might interview every tenth person using a service, weigh every twentieth unit from a production line or count the people in every sixth car passing. Clearly this is not a random sample because every member of the population does not have the same chance of being chosen – and if you interview every tenth person using a service, then members 11, 12, 13 and so on have no chance of being selected.

Unfortunately, a systematic sample can introduce bias. Checking the contents of every twentieth bottle filled by a bottling machine is unreliable if every twentieth bottle is filled by the same head on the machine; collecting data from every thirtieth person leaving a bus station introduces bias if buses carry about 30 people, and you are always interviewing the people who get off last.

WORKED EXAMPLE 4.3

A production line makes 5,000 units a day. How can the quality control department take a systematic sample of 2% of these?

Solution

Quality control checks 2% of 5,000 units, which is 5,000 / 100 × 2 = 100 units a day. A systematic sample checks every 5,000 / 100 = 50th unit – which is units numbered 50, 100, 150, 200 and so on.

Stratified samples

When there are distinct groups – or strata – in the population, it is a good idea to make sure that members from each stratum are fairly represented in a sample. For a **stratified sample** you divide the population into strata and then take a random sample from each, with the number chosen from each stratum ensuring that the overall sample contains the right mix. For example, 60% of people working in a company might be women. To get a stratified sample of views, you divide the population of employees into two strata – women and men – and randomly select 60% of your sample from women and 40% from men.

WORKED EXAMPLE 4.4

In Westmorefield, companies are classified as manufacturers (20%), transport operators (5%), retailers (30%), utilities (10%) and other services (35%). How would you select a stratified sample of 40 companies?

Solution

The strata are the types of company, so you divide the population into these strata and randomly select the appropriate number from each. The population has 20% manufacturers, so you randomly select 40 / 100 × 0.2 = 8 of these for the sample. Similarly, you randomly select 2 transport operators, 12 retailers, 4 utilities and 14 other services.

A problem with stratified samples appears with small groups. In Worked example 4.4, if Westmorefield had very few transport operators, the strata sample would not have suggested collecting data from any of them – but their views might still be important. We could get around this by increasing the sample size, but the sample becomes very large if we include every possible stratum. An alternative is simply to collect views from all strata, even if they are very small. Then small groups are over-represented and the sample is biased – but it does include contributions from all parts.

Quota samples

Quota samples extend the idea of stratified sampling by adding a more rigid structure. They look at the characteristics of the population, and then specify the characteristics needed in the sample to match this exactly. Suppose you want to see how people will vote in an election. For a quota sample you choose a sample that contains exactly the same proportions of people with different characteristics as the population of people eligible to vote. If the population consists of 4% of men who are over 60, retired from manual work and living alone, then the sample is chosen to also have this proportion.

Quota sampling often uses interviewers who are given a number of people with different characteristics to interview. Each interviewer has to fill their quotas, but they choose the actual people, so there is still a significant random element. However, the sample is clearly not random because interviewers who have filled one quota do not interview any more people in it, and they have no chance of being chosen.

WORKED EXAMPLE 4.5

Census records of 56,300 people in a town show the following features.

Age	18 to 25	16%
	26 to 35	27%
	36 to 45	22%
	46 to 55	18%
	56 to 65	12%
	66 and over	5%
Sex	Female	53%
	Male	47%
Socioeconomic group	A	13%
	B	27%
	C1	22%
	C2	15%
	D	23%

How could you organise a quota sample of 1,200 people?

Solution

The sample should contain exactly the same proportion in each category as the population. 16%, or 192 people, should be aged 18 to 25. Of these 192 people, 53%, or 102, should be women. Of these 102 women, 13%, or 13, should be in socioeconomic group A.

Similarly, 5%, or 60 people, should be at least 66 years old; 47%, or 28 of these, should be male; and 23% of these, or 6 people, should be in socioeconomic group D. Repeating these calculations for all other combinations gives the following quotas.

Age		18 to 25	26 to 35	36 to 45	46 to 55	56 to 65	66 and over
Female	A	13	22	18	15	10	4
	B	27	46	38	31	21	9
	C1	22	38	31	25	17	7
	C2	15	26	21	17	11	5
	D	23	40	32	26	18	7
Male	A	12	20	16	13	9	4
	B	24	41	34	27	18	8
	C1	20	34	27	22	15	6
	C2	14	23	19	15	10	4
	D	21	35	29	23	16	6

Rounding to integers introduces small errors in the quotas, but these make little difference with reasonably large samples.

Multi-stage samples

Suppose that you want a sample of people who subscribe to a particular magazine. If you take a random sample, you will probably find that they are spread over a wide geographical area, and it is inconvenient and expensive to travel to interview them. A cheaper option is to use multi-stage sampling, which makes sure that a sample is confined to a smaller geographical area.

The usual approach is to divide the country into a number of geographical regions, such as television or local radio regions. Then select some of these regions at random, and divide them into smaller subdivisions – perhaps parliamentary constituencies or local government areas. Then select some of these subdivisions at random and again divide them into smaller areas – perhaps towns or parliamentary wards. Continue in this way until you have small enough areas, and then identify a sample of individuals from within these areas.

WORKED EXAMPLE 4.6

How would you set about choosing a multi-stage sample of 1,000 people in Scotland?

Solution

One approach is to randomly select two regions, then randomly select three parliamentary constituencies in each of these, then randomly select three wards in each of these and so on. The following table shows an outline plan that gives a sample size of $2 \times 3 \times 3 \times 4 \times 15 = 1,080$. There are obviously other alternatives.

Stage	Area	Number selected
1	Region	2
2	Parliamentary constituency	3
3	Ward	3
4	Street	4
5	Individuals	15

Cluster sampling

Cluster sampling chooses the members in a sample not individually, but in clusters. This is useful when a population naturally falls into distinct groups, and then you randomly select a number of groups and collect information from some, or all of, the members. For example, you might divide the population of a town into households, then select households at random and collect information from everyone within the chosen households. Or you might find that each file of invoices is representative of the whole population, so it is easier to select a file at random and then collect data from random entries within this. This has the benefits of reducing costs and being convenient to organise – and it is especially useful for surveying working practices, when individual companies form the clusters.

Review questions

4.9 Why would you use a sample to collect data?

4.10 It is always difficult to go through the steps of defining the population, designing a sampling frame, identifying actual individuals in this frame and then collecting data from them. Do you agree with this?

4.11 Why is it important to identify the correct population for a survey?

4.12 What types of sampling can you use?

4.13 What is the key feature of a random sample?

Organising data collection

After identifying an appropriate sample, the next stage is to collect the data. There are two ways of doing this. Firstly, you can use direct observation to see what is happening, and secondly you can ask people questions.

Observation

When the population consists of machines, animals, files, documents or any other inanimate objects, the only way to collect data is by direct observation. Then an observer watches some activity and records what happens, typically counting a number of events, taking some measurements or seeing how something works. But the observers do not have to be human because automatic recorders are better for simple tasks like recording Internet use or monitoring traffic conditions. This is the reason why courier services automatically track parcels using bar codes, magnetic stripes or radio frequency identification tags (RFIDs), and why supermarket check-outs collect data about purchases, telephone services record communications data, computers analyse CCTV images and so on.

Observation is usually more reliable than asking for data – but human observers get tired, make mistakes, get distracted and misunderstand, while automatic observers break down and develop faults.

Questionnaires

When you cannot collect data by observation, you have to ask people to supply it. This means interviewing the sample and eliciting data by a series of questions. According to the Gallup organisation,[5] such interviews can reveal:

■ whether or not a respondent is aware of an issue ('Do you know of any plans to develop . . . ?')
■ general feelings for an issue ('Do you think this development is beneficial . . . ?')
■ views about specific points in an issue ('Do you think this development will affect . . . ?')
■ reasons for a respondent's views ('Are you against this development because . . . ?')
■ how strongly these views are held ('On a scale of 1 to 5, how strong are your feelings about this development . . . ?').

A major problem with asking questions is reliability because people tend to give the answers they feel they ought to give – or the answer the interviewer wants – rather than the true answer. For example, fewer people say that they use their mobile phone while driving than is found from direct observation – and more people claim to wash their hands after using a public lavatory, eat healthy food, do exercise, give more to charity, recycle, read books and so on. There are also problems with emotional responses, so asking customers how they liked the food in a restaurant is likely to get replies based on the whole experience, including who they were with, how they felt, what the weather was like, how attractive the servers were and so on.

The usual way of asking questions is to present them in a questionnaire – which is an ordered list of questions. There are several arrangements for administering a questionnaire including personal interview, telephone interview, postal survey, e-mail survey, panel survey and longitudinal survey. Sometimes the questionnaire is given to people to complete themselves (particularly by post or e-mail), and sometimes it is completed by an interviewer.

Personal interviews

These have an interviewer directly asking questions to respondents, and they can be the most reliable way of getting detailed data. They have a high response rate – only about 10% of people refuse to answer on principle, but this depends on circumstances and few people will agree to a long, complicated or inconvenient interview. Quota sampling needs some assessment and selection of the people questioned, so it inevitably uses personal interviews.

In principle, collecting data by personal interviews is easy because it only needs someone to ask questions and record the answers. The reality is more complicated and depends on skilled interviewers. For instance, they must be careful not to direct respondents to a particular answer by their expression, tone of voice or comments. And they should help to sort out questions that are unclear and ask follow-up questions – but they should not explain the questions or offer any help because this would introduce bias.

The main drawback with personal interviews is the high cost. Each interviewer has to be trained, taken to the right place, given somewhere to work, fed, given overnight accommodation and so on. Typically an interviewer spends 40% of their time in travel, 25% in preparation and administration and only 35% in asking questions.

Telephone interviews

These can be used for the 95% of people who own a telephone, and it is cheap and easy, involves no travel and gets a high response rate. On the other hand, it has the disadvantage of bias because it uses only people with telephones, who accept anonymous calls and are willing to give honest answers over the phone. Other weaknesses are that observers cannot see the respondents and phone calls annoy people who object to the intrusion.

The usual procedure for telephone interviews has a computer selecting a phone number at random from a directory listing. Then an interviewer asks the questions presented on a computer screen and types in the answers. This allows the computer to analyse answers interactively and choose an appropriate set of questions – and it prevents errors during the transfer of data.

Postal surveys

These send questionnaires through the post, and ask people to complete it and return the answers. They are cheap and easy to organise, and are suitable for very large samples. But there are drawbacks, such as the inability to observe people or clarify points, and the difficulty of getting a questionnaire to the right people. There are also problems with bias because only certain types of people bother to reply, and those who have had bad experiences are more likely to respond than those who have had good experiences.

The major problem with postal surveys is the low response rate, which is usually lower than 20% and can approach zero. This might be raised by making the questionnaire short and easy to complete, sending it to a named person (or at least a title), enclosing a covering letter to explain the purpose of the survey, including a pre-paid return envelope, promising anonymity of replies, using a follow-up letter or telephone call if replies are slow and promising a summary of results. Many surveys try to increase the response rate by offering some reward – typically a small gift, discount on a future purchase or entry to a prize draw – but this again introduces bias because respondents now feel more kindly towards the questionnaire.

E-mail surveys

These are an extension of postal surveys, and they can contact very large numbers of people at almost no cost. But there are obvious problems with bias because they are limited to people who regularly use e-mail, publish their address, accept unsolicited messages and want to reply. Spam is a huge problem on the Internet and most people use filters that would not allow random questionnaires through. An alternative is to open a website and ask people to visit and give their views – like www.yougov.co.uk. But clearly the replies are rarely representative of the population.

Panel surveys

These assemble a representative panel of respondents who are monitored to see how their opinions change over time. For example, you could monitor the political views of a panel during the lifetime of a government or their awareness of a product during an advertising campaign. Panel surveys are expensive and difficult to administer, so they use very small samples.

One interesting problem is that members of the panel can become so involved in the issues that they change their views and behaviour. For instance, a panel that is looking at the effects of a healthy eating campaign might become more interested in health issues and change their own habits. Another problem is that some panel members inevitably have to leave, and the remainder become less representative of the population.

Longitudinal surveys

These are an extension of panel surveys that monitor a group of respondents over a long period. For example, studies routinely monitor the effects of lifestyles on health over many decades – and find that exercise reduces heart disease, alcohol increases liver disease, smoking reduces life expectancy and so on. Granada TV has been monitoring the progress of a group of 14 children – then adults – since 1964. These studies need a lot of resources and they are generally limited to studies of sociological, health and physical changes.

IDEAS IN PRACTICE Mareco

For 50 years after the Second World War Poland had a centrally planned economy with the government controlling most businesses. However, the economy was reformed in 1990 and newly privatised companies began to approach their customers to find exactly what they wanted. The market research industry grew from nothing in 1990 to $50 million in 1998. This trend continued as the economy evolved and Poland joined the European Union in 2004. By 2008 there were nine major research companies, with Mareco the largest, having won up to 90% of some markets.

Many Polish companies still have little interest in market research, maintaining their traditional view that it is a waste of money. However, foreign companies investing in Poland do not know the country well and they want to learn about the new market. 80% of Mareco's clients are foreign companies starting new operations in Poland.

Mareco aims to conduct research as quickly and as accurately as possible 'to provide the best insights into our clients' markets'. They organise operations from a head office in Warsaw, which has three separate departments.

■ *Opinion polls and market research department* – works at the start of a project, forming relations with customers, preparing research offers, scheduling work, designing questionnaires, selecting samples and so on. It also works at the end of projects, analysing results of surveys and writing reports for clients.
■ *Field research department* – collects the data using a network of 17 coordinators and 200 interviewers throughout Poland.
■ *Data processing department* – takes the data collected in the field research, analyses it and creates databases that are passed back to the Opinion polls and market research department.

Mareco joined Gallup International Association in 1994, allowing it to introduce new ideas and use the experience of other Gallup companies. Mareco's main problem comes from the quality of interviewers, who are often students who want short-term employment. They can do simple data collection, but lack the skills for in-depth interviews or other more demanding jobs.

Sources: Website at www.mareco.pl and company reports, Mareco, Warsaw.

Design of questionnaires

Designing a good questionnaire is far from easy – and many surveys fail because they asked the wrong questions, or asked the right questions in the wrong way. Even subtle differences in wording and layout can have unexpected effects. A lot of research into the design of questionnaires has led to useful guidelines, illustrated in the following list. Many of these are common sense, but they are often overlooked.

■ A questionnaire should ask a series of related questions and should follow a logical sequence.
■ Make the questionnaire as short as possible. People will not answer long or poorly presented questionnaires, and unnecessary questions cost more to collect and analyse.
■ Questions should be short, simple, unambiguous, easy to understand and phrased in everyday terms – if people do not understand a question they will give any response they think of, or none at all.
■ Even simple changes to phrasing can give very different results. For example, people are more impressed by a medical treatment described as having a 60% success rate than by the same treatment described as having a 40% failure rate.

- People are not always objective, so asking 'Do you think that prison sentences would deter speeding drivers?' gets a different response from 'If you are caught driving too fast, should you go to prison?'
- Avoid leading questions such as 'Do you agree with the common view that NBC news is more objective than Fox news?' Such questions encourage conformity rather than truthful answers.
- Use phrases that are as neutral as possible – rephrasing 'Do you like this cake?' to 'How do you rate the taste of this cake on a scale of 1 to 5?'
- Phrase all personal questions carefully – with 'Have you retired from paid work?' being more sensitive than 'Are you an old-age pensioner?'
- Do not give warnings – a question that starts 'We understand if you do not want to answer this, but . . .' will discourage everyone from answering.
- Avoid vague questions like 'Do you usually buy more meat than vegetables?' This raises a series of questions – what does 'usually' mean? What is 'more'? Do frozen meals count as meat or vegetables?
- Ask positive questions like 'Did you buy a Sunday newspaper last week?' rather than the less definite 'Has the number of Sunday newspapers you buy changed?'
- Avoid hypothetical questions such as 'How much would you spend on life insurance if you won a million euros on a lottery?' Any answer will be speculative and probably not based on any real thought.
- Avoid asking two or more questions in one, such as 'Do you think this development should go ahead because it will increase employment in the area and improve facilities?' This will confuse people who think the development should not go ahead, or those who think it will increase employment but not improve facilities.
- Open questions such as 'Have you any other comments?' collect general views, but they favour the articulate and quick thinking, and are difficult to analyse.
- Ask questions with precoded answers, with respondents choosing the most appropriate answer from a set of alternatives. There are many formats for these – examples are given in Figure 4.6.
- Be prepared for unexpected effects, such as sensitivity to the colour and format of the questionnaire, or different types of interviewer getting different responses.
- Always run a pilot survey before starting the whole survey. This is the only way to identify problems and improve the questionnaire design.

Non-responses

Even the best questionnaire will not get a response from everyone in the sample. There are several reasons for this, including:

- People may be genuinely unable to answer the questions, perhaps because of language difficulties or ill health – or they simply do not know the answer.
- They are out when the interviewer called – but careful timing of calls, appointments and repeat visits can reduce this problem.
- They are away for a period, with holidays and business commitments making surveys in the summer particularly difficult.

1 Will you be joining an evening class this term?   YES/NO

2 How many children do you have? (please circle your answer)

           0   1   2   3   4   more

3 Do you use a computer in your office? (please tick a box)

    Yes ☐   No ☐

4 Do you think the government should spend more on education? (please tick a box)

Strongly agree	Agree	Do not know	Disagree	Strongly disagree

5 A proposal has been made to ban all traffic from the town centre. Please circle the number which most accurately reflects your view on this.

| Strongly approve | 1 | 2 | 3 | 4 neutral | 5 | 6 | 7 | Strongly disapprove |

6 Why are you taking this course? (please circle any appropriate answers)
   (a) out of interest
   (b) to get a qualification
   (c) to help in work
   (d) friends are taking it
   (e) to resit a course failed last year
   (f) other reason, please specify ....

7 How old are you? (please tick one answer)
   ☐ less than 18   ☐ 50 to 70
   ☐ 18 to 35   ☐ more than 70
   ☐ 35 to 50

Figure 4.6 Examples of precoded questions

- They have moved and are no longer at the given address – in which case it is rarely worth following up at the new address.
- They refuse to answer – about 10% of people refuse to answer on principle, and nothing can be done about these.

You might be tempted to ignore non-responses. But then you are assuming that the non-respondents make no difference – meaning that actual respondents fairly represent the sample, and this, in turn, represents the population fairly. This is not necessarily true and there may be a systematic reason for the non-responses. Suppose you run a survey and start with the question 'Does your company have any strategic alliances?' Companies that answer 'No' to this question are unlikely to be interested enough to complete the rest of the questionnaire, so replies are biased towards companies that actually have alliances. In an extreme example a postal questionnaire has been used to ask about literacy skills (in the way that people with reading difficulties can pick up information packs when visiting their local library).

To avoid these effects you should always follow up non-respondents. Another well-timed visit, telephone call or letter might encourage non-respondents to reply, but realistically you will get limited success. Then the only option is to examine non-respondents to make sure they do not share some common characteristic that introduces bias.

Summary of data collection

The important point about data collection is that it does not happen by chance, but needs careful planning. Figure 4.2 summarised the main steps in this, and now we can add some details to get the following more-detailed steps in data collection.

1 Define the purpose of the data.
2 Describe the data you need to achieve this purpose.
3 Check available secondary data to see how useful it is.
4 Define the population and sampling frame to give primary data.
5 Choose the best sampling method and sample size.
6 Identify an appropriate sample.
7 Design a questionnaire or other method of data collection.
8 Run a pilot study and check for problems.
9 Train interviewers, observers or experimenters.
10 Do the main data collection.
11 Do follow-up, such as contacting non-respondents.
12 Analyse and present the results.

This seems rather complicated, and you may be tempted to take short-cuts. Remember, though, that every decision in an organisation depends on available information – and this, in turn, depends on reliable data collection. Unfortunately even careful planning cannot eliminate all errors, which typically arise from:

■ failure to identify an appropriate population
■ choosing a sample that does not represent this population
■ mistakes in contacting members of the sample
■ mistakes in collecting data from the sample
■ introducing bias from non-respondents
■ mistakes made during data analysis
■ drawing invalid conclusions from the analysis.

Review questions

4.14 What method of data collection is best for:
    (a) asking how companies use their websites
    (b) asking colleagues for their views on a proposed change to working conditions
    (c) testing the effect of exercise on the incidence of heart disease
    (d) testing the accuracy of invoices?

4.15 What is wrong with the following survey questions?
    (a) 'Most people want higher retirement pensions. Do you agree with them?'
    (b) 'Does watching too much television affect children's school work?'
    (c) 'Should the UK destroy its nuclear arms, reduce spending on conventional arms and increase expenditure on education?'
    (d) 'What is the most likely effect of a single European currency on pensions?'

4.16   What can you do about non-responses in a postal survey?

4.17   Why are non-responses irrelevant for quota sampling?

4.18   'It is best to get some data quickly so that you can start planning the analyses.' Do you agree with this?

IDEAS IN PRACTICE   **PhD research**

In 2003 David Grant was awarded a PhD by the University of Edinburgh, for work on 'A study of customer service, customer satisfaction and service quality in the logistics function of the UK food processing industry'. This won a prestigious award from the Institute for Logistics and Transport. The research needed a lot of data collection, which David undertook in the following stages.

1   Initial review of published material, interviews and discussions to identify a suitable research project.
2   Literature review of published material to find other work in the area and assess its importance.
3   Collection of secondary data to find comparisons for the research.
4   Design and initial testing of a questionnaire for a postal survey, with interviews to gauge reactions to the survey.

5   Pilot study with the questionnaire sent to 380 companies, with follow-up of those who did not initially respond, giving a response rate of 28%.
6   Interviews with respondents to clarify results and refine the questionnaire.
7   Main study with the questionnaire sent to 1,215 companies, with follow-up of those that did not initially reply, giving a response rate of 17%.

The details of every research project vary, but this illustrates a common approach. Initial data collection sets the scene for the research; secondary data identifies work that has already been done; primary data extends the research into new areas.

Sources: Grant D., A study of customer service, customer satisfaction and service quality in the logistics function of the UK food processing industry, unpublished PhD thesis, University of Edinburgh, 2003, and private correspondence.

CHAPTER REVIEW

This chapter described different ways of collecting data.

■ Managers need reliable information to make decisions, and they get this through data collection, analysis and presentation. This means that data collection is an essential requirement for managers in every organisation.

■ Data collection does not just happen – it needs careful planning. This starts by defining the purpose of the data. In principle, there is an optimal amount of data to collect for any purpose.

■ We can classify data in several ways, including quantitative/qualitative, nominal/ordinal/cardinal, and primary/secondary. Data of different types – and with different uses – is collected in different ways.

■ A population consists of all the people or items that could supply data. These are listed in a sampling frame. It can be difficult to choose the right population and find a sampling frame.

■ It is usually too expensive, time-consuming and difficult to collect data from the whole population – giving a census. The alternative collects data from a representative sample of the population and uses this to estimate values for the whole population. There are several types of sample including random, systematic, stratified, quota, multi-stage and cluster samples.

- The two alternatives for collecting data from the sample are observation and questionnaires. Questionnaires can be administered through personal interview, telephone interview, the Internet, postal survey, panel survey or longitudinal survey.

- There are useful guidelines for designing questionnaires.

- You should always run a pilot survey to sort out any problems, and examine non-respondents to make sure they do not introduce bias.

CASE STUDY Natural Wholemeal Biscuits

Natural Wholemeal Biscuits (NWB) make a range of foods that they sell to health food shops around eastern Canada. They divide the country into 13 geographical regions based around major cities. The table shows the number of shops stocking their goods and annual sales in each region.

Region	Shops	Sales ($'000)
Toronto	94	240
Montreal	18	51
Hamilton	8	24
Sudbury	9	18
Windsor	7	23
Québec	12	35
Halifax	8	17
Niagara	6	8
London	5	4
Ottawa	17	66
St John's	8	32
Moncton	4	15
Trois-Rivières	4	25

Sex	Female	64%
	Male	36%
Age	Less than 20	16%
	20 to 30	43%
	30 to 40	28%
	40 to 60	9%
	More than 60	4%
Social class	A	6%
	B	48%
	C1	33%
	C2	10%
	D	3%
Vegetarian	Yes	36% (5% vegan)
	No	60%
	Other response	4%
Reason for buying	Like the taste	35%
	For fibre content	17%
	Never tried before	11%
	Help diet	8%
	Other response	29%
Regular buyer of bar	Yes	32%
	No	31%
	Other response	37%

NWB are about to introduce a 'Vegan Veggie Bar' that is made from a combination of nuts, seeds and dried fruit, and is guaranteed to contain no animal products. The company wants to find likely sales of the new bar and is considering a market survey. They already sell 300,000 similar bars a year at an average price of $1.80, and with an average contribution to profit of 36 cents. An initial survey of 120 customers in three shops gave the following characteristics of customers for these bars.

The company wants as much information as possible, but must limit costs to reasonable levels. Experience suggests that it costs $24 to interview a customer personally, while a postal or telephone survey costs $8 per response. The management information group at NWB can analyse the data relatively cheaply, but management time for reviews and discussion is expensive.

Questions

- How can NWB collect data on potential sales of its Vegan Veggie Bar? What secondary data is available? What primary data do they need, and how should they collect it?

- Design a plan for NWB's data collection including timing, costs and assumptions.

PROBLEMS

4.1 How would you describe the following data?
(a) Weights of books posted to a bookshop
(b) Numbers of pages in books
(c) Position of football teams in a league
(d) Opinions about a new novel.

4.2 What is the appropriate population to give data about the following?
(a) Likely sales of a computer game
(b) Problems facing small shopkeepers
(c) Parking near a new shopping mall
(d) Proposals to close a shopping area to all vehicles.

4.3 Describe a sampling procedure to find reliable data about house values around the country.

4.4 Auditors want to select a sample of 300 invoices from the 9,000 available. How could they do this?

4.5 Use a computer to generate a set of random numbers. Use these to design a sampling scheme to find the views of passengers using a low-cost airline.

4.6 The readership of a Sunday newspaper has the following characteristics.

Age	16 to 25	12%
	26 to 35	22%
	36 to 45	24%
	46 to 55	18%
	56 to 65	12%
	66 to 75	8%
	76 and over	4%
Sex	Female	38%
	Male	62%
Social class	A	24%
	B	36%
	C1	24%
	C2	12%
	D	4%

What are the quotas for a sample of 2,000 readers? Design a spreadsheet to find the quotas in each category for different sample sizes.

4.7 Give some examples of poor questions used in a survey. How could you improve these?

4.8 Give some examples of bias in a survey. What caused the bias and how could it have been avoided?

4.9 Design a questionnaire to collect data on the closure of a shopping area to all vehicles.

4.10 Describe the data collection for a recent survey by the Consumers' Association or an equivalent organisation. How does this compare with data collection at www.yougov.com?

4.11 How could you collect data about the following?
(a) The consumption of cakes and biscuits in a particular country last year
(b) The amount of time people spend on the telephone
(c) Potential sales of a new format for PC data storage
(d) Likely membership of a new running club
(e) Opinions about traffic congestion charges
(f) Satisfaction with government policies
(g) Views on local government expenditure and financing.

RESEARCH PROJECTS

4.1 Design a survey of the way that companies use the Web in your area. What kind of companies form your population? How can you select an unbiased sample from these? What data would you want and how would you collect it? What problems might you meet?

4.2 Use government statistics to see how the gross national product has changed over the past 30 years. How does this compare with other countries? What other international comparisons can you make?

4.3 Run a survey of the way people travel in your area. You might ask basic questions such as how often they make journeys, how far they go and what transport they use. Then you can collect opinions about the quality of their journeys, problems and possible improvements. To make sure your sample is representative you might add some demographic questions about age, gender, occupation etc.

Sources of information

References

1 Browning E.B., *Sonnets from the Portuguese*, Number 1, 1850.

2 Statistical Service, *Monthly Digest of Statistics*, Office for National Statistics, London.

3 Statistical Service, *Annual Abstract of Statistics*, Office for National Statistics, London.

4 Statistical Service, *Guide to Official Statistics*, Office for National Statistics, London.

5 Website at www.gallup.com.

Further reading

Books on sampling often focus on market surveys or statistical analysis. The following give more general material.

Adams J., Khan H., Raeside R. and White D., *Research Methods*, Response Books, New Delhi, 2007.

Barnett V., *Sample Surveys* (3rd edition), Edward Arnold, London, 2002.

Collis J. and Hussey R., *Business Research*, Palgrave Macmillan, Basingstoke, 2003.

Czaja R. and Blair J., *Designing Surveys*, Sage Publications, London, 2005.

Fowler F.J., *Survey Research Methods* (4th edition), Sage Publications, London, 2008.

Francis A., *Working with Data*, Thomson Learning, London, 2003.

Ghauri P. and Gronhaug K., *Research Methods in Business Studies* (4th edition), Financial Times/Prentice Hall, Harlow, 2010.

Rea L.M. and Parker R.A., *Designing and Conducting Survey Research* (3rd edition), Jossey Bass, Hoboken, NJ, 2005.

Starwarski C. and Phillips P., *Data Collection*, Jossey Bass, Hoboken, NJ, 2008.

Wilson J., *Essentials of Business Research*, Sage Publications, London, 2010.

Diagrams for presenting data

Chapter outline

Data collection brings together raw data, but this has to be processed to give useful information. The amount of detail in data sometimes obscures underlying patterns and data reduction clears away the detail and highlights important features and patterns. It enables a view of the data that is concise, but still accurate. There are two approaches to summarising and presenting data. In this chapter we describe diagrams, and Chapter 6 continues the theme by discussing numerical summaries.

After finishing this chapter you should be able to:

- discuss the aims of data reduction and presentation
- design tables of numerical data
- draw frequency distributions of data
- use graphs to show the relationship between two variables
- design pie charts
- draw different kinds of bar chart
- consider pictograms and other formats
- draw histograms for continuous data
- draw ogives and Lorenz curves for cumulative data.

Data reduction and presentation

In Chapter 4 we saw that data are the basic numbers and facts that we process to give useful information. So 78, 64, 36, 70 and 52 are data that we process to give the information that the average mark of five students in an exam is 60%.

Most people can deal with small amounts of numerical data. We happily say, 'this building is 60 metres tall', 'a car travels 15 kilometres on a litre of petrol' and '16% of people use a particular product'. But we have problems when there is a lot of data. For instance, the weekly sales of a product from a website over the past year are:

51 60 58 56 62 69 58 76 80 82 68 90 72
84 91 82 78 76 75 66 57 78 65 50 61 54
49 44 41 45 38 28 37 40 42 22 25 26 21
30 32 30 32 31 29 30 41 45 44 47 53 54

This gives the raw data – which you probably skipped over with hardly a glance. If you put such figures in a report, people would find it boring and jump to something more interesting – even though the figures could be very important. To make things less daunting we could try putting them in the text, starting with 'In the first week sales were 51 units, and they rose by 9 units in the second week, but in the third week they fell back to 58 units, and fell another 2 units in the fourth week . . .'. Clearly, this does not work with so many numbers, and we need a more convenient format.

The problem is that raw data swamps us with detail, obscuring the overall patterns and shape of the data – we cannot see the wood for the trees. So imagine that you have put a lot of effort into collecting data and now want to show it to other people. You really have two jobs – *data reduction* (processing to reduce the amount of detail), and *data presentation* to show the results in a useful format.

- **Data reduction** gives a simplified and accurate view of the data, showing the underlying patterns but not overwhelming us with detail.
- **Data presentation** shows clearly and accurately the characteristics of a set of data and highlights the patterns.

So the sequence of activities for analysing data starts with data collection, moves to data reduction and then data presentation. In practice, there is no clear distinction between data reduction and data presentation, and we usually combine them into a single activity. This combined activity of summarising data has the advantages of:

- showing results in a compact form
- using formats that are easy to understand
- allowing diagrams, graphs or pictures to be produced
- highlighting underlying patterns
- allowing comparisons of different sets of data
- using quantitative measures.

On the other hand, summarising data has the major disadvantage that it loses the detail of the original data and is irreversible.

Diagrams for presenting data

There are essentially two ways of summarising data – using diagrams and numerical descriptions. In this chapter we look at diagrams, with a description of numerical measures following in Chapter 6.

When you look around, there are countless examples of diagrams giving information. A newspaper article adds a diagram to summarise its story; an advertisement uses a picture to get across its message; a company's financial performance is summarised in a graph; a Website uses animation to add interest. Diagrams attract people's attention, and we are more likely to look at them than read the accompanying text – hence the saying, 'One picture is worth a thousand words'. Good diagrams are attractive, they make information more interesting, give a clear summary of data, emphasise underlying patterns and allow us to extract a lot of information in a short time. But they do not happen by chance – they have to be carefully designed.

If you look at a diagram and cannot understand what is happening, it means that the presentation is poor – and it is safe to assume that the fault is with the presenter rather than the viewer. Sometimes there is a more subtle problem – you can look at a diagram quickly and immediately see one pattern, but if you look more closely you find that your initial impression was wrong. To be generous, this might be a simple mistake in presenting the data poorly, but the truth is that many people make a deliberate decision to present data in a form that is misleading and dishonest. Advertisements are notorious for presenting data in a way that gives the *desired* impression, rather than accurately reflecting a situation, and politicians might be more concerned with appearance than with truth. Huff[1] developed this theme in the 1950s with his classic descriptions of 'How to lie with statistics' and this has been followed by similar descriptions, such as those of Kimble[2], Tufte[3] and more recently Wainer.[4,5] The problem is that diagrams are a powerful means of presenting data, but they give only a summary – and this summary can easily be misleading. In this chapter we show how to use diagrams properly, so that they give a fair and honest summary of raw data.

There are many types of diagram for presenting data, with the most common including:

- tables of numerical data and frequency distributions
- graphs to show relationships between variables
- pie charts, bar charts and pictograms showing frequencies
- histograms that show frequencies of continuous data.

The choice of best format is often a matter of personal judgement and preference. But always remember that you want to present information fairly and efficiently – and you are not just looking for the prettiest picture. Some guidelines for choosing the type of diagram include the following, where appropriate:

- choose the most suitable format for the purpose
- always present data fairly and honestly
- make sure all diagrams are clear and easy to understand
- state the source of data
- use consistent units and say what these are

■ include totals, sub-totals and any other useful summaries
■ give each diagram a title
■ add notes to highlight assumptions and reasons for unusual or atypical values.

Review questions

5.1 What is the difference between data and information?

5.2 What is the purpose of data reduction?

5.3 'Data presentation always gives a clear, detailed and accurate view.' Is this true?

5.4 What are the two main methods of presenting data?

Tables of numerical data

Tables are probably the most common way of summarising data. We have already used several in this book, and you can see more in newspapers, magazines, books, reports and websites. Table 5.1 shows the weekly sales of the product mentioned above, and this gives the general format for tables.

Table 5.1 Weekly sales of a product

Week	Quarter 1	Quarter 2	Quarter 3	Quarter 4	Total
1	51	84	49	30	214
2	60	91	44	32	227
3	58	82	41	30	211
4	56	78	45	32	211
5	62	76	38	31	207
6	69	75	28	29	201
7	58	66	37	30	191
8	76	57	40	41	214
9	80	78	42	45	245
10	82	65	22	44	213
11	68	50	25	47	190
12	90	61	26	53	230
13	72	54	21	54	201
Totals	882	917	458	498	2,755

This is clearer than the original list, and you can now see that sales are higher in the first two quarters and lower in the second two. But the table still only shows the raw data – and it does not really give a feel for a typical week's sales, it is difficult to find the minimum and maximum sales and patterns are not clear. We can emphasise the underlying patterns by reducing the data. To start with, we can find that minimum sales are 21, and then count the number of weeks with sales in a range of, say, 20 to 29. There are six weeks in this range. Counting the number of weeks with sales in other ranges gives the summary shown in Table 5.2.

Tables that show the number of values in different ranges are called frequency tables, and the 'ranges' are called classes. Then we can talk about the

Table 5.2 Frequency table of sales

Range of sales	Number of weeks
20–29	6
30–39	8
40–49	10
50–59	9
60–69	7
70–79	6
80–89	4
90–99	2

'class of 20 to 29', where 20 is the lower class limit, 29 is the upper class limit, and the class width is $29 - 20 = 9$. We arbitrarily chose classes of 20–29, 30–39, and so on, but could have used any other reasonable values. This is largely a choice that is guided by the structure of the data and the use of the table, but two guidelines are:

- the classes should all be the same width
- there should be enough classes to make patterns clear, but not too many to obscure them; this usually suggests a minimum of four classes, and a maximum of around ten.

If the eight classes in Table 5.2 seem too many, we could divide the data into, say, four classes and add a note about the source to give the final result shown in Table 5.3.

Table 5.3 Frequency table of weekly sales

Range	Number of weeks
20–39	14
40–59	19
60–79	13
80–99	6

Source: Company Weekly Sales Reports

Tables 5.1 to 5.3 show an inevitable effect of data reduction – if more data is summarised, more detail is lost. For instance, Table 5.3 shows the distribution of weekly sales but it gives no idea of the seasonal variations. We can accept this loss of detail if the result still shows all the information we want and is easier to understand – but not if the details are important. In this example, if we want to plan the number of seasonal employees, we could not use Table 5.3 and would have to return to Table 5.1.

Clearly, you can present a set of data in many different tables – and you always have to compromise between making them too long (when they show lots of detail, but are complicated and obscure underlying patterns) and too short (when they show patterns clearly, but lose most of the detail). Another guideline says that if you repeatedly present data over some period, you should always keep the same format to allow direct comparisons (as you can see in most company reports and government publications).

WORKED EXAMPLE 5.1

Carlson Industries has collected the following monthly performance indicators over the past five years. How would you summarise these in a different table?

	Year 1	Year 2	Year 3	Year 4	Year 5
January	136	135	141	138	143
February	109	112	121	117	118
March	92	100	104	105	121
April	107	116	116	121	135
May	128	127	135	133	136
June	145	132	138	154	147
July	138	146	159	136	150
August	127	130	131	135	144
September	135	127	129	140	140
October	141	156	137	134	142
November	147	136	149	148	147
December	135	141	144	140	147

Solution

There are many different ways of summarising these, with some options shown in the spreadsheet in Figure 5.1.

	A	B	C	D	E	F	G	H
1	**Carlson Industries**							
2								
3	**Range**	**Frequency**		**Monthly averages**			**Annual averages**	
4								
5	< 99	1		January	138.6		Year 1	128.3
6	100–109	5		February	115.4		Year 2	129.8
7	110–119	5		March	104.4		Year 3	133.7
8	120–129	8		April	119		Year 4	133.4
9	130–139	19		May	131.8		Year 5	139.2
10	140–149	18		June	143.2			
11	> 150	4		July	145.8			
12				August	133.4			
13				September	134.2			
14				October	142			
15				November	145.4			
16				December	141.4			

Figure 5.1 Table of results for Carlson Industries

Frequency distributions

The results shown in a frequency table form a frequency distribution. For example, the following table shows the frequency distribution for the number of deliveries made each week to a logistics centre during a typical year.

Number of deliveries	20–39	40–59	60–79	80–99
Number of weeks	14	19	13	6

There are six observations in the highest class of deliveries, 80–99. But suppose that there had been one unusual week with 140 deliveries. In this table we would put it in a class of its own some distance away from the others.

Number of deliveries	20–39	40–59	60–79	80–99	100–119	120–139	140–169
Number of weeks	14	19	13	5	0	0	1

Sometimes it is important to highlight outlying values – but usually it is just confusing. The way to avoid this is to define the highest class so that it includes all the outliers, which we can do here by defining the top class as '80 or more', with 6 entries. Similarly, it is often better to replace the precise 20–39 for the bottom class by the less precise '39 or fewer'.

An obvious point when choosing the boundaries between classes is that there should be no doubt about which class an observation is in. In our example, you could not define adjacent classes of 20–30 and 30–40 because a value of 30 could be in either. Using 20–29 and 30–39 avoids this problem for discrete data, but fails with continuous data. For instance, you could not classify people's ages as 20–29 and 30–39 because this would leave no place for people who are 29.5. Instead you have to use more precise – but rather messy – phrases like 'aged 20 or more and less than 30'.

WORKED EXAMPLE 5.2

The weights of materials (in kilograms) needed for 30 projects are as follows. Draw a frequency distribution of this data.

202 457 310 176 480 277 87 391 325 361
 94 362 221 274 145 240 437 404 398 554
429 216 282 153 470 303 338 209 120 144

Solution

The first decision is the best number of classes. The range is between 87 kg and 554 kg, so a reasonable solution is to use six classes of 'less than 100 kg', '100 kg or more and less than 200 kg', '200 kg or more and less than 300 kg' and so on. Notice that we are careful not to phrase these as 'more than 100 kg and less than 200 kg' because a project needing exactly 100 kg would not fit into any class. Adding the number of observations in each class gives the frequency distribution in Figure 5.2.

	A	B	C
1	**Frequency distribution**		
2			
3	**Class**	**Frequency**	**Percentage frequency**
4	less than 100 kg	2	6.7
5	100 kg or more, and less than 200 kg	5	16.7
6	200 kg or more, and less than 300 kg	8	26.7
7	300 kg or more, and less than 400 kg	9	30.0
8	400 kg or more, and less than 500 kg	5	16.7
9	500 kg or more	1	3.3
10	**Totals**	**30**	**100.0**

Figure 5.2 Frequency distribution for Worked example 5.2

	A	B	C	D	E
1	**Different types of frequency distribution**				
2					
3	**Class**	**Frequency**	**Cumulative frequency**	**Percentage frequency**	**Cumulative percentage frequency**
4	**less than 100 kg**	2	2	6.7	6.7
5	**100 kg or more, and less than 200 kg**	5	7	16.7	23.3
6	**200 kg or more, and less than 300 kg**	8	15	26.7	50.0
7	**300 kg or more, and less than 400 kg**	9	24	30.0	80.0
8	**400 kg or more, and less than 500 kg**	5	29	16.7	96.7
9	**500 kg or more**	1	30	3.3	100.0
10	**Total**	**30**		**100.0**	

Figure 5.3 Different types of frequency distribution

Frequency distributions show the number of observations in each class, but in Figure 5.2 we also calculate a percentage frequency distribution, which shows the percentage of observations in each class. Another useful extension shows cumulative frequencies. Instead of recording the number of observations in a class, cumulative frequency distributions add all observations in lower classes. In Figure 5.2 there were 2 observations in the first class, 5 in the second class and 8 in the third. The cumulative frequency distribution would show 2 observations in the first class, 2 + 5 = 7 in the second class, and 2 + 5 + 8 = 15 in the third. In the same way, we can also present a cumulative percentage frequency distribution, as shown in Figure 5.3.

Review questions

5.5   What are the advantages of using tables of data?

5.6   What is a frequency distribution?

5.7   What is the best number of classes for a table of data?

5.8   Tables of data can seem very dull – so why are they so widely used?

IDEAS IN PRACTICE   **UK cereal production**

Tables range from the very simple to the very complex. For example, we can show the percentages of wheat, barley, oats and other cereals grown in the UK in this simple table:

Cereal	Percentage of cereal-growing land
Wheat	64%
Barley	32%
Oats	3%
Others	1%

Or we can add a lot more detail to get the result in Table 5.4 – and we could continue adding more data until the tables become very complex.

Ideas in practice continued

Table 5.4 Main cereal crops grown in the United Kingdom

	1990	1995	2000	2005	2010
Wheat					
Area ('000 hectares)	2,014 (55.0)	1,859 (58.4)	2,086 (62.3)	1,867 (64.5)	1,814 (58.4)
Harvest ('000 tonnes)	14,033 (62.1)	14,312 (65.4)	16,708 (69.7)	14,863 (71.1)	14,379 (65.6)
Yield (tonnes per hectare)	7.0	7.7	8.0	8.0	7.9
Barley					
Area ('000 hectares)	1,517 (41.4)	1,193 (37.5)	1,128 (33.7)	938 (32.4)	1,160 (37.4)
Harvest ('000 tonnes)	7,911 (35.0)	6,842 (31.3)	6,492 (27.1)	5,495 (26.3)	6,769 (30.9)
Yield (tonnes per hectare)	5.2	5.7	5.8	5.9	5.8
Oats					
Area ('000 hectares)	107 (2.9)	112 (3.5)	109 (3.3)	91 (3.1)	131 (4.2)
Harvest ('000 tonnes)	530 (2.3)	617 (2.8)	640 (2.7)	532 (2.5)	757 (3.5)
Yield (tonnes per hectare)	5.0	5.5	5.9	5.8	5.8
Totals					
Area ('000 hectares)	3,660	3,182	3,348	2,896	3,105
Harvest ('000 tonnes)	22,582	21,870	23,988	20,890	21,905

Sources: Adapted from Department for the Environment, Farming and Rural Affairs, *Agriculture in the UK Annual Report 2010*, London, and website at www.defra.gov.uk.
Notes: Figures in brackets are percentages of annual totals, 2010 figures are current estimates. Rounding means that percentages may not add to 100%.

Diagrams of data

Tables are good at presenting a lot of information, but it can still be difficult to identify underlying patterns. We can see these more clearly in diagrams, such as the graphs we described in Chapter 3. These graphs show the relationship between two variables on a pair of Cartesian axes, with the x-axis showing the independent variable and the y-axis showing corresponding values of a dependent variable. Remember that these terms are often used for convenience. If you plot sales of ice cream against temperature, there is clearly an independent variable (temperature) and a dependent variable (consequent sales of ice cream). But if you plot sales of ice cream against sales of sausages, there is no clear 'dependence' and you can choose to draw the axes either way round.

Formats for graphs

As with tables, there are many different formats for graphs. Returning to the earlier example of weekly sales of a product, we can start by plotting sales (the dependent variable) against the week (the independent variable). Then the simplest graph shows the individual points in a scatter diagram, shown in Figure 5.4(a).

You can see the general pattern here, but this becomes even clearer when we join the points, as shown in Figure 5.4(b). The sales clearly follow a

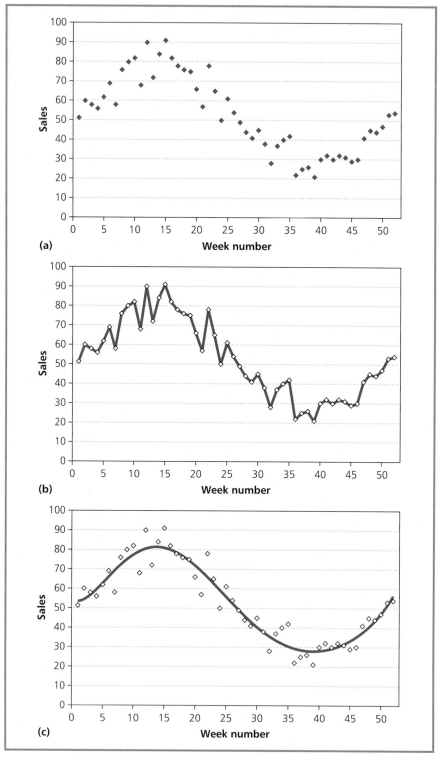

Figure 5.4 Graph of sales figures: (a) scatter diagram, (b) connecting the points to emphasise the pattern, (c) showing the underlying pattern

seasonal cycle, with a peak around week 12 and a trough around week 38. There are small random variations away from this overall pattern, so the graph is not a smooth curve but is rather jagged. We are usually more interested in the underlying patterns than the random variations, and can emphasise this by drawing a smooth trend line through the individual points, as shown in Figure 5.4(c).

The most common difficulty with graphs is choosing the scale for the y-axis. We could redraw the graphs in Figure 5.4 with different scales for the y-axis, and give completely different views. Figure 5.5(a) has a long scale for

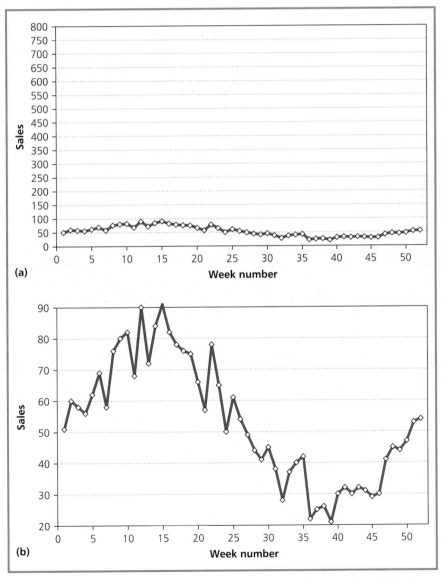

Figure 5.5 Showing poorly drawn graphs: (a) a vertical scale that is too long hides the patterns; (b) part of the vertical scale is omitted, giving a false impression

the *y*-axis, so the graph appears to show stable sales with only small variations; Figure 5.5(b) has a broken scale that omits values 0 to 20, so the graph suggests high sales in the first half and almost no sales in the second half. Both of these views are misleading.

Graphs have a very strong initial impact, so it is important to choose the right scales. Some guidelines for good practice include:

- always label both axes clearly and accurately
- show the scales on both axes
- the maximum of the scale should be slightly above the maximum observation
- wherever possible, the scales on axes should be continuous from zero; if this is too difficult, or hides patterns, show any break clearly in the scale
- where appropriate, give the source of data
- where appropriate, give the graph a title.

Drawing several graphs on the same axes makes it easy to compare different sets of data. For example, we can plot the price of electricity, gas, oil and coal on the same axes to see how they have varied over the past year – or we could compare the price of a single commodity over different years. Figure 5.6 shows the average monthly price of a commodity over five years. As the price differences are small, we have highlighted the pattern by plotting only the relevant part of the *y*-axis.

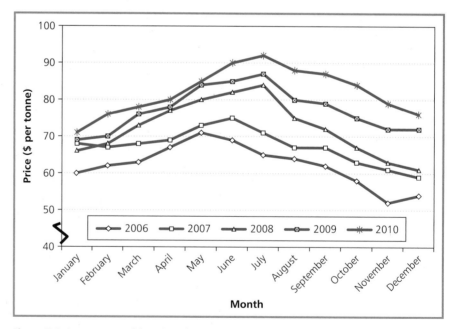

Figure 5.6 Average monthly price of a commodity over a period of five years

WORKED EXAMPLE 5.3

Table 5.5 shows the profit reported by Majestica, Inc. and the corresponding share price. Draw a graph of this data.

Solution

Here there are three variables – quarter, profit and share price – but we can plot only two of these on a graph. We can choose to present the data in several graphs, perhaps showing the vari-ation in share price (or profit) with quarter. However, the most interesting relationship is probably that between profit (as the independent variable) and share price (as the dependent variable) shown in Figure 5.7. In this graph we have chosen the scales to highlight the main areas of interest, and drawn a trend line to suggest the underlying relationship.

Table 5.5 Quarterly company profit and average share price

	Year 1				Year 2				Year 3			
Quarter	1	2	3	4	1	2	3	4	1	2	3	4
Profit	12.1	12.2	11.6	10.8	13.0	13.6	11.9	11.7	14.2	14.5	12.5	13.0
Share price	122	129	89	92	132	135	101	104	154	156	125	136

Source: Company financial reports, New York Stock Exchange and the *Wall Street Journal*.
Note: Profits are in millions of dollars and share prices are in cents.

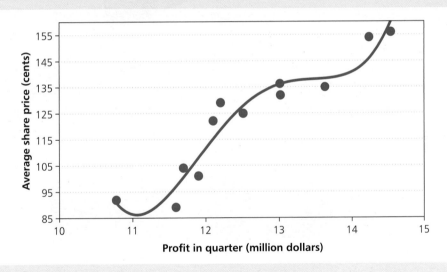

Figure 5.7 Graph of share price against profit for Worked example 5.3

Pie charts

Pie charts are simple diagrams that give a summary of categorical data. To draw a pie chart you draw a circle – the pie – and divide this into slices, each of which represents one category. The area of each slice – and hence the angle at the centre of the circle – is proportional to the number of observations in the category.

WORKED EXAMPLE 5.4

Hambro GmbH has operations in four regions of Europe, with annual sales in millions of euros given in the following table. Draw a pie chart to represent these.

Region	North	South	East	West	Total
Sales	25	10	35	45	115

Solution

There are 360° in a circle, and these represent 115 observations. So each observation is represented by an angle of 360 / 115 = 3.13° at the centre of the circle. Then the sales in the north region are represented by a slice with an angle of 25 × 3.13 = 78.3° at the centre; sales in the south region are represented by a slice with an angle of 10 × 3.13 = 31.3° at the centre, and so on. Figure 5.8(a) shows a basic chart for this data. Of course, you do not actually have to do these calculations – many standard packages draw pie charts automatically. These tools can also improve the presentation, and Figure 5.8(b) shows the same data when it is sorted into order, rotated to put the biggest slice at the back, labelled and given a three-dimensional effect.

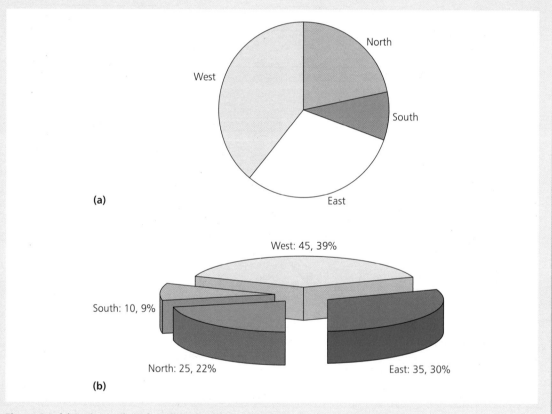

Figure 5.8 (a) Basic pie chart for sales of Hambro GmbH; (b) Adding more features to the pie

Pie charts are very simple and have an immediate impact, but they show only very small amounts of data. When there are more than, say, six or seven slices they become too complicated and confusing. There is also some concern about whether people really understand data presented in this format and whether it gives a misleading view.[6]

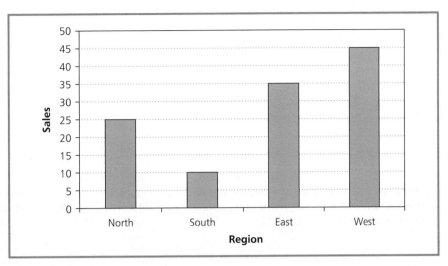

Figure 5.9 Bar chart of results for Hambro GmbH

Bar charts

Like pie charts, **bar charts** show the number of observations in different categories. Each category is represented by its own line or bar, and the length of this bar is proportional to the number of observations. Figure 5.9 shows a bar chart for the data from Hambro GmbH given in Worked example 5.4. Here the bars are vertical, but they could equally be horizontal and – as with pie charts – we can add many variations to enhance the appearance. One constant rule, though, is that you should always start the scale for the bars at zero, and never be tempted to save space by omitting the lower parts of bars. This is sometimes unavoidable in graphs, but in bar charts the result is simply confusing.

WORKED EXAMPLE 5.5

South Middleton Health District has five hospitals, with the following numbers of beds in each. How could you represent this data in bar charts?

	Hospital				
	Foothills	General	Southern	Heathview	St John
Maternity	24	38	6	0	0
Surgical	86	85	45	30	24
Medical	82	55	30	30	35
Psychiatric	25	22	30	65	76

Solution

There are many possible formats here. One shows the number of surgical beds in each hospital – illustrated in Figure 5.10(a). A particular strength of bar charts is that we can show several sets of data in the same diagram to make direct comparisons. For example, Figure 5.10(b) compares the number of beds of each type in each hospital. If we want to highlight the relative sizes of the hospitals, we could combine the bars by 'stacking' them, as shown in Figure 5.10(c). If we want to emphasise type of beds in each hospital, we could describe the percentages of beds, as shown in Figure 5.10(d).

Worked example 5.5 continued

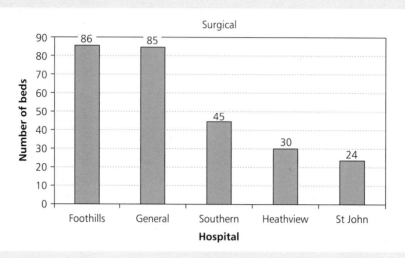

Figure 5.10(a) Bar chart for South Middleton Health District hospitals: number of surgical beds

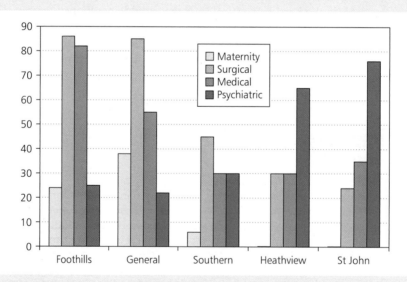

Figure 5.10(b) Comparison of the number of beds of different types in each hospital

Worked example 5.5 continued

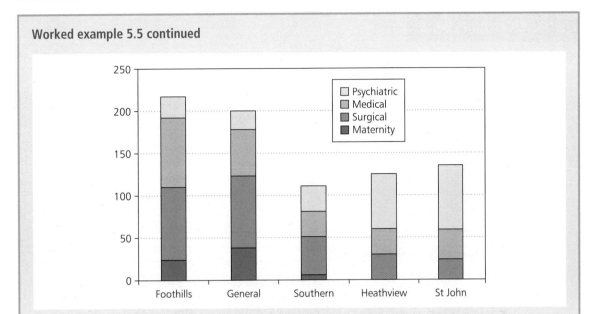

Figure 5.10(c) Stacked bars to emphasise the relative numbers of different types of beds

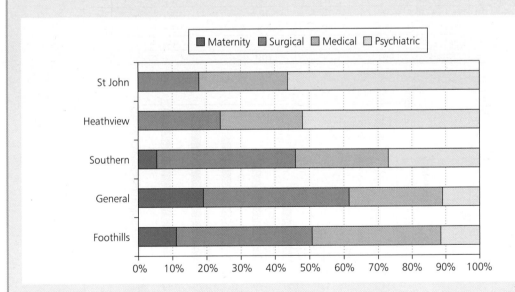

Figure 5.10(d) Percentages of beds of each type

WORKED EXAMPLE 5.6

Draw a frequency distribution for these discrete data:

150 141 158 147 132 153 176 162 180 165
174 133 129 119 133 188 190 165 157 146
161 130 122 169 159 152 173 148 154 171
136 155 141 153 147 168 150 140 161 185

Solution

This illustrates one of the main uses of bar charts, which is to show frequency distributions. We start by defining suitable classes. The values range from 119 to 190, so a class width of 10 gives nine classes. As the values are discrete, we can arbitrarily use 110–119, 120–129, 130–139, and so on. Figure 5.11 shows a spreadsheet calculating a frequency distribution, percentage frequency and cumulative frequencies – and then drawing these in a bar chart.

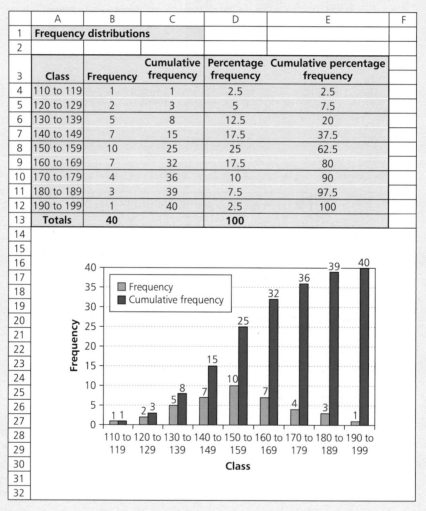

	A	B	C	D	E	F
1	**Frequency distributions**					
2						
3	Class	Frequency	Cumulative frequency	Percentage frequency	Cumulative percentage frequency	
4	110 to 119	1	1	2.5	2.5	
5	120 to 129	2	3	5	7.5	
6	130 to 139	5	8	12.5	20	
7	140 to 149	7	15	17.5	37.5	
8	150 to 159	10	25	25	62.5	
9	160 to 169	7	32	17.5	80	
10	170 to 179	4	36	10	90	
11	180 to 189	3	39	7.5	97.5	
12	190 to 199	1	40	2.5	100	
13	**Totals**	**40**		**100**		

Figure 5.11 Frequency distribution with a spreadsheet

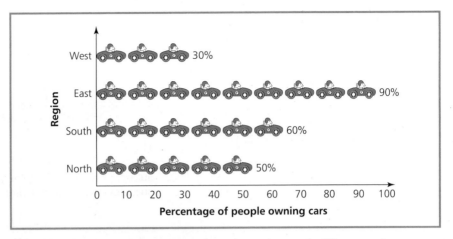

Figure 5.12 Pictogram of percentages of people owning cars in different regions

Pictograms and other images

Basic diagrams can have a considerable impact, but people often want to enhance this by adding even more features. One way of doing this is through pictograms, which are similar to bar charts, except the bars are replaced by sketches of the things being described. For example, Figure 5.12 shows the percentage of people owning cars in different regions by a pictogram. Instead of plain bars we have used pictures of cars, each of which represents 10% of people.

Pictograms are very eye-catching and are good at conveying general impressions, but they are not always accurate. An obvious problem comes with fractional values – if 53% of people owned cars in one region of Figure 5.12, a line of 5.3 cars would be neither clear nor particularly attractive (although it would still give the right impression of 'just over 50%'). A more serious problem comes when the pictures, images and added effects become more important than the charts themselves. Imagine a mushroom farmer who uses the pictogram in Figure 5.13 to show that sales have doubled in the past year. Rather than draw a row of small mushrooms, the farmer uses sketches of single mushrooms. The problem is that we should be concentrating on the height of the sketches, where one is quite rightly twice as high as the other – but it is the area that has immediate impact, and doubling the number of observations increases the area by a factor of four.

Unfortunately, the meaning of many diagrams is hidden by poor design or too much artwork. Unnecessary decoration is sometimes called 'chartjunk' and people refer to the 'ink ratio' – which compares the amount of ink used to describe the data with the amount used in decoration. Remember that the aim of data presentation is not to draw the prettiest picture, but to give the best view of the data. Some useful guidelines for this refer to 'graphical excellence'[6] which has:

- a well-designed presentation that combines significant content, statistical description and design
- clarity, giving results that are easy to understand

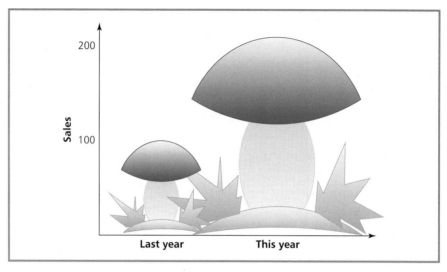

Figure 5.13 Misleading pictogram of increasing mushroom sales

- efficiency, with a precise presentation conveying the largest number of ideas in the shortest possible time
- accuracy, giving a fair and honest representation of the data.

Review questions

5.9   'You should always try to find the best diagram for presenting data.' Do you think this is true?

5.10 Why must you label the axes of graphs?

5.11 'There is only one bar chart that accurately describes a set of data.' Is this true?

5.12 If you wanted to make an impact with some data, what format would you consider?

5.13 What are the problems with pictograms?

5.14 Give some examples of diagrams where the added artwork has hidden or distorted the results.

IDEAS IN PRACTICE   **SAT reasoning test**

In the USA, education is largely organised by state governments. Standard tests are run to allow comparisons, typically when people from one state want to enter university in another. In 1901, the Educational Testing Service started a scholastic aptitude test, and they still administer the latest version of the SAT reasoning test.

In 1995 there was concern that, despite rising public expenditure of education, SAT scores were falling. Some people suggested a link between the two, implying that the way to improve performance was to reduce expenditure. The US Department of Education developed a graph to illustrate this point, shown in Figure 15.14(a).

Paul Cox drew attention to the weaknesses in this presentation, and proposed another view. In particular, he noted that SAT scores ranged from 400 to 1,600, and the full scale should be used.

Ideas in practice continued

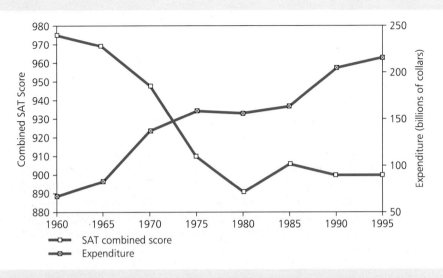

Figure 5.14(a) Published graph of public education expenditure against SAT combined scores

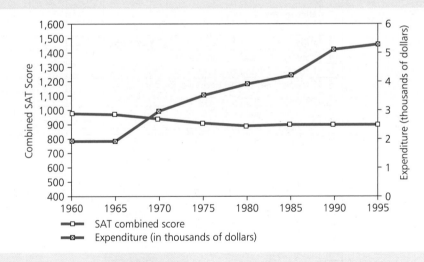

Figure 5.14(b) More accurate view of expenditure per pupil against SAT combined score

And as the number of pupils has risen, a fairer view would show the expenditure per pupil, shown in Figure 5.14(b). The resulting graph is much better, but it is still not perfect – and it cer-tainly suggests a less clear relationship between SAT results and expenditure.

Source: Paul Cox, Glossary of mathematical mistakes at www.members.cox.net/mathmistakes.

Continuous data

Bar charts are easy to use for discrete data, but with continuous data we have already mentioned the messiness of defining classes as '20 units or more and less than 30 units'. This affects the way we draw frequency distributions of continuous data – and it is generally better to use histograms.

Histograms

Histograms are frequency distributions for continuous data. They look very similar to bar charts, but there are important differences. The most important is that histograms are used only for continuous data, so the classes are joined and form a continuous scale. When we draw bars on this scale, their width – as well as their length – has a definite meaning. The width shows the class size, and the area of the bar shows the frequency.

Figure 5.15 shows a frequency distribution for the percentage gain in value of certain unit trusts over the past five years, and the associated histogram. There is a continuous scale along the x-axis for the percentage gain, and each class is the same width, so both the heights of the bars and their areas represent the frequencies.

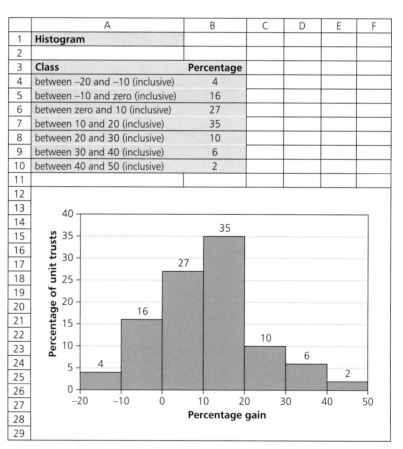

Figure 5.15 Histogram of the percentage gain in value of unit trusts

WORKED EXAMPLE 5.7

Draw a histogram of these continuous data.

Class	Frequency
Less than 10	8
10 or more, and less than 20	10
20 or more, and less than 30	16
30 or more, and less than 40	15
40 or more, and less than 50	11
50 or more, and less than 60	4
60 or more, and less than 70	2
70 or more, and less than 80	1
80 or more, and less than 90	1

Solution

Figure 5.16(a) shows this distribution as a histogram. This has a rather long tail with only 8 observations in the last four classes, and you might be tempted to combine these into one class with 8 observations. But you have to be careful – you cannot change the scale of the x-axis because it is continuous, so the single last class will be 4 times as wide as the other classes. Then you have to remember that in histograms the area of the bar shows the frequency and not the height. So you want to show 8 observations in an area 4 units wide – which means that it must be 2 units high, as shown in Figure 5.16(b). This is not an improvement because the tail of the histogram is now extended even more.

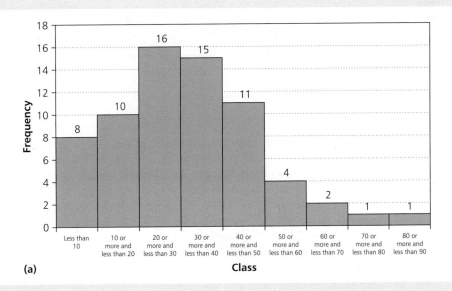

(a)

Figure 5.16(a) Histogram for Worked example 5.7 with nine classes

Worked example 5.7 continued

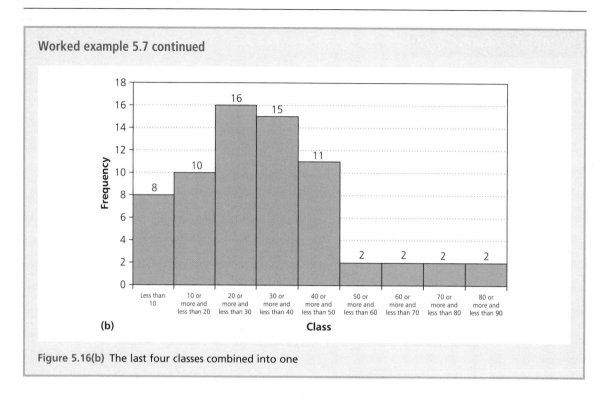

(b)

Figure 5.16(b) The last four classes combined into one

You can see from this example that you have to be careful when drawing histograms. A consistent problem is that the shape of a histogram depends on the way that you define classes. Another problem comes with open-ended classes, where there is no obvious way of dealing with a class like 'greater than 20'. An obvious answer is to avoid such definitions wherever possible; another is to make assumptions about limits, so that we might reasonably interpret 'greater than 20' as 'greater than 20 and less than 24'.

A more subtle problem is that many people do not realise that histograms are different from bar charts. Although bar charts might be less precise, they are easier to draw, and can give better-looking results – so some people suggest avoiding histograms and sticking to bar charts.

Ogives

An ogive is a graph that shows the relationship between class (on the x-axis) and cumulative frequency (on the y-axis) for continuous data. With the cumulative frequency distribution in Table 5.6, you start drawing an ogive by plotting the point (100, 12) to show that 12 observations are in the class '100 or less'. Then you can plot the point (150, 38), which shows that 38 observations are 150 or less; then the point (200, 104) which shows that 104 observations are 200 or less, then (250, 207) and so on. Plotting all these points and joining them gives the result shown in Figure 5.17. Ogives are always drawn vertically, and they have this characteristic elongated 'S'-shape.

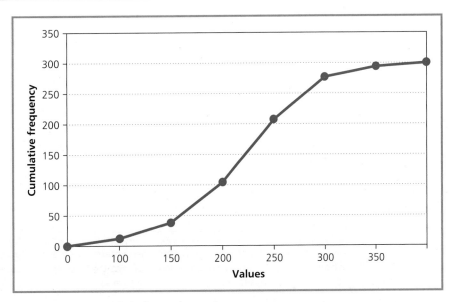

Figure 5.17 Characteristic shape of an ogive

Table 5.6

Class	Frequency	Cumulative frequency
100 or less	12	12
More than 100 and less than or equal to 150	26	38
More than 150 and less than or equal to 200	66	104
More than 200 and less than or equal to 250	103	207
More than 250 and less than or equal to 300	70	277
More than 300 and less than or equal to 350	17	294
More than 350 and less than or equal to 400	6	300

Lorenz curves

A Lorenz curve is an extension of the ogive that is used in economics to show the distribution of income or wealth among a population. It is a graph of cumulative percentage wealth, income or some other measure of wealth, against cumulative percentage of the population. Because a few people have most of the wealth, this is not a standard 'S'-shape, as you can see in Worked example 5.8.

WORKED EXAMPLE 5.8

Tax offices in Chu Nang County calculate the following percentages of total wealth – before and after tax – owned by various percentages of the population. Draw a Lorenz curve of this data.

Percentage of population	Percentage of wealth before tax	Percentage of wealth after tax
45	5	15
20	10	15
15	12	15
10	13	15
5	15	15
3	25	15
2	20	10

Worked example 5.8 continued

Solution
Here a Lorenz curve shows the cumulative percentage of wealth against the cumulative percentage of population. Figure 5.18 shows these calculations in a spreadsheet, followed by the Lorenz curves. Starting with a graph of the cumulative percentage of wealth before tax, the first point is (45, 5), followed by (65, 15), (80, 27) and so on. Similarly, in a graph of the cumulative percentage of wealth after tax, the first point is (45, 15), followed by (65, 30), (80, 45) and so on.

With a perfectly equitable distribution of wealth, a Lorenz curve is a straight line connecting the origin to the point (100, 100). If the graph is significantly below this, the distribution of wealth is unequal, and the further from the straight line the less equitable is the distribution. Here the Lorenz curve for after-tax wealth is considerably closer to the diagonal, and this shows that taxes have had an effect in redistributing wealth.

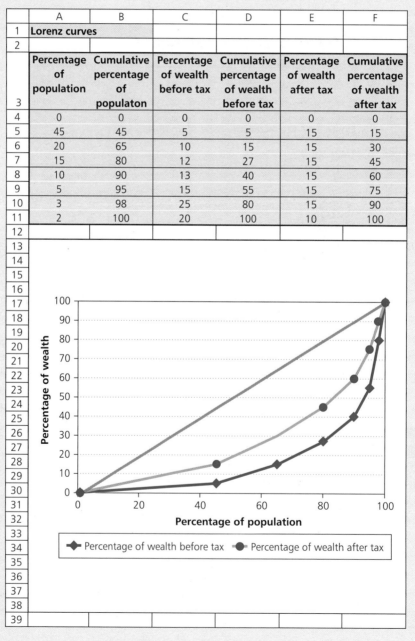

	A	B	C	D	E	F
1	Lorenz curves					
2						
3	Percentage of population	Cumulative percentage of populaton	Percentage of wealth before tax	Cumulative percentage of wealth before tax	Percentage of wealth after tax	Cumulative percentage of wealth after tax
4	0	0	0	0	0	0
5	45	45	5	5	15	15
6	20	65	10	15	15	30
7	15	80	12	27	15	45
8	10	90	13	40	15	60
9	5	95	15	55	15	75
10	3	98	25	80	15	90
11	2	100	20	100	10	100
12						

Figure 5.18 Lorenz curves before and after tax

5.15 'In bar charts and histograms, the height of the bar shows the number of observations in each class.' Is this true?

5.16 If two classes of equal width are combined into one for a histogram, how high is the resulting bar?

5.17 Why would you draw histograms when bar charts are easier and can have more impact?

5.18 What is the purpose of an ogive?

5.19 'A fair Lorenz curve should be a straight line connecting points (0, 0) and (100, 100).' Is this true?

IDEAS IN PRACTICE   Software for drawing diagrams

There is a lot of software available for drawing diagrams, ranging from simple programs that you can download free from websites to specialised graphics packages used by commercial artists. We mentioned some of these in Chapter 3, and can again mention ConceptDraw, CorelDRAW, DrawPlus, Freelance Graphics, Harvard Graphics, PowerPoint, Sigmaplot, SmartDraw and Visio.

Other standard packages include drawing functions – particularly spreadsheets. Excel has a 'chart wizard' that easily turns spreadsheets into diagrams. Figure 5.19 shows some of the formats it offers.

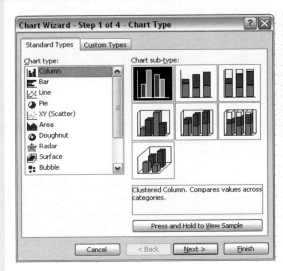
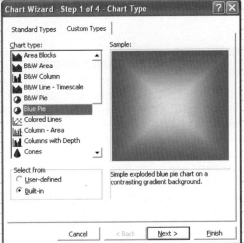

Figure 5.19 Some chart formats offered in Excel

CHAPTER REVIEW

This chapter showed how to summarise data in different types of diagrams.

■ After collecting data, you have to process it into useful information. This starts with data reduction to remove the details and focus on the underlying patterns. Then data presentation shows the results in the best format.

In practice, there is no clear distinction between these two, and they are usually merged into the single task of summarising data.

- Diagrams can have a considerable impact, but you have to design them carefully to give an accurate and fair view. There are many types of diagram and the choice is often a matter of personal preference.

- Tables are the most widely used method of summarising numerical data. They can show a lot of information and be tailored to specific needs.

- Tables are particularly useful for showing frequency distributions, which describe the numbers of observations in different classes. Associated calculations show percentage frequency distributions and cumulative distributions.

- Graphs show relationships between two variables and highlight the underlying patterns.

- Pie charts describe categorical data, representing the frequency of observations by the sectors of a circle.

- Bar charts give more flexible presentations for categorical data, with the length of each bar proportional to the number of observations in the category. Bar charts can be drawn as pictograms, but you have to be careful not to divert attention away from, or obscure, the important figures.

- Histograms are often confused with bar charts, but they show frequency distributions for continuous data and represent the frequency by the area of a bar. These can be extended to show ogives and Lorenz curves.

CASE STUDY High Acclaim Trading

High Acclaim Trading is based in Delhi, from where it has rapidly increased its international operations in recent years. A group of influential shareholders recently asked the finance director to review this international business. In turn, he asked Hari Chandrasan from the audit department to collect some data from company records for his presentation, stressing that he wanted to make an impact with his talk.

At first Hari was worried by the amount of detail available. The company seemed to keep enormous amounts of data on all aspects of its operations. This ranged from transaction records for the movement of virtually every product handled by the company, to subjective management views that nobody ever formally recorded. Often, there seemed no reason for keeping the data and it was rarely summarised or analysed.

Hari did a conscientious job of collecting and summarising data and felt that he had made considerable progress when he approached the finance director and handed over the results in

Table 5.7. He explained, 'This table shows some of our most important trading results. We trade in four main regions, and I have recorded eight key facts about the movements between them. Each element in the table shows, respectively, the number of units shipped (in hundreds), the average income per unit (in dollars), the percentage gross profit, the percentage return on investment, a measure (between 1 and 5) of trading difficulty, potential for growth (again on a scale of 1 to 5), the number of finance administrators employed in each area and the number of agents. I think this gives a good summary of our operations, and should give a useful focus for your presentation.'

The finance director looked at the figures for a few minutes and then asked for some details on how trade had changed over the past 10 years. Hari replied that, in general terms, the volume of trade had risen by 1.5, 3, 2.5, 2.5, 1, 1, 2.5, 3.5, 3 and 2.5% respectively in each of the last 10 years, while the average price had risen by 4, 4.5, 5.5, 7, 3.5, 4.5, 6, 5.5, 5 and 5% respectively.

Case study continued

Table 5.7

		To			
		Africa	America	Asia	Europe
From	Africa	105, 45, 12, 4, 4, 1, 15, 4	85, 75, 14, 7, 3, 2, 20, 3	25, 60, 15, 8, 3, 2, 12, 2	160, 80, 13, 7, 2, 2, 25, 4
	America	45, 75, 12, 3, 4, 1, 15, 3	255, 120, 15, 9, 1, 3, 45, 5	60, 95, 8, 2, 2, 3, 35, 6	345, 115, 10, 7, 1, 4, 65, 5
	Asia	85, 70, 8, 4, 5, 2, 20, 4	334, 145, 10, 5, 2, 4, 55, 6	265, 85, 8, 3, 2, 4, 65, 7	405, 125, 8, 3, 2, 5, 70, 8
	Europe	100, 80, 10, 5, 4, 2, 30, 3	425, 120, 12, 8, 1, 4, 70, 7	380, 105, 9, 4, 2, 3, 45, 5	555, 140, 10, 6, 4, 1, 10, 8

The finance director looked up from the figures and said, 'To be honest I hoped for something with a bit more impact. Could you work these into something more forceful within the next couple of days?'

Question

■ **If you were Hari Chandrasan how would you put the figures into a suitable format for the presentation?**

PROBLEMS

5.1 Find some recent trade statistics published by the UK government and present these in different ways to emphasise different features. Discuss which formats are fairest and which are most misleading.

5.2 A question in a survey gets the answer 'Yes' from 47% of men and 38% of women, 'No' from 32% of men and 53% of women, and 'Do not know' from the remainder. How could you present this effectively?

5.3 The number of students taking a course in the past 10 years is summarised in the following table. Use a selection of graphical methods to summarise this data. Which do you think is the best?

Year	1	2	3	4	5	6	7	8	9	10
Male	21	22	20	18	28	26	29	30	32	29
Female	4	6	3	5	12	16	14	19	17	25

5.4 The following table shows the quarterly profit in millions of dollars reported by the Lebal Corporation, and the corresponding closing share price quoted in cents on the Toronto Stock Exchange. Design suitable formats for presenting this data.

	Year 1				Year 2				Year 3			
Quarter	1	2	3	4	1	2	3	4	1	2	3	4
Profit	36	45	56	55	48	55	62	68	65	65	69	74
Share price	137	145	160	162	160	163	166	172	165	170	175	182

5.5 The following table shows the number of people employed by Testel Electronics over the past 10 years. How can you present this data?

Year	1	2	3	4	5	6	7	8	9	10
Employees	24	27	29	34	38	42	46	51	60	67

5.6 Four regions of Yorkshire classify companies according to primary, manufacturing, transport, retail and service. The number of companies operating in each region in each category is shown in the following table. Show these figures in a number of different bar charts.

	Industry type				
	Primary	Manufacturing	Transport	Retail	Service
Daleside	143	38	10	87	46
Twendale	134	89	15	73	39
Underhill	72	67	11	165	55
Perithorp	54	41	23	287	89

5.7 Jefferson Chang recorded the average wages of 45 people as follows:

221 254 83 320 367 450 292 161 216 410
380 355 502 144 362 112 387 324 576 156
295 77 391 324 126 154 94 350 239 263
276 232 467 413 472 361 132 429 310 272
408 480 253 338 217

Draw a frequency table, histogram, percentage frequency and cumulative frequency table of this data.

5.8 Draw a histogram of the following data.

Class	Frequency
Less than 100	120
100 or more, and less than 200	185
200 or more, and less than 300	285
300 or more, and less than 400	260
400 or more, and less than 500	205
500 or more, and less than 600	150
600 or more, and less than 700	75
700 or more, and less than 800	35
800 or more, and less than 900	15

5.9 Draw an ogive of the data in Problem 5.8.

5.10 The wealth of a population is described in the following frequency distribution. Draw Lorenz curves and other diagrams to represent this data.

Percentage of people	5	10	15	20	20	15	10	5
Percentage of wealth before tax	1	3	6	15	20	20	15	20
Percentage of wealth after tax	3	6	10	16	20	20	10	15

5.11 The following table shows last year's total production and profits (in consistent units) from six factories. Use a graphics package to explore the ways that you can present this data.

Factory	A	B	C	D	E	F
Production	125	53	227	36	215	163
Profit	202	93	501	57	413	296

RESEARCH PROJECTS

5.1 Do a small survey of graphics packages and find one that you prefer. Why do you find this better than the others? Explore the different formats that it can produce for diagrams. Compare this with Excel, which has 30 chart types and many variations.

5.2 Jan Schwartzkopf has collected the following set of data. Explore ways of reducing, manipulating and presenting this data in diagrams.

```
245 487 123 012 159 751 222 035 487 655
197 655 458 766 123 453 493 444 123 537
254 514 324 215 367 557 330 204 506 804
941 354 226 870 652 458 425 248 560 510
```

```
234 542 671 874 710 702 701 540 360 654
323 410 405 531 489 695 409 375 521 624
357 678 809 901 567 481 246 027 310 679
548 227 150 600 845 521 777 304 286 220
667 111 485 266 472 700 705 466 591 398
367 331 458 466 571 489 257 100 874 577
037 682 395 421 233 577 802 190 721 320
444 690 511 103 242 386 400 532 621 144
```

5.3 Governments collect huge amounts of data and present it in long series of tables. Find some figures for transport over the past 20 years and present these in useful formats. Prepare a presentation of your findings suitable for transport managers, general business people and government transport planners.

Sources of information

References

1 Huff D., *How to Lie with Statistics*, Victor Gollancz, New York, 1954.

2 Kimble G.A., *How to Use (and Misuse) Statistics*, Prentice Hall, Englewood Cliffs, NJ, 1978.

3 Tufte E.R., *The Visual Display of Quantitative Information* (2nd edition), Graphics Press, Cheshire, CT, 2001.

4 Wainer H., How to display data badly, *The American Statistician*, Volume 38, pages 137–147, May 1984.

5 Wainer H., *Visual Revelations*, Copernicus/Springer-Verlag, New York, 1997.

6 Cleveland W.S. and McGill R., Graphical perception; theory, experimentation and application to the development of graphical methods, *Journal of the American Statistical Association*, Volume 79, pages 531–554, 1984.

Further reading

Most of the books on mathematics mentioned at the end of Chapter 2 also refer to diagrams. Some other books include:

Chapman M. and Wykes C., *Plain Figures* (2nd edition), HMSO, London, 1996.

Few S., *Show Me the Numbers*, Analytics Press, Oakland, CA, 2004.

Francis A., *Working with Data*, Thomson Learning, London, 2003.

Harris R.L., *Information Graphics*, Oxford University Press, Oxford, 1999.

Hyggett R., *Graphs and Charts*, Palgrave Macmillan, Basingstoke, 1990.

Jelen W., *Charts and Graphs*, Pearson Education, Toronto, 2010.

Koomey J.G., *Turning Numbers into Knowledge*, Analytics Press, Oakland, CA, 2004.

Moon J., *How to Make an Impact*, Financial Times/Prentice Hall, Harlow, 2007.

Robbins N.B., *Creating More Effective Graphs*, John Wiley, Chichester, 2005.

Tufte E.R., *The Visual Display of Quantitative Information* (2nd edition), Graphics Press, Cheshire, CT, 2001.

Zelazny G., *Say it with Charts* (4th edition), McGraw-Hill, New York, 2006.

CHAPTER 6

Using numbers to describe data

Chapter outline

The amount of detail in raw data obscures the underlying patterns. Data reduction and presentation clear away excess detail and highlight the important features. There are two ways of summarising data. Chapter 5 showed how this could be done with different types of diagrams. In this chapter we continue the theme by looking at numerical descriptions. The two most important measures of data describe its average and spread.

After finishing this chapter you should be able to:

- appreciate the need for numerical measures of data
- understand measures of location
- find the arithmetic mean, median and mode of data
- understand measures of data spread
- find the range and quartile deviation of data
- calculate mean absolute deviations, variances and standard deviations
- use coefficients of variation and skewness.

Measuring data

We are usually more interested in the overall patterns of data rather than the minute detail, so we use data reduction and presentation to get a broader picture. Chapter 5 described a series of diagrams for summarising data. These can have considerable impact, and they are very good at giving overall impressions and a 'feel' for the data. But we often want some objective measures of data, and for this we need numerical summaries.

Location and spread

Suppose that you have this set of data, perhaps for weekly sales:

32 33 36 38 37 35 35 34 33 35 34 36 35 34 36 35 37 34 35 33

There are 20 values here, but what measures can you use to describe the data and differentiate it from the following set?

2 8 21 10 17 24 18 12 1 16 12 3 7 8 9 10 9 21 19 6

You could start by drawing frequency distributions, as shown in Figure 6.1. Although each set of data has 20 values, there are two clear differences:

- the second set is lower than the first set, with values centred around 12 rather than 35
- the second set is more spread out than the first set, ranging from 1 to 24 rather than 32 to 38.

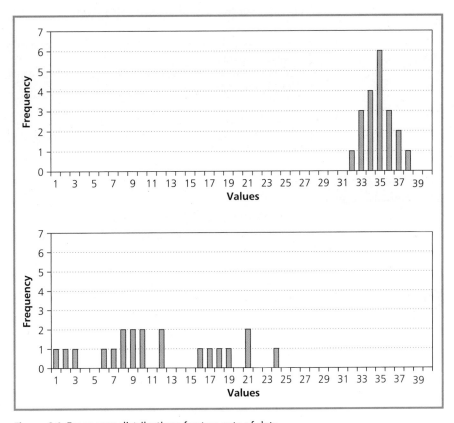

Figure 6.1 Frequency distributions for two sets of data

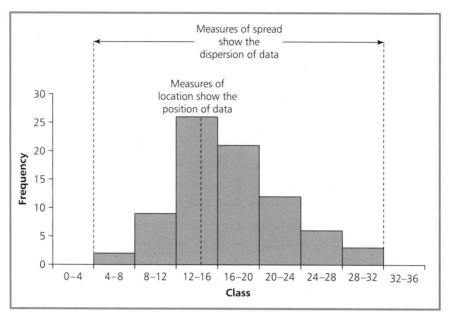

Figure 6.2 Describing the location and spread of data

This suggests two useful measures for data:

- a **measure of location** to show where the centre of the data is, giving some kind of typical or average value
- a **measure of spread** to show how the data is scattered around this centre, giving an idea of the range of values.

In a typical bar chart or histogram, like the one in Figure 6.2, measures of location show where the data lies on the *x*-axis, while measures of spread show how dispersed the data is along the axis.

Review questions

6.1 What is the main weakness of using diagrams to describe data?

6.2 What do we mean by the 'location' of data?

6.3 'You need to measure only location and spread to get a complete description of data.' Do you think this is true?

Measures of location

The most common measure for the location of data is its average. You are probably happy to think of the average as a typical value – and when the average age of students in a night class is 45, you have some feel for what the class looks like; if the average income of a group of people is £140,000 a year, you know they are prosperous; if houses in a village have an average of six bedrooms, you know they are large.

Unfortunately, the simple average can be misleading. For example, the group of people with an average income of £140,000 a year might consist of

10 people, nine of whom have an income of £20,000 a year and one of whom has an income of £1,220,000. The village where houses have an average of six bedrooms might have 99 houses with two bedrooms each, and a stately home with 402 bedrooms. In both of these examples the quoted average is accurate, but it does not represent a typical value or give any real feeling for the data. To get around this problem, we define three different types of average:

■ arithmetic mean, or simple average
■ median, which is the middle value
■ mode, which is the most frequent value.

Arithmetic mean

If you ask a group of people to find the average of 2, 4 and 6, they will usually say 4. This type of average is the most widely used measure of location. It is technically called the arithmetic mean – usually abbreviated mean (there are other types of mean, but they are rarely used).

To find the mean of a set of values you:

■ add all the values together to get the sum
■ divide this sum by the number of values to get the mean.

To find the mean of 2, 4 and 6 you add them together to get $2 + 4 + 6 = 12$, and then divide this sum by the number of values, 3, to calculate the mean as $12 / 3 = 4$.

We can introduce a notation that uses subscripts to describe these calculations much more efficiently. Suppose that we have a set of values – we can call the whole set x, and identify each individual value by a subscript. Then x_1 is the first value, x_2 is the second value, x_3 is the third value and x_n is the nth value. The advantage of this notation is that we can refer to a general value as x_i. Then when $i = 5$, x_i is x_5. At first sight this might not seem very useful, but in practice it saves a lot of effort. For instance, suppose you have four values, x_1, x_2, x_3 and x_4, and want to add them together. You could write an expression for this:

$$y = x_1 + x_2 + x_3 + x_4$$

Alternatively, you could get the same result by writing:

$$y = \text{sum of } x_i \text{ when } i = 1, 2, 3 \text{ and } 4$$

A standard abbreviation replaces 'the sum of' by the Greek capital letter sigma, Σ. Then we get:

$$y = \Sigma x_i \text{ when } i = 1, 2, 3 \text{ and } 4$$

And then we put the values of i around the Σ to give the standard form:

$$y = \sum_{i=1}^{4} x_i$$

The '$i = 1$' below the Σ gives the name of the variable, i, and the initial value, 1. The '4' above the Σ gives the final value for i. The steps between the initial and final values are always assumed to be 1.

WORKED EXAMPLE 6.1

(a) If you have a set of values, x, how would you describe the sum of the first 10?
(b) How would you describe the sum of values numbered 18 to 35 in a set of data?
(c) If you have the following set of data, p, what is the value of $\sum_{i=4}^{8} p_i$?

  5 14 13 6 8 10 3 0 5 1 15 8 0

Solution

(a) You want the sum of x_i when $i = 1$ to 10, which you can write as $\sum_{i=1}^{10} x_i$.

(b) Now you have a set of values, say a, and want the sum of a_i from $i = 18$ to 35. You can write this as $\sum_{i=18}^{35} a_i$.

(c) You want to calculate $p_4 + p_5 + p_6 + p_7 + p_8$. Reading the list of data, p_4 is the fourth number, 6, p_5 is the fifth number, 8 and so on. Then the calculation is $6 + 8 + 10 + 3 + 0 = 27$.

We can use this subscript notation to give a formal definition of the mean of a set of data. For some reason this mean is called $\bar{x}$, which is pronounced 'x bar', defined as:

$$\text{mean} = \bar{x} = \frac{x_1 + x_2 + x_3 + \ldots + x_n}{n} = \frac{\sum_{i=1}^{n} x_i}{n} = \frac{\sum x}{n}$$

Notice that we have used the abbreviation $\sum x$ for the summation. When there can be no misunderstanding, we can replace the rather cumbersome $\sum_{i=1}^{n} x_i$ by the simpler $\sum x$, and assume that the sum includes all values of x_i from $i = 1$ to n. The fuller notation is more precise, but it makes even simple equations appear rather daunting.

WORKED EXAMPLE 6.2

James Wong found the times taken to answer six telephone enquiries to be, in minutes, 3, 4, 1, 5, 7 and 1. What is the mean?

Solution
You find the mean by adding the values, x_i, and dividing by the number of values, n:

$$\text{mean} = \frac{\sum_{i=1}^{n} x_i}{n} = \frac{\sum x}{n}$$

$$= \frac{3 + 4 + 1 + 5 + 7 + 1}{6}$$

$$= \frac{21}{6}$$

$$= 3.5 \text{ minutes}$$

This example shows that the mean of a set of integers is often not an integer itself – for example, an average family might have 1.7 children. So the mean gives an objective calculation for the location of data, but it obviously does not give a typical result. Another problem, which we saw in the discussion at the beginning of the chapter, is that the mean is affected by a few extreme values and can be some distance away from most values. When you hear that the average mark of five students in an exam is 50% you would expect this to represent a typical value – but if the actual marks are 100%, 40%, 40%, 35% and 35%, four results are below the mean and only one is above.

The mean gives the same weight to every value. This is usually reasonable, but it can cause problems. When the three owner/directors of Henderson Associates had to decide how much of their annual profits to retain for future growth, their individual choices were to retain 3%, 7% and 11% of the profits. It might seem that a reasonable compromise takes the mean of the three values, which is 7%. However, the three directors actually hold 10, 10 and 1,000 shares respectively, so this result no longer seems fair. The views of the third director should really be given more weight, and we can do this with a weighted mean.

$$\text{weighted mean} = \frac{\sum w_i x_i}{\sum w_i}, \quad \text{where: } x_i = \text{value } i \\ w_i = \text{weight given to value } i.$$

With Henderson Associates it makes sense to assign weights in proportion to the number of shares each director holds, giving the result:

$$\text{weighted mean} = \frac{\sum wx}{\sum w} = \frac{10 \times 3 + 10 \times 7 + 1{,}000 \times 11}{10 + 10 + 1{,}000}$$
$$= 10.88$$

Usually the weights given to each value are not as clear as this, and they need some discussion and agreement. But this negotiation adds subjectivity to the calculations, and we no longer have a purely objective measure. Largely for this reason, but also because it is difficult to interpret, the weighted mean is not widely used. However, we can extend its reasoning to estimate the mean of data that has already had some processing – typically when data is summarised in a frequency distribution. Then we have grouped data where we do not know the actual values, but do know the number of values in each class. Because we do not have the actual values, we cannot find the true mean – but we can get a reasonable approximation by assuming that all values in a class lie at the midpoint of the class. If we have 10 values in a class 20 to 29, we assume that all 10 have the value $(20 + 29) / 2 = 24.5$. Then we calculate the mean in the usual way.

Imagine that you have a frequency distribution with:

- n values
- f_i values in class i,
- x_i is the midpoint of class i.

The sum of all values is $\sum f_i x_i$ (which is usually abbreviated to $\sum fx$) and the number of values is $\sum f$. So the mean of grouped data is:

$$\text{mean} = \bar{x} = \frac{\sum fx}{\sum f} = \frac{\sum fx}{n}$$

WORKED EXAMPLE 6.3

Estimate the mean of the data in this discrete frequency distribution.

Class	1–3	4–6	7–9	10–12	13–15	16–18	19–21	22–24
Frequency	1	4	8	13	9	5	2	1

Solution

Remember that x_i is the midpoint of class i, so x_1 is the midpoint of the first class which is $(1 + 3) / 2 = 2$, x_2 is the midpoint of the second class which is $(4 + 6) / 2 = 5$, and so on. Figure 6.3 shows a spreadsheet with the calculations. As you can see, $\Sigma f = 43$ and $\Sigma fx = 503$. So the estimated mean is $503 / 43 = 11.7$.

	A	B	C	D	E
1	**Frequency distribution**				
2					
3	**Class**		**Midpoint**	**Frequency**	
4	**From**	**to**	**x**	**f**	**fx**
5	1	3	2	1	2
6	4	6	5	4	20
7	7	9	8	8	64
8	10	12	11	13	143
9	13	15	14	9	126
10	16	18	17	5	85
11	19	21	20	2	40
12	22	24	23	1	23
13	**Totals**			43	503
14	**Mean**				11.70

Figure 6.3 Calculating the arithmetic mean of grouped data

The arithmetic mean usually gives a reasonable measure for location and has the advantages of being:

- objective
- easy to calculate
- familiar and easy to understand
- calculated from all the data
- usually giving a reasonable summary of the data
- useful in a number of other analyses.

However, we have seen that it has weaknesses because it:

- works only with cardinal data
- is affected by outlying values
- can be some distance from most values
- gives fractional values, even for discrete data
- may not give an accurate view.

We really need some other measures to overcome these weaknesses, and the two most common are the median and mode.

Median

When a set of data is arranged in order of increasing size, the median is defined as the middle value. With five values – 10, 20, 30, 40 and 50 – the median is the middle or third value, which is 30. This does not really need any calculation, but we find it by:

- arranging the values in order of size
- counting the number of values
- identifying the middle value – which is the median.

With n values, the median is value number $(n + 1) / 2$ when they are sorted into order. It follows that half of the values are smaller than the median, and half are bigger.

WORKED EXAMPLE 6.4

The annualised percentage returns from a set of low-risk bonds over the past four years have been

4.4	5.3	6.1	7.9	5.6	2.9	2.3	3.0	3.3
5.0	3.6	4.9	5.4	4.5	2.1	7.1	6.8	

What is the median?

Solution

We start by sorting the data into ascending order:

Position	1	2	3	4	5	6	7	8	9	10	11	12	13	14	15	16	17
Value	2.1	2.3	2.9	3.0	3.3	3.6	4.4	4.5	4.9	5.0	5.3	5.4	5.6	6.1	6.8	7.1	7.9

There are 17 values, so the median is number $(17 + 1) / 2 = 9$. This is 4.9, with eight values above it and eight below.

In this last example we deliberately chose an odd number of values, so that we could identify a middle one – but what happens when there is an even number of values? If the example had one more value of 8.1, then the middle point of the 18 values would be number $(18 + 1) / 2 = 9.5$, which is midway between the ninth and tenth. The usual convention is to take the median as the average of these two. The ninth value is 4.9 and the tenth is 5.0, so we describe the median as $(4.9 + 5.0) / 2 = 4.95$. Although this is a value that did not actually occur, it is the best approximation we can get.

When data comes in a frequency distribution, finding the median is a bit more complicated. We start by seeing which class the median is in, and then finding how far up this class it is.

WORKED EXAMPLE 6.5

Find the median of this continuous frequency distribution:

Class	0– 0.99	1.00– 1.99	2.00– 2.99	3.00– 3.99	4.00– 4.99	5.00– 5.99
Frequency	1	4	8	6	3	1

Solution

There are 23 values, so when they are sorted into order the median is number $(n + 1) / 2 = (23 + 1) / 2 = 12$. There is 1 value in the first class, 4 in the second class, and 8 in the third class – so the median is the seventh value in the third class (2.00–2.99). As there are 8 values in this class, it is reasonable

►

Worked example 6.5 continued

to assume that the median is seven-eighths of the way up the class. In other words:

median = lower limit of third class
+ 7 / 8 × class width
= 2.00 + 7 / 8 × (2.99 − 2.00) = 2.87

This calculation is equivalent to drawing an ogive (remembering from Chapter 5 that an ogive plots the class against cumulative frequency for continuous data) and finding the point on the x-axis that corresponds to the 12th value (as shown in Figure 6.4).

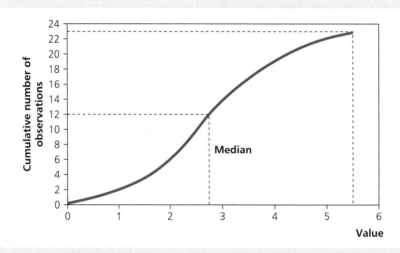

Figure 6.4 Identifying the median from an ogive

The median has the advantages of:

- being easy to understand
- giving a value that actually occurred (except with grouped data or an even number of observations)
- sometimes giving a more reliable measure than the mean
- not being affected by outlying values
- needing no calculation (except for grouped data).

On the other hand it has weaknesses, in that it:

- can be used only with cardinal data
- does not really consider data that is not at the median
- can give values that have not actually occurred (with grouped data or an even number of observations)
- is not so easy to use in other analyses.

Mode

The mode is the value that occurs most often. If we have four values, 5, 7, 7 and 9, the value that occurs most often is 7, so this is the mode. Like the median, the mode relies more on observation than calculation, and we find it by:

- drawing a frequency distribution of the data
- identifying the most frequent value – which is the mode.

WORKED EXAMPLE 6.6

Maria Panelli recorded the number of goals that her local football team scored in the last 12 matches as 3, 4, 3, 1, 5, 2, 3, 3, 2, 4, 3 and 2. What is the mode of the goals?

Solution

The following table shows the frequency distribution for these 12 values. The most frequent value is 3 – as shown in Figure 6.5(a) – so this is the mode. This compares with a mean of 2.9 and a median of 3.

Class	Frequency
1	1
2	3
3	5
4	2
5	1

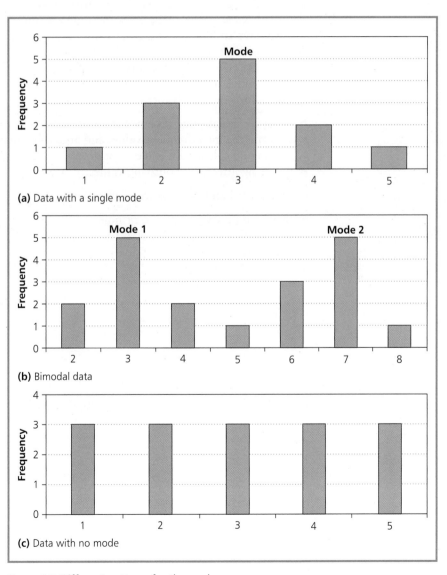

(a) Data with a single mode

(b) Bimodal data

(c) Data with no mode

Figure 6.5 Different patterns for the mode

Unfortunately, data is often not as convenient as in the last example. If the numbers that Maria Panelli recorded were:

3, 5, 3, 7, 6, 7, 4, 3, 7, 6, 7, 3, 2, 3, 2, 4, 6, 7, 8

then the most common values are 3 and 7, which both appear five times. Then the data has two modes – it is bimodal – at 3 and 7, as shown in Figure 6.5(b). Data commonly has several modes, making it multimodal. On the other hand, if you draw a frequency distribution of:

3, 5, 4, 3, 5, 2, 2, 1, 2, 5, 4, 1, 4, 1, 3

you see that each value occurs three times, so there is no mode, as shown in Figure 6.5(c).

It is a bit more difficult to find the mode of data that is grouped in a frequency distribution. We start by identifying the modal class, which is the class with most values. This gives the range within which the mode lies, but we still have to identify an actual value. The easiest way of doing this is to draw two crossing lines, shown in the histogram in Figure 6.6. The point where these two lines cross is the mode. In practice, it is debatable whether this adds much to our understanding of the data, so it is rarely used.

The mode has the advantages of:

■ being an actual value (except for grouped data)
■ showing the most frequent value, and arguably the most typical
■ needing no calculation (except for grouped data)
■ not being affected by outlying values.

On the other hand its weaknesses include:

■ there can be several modes, or none
■ it ignores all data that is not at the mode
■ it cannot be used in further analyses.

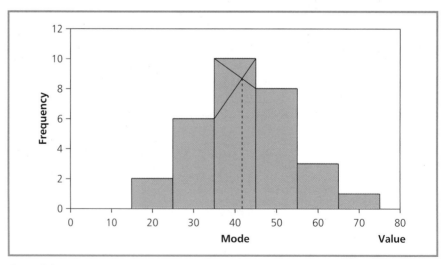

Figure 6.6 Identifying the mode of grouped data

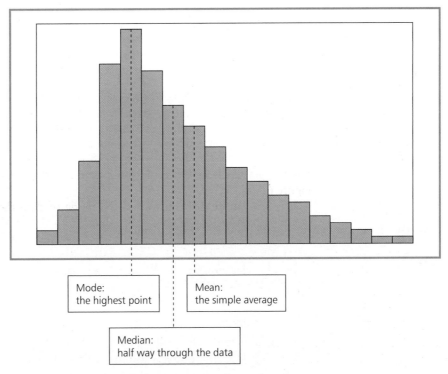

Figure 6.7 Relationship between mean, median and mode

Choice of measure

Each of these three measures for location gives a different view:

- the mean is the simple average
- the median is the middle value
- the mode is the most frequent value.

Figure 6.7 shows the typical relationship between these in a histogram. Usually the measures are quite close to each other – and when the histogram is symmetrical they coincide. Sometimes, though, the histogram is very asymmetrical and the measures are some distance apart.

The mean is certainly the most widely used, but the median often gives a fairer picture. As with diagrams, the choice of 'best' is often a matter of opinion.

Review questions

6.4   What is a 'measure of location'?

6.5   'The average of a set of data has a clear meaning that accurately describes the data.' Do you think this is true?

6.6   Define three measures for the location of a set of data.

6.7   If the mean of 10 values is 34, and the mean of an additional 5 values is 37, what is the mean of all 15 values?

6.8   What functions on a spreadsheet describe the location of data?

Taranangama Village Health Centre

Taranangama Village Health Centre is funded by the local community. Last year there was some discussion about the cost of running the centre. The practice manager wrote a report saying that the average salary of employees was $58,800, which was slightly higher than normal but reflected the greater skills of the staff. The practice nurses were surprised that they all got considerably less than the average pay, while the receptionists pointed out that they got less than a third of the average. The doctors made no comment on the figures.

The practice manager tried to clear things up and produced the spreadsheet shown in Figure 6.8.

This shows a bar chart of the gross salary of the two doctors, one clinical technician, three nurses and four receptionists employed at the centre. The spreadsheet's standard functions AVERAGE, MEDIAN and MODE confirm that the mean salary is $58,800 – but only two people earn more than this, while eight earn less. Only the technician is within $13,800 of the mean. The median is $42,000, which gives a better view of typical pay at the centre. The mode is $16,000 – but, again, this is not a typical value and simply shows that two receptionists are the only people paid the same amount.

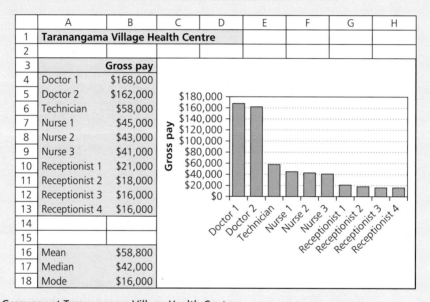

Figure 6.8 Gross pay at Taranangama Village Health Centre

Measures of spread

The mean, median and mode are measures for the location of a set of data, but they give no idea of its spread or dispersion. The mean age of students in a night class might be 45 – but this does not say whether they are all around the same age or their ages range from 5 to 95. The amount of dispersion is often important, as you can imagine with a library that has an average of 300 visitors a day – it is much easier for staff to deal with small variations (from say 290 on quiet days to 310 on busy ones) than large variations (between 0 and 1,000).

Range and quartiles

The simplest measure of spread is the range, which is the difference between the largest and smallest values in a set of data. Clearly, the broader the range the more spread out the data.

---

range = largest value − smallest value

This is usually an easy calculation, but there is a warning for grouped data. If you simply take the range as the difference between the top of the largest class and the bottom of the smallest one, the result depends on the definition of classes rather than on actual values. Another problem is that one or two extreme values can affect the range, making it artificially wide. An obvious way of avoiding this is to ignore extreme values that are a long way from the centre. You can do this using quartiles. When data is sorted into ascending size, quartiles are defined as the values that divide the set of values into quarters. In particular:

- the first quartile, Q_1, is the value a quarter of the way through the data with 25% of values smaller and 75% bigger – it is value number $(n + 1) / 4$
- the second quartile, Q_2, is the value halfway through the data with 50% of values smaller and 50% bigger – this is the median, which is value number $(n + 1) / 2$
- the third quartile, Q_3, is the value three-quarters of the way through the data with 75% of values smaller and 25% bigger – it is value number $3(n + 1) / 4$.

With 11 ordered values:

12, 14, 17, 21, 24, 30, 39, 43, 45, 56, 58

the first quartile is value number $(11 + 1) / 4 = 3$, which is 17. The second quartile, or median, is value number $(11 + 1) / 2 = 6$, which is 30. The third quartile is value number $3 \times (11 + 1) / 4 = 9$, which is 45. Then you can use the quartiles to define a narrower range $Q_3 − Q_1$ that contains 50% of values – giving the interquartile range. Sometimes you will also see a quartile deviation, or semi-interquartile range, which is is defined as half the interquartile range:

Interquartile range = $Q_3 − Q_1$

Quartile deviation = $\dfrac{\text{interquartile range}}{2} = \dfrac{Q_3 − Q_1}{2}$

Figure 6.9 shows these results in a 'box plot' or 'box-and-whisker diagram', where the range between the first and third quartiles is shown by a box, with two whiskers showing the extreme values.

Obviously, we chose 11 values so that the quartiles were easy to find. But what happens if there are, say, 200 values, where the first quartile is value number $(200 + 1) / 4 = 50.25$? When there are many values, the usual convention

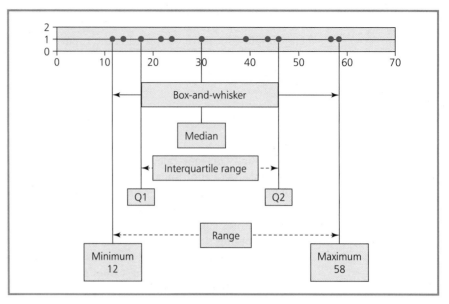

Figure 6.9 Box plot diagram showing the spread of data

is simply to round to the nearest integer. If you want the 50.25th value, you simply round down and approximate it to the 50th; if you want the 50.75th value, you round this up and approximate it to the 51st. And if you want the 50.5th value you might take the average of the 50th and 51st values. In practice, the difference should be small with a reasonable number of values.

WORKED EXAMPLE 6.7

Find the quartile deviation of this continuous frequency distribution:

Class	0– 9.9	10– 19.9	20– 29.9	30– 39.9	40– 49.9	50– 59.9	60– 69.9
Values	5	19	38	43	34	17	4

Solution

There are 160 values, or 40 in each quarter. As this number is fairly large, we can approximate the first quartile by the 40th value, the median by the 80th, and the third quartile by the 120th.

■ There are 24 values in the first two classes, so the first quartile, Q_1, is the 16th value out of 38 in the class 20–29.9. A reasonable estimate has the quartile 16/38 of the way through this class, so:

$Q_1 = 20 + (16 / 38) \times (29.9 - 20)$
$= 24.2$

■ There are 62 values in the first three classes so the median, Q_2, is the 18th value out of 43 in the class 30–39.9. A reasonable estimate puts this 18/43 of the way through this class, so:

$Q_2 = 30 + (18 / 43) \times (39.9 - 30)$
$= 34.1$

■ There are 105 values in the first four classes, so the third quartile, Q_3, is the 15th value out of 34 in the class of 40–49.9. A reasonable estimate for this is:

$Q_3 = 40 + (15 / 34) \times (49.9 - 40)$
$= 44.4$

Then the quartile deviation is:

$(Q_3 - Q_1) / 2 = (44.4 - 24.2) / 2$
$= 10.1$

More detailed variations on the quartile deviation are based on percentiles. For example, the 5th percentile is defined as the value with 5% of values below it, and the 95th percentile is defined as the value with 95% of values below it. Then defining the range between the 5th and 95th percentiles still includes most of the values but ignores any outlying ones.

Mean absolute deviation

The range and quartile deviation focus on a few values and are clearly related to the median. Other measures of spread include more values, and are related to the mean. In particular, they consider the distance that each value is away from the mean, which is called the deviation:

$$\text{deviation} = \text{value} - \text{mean value}$$
$$= x_i - \bar{x}$$

Each value has a deviation, so the mean of these deviations should give a measure of spread. Unfortunately, the mean deviation has the major disadvantage of allowing positive and negative deviations to cancel. If we have the three values 3, 4 and 8, the mean is 5 and the mean deviation is:

$$\text{mean deviation} = \frac{\Sigma(x - \bar{x})}{n}$$
$$= \frac{(3 - 5) + (4 - 5) + (8 - 5)}{3}$$
$$= 0$$

Even dispersed data has a mean deviation of zero, which is why this measure is never used. A more useful alternative is the mean absolute deviation (MAD), which simply takes the absolute values of deviations. In other words, it ignores negative signs and adds all deviations as if they are positive. The result is a measure of the mean distance of observations from the mean – so the larger the mean absolute deviation, the more dispersed the data.

$$\text{mean absolute deviation} = \frac{\Sigma \text{ABS}(x - \bar{x})}{n}$$

$$\text{MAD} = \frac{\Sigma|x - \bar{x}|}{n}$$

where:　x = the values
$\bar{x}$ = mean value
n = number of values
$\text{ABS}(x - \bar{x})$ = the absolute value of $x - \bar{x}$ (that is, ignoring the sign), which is also written as $|x - \bar{x}|$

WORKED EXAMPLE 6.8

What is the mean absolute deviation of 4, 7, 6, 10 and 8?

Solution
The calculation for the mean absolute deviation starts by finding the mean of the numbers, which is:

$$\bar{x} = \frac{4 + 7 + 6 + 10 + 8}{5}$$

$$= 7$$

Then the mean absolute deviation is:

$$MAD = \frac{\Sigma |x - \bar{x}|}{n}$$

$$= \frac{|4 - 7| + |7 - 7| + |6 - 7| + |10 - 7| + |8 - 7|}{5}$$

$$= \frac{|-3| + |0| + |-1| + |3| + |1|}{5}$$

$$= \frac{3 + 0 + 1 + 3 + 1}{5}$$

$$= 1.6$$

This shows that, on average, the values are 1.6 units away from the mean. In practice you will normally use a standard function like AVEDEV in Excel for this calculation.

Calculating the MAD for grouped data is a bit more awkward. To find the mean of grouped data, we took the midpoint of each class and multiplied this by the number of values in the class. Using the same approach to calculate a mean absolute deviation, we approximate the absolute deviation of each class by the difference between its midpoint and the mean of the data. Then the calculation for the mean absolute deviation for grouped data is:

$$\text{mean absolute deviation} = \frac{\Sigma |x - \bar{x}| f}{\Sigma f}$$

$$= \frac{\Sigma |x - \bar{x}| f}{n}$$

where: x = midpoint of a class
f = number of values in the class
$\bar{x}$ = mean value
n = total number of values.

WORKED EXAMPLE 6.9

Find the mean absolute deviation of this set of data:

Class	0–4.9	5–9.9	10–14.9	15–19.9
Frequency	3	5	9	7

Class	20–24.9	25–29.9	30–34.9	35–39.9
Frequency	4	2	1	1

Solution
Figure 6.10 shows the calculations in a spreadsheet (the details are given in full, but you never really have to be this explicit).

There are 32 values with a mean of 15.4. The deviation of each class is the distance its midpoint is away from this mean. Then we find the mean absolute deviation by taking the absolute deviations, multiplying by the frequency, adding the results, and dividing by the number of values. The result is 6.6, which shows that values are, on average, 6.6 away from the mean.

Worked example 6.9 continued

	A	B	C	D	E	F	G	H
1	**Mean absolute deviation**							
2								
3	**Class**		**Midpoint**	**Frequency**	**Product**	**Deviation**	**Absolute deviation**	**Product**
4	**From**	**To**	***x***	***f***	***fx***	**(*x* – mean)**	**|*x* – mean|**	***f*|*x* – mean|**
5	0	4.9	2.5	3	7.4	–13.0	13.0	38.9
6	5	9.9	7.5	5	37.3	–8.0	8.0	39.8
7	10	14.9	12.5	9	112.1	–3.0	3.0	26.7
8	15	19.9	17.5	7	122.2	2.0	2.0	14.2
9	20	24.9	22.5	4	89.8	7.0	7.0	28.1
10	25	29.9	27.5	2	54.9	12.0	12.0	24.1
11	30	34.9	32.5	1	32.5	17.0	17.0	17.0
12	35	39.9	37.5	1	37.5	22.0	22.0	22.0
13	**Sums**			32	493.4			210.9
14	**Means**				15.4			6.6
15								
16	**Mean absolute deviation =**			6.6				

Figure 6.10 Calculation of the mean absolute deviation

The mean absolute deviation is easy to calculate, uses all the data and has a clear meaning. However, it also has weaknesses. For instance, it gives equal weight to all values, and can be affected by a few outlying numbers. Another problem is the difficulty of using it in other analyses. These problems limit its use, and a more widely used alternative is the variance.

Variance and standard deviation

The mean absolute deviation stops positive and negative deviations from cancelling by taking their absolute values. An alternative is to square the deviations and calculate a mean squared deviation – which is always described as the variance.

$$\text{variance} = \frac{\sum (x - \bar{x})^2}{n}$$

This has all the benefits of MAD, but overcomes some of its limitations – with one obvious problem, that the units are the square of the units of the original values. If the values are measured in tonnes, the variance has the meaningless units of tonnes squared; if the values are in dollars, the variance is in dollars squared. To return units to normal, we simply take the square root of the variance. This gives the most widely used measure of spread, which is the standard deviation.

$$\text{standard deviation} = \sqrt{\frac{\sum (x - \bar{x})^2}{n}}$$
$$= \sqrt{\text{variance}}$$

WORKED EXAMPLE 6.10

What are the variance and standard deviation of 2, 3, 7, 8 and 10?

Solution

Again, the calculation starts by finding the mean of the numbers, $\bar{x}$, which is $(2 + 3 + 7 + 8 + 10) / 5 = 6$. The variance is the mean squared deviation, which is:

$$\text{variance} = \frac{\sum (x - \bar{x})^2}{n}$$

$$= \frac{(2 - 6)^2 + (3 - 6)^2 + (7 - 6)^2 + (8 - 6)^2 + (10 - 6)^2}{5}$$

$$= \frac{(-4)^2 + (-3)^2 + 1^2 + 2^2 + 4^2}{5}$$

$$= \frac{16 + 9 + 1 + 4 + 16}{5} = \frac{46}{5}$$

$$= 9.2$$

The standard deviation is the square root of the variance:

$$\text{standard deviation} = \sqrt{9.2}$$
$$= 3.03$$

Again, in practice you are more likely to use a standard spreadsheet function for these calculations, such as VARP and STDEVP.

We can extend the calculations for variance and standard deviation to grouped data, using the same approach as for the MAD, approximating values by the midpoints of classes. Then:

$$\text{variance} = \frac{\sum (x - \bar{x})^2 f}{\sum f} = \frac{\sum (x - \bar{x})^2 f}{n}$$

$$\text{standard deviation} = \sqrt{\text{variance}} = \sqrt{\frac{\sum (x - \bar{x})^2 f}{\sum f}} = \sqrt{\frac{\sum (x - \bar{x})^2 f}{n}}$$

where: x = midpoint of a class
$\quad\quad f$ = number of values in the class
$\quad\quad \bar{x}$ = mean value
$\quad\quad n$ = total number of values

WORKED EXAMPLE 6.11

Find the variance and standard deviation of this set of data:

Class	0–9.9	10–19.9	20–29.9	30–39.9
Frequency	1	4	8	13

Class	40–49.9	50–59.9	60–69.9	70–79.9
Frequency	11	9	5	2

Solution

Figure 6.11 shows the calculations in the same spreadsheet format as Figure 6.10. As you can see, there are 53 values with a mean of 41.2. The deviation of each class is the distance its midpoint is away from the mean. Then we find the variance by taking the square of the deviations, multiplying by the frequency, adding the results, and dividing by the number of values. This gives a value for the variance of 257.5. Taking the square root of this gives the standard deviation of 16.0.

	A	B	C	D	E	F	G	H
1	Variance and standard deviation							
2								
3								
4	Class		Midpoint	Frequency	Product	Deviation	Squared deviation	Product
5	From	To	x	f	fx	$(x - \text{mean})$	$(x - \text{mean})^2$	$f(x - \text{mean})^2$
6	0	9.9	5.0	1	5.0	−36.2	1312.4	1312.4
7	10	19.9	15.0	4	59.8	−26.2	687.8	2751.3
8	20	29.9	25.0	8	199.6	−16.2	263.3	2106.4
9	30	39.9	35.0	13	454.4	−6.2	38.8	504.0
10	40	49.9	45.0	11	494.5	3.8	14.2	156.6
11	50	59.9	55.0	9	494.6	13.8	189.7	1707.4
12	60	69.9	65.0	5	324.8	23.8	565.2	2825.9
13	70	79.9	75.0	2	149.9	33.8	1140.7	2281.3
14	Sums			53	2182.4			13645.3
15	Means				41.2			257.5
16								
17	Variance =			257.5				
18	Standard deviation =			16.0				

Figure 6.11 Calculation of variance and standard deviation for grouped data

Unfortunately, the variance and standard deviation do not have such a clear meaning as the mean absolute deviation. A large variance shows more spread than a smaller one, so data with a variance of 42.5 is more spread out than equivalent data with a variance of 22.5, but we cannot say much more than this. However, they are useful in a variety of other analyses, and this makes them the most widely used measures of dispersion.

Chebyshev made an important observation about standard deviations – a fixed proportion of values is generally within a specified number of standard deviations from the mean. In particular, he found that for data with a standard deviation of s:

- We cannot really say much about values close to the mean, but it is possible that no values will fall within one standard deviation of the mean – which is within the range $(\bar{x} + s)$ to $(\bar{x} - s)$.
- At least three-quarters of values will fall within two standard deviations of the mean – which is within the range $(\bar{x} + 2s)$ to $(\bar{x} - 2s)$.
- At least eight-ninths of values will fall within three standard deviations of the mean – which is within the range $(\bar{x} + 3s)$ to $(\bar{x} - 3s)$.
- In general, at least $1 - \frac{1}{k^2}$ values will fall within k standard deviations of the mean – which is within the range $(\bar{x} + ks)$ to $(\bar{x} + ks)$.

This rule is actually quite conservative, and empirical evidence suggests that for a frequency distribution with a single mode, 68% of values usually fall within one standard deviation of the mean, 95% of values within two standard deviations and almost all values within three standard deviations.

Another important point is that you can sometimes add variances. Provided that two sets of values are completely unrelated (technically described as their covariance being zero), the variance of the sum of data is equal to the sum of the variances of each set. For example, if the daily demand for an item has a variance of 4, while the daily demand for a second item has a variance of 5, the variance of total demand for both items is $4 + 5 = 9$. You can never add standard deviations in this way.

WORKED EXAMPLE 6.12

The mean weight and standard deviation of airline passengers are 72 kg and 6 kg respectively. What is the mean weight and standard deviation of total passenger weight in a 200-seat aeroplane?

Solution

You find the total mean weight of passengers by multiplying the mean weight of each passenger by the number of passengers:

mean $= 200 \times 72$
$\quad\quad = 14,400$ kg

You cannot add the standard deviations like this, but you can add the variances. So the variance in the weight of 200 passengers is the variance in the weight of each passenger multiplied by the number of passengers:

variance $= 200 \times 6^2 = 7,200$ kg^2

The standard deviation in total weight is $\sqrt{7,200} = 84.85$ kg.

Review questions

6.9 List four measures for data spread. Are there any other measures?

6.10 Why is the mean deviation not used to measure data dispersion?

6.11 If the mean of a set of values is 10.37 metres, what are the units of the variance and standard deviation?

6.12 Why is the standard deviation so widely used, when its practical meaning is unclear?

6.13 The number of cars entering a shopping mall car park per hour has a mean of 120 and standard deviation of 10. In one hour, an observer reports 210 cars entering. What can you say about this?

6.14 What functions in a spreadsheet find the dispersion of data?

Tax on house purchase

For many years the UK government has had a policy of encouraging people to own their own houses. In the past, they gave tax relief on mortgage interest, and in the mid-1990s returned almost £3 billion to people who were buying their own homes. However, government policies changed, partly recognising that they were giving benefits to better-off people, who were already gaining from increasing house prices. The government abolished tax relief on mortgages, and the Council for Mortgage Lenders argued that the increasing effects of inheritance tax (paid on inherited property) and stamp duty (paid when buying property) significantly increased the tax burden on homeowners.[1] By 2005, payments in inheritance tax had reached £3 billion (largely because of rising property values) and payments in stamp duty rose to £5 billion.[2,3]

The overall effect was a well-publicised, average increase in tax of £550 a year for each home-owner.[4] However, this average was calculated by dividing the total increase in tax collected by the number of houses in the country, and did not take into account different circumstances or the spread of payments. In reality, only three groups of people were affected:

- people with mortgages no longer had tax relief on the interest and paid extra tax of about 1.5% of their mortgage value a year
- people who bought houses costing more than £120,000 paid 1% of the value in stamp duty
- people who inherited houses in estates valued at more than £275,000, where the inheritance tax rose to 40% of the value.

The real picture is more complicated than the headline suggests – with many people not affected at all, and a few paying a lot.

Other measures of data

One reason why the standard deviation is important is that it is used in other analyses, including the coefficient of variation and the coefficient of skewness.

Coefficient of variation

The measures of spread that we have described give absolute values. This means that they describe a particular set of data, but they cannot really be used to compare different sets of data. One measure that overcomes this problem is the coefficient of variation, which is defined as the ratio of standard deviation over the mean:

$$\text{coefficient of variation} = \frac{\text{standard deviation}}{\text{mean}}$$

The coefficient of variation relates the spread of data to its absolute value, with higher values suggesting more dispersed data. If the cost of operating various facilities in one year has a coefficient of variation of 0.8 and this rises to 0.9 in the following year, it means that the variation in cost has increased, regardless of how the cost has changed in absolute terms.

WORKED EXAMPLE 6.13

Ambrose Financial classify shares in the energy sector as low, medium or high risk. In recent years, these have had mean annual returns of 9.2%, 17.0% and 14.8% respectively. The standard deviations have been 3.9%, 9.8% and 13.6% respectively. What does this tell you?

Solution

The coefficients of variation for share returns are:

■ low risk:

mean = 9.2%, standard deviation = 3.9%
coefficient of variation = 3.9 / 9.2 = 0.42

■ medium risk:

mean = 17.0%, standard deviation = 9.8%
coefficient of variation = 9.8 / 17.0 = 0.58

■ high risk:

mean = 14.8%, standard deviation = 13.6%
coefficient of variation = 13.6 / 14.8 = 0.92

The returns from high-risk shares are more spread out than from lower-risk ones – which is almost a definition of risk. Medium-risk shares had the highest returns, and the relatively low coefficient of variation suggests a comparatively stable performance.

Coefficient of skewness

The coefficient of skewness describes the 'shape' of a set of data. A frequency distribution may be symmetrical about its mean, or it may be skewed. A positive, or right-skewed, distribution has a longer tail to the right (as shown in Figure 6.12(b)); a negative, or left-skewed, distribution has a longer tail to the left (as shown in Figure 6.12(c)).

In a symmetrical distribution the mean, median and mode all have the same value (Figure 6.12(a)). A positive skew means that the mean is bigger than the median, while a negative skew means that the median is bigger than the mean. A formal measure for the amount of skewness comes from Pearson's coefficient of skewness. This has the rather unusual definition of:

$$\text{coefficient of skewness} = \frac{3 \times (\text{mean} - \text{median})}{\text{standard deviation}}$$

This automatically gives the correct sign of the skew, but its precise interpretation is rather difficult. Values around +1 or −1 are generally considered highly skewed.

Review questions

6.15 Why would you use the coefficient of variation?

6.16 What does the coefficient of skewness measure?

6.17 Two sets of data have means 10.2 and 33.4 and variances 4.3 and 18.2. What does this tell you?

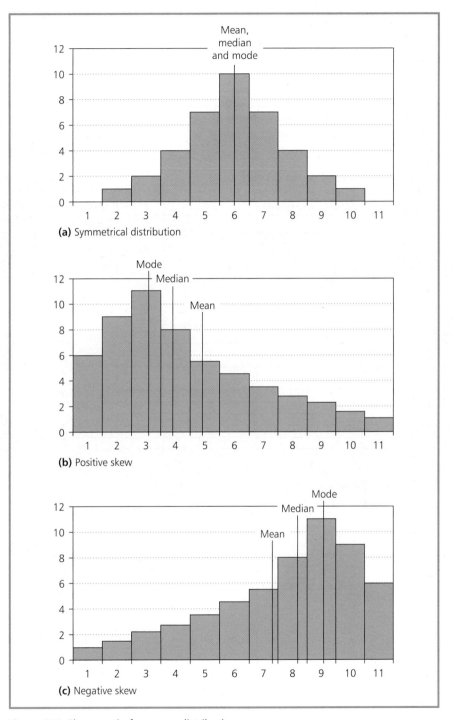

Figure 6.12 Skewness in frequency distributions

IDEAS IN PRACTICE Prinseptia

Prinseptia is a diversified international company operating largely in southern Europe. In 2009 they bought an art auction house in Tuscany. A year later they reviewed operations to see how their investment was developing. At this point they had 44 weeks of contract information and produced their first progress report and planning document.

One part of this document included the figures shown in Figure 6.13 with the aim of giving – when viewed with other information – a review of weekly contract value.

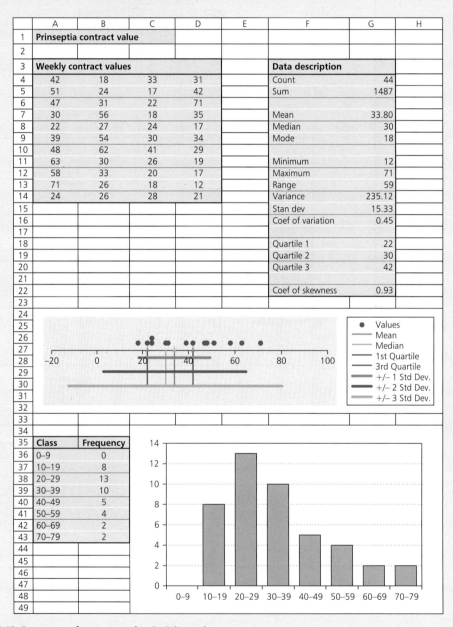

	A	B	C	D	E	F	G	H
1	**Prinseptia contract value**							
2								
3	**Weekly contract values**					**Data description**		
4	42	18	33	31		Count	44	
5	51	24	17	42		Sum	1487	
6	47	31	22	71				
7	30	56	18	35		Mean	33.80	
8	22	27	24	17		Median	30	
9	39	54	30	34		Mode	18	
10	48	62	41	29				
11	63	30	26	19		Minimum	12	
12	58	33	20	17		Maximum	71	
13	71	26	18	12		Range	59	
14	24	26	28	21		Variance	235.12	
15						Stan dev	15.33	
16						Coef of variation	0.45	
17								
18						Quartile 1	22	
19						Quartile 2	30	
20						Quartile 3	42	
21								
22						Coef of skewness	0.93	
23								

Class	Frequency
0–9	0
10–19	8
20–29	13
30–39	10
40–49	5
50–59	4
60–69	2
70–79	2

Figure 6.13 Summary of contract value in Prinseptia

CHAPTER REVIEW

This chapter described a number of numerical measures of data.

- Chapter 5 described some diagrams for summarising data, and this chapter showed how numerical measures give more objective and accurate descriptions. Two key measures describe the location and spread of data.

- Measures of location find the centre of data or a typical value. The (arithmetic) mean is the most widely used measure, giving an average value. Alternatives are the median (which is the middle value, when they are ranked in order of size) and the mode (which is the most frequently occurring value).

- Other measures are needed for the spread of data. The obvious measure is range, but this can be affected by a few outlying results. More reliable values come from the interquartile range or quartile deviation.

- The deviation is the difference between a value and the mean. A basic measure gives the mean absolute deviation. Alternatively, we can square the deviations and calculate the mean squared deviation – or the variance.

- The square root of the variance is the standard deviation, which is the most widely used measure of spread. We can usually estimate the number of observations expected within a certain number of standard deviations of the mean.

- The standard deviation is used for other analyses, such as the coefficient of variation (which gives a relative view of spread) and the coefficient of skewness (which describes the shape of a distribution).

CASE STUDY   Consumer Advice Office

When people buy things, they have a number of statutory rights. A basic right is that the product should be of adequate quality and fit for the purpose intended. When customers think these rights have been infringed, they might contact their local government's trading standards service.

Mary Lomamanu has been working in Auckland as a consumer advice officer for the past 14 months, where her job is to advise people who have complaints against traders. She listens to the complaints, assesses the problem and then takes the follow-up action she thinks is needed. Often she can deal with a client's problem quite quickly – when she thinks the trader has done nothing wrong, or when she advises customers to go back to the place they bought a product and complain to the manager. But some cases are more difficult and need a lot of follow-up, including legal work and appearances in court.

The local government is always looking for ways to reduce costs and improve their service, so it is important for Mary to show that she is doing a good job. She is particularly keen to show that her increasing experience and response to pressures means that she is more efficient and deals with more clients. To help with this, she has kept records of the number of clients she dealt with during her first eight weeks at work, and during the same eight weeks this year.

- Number of customers dealt with each working day in the first eight weeks:

    6 18 22 9 10 14 22 15 28 9 30 26 17 9 11
    25 31 17 25 30 32 17 27 34 15 9 7 10 28 10
    31 12 16 26 21 37 25 7 36 29

- Number of customers dealt with each working day in the last eight weeks:

    30 26 40 19 26 31 28 41 18 27 29 30 33 43 19
    20 44 37 29 22 41 39 15 9 22 26 30 35 38 26
    19 25 33 39 31 30 20 34 43 45

Case study continued

During the past year she estimates that her working hours have increased by an average of 2 hours a week, which is unpaid overtime. Her wages increased by 3% after allowing for inflation.

Question

■ Mary needs a way of presenting these figures to her employers in a form that they will understand. How do you think she should set about this?

PROBLEMS

6.1 When Winnie Mbecu was in hospital for two weeks, the numbers of visitors she received on consecutive days were 4, 2, 1, 5, 1, 3, 3, 5, 2, 1, 6, 4, 1 and 4. How would you describe this data?

6.2 Find the mean, median and mode of the following numbers. What other measures can you use?

> 24 26 23 24 23 24 27 26 28 25 21 22 25 23 26
> 29 27 24 25 24 24 25

6.3 What measures can you use for the following discrete frequency distribution?

Class	0–5	6–10	11–15	16–20
Frequency	1	5	8	11
Class	21–25	26–30	31–35	36–40
Frequency	7	4	2	1

6.4 What measures can you use for the following continuous frequency distribution?

Class	1.00–2.99	3.00–4.99	5.00–6.99	7.00–8.99
Frequency	2	6	15	22
Class	9.00–10.99	11.00–12.99	13.00–14.99	15.00–16.99
Frequency	13	9	5	2

6.5 How would you describe the following data?

> 3 45 28 83 62 44 60 18 73 44 59 67 78 32 74
> 28 67 97 34 44 23 66 25 12 58   9 34 58 29 45
> 37 91 73 50 10 71 72 19 18 27 41 91 90 23 23
> 33

6.6 The Langborne Hotel is concerned about the number of people who book rooms by telephone but do not actually turn up. The following table shows the numbers of people who have done this over the past few weeks. How can they summarise this data?

Day	1	2	3	4	5	6	7	8	9	10	11	12	13	14	15
No-shows	4	5	2	3	3	2	1	4	7	2	0	3	1	4	5
Day	16	17	18	19	20	21	22	23	24	25	26				
No-shows	2	6	2	3	3	4	2	5	5	2	4				
Day	27	28	29	30	31	32	33	34	35	36	37				
No-shows	3	3	1	4	5	3	6	4	3	1	4				
Day	38	39	40	41	42	43	44	45							
No-shows	5	6	3	3	2	4	3	4							

6.7 In Research project 5.2 we described a set of data that had been collected by Jan Schwartzkopf. What numerical summaries can you use for this data?

6.8 Describe the distributions of incomes in a number of different countries.

RESEARCH PROJECTS

6.1 Spreadsheets have procedures for automatically describing data, such as the 'Data Analysis' tool in Excel (if this is missing you have to load the Analysis ToolPac as an add-in). An option in this is 'Descriptive Statistics' which automatically finds 13 measures for a set of data (illustrated in Figure 6.14). Explore the analyses done by these procedures.

6.2 Spreadsheets are not really designed for statistical analysis, but there are many specialised packages. Some of these are commercial packages (such as JMP, Minitab, S-plus, SPSS, STATISTICA and Systat); others are open source (such as PSPP and Statistical Lab); others are add-ins for Excel (such as Analyse-it and SPC XL). Do a small survey of packages that include statistical measures. Compare their features and say which packages you think are most useful.

6.3 Find a set of data about the performance of sports teams, such as last year's results from a football league. Describe the performance of the teams, both numerically and graphically. Include these in a report to the directors of the league to review the year's performance.

6.4 Most organisations try to present data fairly. But some presentations clearly give the wrong impression – perhaps the data is skewed and the median would give a fairer view than the mean; perhaps there are outlying values and the quartile deviation would be fairer than the range. People presenting the data usually argue that they have used objective measures and that readers have interpreted these in the wrong ways. Have a look for summaries of data that you feel are misleading. Say why they are misleading and how you would improve them.

	A	B	C	D
1	**Data description**			
2				
3	**Data**		*Data description*	
4	45			
5	35		Mean	45.41
6	63		Standard error	3.92
7	21		Median	45.00
8	34		Mode	45.00
9	45		Standard deviation	16.15
10	60		Sample variance	260.76
11	19		Kurtosis	−0.75
12	72		Skewness	−0.21
13	54		Range	53.00
14	42		Minimum	19.00
15	67		Maximum	72.00
16	20		Sum	772
17	48		Count	17
18	51			
19	39			
20	57			

Figure 6.14 Data description with Excel

Sources of information

References

1 HM Revenue and Customs, *Income Tax Statistics and Distributions*, HMSO, London, 2006.

2 Websites at www.hmrc.gov.uk and www.statistics.gov.uk.

3 Council for Mortgage Lenders, Inheritance tax and home ownership, *CML News and Views*, London, 24th January 2006.

4 Murray-West R., Home-owners are £550 a year poorer under Labour, *The Daily Telegraph*, 25th January 2006.

Further reading

Most statistics books cover the material in this chapter, and you might find the following useful (some more general statistics books are given in Chapter 14):

Clarke G.M. and Cooke D., *A Basic Course in Statistics* (5th edition), Hodder Arnold, London, 2004.

Levine D.M., Stephan D., Krehbiel T.C. and Berenson M.L., *Statistics for Managers* (6th edition), Pearson Education, New York, 2011.

McClave J., Benson P. and Sincich T., *A First Course in Business Statistics*, Prentice Hall, Englewood Cliffs, NJ, 2000.

Ragsdale C., *Spreadsheet Modelling and Decision Analysis* (5th edition), South-Western College Publishing, Cincinnati, OH, 2008.

Rowntree D., *Statistics Without Tears: a Primer for Non-mathematicians*, Allyn and Bacon, London, 2003.

Runsey C., *Statistics for Dummies*, John Wiley, Chichester, 2003.

Upton G. and Cook I., *Dictionary of Statistics*, Oxford University Press, Oxford, 2008.

Winston W.L. and Albright S., *Spreadsheet Modelling and Applications*, Brooks Cole, Florence, KY, 2004.

Wonnacott R.J. and Wonnacott T.H., *Business Statistics* (5th edition), John Wiley, Chichester, 1999.

Describing changes with index numbers

Chapter outline

Managers often have to monitor the way in which some value changes over time – perhaps the price of raw materials, monthly sales, company share price, number of customers and so on. Index numbers give a way of monitoring such changes. So this chapter continues the theme of data presentation, using index numbers to describe the way that values change over time.

After finishing this chapter you should be able to:

- understand the purpose of index numbers
- calculate indices for changes in the value of a variable
- change the base of an index
- use simple aggregate and mean price relative indices
- calculate aggregate indices using base-weighting and current-weighting
- appreciate the use of the Retail Price Index.

Measuring change

The previous two chapters showed how to summarise data with diagrams and numerical measures. Both take a snapshot of data and describe its features at a specific time. But the values of most variables in business change over time – income, sales, profit, share price, productivity, number of customers and so on. It would be useful to have a way of monitoring these changes and accurately describing the effects over time. Index numbers give a simple way of doing this. In particular, they show how a variable changes over time in relation to its value at some fixed point.

Indices

Suppose that you want to show how the number of crimes committed in an area has changed over time. In the first year you might find that there were 127 crimes, then 142 crimes in the second year, 116 crimes in the third year and 124 in the fourth year. You could say the number of crimes rose by 11.8% between years 1 and 2, and then fell by 18.3% between years 2 and 3, and rose again by 6.9% between years 3 and 4. Although accurate, this description is very messy and does not give direct comparisons of the number of crimes in, say, years 1 and 4. You could plot a graph of the crimes each year and this would certainly show the pattern – but it would not give a measure of the changes. The easiest way of actually measuring such changes is to use an index or index number.

An index is a number that compares the value of a variable at any point in time with its value at a fixed reference point. We call the fixed reference point the base period, and the value of the variable at this point the base value. Then:

$$\text{index for the time} = \frac{\text{value at the time}}{\text{value in base period}}$$
$$= \frac{\text{value at the time}}{\text{base value}}$$

With the crime figures above, we could use the first year as the base period, giving a base value of 127. Then the calculation of each year's index is shown in the following table.

Year	Value	Calculation	Index
1	127	127 / 127	1.00
2	142	142 / 127	1.12
3	116	116 / 127	0.91
4	124	124 / 127	0.98

The index in the base period is 1.00. The index of 1.12 in the second year shows that the number of crimes is 12% higher than the base value, the index of 0.91 in the third year shows that the number of crimes is 9% lower than the base value, and the index of 0.98 in the fourth year shows that the number of crimes is 2% lower than the base value.

We chose the first year as the base period, but this was an arbitrary choice and we could have used any other year. The choice depends on the information you want to present – with the base year chosen as a fixed reference point. If you want to compare the number of crimes in the fourth year with numbers in previous years, you would take year 4 as the base year. Then the base value is 124, and the calculation of each year's index is shown in the following table.

Year	Value	Calculation	Index
1	127	127 / 124	1.02
2	142	142 / 124	1.15
3	116	116 / 124	0.94
4	124	124 / 124	1.00

You can use indices to monitor the value of any variable that changes over time, but one of the most common uses describes the changing price of an item. There are many reasons why prices change – changing costs of raw materials, new suppliers, changes in operations, variable supply (such as seasonal vegetables), variable demand (such as package holidays), changing financial conditions (such as exchange rates), inflation which causes prices to drift upwards and a wide range of other factors. The overall effect is monitored by a price index.

Calculations with indices

You can set an index to 1.00 in the base period, but for convenience it is usually multiplied by 100 to give an index of 100 in the base period. Subsequent indices are defined as the ratio of the current value over the base value multiplied by 100.

$$\text{index in period } N = \frac{\text{value in period } N}{\text{base value}} \times 100$$

This effectively converts the index to a percentage change from the base period. If the base price of a product is €5 and this rises to €7, the price index is $7 / 5 \times 100 = 140$. This shows that the price has risen by $(140 - 100) = 40\%$ since the base period. If the price in the next period is €4, the price index is $4 / 5 \times 100 = 80$, which is a decrease of $(100 - 80) = 20\%$ since the base period.

As well as monitoring changes in one product's price, indices compare price changes in different products, and if the price indices of two products are 125 and 150 then you know that the price of the second product has risen twice as quickly as the price of the first (assuming the same base period is used).

WORKED EXAMPLE 7.1

A shop sells an item for £20 in January, £22 in February, £25 in March and £26 in April. What is the price index in each month using January as the base month?

Solution

The base price is £20 and the price indices for each month are:

- January $\frac{20}{20} \times 100 = 100$ (as expected in the base period)
- February $\frac{22}{20} \times 100 = 110$
- March $\frac{25}{20} \times 100 = 125$
- April $\frac{26}{20} \times 100 = 130$

The price index of 110 in February shows the price has risen by 10% over the base level, an index of 125 in March shows a rise of 25% over the base level and so on. Changes in indices between periods are described as **percentage point changes**. Between February and March the index increased by 125 − 110 = 15 percentage points. Between March and April the price index rose from 125 to 130, giving a rise of 5 percentage points.

Remember that percentage point changes are not the same as percentage changes – and a rise of 15 percentage points is not the same as a rise of 15%. In Worked example 7.1 there is a price rise of 15 percentage points between February and March, but the percentage rise is (25 − 22) / 22 × 100 = 13.6%. Percentage point changes always refer back to the base price and not the current price.

WORKED EXAMPLE 7.2

Amil Gupta's car showroom is giving a special offer on one model. Their advertised price for this model in four consecutive quarters was £10,450, £10,800, £11,450 and £9,999. How would you describe the changes in price?

Solution

You want to show the historical prices in relation to the latest price, so it makes sense to use the fourth quarter as the base period. Then the price indices in other quarters are:

$$\text{price index in quarter} = \frac{\text{price in quarter} \times 100}{\text{price in fourth quarter}}$$

Figure 7.1 shows these calculations, along with the percentage point rise in prices, which is:

percentage point price rise
= index this quarter − index last quarter

The percentage price rise in each quarter is:

percentage price rise
$$= \frac{\text{price this quarter} - \text{price last quarter}}{\text{price last quarter}} \times 100$$

	A	B	C	D	E	F
1	**Price indices**					
2						
3	**Period**	**Price**	**Index**	**Price rise**	**Percentage price rise**	**Percentage point price rise**
4	1	10450	104.5	0.0	0.0	0.0
5	2	10800	108.0	350.0	3.3	3.5
6	3	11450	114.5	650.0	6.0	6.5
7	4	9999	100.0	−1451.0	−12.7	−14.5

Figure 7.1 Price indices for Amil Gupta

If you rearrange the equation for an index in any period n:

$$\text{index for period } n = \frac{\text{value in period } n \times 100}{\text{base value}}$$

you get:

$$\frac{\text{base value}}{100} = \frac{\text{value in period } n}{\text{index for period } n}$$

And because the base value is constant, you can take any other period, m, and say that:

$$\frac{\text{base value}}{100} = \frac{\text{value in period } n}{\text{index for period } n} = \frac{\text{value in period } m}{\text{index for period } m}$$

This is how you compare values at different times, as illustrated in Worked example 7.3.

WORKED EXAMPLE 7.3

The table shows the monthly index for sales of an item.

Month	1	2	3	4	5	6	7	8	9	10	11	12
Index	121	112	98	81	63	57	89	109	131	147	132	126

(a) If sales in month 3 are 240 units, what are sales in month 8?

(b) If sales in month 10 are 1,200 units, what are sales in month 2?

Solution

(a) Using the ratios:

$$\frac{\text{sales in month 8}}{\text{index in month 8}} = \frac{\text{sales in month 3}}{\text{index in month 3}}$$

$$\frac{\text{sales in month 8}}{109} = \frac{240}{98}$$

or

sales in month 8 = 240 × 109 / 98
= 267

(b) Again you can use the indices directly to give:

$$\frac{\text{sales in month 2}}{\text{index in month 2}} = \frac{\text{sales in month 10}}{\text{index in month 10}}$$

or

sales in month 2 = 1,200 × 112 / 147 = 914

We have described a standard format for indices, but remember that:

- You can use an index to measure the way that any variable – not just price – changes over time.
- The usual base value is 100, but this is only for convenience and you can use any other value.
- You can choose the base period as any appropriate point for comparisons. It is usually a typical period with no unusual circumstances – or it might be a period that you are particularly interested in, such as the first period of a financial review.
- You can calculate an index with any convenient frequency, such as monthly indices for unemployment, daily indices for stock market prices, quarterly indices for production and annual indices for GNP.

Review questions

7.1   What is the purpose of an index?

7.2   Indices always use a base value of 100. Why is this?

7.3   What is the difference between a rise of 10% and a rise of 10 percentage points?

IDEAS IN PRACTICE Mohan Dass and Partners

In 2006 Mohan Dass bought out the other partners in a company that distributes medical supplies around the Middle East. He immediately started a programme of improvement and hopes to see the results during the period 2008 to 2013. In particular, he wants the company to expand rapidly, with turnover increasing by 100% a year for the next five years. To achieve this he is focusing on sales through the company website, introducing generic brands, improving logistics flows,

expanding the product range, moving into new geographical areas, forming partnerships with major suppliers and customers and raising the company profile with health service providers.

To monitor his progress, Mohan collects information about operations, illustrated in Figure 7.2 which shows the index of sales over the past year. Mohan continually monitors a set of 82 measures of this kind to show different aspects of company performance.

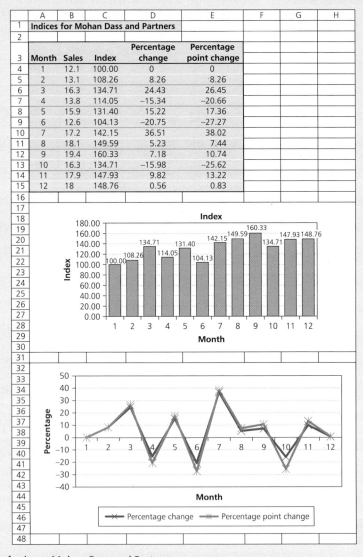

	A	B	C	D	E	F	G	H
1	Indices for Mohan Dass and Partners							
2								
3	Month	Sales	Index	Percentage change	Percentage point change			
4	1	12.1	100.00	0	0			
5	2	13.1	108.26	8.26	8.26			
6	3	16.3	134.71	24.43	26.45			
7	4	13.8	114.05	−15.34	−20.66			
8	5	15.9	131.40	15.22	17.36			
9	6	12.6	104.13	−20.75	−27.27			
10	7	17.2	142.15	36.51	38.02			
11	8	18.1	149.59	5.23	7.44			
12	9	19.4	160.33	7.18	10.74			
13	10	16.3	134.71	−15.98	−25.62			
14	11	17.9	147.93	9.82	13.22			
15	12	18	148.76	0.56	0.83			

Figure 7.2 Index of sales at Mohan Dass and Partners

Source: Richmond E., Internal Report 147/06, Richmond, Parkes and Wright, Cairo, 2006.

Changing the base period

An index can use any convenient base period, but rather than keep the same one for a long time it is often best to update it periodically. There are two reasons for this:

- *Changing circumstances* – you should reset an index whenever there are significant changes that make comparisons with earlier periods meaningless. For example, a service provider might use an index to monitor the number of customers, but should change the base year whenever there are significant changes to the service offered.
- *An index becomes too large* – when an index rises to, say, 5,000 a 10% increase raises it by 500 points, and this seems a much more significant change than a jump from 100 to 110.

On the other hand, changing the base period introduces a discontinuity that makes comparisons over long periods more difficult. This is why people often keep the same base even when it becomes very high (like the Nikkei index of the Tokyo stock exchange which was once approaching 20,000).

In practice, it is easy to convert between indices. When you have an old index that is calculated from an old base value, the old index for period M is:

$$\text{old index} = \frac{\text{value in period } M}{\text{old base value}} \times 100$$

or

$$\text{old index} \times \text{old base value} = \text{value in period } M \times 100$$

Now calculating a new index for period M using a new base period gives:

$$\text{new index} = \frac{\text{value in period } M}{\text{new base value}} \times 100$$

or

$$\text{new index} \times \text{new base value} = \text{value in period } M \times 100$$

These two equations are clearly the same, so we can write:

$$\text{old index} \times \text{old base value} = \text{new index} \times \text{new base value}$$

or

$$\text{new index} = \text{old index} \times \frac{\text{old base value}}{\text{new base value}}$$

As both the old and new base values are fixed, you find the new index by multiplying the old index by a constant. For example, if the old base value was 200 and the new base value is 500, you always find the new index for any period by multiplying the old index by 200 / 500.

WORKED EXAMPLE 7.4

The following indices monitor the annual profits of J.R. Hartman and Associates.

Year	1	2	3	4	5	6	7	8
Index 1	100	138	162	196	220			
Index 2					100	125	140	165

(a) What are the base years for the indices?
(b) If the company had not changed to Index 2, what values would Index 1 have in years 6 to 8?
(c) What values does Index 2 have in years 1 to 4?
(d) If the company made a profit of €4.86 million in year 3, how much did it make in the other years?

Solution

(a) Indices generally have a value of 100 in base periods, so Index 1 uses the base year 1 and Index 2 uses the base year 5.
(b) You find Index 1 by multiplying Index 2 by a constant amount. You can find this constant from year 5, when Index 1 is 220 and Index 2 is 100 – so to convert to Index 1 from Index 2 you multiply by 220 / 100. Then Index 1 for year 6 is 125 × 220 / 100 = 275, and so on, as shown in Figure 7.3.
(c) Using the same reasoning, you change to Index 2 from Index 1 by multiplying by 100 / 220. Index 2 for year 4 is 196 × 100 / 220 = 89.09 and so on, as shown in Figure 7.3.

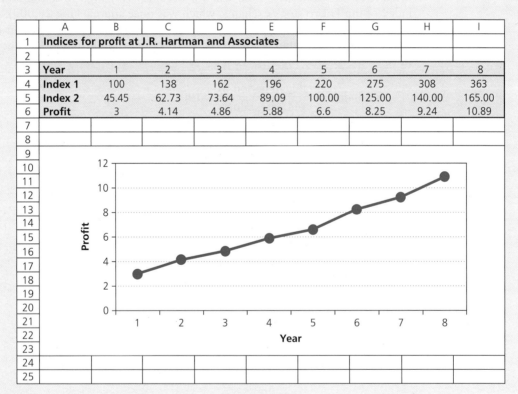

	A	B	C	D	E	F	G	H	I
1	**Indices for profit at J.R. Hartman and Associates**								
2									
3	**Year**	1	2	3	4	5	6	7	8
4	**Index 1**	100	138	162	196	220	275	308	363
5	**Index 2**	45.45	62.73	73.64	89.09	100.00	125.00	140.00	165.00
6	**Profit**	3	4.14	4.86	5.88	6.6	8.25	9.24	10.89
7									
8									

Figure 7.3 Indices for profit at J.R. Hartman and Associates

Worked example 7.4 continued

(d) If the company made a profit of €4.86 million in year 3, you find the profit in any other year from:

$$\frac{\text{profit in year } n}{\text{index in year } n} = \frac{\text{profit in year } m}{\text{index in year } m}$$

We have to use a consistent index in this calculation, so using Index 1 and setting year 3 as year m gives:

$$\text{profit in year } n$$

$$= \text{profit in year } 3 \times \frac{\text{Index 1 in year } n}{\text{Index 1 in year } 3}$$

$$= 4.86 \times \frac{\text{Index 1 in year } n}{162}$$

Then:

$$\text{profit in year } 4 = \frac{4.86 \times \text{Index 1 in year } 4}{162}$$

$$= \frac{4.86 \times 196}{162}$$

$$= 5.88 \text{ or } €5.88 \text{ million}$$

Here we used Index 1, but you can confirm the result using Index 2:

$$\text{profit in year } 4 = \frac{4.86 \times 89.09}{73.64} = 5.88$$

Figure 7.3 shows the profits for other years.

Review questions 7.4   When should you change the base period?

7.5   The old price index for a period is 345, while a new price index is 125. In the following period, the new price index is 132. What would the old index have been?

Indices for more than one variable

Simple indices monitor changes in a single variable, but sometimes you are concerned with changes in a combination of different variables. For instance, a car owner might want to monitor the separate costs of fuel, tax, insurance and maintenance; a company might want to monitor changes in sales of different types of products; a charity might monitor its donations to different types of causes. Indices that measure changes in a number of variables are called aggregate indices.

Aggregate indices

For simplicity we will look at aggregate price indices, but remember that you can use the same reasoning for any other type of index. There are two obvious ways of defining an aggregate price index:

- *The mean of the separate indices for each item* – price indices are sometimes described as the price relatives, so this average of the separate indices is called the mean price relative index:

$$\text{mean price relative index for period } n = \frac{\text{sum of separate indices for period } n}{\text{number of indices}}$$

■ *An index based on the total cost* – this adds all prices together and calculates an index for this total price, called a **simple aggregate index**:

$$\text{simple aggregate index for period } n = \frac{\text{sum of price in period } n}{\text{sum of prices in base period}} \times 100$$

WORKED EXAMPLE 7.5

Last year the prices of coffee, tea and hot chocolate in a café were 55 pence, 28 pence and 72 pence respectively. This year the same items cost 62 pence, 32 pence and 74 pence. What are the mean price relative index and simple aggregate index for this year based on last year?

Solution

■ The mean price relative index uses the price indices for each item, which are:

   coffee: $62 / 55 \times 100 = 112.7$
   tea: $32 / 28 \times 100 = 114.3$
   hot chocolate: $74 / 72 \times 100 = 102.8$

Taking the mean of these gives:

   mean price relative index
   $= (112.7 + 114.3 + 102.8) / 3 = 109.9$

■ For the simple aggregate index we add all the prices:

   sum of base prices $= 55 + 28 + 72$
   $\qquad\qquad\qquad\quad = 155$

   sum of current prices $= 62 + 32 + 74$
   $\qquad\qquad\qquad\qquad = 168$

Then:

   simple aggregate index
   $= \dfrac{\text{sum of current prices}}{\text{sum of base prices}} \times 100$

   $= 168 / 155 \times 100$
   $= 108.4$

These two indices are easy to use, but they do not really give good measures. An obvious criticism – particularly of the simple aggregate index – is that it depends on the units used for each index. An aggregate index that includes the price of, say, butter per kilogram gives a different index from one that includes the price per pound – and if we use the price of butter per tonne, this is so high that it swamps the other costs and effectively ignores them. For example, if the price of a loaf of bread rises from €1 to €1.40 and the price of a tonne of butter rises from €2,684 to €2,713, it makes no sense to calculate a simple aggregate index of $(2{,}713 + 1.40) / (2{,}684 + 1) \times 100 = 101.09$.

Another weakness of the two indices is that they do not consider the relative importance of each product. If people in the café buy more tea than hot chocolate, the index should reflect this. Imagine a service company that spent $1,000 on raw materials and $1 million on wages in the base year, and this year it spends $2,000 on raw materials and $1 million on wages. Again, it makes no sense to say that the price index for raw materials is 200 and for wages is 100, so the mean price relative index is $(200 + 100) / 2 = 150$.

A reasonable aggregate index must take into account two factors:

■ the price paid for each unit of a product
■ the number of units of each product used.

There are several ways of combining these into a weighted index. Suppose that you want to measure changes in the amount a family pays for food. The easiest way of doing this is to look at each week's shopping basket and find the total cost – which depends on both the price of each item and the number of items they buy. Then we can define a weighted price index as:

$$\text{weighted price index} = \frac{\text{current cost of a week's shopping basket}}{\text{cost of the shopping basket in a base period}}$$

At first this seems reasonable, but we soon hit a problem. When the price of, say, cake increases with respect to the price of biscuits, a family may reduce the number of cakes it buys and increase the number of biscuits. Changes in relative price clearly change the amounts that a family buys. Two alternatives allow for this:

- a base-weighted index assumes that quantities purchased do not change from the base period
- a current-weighted index assumes that the current shopping basket was used in the base period.

Base-weighted index

Suppose that in the base period a family's shopping basket contained quantities, Q_0, of different items at prices P_0. The total cost of the basket is the sum of all the quantities multiplied by the prices:

$$\text{total cost in base period} = \text{sum of quantities} \times \text{price}$$
$$= \Sigma Q_0 P_0$$

In another period, n, the prices changed to P_n, but we assume the quantities bought remain unchanged, so the total cost is now $\Sigma Q_0 P_n$. Then the base-weighted index is the ratio of these two costs.

---

base-weighted index

$$= \frac{\text{cost of base period quantities at current prices}}{\text{cost of base period quantities at base period prices}} \times 100$$

$$= \frac{\Sigma Q_0 P_n}{\Sigma Q_0 P_0} \times 100$$

This is sometimes called the Laspeyres index after its inventor, and it has the advantage of reacting to actual price rises. But it assumes that amounts bought do not change over time, and it does not respond to general trends in buying habits or responses to specific changes in price. Base-weighted indices do not notice that people substitute cheaper items for ones whose price is rising, so they tend to be too high.

Current-weighted index

Suppose that in a period, n, a family's shopping basket contains quantities, Q_n, of different items at prices P_n and the total cost is $\Sigma Q_n P_n$. We can compare this with the cost of the same products in the base period, which would have been $\Sigma Q_n P_0$. Then the current-weighted index is the ratio of these two costs.

---

current-weighted index

$$= \frac{\text{cost of current quantities at current prices}}{\text{cost of current quantities at base period prices}} \times 100$$

$$= \frac{\Sigma Q_n P_n}{\Sigma Q_n P_0} \times 100$$

This is sometimes called the Paasche index, which has the advantage of giving an accurate measure of changes in the costs of current purchases. However, the calculation changes each period, so it does not give a direct comparison over time. It also needs more effort in updating it because it relies on constant monitoring of purchasing habits to find the amounts currently purchased. A Paasche index introduces new products that are relatively cheaper than they were in the base period, so it tends to be too low.

WORKED EXAMPLE 7.6

A company buys four products with the following features.

	Number of units bought		Price paid per unit	
Item	Year 1	Year 2	Year 1	Year 2
A	20	24	10	11
B	55	51	23	25
C	63	84	17	17
D	28	34	19	20

(a) What are the price indices for each product in year 2 using year 1 as the base year?
(b) Calculate a base-weighted index for the products.
(c) Calculate a current-weighted index.

Solution

(a) Simple price indices look only at the prices and do not take into account usage of a product, so the values are:

Product A: $11 / 10 \times 100 = 110$
Product B: $25 / 23 \times 100 = 108.7$

Product C: $17 / 17 \times 100 = 100$
Product D: $20 / 19 \times 100 = 105.3$

(b) A base-weighted index compares prices for the basket of items bought in the base period:

$$\text{base-weighted index} = \frac{\Sigma Q_0 P_n}{\Sigma Q_0 P_0} \times 100$$

$$= \frac{20 \times 11 + 55 \times 25 + 63 \times 17 + 28 \times 20}{20 \times 10 + 55 \times 23 + 63 \times 17 + 28 \times 19} \times 100$$

$$= \frac{3{,}226}{3{,}068} \times 100$$

$$= 105.15$$

(c) A current-weighted index compares prices for the basket of items bought in the current period:

$$\text{current-weighted index} = \frac{\Sigma Q_n P_n}{\Sigma Q_n P_0} \times 100$$

$$= \frac{24 \times 11 + 51 \times 25 + 84 \times 17 + 34 \times 20}{24 \times 10 + 51 \times 23 + 84 \times 17 + 34 \times 19} \times 100$$

$$= \frac{3{,}647}{3{,}487} \times 100$$

$$= 104.59$$

La Milla Ferensa

Francesca Birtolli has designed a spreadsheet for calculating price indices for all the materials that La Milla Ferensa buys for its operations. Figure 7.4 shows an outline of this, that is used for training, with calculations for 10 products over four years. The raw data appears at the top of the table as a set of quantities and costs for the 10 products. The spreadsheet calculates individual indices for both the quantities and the prices of each product. Then it calculates four aggregate indices – simple aggregate, mean price relative, base-weighted and current-weighted. You can see that these

aggregate indices give quite different results. The first two do not consider the amounts bought, so they give general impressions but are not too reliable. The second two indices are more reliable, but the base-weighted index tends to be high, while the current-weighted index tends to be low.

The real system in La Milla Ferensa monitors monthly changes in 110 major purchase items and quarterly changes in another 1,500 minor ones. And it produces a series of analyses and reports for company managers.

Source: Company Reports, La Milla Ferensa, Milan, 2010.

	A	B	C	D	E	F	G	H	I
1	Francesca Birtolli – index calculations								
2									
3	Purchases by year								
4		Year 1		Year 2		Year 3		Year 4	
5	Product	Quantity	Cost	Quantity	Cost	Quantity	Cost	Quantity	Cost
6	1	24	16	26	16	30	15	35	15
7	2	3	21	5	21	8	21	10	21
8	3	11	20	11	21	10	22	8	24
9	4	15	9	10	11	5	14	2	16
10	5	8	22	12	21	14	21	16	20
11	6	2	40	2	41	2	40	2	40
12	7	1	36	1	37	1	37	1	37
13	8	1	5	2	7	1	8	1	10
14	9	8	16	6	17	4	19	2	19
15	10	20	12	19	13	15	14	10	15
16									
17	Simple indices								
18		Year 1		Year 2		Year 2		Year 4	
19	Product	Quantity	Cost	Quantity	Cost	Quantity	Cost	Quantity	Cost
20	1	100	100	108.3	100.0	125.0	93.8	145.8	93.8
21	2	100	100	166.7	100.0	266.7	100.0	333.3	100.0
22	3	100	100	100.0	105.0	90.9	110.0	72.7	120.0
23	4	100	100	66.7	122.2	33.3	155.6	13.3	177.8
24	5	100	100	150.0	95.5	175.0	95.5	200.0	90.9
25	6	100	100	100.0	102.5	100.0	100.0	100.0	100.0
26	7	100	100	100.0	102.8	100.0	102.8	100.0	102.8
27	8	100	100	200.0	140.0	100.0	160.0	100.0	200.0
28	9	100	100	75.0	106.3	50.0	118.8	25.0	118.8
29	10	100	100	95.0	108.3	75.0	116.7	50.0	125.0
30									
31	Aggregate indices								
32			Year 1	Year 2	Year 3	Year 4			
33	Simple aggregate		100	104.1	107.1	110.2			
34	Mean price relative		100	108.3	115.3	122.9			
35									
36	Base-weighted		100	104.5	109.1	113.6			
37	Current-weighted		100	100.8	100.3	101.3			

Figure 7.4 Indices calculated by Francesca Birtolli

Other weighted indices

Base-weighting and current-weighting indices both assign weights to prices according to the quantities bought. But sometimes it is better to use other kinds of weighting. For instance, you may be looking at the cost of journeys on public transport. The two indices would consider the costs of travel and the number of journeys – but it would make more sense to include some measure of the distances travelled. We can assign other weights, w, to the prices to reflect some other measure of importance, and define a weighted index as:

$$\text{weighted index} = \frac{\Sigma w P_n / P_0}{\Sigma w} \times 100$$

In principle the weights can take any values, but they are usually related to total expenditure, time, typical value, general importance and so on.

IDEAS IN PRACTICE Retail Price Index

Every month since 1914 the UK government has published figures for the annual rate of inflation[1,2]. It uses several indices to monitor this including the Consumer Price Index, Retail Price Index, Harmonised Index of Consumer Prices, Producer Price Index and Services Producer Price Index.

The Retail Price Index (RPI) originated in 1947 and is the most widely used for giving 'headline inflation rates'. Specifically, it measures changes in the amount spent by a typical household every month. This calculation needs two sets of data – the items that a typical household buys, and the prices that it pays.

To find the items that a family buys, the government runs an expenditure and food survey for which 6,500 families around the country keep a record of their purchases. This identifies 350 major products and services in 14 groups, with the weights (out of 1,000) used in 2010 shown in this table.

Food	118	Clothing and footwear	39
Catering	50	Personal goods and	
Alcoholic drink	63	services	41
Tobacco	27	Motoring expenditure	121
Housing	236	Fares and travel costs	20
Fuel and light	49	Leisure goods	38
Household goods	70	Leisure services	67
Household services	61		

Prices are monitored by collecting 180,000 prices for 700 items on the Tuesday nearest the

middle of each month. Some of these are collected centrally (from websites, catalogues, advertisements etc.) but accurate figures have to allow for price variations around the country, so around 100,000 prices for 550 items are collected by personal visits to 20,000 shops in 150 representative shopping areas.

The weights and current values are used to calculate a broad aggregate index of prices that is used for many purposes, including wage bargaining, calculating index-linked benefits, raising insurance values and adjusting pensions. But it is not a perfect answer, and it does not represent the true rate of inflation felt by certain groups whose buying habits are not 'typical'. The government takes some of these into account with special indices for pensioners and very prosperous households – and it also publishes specific indices for each type of item, such as fruit, electricity, garden equipment and so on.

In an attempt to save money, the government announced that it would stop using the RPI to adjust pensions and other benefits in 2011 and would switch to the CPI (consumer price index). This excludes the costs of housing and is usually lower than the RPI. For example, in June 2010 the annual rate of inflation reported by the RPI was 5.0%, while the CPI recorded 3.2%.

It can be very important to interpret the indices properly. For instance, if someone's pay doubled over five years they would expect to be much better off. However, the period 1974 to 1979 had

Ideas in practice continued

high inflation and the RPI was 206 in 1979, with 1974 as the base year; in real terms a doubling of salary would leave someone worse off. Similarly, after the financial crisis around 2009, banks

offered depositors interest rates of less than 2%. As the RPI rose to more than 3%, any money invested would actually lose value.

Sources: www.statistics.gov.uk

Review questions

7.6   What are the mean price relative index and simple aggregate index?

7.7   What are the weaknesses in these measures?

7.8   What is the difference between base-period weighting and current-period weighting for aggregate indices?

7.9   Why does base-weighting give a higher index than current-weighting?

7.10 Is it possible to use a weighting other than base period or current period?

7.11 'The retail price index gives an accurate measure of the cost of living.' Do you think this is true?

CHAPTER REVIEW

This chapter showed how indices can monitor changing values over time.

■ The values of most variables – like prices, output, employment, sales, rainfall etc. – change over time. You can use an index to monitor these changes.

■ An index is defined as the ratio of the current value of a variable over its base value – which is its value in the base period. This is normally multiplied by 100 to give a more convenient figure.

■ The difference in an index between periods shows the percentage point change.

■ The base period of an index can be any convenient point, but it should be revised periodically. To calculate a new index you multiply the old index by a constant.

■ As well as measuring changes in a single variable, you can also monitor changes in a combination of related variables using aggregate indices. Two basic aggregate indices are the simple aggregate index and the mean price relative index. But both of these have weaknesses – in particular, they do not reflect the quantities bought.

■ Better options use base-period weighting (which assumes that the items bought in the base period continue to be bought) and current-period weighting (which assumes that items currently bought have always been bought).

■ The Retail Price Index is a widely accepted measure of price increase based on the expenditure of a typical family.

CASE STUDY Heinz Muller Engineering

In 2003 Heinz Muller Engineering had some problems with industrial relations and productivity. By 2010 it tried hard to overcome these and made a series of changes in the way that employees were rewarded and involved in decision-making. Some of these changes included profit sharing, quality circles, reducing the number of layers of management from 13 to 6, more flexible working practices, improved communications and the same basic pay rise for all employees.

As part of these changes, the company negotiates an annual basic pay rise, which is proposed by a committee of representatives from all parts of the company along with a number of independent members. The independent members give an impartial view in a process which, by its nature, generates strong feelings. Turek Camalli is one of these independent members, which means that he cannot be connected with Heinz Muller in any way. He is an accountant working at the head office of a major bank and his employers have no connection with Heinz Muller or with engineering work.

Recently Turek has started preparing for the first meeting to set this year's annual wage rise. He has some data about Heinz Muller for the past

10 years, shown in the following table, but unfortunately he does not know how well the company is doing at the moment, nor how well it is likely to do next year. He has to work out some initial ideas, based only on this limited data.

Year	Average weekly earnings	Average hours worked	Company revenue (€million)	Gross company profit (€'000)	Index of industry wages	Retail Price Index
1	80.45	44	24.0	2,410	85.5	84.5
2	104.32	43	30.2	2,900	100.0	100.0
3	124.21	45	34.6	3,300	115.6	113.5
4	140.56	46	41.6	3,840	130.2	126.4
5	152.80	46	43.2	4,300	141.1	139.8
6	182.90	45	44.6	4,580	158.3	156.2
7	214.33	44	58.6	5,900	168.1	168.8
8	242.75	43	69.0	4,420	182.5	185.6
9	254.16	43	85.2	5,780	190.7	198.9
10	264.34	42	89.0	7,740	201.3	218.4

Questions

- If you were Turek Camalli, how would you start thinking about this problem?
- What other data would you like to see and how can this be collected?

PROBLEMS

7.1 The price of an item in consecutive months has been £106, £108, £111, £112, £118, £125, £130 and £132. Use an index based on the first month to describe these changes. How would this compare with an index based on the final month?

7.2 The numbers of fishing boats operating from Porto Novapietro over the past 10 years were:

325 321 316 294 263 241 197 148 102 70

Describe these changes by indices based on the first and last year's figures.

7.3 The number of people employed by Westbury Cladding over the past 12 months is as follows. Use an index to describe these figures.

Month	1	2	3	4	5	6	7	8	9	10	11	12
Number	121	115	97	112	127	135	152	155	161	147	133	131

7.4 The annual output of a company is described by the following indices:

Year	1	2	3	4	5	6	7	8
Index 1	100	125	153	167				
Index 2				100	109	125	140	165

If the company made 23,850 units in year 2, how many did it make in the other years? What is the percentage increase in output each year?

7.5 ARP insurance company uses an index to describe the number of agents working for it. This index was revised five years ago, and had the following values over the past 10 years:

Year	1	2	3	4	5	6	7	8	9	10
Index 1	106	129	154	173	195	231				
Index 2						100	113	126	153	172

If the company had 645 agents in year 4, how many did it have in the other years?

7.6 Employees in a company are put into four wage groups. During a three-year period the numbers employed in each group and the average weekly wage are as follows.

	Year 1		Year 2		Year 3	
Group	Number	Wage	Number	Wage	Number	Wage
1	45	125	55	133	60	143
2	122	205	125	211	132	224
3	63	245	66	268	71	293
4	7	408	9	473	13	521

Use different indices to describe the changes in wages paid and the numbers employed.

7.7 The following table shows the price of drinks served in The Lion Inn. How would you describe the price changes?

	Wine	Spirits	Beer	Soft drinks
Year 1	91	95	78	35
Year 1	97	105	85	39
Year 3	102	112	88	42
Year 4	107	125	93	47

7.8 A company buys four products with the following characteristics.

	Number of units bought		Price paid per unit	
Product	Year 1	Year 2	Year 1	Year 2
A	121	141	9	10
B	149	163	21	23
C	173	182	26	27
D	194	103	31	33

Calculate a base-weighted index and a current-weighted index for the products.

7.9 The average prices for four items over four years are as follows.

Item	Year 1	Year 2	Year 3	Year 4
A	25	26	30	32
B	56	61	67	74
C	20	25	30	36
D	110	115	130	150

A company annually bought 400, 300, 800 and 200 units of each item respectively. Calculate weighted price indices for years 2 to 4, taking year 1 as the base year.

7.10 Calculate appropriate indices for the data in the table below.

	Year 1		Year 2		Year 3		Year 4	
Item	Price	Quantity	Price	Quantity	Price	Quantity	Price	Quantity
AL403	142	27	147	26	155	32	165	32
ML127	54	284	58	295	65	306	75	285
FE872	1,026	5	1,026	8	1,250	2	1,250	3
KP332	687	25	699	25	749	20	735	55
KP333	29	1,045	31	1,024	32	1,125	36	1,254
CG196	58	754	64	788	72	798	81	801
CG197	529	102	599	110	675	120	750	108
CG404	254	306	275	310	289	305	329	299
CG405	109	58	115	62	130	59	140	57
NA112	86	257	83	350	85	366	90	360
QF016	220	86	220	86	225	86	225	86
QT195	850	10	899	9	949	12	999	16
LJ878	336	29	359	38	499	11	499	25

RESEARCH PROJECTS

7.1 The following table shows the UK's Retail Price Index from 1970 to 2009. As you can see, the index was reset to 100 in January 1974, and again in January 1987.

Year	Index	Year	Index	Year	Index	Year	Index	Year	Index
1970	140	1979	224	1988	107	1997	158	2006	198
1971	153	1980	264	1989	115	1998	163	2007	207
1972	164	1981	295	1990	126	1999	165	2008	215
1973	179	1982	320	1991	134	2000	170	2009	214
1974	109	1983	335	1992	139	2001	173		
1975	135	1984	352	1993	141	2002	176		
1976	157	1985	373	1994	144	2003	181		
1977	182	1986	386	1995	149	2004	187		
1978	197	1987	102	1996	153	2005	192		

What is the annual rate of inflation for each year? The UK government publishes several values for inflation, each of which is calculated in a different way. How do the figures above compare with other published results? Why are there differences? How do these figures compare with those from other countries?

7.2 The following table shows the gross domestic product of Germany at current prices for a period of 10 years[3,4]. What indices could you use to describe these figures? Collect information to show how these would compare with other European countries. Write a report summarising your findings in different formats.

Year	Quarter	GDP
2009	IV	624.00
	III	616.00
	II	589.60
	I	579.50
2008	IV	626.10
	III	634.40
	II	625.60
	I	609.70
2007	IV	624.60
	III	617.20
	II	596.70
	I	589.70

Year	Quarter	GDP
2006	IV	603.80
	III	590.30
	II	571.10
	I	559.90
2005	IV	576.30
	III	570.50
	II	557.60
	I	537.80
2004	IV	566.40
	III	560.10
	II	547.10
	I	537.30
2003	IV	557.00
	III	552.00
	II	531.80
	I	523.00
2002	IV	551.25
	III	546.30
	II	528.97
	I	516.66
2001	IV	546.11
	III	532.61
	II	521.43
	I	513.01
2000	IV	529.67
	III	521.21
	II	510.69
	I	500.93

Sources of information

References

1 *Measuring the Cost of Living*, Office for National Statistics, London, 2010.

2 www.statistics.gov.uk.

3 *Statistisches Jahrbuch 2009*, Statistisches Bundesamt Deutschland, Berlin, 2010.

4 www.destatis.de

Further reading

There are not really any books exclusively about indices, except the odd comprehensive one such as:

Balk B.M., *Price and quantity index numbers*, Cambridge University Press, Cambridge, 2008.

Most statistics books discuss indices, and some useful titles are given in Chapter 12.

PART THREE

Solving management problems

This book is divided into five parts. The first part looked at the background and context for quantitative methods. The second part showed how to collect, summarise and present data. These two parts gave the context for the rest of the book. Now you should understand the importance of quantitative methods, know how to work with numbers and be able to collect and process the necessary data. The next stage is to use these tools for some real problems.

This is the third part of the book, which looks at a number of common – and even universal – management problems. The problems tackled in this part are deterministic, which means that we are dealing with conditions of certainty. The fourth part of the book introduces uncertainty through probability and statistical analyses. Then the last part shows how to solve some management problems that include uncertainty.

There are four chapters in this part. Chapter 8 describes some calculations for finance and performance. Chapter 9 uses regression to describe the relationship between variables and Chapter 10 extends these ideas into forecasting. Then Chapter 11 introduces the ideas of 'constrained optimisation' through linear programming.

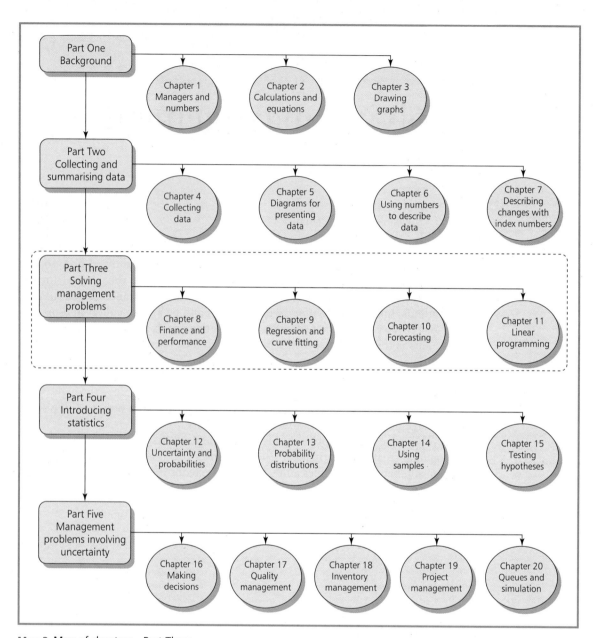

Map 3 Map of chapters – Part Three

Finance and performance

Chapter outline

Managers use a range of different measures to monitor the performance of their organisations. For instance, they look at productivity to see how efficiently resources are being used, or capacity to find maximum production levels. Such measures are essential for showing how well the organisation is working, whether it is meeting targets, how it compares with competitors and how performance has changed in the past. Many measures are phrased in financial terms, as you can see from company annual reports. This chapter describes a number of calculations for measuring performance – particularly financial returns and the flows of money.

After finishing this chapter you should be able to:

- appreciate the importance of measuring performance
- calculate a number of performance ratios
- find break-even points
- understand the reasons for economies of scale
- do calculations for compound interest
- discount amounts of money to their present value
- calculate net present values and internal rates of return
- depreciate the value of assets
- calculate the payments for sinking funds, mortgages and annuities.

Measures of performance

Managers have to monitor the performance of their organisations. If they fail to do this basic task, they have no idea how well the organisation is working, whether it is meeting targets or not, how it compares with competitors, how performance has changed in the past, how operations can be improved, whether investments are channelled to the right areas, whether all areas are profitable and a host of other questions. The only way to answer such questions is to make a series of different measures of performance. These typically monitor sales, profit, output, number of customers, growth, share price, productivity, capacity and so on.

We can start looking at these measures with a basic measure of performance – capacity. This is the maximum output from a process in a specified time. For instance, the capacity of a bottling plant is its maximum output of 1,000 bottles an hour, the capacity of a call centre is 2,000 calls a day, and the capacity of a theatre is 1,200 people for a performance.

At first it seems strange to describe capacity as a measure of performance rather than a fixed constraint. But we can make two observations:

- Firstly, the capacity of a process depends on the way in which resources are organised and managed, so that two organisations can use identical resources in different ways and have different capacities.
- Secondly, the capacity of a process varies over time. You can imagine this with a team of people who are shovelling sand – at eight o'clock in the morning they are fresh and working hard, but by six o'clock in the evening they are tired and working more slowly. So their capacity has changed, even though the operations are the same.

Even an apparently simple measure like capacity can need some interpretation – and it depends on assumptions, approximations and opinions. Another problem is that absolute measures do not really say much. When you hear that a company made a profit of €1 million last year, this does not really say much about its performance. It would certainly be an excellent performance for Jane's Bespoke Software – but it would be a disaster for Microsoft. And when a company increases annual productivity by 10% this would be a good result for a company that is already highly productive, but a poor result for one that is swamped by inefficiencies. We really need more information about the context of a measure, and the easiest way of getting this uses a performance ratio.

Performance ratios

A performance ratio means that you take one direct measure of performance, and divide this by another reference value that sets the context. For example, you can take a figure for profit and put this into context by dividing it by sales volume to get a profit per unit; or you can find the ratio of profit over assets to find the return on investment; or you can measure the output over machine time used, production over the number of employees, accidents per man year, deliveries per vehicle and so on.

One of the most widely used performance ratios is utilisation, which shows how much of the available capacity is actually used. If a process has a capacity of 100 units a week but makes only 60 units, then:

$$\text{utilisation} = \frac{\text{amount of capacity used}}{\text{available capacity}} = \frac{60}{100}$$
$$= 0.6 \text{ or } 60\%$$

Managers like to use resources as fully as possible and generally aim for high utilisation. There are only two ways of achieving this – either by raising the top line (the level of performance) or by reducing the bottom line (the standard for comparison). RyanAir's utilisation of seats is defined as:

$$\text{utilisation} = \frac{\text{number of seats used}}{\text{number of seats available}}$$

The company makes more profit by having high utilisation, and the only ways of raising this are to get more passengers sitting on seats (adjusting the demand) or to reduce the number of seats available (adjusting the supply).

Another widely used performance ratio is productivity. People often assume that this is the amount produced per person, but it is more general than this and measures the amount of output for each unit of any specified resource used. For instance, it might measure the output per tonne of raw material, production per barrel of oil, output per machine and so on. This is really described as a partial productivity, which is defined as:

$$\text{partial productivity} = \frac{\text{amount of products made}}{\text{units of a single resource used}}$$

Each process can have several measures of partial productivity. If it uses 25 hours of machine time to make 50 units, the productivity is 2 units per machine-hour; if it employs 5 people the productivity is 10 units per person; if it uses 50 tonnes of raw material the productivity is 1 unit per tonne. There are four main types of partial productivity:

- *equipment productivity* – such as the number of units made per machine
- *labour productivity* – typically the output from each employee
- *capital productivity* – such as the production for each pound invested
- *energy productivity* – such as the amount produced from each barrel of oil.

WORKED EXAMPLE 8.1

Peter Keller collected this data for a process over two consecutive years. What can you say about performance?

	2009	2010
Number of units made	1,000	1,200
Selling price	£100	£100
Raw materials used	5,100 kg	5,800 kg
Cost of raw materials	£20,500	£25,500
Hours worked	4,300	4,500
Direct labour costs	£52,000	£58,000
Energy used	10,000 kWh	14,000 kWh
Energy cost	£1,000	£1,500
Other costs	£10,000	£10,000

Solution

You can consider various ratios, such as the units of output per kilogram of raw material. In 2009 this was 1,000 / 5,100 = 0.196, and in 2010 it had risen to 1,200 / 5,800 = 0.207. Some other measures are:

	2009	2010	Percentage increase
Units / kg of raw material	0.196	0.207	5.6
Units / £ of raw material	0.049	0.047	−4.1
Units / hour	0.233	0.267	14.6
Units / £ of labour	0.019	0.021	10.5
Units / kWh	0.100	0.086	−14.0
Units / £ of energy	1.000	0.800	−20

Worked example 8.1 continued

In general, labour productivity has risen, raw materials productivity has stayed about the same and energy productivity has fallen.

An alternative measure of productivity would look at the value of the output (the number of units produced multiplied by the selling price) divided by the value of inputs (the sum of the costs of all inputs). This figure for 2009 is:

$$\frac{\text{total output}}{\text{total input}} = \frac{100 \times 1,000}{20,000 + 52,000 + 1,000 + 10,000}$$
$$= 1.2$$

By 2010 this had risen to 120,000 / 95,000 = 1.26, an increase of 5%.

Financial ratios

For many organisations the crucial measure of performance is profit. If you subtract all the costs of running a business from the income generated by sales, you are left with the profit. If the income is less than the costs, the organisation makes a loss.

profit = revenue − costs

This seems straightforward, but remember that any financial data depends on accounting conventions and does not necessarily give an objective view (as illustrated by some well-known examples of 'financial irregularities'[1,2,3]). Again, absolute measures do not really say much, and managers usually calculate a range of different ratios, including:

■ Profit margin – the profit before tax and interest as a percentage of sales:

$$\text{profit margin} = \frac{\text{profit before tax and interest}}{\text{sales}} \times 100$$

■ Return on assets (ROA) – profit as a percentage of the organisation's assets:

$$\text{return on assets} = \frac{\text{profit before interest and tax}}{\text{fix assets + current assets}} \times 100$$

This is arguably the most comprehensive measure of business performance. From a purely financial point of view, the ROA should be as high as possible – but remember that different types of organisation need very different amounts of assets. An advertising agency needs few assets and should have a much higher ROA than, say, a power station or a car assembly plant.

■ Acid test – the ratio of liquid assets (which are cash and those assets that are readily saleable or can easily be turned into cash) and liabilities:

$$\text{acid test} = \frac{\text{liquid assets}}{\text{current liabilities}}$$

Some other ratios that are particularly important for investors include:

$$\text{return on equity} = \frac{\text{profit after tax}}{\text{shareholders' money}} \times 100$$

$$\text{gearing} = \frac{\text{borrowed money}}{\text{shareholders' money}}$$

$$\text{earnings per share} = \frac{\text{profit after tax}}{\text{number of shares}}$$

$$\text{dividends per share} = \frac{\text{amount distributed as dividends}}{\text{number of shares}}$$

$$\text{price–earnings ratio} = \frac{\text{share price}}{\text{earnings per share}}$$

$$\text{dividend cover} = \frac{\text{profit after tax}}{\text{profit distributed to shareholders}}$$

$$\text{yield} = \frac{\text{dividend}}{\text{share price}} \times 100\%$$

IDEAS IN PRACTICE   AstraZeneca

AstraZeneca is one of the world's major pharmaceutical companies, with sales of more than $30 billion. It has 63,000 employees, works in more than 100 countries and has 20 major manufacturing sites. Its operations range from basic research to find new medicines, through manufacturing and distribution, to after-sales service and social health. The company uses thousands of measures for different aspects of its performance. The table illustrates some calculations it might include, based on figures for 2009.

Measures	$ million	
Sales		32,804
Cost of sales		5,775
Gross profit	32,804 – 5,775	= 27,029
Distribution, research, development, selling, general and administrative costs		16,039
Other operating income		553
Operating profit	27,029 + 553 – 16,039 = 11,543	
Financial expenses and tax	736 + 3,263	= 3,999

Measures	$ million	
Profit	11,543 – 3,999	= 7,544
Dividends paid		3,336
Total assets at end of financial year		54,920
Number of ordinary shares issued		1,451 million
Share price at end of financial year		$42.19

Financial ratios

Earnings per share	$5.19	($7,544 million / 1,451 million)
Dividend per share	$2.30	($3,336 million / 1,451 million)
Gross return on sales	35.2%	($11,543 million / $32,804 million)
Gross return on assets	21.0%	($11,543 million / $54,920 million)
Share price to earnings	8.1	($42.19 / $5.19)
Yield	5.5%	($2.30 / $42.19)

Sources: AstraZeneca Annual Report 2009; www.astrazeneca.com; www.uk.finance.yahoo.com; www.lse.co.uk.

8.1 Why is it often better to use ratios rather than absolute measures of performance?

8.2 'Productivity gives an overall measure for the profit made per employee.' Is this true?

8.3 Is it possible for some measures of performance to rise while others fall?

8.4 Are profit-making companies the only ones concerned with their finances?

Break-even point

When an organisation sells a product – which might be either services or goods – it has to cover all its costs, including the fixed costs and overheads. Each unit sold makes a contribution to the fixed costs, so a key piece of information is the break-even point. This is the number of units that must be sold to cover all costs and start making a profit. You can calculate this using the following argument.

The revenue from a product is:

revenue = price charged per unit × number of units sold

The total production costs are a bit different because some vary with the number of units made while others are fixed. For instance, when a company makes a product in a rented factory, the cost of raw materials rises with the number of units made, but the rental charge is fixed regardless of production. You see the same effect with a car, where some costs are fixed (repayment of purchase loan, road tax, insurance etc.) and others vary with the distance travelled (petrol, oil, tyres, depreciation etc.). Then we have:

total cost = fixed cost + variable cost
            = fixed cost + (cost per unit × number of units made)

The break-even point is defined as the point where revenue covers the total cost, so that:

revenue = total cost

$$\frac{\text{price per}}{\text{unit}} \times \frac{\text{number of}}{\text{units sold}} = \text{fixed cost} + \frac{\text{cost per}}{\text{unit}} \times \frac{\text{number of}}{\text{units made}}$$

Both the revenue and total cost rise linearly with the number of units, and we can plot the relationship in Figure 8.1.

If we let P = price charged per unit, C = production cost per unit, F = fixed cost and N = number of units sold (assuming this is the same as the number of units made), the break-even point has:

$$PN = F + CN$$

Rearranging this gives:

$$N(P - C) = F$$

or:

$$\text{break-even point} = N = \frac{F}{P - C}$$

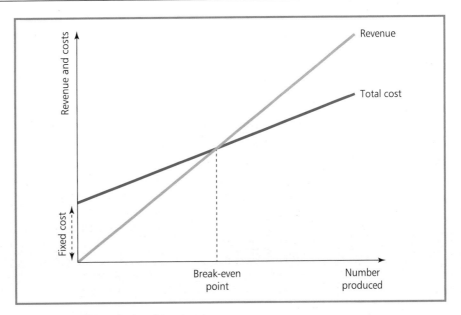

Figure 8.1 Defining the break-even point

Suppose a company spends £500,000 on research, development, equipment and other fixed costs before it starts making a new product. If each unit of the product costs £30 to make and sells for £50, the break-even point is:

$$N = F / (P - C)$$
$$= 500,000 / (50 - 30)$$
$$= 25,000 \text{ units}$$

Here, the company makes a profit only when it recovers the initial investment and, because each unit contributes £50 – £30 = £20 the company has to sell 25,000 units before this happens. If production is less than 25,000 units the revenue does not cover fixed costs and the company makes a loss; if production is more than 25,000 all costs are covered and the excess revenue gives a profit. We can calculate the profit and loss as follows.

- When the number of units sold is higher than the break-even point, revenue is greater than total cost and there is a profit (shown in Figure 8.2):

  $$\text{profit} = N(P - C) - F$$

- When the number of units sold equals the break-even point, revenue exactly equals total cost:

  $$N(P - C) = F$$

- When the number of units sold is less than the break-even point, total cost is higher than revenue and there is a loss:

  $$\text{loss} = F - N(P - C)$$

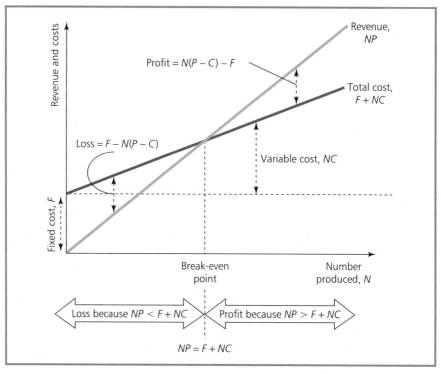

Figure 8.2 Profit and loss around the break-even point

WORKED EXAMPLE 8.2

A company sells 200 units of a product every week. The fixed costs for buildings, machines and employees are €12,000 a week, while raw material and other variable costs are €50 a unit.

(a) What is the profit if the selling price is €130 a unit?
(b) What is the profit if the selling price is €80 a unit?
(c) What is the profit if the selling price is fixed at €80 but sales rise to 450 units a week?

Solution

(a) We know that:

N = 200 units = number of units sold each week
F = €12,000 a week = fixed cost each week
C = €50 a unit = variable cost per unit

With a selling price, P, of €130 the break-even point is:

$$N = \frac{F}{P - C} = \frac{12,000}{130 - 50} = 150 \text{ units}$$

Actual sales are more than this, so the product makes a profit of:

$$\text{profit} = N(P - C) - F = 200 \times (130 - 50) - 12,000$$
$$= €4,000 \text{ a week}$$

(b) With a selling price, P, of €80 the break-even point is:

$$N = \frac{F}{P - C} = \frac{12,000}{80 - 50} = 400 \text{ units}$$

Actual sales are less than this, so the product makes a loss of:

$$\text{loss} = F - N(P - C) = 12,000 - 200 \times (80 - 50)$$
$$= €6,000 \text{ a week}$$

(c) With a selling price of €80 we know that the break-even point is 400 units. If sales increase to 450 units a week, the product makes a profit of:

$$\text{profit} = N(P - C) - F = 450 \times (80 - 50) - 12,000$$
$$= €1,500 \text{ a week}$$

The company can still make a profit with a lower selling price, provided that sales are high enough.

Apart from its basic purpose of analysing profitability, break-even analyses are useful in considering decisions about buying or leasing equipment, setting the capacity of new equipment, deciding whether to buy an item or make it within the company, comparing competitive tenders, funding new projects and so on. However, we should mention the most common difficulty of finding break-even points, which is assigning a reasonable proportion of overheads to the fixed cost of each product. This depends on the accounting conventions used – with the problem becoming worse when the product mix is continually changing, and a changing amount of overheads is assigned to each product. Then the costs of making a particular product can apparently change, even though there is no change in the product itself or the way it is made.

WORKED EXAMPLE 8.3

NorElec offers two prices to domestic consumers. The normal rate has a standing charge of £18.20 a quarter, and each unit of electricity used costs £0.142. A special economy rate has a standing charge of £22.70 a quarter, with each unit of electricity used during the day costing £0.162, but each unit used during the night costing only £0.082. What pattern of consumption makes it cheaper to use the economy rate?

Solution

If a customer uses an average of D units a quarter during the day and N units a quarter during the night, their costs are:

normal rate: $18.20 + 0.142 \times (D + N)$
economy rate: $22.70 + 0.162 \times D + 0.082 \times N$

It is cheaper to use the economy rate when:

$$22.7 + 0.162D + 0.082N < 18.2 + 0.142(D + N)$$

i.e.

$$4.5 < 0.06N - 0.02D$$

or

$$D < 3N - 225$$

When consumption during the day is less than three times consumption during the night minus 225 units, it is cheaper to use the economy rate – otherwise it is cheaper to use the standard rate (as shown in Figure 8.3).

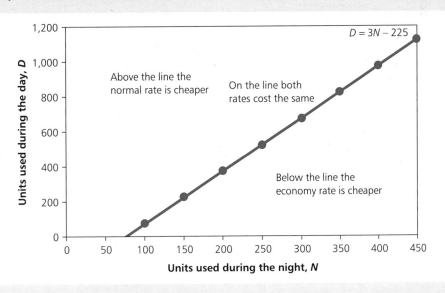

Figure 8.3 Identifying the cheapest options with NorElec

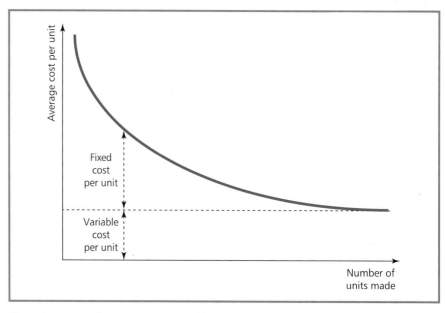

Figure 8.4 Decreasing average cost with increasing production

Economies of scale

Organisations often use very large facilities so that they can get economies of scale. This is the effect where the average cost per unit declines as the number of units produced increases. You can see one reason for this from the break-even analysis, where:

total cost = fixed cost + variable cost = $F + NC$

Dividing this total cost by the number of units made, N, gives the average cost per unit:

average cost per unit = $(F + NC) / N = F / N + C$

As N increases, the value of F / N decreases – meaning that the proportion of the fixed cost recovered by each unit falls, and the average cost per unit also falls (as shown in Figure 8.4).

WORKED EXAMPLE 8.4

Jane's Seafood Diner serves 200 meals a day at an average price of €20. The variable cost of each meal is €10, and the fixed costs of running the restaurant are €1,750 a day.

(a) What profit does the restaurant make?
(b) What is the average cost of a meal?
(c) By how much would the average cost of a meal fall if the number of meals served rose to 250 a day?

Solution

(a) The break-even point is:

$$N = F / (P - C) = 1,750 / (20 - 10)$$
$$= 175 \text{ meals}$$

Actual sales are above this, so there is a profit of:

$$\text{profit} = N(P - C) - F$$
$$= 200 \times (20 - 10) - 1,750$$
$$= €250 \text{ a day}$$

Worked example 8.4 continued

(b) The average cost of a meal is:

average cost = (fixed cost + variable cost) /
                    number of meals
             = (1,750 + 200 × 10) / 200
             = €18.75 a meal

(c) Serving 250 meals a day would give:

average cost = (1,750 + 250 × 10) / 250
             = €17 a meal

Spreading the fixed costs over more units is only one reason for economies of scale. The unit cost can also fall because operations become more efficient, people get more familiar with the work and take less time, problems are sorted out, disruptions are eliminated, planning becomes routine and so on. These effects seem to suggest that facilities should always be as big as possible. This is certainly the reason why mobile phone companies, banks and oil companies have become so big.

But there can also be diseconomies of scale. Here the benefits of larger operations are more than offset by the problems, which include more bureaucracy, difficulties of communication, more complex management hierarchies, increased costs of supervision and perceived reduction in importance of individuals. These effects usually lead to economies of scale up to an optimal size, and then diseconomies of scale, as shown in Figure 8.5.

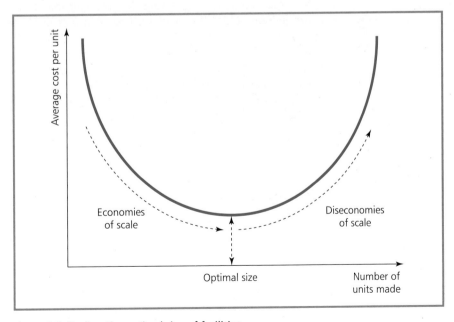

Figure 8.5 Finding the optimal size of facilities

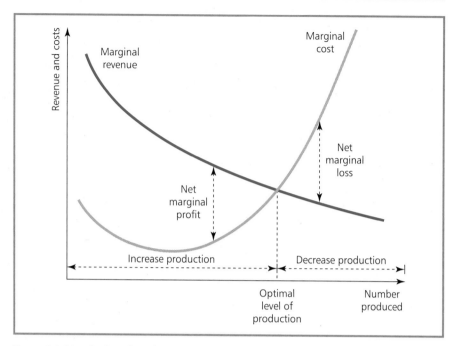

Figure 8.6 Marginal analysis finds the best level of production

Marginal values

The break-even model assumes that the variable cost is constant, regardless of the number of units made. But we have just said that larger operations can be more efficient – suggesting that the variable cost can fall with increasing production. This effect is described by a **marginal cost** – the cost of making one extra unit of a product. The marginal cost is generally high when small numbers are produced, but falls as production increases. But again there comes a point where diseconomies of scale come into play, making the marginal cost rise as shown in Figure 8.6.

We can also define a **marginal revenue**, which is the revenue generated by selling one extra unit of a product. The break-even analysis again assumes that customers pay a constant price, regardless of sales. But the price they are willing to pay often varies with production, and customers generally expect to pay less for mass-produced items. In other words, the marginal revenue falls with increasing production.

Now Figure 8.6 shows an important pattern. With low production levels, the marginal cost is less than the marginal revenue, so there is a net profit on every extra unit made. This encourages the company to increase production. As production increases, the marginal revenue declines, and after an initial fall the marginal cost begins to rise. So with high production levels the marginal cost is more than the marginal revenue, and there is a net loss on every extra unit made. This encourages the company to reduce production. The overall effect has organisations always moving towards the point where the marginal revenue exactly matches the marginal cost. This defines their optimal production level. Below this they are missing out on potential profits, and above it they are making unnecessary losses.

8.5   What does the variable cost vary with?

8.6   What exactly is the break-even point?

8.7   'Because of economies of scale, it is always better to have a single large office than a number of smaller ones.' Is this true?

8.8   What is the significance of marginal cost and revenue?

IDEAS IN PRACTICE   **Start-up business**

Many new businesses fail because the owners do not do enough financial analysis. A basic approach might start with the expected gross profit margin. Many industries work with standard figures for this – a supermarket might make 3%, a newsagent 15%, a carpet wholesaler 20% and a guesthouse 60%. The gross profit margin is defined as:

$$\frac{\text{gross profit}}{\text{margin}} = \frac{\text{selling price} - \text{direct costs per unit}}{\text{selling price}} \times 100$$

The gross profit margin has to cover overheads and other fixed costs, so if you divide the overheads by the gross profit margin, you find the sales value that the business has to achieve.

For example, if you are a retailer who buys an item for €16 and adds a mark-up of 150%, you sell the item for (16 × 2.5) = €40. Your gross profit margin is (40 − 16) / 40 = 0.6 or 60%. If your overheads are £34,000 a year, you divide this by 0.6 to get a required turnover of (34,000 / 0.6) = €56,667. If your forecast sales are less than this, you have to make some adjustments, either by reducing costs and overheads or increasing sales and prices.

Source: www.fastlinksolutions.co.uk

Value of money over time

If you want to buy a house, you can try saving enough money to pay cash – but this will take a very long time, and experience suggests that house prices rise a lot faster than savings. A better option is to save a deposit and then borrow the rest of the money as a mortgage, which you repay over a long period, typically around 25 years. If you add up all your repayments, they are much higher than the amount you originally borrowed, with the difference due to interest.

Interest

When someone borrows money, the amount they borrow is the principal. The borrower agrees both to repay the loan over some period and to pay an additional amount of interest. The interest is the lender's reward for lending money – and the borrower's penalty – and is usually quoted as a percentage of the principal, so you might pay interest of 7% a year.

Suppose you have some money to spare and put it into a bank account – effectively lending your money to the bank. If you leave £1,000 in an account offering interest of 8% a year, it earns $1,000 \times 8 / 100 = £80$ at the end of the year. If you take the interest earned out of the account, the initial deposit stays unchanged at £1,000. This is the principle of simple interest, which pays interest only on the initial deposit, and the amount of interest paid each year remains the same. If the original investment is A_0 and the interest rate is I, the amount of interest paid each year is $A_0 I / 100$. It is easier to do calculations with the interest rate described as a decimal fraction, i, rather than a percentage, I. Then $i = I / 100$, and an interest rate of 10% means that $i = 0.1$, an interest rate of 15% has $i = 0.15$, and so on. The amount of interest paid each year is $A_0 i$.

In practice, loans rarely use simple interest, and almost invariably offer compound interest. This pays interest both on the original investment and on interest earned previously and left in the account. If you put an amount of money A_0 into a bank account and leave it untouched for a year, earning interest at an annual rate i, at the end of the year you have an amount A_1, where:

$$A_1 = A_0 \times (1 + i)$$

So if you put €1,000 in a bank earning 5% a year at the end of the year you would get:

$$A_1 = A_0 \times (1 + i) = 1,000 \times (1 + 0.05) = 1,000 \times 1.05$$
$$= €1,050$$

If you leave the amount A_1 untouched for a second year, it will earn interest not only on the initial amount deposited, but also on the interest earned in the first year. Then, if A_2 is the amount in the account at the end of the second year:

$$A_2 = A_1 \times (1 + i)$$

But we can substitute the value for A_1 and find that:

$$A_2 = [A_0 \times (1 + i)] \times (1 + i)$$
$$= A_0 \times (1 + i)^2$$

If you leave the amount A_2 untouched for a third year, you have:

$$A_3 = A_2 \times (1 + i)$$

and substituting for A_2:

$$A_3 = A_0 \times (1 + i)^3$$

Your money increases in this compound way, and at the end of n years you have A_n, where:

for compound interest

$$A_n = A_0 \times (1 + i)^n$$

The longer you leave money in the account, the greater the annual interest it earns. Figure 8.7 shows this cumulative effect on the value of €1 invested over time with interest rates between 3% and 25%.

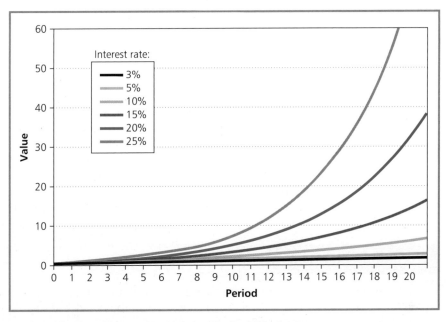

Figure 8.7 The increasing value of €1 invested at different interest rates

WORKED EXAMPLE 8.5

If you leave £1,000 in a bank account earning 5% compound interest a year, how much will be in your account at the end of 5 years? How much will there be at the end of 20 years?

Solution

We know that:

$A_0 = £1,000$

$i = 0.05$

With compound interest, the amount in the account is:

$A_n = A_0 \times (1 + i)^n$

At the end of 5 years you will have:

$A_5 = 1,000 \times (1 + 0.05)^5 = 1,000 \times 1.2763$
$\quad = £1,276$

At the end of 20 years you will have:

$A_{20} = 1,000 \times (1 + 0.05)^{20} = 1,000 \times 2.6533$
$\quad = £2,653$

Interest is often paid more regularly than each year, but you can use the same approach to the calculations. Leaving $100 in a bank for twelve months at 1% a month gives you $100 \times (1.01)^{12} = \$112.68$.

Suppose that you borrow £100 with interest of 2% payable at the end of each month. You might do a quick calculation and assume that this is equal to $2 \times 12 = 24\%$ a year – but this is not quite right, as you can see from this comparison:

■ borrowing £100 at 24% a year raises the debt to $100 \times (1 + 0.24) = £124$ at the end of the year

■ borrowing £100 at 2% a month, and using compound interest to calculate the debt at the end of 12 months, gives:

$$A_n = A_0 \times (1 + i)^n = 100 \times (1 + 0.02)^{12}$$
$$= £126.82$$

This effect might be confusing when banks typically quote annual interest rates, but actually calculate interest daily. To avoid this confusion, many countries have a legal requirement to quote an effective or real annual interest rate. This is commonly called an **annual percentage rate** (APR), which gives the true cost of borrowing (including any fees etc). When a lender offers an APR of 12%, by the end of the year interest payments will be exactly 12% of the principal.

WORKED EXAMPLE 8.6

If you invest €2,000 how much will you have after 3 years if the interest rate is 12% a year? How does this differ from rates of 3% a quarter, 1% a month, or (12 / 52 =) 0.23% a week?

Solution

■ With annual payments the interest rate, *i*, is 0.12 and after 3 years you have

$$2,000 \times (1 + 0.12)^3 = €2,809.86.$$

■ With quarterly payments the interest rate, *i*, is 0.03 and after 12 quarters you have

$$2,000 \times (1 + 0.03)^{12} = €2,851.52.$$

■ With monthly payments the interest rate, *i*, is 0.01 and after 36 months you have

$$2,000 \times (1 + 0.01)^{36} = €2,861.54.$$

■ With weekly payments the interest rate, *i*, is 0.12 / 52 = 0.0023 and after 156 weeks you have

$$2,000 \times (1 + 0.0023)^{156} = €2,862.04.$$

The differences may be small, but they do accumulate. You can also see that shorter times between interest payments give larger returns, because interest already earned is added more quickly to the principal, and starts earning its own interest sooner.

One problem with these interest calculations is that they can become rather messy. For instance, if you want to find the value of an initial investment of £10,000 earning nominal interest of 0.19% a week for ten years, you calculate:

$$A_{10} = A_0 \times (1 + i)^n = 10,000 \times (1 + 0.0019)^{10 \times 52}$$
$$= £26,833.41$$

If the interest is paid daily, *i* would be around 0.0019 / 7 = 0.0002714 and you would have to calculate $10,000 \times (1.0002714)^{365 \times 10} = £26,928$. It is easy to get errors in such calculations (or even to forget leap years).

Review questions

8.9 Would you rather have £1,000 now or in five years' time?

8.10 If you leave an amount of money in a bank account, why does its value not rise linearly?

8.11 Is an interest rate of 12% a year the same as 1% a month?

Discounting to present value

We know that an amount of money A_0 invested now will earn interest and have a value of $A_n = A_0 \times (1 + i)^n$ at a point n periods in the future. So £1,000 invested now at 8% a year will be worth £1,469 in 5 years' time. We can turn this the other way around and say that £1,469 in 5 years' time is worth £1,000 now. And in general an amount, A_n, n periods in the future has a present value of A_0, where:

$$A_0 = A_n / (1 + i)^n$$
$$= A_n \times (1 + i)^{-n}$$

Calculating the present value of an amount in the future is called discounting to present value. Then the value of i becomes a discount rate and $(1 + i)^{-n}$ is the discount factor. The benefit of present values is that they allow you to compare amounts of money that become available at different points in the future.

WORKED EXAMPLE 8.7

Rockwall Trust is thinking of investing in a new technology company. There are two possible investments, whose profits can be summarised as follows:

- Option 1 gives a profit of €300,000 in 5 years' time.
- Option 2 gives a profit of €500,000 in 10 years' time.

Which option should the company choose if it uses a discount rate of 20% a year for future profits?

Solution

Rockwall has to compare amounts of money generated at different times, and can do this by comparing the present value of each.

- Option 1 has $i = 0.2$, $n = 5$ and $A_5 = 300,000$.

$$A_0 = A_n \times (1 + i)^{-n} = A_5 \times (1 + i)^{-5}$$
$$= 300,000 \times (1 + 0.2)^{-5}$$
$$= €120,563$$

- Option 2 has $i = 0.2$, $n = 10$ and $A_{10} = 500,000$.

$$A_0 = A_n \times (1 + i)^{-n} = A_{10} \times (1 + i)^{-10}$$
$$= 500,000 \times (1 + 0.2)^{-10}$$
$$= €80,753$$

Option 1 has the higher present value and on this evidence is the better alternative.

Discounting to present value is particularly useful with large projects that have payments and incomes spread over varying periods. Then you can compare all the costs and incomes by discounting them to their present value – and subtracting the present value of all costs from the present value of all revenues gives a net present value.

net present value = sum of discounted revenues – sum of discounted costs

If the net present value (NPV) is negative, a project will make a loss and should not be started; if alternative projects all have positive net present values, the best is the highest.

WORKED EXAMPLE 8.8

FHP Construction is considering three alternative projects with initial costs and projected revenues (each in thousands of dollars) over the next 5 years as shown in the following table. If the company has enough resources to start only one project, use a discount rate of 10% to suggest the best.

		Initial cost	Net revenue generated in each year				
			1	2	3	4	5
Project	A	1,000	500	400	300	200	100
	B	1,000	200	200	300	400	400
	C	500	50	200	200	100	50

Solution

The revenues for each project vary over time, with A offering more in the early years and B offering more later on. To get a valid comparison we can transform all amounts to present values and compare the NPV of each project. So for project A:

- 500 in year 1 has a present value of 500 / 1.1 = 454.545
- 400 in year 2 has a present value of 400 / 1.1^2 = 330.579
- 300 in year 3 has a present value of 300 / 1.1^3 = 225.394 and so on.

Figure 8.8 shows the details of these calculations. Adding the present values of revenues and then subtracting the costs (in this case the single initial project cost) gives the net present values.

Project A has the highest NPV and is the one that FHP should choose (all things being equal). Project C has a negative NPV showing a loss, so the company should clearly avoid this one. Another consideration is that the revenues from A are declining, suggesting that the project has a limited life span of around 5 years; revenues from project B are rising, implying a longer potential life.

	A	B	C	D	E	F	G	H
1	Net present value							
2								
3	Discount rate	0.1						
4								
5	Year	Discount factor		Project A		Project B		Project C
6			Revenue	Present value	Revenue	Present value	Revenue	Present value
7	1	1.1	$500.00	$454.55	$200.00	$181.82	$50.00	$45.45
8	2	1.21	$400.00	$330.58	$200.00	$165.29	$200.00	$165.29
9	3	1.331	$300.00	$225.39	$300.00	$225.39	$200.00	$150.26
10	4	1.4641	$200.00	$136.60	$400.00	$273.21	$100.00	$68.30
11	5	1.61051	$100.00	$62.09	$400.00	$248.37	$50.00	$31.05
12	Totals		$1,500.00	$1,209.21	$1,500.00	$1,094.08	$600.00	$460.35
13								
14	Present values							
15		Revenues		$1,209.21		$1,094.08		$460.35
16		Costs		$1,000.00		$1,000.00		$500.00
17								
18	Net present value			$209.21		$94.08		−$39.65

Figure 8.8 Calculation of net present values for the three projects in Worked example 8.8

WORKED EXAMPLE 8.9

Use an annual discount rate of 15% to find the NPV of a project with the following returns (in thousands of euros) at the end of each year:

Year	1	2	3	4	5	6	7	8	9	10	11
Revenue	−70	−30	5	15	25	40	60	50	40	30	10

Solution

Spreadsheets have standard functions to calculate net present values – such as Excel's NPV or XNPV. These functions use slightly different assumptions about the time of payments, so you have to be a bit careful. Figure 8.9 shows two ways of doing the calculations. The first uses the standard NPV function to find the net present value of €17,870. The second does the full calculations to check this value.

	A	B	C	D	E	F	G	H	I	J	K	L
1	Net present value											
2												
3	Discount rate		0.15									
4												
5	Year	1	2	3	4	5	6	7	8	9	10	11
6	Revenue	−70	−30	5	15	25	40	60	50	40	30	10
7												
8	Function, NPV											
9	Net present value	€17.87										
10												
11	Calculation to check											
12	Discount factor	1.15	1.32	1.52	1.75	2.01	2.31	2.66	3.06	3.52	4.05	4.65
13	Discounted revenue	−60.87	−22.68	−3.29	8.58	12.43	17.29	22.56	16.35	11.37	7.42	2.15
14	Net present value	€17.87										

Figure 8.9 Using the function NPV to calculate net present value in Worked example 8.9

Traditional accounting uses two other measures to evaluate projects. The first is an average rate of return, which is the average annual revenue as a percentage of the initial investment. In Worked example 8.9 there was an initial investment of €100,000 in the first 2 years, followed by average revenues in the next 9 years of €30,556, so the average rate of return is 30,566 / 100,000 = 0.31 or 31%. This makes the project seem more attractive than the net present value because it does not discount future values. To get a more accurate value we would have to find the average discounted rate of return.

The second measure is the payback period, which shows the time before the project will make a net profit. Here the initial investment of €100,000 is repaid sometime in year 7 – but a more accurate figure would again have to include discounting to reduce the value of future income.

Internal rate of return

An obvious problem with the net present value is setting a realistic discount rate. This has to consider interest payable and any other factors that will affect future values, such as inflation, taxes, opportunity costs, target returns, exchange rates, risk, competition and so on. If the rate is set too high, good long-term projects have future incomes heavily discounted and become less attractive; if the rate is set too low, risky projects with speculative benefits far into the future seem unrealistically attractive.

However, there is an alternative to setting a discount rate. Rather than choosing a discount rate and using this to calculate the net present value, we can set a target present value and calculate the discount rate that gives this. Then to compare projects, rather than using the same discount rate to get different present values, we find the discount rate for each project that leads to a specified net present value. In practice, the target net present value is invariably set to zero, and the discount rate that achieves this is the internal rate of return.

> The **internal rate of return** (IRR) is the discount rate that gives a net present value of zero.

Projects with better financial performance have higher internal rates of return – so to compare projects we find the internal rate of return for each, and choose the one with the highest IRR. Unfortunately, there is no straightforward equation for calculating the IRR, but you can easily use standard spreadsheet function like Excel's IRR, MIRR or XIRR.

WORKED EXAMPLE 8.10

What is the internal rate of return of a project with these cash flows?

Year	1	2	3	4	5	6	7	8	9
Net cash flow (£)	−1,800	−500	−200	800	1,800	1,600	1,500	200	100

Solution

Figure 8.10 shows the net present values for a range of discount rates. In particular, a rate of 20% gives an NPV of £167, while a rate of 25% gives an NPV of −£164. In other words, a discount rate of 20% gives a positive NPV, and a discount rate of 25% gives a negative NPV. We want the discount rate that gives an NPV of zero, so it must be somewhere between these two, in the range 20–25%. If we try 22% the NPV is £21 and we are getting closer. Continuing in this haphazard way, we guess a value around 22.3%.

Of course, you do not really have to do this repetitive calculation, and cell D10 uses the standard function IRR to give the actual internal rate of return as just over 22.32%.

	A	B	C	D	E	F	G	H	I	J	K
1	Internal rate of return										
2											
3	Year		1	2	3	4	5	6	7	8	9
4	Net revenue		−£1,800	−£500	−£200	£800	£1,800	£1,600	£1,500	£200	£100
5											
6	Iterative calculation										
7	Discount rate		0.15	0.2	0.25	0.22	0.225	0.223			
8	NPV		£626.96	£166.57	−£163.93	£21.22	−£12.22	£1.02			
9											
10	Standard function IRR =			22.32%							

Figure 8.10 Iterative calculation of IRR, and standard function, in Worked example 8.10

IDEAS IN PRACTICE Melchior Trust 'E'

Melchior Trust 'E' is based in New York and funds new companies in the Balkan countries with the aim of helping them to expand and contribute to their national economies. Part of its 2009 round of investment decisions considered five alternative companies in Croatia. Figure 8.11 shows the esti- mated returns from each company, in thousands of dollars a year. The internal rates of return are between –2% and 14%, with the highest value from company 3. Melchior considered this – along with a lot of other information – before coming to their final decision.

	A	B	C	D	E	F
1	Melchior Trust 'E'					
2						
3	Year	Company 1	Company 2	Company 3	Company 4	Company 5
4	1	−80	−100	−50	−35	0
5	2	−30	−50	−40	−15	−10
6	3	−15	−20	−10	−5	−15
7	4	0	−10	0	15	10
8	5	10	0	20	15	10
9	6	25	10	40	−5	10
10	7	50	50	40	−15	−15
11	8	55	70	40	10	−15
12	9	60	90	40	20	10
13	10	60	100	40	10	20
14	IRR	12%	9%	14%	−2%	4%

Figure 8.11 IRRs of five projects considered by Melchior Trust 'E'

Depreciation

When people buy a car, they expect to drive it for a few years and then replace it. This is because maintenance and repair costs rise, the car breaks down more often, new cars are more efficient, they are more comfortable and so on. Not surprisingly, the value of a car declines as it gets older. In the same way, a company buys a piece of equipment, uses it for some time and then replaces it – and the value of equipment declines over time. But equip- ment forms part of a company's assets and the balance sheet must always show a reasonable valuation. So organisations write-down the value of their assets each year – meaning that they reduce the book value by an amount of depreciation.

There are two widely used ways of calculating depreciation – straight-line and reducing-balance methods.

Straight-line depreciation

This reduces the value of equipment by a fixed amount each year. If we assume that equipment is bought, works for its expected life and is then sold for scrap:

$$\text{annual depreciation} = \frac{\text{cost of equipment} - \text{scrap value}}{\text{life of equipment}}$$

Here the scrap value is normally the resale value and does not imply that the equipment is actually scrapped – better terms are perhaps residual or resale value. A machine costing £20,000 with an estimated resale value of £5,000 after a useful life of 5 years has an annual depreciation of:

$$\text{annual depreciation} = \frac{20{,}000 - 5{,}000}{5}$$

$$= £3{,}000$$

Straight-line depreciation is easy to calculate, but it does not reflect actual values. Most equipment loses a lot of value in the first years of operation, and it is actually worth less than its depreciated value.

Reducing-balance depreciation

This reduces the value of equipment by a fixed percentage of its residual value each year – so an organisation might write-off 20% of book value each year. Then if a machine has a residual value of £2,000 at the end of a year, 20% of this is written-off for the next year to give a new residual value of $2{,}000 \times 0.8 = £1{,}600$. This has the benefit of giving more depreciation in the first few years, and a more accurate view of equipment's value.

Calculations for the reducing-balance method are a simple extension of compound interest. With interest we know that an amount A_0 increases at a fixed rate, i, each period and after n periods has a value of:

$$A_n = A_0 \times (1 + i)^n$$

With depreciation the amount is decreasing at a fixed rate, so we simply subtract the rate i instead of adding it. Then for a depreciation rate of i, equipment whose initial cost is A_0 has a depreciated value after n periods of:

$$A_n = A_0 \times (1 - i)^n$$

WORKED EXAMPLE 8.11

David Krishnan bought a machine for €10,000 and now has to consider its depreciation.

(a) If the machine has an expected life of 5 years and a scrap value of €1,000, what is the annual rate of straight-line depreciation?

(b) What is the value of the machine after 5 years with the reducing-balance method and a depreciation rate of 30%?

(c) What depreciation rate would reduce the machine's value to €2,000 after 3 years?

Solution

(a) For straight-line depreciation:

annual depreciation

$$= \frac{\text{cost of equipment} - \text{scrap value}}{\text{life of equipment}}$$

$$= \frac{10{,}000 - 1{,}000}{5}$$

$$= €1{,}800$$

Worked example 8.11 continued

(b) For reducing-balance depreciation:

$$A_n = A_0 \times (1 - i)^n$$

Then after 5 years:

$$A_5 = 10,000 \times (1 - 0.3)^5$$
$$= €1,681$$

(c) With straight-line depreciation and a final value of €2,000 after 3 years, the annual depreciation is:

$$\text{annual depreciation} = \frac{10,000 - 2,000}{3}$$
$$= €2,667$$

With reducing-balance we want A_3 to be €2,000, so:

$$A_3 = A_0 \times (1 - i)^3$$

or

$$2,000 = 10,000 \times (1 - i)^3$$

Then:

$$0.2 = (1 - i)^3$$
$$1 - i = 0.585$$
$$i = 0.415$$

giving a depreciation rate of 41.5%.

WORKED EXAMPLE 8.12

Hamil Leasing buys vans for €50,000 and expects to use them for 5 years. Then the suppliers buy them back for €10,000 and offer a replacement. If Hamil uses straight-line depreciation, what is the book value of a van each year? What depreciation rate should the company use with the reducing-balance method, and what is a van's book value each year? If Hamil discounts future amounts by 10% a year, what are the current values of all these amounts?

Solution

Figure 8.12 shows a spreadsheet of these calculations. Straight-line depreciation reduces the book value of the machine by $(50,000 - 10,000) / 5 = €8,000$ a year (shown in cell D4), with depreciated values shown in column D. For the reducing balance method, $50,000 \times (1 - i)^5 = 10,000$, so $i = 0.2752203$ (calculated in cell F4), with depreciated values shown in column F. Discounting book values to present values in the usual way gives the results in columns E and G.

	A	B	C	D	E	F	G
1	**Depreciation**						
2							
3				**Straight line**		**Reducing balance**	
4	**Rate**	10%		€8,000.00		0.2752203	
5	**Year**	**Discount factor**		**Book value**	**Present value**	**Book value**	**Present value**
6	0	1		€50,000.00	€50,000.00	€50,000.00	€50,000.00
7	1	1.1		€42,000.00	€38,181.82	€36,238.99	€32,944.53
8	2	1.21		€34,000.00	€28,099.17	€26,265.28	€21,706.84
9	3	1.331		€26,000.00	€19,534.18	€19,036.54	€14,302.44
10	4	1.4641		€18,000.00	€12,294.24	€13,797.30	€9,423.74
11	5	1.61051		€10,000.00	€6,209.21	€10,000.00	€6,209.21

Figure 8.12 Depreciated value of vans at Hamil Leasing in Worked example 8.12

8.12 How could you compare the net benefits of two projects, one of which lasts for 5 years and the other for 7 years?

8.13 What is a discount rate?

8.14 What is the difference between NPV and IRR?

8.15 What is the difference between the straight-line and reducing-balance methods of depreciation?

Mortgages, annuities and sinking funds

If you invest an initial amount A_0, at the end of n periods you have $A_0 \times (1 + i)^n$. But suppose that you add regular savings, paying in an extra amount F at the end of each period. A standard result then gives the amount invested after n periods as:

$$A_n = A_0 \times (1 + i)^n + \frac{F \times (1 + i)^n - F}{i}$$

The first part of this equation shows the income from the original investment, and the second part shows the amount accumulated by regular payments (you can find the derivation of this on the companion website **www.pearsoned.co.uk/waters**).

WORKED EXAMPLE 8.13

Gaynor Johnson puts £1,000 into a building society account that earns 10% interest a year.

(a) How much will be in her account at the end of 5 years?
(b) How much will there be if she adds an extra £500 at the end of each year?

Solution

(a) Without additional payments the standard result is:

$$A_n = A_0 \times (1 + i)^n$$

Substituting $A_0 = £1,000$, $i = 0.1$ and $n = 5$ gives:

$$\begin{aligned} A_5 &= 1{,}000 \times (1 + 0.1)^5 \\ &= £1{,}611 \end{aligned}$$

(b) With additional payments the revised equation gives:

$$A_n = A_0 \times (1 + i)^n + \frac{F \times (1 + i)^n - F}{i}$$

Then with $F = £500$:

$$\begin{aligned} A_5 &= 1{,}000 \times (1 + 0.1)^5 + \frac{500 \times (1 + 0.1)^5 - 500}{0.1} \\ &= £4{,}663 \end{aligned}$$

The rather unpleasant equation for finding the value of an investment has five variables: i, n, A_0, A_n and F. The Worked example 8.13 showed how to find the unknown value A_n by substituting known values for the other four – but if you know any four values, you can find a value for the fifth. For example, you may want to do the calculations the other way around and see how much you have to set aside in regular payments to accumulate a certain amount at the end of some period. Then i, n, A_0 and A_n are fixed and you want to find the value of F. Managers often meet this calculation with sinking funds which are typically set up to replace equipment at the end of its life. If you want to replace your computer every 3 years, you might put regular payments into a sinking fund to accumulate enough for its replacement.

WORKED EXAMPLE 8.14

How much should you invest each year to get £40,000 in a sinking fund at the end of 10 years when expected interest rates are 12%? How would the payments differ if you could put an initial £5,000 into the fund?

Solution

The variables are:

- final value, $A_n = £40,000$
- no initial payment, so $A_0 = £0$
- interest rate, $i = 0.12$
- number of years, $n = 10$.

Substituting these values into the equation

$$A_n = A_0 \times (1 + i)^n + \frac{F \times (1 + i)^n - F}{i}$$

gives:

$$40,000 = 0 + \frac{F \times (1 + 0.12)^{10} - F}{0.12}$$

$$4,800 = F \times 3.106 - F$$

$$F = £2,280$$

If you invest £2,280 each year you actually pay £22,800 and this earns interest of £17,200 to give the total of £40,000 needed.

With an initial investment of $A_0 = £5,000$ the calculation becomes:

$$40,000 = 5,000 \times (1 + 0.12)^{10} + \frac{F \times (1 + 0.12)^{10} - F}{0.12}$$

or

$$4,800 = 1,863.51 + F \times (3.106 - 1)$$

$$F = £1,394$$

The initial payment of £5,000 reduces the annual payments by $(2,280 - 1,394) = £886$, saving £8,860 over the 10 years.

Spreadsheets have standard functions for these calculations, and Excel includes FV to find the future value of an investment, PV to find the present value of an investment, PMT to find the regular payments needed to accumulate an amount, and NPER to show how many periods it will take to accumulate a certain amount.

Repaying loans

Another variation of this calculation concerns loans instead of investments. The only difference is that you have to be careful with the positive and negative signs. We have assumed that all payments are positive, showing the benefits of investing, but if payments are negative they become loans rather than investments. $A_0 = £10$ shows that you invest some money; $A_0 = -£10$ shows that you borrow it.

For most people, their biggest debt comes from buying a house. These purchases are financed by a mortgage, which is repaid by regular payments over some extended period. The initial payment A_0 is negative, showing that you borrow money, and the value after n periods must be zero, showing that you have repaid it.

WORKED EXAMPLE 8.15

Hans Larsson borrowed £120,000 over 25 years at 8% annual interest to set up his own business. He repays this by regular instalments at the end of every year. How much is each instalment?

Solution
We know that:

$A_0 = -£120,000$
$A_{25} = £0$
$i = 0.08$
$n = 25$

and want to find F from the equation:

$$A_n = A_0 \times (1 + i)^n + \frac{F \times (1 + i)^n - F}{i}$$

Substituting the values we know:

$$0 = -120,000 \times (1 + 0.08)^{25} + \frac{F \times (1 + 0.08)^{25} - F}{0.08}$$

Then:

$$120,000 \times 6.848 = \frac{5.848 \times F}{0.08}$$

$$F = £11,241 \text{ per year}$$

After 25 annual payments of £11,241 the original debt is repaid. Notice that Hans has to pay a total of $25 \times 11,241 = £281,025$, which is 2.34 times the original loan.

An **annuity** is the reverse of a mortgage, and allows someone with a lump sum to invest it and receive regular income over some period in the future. This kind of arrangement is popular with retired people who convert their savings into a regular income.

WORKED EXAMPLE 8.16

Rohan Kalaran wants an annuity that will pay £10,000 a year for the next 10 years. If the prevailing interest rate is 12%, how much will this cost?

Solution
Rohan wants to find the initial payment, A_0, that gives $F = -£10,000$ (the negative sign showing a receipt rather than a payment) with $i = 0.12$. The arrangement lasts for 10 years, so $n = 10$, and after this the annuity has no value, so $A_{10} = 0$. Substituting into the standard equation:

$$A_n = A_0 \times (1 + i)^n + \frac{F \times (1 + i)^n - F}{i}$$

gives:

$$A_{10} = 0$$

$$= A_0 \times (1 + 0.12)^{10} - \frac{10,000 \times (1 + 0.12)^{10} - 10,000}{0.12}$$

$$= A_0 \times 3.1059 - 175,487.35$$

or

$$A_0 = £56,502$$

Review questions

8.16 What is a sinking fund?

8.17 How would you calculate the payment worth making for an annuity?

8.18 The best value of i is the current interest rate. Do you think this is true?

Retirement annuity

In 1990 Heather Blackburn started paying £150 a month into a free-standing pension scheme run by a life insurance company. This was a significant part of her take-home pay, but she felt that it would allow her to retire on her sixtieth birthday in 2010. It was an efficient investment because the government gave tax relief on the contributions, and her investment was linked to stock market prices that had shown continuous long-term growth.

When Heather started her pension scheme, the insurance company quoted illustrations of what returns she might expect when she retired – but these were not guarantees. One illustration said that with certain assumptions Heather might accumulate a fund of £94,400 and she could use this to buy an annuity earning £80 per thousand, giving a pension of £7,552 a year.

The insurance company provided regular performance reviews, but Heather was usually disappointed. The stock market did not give consistently high returns, exemplified by the economic recession in 2008. And the fund in which she invested had below average returns. When she bought an annuity in 2010, her retirement fund stood at £44,176 (£36,000 from her contributions and £8,176 from interest). She could take 25% of this as a tax-free lump sum, leaving £33,132 for which the insurance company offered a pension of £1,741 a year.

Since Heather started her calculations, the government has begun raising the age for women to receive a state retirement pension from 60 to 65 (the same age as men) and this will slowly rise to 68. Heather is now hoping that she can retire at 65.

CHAPTER REVIEW

This chapter described a range of common performance measures and financial calculations.

- Managers have to measure performance to see how well their organisation is functioning, whether it is reaching targets, the rate of improvement and so on.
- There is a huge number of measures for different aspects of performance. Common measures directly monitor operations (such as capacity and output) while others are related to finance (such as profit and share price).
- Absolute measures are the most straightforward, but they give a limited view. More useful figures add some context, usually by calculating a performance ratio, such as sales per employee. There are many standard performance ratios, again notably relating to operations (such as productivity and utilisation) and finance (such as profit margins and return on assets).
- The break-even point is the production quantity at which revenue covers all the costs of production and the organisation begins to make a profit. Extensions of this analysis consider economies of scale, average and marginal costs.
- People can invest (or borrow) money to earn (or pay) interest. An amount available now can earn interest and grow over time, usually by compound interest. This suggests that the value of money changes over time.
- You can compare amounts of money available at different times by discounting to their present values. Subtracting the present value of all costs from the present value of all revenues gives a net present value.

- It is difficult to set a reliable discount rate, so an alternative calculates an internal rate of return.
- Using similar reasoning you can depreciate the value of assets to give a reducing value over time. Other extensions consider sinking funds, annuities and mortgages.

CASE STUDY OnlineInkCartridges.com

Janet Simmons used to work from home and did a lot of printing from her computer. Over the years, the price of high-quality printers fell, but the replacement ink cartridges always seemed expensive. Ten years ago she formed OnlineInkCartridges.com to buy low-cost generic cartridges from China and sell them through the company website. Seven years ago, she added a recycling unit to refill customers' old cartridges.

At first the business made a steady loss, but now sales are climbing steadily by around 10% a year. The last financial year showed a gross profit of €80,000, giving a margin of 7% and a return on investment of almost 5%.

The long-term prospects for the company seem good, and Janet has to make some major decisions. Firstly, she can stay with the company and take it through a period of continuing growth. Her financial backers already own 35% of the shares, and her second option is to sell the rest of the company to them and either invest the money or start up another business. Her skills undoubtedly form part of the company's assets, and if she leaves then the remaining shareholders are likely to discount the company's value by about 50%. Her third option is a compromise in which she will sell some of the shares – perhaps 15–20%. This will have less effect on the share value, and still give her a lump sum to pay off her debts and invest for the future.

Janet's aim is to maximise the value of her assets over the next 10 or 15 years, by which time she will be ready to take early retirement. Her accountant is adamant that her best future lies in running the company. This has the disadvantages, though, of putting all her assets in one place. Her bank's business advisor recommended the middle option of selling some shares to release money for other opportunities. She could add another €5,000 a year from her salary and build up a reasonable amount, perhaps using:

- a savings account which gives a return of 4.5% a year
- a gold account for the fixed sum, which gives a return of 6.5% but leaves the money tied up for at least a year; the additional savings could go into a savings account
- a personal accumulator which gives 5% interest on a minimum of €50,000, but 10% on any additional savings.

Janet also visited a building society manager who gave similar advice, but offered two other options. She could put the money into an 'inflation fighter' account, which links the interest rate to the Retail Price Index and guarantees a return of 1% above inflation. Alternatively she could buy another house as an investment. The manager explained that the rent-to-own market has been very unsettled lately. But taking a long-term view, house prices have risen by 10% to 15% a year for the past 20 years, while inflation has become progressively lower. Janet could also generate income from rent – usually about 0.5% of the value of the house per month, a quarter of which is needed for repairs and maintenance.

Janet thought about these alternatives, but found them all a bit boring. Perhaps she should go for the excitement of starting a new business and seeing it grow over time.

Questions

- If Janet asks for your advice, how would you summarise her main options? What analyses would help her?

- Based on the information available, what recommendations would you make?

- What other information would you need to make a reasoned decision?

PROBLEMS

8.1 A family doctor sees patients for an average of 10 minutes each. There is an additional 5 minutes of paperwork for each visit, so she makes appointments at 15-minute intervals for 5 hours a day. During one surgery the doctor was called away for an emergency that lasted an hour and patients who had appointments during this time were told to come back later. How can you measure the doctor's performance in the surgery?

8.2 ABC Taxis has an average fixed cost of £9,000 a year for each car. Each kilometre driven has variable costs of 40 pence and collects fares of 60 pence. How many kilometres a year does each car have to travel before making a profit? Last year each car drove 160,000 kilometres. What does this tell you? How would the distance travelled have to change to reduce the average cost per kilometre by 5%?

8.3 Air Atlantic is considering a new service between Paris and Calgary. It can use existing aeroplanes, each of which has a capacity of 240 passengers, for one flight a week with fixed costs of $90,000 and variable costs amounting to 50% of ticket price. If the airline plans to sell tickets at $600 each, what can you say about their proposed service?

8.4 A company can introduce only one new product from three available. If it estimates the following data, which product would you recommend?

	Product A	Product B	Product C
Annual sales	600	900	1,200
Unit cost	680	900	1,200
Fixed cost	200,000	350,000	500,000
Product life	3 years	5 years	8 years
Selling price	760	1,000	1,290

8.5 How much will an initial investment of $1,000 earning interest of 8% a year be worth at the end of 20 years? How does this change if the interest is paid more frequently?

8.6 Several years ago John McGregor bought an endowment insurance policy that is about to mature. He has the option of receiving £20,000 now or £40,000 in 10 years' time. Because he has retired and pays no income tax, he could invest the money with a real interest rate expected to remain at 10% a year for the foreseeable future. Which option should he take?

8.7 Mitsushama Systems buys new development machines for ¥150,000 each, and these are used within the company for 6 years. If they have a resale value of ¥40,000, what is their value at the end of each year with straight-line depreciation? How does this compare with the values from reducing-balance depreciation at a rate of 25%? What depreciation rate would reduce the machine's value to ¥10,000 after 4 years?

8.8 A company makes fixed annual payments to a sinking fund to replace equipment in 5 years' time. The equipment is valued at £100,000 and interest rates are 12%. How much should each payment be? How would these payments change if the company could put an initial £10,000 into the fund?

8.9 How much would the monthly repayments be on a mortgage of €100,000 taken out for 25 years at an interest rate of 12% a year?

8.10 Suppose that you are about to buy a new car. You have decided on the model, which costs £12,000. The supplier gives you an option of either a 5-year car loan at a reduced APR of 7%, or £1,250 in cash and a 5-year car loan with an APR of 10%. Which choice is the better? If you depreciate the car at 20% a year, what is its value in 10 years' time?

8.11 Given the following cash flows for four projects, calculate the net present value using a discount rate of 12% a year. What are the internal rates of return for the projects?

Year	Project A Income	Project A Expenditure	Project B Income	Project B Expenditure	Project C Income	Project C Expenditure	Project D Income	Project D Expenditure
0	0	18,000	0	5,000	0	24,000	0	21,000
1	2,500	0	0	10,000	2,000	10,000	0	12,000
2	13,500	6,000	0	20,000	10,000	6,000	20,000	5,000
3	18,000	0	10,000	20,000	20,000	2,000	20,000	1,000
4	9,000	2,000	30,000	10,000	30,000	2,000	30,000	0
5	5,000	0	50,000	5,000	25,000	2,000	25,000	0
6	3,000	0	60,000	5,000	15,000	2,000	20,000	5,000
7	1,000	0	60,000	5,000	10,000	1,000	20,000	1,000

8.12 How does the net present value of the following net cash flows change with discount rate? What is the internal rate of return?

Year	1	2	3	4	5	6	7	8	9	10	11	12
Net cash flow	−6,000	−1,500	−500	600	1,800	2,000	1,800	1,300	900	500	300	100

RESEARCH PROJECTS

8.1 Spreadsheets have a range of standard functions and procedures for financial calculations. We have already mentioned some of these, including Excel's NPV, IRR, FV, PV, PMT and NPER. Explore the financial functions that are available in a spreadsheet. Check the calculations in this chapter and describe the effects of changing parameter values. What assumptions do the functions make? What improvements would you like?

8.2 The following table shows the net cash flows for six projects over the next 15 years. How would you compare these projects?

Year	Project A	Project B	Project C	Project D	Project E	Project F
1	−140	−200	−80	0	−500	−50
2	−80	0	30	10	−200	50
3	−15	100	30	20	−100	100
4	15	80	30	30	50	50
5	35	60	30	20	100	−50
6	55	50	−40	15	150	60
7	65	40	30	−100	200	100
8	65	35	30	50	250	70
9	60	30	30	40	300	−50
10	50	30	30	30	300	70
11	40	25	−40	20	300	110
12	30	20	30	10	250	70
13	10	20	30	−100	150	−50
14	0	15	30	50	100	80
15	0	10	30	40	100	120

8.3 Imagine that you want a mortgage to buy a house. Many finance companies can lend you the money, but they quote widely differing terms and conditions. Collect information about offers currently advertised. How can you compare these? Which seems to be the best?

Sources of information

References

1 Tran M., Enron chief 'ignored financial irregularities', *Guardian*, 26th February 2002.

2 Gordon M., WorldCom unveils new irregularities, *The Standard Times*, 2nd July 2002.

3 Dunne H., SFO probes 'irregularities at city firm', *The Daily Telegraph*, 23rd January 1999.

Further reading

Financial models are described in many accounting and economics books; performance measures are described in operations management books. Some more specific sources are:

Bhattacharya H., *Total Management by Ratios* (2nd edition), Sage Publications, New Delhi, 2007.

Harvard Business School, *Measuring Performance*, HBS Press, Cambridge, MA, 2009.

Klammer T.P., *Capacity Measurement and Improvement*, Mount Valley Publishers, Martinsville, NJ, 2010.

Moore J.H. and Weatherford L.R., *Decision Modelling with Microsoft Excel* (6th edition), Prentice Hall, Upper Saddle River, NJ, 2001.

Neely A., *Measuring Business Performance* (2nd edition), Economist Books, London, 2005.

Phelps B., *Smart Business Metrics*, FT-Prentice Hall, Harlow, 2003.

Ragsdale C., *Spreadsheet Modelling and Decision Analysis* (5th edition), South-Western College Publishing, Cincinnati, OH, 2008.

Reid W. and Middleton D.R., *The Meaning of Company Accounts*, Gower, London, 2005.

Spitzer D., *Transforming Performance Measurement*, Amacom Books, New York, 2007.

Walsh C., *Key Management Ratios* (5th edition), FT-Prentice Hall, Harlow, 2008.

Waters D., *Operations Management*, FT-Prentice Hall, Harlow, 2002.

Winston W.L. and Albright S., *Spreadsheet Modelling and Applications*, Brooks Cole, Florence, KY, 2004.

Wood F. and Sangster A., *Business Accounting* (10th edition), Pitman, London, 2005.

CHAPTER 9

Regression and curve fitting

Chapter outline

This chapter considers relationships between variables. Often there is not an exact relationship – but there is an underlying pattern to observations with superimposed variations. These variations can make it difficult to identify the underlying patterns, but with pairs of observations we can do this using regression. In particular, linear regression draws a line of best fit through a set of data, and the amount of variation around this line shows how good the fit is.

After finishing this chapter you should be able to:

- understand the purpose of regression
- see how the strength of a relationship is related to the amount of noise
- measure the errors introduced by noise
- use linear regression to find the line of best fit through a set of data
- use this line of best fit for causal forecasting
- calculate and interpret coefficients of determination and correlation
- use Spearman's coefficient of rank correlation
- understand the results of multiple regression
- use curve fitting for more complex functions.

Measuring relationships

Chapter 3 showed how to draw a relationship between two variables as a graph. Here we look at this idea again, but now consider relationships that are not perfect. In other words, the observations do not all fall exactly on a line but are somewhere close. For instance, the number of people visiting an office in four consecutive days might be 22, 18, 19 and 21. The number visiting is around 20, but there is some unexplained variation. So you would expect the number visiting on the fifth day to be around 20, but would not be surprised by a small difference between the actual number and the expected one. This raises two questions:

■ How can you identify the underlying pattern, finding the equation that best describes a relationship? This is called regression.
■ How well does this relationship fit the data?

The answers to both of these depend on the errors that appear in actual observations.

Errors

Suppose you have the following data for the average daily temperature in a town and the corresponding consumption of electricity.

Temperature	0	2	5	7	10	12	15	17
Electricity	5	9	15	19	25	29	35	39

Figure 9.1 shows a graph of this, and you can see that there is a perfect relationship, with the consumption of electricity (the dependent variable) related perfectly to the temperature (the independent variable). In fact:

consumption of electricity = 2 × average temperature + 5

In reality, you rarely find such a perfect relationship and there is usually some variation around the expected values. You are more likely to find the

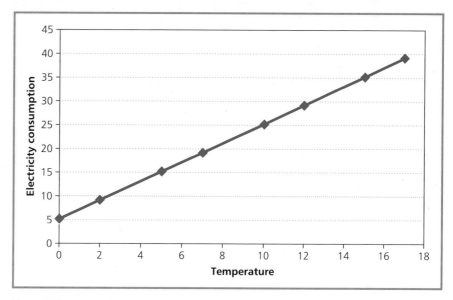

Figure 9.1 Relationship between electricity consumption and average daily temperature

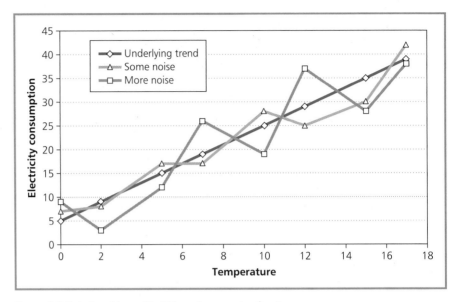

Figure 9.2 Relationships with different amounts of noise

following pattern of electricity consumption, which was recorded in the USA in January 2006.

Temperature	0	2	5	7	10	12	15	17
Electricity	7	8	17	17	26	24	30	42

There is still a clear linear relationship, but superimposed on this underlying pattern is a random variation called **noise**. We cannot explain the noise, but have to accept it as an inherent part of most observations. Then we have:

actual value = underlying pattern + random noise

There might be even more noise, with varying amounts shown in Figure 9.2.
    The amount of random noise determines the strength of a relationship:

- When there is no noise – as in the first set of figures above – the relationship is perfect.
- When there is some noise the relationship is weaker.
- When there is a lot of noise, the relationship becomes even weaker and more difficult to identify.
- When the noise is overwhelming, it hides any underlying relationship and data appears to be random.

Measuring the noise

To find the strength of a relationship between two variables we need some way of measuring the noise. For each value of the independent variable there is a corresponding value of the dependent variable. But the noise means that

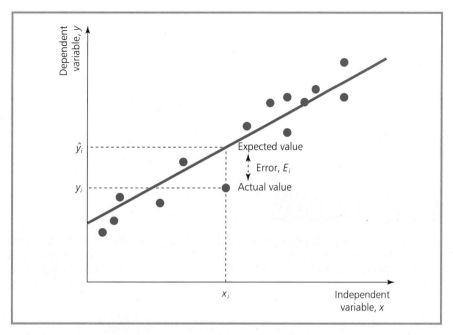

Figure 9.3 Noise introduces errors in observations

there is a difference between the actual value of the dependent variable and the expected value. You can think of the noise as an error in each observation.

For each observation i,

  error, E_i = actual value – expected value from the relationship

Figure 9.3 shows a linear relationship between two variables, with super-imposed noise. The noise means that each observation has an error, which is its vertical distance from the line. Then:

$$E_i = y_i - \hat{y}_i$$

where: y_i = actual value

$\hat{y}_i$ = value suggested by the relationship (which is pronounced 'y hat').

Each observation has an error, so in principle we can find the mean of these from:

$$\text{mean error} = \frac{\Sigma E_i}{n}$$
$$= \frac{\Sigma(y_i - \hat{y}_i)}{n}$$

But the mean error has the major drawback (which we met with variance in Chapter 6) of allowing positive and negative errors to cancel. So data with very large errors can still have a mean error of zero. The usual ways around this either take the absolute values of errors (and calculate the mean absolute error), or square the errors (and calculate the mean squared error).

$$\text{mean absolute error} = \frac{\Sigma |E_i|}{n} = \frac{\Sigma |y_i - \hat{y}_i|}{n}$$

$$\text{mean squared error} = \frac{\Sigma (E_i)^2}{n} = \frac{\Sigma (y_i - \hat{y}_i)^2}{n}$$

The mean absolute error has an obvious meaning – when it takes a value of 1.5, the actual value is on average 1.5 away from the expected value. The mean squared error has a less clear meaning, but is useful for other analyses. Whichever measure we use, smaller values show that there is less noise in the observations and a stronger relationship between variables.

WORKED EXAMPLE 9.1

Sonja Prizniscz collects eight pairs of observations that she thinks are related by the equation $y = 3x + 3$. What are the errors in these observations?

x	3	6	10	15	8	4	1	12
y	10	24	29	48	25	12	5	41

Solution

Sonja has to calculate the values of E_i by substituting values for x into the equation $y = 3x + 3$, and

then the error in each observation is $E_i = y_i - \hat{y}_i$. For the first observation x is 3, so $y = 3x + 3 = 3 \times 3 + 3 = 12$. The actual observation is 10, so the error is $10 - 12 = -2$, the absolute error is 2 and the error squared is 4. Figure 9.4 shows all the calculations in a spreadsheet. The mean error = –0.88 (showing that actual values are, on average, a bit lower than expected), the mean absolute error = 2.13 (showing that actual values are, on average, 2.13 away from expected ones) and the mean squared error = 5.88.

	A	B	C	D	E	F
1	**Measuring errors**					
2						
3	*x*	Actual *y*	Calculated *y*	Error	Absolute error	Squared error
4	3	10	12	−2	2	4
5	6	24	21	3	3	9
6	10	29	33	−4	4	16
7	15	48	48	0	0	0
8	8	25	27	−2	2	4
9	4	12	15	−3	3	9
10	1	5	6	−1	1	1
11	12	41	39	2	2	4
12	**Sums**			−7	17	47
13	**Means**			−0.88	2.13	5.88

Figure 9.4 Different measures for average errors

Review questions

9.1 What is the 'noise' in a relationship?

9.2 Why do almost all relationships contain errors?

9.3 What is the mean error and why is it rarely used?

9.4 Define two other measures of error.

9.5 Two people suggest different equations for describing the relationship between two variables. How can you tell which is better?

Linear relationships

Many relationships have this basic form of an underlying pattern with superimposed noise – such as the sales of a product falling with increasing price, demand for a service rising with advertising expenditure, productivity rising with bonus payments, borrowings falling with rising interest rates and crop yield depending on the amount of fertiliser used. These are examples of causal relationships where changes in the first (dependent) variable are actually caused by changes in the second (independent) variable. People often assume that because there is a relationship there must be some cause and effect – but this is not true. Sales of ice-cream are directly related to sales of sunglasses, but there is no cause and effect – and the way to increase sales of ice-cream is not to sell more sunglasses. Here the weather clearly affects the sales of both ice-cream and sunglasses. It is easy to spot ridiculous examples of assumed cause and effect – the number of lamp posts is related to prosecutions for drunken driving, the number of storks nesting in Sweden is related to the birth rate in Northern Europe, the number of people in higher education is related to life expectancy and in the nineteenth century the number of asses in America was related to the number of PhD graduates!

Unfortunately, not all mistakes of this kind are as easy to spot. For example, the productivity of a coal mine declines with increasing investment (because of the age of the mine and increasing difficulty of extracting coal); an economist says that high wages cause inflation (ignoring the fact that countries with the highest wages often have the lowest inflation); the revenue of a bus company is related to the fares charged (but increasing fares deters passengers and reduces long-term income).

So we are looking at relationships between variables, but not implying any cause and effect. In particular, we start by looking at linear relationships where the underlying pattern is a straight line. The process that finds the equation for the straight line that best fits a set of data is called linear regression.

WORKED EXAMPLE 9.2

The table shows the number of shifts worked each month and the production at Van Hofen, Inc. If the company plans 50 shifts for next month, what is their expected production?

Month	1	2	3	4	5	6	7	8	9
Shifts worked	50	70	25	55	20	60	40	25	35
Output	352	555	207	508	48	498	310	153	264

Solution

Figure 9.5 shows a scatter diagram of shifts worked (the independent variable, x) and production (the dependent variable, y). There is a clear linear relationship, and we can draw by eye a reasonable straight line through the data. This line shows that with 50 shifts worked, the output will be around 400 units.

Worked example 9.2 continued

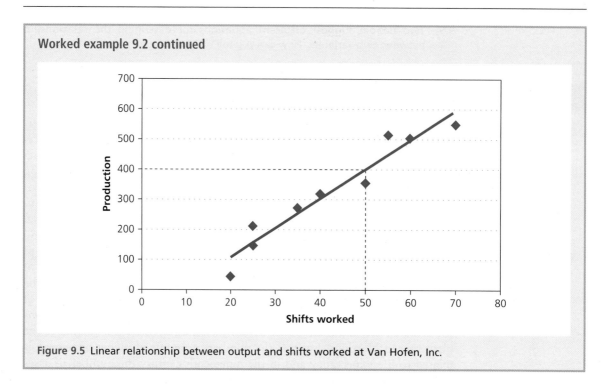

Figure 9.5 Linear relationship between output and shifts worked at Van Hofen, Inc.

Worked example 9.2 illustrates the basic approach of linear regression:

1 Draw a scatter diagram.
2 Identify a linear relationship.
3 Find the equation for the line of best fit through the data.
4 Use this line to predict a value for the dependent variable from a known value of the independent variable.

The third step is the crucial one, finding the line of best fit through the data. We approach this by using the equation of a straight line that we found in Chapter 3:

$$y = a + bx$$

where x is the independent variable, y is the dependent variable, a is the intercept on the y-axis and b is the gradient. Noise means that even the best line is unlikely to fit the data perfectly, so there is an error at each point and we really have:

$$y_i = a + bx_i + E_i$$

And we can define the line of best fit as the line that minimises some measure of this error. In practice, this means that we look for the line that minimises the mean squared error. Then we can say that:

Linear regression finds values for the constants a and b that define the line of best fit through a set of points, and minimises the mean squared error.

A standard result (derived in the companion website at **www.pearsoned. co.uk/waters**) shows that the equation for the line of best fit is:

$$y = a + bx$$

where:

$$b = \frac{n\Sigma xy - \Sigma x\Sigma y}{n\Sigma x^2 - (\Sigma x)^2}$$

$$a = \bar{y} - b\bar{x}$$

(Remember that $\bar{x}$ and $\bar{y}$ are the mean values of x and y.)

WORKED EXAMPLE 9.3

Find the line of best fit through the following data for an advertising budget (in thousands of euros) and units sold. Forecast the number of units sold with an advertising budget of €70,000.

Advertising budget	20	40	60	80	90	110
Units sold	110	150	230	230	300	360

Solution
Figure 9.6 shows that there is a clear linear relationship, with:

units sold (y) = $a + b \times$ advertising budget (x)

We can do the calculations in a number of ways. The equations are fairly messy, but Figure 9.7 shows the values of n, Σx, Σy, Σxy and Σx^2. Substituting these into the standard equations gives:

$$b = \frac{\Sigma xy - \Sigma x\Sigma y}{n\Sigma x^2 - (\Sigma x)^2} = \frac{6 \times 107{,}000 - 400 \times 1{,}380}{6 \times 32{,}200 - 400 \times 400}$$

$$= 2.71$$

$$a = \bar{y} - b\bar{x}$$
$$= 230 - 2.71 \times 66.67 = 49.28$$

So the line of best fit is:

units sold = 49.28 + 2.71 × advertising budget

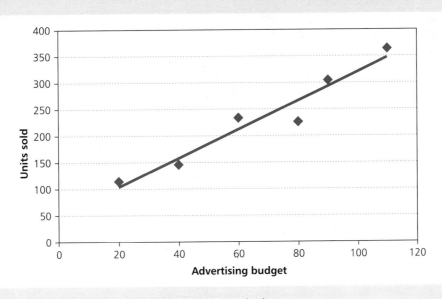

Figure 9.6 Relationship between units sold and advertising budget

Worked example 9.3 continued

With an advertising budget of €70,000, $x = 70$ and:

$$\text{units sold} = 49.28 + 2.71 \times 70$$
$$= 239 \text{ units}$$

Spreadsheets have standard functions for these calculations, and you can see these in the second part of Figure 9.7. Here Excel's INTERCEPT function gives the intercept of the line, a, the SLOPE function gives the gradient, b, and the FORECAST function substitutes these values and predicts the number of sales with €70,000 of advertising.

The third part of Figure 9.7 shows another option, which is to use a spreadsheet's Data Analysis ToolPak. Here the 'Regression' option automatically finds the line of best fit. These tools often give more information than we really want, so we have given only the main results. The 'Regression statistics' show how well the line fits the data (which we discuss later in the chapter), the 'ANOVA' (analysis of variance) describes the errors, and the last table in rows 37–39 shows the information we want – in particular the 'intercept' value in cell B38 and the 'X variable 1' value in cell B39 are the values of a and b respectively.

	A	B	C	D	E
1	Linear regression				
2					
3	1. Calculation				
4	Data			Calculation	
5		x	y	xy	x^2
6		20	110	2200	400
7		40	150	6000	1600
8		60	230	13800	3600
9		80	230	18400	6400
10		90	300	27000	8100
11		110	360	39600	12100
12	Sum	400	1380	107000	32200
13	Mean	66.67	230.00	17833.33	5366.67
14	$n =$	6			
15	Substitution	$a =$	49.28	$b =$	2.71
16	Forecast	$x =$	70	$y =$	239.04
17					
18	2. Standard function				
19	Intercept	49.28			
20	Slope	2.71			
21	Forecast	239.04			
22					
23	3. Data analysis				
24	Regression Statistics				
25	Multiple R	0.98			
26	R Square	0.95			
27	Adjust R Square	0.94			
28	Standard Error	22.01			
29	Observations	6			
30					
31	ANOVA				
32		df	SS	MS	
33	Regression	1	40662.65	40662.65	
34	Residual	4	1937.35	484.34	
35	Total	5	42600		
36					
37		Coefficients	Stand error		
38	Intercept	49.28	21.67		
39	X Variable 1	2.71	0.30		

Figure 9.7 Three ways of doing the regression calculations in a spreadsheet

Using linear regression to forecast

The main purpose of linear regression is to predict the value of a dependent variable that corresponds to a known value of an independent variable. In Worked example 9.3 we found a relationship between advertising budget and sales, and then used this to forecast expected sales for a particular advertising budget. In Worked example 9.4 we forecast the number of mistakes with a planned level of quality control. This approach is known as causal forecasting, even though changes in the independent variable may not actually cause changes in the dependent variable.

Worked example 9.4 shows that the line of best fit is only really valid within the range of x used to find it – and there is no evidence that the same relationship holds outside this range. Using a value of x outside the range to find a corresponding value of y is called extrapolation, and you cannot rely on the result. In practice extrapolated results are generally acceptable provided the values of x are not too far outside the range. This is an important point – managers often use time-period as the independent variable, with linear regression finding the line of best fit through historical data. Then they use the equation to forecast values for the future. This is clearly extrapolation, but provided they do not forecast too far into the future the results should be fairly reliable.

WORKED EXAMPLE 9.4

Olfentia Travel arrange a large number of holidays, and in some of these they make administrative mistakes. They are about to change their quality control procedures, and have run some experiments to see how the number of mistakes varies with the number of checks. The table summarises their findings. How many mistakes should Olfentia expect with 6 checks? How many would they expect with 20 checks?

Checks	0	1	2	3	4	5	6	7	8	9	10
Mistakes	92	86	81	72	67	59	53	43	32	24	12

Solution

The independent variable, x, is the number of checks and the dependent variable, y, is the consequent mistakes. Figure 9.8 shows that there is a clear linear relationship between these. If you do the calculations, you find that $n = 11$, $\Sigma x = 55$, $\Sigma y = 621$, $\Sigma xy = 2{,}238$ and $\Sigma x^2 = 385$. Substituting these values gives:

$$b = \frac{\Sigma xy - \Sigma x \Sigma y}{n\Sigma x^2 - (\Sigma x)^2} = \frac{11 \times 2{,}238 - 55 \times 621}{11 \times 385 - 55 \times 55}$$

$$= -7.88$$

$$a = \bar{y} - b\bar{x} = 621 / 11 + 7.88 \times 55 / 11$$
$$= 95.86$$

This confirms the results given directly in Figure 9.8 by the standard 'Regression' tool, that the line of best fit is:

number of mistakes = 95.86 − 7.88 × number of checks

With 6 inspections Olfentia can forecast 95.86 − 7.88 × 6 = 48.58 mistakes. With 20 inspections they have to be a bit more careful because substitution gives 95.86 − 7.88 × 20 = −61.74. It is impossible to have a negative number of mistakes, so they should simply forecast zero.

Worked example 9.4 continued

	A	B	C	D	E	F	G	H
1	**Quality control at Olfentia Travel**							
2								
3	**Checks**	**Mistakes**		**SUMMARY OUTPUT**				
4	0	92						
5	1	86		Regression Statistics				
6	2	81		Multiple R	0.994			
7	3	72		R Square	0.988			
8	4	67		Adjusted R Square	0.986			
9	5	59		Standard error	3.077			
10	6	53		Observations	11			
11	7	43						
12	8	32		ANOVA				
13	9	24			df	SS	MS	
14	10	12		Regression	1	6833.536	6833.536	
15				Residual	9	85.191	9.466	
16				Total	10	6918.727		
17								
18				Coefficient standard error				
19				Intercept	95.864	1.735		
20				X Variable 1	−7.882	0.293		
21								
22								

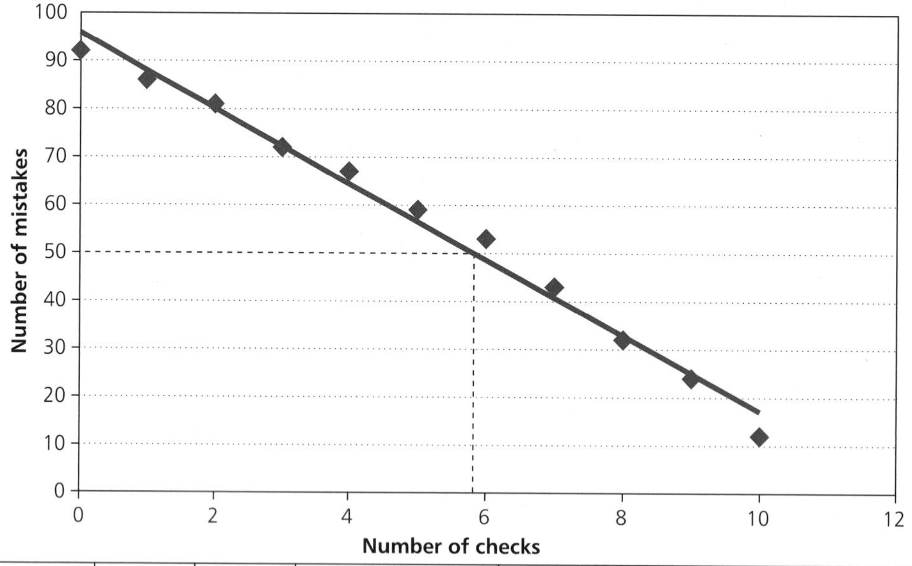

Figure 9.8 Linear relationship between the number of mistakes and checks at Olfentia Travel

WORKED EXAMPLE 9.5

Sales of a product over the last 10 weeks have been 17, 23, 41, 38, 42, 47, 51, 56, 63 and 71. Use linear regression to forecast demand for the next three weeks, and for week 30.

Solution

Here time – or week number – is the independent variable, and the dependent variable is sales. Figure 9.9 shows the line of best fit calculated by the standard Excel functions INTERCEPT and SLOPE to be:

$$sales = 15.4 + 5.36 \times week$$

Substituting week numbers into this equation gives:

Week 11: sales $= 15.4 + 5.36 \times 11 = 74.4$
Week 12: sales $= 15.4 + 5.36 \times 12 = 79.8$
Week 13: sales $= 15.4 + 5.36 \times 13 = 85.1$
Week 30: sales $= 15.4 + 5.36 \times 30 = 176.2$

The relationship is only really valid for weeks 1 to 10, and we are fairly safe in extrapolating to week 13 – but we must be far more cautious when extrapolating to week 30.

	A	B	C	D	E	F
1	Linear regression					
2						
3	Week	Sales	Forecast		Intercept =	15.40
4	1	17	20.8		Gradient =	5.36
5	2	23	26.1			
6	3	41	31.5			
7	4	38	36.9			
8	5	42	42.2			
9	6	47	47.6			
10	7	51	52.9			
11	8	56	58.3			
12	9	63	63.7			
13	10	71	69.0			
14	11		74.4			
15	12		79.8			
16	13		85.1			
17						
18	30		176.3			

Figure 9.9 Using linear regression with time as the independent variable

IDEAS IN PRACTICE Long Barrow Farm

Geoff Harris has been running a cereal farm for the past 20 years. He has to consider many different factors for his crops, especially in the use of chemical fertilisers and pesticides. However, with his current methods Geoff's profit per hectare is directly affected by the amount he spends on fertiliser.

Farming has also become a major user of information technology, and Geoff can fairly readily measure the relationship shown in Figure 9.10, where:

$$profit\ per\ hectare = -4.09 + 0.078 \times cost\ of\ fertiliser$$

▶

Ideas in practice continued

Geoff used this result to evaluate four options for expenditure next year. He wants to reduce his use of chemicals, but must make significant changes to operations before this is a feasible option. The financial analysis (omitted from the spreadsheet) shows the broader effects of changes to operations. Overall, Geoff concluded that he could reduce expenditure on chemicals by 50% over the next five years – while potentially increasing his profit margins by 20%.

	A	B	C	D	E	F	G	H	I	J	K	L	M
1	Long Barrow Farm												
2													
3	Cost of fertiliser	500	1000	1500	2000	2500	3000	3500	4000	4500	5000	5500	6000
4	Profit per hectare	35	70	110	160	200	220	260	310	350	380	430	460
5													
6	Regression results												
7	Intercept, a =	−4.09											
8	gradient, b =	0.078											
9													
10	Options	1	2	3	4								
11	Cost of fertiliser	0	1500	3000	4500								
12	Profit per hectare	−4	113	229	346								
13													
14	Financial analysis												

Figure 9.10 Start of financial analysis for Long Barrow Farm

Review questions

9.6 What is the purpose of linear regression?

9.7 Define each of the terms in the regression equation $y_i = a + b \times x_i + E_i$

9.8 If you want to forecast future values, what is the most commonly used independent variable?

9.9 'Linear regression means that changes in the independent variable cause changes in the dependent variable.' Is this is true?

9.10 What are 'interpolation' and 'extrapolation'?

Measuring the strength of a relationship

Linear regression finds the line of best fit through a set of data – but we really need to measure how good the fit is. If observations are close to the line, the errors are small and the line is a good fit to the data; but if observations are some way away from the line, errors are large and even the best line is not very good.

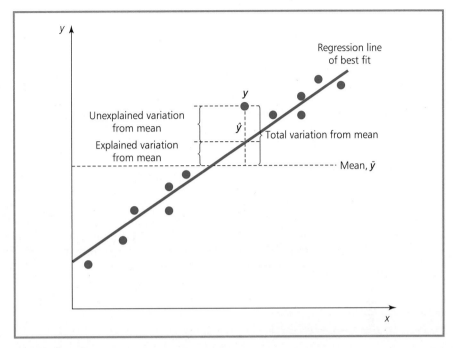

Figure 9.11 Explained and unexplained variation from the mean

Coefficient of determination

Suppose you have a number of observations of y_i and calculate the mean, $\bar{y}$. Actual values vary around this mean, and you can measure the variation by the total sum of squared errors:

$$\text{total SSE} = \Sigma(y_i - \bar{y})^2$$

If you look carefully at this sum of squared errors (SSE) you can separate it into different components (as illustrated in Figure 9.11). When you build a regression model you estimate values, $\hat{y}_i$, which show what the observations would be if there were no noise. So the regression model explains some of the variation of actual observations from the mean:

$$\text{explained SSE} = \Sigma(\hat{y}_i - \bar{y})^2$$

But there is also random noise, so the regression model does not explain all the variation and there is some residual left unexplained:

$$\text{unexplained SSE} = \Sigma(y_i - \hat{y}_i)^2$$

Using a bit of algebra you can find that:

$$\text{total SSE} = \text{explained SSE} + \text{unexplained SSE}$$

The more of the variation that is explained by the regression, the better the line of best fit. So a measure of the goodness of fit is the proportion of total SSE that is explained by the regression model. This is the coefficient of determination:

$$\text{coefficient of determination} = \frac{\text{explained SSE}}{\text{total SSE}}$$

This measure has a value between 0 and 1. If it is near to 1 then most of the variation is explained by the regression, there is little unexplained variation and the line is a good fit for the data. If the value is near to 0 then most of the variation is unexplained and the line is not a good fit.

If you are keen, you can calculate the coefficient of determination from the rather messy equation:

$$\text{coefficient of determination} = \left[\frac{n\Sigma xy - \Sigma x \Sigma y}{\sqrt{[n\Sigma x^2 - (\Sigma x)^2] \times [n\Sigma y^2 - (\Sigma y)^2]}} \right]^2$$

The coefficient of determination is called r^2, and it is much better to let a computer do the calculation. If you look back at Figure 9.7 you can see that this is one of the values calculated by the regression tool, with the result given as 'R Square 0.95'. This is a high value and shows a strong linear relationship, with 95% of all the variation from the mean explained by the regression and only 5% due to noise.

WORKED EXAMPLE 9.6

Calculate the coefficient of determination for the data from Long Barrow Farm. What does this tell you?

Solution
We know that:

coefficient of determination

$$= \left[\frac{n\Sigma xy - \Sigma x \Sigma y}{\sqrt{[n\Sigma x^2 - (\Sigma x)^2] \times [n\Sigma y^2 - (\Sigma y)^2]}} \right]^2$$

If you do the calculations, you find that $n = 12$, $\Sigma x = 39,000$, $\Sigma y = 2,985$, $\Sigma xy = 12,482,500$, $\Sigma x^2 = 162,500,000$ and $\Sigma y^2 = 959,325$. Then:

$$r^2 = \left[\frac{12 \times 12,482,500 - 39,000 \times 2,985}{\sqrt{[12 \times 162,500,000 - 39,000^2] \times [12 \times 959,325 - 2,985^2]}} \right]^2$$

$$= 0.998$$

This tells us two things. Firstly, this is very close to 1, so almost all the variation is explained by the regression and there is virtually no noise – there is a very strong linear relationship between the cost of fertiliser and the profit per hectare. Secondly, it shows that the arithmetic is messy, and it is always better to use a computer.

Normally any value for the coefficient of determination above about 0.5 is considered a good fit. If the coefficient of determination is lower, say closer to 0.2, then most of the variation is left unexplained by the regression and there is not a strong relationship. However, we should give a word of warning about outliers – single observations that are some distance away from the regression line. Even the odd outlier can influence the regression result and give a lower coefficient of determination, so there is always a temptation to assume they are mistakes and simply ignore them. But you should not do this! You should ignore a point only when there is a genuine reason, like a mistake or because the point is not strictly comparable with the rest of the data. Deciding to arbitrarily ignore some observations because they spoil a pattern is missing the whole point of the analysis – to see whether there really is an underlying pattern and measure the strength of a relationship.

Coefficient of correlation

A second measure for regression is the coefficient of correlation, which answers the basic question 'are x and y linearly related?' The coefficients of correlation and determination obviously answer very similar questions and a standard result shows that:

coefficient of correlation $= \sqrt{\text{coefficient of determination}}$

Now you can see why we refer to the coefficient of determination as r^2 – so that we can refer to the coefficient of correlation as r. This correlation co-efficient is also called Pearson's coefficient and it has a value between +1 and −1.

■ A value of $r = 1$ shows that the two variables have a perfect linear rela-tionship with no noise at all, and as one increases so does the other (shown in Figure 9.12).

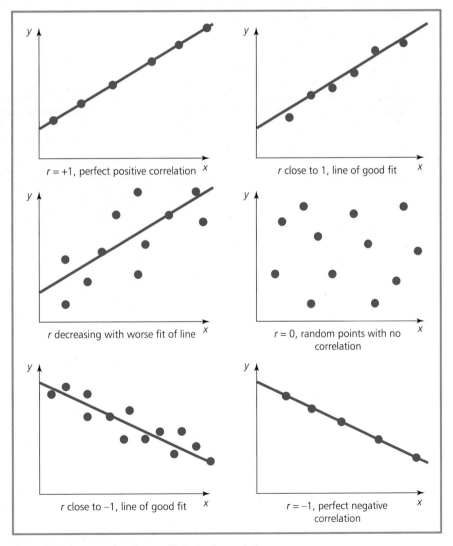

Figure 9.12 Interpreting the coefficient of correlation

- A value of r close to 1 shows a line of good fit but with some noise.
- A lower positive value of r shows that the linear relationship is weaker.
- A value of $r = 0$ shows that there is no correlation at all between the two variables, and no linear relationship.
- A low negative value of r shows a weak linear relationship, and as one increases the other decreases. As r gets closer to -1 the relationship gets stronger.
- A value of $r = -1$ shows that the two variables have a perfect negative linear relationship.

With a correlation coefficient, r, near to $+1$ or -1 there is a strong linear relationship between the two variables. However, when r falls to 0.7 or -0.7 the coefficient of determination, r^2, is 0.49, meaning that less than half the variation from the mean is explained by the regression model. We can conclude that values of r between 0.7 and -0.7 suggest that there is, at best, a relatively weak linear relationship.

WORKED EXAMPLE 9.7

Calculate the coefficients of correlation and determination for the data in the table. What conclusions can you draw from these? What is the line of best fit?

x	4	17	3	21	10	8	4	9	13	12	2	6	15	8	19
y	13	47	24	41	29	33	28	38	46	32	14	22	26	21	50

Solution

Figure 9.13 shows the results from the 'Regression' option in Excel's Data Analysis ToolPak (actually this gives a lot more detail, but we have focused on a limited part). The key points are as follows:

- There are 15 observations.
- The intercept = 15.376.

	A	B	C	D	E	F
1	**Correlation and determination**					
2						
3	x	y		SUMMARY OUTPUT		
4	4	13				
5	17	47		Regression statistics		
6	3	24		Multiple R	0.797	
7	21	41		R Square	0.635	
8	10	29		Adjusted R Square	0.607	
9	8	33		Standard error	7.261	
10	4	28		Observations	15	
11	9	38				
12	13	46		ANOVA		
13	12	32			*df*	*SS*
14	2	14		Regression	1	1191.630
15	6	22		Residual	13	685.304
16	15	26		Total	14	1876.933
17	8	21				
18	19	50			**Coefficients**	
19				Intercept	15.376	
20				X Variable 1	1.545	

Figure 9.13 Results from the 'Regression' data analysis tool

Worked example 9.7 continued

- The gradient = 1.545, so the line of best fit is:

  $y = 15.376 + 1.545x$

- The coefficient of correlation, described as 'Multiple R' = 0.797. This shows a reasonably strong linear relationship.
- The coefficient of determination, described as 'R Square' = 0.635. This is the square of the coefficient of correlation and shows that 63.5% of variation from the mean is explained by the linear relationship, and only 36.5% is unexplained.
- The coefficient of correlation is sometimes rather optimistic, especially when there are only a few observations. To overcome any bias, the spreadsheet calculates an adjusted figure of 0.607. This might give a more realistic view, but it should usually be close to the calculated value.
- ANOVA – analysis of variance – shows the sum of squared errors from the mean. The total SSE = 1876.933.
- Of this, the regression explains 1191.630, giving the explained SSE. Dividing this by the total SSE gives the coefficient of determination: 1191.630 / 1876.933 = 0.635.
- The residual or unexplained SSE = 685.304, confirming that total SSE (1876.933) = explained SSE (1191.630) + unexplained SSE (685.304).
- The standard error = 7.261, and this gives a measure of the error in the predicted value of each y.

Rank correlation

Pearson's coefficient is the most widely used measure of correlation, but it works only for cardinal data (that is, numerical values). Sometimes we want to measure the strength of a relationship between ordinal data (data that is ranked but whose values are unknown). You can imagine this with a market survey that asks people to specify an order of preference for different alternatives. For example, a survey might ask customers to rank different Internet service providers (ISPs) according to the quality of their service. The survey might also rank the prices charged for these services. So a useful analysis would test if there is a relationship between two rankings – service quality and price. You can do this using Spearman's coefficient of rank correlation, which is called r_s.

Spearman's coefficient $= r_s = 1 - \dfrac{6\sum D^2}{n(n^2 - 1)}$

where: n = number of paired observations
D = difference in rankings
= first ranking − second ranking

WORKED EXAMPLE 9.8

A company offers five services (labelled V to Z) and asks customers to rank them according to quality and cost. What can you find from the following results?

Service	V	W	X	Y	Z
Quality ranking	2	5	1	3	4
Cost ranking	1	3	2	4	5

Solution

You can use Spearman's rank correlation coefficient to see if there is a relationship between quality and cost. Then:

$$D = \text{quality ranking} - \text{cost ranking}$$

In this case there are five rankings, so $n = 5$ and the sum of D^2 is:

$$(2 - 1)^2 + (5 - 3)^2 + (1 - 2)^2 + (3 - 4)^2 + (4 - 5)^2$$
$$= 1 + 4 + 1 + 1 + 1$$
$$= 8$$

Spearman's coefficient is:

$$r_s = 1 - \frac{6\sum D^2}{n(n^2 - 1)} = 1 - \frac{6 \times 8}{5 \times (25 - 1)}$$
$$= 0.6$$

Although it looks completely different to Pearson's coefficient, Spearman's coefficient is derived from similar principles and is interpreted in exactly the same way. A value of 0.6 suggests some relationship between quality and cost – but not a very strong one.

It is worth remembering that ordinal data is far less precise than cardinal. This means that an item ranked first may be slightly better than the item ranked second, or it may be a lot better. It follows that the results of regressions are also less precise, and wherever possible you should use cardinal data and Pearson's coefficient.

WORKED EXAMPLE 9.9

Kipram Jansaporanam runs an apprentice scheme that judges the performance of trainees by a combination of interviews and job performance. Last year she had seven trainees and ranked them as follows.

Trainee	A	B	C	D	E	F	G
Interview	3	2	6	4	1	7	5
Job performance	1	3	5	2	4	6	7

Is there a link between the results of interviews and job performance?

Solution

For each trainee we can find D, the difference between each ranking. Then:

$$\sum D^2 = (3 - 1)^2 + (2 - 3)^2 + (6 - 5)^2 + (4 - 2)^2$$
$$+ (1 - 4)^2 + (7 - 6)^2 + (5 - 7)^2$$
$$= 4 + 1 + 1 + 4 + 9 + 1 + 4$$
$$= 24$$

Spearman's coefficient is:

$$r_s = 1 - \frac{6\sum D^2}{n(n^2 - 1)} = 1 - \frac{6 \times 24}{7(49 - 1)} = 0.57$$

This is not very high and does not suggest a strong relationship.

9.11   What is measured by the coefficient of determination?

9.12   What values can the coefficient of correlation take?

9.13   Is the coefficient of correlation related to the coefficient of determination?

9.14   What is the difference between Pearson's and Spearman's coefficients of correlation?

9.15   'A coefficient of determination of 0.9 shows that 10% of variation in the dependent variable is caused by change in the independent variable.' Is this true?

Multiple regression

There are several extensions to linear regression, with the most common relating a dependent variable to more than one independent variable. You can imagine this with, say, the sales of a product that might be related to the advertising budget, price, unemployment rates, average incomes, competition and so on. In other words, the dependent variable, y, is not set by a single independent variable, x, but by a number of separate independent variables x_i. Specifically, we can write this relationship as:

$$y = a + b_1x_1 + b_2x_2 + b_3x_3 + b_4x_4 + b_5x_5 + \cdots$$

In our illustration, this might mean that:

$$\text{sales} = a + b_1 \times \text{advertising} + b_2 \times \text{price} + b_3 \times \text{unemployment rate} + b_4 \times \text{income} + b_5 \times \text{competition}$$

By adding more independent variables we are trying to get a more accurate model. Then we might find that advertising explains 60% of the variation in sales, but adding a second term for price explains 75% of the variation, and adding a third term for unemployment explains 85% of the variation and so on.

Because we are looking for a linear relationship between a dependent variable and a set of independent ones, we should really call this multiple linear regression – but it is always abbreviated to multiple regression.

- **Multiple regression** finds the line of best fit through a set of dependent variables.
- It finds the best values for a and b_i in the equation:

  $$y = a + b_1x_1 + b_2x_2 + b_3x_3 + b_4x_4 + b_5x_5 + \cdots$$

We have to calculate the coefficients a and b_i, but after seeing the arithmetic for linear regression you might guess, quite rightly, that the arithmetic is even more messy. This is why multiple regression is never tackled by hand. Thankfully, a lot of standard software includes multiple regression as a standard function.

WORKED EXAMPLE 9.10

The data section in Figure 9.14 shows sales, advertising costs and prices for a product at Soo Yueng Commercial. The rest of this figure shows some results when the 'Regression' function in Excel's Data Analysis ToolPak automatically does multiple regression. What do these figures show? What are the expected sales with a price of 60 and advertising of 200?

Solution

There is data for two independent variables – advertising and price – and one dependent variable – sales. So we are looking for a relationship of the form:

sales = $a + b_1 \times$ advertising + $b_2 \times$ price

Rows 26 to 29 of the spreadsheet show the values for the intercept and variables, with the line of best fit identified as:

sales = 585.96 + 9.92 × advertising + 19.11 × price

The coefficient of correlation $r = 0.996$. This shows a very strong linear relationship. This is confirmed by the coefficient of determination, r^2, which shows that 99.2% of the variation is explained by the relationship. Row 16 shows the adjusted r^2, which removes bias but is only slightly lower than the calculated value.

To find the expected sales, we substitute values for advertising and price into the regression equation. With advertising of 200 and price of 60, the expected sales are:

sales = 585.96 + 9.92 × advertising + 19.11 × price
= 585.96 + 9.92 × 200 + 19.11 × 60
= 3,717

	A	B	C
1	**Multiple regression**		
2			
3	**DATA**		
4	**Sales**	**Advertising**	**Price**
5	2450	100	50
6	3010	130	56
7	3090	160	45
8	3700	190	63
9	3550	210	48
10	4280	240	70
11			
12	**SUMMARY OUTPUT**		
13		Regression statistics	
14	Multiple R	0.996	
15	R Square	0.992	
16	Adjusted R Square	0.986	
17	Standard error	75.055	
18	Observations	6	
19			
20	ANOVA		
21		*df*	*SS*
22	Regression	2	2003633.452
23	Residual	3	16899.882
24	Total	5	2020533.333
25			
26		Coefficients	Standard error
27	Intercept	585.96	195.57
28	X Variable 1	9.92	0.76
29	X Variable 2	19.11	4.13

Figure 9.14 Multiple regression results for Worked example 9.10

With multiple regression, you have to take a few precautions to make sure that the results are reliable. To start with, you have to make sure that there is enough data. In principle, you can draw a regression line with only two observations, but you need a lot more data to get useful results. A rule of thumb suggests that there should be at least five observations for each variable fitted into the equation – so linear regression needs at least five observations, multiple regression with two variables needs at least 10 observations, and so on.

A second problem is that the method works properly only when there is no linear relationship between the independent variables. So in Worked example 9.10 there should be no relationship between the advertising costs and price. Obviously, if the two independent variables are related in some way then they are not – by definition – independent. But these relationships often exist in real problems, and there might well be a relationship between advertising costs and price. In general, we accept the results if the relationships are not too strong. We can measure the strengths of relationships between independent variables by the coefficient of correlation between them. If the correlations are more than about 0.7 or less than about –0.7, we have to say that the relationships are too strong and we cannot rely on the multiple regression results. The technical term for a relationship between the independent variables is multicollinearity.

WORKED EXAMPLE 9.11

Are the advertising and price in Worked example 9.10 really independent?

Solution

The coefficients of correlation between the variables are shown in the spreadsheet in Figure 9.15. These results come from the 'Correlation' tool in Excel's 'Data Analysis ToolPak'. Not surprisingly, there is a perfect correlation between each variable and itself. We want a very high correlation between sales and each of the independent variables – so the correlations of 0.965 between sales and advertising, and 0.723 between sales and price are both good. We also want the correlation between advertising and price to be low, ideally less than its value of 0.535. Nonetheless, the results seem reasonably good.

These coefficients of correlation show that a simple linear regression model relating sales to advertising explains 93.2% of the variation in sales – this is the value of r^2 when $r = 0.965$. But we saw in Figure 9.14 that adding price as a second variable increases this to 99.2%, showing an even better model. The result is now so good that we are unlikely to improve it any further. It is always tempting to keep adding another independent variable to see if we can raise the coefficient of correlation a bit higher, but this soon becomes both pointless and misleading. Adding more independent variables can give small increases in correlation, even though the effects are not really significant. In general, it pays to be cautious and add only variables that have an obvious effect.

	A	B	C	D	E	F	G	H
1	**Coefficients of correlation**							
2								
3	**DATA**				**CORRELATIONS**			
4	**Sales**	**Advertising**	**Price**					
5	2450	100	50			**Sales**	**Advertising**	**Price**
6	3010	130	56		**Sales**	1		
7	3090	160	45		**Advertising**	0.965	1	
8	3700	190	63		**Price**	0.723	0.535	1
9	3550	210	48					
10	4280	240	70					

Figure 9.15 Correlations between the variables in Worked example 9.11 (from 9.10)

A third problem with multiple regression is that it only really works when the errors are all independent. This might seem strange, but there can actually be a relationship between errors. For example, there might be regular seasonal variations that give a correlation between the error terms – perhaps with a low error in November always followed by a high error in December. When there is a relationship between the errors it is called autocorrelation.

WORKED EXAMPLE 9.12

Elsom Service Corporation is trying to see how the number of shifts worked, bonus rates paid to employees, average hours of overtime and staff morale all affect production. They have collected the following data, using consistent units. What conclusions can they reach from this data?

Production	2,810	2,620	3,080	4,200	1,500	3,160	4,680	2,330	1,780	3,910
Shifts	6	3	3	4	1	2	2	7	1	8
Bonus	15	20	5	5	7	12	25	10	12	3
Overtime	8	10	22	31	9	22	30	5	7	20
Morale	5	6	3	2	8	10	7	7	5	3

Solution

Figure 9.16 shows the calculations for this problem. You can see from rows 37 to 42 that the intercept is 346.33, and the line of best fit is:

$$\text{production} = 346.33 + 181.80 \times \text{shifts} + 50.13 \times \text{bonus} + 96.17 \times \text{overtime} - 28.70 \times \text{morale}$$

This model fits the data very well, with a coefficient of correlation of 0.997. The coefficient of determination of 0.995 means that 99.5% of the variation in production is explained, and only 0.5% is unexplained. The separate coefficients of correlation between each pair of independent variables are low, so Elsom do not need to worry about multicollinearity. The coefficients of correlation between production and the independent variables also seem low – apart from the correlation between production and overtime – and there is surprisingly slight negative correlation between production and morale.

Elsom can use this model to forecast future production. For example, with 5 shifts, bonus of 10, overtime of 20 and morale of 6, their expected production is:

$$\text{production} = 346.33 + 181.80 \times 5 + 50.13 \times 10 + 96.17 \times 20 - 28.70 \times 6$$
$$= 3,508$$

However, they should investigate the data to see if there really is a significant relationship between, say, production and bonus.

Worked example 9.12 continued

	A	B	C	D	E	F
1	**Multiple regression**					
2						
3						
4	**Production**	**Shifts**	**Bonus**	**Overtime**	**Morale**	
5	2810	6	15	8	5	
6	2620	3	20	10	6	
7	3080	3	5	22	3	
8	4200	4	5	31	2	
9	1500	1	7	9	8	
10	3160	2	12	22	10	
11	4680	2	25	30	7	
12	2330	7	10	5	7	
13	1780	1	12	7	5	
14	3910	8	3	20	3	
15						
16	**Correlations**					
17		**Production**	**Shifts**	**Bonus**	**Overtime**	**Morale**
18	**Production**	1				
19	**Shifts**	0.262	1			
20	**Bonus**	0.153	−0.315	1		
21	**Overtime**	0.878	−0.108	−0.022	1	
22	**Morale**	−0.332	−0.395	0.451	−0.265	1
23						
24	**Regression**					
25	Multiple R	0.997				
26	R Square	0.995				
27	Adjusted R Square	0.990				
28	Standard error	100.807				
29	Observations	10				
30						
31	**ANOVA**					
32		*df*	*SS*			
33	Regression	4	9439000			
34	Residual	5	50810			
35	Total	9	9489810			
36						
37		**Coefficients**	**Standard error**			
38	Intercept	346.33	160.22			
39	X Variable 1	181.80	15.25			
40	X Variable 2	50.13	5.44			
41	X Variable 3	96.17	3.69			
42	X Variable 4	−28.70	16.76			

Figure 9.16 Multiple regression results for Elsom Service Corporation

9.16 What are the most common extensions to linear regression?

9.17 'Multiple regression considers linear relationships between an independent variable and several dependent ones.' Is this true?

9.18 How can you tell whether multiple regression will find a better fit to a set of data than simple linear regression?

IDEAS IN PRACTICE **Richmond, Parkes and Wright**

Richmond, Parkes and Wright is a private company whose interests are in management research, analysis and education. They frequently use regression to describe the relationships between different variables, and they suggest a general approach with these steps.

1 Collect and check relevant data.
2 Draw a graph of the data and see if it suggests a linear relationship.
3 If there seems to be a linear relationship, find the line of best fit.

4 Calculate the coefficients of correlation and determination to see how well this line fits the data.
5 If there is a good fit, substitute appropriate values for the independent variable to predict corresponding values for the dependent variable.
6 If there is not a good fit – or there is some other problem – basic linear regression does not work.
7 Either look for some other approach or refine the model to see if multiple regression or non-linear regression gives better results.

Curve fitting

When you plot a set of points on a graph, there may be a clear pattern but it may not necessarily be linear. For instance, there may be a clear quadratic relationship or a constant rate of growth. To fit a more complicated function through a set of data we use **non-linear regression** – or more generally **curve fitting**. In principle, this is the same as linear regression and we look for an equation that minimises the mean squared error. But, as you would expect, the arithmetic becomes more complicated. So there are realistically two options:

■ use a computer package that automatically finds more complicated lines of best fit
■ transform the data into a linear form.

Many packages have functions for fitting more complicated curves to data, and spreadsheets typically fit:

■ linear models: $y = a + bx$
■ multiple linear curves: $y = a + b_1x_1 + b_2x_2 + b_3x_3 + \ldots$
■ polynomials: $y = a + bx + cx^2 + dx^3 + \ldots$
■ exponential curves: $y = ax^b$
■ growth curves: $y = ab^x$

Such models can give basic information about the types of relationship within a set of data.

WORKED EXAMPLE 9.13

John Mbulu is convinced that his accountant has raised prices by more than the cost of inflation. Over the past 11 years he has noticed that the cost of doing his accounts (in thousands of Rand) is as follows. What does this data show?

Year	1	2	3	4	5	6	7	8	9	10	11
Cost	0.8	1.0	1.3	1.7	2.0	2.4	2.9	3.8	4.7	6.2	7.5

Solution

You can see, without drawing a graph or calculating the correlation, that the data does not form a straight line, but is rising quickly. This kind of data can follow a growth curve of the form $y = ab^x$, where x is the independent variable, y is the dependent variable, and both a and b are constants. In Excel, the function LOGEST does this automatically, with results shown in Figure 9.17. The line of best fit is:

$$y = ab^x \text{ or } y = 0.6541 \times 1.2457^x$$

The value of $b = 1.2475$ suggests that the accountant's charges are rising by almost 25% a year. Substituting values for the year into the equation gives the predictions in column C, which are very close to the actual values suggesting a good fit to the data.

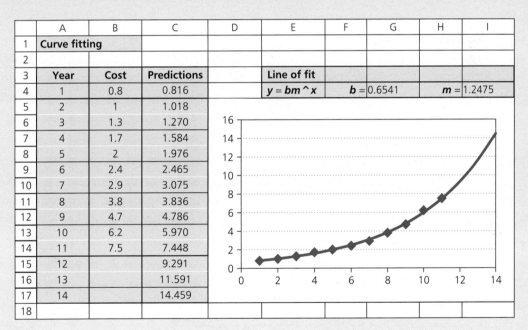

Figure 9.17 Curve fitting for John Mbulu's accountant's costs

An alternative to using appropriate software is to see if the data can be transformed into a linear form. We can illustrate this with data that follows a growth curve of type described in Worked example 9.13. Here we have $y = ab^x$, but taking the logarithms of both sides (have another look at Chapter 2 if you are not sure about this) gives:

$$\log y = \log a + x \log b$$

As both $\log a$ and $\log b$ are constants, we have a linear relationship between x and $\log y$.

WORKED EXAMPLE 9.14

Figure 9.18 shows Janet Curnow's local council tax over the past seven years. How much should she expect to pay next year?

Solution

The council tax is rising quickly, and we can try to fit a curve of the form:

$y = ab^x$, or tax $= a \times b^{year}$

Then:

$\log(tax) = \log a + year \times \log b$

As both log a and log b are constants, we have a linear relationship between log(tax) and year. Then we can use linear regression to find the line of best fit, as shown in Figure 9.18. Here rows 25 and 26 show the result:

$\log(tax) = -159.432 + year \times 0.081$

These numbers have been rounded for display, and the more exact values used in the calculation are -159.4323 and 0.0811909. Then substituting 2007 for the year gives:

$\log(tax) = -159.4323 + 2,007 \times 0.0811909$
$= 3.5178$

To find the tax from this, you have remember the definition of a logarithm. When log(tax) = 3.5178 it means that tax $= 10^{3.5178} = 3,294$. You can see this result in cell D12.

	A	B	C	D	E	F	G
1	Janet Curnow's Council Tax						
2							
3	Year	Tax	log(tax)	Forecast			
4	1999	850	2.9294				
5	2000	923	2.9652				
6	2001	1015	3.0065				
7	2002	1130	3.0531				
8	2003	1370	3.1367				
9	2004	1856	3.2686				
10	2005	2334	3.3681				
11	2006	3102	3.4916				
12	2007		3.5178	3294			
13	2008		3.5990	3971			
14							
15	SUMMARY OUTPUT						
16							
17	Regression statistics						
18	Multiple R	0.975					
19	R Square	0.951					
20	Adjusted R Square	0.942					
21	Standard error	0.049					
22	Observations		8				
23							
24		Coefficients					
25	Intercept	-159.432					
26	X Variable 1	0.081					

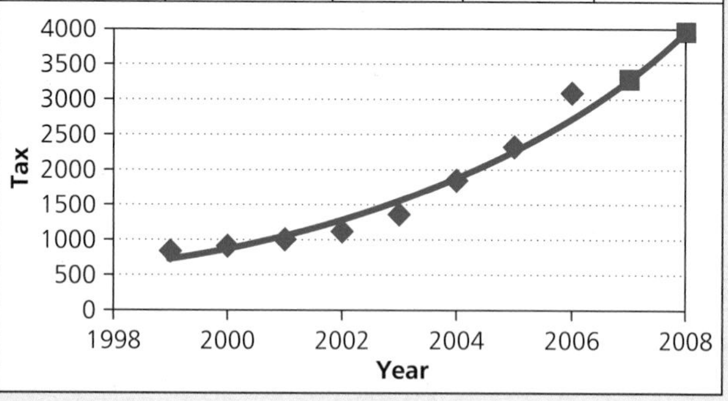

Figure 9.18 Calculations for Janet Curnow's council tax

Another instance when we can transform curves into linear forms is with polynomial expressions. Suppose you want to fit a quadratic equation through a set of points and are looking for a relationship of the form $y = a + b_1 x + b_2 x^2$. If you define one variable as x and a second variable as x^2 then you can use multiple regression to find the best values for a, b_1 and b_2.

WORKED EXAMPLE 9.15

Fit a quadratic curve through the points:

x	1	2	3	4	5	6	7	8	9	10
y	13	38	91	142	230	355	471	603	769	952

Solution

We can transform this into a multiple regression problem of the form:

$$y = a + b_1x_1 + b_2x_2$$

Now we define one variable, x_1, as the values of x and a second variable, x_2, as the values of x^2. Then we can use multiple regression to find the values of a, b_1 and b_2, Figure 9.19 shows these results, and in rows 15 to 18 you can see that the line of best fit is:

$$y = 2.65 - 0.97x_1 + 9.59x_2$$

or

$$y = 2.65 - 0.97x + 9.59x^2$$

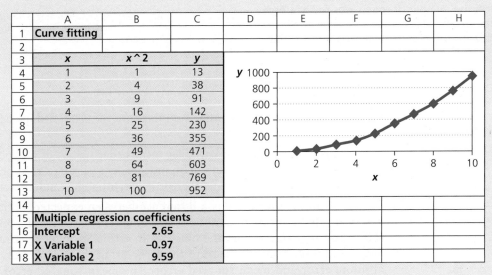

Figure 9.19 Using multiple regression for fitting a quadratic equation

The spreadsheet contents:

	A	B	C
1	Curve fitting		
2			
3	x	x^2	y
4	1	1	13
5	2	4	38
6	3	9	91
7	4	16	142
8	5	25	230
9	6	36	355
10	7	49	471
11	8	64	603
12	9	81	769
13	10	100	952
14			
15	Multiple regression coefficients		
16	Intercept	2.65	
17	X Variable 1	−0.97	
18	X Variable 2	9.59	

Review questions

9.19 What is the difference between non-linear regression and curve fitting?

9.20 'In practice, the more complex forms of curve fitting are used much less widely than basic linear regression.' Do you think this is true?

IDEAS IN PRACTICE   Hotel costing

Hotels are businesses that are widely bought and sold, so an obvious question asks how much a hotel is worth. There are several traditional ways of suggesting answers. One is income capitalisation, where the net operating income is translated into a corresponding capital value. Another approach uses market comparisons to see how much similar hotels have sold for and then to make subjective adjustments. A third approach looks for factors that influence the cost, and then builds a regression model based on these.

O'Neil used this third approach to study more than 300 hotel purchases, to find the factors that affect value and put them into an automated valuation model. He looked at the purchase cost per room and found that the four key factors were net operating income per room (NOI), average daily room price, number of rooms and occupancy

Ideas in practice continued

rate. A simple regression model relating the NOI to the hotel cost per room had a coefficient of determination of 0.791; when the daily room price was added, the coefficient rose to 0.892; when the number of rooms was added, the coefficient rose to 0.897; and when the occupancy rate was included the coefficient rose to 0.9.

It is not surprising that the NOI is the most significant factor, reflecting the link between capital cost and projected income. The hotel's average room price gave an indication of the quality of service; the number of rooms was really a proxy for the extent of facilities and services (such as restaurants, conference rooms, recreation facilities

and infrastructure); the occupancy rate suggests the utilisation of available facilities.

When this model was used to value the 57-room Hampton Inn in Ohio, with an NOI of $450,000, average daily room price of $76.81 and occupancy rate of 72.8 per cent, it suggested a price of $67,718 per room – or a total value of approximately $3,860,000. The hotel actually sold for $64,912 per room, within 5% of the estimated price.

Sources: O'Neil J., An automated valuation model for hotels, *Cornell Hotel & Restaurant Administration Quarterly*, August, 2004; www.entrepreneur.com.

CHAPTER REVIEW

This chapter has shown how to find and measure the relationships between variables.

- A relationship between two variables means that values of a dependent variable, y, are related to values of an independent variable, x. In practice, few relationships are perfect and there is inevitably some random noise.

- The noise means that there is a difference between expected values and observed values. The amount of noise determines the strength of a relationship – and we can consider the noise as an error. Stronger relationships have less noise. You can measure the error using the mean error, mean absolute error and mean squared error. The mean squared error is the most widely used.

- Linear regression finds the line of best fit through a set of data. This line is defined as the one that minimises the sum of squared errors. The main use of linear regression is to predict the value of a dependent variable for a known value of an independent variable.

- The coefficient of determination measures the proportion of the total variation from the mean explained by the regression line. A value close to 1 shows that the regression line gives a good fit, while a value close to zero shows a poor fit.

- Pearson's correlation coefficient shows how strong the linear relationship is between two variables. A value close to 1 or –1 shows a strong relationship, while a value close to zero shows a weak one. Spearman's coefficient gives a correlation for ranked data.

- Sometimes a dependent variable is related to several independent variables. Then multiple regression finds the best values for the constants a and b_i. Many packages do these calculations automatically, but the interpretation of results can be difficult.

- Sometimes relationships are clearly not linear – you can use curve fitting to find more complex functions through data.

CASE STUDY   Western General Hospital

Each term, the Western General Hospital accepts a batch of 50 new student nurses. Their training lasts for several years before they become state registered or state enrolled. The hospital invests a lot of money in nurse training, and it wants to make sure that this is used efficiently.

A continuing problem is the number of nurses who fail exams and do not complete their training. One suggestion for reducing this number is to improve recruitment and select only students who are more likely to complete the course. For instance, the hospital might look for relationships between students' likely performance in nursing exams and their performance in school exams. But nurses come from a variety of backgrounds and start training at different ages, so their performance at school may not be relevant. Other possible factors are age and number of previous jobs.

The following table shows some results for last term's nurses. Grades in exams have been converted to numbers (A = 5, B = 4 and so on), and average marks are given.

Nurse	Year of birth	Nursing grade	School grade	Number of jobs	Nurse	Year of birth	Nursing grade	School grade	Number of jobs
1	82	2.3	3.2	0	26	70	4.1	3.7	4
2	75	3.2	4.5	1	27	84	2.6	2.3	1
3	82	2.8	2.1	1	28	84	2.3	2.7	1
4	72	4.1	1.6	4	29	82	1.8	1.9	2
5	80	4.0	3.7	2	30	81	3.1	1.0	0
6	83	3.7	2.0	1	31	72	4.8	1.2	3
7	75	3.5	1.5	0	32	78	2.3	3.0	1
8	73	4.8	3.6	0	33	80	3.1	2.1	5
9	83	2.8	3.4	2	34	81	2.2	4.0	2
10	84	1.9	1.2	1	35	82	3.0	4.5	3
11	84	2.3	4.8	2	36	72	4.3	3.3	0
12	83	2.5	4.5	0	37	82	2.4	3.1	1
13	76	2.8	1.0	0	38	78	3.2	2.9	0
14	69	4.5	2.2	3	39	84	1.1	2.5	0
15	84	2.0	3.0	1	40	69	4.2	1.9	2
16	80	3.4	4.0	0	41	78	2.0	1.2	1
17	78	3.0	3.9	2	42	84	1.0	4.1	0
18	78	2.5	2.9	2	43	77	3.0	3.0	0
19	79	2.8	2.0	1	44	80	2.0	2.2	0
20	81	2.8	2.1	1	45	76	2.3	2.0	2
21	78	2.7	3.8	0	46	76	3.7	3.7	4
22	71	4.5	1.4	3	47	68	4.7	4.0	5
23	75	3.7	1.8	2	48	75	4.0	1.9	2
24	80	3.0	2.4	6	49	75	3.8	3.1	0
25	81	2.9	3.0	0	50	79	2.5	4.6	1

The hospital collected data on the number of nurses who did not finish training in the past 10 terms, with the following results.

Term	1	2	3	4	5	6	7	8	9	10
Number	4	7	3	6	9	11	10	15	13	17

Questions

■ Having collected this data, how can the hospital present it in a useful format that is clear and easy to understand?

■ Which factors can it use to predict nurses' grades? What other factors might be relevant?

■ What do you think the hospital should do next?

PROBLEMS

9.1 The productivity of a factory has been recorded over 10 months, together with forecasts made the previous month by the production manager, the foreman and the Management Services Department. Compare the accuracy of the three sets of forecasts.

Month	1	2	3	4	5	6	7	8	9	10
Productivity	22	24	28	27	23	24	20	18	20	23
Production manager	23	26	32	28	20	26	24	16	21	23
Foreman	22	28	29	29	24	26	21	21	24	25
Management Services	21	25	26	27	24	23	20	20	19	24

9.2 Find the line of best fit through the following data. How good is this fit?

x	10	19	29	42	51	60	73	79	90	101
y	69	114	163	231	272	299	361	411	483	522

9.3 Blaymount Amateur Dramatic Society is staging a play and wants to know how much to spend on advertising. Its objective is to attract as many people as possible, up to the hall capacity. For the past 11 productions their spending on advertising (in hundreds of pounds) and total audience are shown in the following table. If the hall capacity is now 300 people, how much should Blaymount spend on advertising?

Spending	3	5	1	7	2	4	4	2	6	6	4
Audience	200	250	75	425	125	300	225	200	300	400	275

9.4 Ten experiments were done to find the effects of bonus rates paid to the sales team. What is the line of best fit through the following results? How good is the fit?

% Bonus	0	1	2	3	4	5	6	7	8	9
Sales ('00s)	3	4	8	10	15	18	20	22	27	28

9.5 Monthly sales for Sengler Marketing for the past year are:

6 21 41 75 98 132 153 189 211 243 267 301

Use linear regression to forecast sales for the next year. How reliable are these figures?

9.6 Jamie O'Connor appraises his employees using the views of two managers. In one department the two managers rank staff as follows. How reliable does this scheme seem?

Person	A	B	C	D	E	F	G	H	I	J	K	L
Rank 1	5	10	12	4	9	1	3	7	2	11	8	6
Rank 2	8	7	10	1	12	2	4	6	5	9	11	3

9.7 A food company wanted to know if the amount of taste enhancer added to one of its products has any effect. It ran a test by adding eight different amounts and asking a panel of tasters to rank the results. Does there seem to be a relationship between the amount of enhancer and taste?

Test	A	B	C	D	E	F	G	H
Amount of enhancer	22	17	67	35	68	10	37	50
Rank	3	2	8	5	7	1	4	6

9.8 Use multiple regression to find the line of best fit through the following data. What does this tell you?

y	420	520	860	740	510	630	650	760	590	680
a	1	2	3	4	5	6	7	8	9	10
b	3	7	9	3	1	6	2	9	6	6
c	23	15	64	52	13	40	36	20	19	24
d	109	121	160	155	175	90	132	145	97	107

9.9 What is the best line through the following data?

X	1	2	3	4	5	6	7	8	9	10
Y	9	14	20	28	40	60	90	130	180	250

9.10 How could you fit a curve through the following points?

Time	1	2	3	4	5	6	7	8	9	10	11	12
Value	25	18	8	−6	−21	−31	−29	−24	−9	22	68	35

9.11 A company records sales of four products over a 10-month period. What can you say about these?

Month	1	2	3	4	5
P	24	36	45	52	61
Q	2,500	2,437	2,301	2,290	2,101
R	150	204	167	254	167
S	102	168	205	221	301

Month	6	7	8	9	10
P	72	80	94	105	110
Q	2,001	1,995	1,847	1,732	1,695
R	241	203	224	167	219
S	302	310	459	519	527

RESEARCH PROJECTS

9.1 The daily number of flights from Skorgaard Airport over a typical summer period are as follows:

24 23 25 24 27 29 32 30
35 34 34 39 41 40 38 46
41 51 48 46 41 57 56 62
61 62 68 74 80 81 76 80
93 82 88 91 95 99 97 98

Analyse these figures and forecast the future numbers of flights. How does this pattern compare with the numbers of flights from other airports?

9.2 Emilio Gaspin provides an information back-up service to industrial users. Over 19 typical months he records the following data. How useful would multiple regression be in analysing these results? In general, what problems are there likely to be with using multiple regression?

Month	Output	Shifts	Advertising	Bonuses	Faults
1	1,120	10	1,056	0	241
2	131	10	1,050	0	236
3	144	11	1,200	0	233
4	152	11	1,250	10	228
5	166	11	1,290	15	210
6	174	12	1,400	20	209
7	180	12	1,510	20	225
8	189	12	1,690	20	167
9	201	12	1,610	25	210
10	225	12	1,802	30	128
11	236	13	1,806	35	201
12	245	13	1,988	40	165
13	261	13	1,968	40	132
14	266	13	2,045	40	108
15	270	14	2,163	45	98
16	289	15	2,138	50	134
17	291	16	2,431	50	158
18	300	16	2,560	55	109
19	314	16	2,570	55	65

9.3 A Malaga tourist agency has been looking at the prices charged for hotel rooms in the city. They have collected the following data from a sample of hotels. What information can they get from this? What other data could they collect and analyse?

Cost (€)	Rating	Rooms	Location	Facilities	Meals	Staff
90	1	45	2	4	10	70
170	3	90	4	6	8	70
80	2	120	1	5	6	120
130	4	30	1	2	4	8
70	3	40	5	9	5	8
240	5	240	3	12	12	140
30	1	8	5	2	2	4
32	1	12	4	2	2	5
56	2	40	2	6	6	18
120	4	100	1	8	10	45
240	5	60	3	12	12	100
190	3	80	3	8	8	30
110	2	50	4	2	10	20
120	2	45	1	2	8	15
36	1	40	1	12	2	30
56	3	30	4	4	6	8

Sources of information

Further reading

There are some books specifically about regression, but they tend to get very complicated. It is generally better to look up the topic in books on forecasting (there are examples in the next chapter) or statistics (examples in Chapter 12). Some books specifically on regression are:

Betenuth C. and Betenuth G., *Examples for the Application of Linear Regression*, QED Books, 2005.

Fox J., *Applied Regression Analysis, Linear Models and Related Methods* (2nd edition), Sage Publications, London, 2008.

Kutner M.H., Nachsheim C.J. and Li W., *Applied Linear Regression Models*, McGraw-Hill, New York, 2010.

Montgomery D.C., Peck E.A. and Vining G.G., *An Introduction to Linear Regression Analysis*, John Wiley, Chichester, 2006.

Ragsdale C., *Spreadsheet Modelling and Decision Analysis* (5th edition), South-Western College Publishing, Cincinnati, OH, 2008.

Weisberg S., *Applied Linear Regression*, John Wiley, Chichester, 2005.

Winston W.L. and Albright S., *Spreadsheet Modelling and Applications*, Brooks Cole, Florence, KY, 2004.

Forecasting

Chapter outline

All decisions become effective at some point in the future. So managers should not base their decisions on present circumstances, but on conditions as they will be when the decisions become effective. These conditions must be forecast – and this suggests that forecasting is a core concern of every organisation. Unfortunately, there is no single best way to prepare forecasts, and managers have to choose the method that best suits their needs. This chapter describes a range of the most widely used approaches to forecasting.

After finishing this chapter you should be able to:

- appreciate the importance of forecasting to every organisation
- list different types of forecasting methods
- discuss the characteristics of judgemental forecasting
- use a variety of approaches to judgemental forecasting
- describe the characteristics of projective forecasting
- understand the importance of time series
- calculate errors and a tracking signal for forecasts
- forecast using simple averages, moving averages and exponential smoothing
- forecast time series with seasonality and trend.

Forecasting in organisations

In Chapter 8 we described a break-even analysis to find the number of units of a product that a firm must sell before it begins to make a profit. If sales of a new product are unlikely to reach the break-even point, the firm should not bother making it. Unfortunately, there is no way of knowing exactly what future sales will be – so the only option is to make a forecast. In other words, a central decision about products offered depends on a forecast of likely future sales. If you continue thinking along these lines, it becomes clear that virtually every decision made by managers depends on forecasts of future conditions. All their decisions become effective at some point in the future – so managers should not base decisions on current circumstances, but on the circumstances prevailing when their decisions become effective. Information about these future conditions comes from forecasts. If you have any doubts about the central role of forecasting in every organisation, try thinking of a decision that does not involve a forecast – or imagine the consequences when a forecast is wildly wrong!

Much of the following discussion talks of 'forecasting demand', but this is only a convenient label. In practice, virtually everything has to be forecast – demand, costs, availability of resources, weather, staff turnover, competitors' actions, exchange rates, taxes, inflation, energy consumption, traffic levels, customer complaints – and just about anything else.

Methods of forecasting

It would be reassuring to say 'a lot of work has been done on forecasting and the best method is . . .'. Unfortunately, we cannot do this. Because of the range of different things to be forecast and the conditions in which forecasts are needed, there is no single best method. In reality, there are many different ways of forecasting – sometimes one method works best, sometimes another method is better. As a result, managers have to look at the forecasting methods available for any specific decision and choose the most appropriate.

Unfortunately even when managers choose the best available method the result is rarely entirely accurate, and there are differences between the forecast and actual results. If this were not true we could rely on weather forecasts, predict the winner of a horse race, become rich by speculating on the stock market, not buy too much food for a dinner party, never arrive late for anything and so on.

> The aim of forecasting is to make the best possible predictions for future events, minimise errors and provide the most reliable information possible.

One classification of forecasting methods is based on the time in the future they cover. In particular:

- *long-term forecasts* look ahead several years – the time typically needed to build a new factory
- *medium-term forecasts* look ahead between three months and two years – the time typically needed to replace an old product with a new one
- *short-term forecasts* cover the next few weeks – describing the continuing demand for a product.

The time horizon affects the choice of forecasting method because of the availability and relevance of historical data, time available to make the

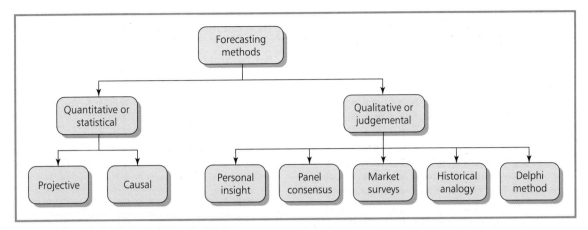

Figure 10.1 Classification of forecasting methods

forecast, cost involved, seriousness of errors, effort considered worthwhile and so on.

Another classification of methods draws a distinction between qualitative and quantitative approaches (as shown in Figure 10.1).

When a company is already making a product, it has records of past sales and knows the factors that affect them. Then it can use a quantitative method to forecast future demand. There are two ways of doing this:

- **Causal methods** analyse the effects of outside influences and use these to produce forecasts. The demand for mortgages might depend on the interest rate charged, so lenders could use the proposed interest rate to forecast likely demand. This is the approach of linear regression that we described in Chapter 9.
- **Projective methods** examine the pattern of past demand and extend this into the future. If demand in the past five weeks has been 10, 20, 30, 40 and 50, it seems reasonable to project this pattern into the future and suggest that demand in the next week will be 60.

Both of these methods need accurate, quantified data. But suppose that a company is introducing an entirely new product. There are no figures of past demand to project forward, and no one can say what factors really affect demand for a causal forecast. Because there is no reliable quantitative data, the company must use a qualitative forecast that relies on subjective assessments and opinions. Such methods are generally described as judgemental.

We described causal forecasting with regression in Chapter 9, so here we concentrate on the other methods, starting with qualitative or judgemental methods.

Review questions

10.1   Why do managers use forecasts?

10.2   'Forecasting is a specialised function, where experts use mathematical techniques to project historical trends.' Is this is true?

10.3   List three fundamentally different approaches to forecasting.

10.4   What factors should you consider when choosing a forecasting method?

IDEAS IN PRACTICE   Forecasting demand for new businesses

New businesses have a particularly difficult job in forecasting demand for their products. Often they simply give up and ask, 'Why bother forecasting at all – when the results may be little more than guesses, and even established businesses make mistakes?' Of course, without forecasts all decisions are effectively made in ignorance of conditions, giving no idea what to do, where to spend money, how much to make, what resources are needed, what the cash flows will be – or anything else.

Fastlinksolutions say that there are three fundamental concerns for new businesses making sales forecasts:

- *Value-based* – focusing on the production and sales levels that must be achieved to cover all costs. In particular, a business must calculate the sales and profit margins needed to at least break-even, and test if these are feasible.
- *Market-based* – using the result of market surveys to find likely sales levels. Then the business

has to confirm that these give a reasonable number of customers and level of income.
- *Resource-based* – to find the level of business that could be achieved with available resources. All businesses have limited resources and if the constraints are too tight they may prevent a business meeting its target output, taking advantage of opportunities or even covering costs.

For example, in a new restaurant, a value-based sales forecast would look at the profit margins needed to cover all costs, and see if this is in line with the current performance of local businesses. A market-based forecast would do a local survey to test likely customer levels, and check that this would give enough income. A resource-based forecast would look at the capacity limitations on the service and ensure that these are high enough to cover costs.

Source: www.fastlinksolutions.co.uk.

Judgemental forecasts

Suppose a company is about to market an entirely new product, or a medical team is considering a new type of organ transplant, or a board of directors is considering plans for 25 years in the future. In such circumstances there is no historical data that the company can use to make a quantitative forecast. This is either because there really is no data available or because there is some data but it is unreliable or irrelevant to the future. When managers have no numerical data they cannot use a quantitative forecasting method, and their only alternative is a judgemental forecast.

The key feature of judgemental forecasts is that they use opinions and subjective views of informed people. The most widely used methods are:

- personal insight
- panel consensus
- market surveys
- historical analogy
- the Delphi method.

Personal insight

This has a single expert who is familiar with the situation producing a forecast based on their own judgement. This is the most widely used forecasting method – and is the one that you should avoid. It relies entirely on one person's judgement – as well as their opinions, bias, objectives, prejudices, hidden agendas and ignorance. Sometimes personal insight gives good forecasts, but more often it gives very bad ones – and there are countless examples of experts being totally wrong. So its main weakness is unreliability. This may not matter for minor decisions, but when errors have serious consequences it is better to use a more dependable method.

Comparisons of forecasting methods consistently show that someone who is familiar with a situation, using their experience and knowledge, will produce *worse* forecasts than someone who knows nothing about the situation but uses a more formal method.

Panel consensus

A single expert can easily make mistakes, but collecting together a panel of experts and allowing them to talk freely and exchange ideas should lead to a more reliable consensus. If the panel works well, with open discussions and no secrecy or hidden agendas, it can reach a genuine consensus. On the other hand, there can be difficulties in combining the views of different experts when they cannot reach a consensus.

Although it is more reliable than one person's insight, panel consensus still has the major weakness that even experts make mistakes. There are also problems of group working, where 'he who shouts loudest gets his way', everyone tries to please the boss, some people do not speak well in groups and so on. Overall, panel consensus is an improvement on personal insight, but you should view results from either method with caution.

Market surveys

Even panels of experts may not have enough knowledge to make a convincing forecast. For instance, when a company is about to launch a new product they would be sensible to get the views of potential customers rather than appointed 'experts'. As we saw in Chapter 4, market surveys collect data from representative samples of customers and analyse this to show likely behaviour of the whole population.

Some market surveys give useful information, but they tend to be expensive and time-consuming. They can also be wrong because they rely on:

- identifying the right population
- choosing a sample of customers that accurately represents the whole population
- properly identifying and contacting the sample
- fair and unbiased data collection from the sample
- accurate analyses of the responses
- valid conclusions drawn from the analyses.

Historical analogy

When a company introduces a new product, it may have a similar product that it launched recently and can assume that demand will follow a similar pattern. For example, when a publisher introduces a new book, it forecasts likely sales from the demand for similar books that it published recently.

To use historical analogy, managers must have a product that is similar enough to the new one, that was launched recently and for which they have reliable information. In practice, it is difficult to get all of these – but there is often enough data to give reasonable guidelines.

The Delphi method

This is the most formal of the judgemental methods and has a well-defined procedure. A number of experts are contacted by post and each is given a questionnaire to complete – so data is collected from a group of experts away from problems of face-to-face discussions. The replies are analysed and summaries passed back to the experts – with everything done anonymously to avoid undue influence of status etc. Then each expert is asked to reconsider their original reply in the light of the summarised replies from others, and perhaps to adjust their responses. This process of modifying responses in the light of replies made by the rest of the group is repeated several times – usually between three and six. By this time, the range of opinions should have narrowed enough to help with decision-making.

We can illustrate this process using an example from offshore oil fields. A company wants to know when underwater inspections on platforms will be done entirely by robots rather than divers. To start the Delphi forecast, the company contacts a number of experts from various backgrounds including divers, technical staff from oil companies, ships' captains, maintenance engineers and robot designers. The overall problem is explained, and each expert is asked when they think robots will replace divers. The initial returns will probably give a wide range of dates from, say, 2015 to 2050 and these views are summarised and passed back to the group. Each expert is then asked if they would like to reassess their answer in the light of other replies. After repeating this several times, views might converge so that 80% of replies suggest a date between 2015 and 2020, and this is enough to help with planning.

10.5   What are judgemental forecasts?

10.6   List five types of judgemental forecast.

10.7   What are the main problems and benefits of judgemental forecasting?

IDEAS IN PRACTICE   Forecasting oil prices

In March 1996 the California Energy Commission[1] published the results of their latest Delphi forecasts of oil prices. For this they used a panel of 21 experts from government, academia, consulting firms, industry and financial institutions. They asked seven questions about the likely price of oil up to 2016 and the factors that would affect this price. Starting from a base price of $15.96 a barrel in 1995, the Delphi forecasts gave an expected price (in 1996 dollars) of $19.93 by 2016, with a low estimate (the tenth percentile) of $13.33 and a high estimate (the 90th percentile) of $30.00.

Ideas in practice continued

In 2004 the state of Alaska forecast that the price of oil would reach $57.30 in 2006 and then fall back to $25.50 beyond 2008.[2]

Perhaps the most authoritative view of oil prices comes from the US Government's Energy Information Administration that uses huge statistical models to forecast energy prices. In 2006, they suggested that the price of oil in 2016 would be $43.39 (in 2004 dollars) rising to $49.99 by 2030 (compared with the 2004 price of $46).[3]

In 2006 World in Turmoil[4] suggested that world oil production had already peaked and would move into a rapid decline. This would cause oil shortages and a rapid increase in the price, moving beyond $100 by 2008 and rapidly higher afterwards.

There seems little agreement even on the price of the world's most important commodity. The actual price of crude oil reached $70 a barrel in 2006, peaked at $107 in 2008, fell sharply and then returned to $75 in 2010.

Projective forecasts

Projective forecasting takes historical observations and uses them to forecast future values. If the average cost of motor insurance in the past four years has been €300, €350, €400 and €450 we can project this pattern into the future and forecast the likely cost for next year as €500. This approach ignores any external influences and looks only at past values of demand to suggest future values.

Time series

Projective forecasts often work with time series, which are series of observations taken at regular intervals – such as monthly unemployment figures, daily rainfall, weekly sales, quarterly profit and annual fuel consumption. When you have a time series it is always useful to draw a graph, and a simple scatter diagram shows any underlying patterns. The three most common patterns in time series (shown in Figure 10.2) are:

- *constant series* – with observations taking roughly the same value over time, such as annual rainfall
- *series with a trend* – with values either rising or falling steadily, such as a country's gross national product
- *seasonal series* – which have a cyclical component, such as the weekly sales of soft drinks.

If observations followed such simple patterns, there would be no problems with forecasting. Unfortunately, there are inevitably differences between actual observations and the underlying pattern. In particular, random noise is superimposed on an underlying pattern (illustrated in Figure 10.3) so that a constant series, for example, does not always take exactly the same value but is somewhere close. Then:

200 205 194 195 208 203 200 193 201 198

is a constant series of 200 with superimposed noise.

actual value = underlying pattern + random noise

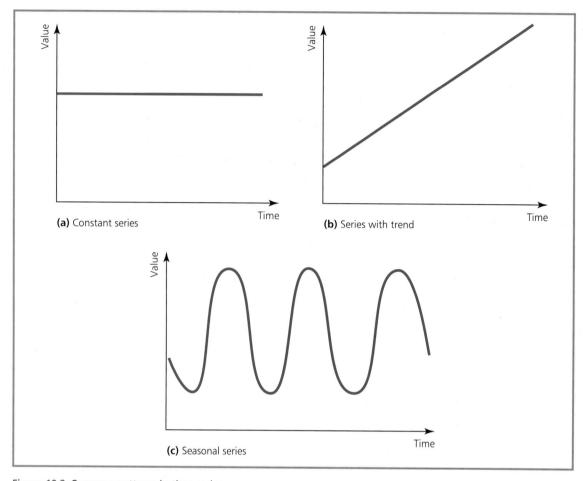

Figure 10.2 Common patterns in time series

We met the idea of noise when considering regression in Chapter 9, and it is these random effects that make forecasting so difficult. When there is little noise, forecasting is relatively easy and we can get good results, but when there is a lot of noise it hides the underlying pattern and forecasting becomes more difficult.

We can define the difference between a forecast value, or expected value, for a period and the value that actually occurs as an error. Then in each period:

E_t = error in the forecast in period t
   = actual observation in period t – forecast value

or $E_t = y_t - F_t$

where: F_t is the forecast for period t
and y_t is the value that actually occurs

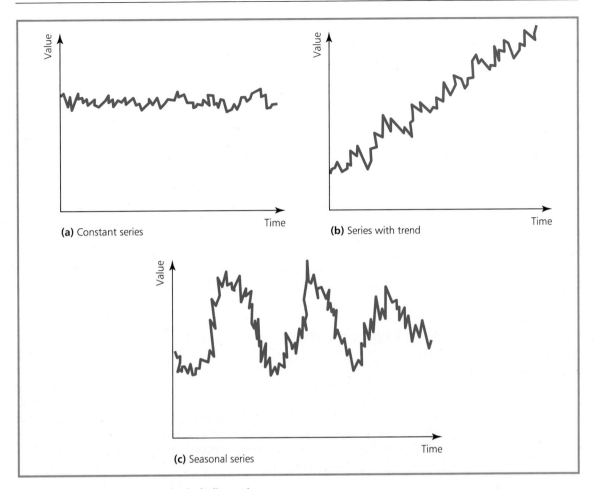

Figure 10.3 Patterns in time series including noise

Figure 10.4 shows this effect when there is an underlying trend, and the error in each observation is the vertical distance between the line and the actual observation.

Doing this calculation for each period allows us to calculate a mean error:

$$\text{mean error} = \frac{\Sigma E_t}{n} = \frac{\Sigma(y_t - E_t)}{n}$$

But we know that the mean error allows positive and negative errors to cancel, and data that has very large errors can have zero mean error. In the following table the demand pattern is clear, and the forecasts are obviously very poor.

Period, t	1	2	3	4
Observation, y_t	100	200	300	400
Forecast, F_t	0	0	0	1,000
Error, E_t	−100	−200	−300	600

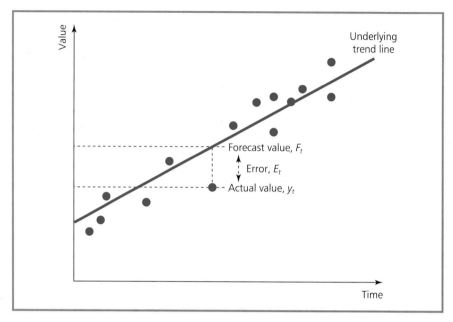

Figure 10.4 Errors in forecasts

Despite this, the mean error is zero. In reality, the mean error does not measure forecast accuracy, but measures bias. If the mean error is positive, the forecast is consistently too low; if the mean error is negative, the forecast is consistently too high.

The two alternatives for measuring forecast errors are the mean absolute error and the mean squared error:

$$\text{mean absolute error} = \frac{\Sigma |E_t|}{n} = \frac{\Sigma |y_t - F_t|}{n}$$

$$\text{mean squared error} = \frac{\Sigma (E_t)^2}{n} = \frac{\Sigma (y_t - F_t)^2}{n}$$

WORKED EXAMPLE 10.1

Two managers produce the following results for a time series. Which manager gets better results?

T	1	2	3	4	5
y_t	20	22	26	19	14
F_t by manager 1	17	23	24	22	17
F_t by manager 2	15	20	22	24	19

Solution

Manager 1 gives forecasts that are always nearer to actual demand than manager 2, so in this case the decision is easy. We can confirm this by calculating the errors.

Worked example 10.1 continued

Manager 1

T	1	2	3	4	5	Total	Mean
y_t	20	22	26	19	14	101	20.2
F_t	17	23	24	22	17	103	20.6
E_t	3	−1	2	−3	−3	−2	−0.4
$|E_t|$	3	1	2	3	3	12	2.4
$(E_t)^2$	9	1	4	9	9	32	6.4

■ The mean error is −0.4, showing that the forecasts are slightly biased, being an average of 0.4 too high.
■ The mean absolute error is 2.4, showing that forecasts are an average of 2.4 away from actual demand.
■ The mean squared error is 6.4, which does not have such a clear meaning but is useful for other analyses.

Manager 2

T	1	2	3	4	5	Total	Mean
y_t	20	22	26	19	14	101	20.2
F_t	15	20	22	24	19	100	20
E_t	5	2	4	−5	−5	1	0.2
$|E_t|$	5	2	4	5	5	21	4.2
$(E_t)^2$	25	4	16	25	25	95	19

■ The mean error is 0.2, showing that each forecast is slightly biased, being an average of 0.2 too low.
■ The mean absolute error is 4.2, so the forecast is an average of 4.2 away from actual demand.
■ The mean squared error is 19.0.

Manager 1 has lower mean absolute error and mean squared error, and is the better choice. Manager 2 has slightly less bias, measured by the mean error.

Simple averages

The four main methods of projective forecasting are using:

■ simple averages
■ moving averages
■ exponential smoothing
■ models for seasonality and trend.

Suppose you are going away on holiday and want to know the temperature at your destination. The easiest way of finding this is to look up records for past years and take an average. If your holiday starts on 1st July you could find the average temperature on 1st July over, say, the past 20 years. This is an example of forecasting using simple averages, where:

$$\text{forecast} = F_{t+1} = \frac{\Sigma y_t}{n}$$

where: t = time period
F_{t+1} = forecast for period $t + 1$
y_t = observation for period t
n = number of periods of historical data.

WORKED EXAMPLE 10.2

John Butler runs two dental surgeries, with the following numbers of patients visiting each over the past 5 weeks. Use simple averages to forecast the numbers of patients visiting in week 6. How accurate are the forecasts? What are the forecasts for week 24?

Week	1	2	3	4	5
Surgery 1	98	100	98	104	100
Surgery 2	140	66	152	58	84

Solution

Calculating the simple averages:

- Surgery 1: $F_6 = (\Sigma y_t) / 5 = 500 / 5 = 100$
- Surgery 2: $F_6 = (\Sigma y_t) / 5 = 500 / 5 = 100$

Although the forecasts are the same, there is clearly less noise in the figures for Surgery 1 than for Surgery 2, so you should expect smaller errors in this forecast and be more confident in the results.

Simple averages assume that the underlying pattern is constant, so the forecasts for week 24 are the same as the forecasts for week 6, that is 100.

Simple averages can give good forecasts for constant series, and they are easy to use and understand. But they do not work well when the underlying pattern changes. The problem is that older data tends to swamp the latest figures and the forecast is very slow to follow the changing pattern. Suppose that demand for an item has been constant at 100 units a week for the past 2 years (104 weeks). Simple averages give a forecast demand for week 105 of 100 units. But if the actual demand in week 105 suddenly rises to 200 units, simple averages give a forecast for week 106 of:

$$F_{106} = (104 \times 100 + 200) / 105$$
$$= 100.95$$

A rise in demand of 100 gives an increase of only 0.95 in the forecast. If demand continues at 200 units a week, following forecasts are $F_{107} = 101.89$, $F_{108} = 102.80$, $F_{109} = 103.70$, $F_{110} = 104.59$, ... etc.

The forecasts are rising to reflect the higher demand, but the response is very slow. Simple averages are so unresponsive that they only really work for constant series. In reality, very few time series are stable over long periods, so this restriction makes the method have limited value.

Moving averages

Patterns of demand tend to vary over time, so only a certain amount of historical data is relevant to future forecasts. The problem with simple averages is that old, out-of-date data tends to swamp newer, more relevant data. One way around this is to ignore old data and use only a few of the most recent observations – this is the principle of moving averages.

If you decide that only the last n observations are relevant, and you can ignore all data older than this, you can calculate a moving average forecast from:

$$F_{t+1} = \text{average of } n \text{ most recent observations}$$
$$= \frac{\text{latest demand} + \text{next latest} + \ldots + n\text{th latest}}{n}$$
$$= \frac{y_t + y_{t-1} + \ldots + y_{t-n+1}}{n}$$

WORKED EXAMPLE 10.3

Epsilan Court Co. has recorded the numbers of customer complaints each month:

Month, t	1	2	3	4	5	6	7
Complaints, y_t	135	130	125	135	115	80	105

Continuously changing conditions mean that any data over three months old is no longer reliable. Use a moving average to forecast the number of complaints for the future.

Solution

Only data more recent than three months is reliable, so we can use a 3-month moving average to forecast. Consider the situation at the end of month 3, when we can calculate the forecast for month 4 as:

$$F_4 = (y_1 + y_2 + y_3) / 3 = (135 + 130 + 125) / 3$$
$$= 130$$

At the end of month 4 we know that the actual number is 135, so the forecast for month 5 is:

$$F_5 = (y_2 + y_3 + y_4) / 3 = (130 + 125 + 135) / 3$$
$$= 130$$

Similarly,

$$F_6 = (y_3 + y_4 + y_5) / 3 = (125 + 135 + 115) / 3 = 125$$
$$F_7 = (y_4 + y_5 + y_6) / 3 = (135 + 115 + 80) / 3 = 110$$
$$F_8 = (y_5 + y_6 + y_7) / 3 = (115 + 80 + 105) / 3 = 100$$

In this example, you can see that the forecast is clearly responding to changes, with a high number of complaints moving the forecast upwards, and a low number moving it downwards. This ability of a forecast to respond to changing demand is important. We want a forecast to respond to real changes – but not to follow random variations in the data. With most forecasting methods we can adjust the speed of response, or sensitivity. In a moving average we do this by altering n, the number of periods averaged. A high value of n takes the average of a large number of observations and the forecast is unresponsive – it smoothes out random variations, but may not follow genuine changes. On the other hand, a low value of n takes the average of a few observations giving a responsive forecast that follows genuine changes, but it may be too sensitive to random fluctuations. We need a compromise between these two and this often means a value of n around six periods.

WORKED EXAMPLE 10.4

Column B in Figure 10.5 shows the monthly demand for a product. Use moving averages of three, six and nine months to give forecasts one month ahead.

Solution

Figure 10.5 also shows the calculations for moving average forecasts. With a 3-month moving average (that is $n = 3$), the earliest forecast we can make is for month 4, with $F_4 = (y_1 + y_2 + y_3) / 3$. Similarly, the earliest forecasts for 6- and 9-month moving averages are for F_7 and F_{10} respectively.

You can see from the graphs that for the first 10 months the pattern is fairly stable. All three forecasts do reasonably well here, smoothing out variations and following the underlying trends. The 3-month moving average follows changes quite quickly, while the 9-month moving average is most stable. This is clearer after month 10 when there is a rising trend, and now the 3-month moving average is much quicker to respond, while the 9-month moving average is least responsive.

Worked example 10.4 continued

	A	B	C	D	E	F	G	H
1	**Moving averages**							
2								
3	**Month**	**Demand**	**Forecasts**					
4			*n* = 3	*n* = 6	*n* = 9			
5	1	16						
6	2	13						
7	3	11						
8	4	15	13.33					
9	5	17	13.00					
10	6	14	14.33					
11	7	12	15.33	14.33				
12	8	15	14.33	13.67				
13	9	10	13.67	14.00				
14	10	12	12.33	13.83	13.67			
15	11	18	12.33	13.33	13.22			
16	12	21	13.33	13.50	13.78			
17	13	25	17.00	14.67	14.89			
18	14	30	21.33	16.83	16.00			
19	15	28	25.33	19.33	17.44			
20	16	26	27.67	22.33	19.00			
21	17	34	28.00	24.67	20.56			
22	18	36	29.33	27.33	22.67			
23	19		32.00	29.83	25.56			
24								

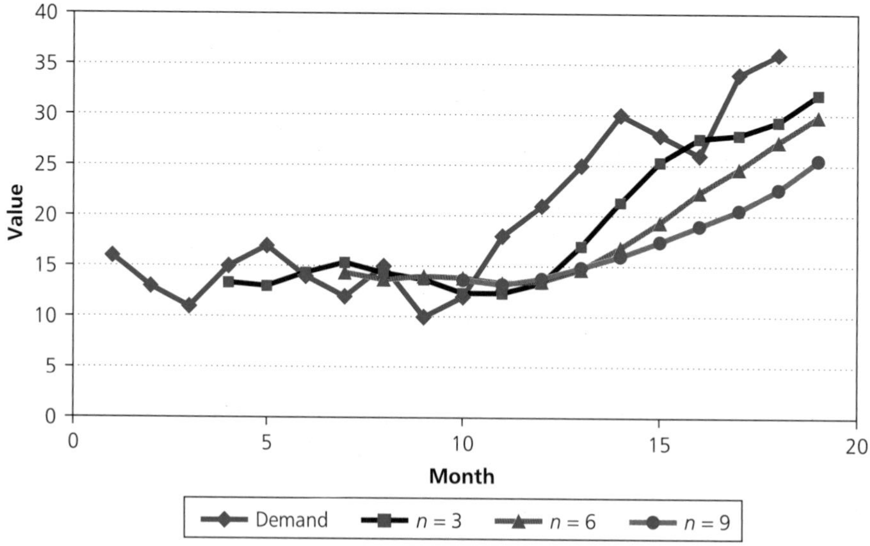

Figure 10.5 Moving average forecasts with different periods

You can see from Worked example 10.4 that moving averages give good results for stable patterns, but they tend to fall behind trends. However, they have a very useful property for data with strong seasonal variations – when you choose *n* equal to the number of periods in a season, a moving average will completely deseasonalise the data. You can see this effect in Worked example 10.5.

WORKED EXAMPLE 10.5

Use a moving average with two, four and six periods to calculate the forecasts one period ahead for this set of data.

Quarter	1	2	3	4	5	6	7	8	9	10	11	12
Demand	100	50	20	150	110	55	25	140	95	45	30	145

Solution

This data has a clear seasonal pattern, with a peak in the fourth quarter of every year. Figure 10.6 shows the moving averages and you can clearly see the patterns. The moving averages with both $n = 2$ and $n = 6$ have responded to the peaks and troughs of demand, but neither has got the timing right – both forecasts lag behind demand. As you would expect, the 2-month moving average is much more responsive than the 6-month one. But the most interesting result is the 4-month moving average, which has completely deseasonalised the data.

Although moving averages overcome some of the problems of simple averages, the method still has defects, including:

- it gives all recent observations the same weight
- it only works well with constant time series – as we have seen, it lags behind trends and either removes seasonal factors or gets the timing wrong
- it needs a lot of historical data to update the forecast
- the choice of *n* is often arbitrary
- there is a distinct point at which information is reclassified as valueless.

We can overcome the first of these problems by assigning different weights to observations. For example, a three-period moving average gives equal weight to the last three observations, so each is given a weight of 0.33. We can adjust these weights to put more emphasis on later results, perhaps using:

$$F_4 = 0.2 \times y_1 + 0.3 \times y_2 + 0.5 \times y_3$$

In practice, it is difficult to assign valid weights, and a more convenient approach to changing the weights uses exponential smoothing.

Worked example 10.5 continued

	A	B	C	D	E	F	G	H
1	Moving averages							
2								
3								
4	Year	Quarter	Demand	Forecasts				
5				$n = 2$	$n = 4$	$n = 6$		
6	1	1	100					
7		2	50					
8		3	20	75.0				
9		4	150	35.0				
10	2	1	110	85.0	80.00			
11		2	55	130.0	82.50			
12		3	25	82.5	83.75	80.83		
13		4	140	40.0	85.00	68.33		
14	3	1	95	82.5	82.50	83.33		
15		2	45	117.5	78.75	95.83		
16		3	30	70.0	76.25	78.33		
17		4	145	37.5	77.75	65.00		
18	4	1		73.3	78.75	80.00		
19								
20								

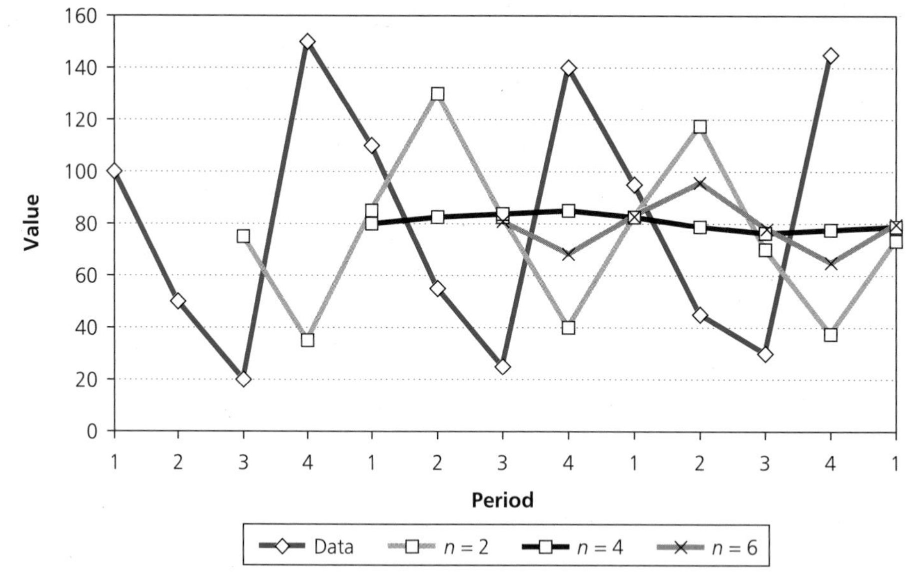

Figure 10.6 Using a moving average to deseasonalise data

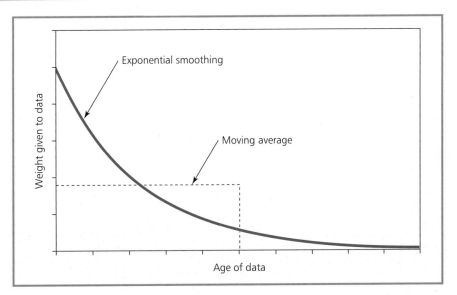

Figure 10.7 Weights given to data with exponential smoothing and moving average

Exponential smoothing

Exponential smoothing is based on the idea that as data gets older it becomes less relevant and should be given less weight. In particular, it gives an exponentially declining weight to observations (as shown in Figure 10.7). You might think it is difficult to organise this weighting, but in practice we can do it by using the latest observation to update a previous forecast. The calculation for this takes a proportion, α, of the latest observation and adds a proportion, $1 - \alpha$, of the previous forecast (α is the Greek letter 'alpha').

new forecast = $\alpha \times$ latest observation + $(1 - \alpha) \times$ last forecast

$$F_{t+1} = \alpha y_t + (1 - \alpha)F_t$$

Here α is a **smoothing constant** that typically has a value between 0.1 and 0.2. This determines the sensitivity of the forecast.

Exponential smoothing adds a part of the latest observation to a forecast, so it automatically responds to changing values. Suppose a forecast is optimistic and suggests a value of 200 for an observation that actually turns out to be 180. Taking a value of $\alpha = 0.2$, the forecast for the next period is:

$$F_{t+1} = \alpha y_t + (1 - \alpha)F_t = 0.2 \times 180 + (1 - 0.2) \times 200$$
$$= 196$$

The method notices the optimistic forecast and adjusts the forecast for the next period downwards. If we rearrange the exponential smoothing formula:

$$F_{t+1} = \alpha y_t + (1 - \alpha)F_t$$
$$= F_t + \alpha(y_t - F_t)$$

We define the error in a forecast as $E_t = y_t - F_t$, so the forecast is:

$$F_{t+1} = F_t + \alpha E_t$$

In other words, exponential smoothing takes the error in the last forecast, and adds a proportion of this to get the next forecast. The larger the error in the last forecast, the greater is the adjustment to the next forecast.

Exponential smoothing works by updating a previous forecast, so it needs an initial starting value. In principle, you can choose any convenient value for this, but to reduce early errors it should be a reasonable estimate. For instance, you could use the average demand in recent periods.

WORKED EXAMPLE 10.6

Use exponential smoothing with $\alpha = 0.2$ and an initial value of $F_1 = 170$ to get forecasts for this time series.

Month	1	2	3	4	5	6	7	8
Demand	178	180	156	150	162	158	154	132

Solution

We know that $F_1 = 170$ and $\alpha = 0.2$. Substituting these values gives a forecast for the second period:

$$F_2 = \alpha y_1 + (1 - \alpha)F_1 = 0.2 \times 178 + 0.8 \times 170$$
$$= 171.6$$

Then substituting for F_2 gives:

$$F_3 = \alpha y_2 + (1 - \alpha)F_2 = 0.2 \times 180 + 0.8 \times 171.6$$
$$= 173.3$$

$$F_4 = \alpha y_3 + (1 - \alpha)F_3 = 0.2 \times 156 + 0.8 \times 173.3$$
$$= 169.8$$

and so on, giving these results.

Month, t	1	2	3	4	5	6	7	8	9
Demand, y_t	178	180	156	150	162	158	154	132	
Forecast, F_t	170	171.6	173.3	169.8	165.8	165	163.6	161.7	155.8

It may not be obvious that the exponential smoothing calculations actually do give less weight to data as it gets older. However, we can demonstrate this by taking an arbitrary value for α, say 0.2. Then we know that:

$$F_{t+1} = 0.2y_t + 0.8F_t$$

Substituting $t - 1$ for t gives:

$$F_t = 0.2y_{t-1} + 0.8F_{t-1}$$

and substituting this in the equation for F_{t+1} gives:

$$F_{t+1} = 0.2y_t + 0.8 \times (0.2y_{t-1} + 0.8F_{t-1})$$
$$= 0.2y_t + 0.16y_{t-1} + 0.64F_{t-1}$$

This version now includes both y_t and y_{t-1}. But we can go further because we know that:

$$F_{t-1} = 0.2y_{t-2} + 0.8F_{t-2}$$

so we can substitute this into the equation for F_{t+1} and get:

$$F_{t+1} = 0.2y_t + 0.16y_{t-1} + 0.64 \times (0.2y_{t-2} + 0.8F_{t-2})$$
$$= 0.2y_t + 0.16y_{t-1} + 0.128y_{t-2} + 0.512F_{t-2}$$

We could carry on with this, but it is clear that the equation actually includes all previous demands, and puts progressively less weight on each as it gets older. If you do the calculations you can find that with a smoothing constant of α equal to 0.2, the weights are:

Age of data	1	2	3	4	5	6	7
Weight	0.2	0.16	0.128	0.1024	0.08192	0.065536	0.0524288

The choice of α is important because it sets the balance between the previous forecast and the latest observation – and hence the sensitivity of the forecasts. A high value of α, say more than 0.3, gives a responsive forecast; a low value, say 0.05 to 0.1, gives an unresponsive forecast. Again, we want a compromise between forecasts that are too sensitive and follow random fluctuations, and ones that are not sensitive enough and do not follow real patterns. A useful way of achieving this is to test several values for α over a trial period, and choose the one that gives smallest errors.

You can monitor the performance of a forecast using a tracking signal. This will show whether results continue to be good, or they are getting worse and it is time to take some remedial action. For instance, you can monitor the mean absolute error and when it gets too big adjust the value of α. A more informative signal than the mean absolute error is defined as:

$$\text{tracking signal} = \frac{\text{sum of errors}}{\text{mean absolute error}}$$

A good forecast is likely to have as many positive errors as negative ones, so these should cancel giving a sum around zero. While the tracking signal remains close to zero, the forecasts remain good – but if it increases to, say, 2.5 the errors are getting bigger and some remedial action is needed. For this you might change the value of α or make more radical changes.

WORKED EXAMPLE 10.7

Remko van Rijn collected the demand figures shown in Figure 10.8. Use an initial forecast of 500 to compare exponential smoothing forecasts with different values of α.

Solution

You can start the calculations at the end of month 1, and taking a value of $\alpha = 0.1$ gives:

$$F_2 = \alpha y_1 + (1 - \alpha)F_1 = 0.1 \times 470 + 0.9 \times 500$$
$$= 497$$

Then

$$F_3 = \alpha y_2 + (1 - \alpha)F_2 = 0.1 \times 510 + 0.9 \times 497$$
$$= 498.3$$

When $\alpha = 0.2$ you get:

$$F_2 = \alpha y_1 + (1 - \alpha)F_1 = 0.2 \times 470 + 0.8 \times 500$$
$$= 494$$

Then

$$F_3 = \alpha y_2 + (1 - \alpha)F_2 = 0.2 \times 510 + 0.8 \times 494$$
$$= 497.2$$

Continuing these calculations gives the results in Figure 10.8.

You can see that demand is relatively stable for the first six months, and there is a sharp rise in month 7. The graph shows how differing values of α respond to this. All values follow the steady pattern well, and they all move upwards with the step in demand – but higher values of α make this adjustment more quickly and give a more responsive forecast. Eventually, all forecasts would home in on the new level of demand.

Worked example 10.7 continued

	A	B	C	D	E	F	G	H
1	**Exponential smoothing**							
2								
3			Forecast					
4	**Month**	**Demand**	$\alpha = 0.1$	$\alpha = 0.2$	$\alpha = 0.3$	$\alpha = 0.4$		
5	1	470	500.0	500.0	500.0	500.0		
6	2	510	497.0	494.0	491.0	488.0		
7	3	460	498.3	497.2	496.7	496.8		
8	4	490	494.5	489.8	485.7	482.1		
9	5	520	494.0	489.8	487.0	485.2		
10	6	460	496.6	495.8	496.9	499.1		
11	7	1500	493.0	488.7	485.8	483.5		
12	8	1450	593.7	690.9	790.1	890.1		
13	9	1550	679.3	842.8	988.1	1114.1		
14	10	1500	766.4	984.2	1156.6	1288.4		
15	11	1480	839.7	1087.4	1259.6	1373.1		
16	12	1520	903.8	1165.9	1325.8	1415.8		
17	13	1500	965.4	1236.7	1384.0	1457.5		
18	14	1490	1018.8	1289.4	1418.8	1474.5		
19	15	1500	1066.0	1329.5	1440.2	1480.7		
20	16		1109.4	1363.6	1458.1	1488.4		

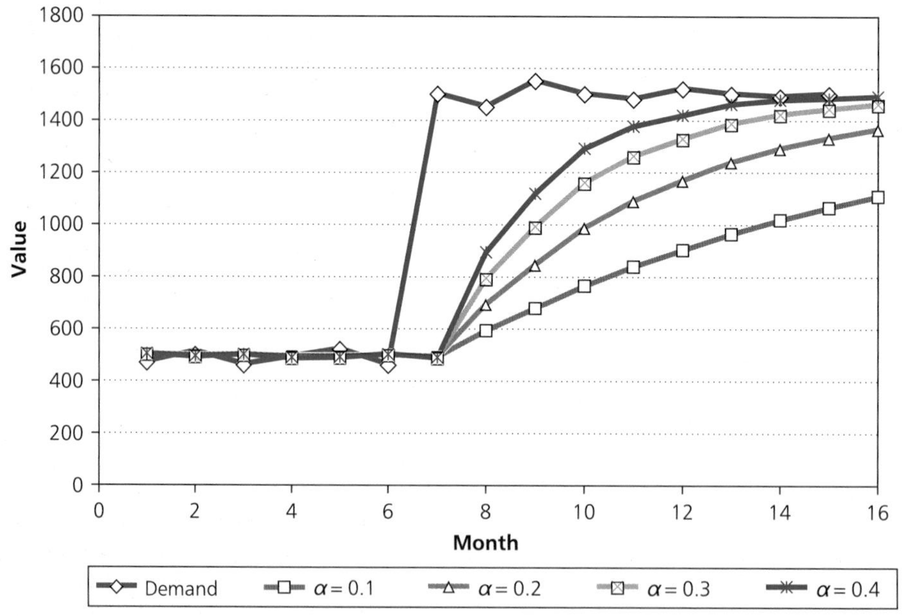

Figure 10.8 Exponential smoothing with varying values of alpha

10.8   Why do virtually all forecasts contain errors?

10.9   How would you compare the results from two forecasting methods?

10.10 Why are simple averages of limited use for forecasting?

10.11 How can you make a moving average forecast more responsive?

10.12 What is the drawback with a responsive forecast?

10.13 How can you deseasonalise data?

10.14 Why is the forecasting method called 'exponential smoothing'?

10.15 How can you make exponential smoothing more responsive?

IDEAS IN PRACTICE   SaskPower

In practice, it is often very difficult to get good forecasts – as you can see with people trying to forecast the winner of a horse race, lottery numbers, price of oil, interest rates or the weather.

One of the most difficult problems of forecasting is the demand for electricity. Electricity cannot be stored – except in very small quantities using batteries – so the supply from power stations and generators must exactly match the total demand. Any shortages in electricity give power cuts, which customers do not accept, while excess capacity wastes expensive resources.

In Saskatchewan, Canada the main supplier of electricity is SaskPower. They run three coal-fired power stations, seven hydro-electric, five natural gas and two wind farms – along with joint ventures – to generate 3.3 gigawatts of electricity for their half-million customers. The long-term demand for electricity is rising so SaskPower has to build enough capacity to meet this increase. Planning and building major facilities takes many years, so decisions are based on forecast demand 20 or more years in the future.

In the shorter term, demand for electricity follows an annual cycle, with demand higher in winter when people turn on their heating. There are also short, irregular periods of especially high demand during very cold spells. There are weekly cycles, with lower demand at weekends when industry is not working so intensely. On top of this there are daily cycles with lighter demand during the night when most people are asleep. Finally, there are irregular peaks during the day, perhaps corresponding to breaks in television programmes when people turn on electric coffee pots and kettles.

Power stations need 'warming-up' before they start supplying electricity, so a stable demand would make operations much easier. In practice, though, they have to forecast demands with long-term trend, annual cycle, short-term peak, weekly cycle, daily cycle and short-term variations.

Source: www.saskpower.com.

Forecasts with seasonality and trend

The methods we have described so far give good results for constant time series, but they need adjusting for other patterns. The easiest way of doing this is to divide the underlying pattern into separate components, and forecast each component separately. Then we get the final forecast by recombining the separate components. To be specific, we assume that an observation is made up of three components:

- *trend* (T) – the long-term direction of a time series, typically a steady upward or downward movement.
- *seasonal factor* (S) – the regular variation around the trend, which shows the variation in demand over a year or some other period.
- *residual* (R) – the random noise that we cannot explain properly.

Adding these three components gives an 'additive model' that assumes that an observation, y, is:

$$y = T + S + R$$

The seasonal factor, S, is an amount we add to the trend to allow for the season. If summer sales are 100 units higher than the trend, S has a value of 100; if winter sales are 100 units lower than the trend, S has a value of -100.

This additive model is easy to organise but it can underestimate variations, particularly when there is a significant trend. Then it is better to use indices for seasonal variations and put these into a 'multiplicative model' where:

$$y = T \times S \times R$$

If summer sales are 50% higher than the trend, S has a value of 1.5; if winter sales are 50% lower than the trend, S has a value of 0.5. Because we do not know the random elements, R, we cannot include this in forecasts, which become:

- Additive model: $F = T + S$
- Multiplicative model: $F = T \times S$

WORKED EXAMPLE 10.8

(a) What is the forecast for an additive model where the trend is 20 and the seasonal factor is 5?

(b) What is the forecast for a multiplicative model where the trend is 20 and the seasonal index is 1.25?

Solution

(a) The additive model forecasts by adding the factors, giving:

$$F = T + S = 20 + 5 = 25$$

(b) The multiplicative model forecasts by multiplying the factors, giving:

$$F = T \times S = 20 \times 1.25 = 25$$

The multiplicative model gives better results when there is a trend, so this is more widely used. We will describe the details of this and remember that the additive model is very similar. The steps needed for this forecast are:

1 Deseasonalise historical data and find the underlying trend, T.
2 Find the seasonal indices, S.
3 Use the calculated trend and seasonal indices to forecast future values, using $F = T \times S$.

Finding the underlying trend

There are two ways of deseasonalising data to find the trend, T, both of which we have already met:

- linear regression with time as the independent variable
- moving averages with a period equal to the length of a season.

If the trend is clearly linear, regression is probably better becasue it gives more information; if the trend is not so clear, moving averages may be better.

WORKED EXAMPLE 10.9

Find the deseasonalised trend in the following set of observations using:

(a) linear regression
(b) moving averages.

Period	1	2	3	4	5	6	7	8	9	10	11	12
Observation	291	320	142	198	389	412	271	305	492	518	363	388

Solution

(a) Figure 10.9 shows a spreadsheet that finds the line of best fit – the deseasonalised trend line – as:

$$observation = 223.41 + 18.05 \times period$$

You can confirm this result by doing the calculations: $n = 12$, $\Sigma x = 78$, $\Sigma y = 4{,}089$, $\Sigma x^2 = 650$, $\Sigma(xy) = 29{,}160$. Substituting these in the standard linear regression equations gives:

$$b = \frac{n\Sigma(xy) - \Sigma x \Sigma y}{n\Sigma x^2 - (\Sigma x)^2}$$

$$= \frac{12 \times 29{,}160 - 78 \times 4{,}089}{12 \times 650 - 78 \times 78}$$

$$= 18.05$$

$$a = \bar{y} - b \times \bar{x} = 4{,}089 / 12 - 18.05 \times 78 / 12$$
$$= 223.41$$

Substituting values for the period into this equation gives the deseasonalised trend shown in column C. The deseasonalised value for period 1 is $223.41 + 1 \times 18.05 = 241.46$, and so on.

One point about this regression line is that the coefficient of determination is only 0.35. This is because a lot of the variation is explained not by the trend, but by the seasonality. When using linear regression to deseasonalise data, a low coefficient of determination does not necessarily mean that the results are poor.

(b) You can see from Figure 10.9 that the observations have a season that is four periods long, and we have data for three complete cycles. This means that we can also deseasonalise the data by using a four-period moving average. However, there is an immediate problem; when we find the average values, they occur at the average times. In other words, taking the first four periods gives an average value of $(291 + 320 + 142 + 198) / 4 = 237.75$, which occurs at the average time of $(1 + 2 + 3 + 4) / 4 = 2.5$. In other words, it occurs halfway through a period. Whenever a season has an even number of periods, we have to work with 'half periods' (but obviously not when the season has an odd number of periods). Figure 10.10 shows a spreadsheet of the four-period moving averages, and the times at which they occur.

Now we have to return these deseasonalised values that occur halfway through periods to values for whole periods. The easiest way of doing this is to take the deseasonalised value for a period as the average of the two values either side of it. Then the deseasonalised value for period 3 is the average of the deseasonalised values at times 2.5 and 3.5, or $(237.75 + 262.25) / 2 = 250$. Repeating this calculation gives the deseasonalised values for periods 3 to 10, shown in column D.

Unfortunately, we now have deseasonalised data for only eight periods, rather than the original 12. This is just enough to find the patterns, but it gives another reason why it is generally better to use regression. The two methods give similar – but not identical – results.

Worked example 10.9 continued

	A	B	C	D	E	F	G
1	**Deseasonalised trend**						
2							
3	**Period**	**Observation**	**Deseasonalised trend**		SUMMARY OUTPUT		
4	1	291	241.46				
5	2	320	259.51		Regression statistics		
6	3	142	277.57		Multiple R	0.59	
7	4	198	295.62		R Square	0.35	
8	5	389	313.67		Adjusted R Square	0.28	
9	6	412	331.72		Standard error	93.14	
10	7	271	349.78		Observations	12	
11	8	305	367.83				
12	9	492	385.88				
13	10	518	403.93		Coefficients		
14	11	363	421.99		Intercept	223.41	
15	12	388	440.04		X Variable 1	18.05	
16							

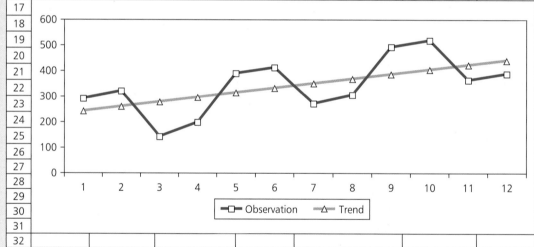

Figure 10.9 Deseasonalising data with linear regression

Worked example 10.9 continued

	A	B	C	D	E	F	G
1	**Deseasonalised trend**						
2							
3	**Period**	**Observation**	**4-period moving average**	**Deseasonalised values**			
4	1	291					
5	1.5						
6	2	320					
7	2.5		237.75				
8	3	142		250.00			
9	3.5		262.25				
10	4	198		273.75			
11	4.5		285.25				
12	5	389		301.38			
13	5.5		317.50				
14	6	412		330.88			
15	6.5		344.25				
16	7	271		357.13			
17	7.5		370.00				
18	8	305		383.25			
19	8.5		396.50				
20	9	492		408.00			
21	9.5		419.50				
22	10	518		429.88			
23	10.5		440.25				
24	11	363					
25	11.5						
26	12	388					
27							

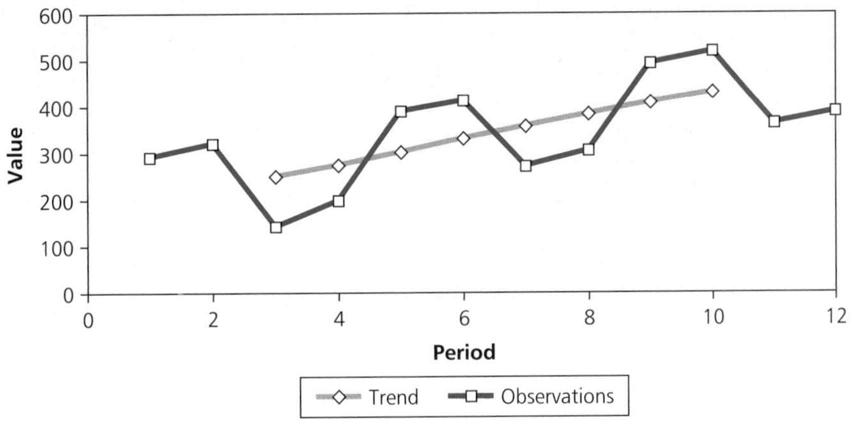

Figure 10.10 Deseasonalising data with moving averages

Finding the seasonal indices

In multiplicative models, seasonal variations are measured by seasonal indices, S. These are defined as the amounts by which deseasonalised values are multiplied to get seasonal values.

$$\text{seasonal index, } S = \frac{\text{seasonal value}}{\text{deseasonalised value}}$$

Suppose a newspaper sells an average of 1,000 copies a day in a town, but this rises to 2,000 copies on Saturday and falls to 500 copies on Monday and Tuesday. The deseasonalised value is 1,000, the seasonal index for Saturday is 2,000 / 1,000 = 2.0, the seasonal indices for Monday and Tuesday are 500 / 1,000 = 0.5, and the seasonal indices for other days are 1,000 / 1,000 = 1.0.

WORKED EXAMPLE 10.10

Worked example 10.9 found the deseasonalised trend using linear regression. What is the seasonal index for each period?

Solution

Figure 10.11 shows the actual observations and the deseasonalised trend values from the regression in columns B and C. To find the seasonal index for each period, you divide the actual observation by the trend value. For example, period 4 has an actual observation of 198 and a deseasonalised value of 295.62, so the seasonal index = 198/295.62 = 0.67. Repeating these calculations for other periods gives the indices in column D.

Each index is affected by noise in the data, so it is only an approximation. But if you take several complete seasons, you can find average indices that are more reliable. The graphs in Figures 10.9

	A	B	C	D	E	F
1	Seasonal indices					
2						
3	Period	Observation	Deseasonalised trend value	Seasonal index	Period in season	Average seasonal index
4	1	291	241.46	1.205	1	1.240
5	2	320	259.51	1.233	2	1.252
6	3	142	277.57	0.512	3	0.716
7	4	198	295.62	0.670	4	0.794
8	5	389	313.67	1.240	1	1.240
9	6	412	331.72	1.242	2	1.252
10	7	271	349.78	0.775	3	0.716
11	8	305	367.83	0.829	4	0.794
12	9	492	385.88	1.275	1	1.240
13	10	518	403.93	1.282	2	1.252
14	11	363	421.99	0.860	3	0.716
15	12	388	440.04	0.882	4	0.794
16						

Figure 10.11 Calculating seasonal indices

Worked example 10.10 continued

and 10.10 clearly show that there are four periods in a season – so you need to calculate four seasonal indices. Then periods 1, 5 and 9 are the first periods in consecutive seasons, and you can find an average index of (1.205 + 1.240 + 1.275) / 3 = 1.240. Then periods 2, 6 and 10 are the second periods in consecutive seasons, and so on. The average indices for all the periods in a season are:

- first period in a season: (1.205 + 1.240 + 1.275) / 3 = 1.240
- second period in a season: (1.233 + 1.242 + 1.282) / 3 = 1.252
- third period in a season: (0.512 + 0.775 + 0.860) / 3 = 0.716
- fourth period in a season: (0.670 + 0.829 + 0.882) / 3 = 0.794

Making forecasts

Now we have both the trend and seasonal indices, and can start forecasting. For this we:

1 Project the trend into the future to find the deseasonalised values.
2 Multiply this by the appropriate seasonal index.

WORKED EXAMPLE 10.11

Forecast values for periods 13 to 17 for the time series in Worked example 10.9.

Solution

We found the equation for the underlying trend to be:

value = 223.41 + 18.05 × period

Substituting values for future periods into this equation gives deseasonalised values. For period 13 the deseasonalised trend is 223.41 + 13 × 18.05 = 458.06. We also know that period 13 is the first period in a season, and the seasonal index is 1.240. Multiplying the deseasonalised trend by the seasonal index gives the forecast for period 13:

forecast = 458.06 × 1.240 = 568

Repeating this calculation for the other periods gives these forecasts.

- *Period 14*

    deseasonalised trend = 223.41 + 18.05 × 14
                                    = 476.11
    seasonal index = 1.252 (second period in a season)
    forecast = 476.11 × 1.252
                    = 596

- *Period 15*

    deseasonalised trend = 223.41 + 18.05 × 15
                                    = 494.16
    seasonal index = 0.716 (third period in a season)
    forecast = 494.16 × 0.716
                    = 354

- *Period 16*

    deseasonalised trend = 223.41 + 18.05 × 16
                                    = 512.21
    seasonal index = 0.794 (fourth period in a season)
    forecast = 512.21 × 0.794
                    = 407

- *Period 17*

    deseasonalised trend = 223.41 + 18.05 × 17
                                    = 530.26
    seasonal index = 1.240 (first period in a season)
    forecast = 530.26 × 1.240
                    = 658

WORKED EXAMPLE 10.12

Forecast values for the next four periods of this time series:

T	1	2	3	4	5	6	7	8
Y	986	1,245	902	704	812	1,048	706	514

Solution

For this we have to combine all the steps for forecasting, finding the deseasonalised trend, calculating a seasonal index for each period, projecting the trend and then using the indices to get a forecast.

If you draw a graph of the data (shown in Figure 10.12), you can see that there is a linear trend with a season of four periods. Linear regression (with results in rows 24 to 26) shows that the deseasonalised trend line is:

$$Y = 1{,}156.75 - 64.92T$$

	A	B	C	D	E	F	G	H
1	**Forecasting with seasonality and trend**							
2								
3	**Period (T)**	**Observation (Y)**	**Regression value**	**Seasonal index**	**Period in season**	**Average seasonal index**	**Forecast**	
4	1	986	1091.83	0.903	1	0.939		
5	2	1245	1026.92	1.212	2	1.289		
6	3	902	962.00	0.938	3	0.971		
7	4	704	897.08	0.785	4	0.796		
8	5	812	832.17	0.976	1	0.939		
9	6	1048	767.25	1.366	2	1.289		
10	7	706	702.33	1.005	3	0.971		
11	8	514	637.42	0.806	4	0.796		
12	9		572.50		1	0.939	538	
13	10		507.58		2	1.289	654	
14	11		442.67		3	0.971	430	
15	12		377.75		4	0.796	301	
16								
17	**SUMMARY OUTPUT**							
18	Regression statistics							
19	Multiple R	0.691						
20	R Square	0.477						
21	Adjusted R Square	0.390						
22	Observation	8						
23								
24		Coefficients						
25	Intercept	1156.75						
26	X Variable 1	−64.92						
27								
28								
29								
30								

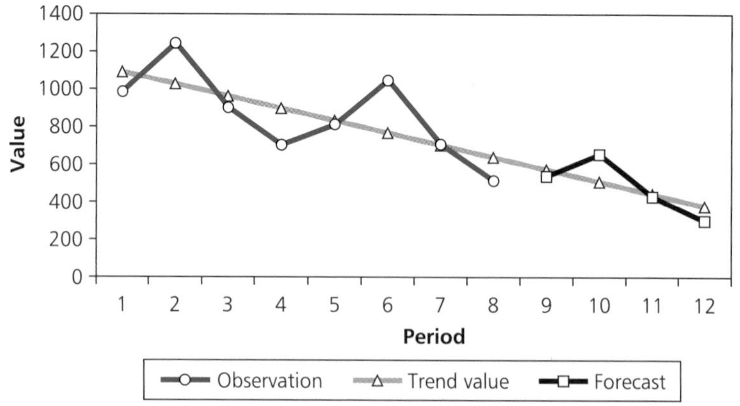

Figure 10.12 Calculations for Worked example 10.12

Worked example 10.12 continued

This equation gives the deseasonalised values in column C. Dividing observations in column B by the corresponding values in column C gives the seasonal indices in column D. Taking average indices for each of the four periods in a season gives the results in column F of 0.939, 1.289, 0.971 and 0.796. The forecast for period 9 is:

deseasonalised value × seasonal index
= $(1,156.75 - 64.92 \times 9) \times 0.939$
= 538

Similarly the other forecasts are:

- Period 10: $(1,156.75 - 64.92 \times 10) \times 1.289 = 654$
- Period 11: $(1,156.75 - 64.92 \times 11) \times 0.971 = 430$
- Period 12: $(1,156.75 - 64.92 \times 12) \times 0.796 = 301$

Review questions

10.16 What are the steps in forecasting for data with seasonality and trend?

10.17 What is the difference between an additive and a multiplicative forecasting model?

10.18 Would you prefer to use regression or moving averages to deseasonalise data?

IDEAS IN PRACTICE **ExcelEst Education**

ExcelEst Education run many training courses in Europe, including reviews of management forecasting. Figure 10.13 shows one of the examples used in their courses, with the calculations for an additive model to forecast demand when there is seasonality and trend.

Additive models work in virtually the same way as multiplicative models, except that seasonal adjustments are amounts added to the deseasonalised value (rather than an index to be multiplied). In Figure 10.13 the regression equation is 63.363 + 1.609 × period, and this gives the deseasonalised values in column C. Then there are seasonal adjustments, which are defined as:

seasonal adjustment = observation −
deseasonalised value

Column D shows these results by subtracting entries in column C from corresponding observations in column B.

The data shows weekly sales, so there are seven periods in a season. Then the average seasonal adjustment for the first period is $(-22.971 - 13.233) / 2 = -18.102$. Adjustments for the other seasons are calculated in the same way, with the results in column F. The average adjustment for each period is shown in rows 18 to 24. Then the forecasts come from the regression line trend and the seasonal adjustments:

forecast = deseasonalised trend
+ seasonal adjustment

For period 15:

forecast = $(63.363 + 1.609 \times 15) - 18.102$
= 69.396

Repeating these calculations for the six periods gives the forecasts in column G.

Source: ExcelEst Education, *Management Forecasting Course Material*, Geneva, 2010.

▶

Ideas in practice continued

	A	B	C	D	E	F	G
1	Forecasting with seasonality and trend						
2							
3	Period	Observation	Regression value	Seasonal adjustment	Period in season	Average seasonal adjustment	Forecast
4	1	42	64.97	−22.971	1	−18.102	
5	2	61	66.58	−5.580	2	−2.211	
6	3	83	68.19	14.811	3	22.680	
7	4	102	69.80	32.202	4	25.571	
8	5	79	71.41	7.593	5	8.463	
9	6	65	73.02	−8.015	6	−3.146	
10	7	39	74.62	−35.624	7	−33.255	
11	8	63	76.23	−13.233	1	−18.102	
12	9	79	77.84	1.158	2	−2.211	
13	10	110	79.45	30.549	3	22.680	
14	11	100	81.06	18.941	4	25.571	
15	12	92	82.67	9.332	5	8.463	
16	13	86	84.28	1.723	6	−3.146	
17	14	55	85.89	−30.886	7	−33.255	
18	15		87.49		1	−18.102	69
19	16		89.10		2	−2.211	87
20	17		90.71		3	22.680	113
21	18		92.32		4	25.571	118
22	19		93.93		5	8.463	102
23	20		95.54		6	−3.146	92
24	21		97.15		7	−33.255	64
25							
26	SUMMARY OUTPUT						
27							
28	Regression Statistics						
29	Multiple R	0.306					
30	R Square	0.093					
31	Adjusted R Square	0.018					
32	Standard error	21.830					
33	Observations	14					
34	Intercept	63.363					
35	X Variable 1	1.609					
36							
37							
38							
39							
40							

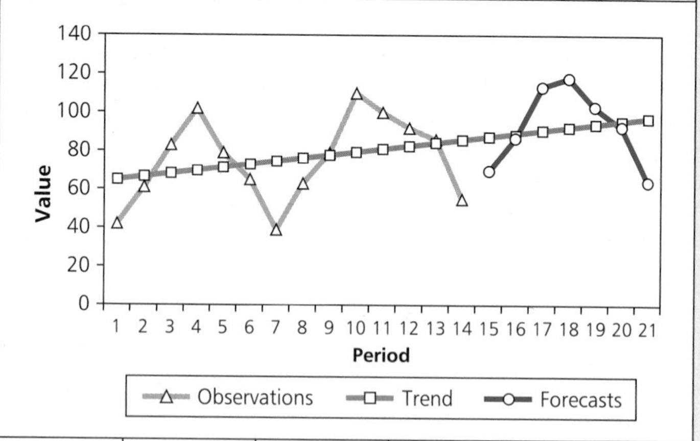

Figure 10.13 Example of forecasting with ExcelEst Education

CHAPTER REVIEW

This chapter discussed methods of forecasting, which is an essential function in every organisation.

- There are many different ways of forecasting. No method is always best, and managers have to choose the most appropriate for particular circumstances.

- Forecasting methods can be classified in several ways, including the length of time they cover in the future. The most useful classification refers to causal, judgemental and projective methods.

- Causal forecasting looks for a relationship between variables, and then forecasts values for a dependent variable from known values of the independent variable. We discussed this in terms of regression in Chapter 9.

- Judgemental, or qualitative, forecasts are the only option when there is no accurate or relevant historical data. They rely on subjective views and opinions, as demonstrated by personal insight, panel consensus, market surveys, historical analogy and the Delphi method.

- It is always better to use quantitative forecasts when data is available. This data often appears as time series, with observations taken at regular intervals. Then observations often follow an underlying pattern with superimposed noise.

- Projective forecasts look only at historical observations and project the underlying patterns into the future. A basic form of projective forecasting uses simple averages, but this is insensitive and has limited practical use. Moving averages are more flexible, setting forecasts as the average of the latest n observations, and ignoring all older values.

- Exponential smoothing is an efficient forecasting method which adds portions of the latest observation to the previous forecast. This automatically reduces the weight given to data as it gets older.

- Data that is not stable but has some underlying patterns needs special attention. The best way to forecast time series with seasonality and trend is to divide observations into distinct components, forecast each of these separately and then combine the results into a final forecast.

CASE STUDY   Workload planning

Maria Castigliani is head of the purchasing department of Ambrosiana Merceti, a medium-sized construction company. One morning she walked into the office and said, 'The main problem in this office is lack of planning. I have read a few articles about planning, and it seems that forecasting is the key to an efficient business. We have never done any forecasting, but simply rely on experience to guess our future workload. I think we should start using exponential smoothing and then we can foresee problems and schedule our time more efficiently.'

Unfortunately, the purchasing department was particularly busy and nobody in the office had time to develop Maria's ideas. A month later nothing had happened. Maria was not pleased and said that their current high workload was caused by lack of planning – and hence forecasting – and

▶

Case study continued

things would be much better if they organised their time more effectively. In particular, they could level their workload and would not be overwhelmed by periodic surges.

To make some progress with the forecasting, Maria seconded Piotr Zemlinski, a management trainee, to work on some figures. Piotr examined their work and divided it into seven categories, including searching for business, preparing estimates, submitting tenders, finding suppliers and so on. For each of these categories he added the number of distinct tasks the office had completed in each quarter of the past three years. Collecting the data took six weeks, and Piotr summarised it in this table.

	Category						
Quarter	1	2	3	4	5	6	7
1,1	129	74	1,000	755	1,210	204	24
2,1	138	68	1,230	455	1,520	110	53
3,1	110	99	890	810	1,390	105	42
4,1	118	119	700	475	1,170	185	21
1,2	121	75	790	785	1,640	154	67
2,2	137	93	1,040	460	1,900	127	83
3,2	121	123	710	805	1,860	187	80
4,2	131	182	490	475	1,620	133	59
1,3	115	103	610	775	2,010	166	105
2,3	126	147	840	500	2,340	140	128
3,3	131	141	520	810	2,210	179	126
4,3	131	112	290	450	1,990	197	101

Now Piotr wants to forecast the likely workload for the next two years. He knows a little about forecasting, and feels that exponential smoothing may not be the answer. He is not sure that the data is accurate enough, or that the results will be reliable. He feels that it would be better to link the forecasts directly to planning, overall workload and capacity. To help with this, he converted the effort involved with different tasks into 'standard work units'. After some discussion he allocated the following number of work units to a typical task in each category of work.

- Category 1 – 2 work units
- Category 2 – 1.5 work units
- Category 3 – 1 work unit
- Category 4 – 0.7 work units
- Category 5 – 0.4 work units
- Category 6 – 3 work units
- Category 7 – 2.5 work units.

Questions

- What information has Piotr collected and how useful is it? What other information does he need?
- How can Piotr forecast future workloads in the purchasing department? How reliable are the results? Do they suggest any patterns of workload?
- What are the implications of Piotr's work, and what should he do now?

PROBLEMS

10.1 Use linear regression to forecast values for periods 11 to 13 for the following time series.

Period	1	2	3	4	5	6	7	8	9	10
Observation	121	133	142	150	159	167	185	187	192	208

10.2 Use simple averages to forecast values for the data in Problem 10.1. Which method gives better results?

10.3 Use a 4-period moving average to forecast values for the data in Problem 10.1.

10.4 Find the 2-, 3- and 4-period moving averages for the following time series, and use the errors to say which gives the best results.

T	1	2	3	4	5	6	7	8	9	10
Y	280	240	360	340	300	220	200	360	410	280

10.5 Use exponential smoothing with $\alpha = 0.1$ and 0.2 to forecast values for the data in Problem 10.4. Which smoothing constant gives better forecasts? How would you monitor the results with a tracking signal?

10.6 Use exponential smoothing with α between 0.1 and 0.4 to get forecasts one period ahead for the following time series. Use an initial value of $F_1 = 208$ and say which value of α is best.

t	1	2	3	4	5	6	7	8	9	10
Demand	212	216	424	486	212	208	208	204	220	200

10.7 Balliol.com recorded their opening share price for 12 consecutive weeks. Deseasonalise their results and identify the underlying trend. Forecast values for the next 6 weeks.

Week	1	2	3	4	5	6	7	8	9	10	11	12
Share price (pence)	75	30	52	88	32	53	90	30	56	96	38	62

10.8 Use a multiplicative model to forecast values for the next 6 periods of the following time series.

t	1	2	3	4	5	6
y	100	160	95	140	115	170

10.9 Use a multiplicative model to forecast values for the next eight periods of the following time series.

t	1	2	3	4	5	6	7	8	9	10
y	101	125	121	110	145	165	160	154	186	210

10.10 Use additive models to forecast values for the time series in Problems 10.8 and 10.9.

RESEARCH PROJECTS

10.1 In this chapter we have used spreadsheets for doing most of the calculations. Spreadsheets – or specialised add-ins – have standard functions for forecasting, typically including regression, simple averages, moving averages and exponential smoothing. Design a spreadsheet that uses these for a variety of forecasting methods. Specialised software may be better, so do a small survey of available forecasting packages. What extra features do these have?

10.2 Governments routinely collect huge amounts of data that they often present in extended time series – giving figures for populations, gross domestic product, employment etc. Collect a reasonably long set of data, and see how well standard forecasting methods work. How can the forecasts be improved?

10.3 Energy consumption around the world is rising. Find some figures to describe this growth. Now forecast the future demand for electricity. How accurate are your results? What other factors should be taken into account? What are the implications of your findings?

Sources of information

References

1 Nelson Y. and Stoner S., *Results of the Delphi VIII Survey of Oil Price Forecasts*, California Energy Commission, Sacramento, CA, 1996.

2 Department of Revenue, *Oil Revenue Forecasts, State of Alaska*, Juneau, AK, 2005.

3 EIA, *Annual Energy Outlook*, Energy Information Administration, Washington, DC, 2006.

4 WiT, *Oil Production in Terminal Decline*, World in Turmoil, San Francisco, CA, 2006.

Further reading

You can find material on forecasting in most operations management and marketing books. The following list gives some more specialised books.

Carlberg C., *Excel Sales Forecasting for Dummies*, John Wiley, New York, 2005.

Diebold F.X., *Elements of Forecasting* (4th edition), South Western, Cincinnati, OH, 2006.

Evans M.K., *Practical Business Forecasting*, Blackwell, London, 2002.

Hanke J.E., Reitsch A.G. and Wichern D., *Business Forecasting* (9th edition), Pearson Education, Englewood Cliffs, NJ, 2009.

Lawrence K.D., Klimberg R.K. and Lawrence S.M., *Fundamentals of Forecasting Using Excel*, Industrial Press, New York, 2009.

Moore J.H. and Weatherford L.R., *Decision Modelling with Microsoft Excel* (6th edition), Prentice Hall, Upper Saddle River, NJ, 2001.

Morlidge S. and Player S., *How to Master Business Forecasting*, John Wiley, Chichester, 2009.

Ragsdale C., *Spreadsheet Modelling and Decision Analysis* (5th edition), South-Western College Publishing, Cincinnati, OH, 2008.

Shim J.K., *Strategic Business Forecasting*, St. Lucie Press, Boca Raton, FL, 2000.

Wilson J.H. and Keating B., *Business Forecasting* (5th edition), McGraw Hill, New York, 2006.

Winston W.L. and Albright S., *Spreadsheet Modelling and Applications*, Brooks Cole, Florence, KY, 2004.

Linear programming

Chapter outline

Managers often face problems of allocating scarce resources in the best possible way to achieve their objectives. As there are constraints on the options available, these problems are described as 'constrained optimisation'. This chapter describes linear programming, which is a widely used method of solving problems of constrained optimisation. It builds on the ideas of simultaneous equations discussed earlier – with 'programming' used in its broad sense of planning.

After finishing this chapter you should be able to:

- appreciate the concept of constrained optimisation
- describe the stages in solving a linear programme
- formulate linear programmes and understand the basic assumptions
- use graphs to solve linear programmes with two variables
- calculate marginal values for resources
- calculate the effect of changing an objective function
- interpret printouts from computer packages.

Constrained optimisation

Managers search for the best possible solutions to their problems – but there are inevitably constraints on their options, often set by the resources available.

For instance, an operations manager wants to maximise production, but has facilities with limited capacity; a marketing manager wants to maximise the impact of an advertising campaign, but cannot exceed a specified budget; a finance manager wants to maximise returns, but has limited funds; a construction manager wants to minimise the cost of a project, but has to finish within a specified time.

These problems are characterised by:

- an aim of optimising – that is either maximising or minimising – some objective
- a set of constraints that limit the possible solutions.

For this reason they are called problems of constrained optimisation.

Linear programming (LP) is a method of solving certain problems of constrained optimisation. And we should say straight away that linear programming has nothing to do with computer programming – its name comes from the more general meaning of planning.

> There are three distinct stages to solving a linear programme:
> - **formulation** – getting the problem in the right form
> - **solution** – finding an optimal solution to the problem
> - **sensitivity analysis** – seeing what happens when the problem is changed slightly.

Of these, formulation is often the most difficult. It needs an accurate description of the problem and a lot of data – and the resulting model can be very bulky. But when a problem is in the right form, getting a solution can be relatively straightforward. This is because the solution procedures need a very large number of repetitive calculations, and in practice these are *always* done by computer. So we are going to demonstrate the principles with simple examples showing how to approach a formulation, how computers get optimal solutions and what the sensitivity analysis does.

Review questions

11.1 What is constrained optimisation?

11.2 What is linear programming?

Formulation

The first stage of solving a linear programme is to describe the problem in a standard format. It is easiest to illustrate this formulation with an example, and for this we use a problem from production planning.

Suppose a small factory makes two types of liquid fertiliser, Growbig and Thrive. It makes these by similar processes, using the same equipment for blending raw materials, distilling the mix and finishing (bottling, testing, weighing etc.). Because the factory has a limited amount of equipment, there are constraints on the time available for each process. In particular, there are only 40 hours of blending available in a week, 40 hours of distilling and

25 hours of finishing. We assume that these are the only constraints and there are none on, say, sales or availability of raw materials.

The fertilisers are made in batches, and each batch needs the following hours for each process.

	Growbig	Thrive
Blending	1	2
Distilling	2	1
Finishing	1	1

If the factory makes a net profit of €300 on each batch of Growbig and €200 on each batch of Thrive, how many batches of each should it make in a week?

This is clearly a problem of constrained optimisation – we want to optimise an objective (maximising profit) subject to constraints (production capacity), as shown in Figure 11.1. The variables that the company can control are the

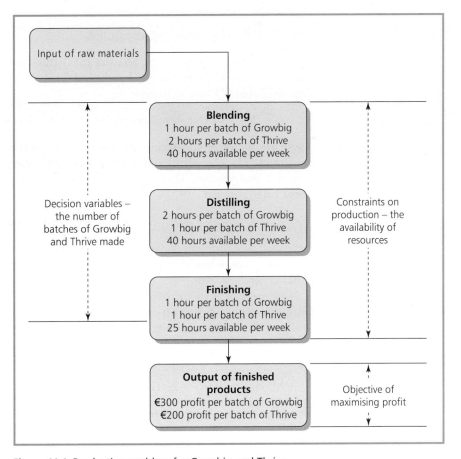

Figure 11.1 Production problem for Growbig and Thrive

number of batches of Growbig and Thrive they make, so these are the decision variables. Then we can define:

- G is the number of batches of Growbig made in a week
- T is the number of batches of Thrive made in a week.

Now consider the time available for blending. Each batch of Growbig uses 1 hour of blending, so G batches use G hours; each batch of Thrive uses 2 hours of blending, so T batches use $2T$ hours. Adding these together gives the total amount of blending used as $G + 2T$. The maximum amount of blending available is 40 hours, so the time used must be less than, or at worst equal to, this. So this gives the first constraint:

$G + 2T \leq 40$ (blending constraint)

(Remember that $\leq$ means 'less than or equal to'.)

Turning to the distilling constraint, each batch of Growbig uses 2 hours of distilling, so G batches use $2G$ hours; each batch of Thrive uses 1 hour of distilling, so T batches use T hours. Adding these together gives the total amount of distilling used and this must be less than, or at worst equal to, the amount of distilling available (40 hours). So this gives the second constraint:

$2G + T \leq 40$ (distilling constraint)

Now the finishing constraint has the total time used for finishing (G for batches of Growbig plus T for batches of Thrive) less than or equal to the time available (25 hours) to give:

$G + T \leq 25$ (finishing constraint)

These are the three constraints for the process – but there is another implicit constraint. The company cannot make a negative number of batches, so both G and T are positive. This **non-negativity constraint** is a standard feature of linear programmes:

$G \geq 0$ and $T \geq 0$ (non-negativity constraints)

Here the three problem constraints are all 'less than or equal to', but they can be of any type – less than; less than or equal to; equal to; greater than or equal to; greater than.

Now we can turn to the objective, which is maximising the profit. The company makes €300 on each batch of Growbig, so with G batches the profit is $300G$; they make €200 on each batch of Thrive, so with T batches the profit is $200T$. Adding these gives the total profit that is to be maximised – this is the objective function.

Maximise $300G + 200T$ (objective function)

This objective is phrased in terms of maximising an objective. The alternative for LPs is to minimise an objective (typically phrased in terms of minimising costs).

This completes the linear programming formulation which we can summarise as:

Decision variables:

- G is the number of batches of Growbig made in a week
- T is the number of batches of Thrive made in a week.

Maximise:

$300G + 200T$ objective function

subject to:

$$\left. \begin{array}{l} G + 2T \leq 40 \\ 2G + T \leq 40 \\ G + T \leq 25 \end{array} \right\} \text{ constraints}$$

with

$G \geq 0$ and $T \geq 0$ non-negativity constraints

This illustrates the features of all linear programming formulations, which consist of:

- decision variables
- an objective function
- a set of constraints
- a non-negativity constraint.

This formulation makes a number of assumptions that are implicit in all LPs. Most importantly, the objective function and constraints are all linear functions of the decision variables. This means that the use of resources is proportional to the quantity being produced and if, say, production is doubled then the use of resources is also doubled. This is usually a reasonable assumption, but it is not always true. For example, increasing production may give longer production runs that reduce setup times and running-in problems. On the other hand, higher production might mean faster working that creates more faults, and more units scrapped as defective.

A second assumption is that adding the resources used for each product gives the total amount of resources used. Again, this is not always true. For instance, a craft manufacturer will use the most skilled craftsmen for the most complex jobs – but if there are no complex jobs in one period then the skilled craftsmen do fewer complex jobs, and they do them better or faster than usual.

WORKED EXAMPLE 11.1

A political campaign wants to hire photocopiers to make leaflets for a local election. There are two suitable machines:

- ACTO costs £120 a month to rent, occupies 2.5 square metres of floor space and can produce 15,000 copies a day.
- ZENMAT costs £150 a month to rent, occupies 1.8 square metres of floor space and can produce 18,500 copies a day.

The campaign has allowed up to £1,200 a month for copying machines which will be put in a room of 19.2 square metres. Formulate this problem as a linear programme.

Solution

The problem variables are the things we can vary, which are the number of ACTO and ZENMAT machines rented. Let:

- A be the number of ACTO machines rented
- Z be the number of ZENMAT machines rented.

The objective is to make as many copies as possible.

Maximise $15,00A + 18,500Z$ (objective function)

There are constraints on floor space and costs:

$$120A + 150Z \leq 1,200 \quad \text{(cost constraint)}$$
$$2.5A + 1.8Z \leq 19.5 \quad \text{(space constraint)}$$

with

$$A \geq 0 \text{ and } Z \geq 0 \quad \text{(non-negativity constraint)}$$

WORKED EXAMPLE 11.2

Foreshore Investment Trust has £1 million to invest. After consulting its financial advisers it considers six possible investments with these characteristics:

Investment	% Risk	% Dividend	% Growth	Rating
1	18	4	22	4
2	6	5	7	10
3	10	9	12	2
4	4	7	8	10
5	12	6	15	4
6	8	8	8	6

The trust wants to invest the £1 million with minimum risk, but with a dividend of at least £70,000 a year, average growth of at least 12% and an average rating of at least 7. Formulate this as a linear programme.

Solution

The decision variables are the amount of money put into each investment. Let:

- X_1 be the amount of money put into investment 1
- X_2 be the amount of money put into investment 2

- and so on, so that X_i is the amount of money put into investment i.

The objective is to minimise risk.

Minimise $0.18X_1 + 0.06X_2 + 0.10X_3 + 0.04X_4$
$+ 0.12X_5 + 0.08X_6$

There are constraints on the amount of:

- money – the total invested must equal £1 million:

$$X_1 + X_2 + X_3 + X_4 + X_5 + X_6 = 1,000,000$$

- dividend – must be at least 7% of £1 million:

$$0.04X_1 + 0.05X_2 + 0.09X_3 + 0.07X_4 + 0.06X_5$$
$$+ 0.08X_6 \geq 70,000$$

- average growth – at least 12% of £1 million:

$$0.22X_1 + 0.07X_2 + 0.12X_3 + 0.08X_4 + 0.15X_5$$
$$+ 0.08X_6 \geq 120,000$$

- rating – the average (weighted by the amount invested) must be at least 7:

$$4X_1 + 10X_2 + 2X_3 + 10X_4 + 4X_5 + 6X_6$$
$$\geq 7,000,000$$

The non-negativity constraints X_1, X_2, X_3, X_4, X_5 and $X_6 \geq 0$ complete the formulation.

WORKED EXAMPLE 11.3

StatFunt Oil makes two blends of fuel by mixing three oils. The costs and daily availability of the oils are:

Oil	Cost (€/litre)	Amount available (litres)
A	2.5	10,000
B	2.8	15,000
C	3.5	20,000

The blends of fuel contain:

Blend 1	at most 25% of A
	at least 30% of B
	at most 40% of C
Blend 2	at least 20% of A
	at most 50% of B
	at least 30% of C

Each litre of Blend 1 sells for €6 and each litre of Blend 2 sells for €7. Long-term contracts mean that at least 10,000 litres of each blend must be produced. The company has to decide the best mixture of oils for each blend. Formulate this as a linear programme.

Solution

The decision variables are the amount of each type of oil that the company puts into each blend:

- Let A_1 be the amount of oil A put into Blend 1.
- Let A_2 be the amount of oil A put into Blend 2.
- Let B_1 be the amount of oil B put into Blend 1
- etc.

The total amounts of Blend 1 and Blend 2 produced are:

Blend 1: $A_1 + B_1 + C_1$
Blend 2: $A_2 + B_2 + C_2$

and the amounts of each oil used are:

oil A: $A_1 + A_2$
oil B: $B_1 + B_2$
oil C: $C_1 + C_2$

The objective is to maximise profit. We know that the income from selling blends is:

$$6 \times (A_1 + B_1 + C_1) + 7 \times (A_2 + B_2 + C_2)$$

while the cost of buying oil is:

$$2.5 \times (A_1 + A_2) + 2.8 \times (B_1 + B_2) + 3.5 \times (C_1 + C_2)$$

The profit is the difference between the income and the cost:

$$6A_1 + 6B_1 + 6C_1 + 7A_2 + 7B_2 + 7C_2 - 2.5A_1 - 2.5A_2 - 2.8B_1 - 2.8B_2 - 3.5C_1 - 3.5C_2$$

which we can rearrange to give the objective function:

Maximise $3.5A_1 + 4.5A_2 + 3.2B_1 + 4.2B_2 + 2.5C_1 + 3.5C_2$

There are constraints on the availability of oils:

$$A_1 + A_2 \le 10,000$$
$$B_1 + B_2 \le 15,000$$
$$C_1 + C_2 \le 20,000$$

There are also six blending constraints. The first of these says that Blend 1 must be at most 25% of oil A. In other words:

$$A_1 \le 0.25 \times (A_1 + B_1 + C_1) \quad \text{or}$$
$$0.75A_1 - 0.25B_1 - 0.25C_1 \le 0$$

Similarly for the other blends:

$$B_1 \ge 0.3 \times (A_1 + B_1 + C_1) \quad \text{or}$$
$$0.3A_1 - 0.7B_1 + 0.3C_1 \le 0$$
$$C_1 \le 0.4 \times (A_1 + B_1 + C_1) \quad \text{or}$$
$$-0.4A_1 - 0.4B_1 + 0.6C_1 \le 0$$
$$A_2 \ge 0.2 \times (A_2 + B_2 + C_2) \quad \text{or}$$
$$-0.8A_2 + 0.2B_1 + 0.2C_1 \le 0$$
$$B_2 \le 0.5 \times (A_2 + B_2 + C_2) \quad \text{or}$$
$$-0.5A_2 + 0.5B_2 - 0.5C_2 \le 0$$
$$C_2 \ge 0.3 \times (A_2 + B_2 + C_2) \quad \text{or}$$
$$0.3A_2 + 0.3B_2 - 0.7C_2 \le 0$$

Long-term contracts add the conditions that:

$$A_1 + B_1 + C_1 \ge 10,000$$
$$A_2 + B_2 + C_2 \ge 10,000$$

The non-negativity conditions that all variables, A_1, A_2, B_1, etc., are greater than or equal to 0 completes the formulation.

Review questions
11.3   What are the main assumptions of linear programming?

11.4   What happens when you formulate a linear programme?

11.5   What are the parts of an LP formulation?

IDEAS IN PRACTICE   Argentia Life Assurance

In 2009 the financial crisis meant that Argentia Life Assurance reserves were not earning enough to cover their life insurance commitments. They had transferred an additional $20 million into their life policy reserves in 2004, but now felt that they should add another $30 million. The company wanted to maximise its returns on this new investment, but there were regulations and guidelines on the types of investment they could make. This was clearly a problem of constrained optimisation and the company used linear programming to suggest the best investment.

The main constraint was on the amount invested. Other constraints concerned the types of investment available – or that Argentia wanted to use. They would not make any investment that had significant risk, so their choice was limited to government and corporate bonds, shares in blue-chip companies, property, mortgages and some unclassified investments. Even these were not as safe as they had been in the past. Guidelines prevented them from buying shares with a value greater than 25% of the total assets of the company. Similarly, property was limited to 15%, and unclassified investments to 2% of the total assets of the company. Other constraints limited the maximum amounts in each investment, spread of risk and so on.

The final formulation had over 1,000 variables and 12,000 constraints. The solution gave the best options at a particular time. But financial markets change very quickly, and the data used in the model had to be updated frequently.

Source: Scarborough J., *Investment Policies*, Argentia Corp., New York, 2010.

Using graphs to solve linear programmes

It takes many repetitive calculations to solve a real linear programme and these are always done by a computer. But we can illustrate the principles with a simple example, and for this we return to the previous example of Growbig and Thrive.

Maximise:

$$300G + 200T \qquad \text{(objective function)}$$

subject to:

$$
\begin{aligned}
G + 2T &\leq 40 && \text{(blending constraint)}\\
2G + T &\leq 40 && \text{(distilling constraint)}\\
G + T &\leq 25 && \text{(finishing constraint)}
\end{aligned}
$$

and

$$G \geq 0 \text{ and } T \geq 0 \quad \text{(non-negativity constraints)}$$

Take the blending constraint, which is $G + 2T \leq 40$. We can draw the equation $G + 2T = 40$ as a straight line on a graph of G against T as shown in Figure 11.2. (If you are not sure about this, have another look at Chapter 3.)

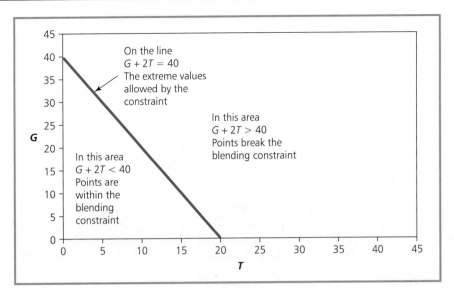

Figure 11.2 Graph of the blending constraint

Remember that the easiest way to draw lines is to take two convenient points and draw a straight line through them. Here, setting $G = 0$ gives $2T = 40$ or $T = 20$, and setting $T = 0$ gives $G = 40$. Then we can draw the line of the equation through the points (0, 20) and (40, 0). The non-negativity constraints mean that we have to consider this only in the positive quadrant – where both G and T are positive.

The important fact here is that any point above this line breaks the blending constraint, while any point on or below the line does not break the constraint. You can check this by taking any points at random. For instance, the point $G = 10$, $T = 10$ is below the line and substituting into the constraint gives:

$$1 \times 10 + 2 \times 10 \leq 40 \quad ✓$$

This is true and the constraint is not broken.

On the other hand, the point $G = 20$, $T = 20$ is above the line and substitution gives:

$$1 \times 20 + 2 \times 20 \leq 40 \quad ✗$$

This is not true and the constraint is broken.

Points that are actually on the line satisfy the equality. For example, the point $G = 20$, $T = 10$ is on the line and substitution gives:

$$1 \times 20 + 2 \times 10 \leq 40 \quad ✓$$

This is true and shows the extreme values allowed by the constraint. So the line divides the graph into two areas – all points above the line break the constraint, and all points on or below the line do not break the constraint.

We can add the other two constraints in the same way (shown in Figure 11.3). The distilling constraint ($2G + T \leq 40$) is the straight line through $G = 20$, $T = 0$ and $G = 0$, $T = 40$. As before, any point above the line breaks the

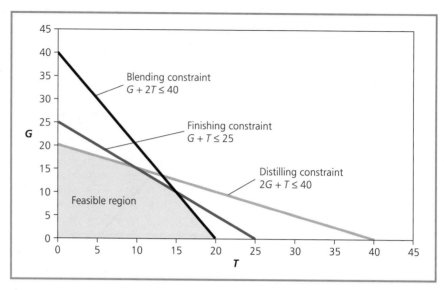

Figure 11.3 Graph of the three constraints defining a feasible region

constraint, and any point on or below the line does not break the constraint. The finishing constraint $(G + T \leq 25)$ is the straight line through the points $G = 0$, $T = 25$ and $G = 25$, $T = 0$, and again any point above the line breaks the constraint, and any point on or below the line does not break the constraint.

Any point that is below *all three* of the constraint lines represents a valid, feasible solution – but a point that is above *any* of the lines breaks at least one of the constraints and does not represent a feasible solution. So this defines a feasible region, which is the area in which all feasible solutions lie. Any point inside the feasible region represents a valid solution to the problem, but any point outside breaks at least one of the constraints.

Now we know the area in which feasible solutions lie, the next stage is to examine all feasible solutions and identify the best or optimal. For this we use the objective function, which is to maximise profit of $300G + 200T$. We can also draw this profit line on the graph of G against T. Although we do not know the optimal value of the profit, we can start looking at an arbitrary trial value of, say, €6,000. Then we can draw the graph of $300G + 200T = 6,000$ through two convenient points, say $G = 0$, $T = 30$ and $G = 20$, $T = 0$. In the same way, we can draw a number of other arbitrary values for profit, with the results shown in Figure 11.4.

As you can see, the lines for different profits are all parallel. This is not surprising because we can write the objective function in the standard form, $y = ax + b$:

$$300G = -200T + \text{profit}$$

or:

$$G = \frac{-200T}{300} + \frac{\text{profit}}{300}$$

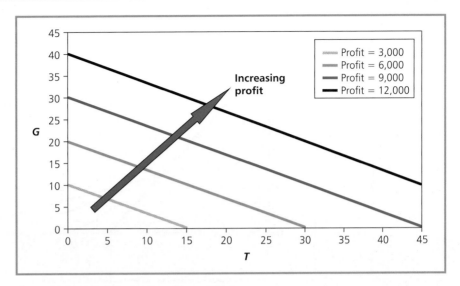

Figure 11.4 Profit lines for Growbig and Thrive

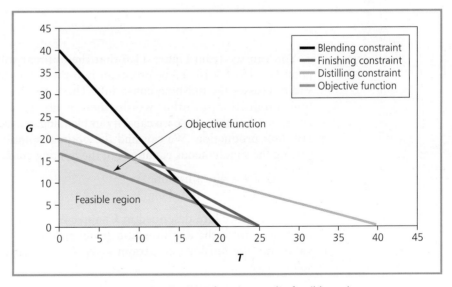

Figure 11.5 Superimposing the objective function on the feasible region

This shows that the gradient of the profit line is constant at −200/300, and the line crosses the G axis at the point profit/300. Another critical observation is that the further the line is away from the origin, the higher is the value of the objective function. This suggests a way of finding the optimal solution. For this we superimpose an objective function line onto the graph of constraints, so that it passes through the feasible region (as shown in Figure 11.5). Then we move the objective function line away from the origin – the further we move it out, the higher is the profit. As the objective function line moves away from the origin, it passes through a smaller part of the feasible region, and eventually it passes through only a single point (as shown in Figure 11.6) – this single point is the optimal solution.

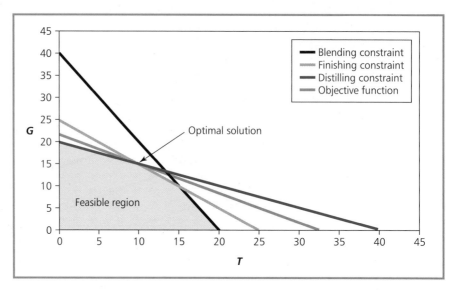

Figure 11.6 Moving the objective function line as far as possible away from the origin identifies the optimal solution

You can see from Figure 11.6 that the optimal solution is at about the point $G = 15$, $T = 10$. To be precise, it is at the point where the distilling constraint crosses the finishing constraint. These are the active constraints that limit production. In other words, there is no spare distilling or finishing capacity – but there is spare capacity in blending because this constraint does not limit production. We can find the optimal solution more accurately by solving the simultaneous equations of the limiting constraints.

$$2G + T = 40 \quad \text{(distilling)}$$
$$G + T = 25 \quad \text{(finishing)}$$

Using the procedure described in Chapter 2, you can subtract the finishing constraint from the distilling constraint to give $G = 15$. Substituting this value into the finishing constraint gives $T = 10$. This confirms the optimal solution as:

$$G = 15 \quad \text{and} \quad T = 10$$

Substituting these optimal values into the objective function gives the maximum profit:

$$300G + 200T = 300 \times 15 + 200 \times 10$$
$$= €6,500$$

We can find the resources used by substituting $G = 15$ and $T = 10$ into the constraints:

■ Blending –   time available = 40 hours
                time used = $G + 2T = 15 + 2 \times 10$
                              = 35
             spare capacity = 5 hours

■ Distilling –   time available = 40 hours
                  time used = $2G + T = 2 \times 15 + 10$
                                     $= 40$
                  spare capacity = 0

■ Finishing –   time available = 25 hours
                  time used = $G + T = 1 \times 15 + 1 \times 10$
                                   $= 25$
                  spare capacity = 0

WORKED EXAMPLE 11.4

Find the optimal solution to this linear programme:

Minimise: $2X + Y$

subject to: $X + T \leq 10$ (1)

$X - Y \leq 2$ (2)

$X \geq 4$ (3)

$Y \geq 5$ (4)

with X and Y greater than or equal to zero.

Solution

This problem has already been formulated, so we can immediately draw a graph (shown in Figure 11.7). Sometimes it is not obvious whether a constraint restricts solutions to points above the line or below it (constraint 2, for example). Then you simply take random points either side of the line and see which ones break the constraint.

In this problem we want to *minimise* the objective function, so instead of moving its line as far away from the origin as possible, we move it as close in as possible. As the line moves towards the origin the last point it passes through in the feasible region is the point where constraints (2) and (3) cross. These are the active constraints, and there must be some slack in the other constraints.

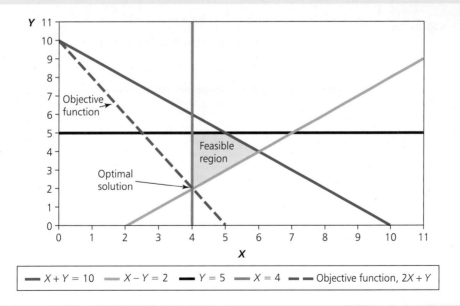

Figure 11.7 Identifying the optimal solution for Worked example 11.4

Worked example 11.4 continued

Here:

$X - T = 2$ (2)

$X = 4$ (3)

Solving these gives the optimal solution of $X = 4$ and $Y = 2$.

Substituting these optimal values into the objective function gives a minimum value of $Y =$

$2 \times 4 + 1 \times 2 = 10$. Substituting the optimal values into the constraints gives:

(1) $X + Y \le 10$ $X + Y = 4 + 2 = 6$, giving spare capacity of $10 - 6 = 4$

(2) $X - Y \le 2$ $X - Y = 4 - 2 = 2$, giving no spare capacity and an active constraint

(3) $X \ge 4$ $X = 4$, giving no spare capacity and an active constraint

(4) $Y \le 5$ $Y = 2$, giving spare capacity of $5 - 2 = 3$

You can see from these examples that the feasible region is always a polygon without any indentations, and the optimal solution is always at a corner or **extreme point**. This is not a coincidence but is a fundamental property of all linear programmes.

> If an optimal solution exists for a linear programme, it is at an extreme point of the feasible region.

This is a very useful property because it shows how computers can tackle large problems. Essentially they identify the feasible region and then search the extreme points around the edge until they find an optimum.

Review questions

11.6   What is the feasible region for a problem?

11.7   What is the role of the objective function in an LP model?

11.8   What are the extreme points of a feasible region and why are they important?

11.9   How can you identify the optimal solution on a graph?

Sensitivity of solutions to changes

Linear programming finds an optimal solution to a problem, but managers might prefer to use a slightly different answer. For instance, they may want to take into account future conditions, use their experience with similar problems, allow for non-quantifiable factors, recognise that assumptions in the model are not entirely accurate – or simply adjust optimal solutions to give more convenient amounts. So it is important to know how sensitive the optimal solution is to changes. If an LP solution suggests a production quantity of 217 units but managers feel that 250 units would be better, they need to know what effects this will have on profits. This is done in the third stage of solving an LP, which does a sensitivity analysis on the solution.

Sensitivity analyses answer two important questions:

- What happens when resources change?
- What happens when the objective function changes?

Changes in resources

Returning to our original problem of Growbig and Thrive, the limiting constraints were distilling and finishing, and we found the optimal solution by solving:

$$2G + T = 40 \quad \text{(distilling constraint)}$$
$$G + T = 25 \quad \text{(finishing constraint)}$$

Suppose that the company could buy an extra unit of distilling – how much is it worth? For small changes we can simply replace the original distilling constraint by a revised one with an extra unit available, and then find the new optimal solution from:

$$2G + T = 41 \quad \text{(new distilling constraint)}$$
$$G + T = 25 \quad \text{(finishing constraint)}$$

The solution here is $G = 16$ and $T = 9$, and substituting these values into the objective function gives a new maximum profit of $300 \times 16 + 200 \times 9 =$ €6,600. The extra hour of distilling has raised the profit from €6,500 to €6,600. To put it another way, distilling has a marginal value of €100. For some reason, in LP this marginal value is called a shadow price, and it is the maximum amount that you would pay for one extra unit of a resource. Conversely, if an hour of distilling is lost for any reason, the profit falls by €100.

The shadow price is valid only for relatively small changes. We found that an extra hour of distilling is worth €100, but there are limits and an extra 1,000 hours would certainly not be worth €100,000. The other two constraints would become active long before this, and they would limit production and leave spare distilling.

We can repeat this analysis to find a shadow price for finishing, by using a new finishing constraint:

$$2G + T = 40 \quad \text{(distilling constraint)}$$
$$G + T = 26 \quad \text{(new finishing constraint)}$$

Solving these equations gives $G = 14$ and $T = 12$, and substituting these values in the objective function gives a new maximum profit of $12 \times 200 + 14 \times 300$ = €6,600. This is again an increase of €100 over the original profit, showing that the shadow price for finishing – which is the most you should pay for an extra hour of finishing – is €100. (It is simply coincidence that this is the same as the shadow price for distilling.) Again, this value holds for small changes, but if the capacity for finishing changes markedly, the other constraints become limiting.

If a process already has spare capacity, there is no point in adding even more capacity – this would just give more spare. It follows that shadow prices of non-limiting resources are zero. In this example, there is spare capacity in blending so its shadow price is zero.

Now we have shadow prices for all three processes: €0 an hour for blending, €100 an hour for distilling and €100 an hour for finishing. But it would be interesting to see what happens when several resources are increased at the same time. For instance, we can find the effect of an extra hour of both distilling and finishing by replacing the original constraints by:

$$2G + T = 41 \quad \text{(new distilling constraint)}$$
$$G + T = 26 \quad \text{(new finishing constraint)}$$

Solving these gives $G = 15$ and $T = 11$ and substitution in the objective function gives a maximum profit of €6,700. This is €200 more than the original solution – and is also the sum of the two individual shadow prices. In other words, for small changes the total benefit is the sum of the separate benefits of increasing each resource separately.

WORKED EXAMPLE 11.5

Suppose a new fertiliser, Vegup, can be made in addition to Growbig and Thrive. Vegup uses 2 hours of blending, 2 hours of distilling and 2 hours of finishing for each batch and contributes €500 to profits. Should the company introduce this new product?

Solution

You can answer this by looking at the shadow prices. If the company makes a batch of Vegup, it must make fewer batches of Growbig and Thrive. You can use the shadow prices to see how much the profit will decline from fewer batches of Growbig and Thrive, and compare this with the extra profit from a batch of Vegup.

A batch of Vegup uses 2 hours of distilling with a shadow price of €100 an hour, so this costs €200. The batch also uses 2 hours of finishing with a shadow price of €100 an hour, so this also costs €200. The 2 hours of finishing has zero shadow price, so this does not cost anything. So making a batch of Vegup reduces the profit from Growbig and Thrive by a total of €400. But the batch of Vegup makes a profit of €500 so there is a net benefit of €100. It is clearly in the company's interest to make Vegup. The next obvious question is how much to make? Unfortunately you cannot find this from the original solution and have to add Vegup to the formulation and solve a new LP problem.

Changes in the objective function

The other aspect of sensitivity analysis considers changes to the objective function. How would changing the profit on batches of Growbig and Thrive affect the optimal solution? The general answer is that provided the changes are small, the optimal solution – that is the numbers of batches of Growbig and Thrive made – does not change. If the profit on each batch of Growbig rises by €10 from €300 to €310, the optimal solution still makes 15 batches of Growbig, so the profit simply rises by $15 \times 10 = €150$. But this argument is not valid for bigger changes. For example, raising the profit on each batch of Growbig from €300 to €600 would not raise the profit by 15 × 300 = €4,500. What happens is that the gradient of the objective function changes and the optimal solution moves to another extreme point. We could calculate these effects in detail but it is much easier to use a computer, as we shall see in the next section.

11.10 What is the 'sensitivity analysis' in LP problems?

11.11 What is the shadow price of a resource?

11.12 Within what limits are shadow prices valid?

Solving real problems

We can solve problems with two variables using a graph, but real problems commonly have hundreds or even thousands of variables. There are standard procedures for solving large problems, usually based on the 'simplex method', but they need so much arithmetic that computers are always used. Many specialised programs are available for solving LPs and Figure 11.8 shows the results when the Growbig and Thrive problem is solved by a simple package. The output has three parts – the first shows the data, to confirm that it was entered properly; the second shows the main results, with optimal values, profits, spare resources and shadow prices; and the third part shows a sensitivity analysis.

The results in this printout confirm our optimal solution and give more information about sensitivity. For example, they confirm that the shadow price for distilling is €100, but this is valid only when the amount of distilling is in the range 35 to 50 hours – outside this range the shadow price changes. Similarly, the shadow price for finishing is €100, but this is valid only when the amount of finishing is in the range 20 to 26.67 hours. The shadow price for blending is zero, but if there are less than 35 hours available it becomes limiting and the shadow price rises.

The sensitivity analysis also considers the objective function. The original profit on each batch of Growbig is €300 but this can vary between €200 and €400 without changing the location of the optimal solution (provided the profit on each batch of Thrive remains at €200). Similarly the profit on each batch of Thrive can vary between €150 and €300 without changing the location of the optimal solution (provided the profit on each batch of Growbig remains at €300).

Specialised computer programs are generally the best ways of solving LPs. Examples of this are ILOG's CPLEX, GAM, GLPX, LINDO and many others. As usual, the scope and quality of this software varies, and it can be either free or very expensive. An alternative for small problems is to use a spreadsheet, but these are not really designed for such specialised use.

-=*=- **INFORMATION ENTERED** -=*=-

PROBLEM NAME : GROWBIG AND THRIVE

NUMBER OF VARIABLES : 2
    G   =   batches of Growbig
    T   =   batches of Thrive

NUMBER OF <= CONSTRAINTS : 3
NUMBER OF = CONSTRAINTS : 0
NUMBER OF >= CONSTRAINTS : 0

MAXIMISE: Profit = 300 G + 200 T

SUBJECT TO:
Blending   1 G + 2 T <= 40
Distilling   2 G + 1 T <= 40
Finishing   1 G + 1 T <= 25

-=*=- **RESULTS** -=*=-

Optimal solution found after 3 iterations

OBJECTIVE FUNCTION VALUE: 6500

VARIABLE	OPTIMAL VALUE
G	15
T	10

CONSTRAINT	ORIGINAL RIGHT-HAND VALUE	USED	SLACK OR SURPLUS	SHADOW PRICE
Blending	40	35	5	0
Distilling	40	40	0	100
Finishing	25	25	0	100

-=*=- **SENSITIVITY ANALYSIS** -=*=-

OBJECTIVE FUNCTION COEFFICIENTS

VARIABLE	LOWER LIMIT	ORIGINAL COEFFICIENT	UPPER LIMIT
G	200	300	400
T	150	200	300

SHADOW PRICES VALID IN RHS RANGES

CONSTRAINT	LOWER LIMIT	ORIGINAL VALUE	UPPER LIMIT
Blending	35	40	NO LIMIT
Distilling	35	40	50
Finishing	20	25	26.667

-=*=- **END OF ANALYSIS** -=*=-

Figure 11.8 Printout for the Growbig and Thrive problem

IDEAS IN PRACTICE   Microsoft Excel's Solver

In Excel you can use 'Solver' in the tools options to tackle linear programmes. Figure 11.9 shows how this works for the problem of Growbig and Thrive. Essentially you have to describe the details of a problem in the body of a spreadsheet, and then transfer information to the 'solver parameters' form.

Here we name the variables, G and T, in cells D4 and E4.

Then cells D5 and E5 contain values for the decision variables, G and T. Initially you estimate a reasonable solution and then Solver iteratively changes the values until it finds the optimal solution.

The constraints are written explicitly in cells D6 to G8. Specifically, cells D6 to E8 contain the left-hand side coefficients, the type of constraint is shown in cells F6 to F8, and the right-hand side

limits are given in cells G6 to G8. The precise calculations using these are described in cells H6 to H8.

The objective function coefficients are given in cells D9 and E9, and the precise calculation is shown in cell H9. Solver uses this as its 'target cell' whose value is to be, in this case, maximised.

This gives the structure of the problem in the body of the spreadsheet. Now you open Excel Tools and select Solver (which is an add-in that must be loaded). Then you set the Target Cell (H9), specify their values (D5 and E5), and give the constraints (left-hand sides in H6 to H8 and right-hand sides from G6 to G8). Then press 'Solve' and the optimal answer appears in cells D5 and E5. Solver gives three results – the optimal solution, a sensitivity analysis and a limits report that shows the ranges within which the sensitivity analysis is valid.

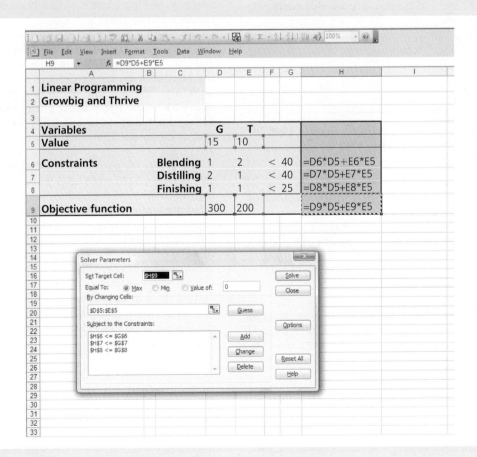

Figure 11.9 Using 'Solver' for a linear programme

WORKED EXAMPLE 11.6

West Coast Wood Products Ltd make four types of pressed panels from pine and spruce. Each panel must be cut and pressed. The panels are made in batches with the following table showing the number of hours needed to produce a batch of each type of panel and the hours available each week.

Panel type	Hours of cutting	Hours of pressing
Classic	1	1
Western	1	4
Nouveau	2	3
East Coast	2	2
Available	**80**	**100**

There is a limited amount of suitable wood available. The amounts needed for a batch of each type of panel and the maximum weekly availability are as follows.

	Classic	Western	Nouveau	East Coast	Availability
Pine	50	40	30	40	2,500
Spruce	20	30	50	20	2,000

The profit on each batch of panels is $400 for Classic, $1,100 for Western, $750 for Nouveau and $350 for East Coast.

(a) Formulate this as a linear programme.
(b) Explain the results given in the printout of Figure 11.10.
(c) Should the company start making a new type of panel that needs 3 hours of cutting and 2 hours of pressing, uses 40 units of pine and 30 units of spruce, and makes a profit of $750?

Solution

(a) We start by defining the decision variables as the number of batches of each type of panelling made a week (CLS, WST, NOU and EST). Then the formulation is:

Maximise:

$$400 \, CLS + 1{,}100 \, WST + 750 \, NOU + 350 \, EST$$

subject to

$$50 \, CLS + 40 \, WST + 30 \, NOU + 40 \, EST \leq 2{,}500$$
(pine)

$$20 \, CLS + 30 \, WST + 50 \, NOU + 20 \, EST \leq 2{,}000$$
(spruce)
$$1 \, CLS + 1 \, WST + 2 \, NOU + 2 \, EST \leq 80$$
(cutting)
$$1 \, CLS + 4 \, WST + 3 \, NOU + 2 \, EST \leq 100$$
(pressing)

with CLS, WST, NOU and EST ≥ 0.

(b) The computer package identifies the optimal solution and does a sensitivity analysis.

The optimal solution is to make 37.5 batches of Classic a week, 15.6 batches of Western and none of the others. This gives a profit of $32,188. If a batch of Nouveau is made it would reduce profit by $75, so this is the amount the profit on a batch would have to increase before it becomes profitable. Similarly, making a batch of East Coast would reduce profit by $263.

The limiting constraints are pine and pressing, with spare capacity in spruce (781 units) and cutting (27 hours). This remains true while the constraint on spruce remains over 1,219 units and the amount of cutting remains above 53 hours. The shadow price of pine is $3 (valid between 1,000 and 3,933 units) and that of pressing is $244 (valid between 50 and 250 hours).

The profit for each batch of Classic could vary between $275 and $1,375 without changing the position of the optimal solution (provided the profits on the other panels remained unchanged). Similarly, the optimal solution remains at the same extreme point provided that the profit on Western is between $1,000 and $1,600, Nouveau is below $825 and East Coast is below $613.

(c) To find the cost of producing one unit of the new panel, we multiply each requirement by the shadow price and add the results:

cutting: 3×0; pressing: 2×244;
pine: 40×3; spruce: 30×0.

So the total cost of making one unit is 488 + 120 = $608. But the profit is $750, so the company should start making the new panel. To find the revised, optimal production numbers, the compay would have to formulate and solve a new linear programme.

Worked example 11.6 continued

-=*=-   INFORMATION ENTERED   -=*=-

PROBLEM NAME   :   WEST COAST WOOD PRODUCTS LTD

NUMBER OF VARIABLES   :   4
    CLS   =   batches of classic
    WST   =   batches of western
    NOU   =   batches of nouveau
    EST   =   batches of east coast

NUMBER OF <= CONSTRAINTS   :   4
NUMBER OF = CONSTRAINTS   :   0
NUMBER OF >= CONSTRAINTS   :   0

MAXIMISE Profit   =   400 CLS   +   1,100 WST   +   750 NOU   +   350 EST

SUBJECT TO:
pine   50 CLS   +   40 WST   +   30 NOU   +   40 EST   <=   2,500
spruce   20 CLS   +   30 WST   +   50 NOU   +   20 EST   <=   2,000
cutting   1 CLS   +   1 WST   +   2 NOU   +   2 EST   <=   80
pressing   1 CLS   +   4 WST   +   3 NOU   +   2 EST   <=   100

-=*=-   RESULTS   -=*=-

Optimal solution found after   6   iterations

OBJECTIVE FUNCTION VALUE: 32188

VARIABLE	OPTIMAL VALUE	ORIGINAL PROFIT	INCREASE NEEDED
CLS	37.5	400	0
WST	15.6	1,100	0
NOU	0	750	75
EST	0	350	263

CONSTRAINT	ORIGINAL RIGHT-HAND VALUE	USED	SLACK OR SURPLUS	SHADOW PRICE
pine	2,500	2,500	0	3
spruce	2,000	1,219	781	0
cutting	80	53	27	0
pressing	100	100	0	244

-=*=-   SENSITIVITY ANALYSIS   -=*=-

OBJECTIVE FUNCTION COEFFICIENTS

VARIABLE	LOWER LIMIT	ORIGINAL COEFFICIENT	UPPER LIMIT
CLS	275	400	1,375
WST	100	1,100	1600
NOU	no limit	750	825
EST	no limit	350	613

SHADOW PRICES VALID IN RHS RANGES

CONSTRAINT	LOWER LIMIT	ORIGINAL VALUE	UPPER LIMIT
pine	1,000	2,500	3,933
spruce	1,219	2,000	no limit
cutting	53	80	no limit
pressing	50	100	250

-=*=-   E N D   O F   A N A L Y S I S   -=*=-

Figure 11.10 Printout for West Coast Wood Products, Worked example 11.6

In practice, LP formulations can be very large and complex, and commonly have tens of thousands of constraints. It is very easy to make mistakes with such large models, and three particular concerns are:

- **Unbound solutions** – the constraints do not limit the solution, and the feasible region effectively extends to infinity.
- **Infeasible solutions** – the constraints are so tight that they have left no feasible region.
- **Degeneracy** – there are many solutions that give the same optimal value.

If you get any of these, you should check the input data carefully for mistakes.

Review questions

11.13 Why are computers always used to solve LPs?

11.14 What information might an LP package give?

11.15 'Spreadsheets are the best way of getting solutions to LP problems.' Is this true?

IDEAS IN PRACTICE Goolongon Smelting

In recent years the demand for lead has fallen because substitutes are used in petrol, paint and construction. Prices have fallen putting pressure on supplier profits. Goolongon Smelting are major producers of lead in Australia. They use linear programming in several ways to maximise profit, with one model looking at production planning.

Goolongon mine their own ore and buy smaller amounts from other suppliers. The ores have variable composition and costs, but are processed in the same way. They are crushed and prepared before a sintering plant removes sulphur and replaces it with oxygen. Then a blast furnace removes the oxygen and other impurities to leave lead bullion. This bullion still contains metallic impurities, which are removed in a refinery. Goolongon can sell the impurities – which include copper, silver, arsenic and bismuth – along with other by-products like sulphuric acid.

The model of production plans has three types of decision variables:

- There are 22 different grades of ore, and the first type of variable considers the amount of each ore used.
- There are 25 major products, and the second type of variable considers the amount of each product made.

- The third type of variable describes other conditions, such as the chemical composition of each ore.

The variables are combined into four types of constraint:

- The first type is on the preparation of the ores. There is always some variation in the incoming ores, but the smelters work best with fixed conditions – so the preparation of the ores includes blending to give consistent inputs.
- The second type is the availability of different types of ore. It makes sure that the amount of each ore used matches the supply.
- The third type looks at the different products. There is a varying demand for products, and Goolongon varies its supply to meet these.
- Finally, there are constraints to match the total composition of the input to the outputs – so that no materials are lost in the process.

Goolongon find their gross profit by subtracting the costs of all inputs from the revenues for all products.

Their objective is to maximise this profit. This basic production planning model has 214 decision variables and over 1,000 constraints. Goolongon have several versions of the model for different time periods and production assumptions. The larger models have several hundred variables and thousands of constraints.

CHAPTER REVIEW

This chapter described linear programming (LP) as a way of solving some types of problem with constrained optimisation.

- With problems of constrained optimisation, managers want to get an optimal solution, but there are constraints on their choices.

- Linear programming is a method of tackling problems of constrained optimisation, where the objective function and constraints are linear functions of the decision variables. There are three stages in solving such problems.

- The first stage is to describe a problem in a standard form. The resulting formulation consists of decision variables, an objective function, problem constraints and non-negativity constraints.

- The constraints of a problem define a feasible region, which is a convex space surrounded by extreme points. The optimal solution is at one of the extreme points of the feasible region. The second stage of solving a linear programme is to identify the optimal solution. For small problems you can do this graphically but real problems always need a computer.

- The third stage does a sensitivity analysis to examine the effects of small changes to the problem. In particular, it calculates shadow prices and looks at the effects of changing constraints and the objective function.

- The easiest way of solving linear programmes is to use a standard software package, but you can use spreadsheets. All packages give similar results, but they need careful analysis and interpretation.

CASE STUDY Elemental Electronics

Elemental Electronics assembles microcomputers and acts as wholesalers for some components. For the manufacturing business, they buy components from a number of suppliers and assemble them in a well-tried design. They do virtually no research and development, and are happy to use designs that have been tested by other manufacturers. They also spend little on advertising, preferring to sell computers through their website and a few specialised retailers. As a result they have very low overheads and can sell their machines at a much lower cost than major competitors.

A typical component that Elemental buys is a standard motherboard. There are at least six suppliers of equivalent boards in America, Europe and the Far East. Elemental acts as a wholesaler for two of these – one in the Far East and one in South America. The boards are delivered in bulk

and Elemental tests and repackages them to sell to a number of small manufacturers. Each board from the Far East takes 2 hours to test and 2 hours to repackage, while each board from South America takes 3 hours to test and 1 hour to repackage. Elemental has enough facilities to provide up to 8,000 hours a week for testing and 4,000 hours a week for repackaging. There are maximum sales of 1,500 a week for the board from the Far East and each board gives a profit of €20 when sold.

On the production side, Elemental manufactures 4 models of computer (A to D). Each of these has 4 stages in manufacturing – sub-assembly, main assembly, final assembly and finishing. The following table shows the times needed for each stage, total availability each week and some related costs.

Case study continued

	Hours needed per unit				Number of machines	Hours available per machine per week	Time needed for maintenance
	Model A	Model B	Model C	Model D			
Sub-assembly	2	3	4	4	10	40	10%
Main assembly	1	2	2	3	6	36	16.7%
Final assembly	3	3	2	4	12	38	25%
Finishing	2	3	3	3	8	40	10%
Direct costs	€1,600	€1,800	€2,200	€2,500			
Selling price	€2,500	€2,800	€3,400	€4,000			

Fixed costs of production are €3 million a year and Elemental works a standard 48-hour week.

Question

■ Elemental Electronics works in a very competitive industry. Their operations manager has suggested that they should use linear programming more explicitly in their production planning. With the limited information about their operations, could you build a case to support the operations manager's position?

PROBLEMS

11.1 Two additives, X1 and X2, can be used to increase the octane number of petrol. 1 kilogram of X1 in 5,000 litres of petrol increases the octane number by 10, while 1 kilogram of X2 in 5,000 litres increases the octane number by 20. The total additives must increase the octane number by at least 5, but a total of no more than 500 grams can be added to 5,000 litres, and the amount of X2 plus twice the amount of X1 must be at least 500 grams. If X1 costs €30 a kilogram and X2 costs €40 a kilogram, formulate this problem as a linear programme. Use a graphical method to find an optimal solution.

11.2 North Penberthy Housing Association is planning a number of blocks of flats. Five types of block have been designed, containing flats of four categories (1 – senior citizens, 2 – single person, 3 – small family and 4–large family). The number of flats in each block, and other relevant information, is as follows:

Type of block	Number of flats in category				Number of storeys	Plan area	Cost per block ($million)
	1	2	3	4			
A	1	2	4	0	3	5	2.08
B	0	3	6	0	6	5	3.2
C	2	2	2	4	2	8	3.0
D	0	6	0	8	8	6	4.8
E	0	0	10	5	3	4	4.8

The association wants to build a total of 500 flats with at least 40 in category 1 and 125 in each of the other categories. In the past, high-rise flats have proved unpopular and the association wants to limit the number of storeys in the development – with the average number of storeys at most five, and at least half the flats in blocks of three or fewer storeys. An area of 300 units has been set aside for the development and any spare land will be used as a park. Formulate this problem as a linear programme.

11.3 Jane MacFarlane wants a weekly schedule for two business services, X and Y. Each 'unit' of X delivered to customers needs one service package, while each unit of Y uses two of the packages, and Jane has a maximum of 80 packages available a week. Each unit of X and Y needs 10 hours of subcontracted work, and Jane has signed agreements with subcontractors for a weekly minimum of 200 hours and a maximum of 600 hours. Jane knows from market surveys that demand for Y is high, and she will have no trouble selling any number of units. However, there is a maximum demand of 50 units of X, despite a long-term contract to supply 10 units to one customer. The net profit on each unit of X and Y is €2,000 and €3,000 respectively. Formulate this problem as a linear programme. Use a graphical method to find an optimal solution. Use a suitable program to check your results.

11.4 Novacook Ltd makes two types of cooker, one electric and one gas. There are four stages in the production of each of these, with the following features:

Manufacturing stage	Time needed (hours per unit)		Total time available (hours a week)
	Electric	Gas	
Forming	4	2	3,600
Machine shop	10	8	12,000
Assembly	6	4	6,000
Testing	2	2	2,800

Each electric cooker has a variable cost of £200 and a selling price of £300, and each gas cooker has a variable cost of £160 and a selling price of £240. Fixed overheads are £60,000 a week and the company works a 50-week year. The marketing department suggest maximum sales of 800 electric and 1,250 gas cookers a week.

(a) Formulate this as a linear programme.
(b) Find the optimal solution to the problem, and draw a graph to illustrate its features.
(c) A company offers testing services to Novacook. What price should they be prepared to pay for this service, and how much should they buy?
(d) A new cooker is planned that would use the manufacturing stages for 4, 6, 6 and 2 hours respectively. At what selling price should Novacook consider making this cooker if the other variable costs are £168 a unit?

11.5 Tarsands Oil make two blends of fuel by mixing three crude oils. The costs and daily availability of the oils are:

Oil	Cost ($/litre)	Amount available (litres)
A	0.33	5,000
B	0.40	10,000
C	0.48	15,000

The requirements of the blends of fuel are:

Blend 1	at least 30% of A
	at most 45% of B
	at least 25% of C
Blend 2	at most 35% of A
	at least 30% of B
	at most 40% of C

Tarsands sell each litre of Blend 1 for $1.00 and each litre of Blend 2 for $1.20. Long-term contracts require at least 10,000 litres of each blend to be produced. What should Tarsands do?

11.6 Amalgamated Engineering makes two kinds of gearbox – manual and automatic. There are four stages in the production of these, with details of times needed and weekly availabilities given below. The company makes a profit of £64 on each manual gearbox sold and £100 on each automatic gearbox.

Stage in manufacture	Time needed (hours per unit)		Time available (hours per week)
	Manual	Automatic	
Foundry	3	5	7,500
Machine shop	5	4	10,000
Assembly	2	1	3,500
Testing	1	1	2,000

(a) Find an optimal solution to the problem.
(b) The company can start making a new semiautomatic gearbox that needs 4, 4, 1 and 1 hour respectively in each manufacturing stage, and gives a profit of £80 a unit. Should they make this new gearbox?

11.7 Figure 11.11 shows a printout from a linear programming package. Explain what these results show. How could the format of the results be improved?

-=*=- **INFORMATION ENTERED** -=*=-

PROBLEM NAME   :   Manheim Service

NUMBER OF VARIABLES   :   3
    PrA   =   batches of Service Product A
    PrB   =   batches of Service Product B
    PrC   =   batches of Service Product C

NUMBER OF <= CONSTRAINTS   :   1
NUMBER OF = CONSTRAINTS   :   0
NUMBER OF >= CONSTRAINTS   :   2

MAXIMISE Profit   =   10 PrA   +   5 PrB   +   3 PrC

SUBJECT TO:
Constraint 1   120 PrA   +   23 PrB   +   10 PrC   <=   1,545
Constraint 2   150 PrA   +   35 PrB   +   10 PrC   <=   550
Constraint 3   100 PrA   +   15 PrB   +   55 PrC   <=   675

-=*=- **RESULTS** -=*=-

Optimal solution found after   4   iterations

OBJECTIVE FUNCTION VALUE: 51.55

VARIABLE	OPTIMAL VALUE	ORIGINAL PROFIT	INCREASE NEEDED
PrA	3.24	10	0
PrB	0	5	3.07
PrC	6.38	3	0

CONSTRAINT	ORIGINAL RIGHT-HAND VALUE	USED	SLACK OR SURPLUS	SHADOW PRICE
Constraint 1	1,545	452.76	1,092.24	0
Constraint 2	550	550	0	0.034
Constraint 3	675	675	0	0.048

-=*=- **SENSITIVITY ANALYSIS** -=*=-

OBJECTIVE FUNCTION COEFFICIENTS

VARIABLE	LOWER LIMIT	ORIGINAL COEFFICIENT	UPPER LIMIT
PrA	5.46	10	22.54
PrB	1.93	5	no limit
PrC	0.67	3	5.5

SHADOW PRICES VALID IN RHS RANGES

CONSTRAINT	LOWER LIMIT	ORIGINAL VALUE	UPPER LIMIT
Constraint 1	452.76	1,545	no limit
Constraint 2	122.73	550	1,012.5
Constraint 3	366.67	675	3,025

-=*=- **END OF ANALYSIS** -=*=-

Figure 11.11 Printout for Problem 11.7

RESEARCH PROJECTS

11.1 Most spreadsheets have procedures – either as standard or as add-ins – that can solve linear programmes. The best known is Microsoft Excel's Solver. Unfortunately, these can be rather awkward to use. Have a look at the facilities offered by a spreadsheet and explore its features. How could it be made easier to use? What features do you think a reasonable spreadsheet function should have?

11.2 There are many specialised LP packages, ranging from the very basic (and free) to the very sophisticated (and expensive). See what packages you have access to and compare their features. Then use a package to check the results given in this chapter.

11.3 Linear programming is part of a family of methods for solving different types of constrained optimisation problems. Members of this family include integer, zero-one, non-linear and goal programming. Describe the features of other kinds of programming, and the kinds of problem that they tackle.

11.4 The demand in all branches of banks varies during the day. The AIBC International branch in Toronto has a peak demand for domestic transactions around lunchtime. When this is translated into the number of employees needed in the branch, it gives the following pattern.

Period	Number of employees	Period	Number of employees
0900–1000	20	1400–1500	85
1000–1100	35	1500–1600	70
1100–1200	40	1600–1700	45
1200–1300	55	1700–1800	20
1300–1400	75	1800–1900	10

This demand is met by a combination of normal work by full-time staff and overtime by full-time staff and part-time staff. Approximate hourly costs for these are $20, $25 and $15 respectively. The bank aims to provide at least the number of people required at minimum cost. But there are a number of constraints. These include:

- The bank does not work outside the 0900 to 1900 time slot.
- Full-time staff are available for 35 hours a week, and anything beyond this is overtime.
- Full-time staff rarely like to work more than 5 hours of overtime a week.
- All full-time staff have an hour's lunch break at an agreed time between 1100 and 1300.
- Part-time staff work between 4 and 8 hours a day without a lunch break.
- A company policy limits part-time staff to a maximum of 40% of hours worked.

Can LP tackle this kind of scheduling problem?

Sources of information

Further reading

Linear programming appears in books on management science and operational research. The following list gives some more specific references, but these often become very technical.

Basaraa M.S., Jarvis J.J. and Sherali H.D., *Linear Programming and Network Flows* (4th edition), Wiley-Blackwell, New York, 2010.

Derhy M., *Linear Programming, Sensitivity Analysis and Related Topics*, Prentice Hall, Harlow, 2010.

Eiselt H.A. and Sandblom C., *Linear Programming and its Applications*, Springer, Berlin, 2007.

Gass S., *Linear Programming* (5th edition), Dover Publications, New York, 2003.

Grosh D.L., *Linear Programming for Beginners*, Luku.com, 2010.

Kolman B. and Beck R.E., *Elementary Linear Programming with Applications* (2nd edition), Academic Press, London, 1995.

Matousec J. and Gartner B., *Understanding and Using Linear Programming*, Springer, Berlin, 2007.

Moore J.H. and Weatherford L.R., *Decision Modelling with Microsoft Excel* (6th edition), Prentice Hall, Upper Saddle River, NJ, 2001.

Pannell D., *Introduction to Practical Linear Programming*, John Wiley, New York, 1996.

Ragsdale C., *Spreadsheet Modelling and Decision Analysis* (5th edition), South-Western College Publishing, Cincinnati, OH, 2008.

Walker R.C., *Introduction to Mathematical Programming*, Pearson Education, Harlow, 1999.

Williams P., *Model Building in Mathematical Programming* (4th edition), John Wiley, Chichester, 1999.

Winston W.L. and Albright S., *Spreadsheet Modelling and Applications*, Brooks Cole, Florence, KY, 2004.

PART FOUR

Introducing statistics

So far we have looked at problems where there is certainty – which means we know that variables have fixed values, understand the effects of changes, know the constraints on a process and so on. In reality most problems include a lot of uncertainty. Managers do not really know what customers will buy next year, how much oil will cost, what interest rates will be or what competitors will do. We introduced the idea of uncertainty with noise in forecasting and regression. In this part of the book we look more formally at ways of dealing with uncertainty. Specifically, we start developing some ideas of statistics.

This is the fourth part of the book. The first part gave the background and context for the rest of the book. The second part showed how to collect, summarise and present data, and the third part used this data to solve some common business problems. These problems were deterministic, which means that they dealt with certainties. This fourth part considers ways of dealing with uncertainty, introducing the ideas of probability and statistics. The final part uses these to solve some common management problems with uncertainty.

There are four chapters in this fourth part. Chapter 12 introduces the ideas of probability as a way of measuring uncertainty. This is the core idea that is developed in the following chapters. Chapter 13 looks at probability distributions, which describe some common patterns in uncertain data. Chapter 14 returns to the theme of using samples for collecting data and Chapter 15 introduces the ideas of statistical testing, focusing on hypothesis testing.

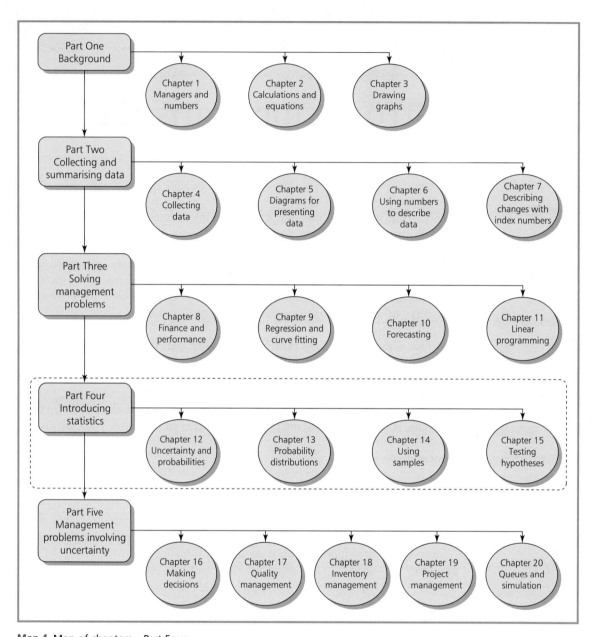

Map 4 Map of chapters – Part Four

CHAPTER 12

Uncertainty and probabilities

Chapter outline

Previous chapters have assumed that we can describe a problem with certainty. This chapter looks at situations where this is not true, and there is some level of uncertainty. We can measure uncertainty with probabilities, where the probability of an event is its likelihood or relative frequency. This basic measure is used in many types of analyses.

Probabilities are used in all the following chapters, so it is important that you understand the basic ideas before moving on. If you have any difficulties it is worth spending the time to sort them out. If you want more information you might find some of the further reading at the end of the chapter useful.

After finishing this chapter you should be able to:

- appreciate the difference between deterministic and stochastic problems
- define probability and appreciate its importance
- calculate probabilities for independent events
- calculate probabilities for mutually exclusive events
- understand the concept of dependent events and conditional probabilities
- use Bayes' theorem to calculate conditional probabilities
- draw probability trees.

Measuring uncertainty

So far, in this book we have largely assumed that we can describe a problem with certainty. We know the number of sales and the prices charged with certainty and can say, 'PhoneLoft sells 1,000 units a year'. When you look at production you can say with certainty, 'Bionorm makes 120,000 units a year at an average cost of $8 a unit'; when you look at employees you know how many are employed, their hours of work, the number of customers they serve and so on. Such situations are called deterministic.

In reality we can never be so confident. We have already seen that random noise makes forecasts wrong. When you spin a coin, you do not know whether it will come down heads or tails; a company launching a new service does not know how many customers it will attract; someone selling a house does not know exactly how much a buyer will pay; a manufacturer does not know exactly how many units it will make. Each of these has some uncertainty, and such situations are described as stochastic or probabilistic.

Although stochastic problems contain uncertainty, this is not the same as ignorance. When you spin a coin the outcome is uncertain – but you know that it will come down either heads or tails, and you know that each of these outcomes is equally likely. When a company launches a new service it does not know exactly how many customers it will attract, but market research should give a reasonable estimate. So managers often have to make decisions when they have some information – but there is still a significant amount of uncertainty. In this chapter we discuss ways of measuring and dealing with uncertainty – and for this we use probabilities.

Defining probability

Probabilities give a measure of uncertainty. To be more precise, the probability of an event is a measure of its likelihood or relative frequency.

Experience leads us to believe that when we toss a fair coin it comes down heads half the time and tails half the time. From this observation we can say, 'the probability that a fair coin comes down heads is 0.5'. This uses a definition of the probability of an event as the proportion of times the event occurs:

$$\text{probability of an event} = \frac{\text{number of ways that the event can occur}}{\text{number of possible outcomes}}$$

When you spin a coin, there are two possible outcomes (heads and tails) and one of these is a head, so the probability of a head is 1/2. Similarly, there are 52 cards in a pack of cards and 1 ace of hearts, so the probability that a card chosen at random is the ace of hearts (or any other specified card) is 1/52. In the last 500 days, the train to work has broken down 10 times, so the probability it broke down on any particular day is 10/500 or 0.02. For 200 of the last 240 trading days the New York Stock Exchange has had more advances than declines, so there is a probability of 200/240 or 0.83 that the stock exchange advanced on a particular day.

Probability measures the proportion of times an event occurs, so its value is defined only in the range 0 to 1:

- Probability = 0 means the event will never occur.
- Probability = 1 means the event will always occur.
- Probability between 0 and 1 gives the relative frequency or likelihood.
- Probabilities outside the range 0 to 1 have no meaning.

An event with a probability of 0.8 is quite likely (it happens 8 times out of 10); an event with a probability of 0.5 is as equally likely to happen as not; an event with a probability of 0.2 is quite unlikely (it happens 2 times out of 10).

Rather than keep saying 'the probability of an event is 0.8', we can abbreviate this to P(event) = 0.8. Then when spinning a coin P(head) = P(tail) = 0.5.

WORKED EXAMPLE 12.1

The *Monthly Gazette* advertised a prize draw with one first prize, five second prizes, 100 third prizes and 1,000 fourth prizes. Prize winners were drawn at random from entries, and after each draw the winning ticket was returned to the draw. By the closing date there were 10,000 entries, and at the draw no entry won more than one prize. What is the probability that a given ticket won first prize, or that it won any prize?

Solution

There were 10,000 entries and 1 first prize, so the probability that a given ticket wins first prize is 1 / 10,000 or P(first prize) = 0.0001.

There are five second prizes, so the probability of a given ticket winning one of these is 5 / 10,000 = 0.0005. The probabilities of winning third or fourth prizes are 100 / 10,000 (= 0.01) and 1,000 / 10,000 (= 0.1) respectively.

There are a total of 1,106 prizes, so the probability of a ticket winning one of these is 1,106 / 10,000 = 0.1106. Conversely 8,894 tickets did not win a prize, so the probability of not winning a prize is 8,894 / 10,000 = 0.8894.

WORKED EXAMPLE 12.2

An office has the following types of employees.

	Female	Male
Administrators	25	15
Operators	35	25

If one person from the office is chosen at random, what is the probability that the person is (a) a male administrator, (b) a female operator, (c) male, (d) an operator?

Solution

(a) Adding the numbers shows that there are 100 people in the office. Of these, 15 are male administrators, so:

P(male administrator) = 15 / 100 = 0.15

(b) 35 people in the office are female operators, so:

P(female operator) = 35 / 100 = 0.35

(c) A total of 40 people in the office are male, so:

P(male) = 40 / 100 = 0.4

(d) A total of 60 people in the office are operators, so:

P(operator) = 60 / 100 = 0.6

These worked examples have suggested two different ways of finding probabilities:

1 **Calculation** – in Worked example 12.1 we used the available information to calculate the probabilities. You can do this when you have enough knowledge of a situation to calculate theoretical or *a priori* probabilities

(called *a priori* because you calculate the probability of an event before it actually happens):

$$\text{probability of an event} = \frac{\text{number of ways that the event can occur}}{\text{number of possible outcomes}}$$

The probability that two people share the same birthday is 1 / 365 (ignoring leap years). This is an *a priori* probability calculated by saying that there are 365 days on which the second person can have any birthday, but only one of these corresponds to the birthday of the first person.

2 **Observation** – in Worked example 12.2 we looked at data for what has actually happened in the past. Then by seeing how often an event actually happened we can get experimental or empirical probabilities:

$$\text{probability of an event} = \frac{\text{number of times that the event occurred}}{\text{number of observations}}$$

In the last 100 matches that a football team played at home, it attracted a crowd of more than 10,000 on 62 occasions. This gives an empirical probability of 62 / 100 = 0.62 that the team attracts a crowd of more than 10,000.

A warning about empirical values is that the historical data must be representative. If a fair coin is tossed five times and comes down heads each time, the empirical evidence suggests that it will always come down heads. This is clearly wrong, and it shows that empirical values must be based on typical values that are collected over a sufficiently long period. Tossing a fair coin 5,000 times will give a more accurate empirical value for the probability of coming down heads.

There is a third way of getting probabilities, which is not generally recommended. This asks people to give their subjective views about probabilities. For instance, you might ask a financial advisor to give a probability that a company will make a profit next year. This is equivalent to judgemental forecasting – and it has the same drawbacks of using personal opinions that are unreliable. If someone tells you that they think a horse has a probability of 0.8 of winning a race, you would still be foolish to back it.

Probability measures the relative likelihood of an event. If you spin a coin 1,000 times, the probability of a head is 0.5, so you would expect 1,000 × 0.5 = 500 heads; if the probability of a bus arriving on time is 0.2, during a working week you would expect 5 × 0.2 = 1 to arrive on time; if the probability of an IT company making a loss is 0.1, you would expect a survey of 100 companies to find 100 × 0.1 = 10 making a loss.

Review questions

12.1 'You cannot tell what is going to happen in the future, so all decisions contain uncertainty.' Do you think this is true?

12.2 What is the probability of an event?

12.3 Does uncertainty mean the same as ignorance?

12.4 Is the probability of an event the same as its relative frequency?

12.5 If the probability of a new car having a fault is 0.01, how many cars with defects would you expect in a sample of 10,000?

CIS personal pensions

Investing in the stock market is risky. Sometimes share prices rise quickly and lucky investors make a fortune; at other times, share prices plummet and unlucky investors lose their shirt. Unfortunately, there seems little underlying logic behind these variations. The 'value' of a company can collapse one day, and then soar the next day. A commentator for the Royal Bank of Canada looked at the wild fluctuations in the stock market and said, 'Market volatility continued in the second quarter of 2000 due to concerns about strong economic growth, inflationary pressures, currency fluctuations and valuations in general'.[1]

Financial managers often try to disguise the fact that they do not know what will happen by talking of uncertainty, difficult conditions, volatility, effects of distortions, cyclical factors and so on. The sensible response of investors is to spread their risk by putting money into a wide range of options. There are several ways of organising this, including unit trusts, managed funds – and in long-term personal pensions. But finance companies

have a fundamental problem, because they want their products to be attractive but they have little idea of long-term returns. Companies such as CIS can say how well they did in the past, and how much you will get if they achieve annual growth of 5%, 7% or 9% in the future, but they have to add cautionary notes such as:[2]

- 'These figures are only examples and are not guaranteed – they are not minimum or maximum amounts. What you get back depends on how your investment works.'
- 'You could get back more or less than this.'
- 'All insurance companies use the same rates of growth for illustrations but their charges vary.'
- 'Do not forget that inflation would reduce what you could buy in the future with the amounts shown.'

In practice, all organisations have to work with uncertainty. They do not know what will happen in the future and have to allow for uncertainty.

Calculations with probabilities

An important concept for probabilities is the independence of events. When the occurrence of one event does not affect the occurrence of a second event, the two events are said to be independent. The fact that a person works in a bank is independent of the fact that they are left-handed; the event that a company has a shipment of raw materials delayed is independent of the event that they increased their marketing budget. Using the notation:

$P(a)$ = the probability of event a
$P(a / b)$ = the probability of event a given that b has already occurred
$P(a / \bar{b})$ = the probability of event of event a given that b has not occurred

two events, a and b, are independent if:

$$P(a) = P(a / b) = P(a / \bar{b})$$

The probability that a person buys a particular newspaper is independent of the probability that they suffer from hay fever, and:

$$P(\text{buys } The\ Times) = P(\text{buys } The\ Times / \text{suffers from hay fever})$$
$$= P(\text{buys } The\ Times / \text{does not suffer from hay fever})$$

For independent events, you find the probability that several events happen by *multiplying* the probabilities of the separate events:

> **For independent events**
> **AND** means that you **multiply** separate probabilities:
> - $P(a \text{ AND } b) = P(a) \times P(b)$
> - $P(a \text{ AND } b \text{ AND } c) = P(a) \times P(b) \times P(c)$
> - $P(a \text{ AND } b \text{ AND } c \text{ AND } d) = P(a) \times P(b) \times P(c) \times P(d)$
> - etc.

WORKED EXAMPLE 12.3

Maxed Mail-order puts a product and the associated invoice into each box they deliver. An average of 3% of products are defective, and an average of 5% of invoices are faulty. What is the probability that a delivery has faults in both the product and the invoice?

Solution
We actually know four probabilities here:

$$P(\text{defective product}) = 3 / 100$$
$$= 0.03$$

$$P(\text{good product}) = 97 / 100$$
$$= 0.97$$

$$P(\text{faulty invoice}) = 5 / 100$$
$$= 0.05$$

$$P(\text{good invoice}) = 95 / 100$$
$$= 0.95$$

Assuming that defects in products and invoices are independent:

$$P(\text{defective product AND faulty invoice})$$
$$= P(\text{defective product}) \times P(\text{faulty invoice})$$
$$= 0.03 \times 0.05 = 0.0015$$

Similarly:

$$P(\text{defective product AND good invoice})$$
$$= 0.03 \times 0.95 = 0.0285$$
$$P(\text{good product AND faulty invoice})$$
$$= 0.97 \times 0.05 = 0.0485$$
$$P(\text{good product AND good invoice})$$
$$= 0.97 \times 0.95 = 0.9215$$

These are the only four possible combinations, so it is not surprising that the probabilities add to 1 – meaning that one of them is certain to happen.

WORKED EXAMPLE 12.4

A warehouse classifies stock into three categories A, B and C. On all category A items it promises a service level of 97% (in other words, there is a probability of 0.97 that the warehouse can meet demand from stock). On category B and C items it promises service levels of 94% and 90% respectively. What are the probabilities that the warehouse can immediately supply an order for:

(a) one item of category A and one item of category B
(b) one item from each category
(c) two different items from A, one from B and three from C
(d) three different items from each category?

Solution
(a) Take P(one A) as the probability that one item of category A is in stock, P(two A) the probability that two items of category A are in stock etc. And assuming that the service levels of each item are independent, you multiply the separate probabilities to get

$$P(\text{one A AND one B}) = P(\text{one A}) \times P(\text{one B})$$
$$= 0.97 \times 0.94$$
$$= 0.912$$

(b) Similarly:

$$P(\text{one A AND one B AND one C})$$
$$= P(\text{one A}) \times P(\text{one B}) \times P(\text{one C})$$
$$= 0.97 \times 0.94 \times 0.90$$
$$= 0.821$$

> **Worked example 12.4 continued**
>
> (c) P(two A AND one B AND three C) = P(two A) × P(one B) × P(three C)
>
> You have to break this down a bit further by noting that the probability of two items of category A being in stock is the probability that the first is there AND the probability that the second is there. In other words:
>
> P(two A) = P(one A AND one A) = P(one A) × P(one A) = P(one A)^2
>
> Similarly:
>
> P(three C) = P(one C AND one C AND one C)
> = P(one C) × P(one C) × P(one C)
> = P(one C)^3
>
> Then the answer becomes:
>
> P(one A)^2 × P(one B) × P(one C)^3
> = $0.97^2 × 0.94 × 0.9^3$
> = 0.645
>
> (d) Similarly:
>
> P(three A AND three B AND three C)
> = P(one A)^3 × P(one B)^3 × P(one C)^3
> = $0.97^3 × 0.94^3 × 0.9^3$
> = 0.553

Mutually exclusive events

Another important idea for probabilities is **mutually exclusive events**. Two events are mutually exclusive when they cannot both happen – and if one of the events happens, then the other event cannot happen. When you toss a coin, having it come down heads is mutually exclusive with having it come down tails; the event that a company makes a profit is mutually exclusive with the event that it makes a loss; the events that sales both increase and decrease are mutually exclusive.

For mutually exclusive events, you can find the probabilities of one or another happening by *adding* the separate probabilities.

> **For mutually exclusive events**
> **OR** means that you **add** separate probabilities:
>
> - P(a OR b) = P(a) + P(b)
> - P(a OR b OR c) = P(a) + P(b) + P(c)
> - P(a OR b OR c OR d) = P(a) + P(b) + P(c) + P(d)
> - etc.

We have already met examples of this, for instance with the *Monthly Gazette*'s prize draw. There the probability that a particular ticket won a prize was 1,106 / 10,000, and the probability that it did not win was 8,894 / 10,000. Each ticket must either win or lose, and these two events are mutually exclusive, so:

$$P(\text{win OR lose}) = P(\text{win}) + P(\text{lose})$$
$$= 0.1106 + 0.8894$$
$$= 1$$

and

$$P(\text{lose}) = 1 - P(\text{win})$$

WORKED EXAMPLE 12.5

Santos Domestica make 40,000 washing machines a year. Of these 10,000 are for the home market, 12,000 are exported to the Americas, 8,000 to Europe, 4,000 to the Far East, and 6,000 to other markets.

(a) What are the probabilities that a particular machine is sold in each of the markets?

(b) What is the probability that a machine is exported?

(c) What is the probability that a machine is exported to either the Americas or Europe?

(d) What is the probability that a machine is sold in either the home or Far East markets?

Solution

(a) The probability that a machine is sold on the home market is:

$$P(home) = \frac{\text{number sold on home market}}{\text{told number sold}}$$

$$= \frac{10,000}{40,000} = 0.25$$

Similarly for the other markets:

$$P(Americas) = 12,000 / 40,000$$
$$= 0.3$$

$$P(Europe) = 8,000 / 40,000$$
$$= 0.2$$

$$P(Far East) = 4,000 / 40,000$$
$$= 0.1$$

$$P(others) = 6,000 / 40,000$$
$$= 0.15$$

These are the only options, and the events – or areas of sales – are mutually exclusive. The probability that a machine is sold somewhere is $0.25 + 0.3 + 0.2 + 0.1 + 0.15 = 1.0$, showing that it must be sold in one of the markets.

(b) As the events are mutually exclusive, you can find the probability that a machine is exported by adding the probabilities that it is sent to each export market:

$$P(exported) = P(\text{Americas OR Europe OR Far East OR others})$$
$$= P(Americas) + P(Europe) + P(Far East) + P(others)$$
$$= 0.3 + 0.2 + 0.1 + 0.15$$
$$= 0.75$$

Alternatively, you can say that all machines are sold somewhere, so the probability that a machine is sold is 1.0. It is either sold on the home market or exported, so:

$$P(\text{exported OR home}) = 1$$
$$= P(exported) + P(home)$$

and

$$P(exported) = 1 - P(home)$$
$$= 1 - 0.25$$
$$= 0.75$$

(c) $P(\text{Americas OR Europe}) = P(Americas) + P(Europe)$
$$= 0.3 + 0.2$$
$$= 0.5$$

(d) $P(\text{home OR Far East}) = P(home) + P(Far East)$
$$= 0.25 + 0.1$$
$$= 0.35$$

Clearly, not all events are mutually exclusive. The event that someone has a blue car is not mutually exclusive with the event that they work in Paris; the event that a company makes a profit is not mutually exclusive with the event that they offer banking services. Suppose you pick a single card from a pack. What is the probability that it is an ace or a heart? Clearly these two are not mutually exclusive because your card can be both an ace and a heart. So you cannot say that:

$$P(\text{ace OR heart}) = P(ace) + P(heart) \quad ✗$$

Venn diagrams give a useful way of illustrating this point. These show the probabilities of events as circles. If two events are mutually exclusive, the Venn diagram shows completely separate circles, as shown in Figure 12.1.

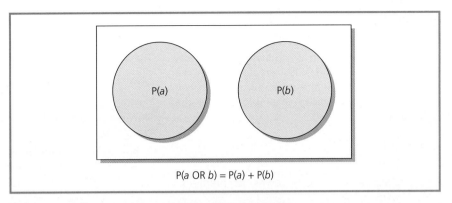

$$P(a \text{ OR } b) = P(a) + P(b)$$

Figure 12.1 Venn diagram for mutually exclusive events

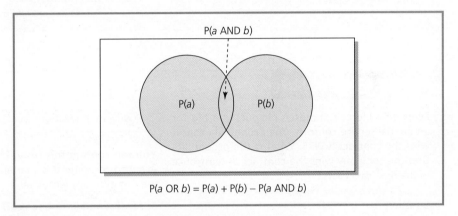

$$P(a \text{ OR } b) = P(a) + P(b) - P(a \text{ AND } b)$$

Figure 12.2 Venn diagram for non-mutually exclusive events

If two events are *not* mutually exclusive, there is a probability they can both occur, as shown in Figure 12.2. The circles now overlap – with the overlap representing the probability that both events occur.

In Venn diagrams the overlap area represents the probability that one or another event occurs. But in Figure 12.2, if you add the probabilities of two events that are not mutually exclusive, you actually add the overlap twice. To correct this, you have to subtract the probability of both events occurring.

> **For events that are not mutually exclusive:**
>
> $P(a \text{ OR } b) = P(a) + P(b) - P(a \text{ AND } b)$

When you pick a single card from a pack, the probability that it is an ace or a heart is:

$$
\begin{aligned}
P(\text{ace OR heart}) &= P(\text{ace}) + P(\text{heart}) - P(\text{ace AND heart}) \\
&= 4 / 52 + 13 / 52 - 1 / 52 \\
&= 16 / 52 \\
&= 0.31
\end{aligned}
$$

WORKED EXAMPLE 12.6

60% of companies in an industrial estate own their premises, and 40% employ more than 30 people. What is the probability that a company owns its premises or employs more than 30 people?

Solution

We know that:

probability a company owns its premises = P(owns) = 0.6

probability a company employs more than 30 = P(employs) = 0.4

These are not mutually exclusive, so:

$$P(\text{owns OR employs}) = P(\text{owns}) + P(\text{employs}) - P(\text{owns AND employs})$$

Now we need P(owns AND employs), and assuming that these two are independent:

$$P(\text{owns AND employs}) = P(\text{owns}) \times P(\text{employs})$$
$$= 0.6 \times 0.4$$
$$= 0.24$$

So:

$$P(\text{owns OR employs}) = 0.6 + 0.4 - 0.24$$
$$= 0.76$$

WORKED EXAMPLE 12.7

Every year Pieter Amundsen plc puts in a bid for an annual service contract. The probability that it wins the contract is 0.75. What is the probability that the company wins the contract at least once in the next two years?

Solution

The probability that the company wins the contract in at least one year is:

$$1 - P(\text{loses in both years}) = 1 - P(\text{loses this year AND loses next year})$$

Assuming that the probability of losing the contract this year is independent of the probability of losing next year (for convenience rather than reality):

$$P(\text{loses this year AND loses next year}) = 0.25 \times 0.25$$
$$= 0.0625$$

$$P(\text{wins in at least one year}) = 1 - 0.0625$$
$$= 0.9375$$

You can confirm this result by assuming that the events of winning this year and winning next year are not mutually exclusive:

P(wins in at least one year)
= P(wins this year OR wins next year)
= P(wins this year) + P(wins next year) − P(wins this year AND wins next year)

Now:

$$P(\text{wins this year AND wins next year}) = 0.75 \times 0.75$$
$$= 0.5625$$

So:

$$P(\text{wins in at least one year}) = 0.75 + 0.75 - 0.5625$$
$$= 0.9375$$

Review questions

12.6 What are independent events?

12.7 What are mutually exclusive events?

12.8 How would you find the probability that one of several mutually exclusive events occurs?

12.9 How would you find the probability that all of several independent events occur?

12.10 If events X and Y are not mutually exclusive, what is P(X or Y)?

IDEAS IN PRACTICE   Medical testing

Many medical conditions can be treated much more effectively if they are detected early. For example, when certain heart conditions are caught early, they can be treated with mild medicines – but if they are not detected until later, both the conditions and the treatment are much more severe. The problem is detecting conditions at an early stage, when there are no significant symptoms.

Many health services routinely screen populations to detect some conditions (such as breast cancer) as early as possible. Unfortunately, these tests do not give a simple result of 'problem' or 'no problem' that is guaranteed to be accurate.

In one area – and you do not need to worry about the details – it is estimated that 0.5% of the population will contract a certain type of cancer. A simple and established test for detecting this cancer is said to be 98% accurate. It is very good to have such a reliable test – but it is not used for routine screening. You can see the arguments for not using it by doing some calculations.

If a screening programme tests 10,000 people, 50 are likely to actually have the cancer. Of these 50, 98%, or 49, will give a correct positive response to the test, and one will be missed. Of the remaining 9,950 people, 2%, or 199, will give an incorrect positive response. So there is a total of 248 positive responses, of which 49 are correct. The remainder face a mixture of unnecessary anguish, further tests and possibly unneeded treatment.

Conditional probabilities

Many events are not independent, and the occurrence of one event can directly affect the probability of another. For example, the fact that someone is employed in one of the professions is not independent of their having had higher education; the probability that a machine breaks down this week is not independent of whether or not it was maintained last week; the probability that a train arrives late is not independent of the service operator.

For **dependent events**, the fact that one event has occurred or not changes the probability that a second event occurs. Again using:

P(a) = the probability of event a
P(a / b) = the probability of event a given that b has already occurred
P($a / \bar{b}$) = the probability of event a given that b has not occurred

two events, a and b, are dependent if:

P(a) ≠ P(a / b) ≠ P($a / \bar{b}$)

(Remember that the symbol ≠ means 'is not equal to'.)

The probability that the price of a company's shares rises is dependent on whether or not the company announces a profit or a loss. Then:

P(share price rises) ≠ P(share price rises / announce profit)
≠ P(share price rises / announce loss)

Probabilities with the form P(a / b) are called conditional probabilities – because the probability of a occurring is conditional on whether or not b has already occurred.

The most important rule for conditional probabilities is that the probability of two dependent events occurring is the probability of the first, multiplied by the conditional probability that the second occurs given that the first has already occurred. We can write this rather clumsy statement as:

$$P(a \text{ AND } b) = P(a) \times P(b / a)$$

With a bit of thought, you can extend this to the obvious result:

$$P(a \text{ AND } b) = P(a) \times P(b / a)$$
$$= P(b) \times P(a / b)$$

Rearranging these gives the most important calculation for conditional probabilities, which is known as **Bayes' theorem**:

$$P(a / b) = \frac{P(b / a) \times P(a)}{P(b)} = \frac{P(a \text{ AND } b)}{P(b)}$$

To put it simply, when you have a conditional probability $P(b / a)$, Bayes' theorem lets you do the reverse calculation to find $P(a / b)$.

WORKED EXAMPLE 12.8

The students in a class can be described as follows:

	Home	Overseas
Male	66	29
Female	102	3

(a) If you choose a student from the class at random and she is female, what is the probability that she is from overseas?

(b) If the student is from overseas, what is the probability that the student is female?

Solution

(a) The make-up of the class suggests that the event that a student is female is not independent of the fact that they are from overseas. So we want P(overseas / female) and can calculate this from Bayes' theorem:

$$P(a / b) = \frac{P(a \text{ AND } b)}{P(b)}$$

so

$$P(\text{overseas / female}) = \frac{P(\text{overseas AND female})}{P(\text{female})}$$

There are 200 students, with 105 females and 3 females from overseas, so:

$$P(\text{overseas AND female}) = 3 / 200$$
$$= 0.015$$
$$P(\text{female}) = 105 / 200$$
$$= 0.525$$

so:

$$P(\text{overseas / female}) = 0.015 / 0.525$$
$$= 0.029$$

You can check this by considering the 105 female students, and see that 3 are from overseas, so:

P(overseas / female) = number of overseas females / number of females
$$= 3/105$$
$$= 0.029.$$

The related calculation shows that:

$$P(\text{overseas / male}) = \frac{P(\text{overseas AND male})}{P(\text{male})}$$
$$= 0.145 / 0.475$$
$$= 0.305$$

You can also calculate:

P(overseas) = number from overseas / number of students
$$= 32 / 200$$
$$= 0.16$$

Worked example 12.8 continued

These results confirm that 'female' and 'from overseas' are not independent because:

$$P(overseas) \neq P(overseas / female)$$
$$\neq P(overseas / male)$$

(b) Now we want P(female / overseas) and can again calculate this from Bayes' theorem:

$$P(a / b) = \frac{P(b / a) \times P(a)}{P(b)}$$

so

$$P(female / overseas)$$
$$= \frac{P(overseas / female) \times P(female)}{P(overseas)}$$

We have just calculated P(overseas / female) = 0.029, and we know that P(female) = 0.525 and P(overseas) = 0.16. So:

$$P(female / overseas) = 0.029 \times 0.525 / 0.016$$
$$= 0.094$$

You can check this by considering the 32 overseas students and see that 3 of them are female, so:

$$P(female / overseas) = number\ of\ overseas$$
$$females / number\ of\ overseas\ students$$
$$= 3 / 32$$
$$= 0.094$$

WORKED EXAMPLE 12.9

Two machines make identical parts that are combined on a production line. The older machine makes 40% of the parts, of which 85% are of good quality; the newer machine makes 60% of the parts, of which 92% are good. A random check further down the production line shows an unusual fault, which suggests the particular machine that made the part needs adjusting. What is the probability that the older machine made the part?

Solution
Figure 12.3 gives a summary of this problem. Using the abbreviations O for the older machine, N for the newer machine, G for good units and F for faulty ones, we have P(F / O) etc. and want to find P(O / F). For this we use Bayes' theorem:

$$P(a / b) = \frac{P(b / a) \times P(a)}{P(b)}$$

Then:

$$P(O / F) = \frac{P(F / O) \times P(O)}{P(F)}$$

We know that P(O) = 0.4 and P(F / O) = 0.15, so the remaining value we need is P(F), the probability that a unit is faulty. With a bit of thought you can see that:

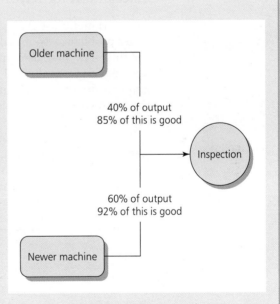

Figure 12.3 Process for Worked example 12.9

probability (a unit is faulty) = probability (it is faulty from the old machine OR it is faulty from the new machine)

or:

$$P(F) = P(F\ AND\ O) + P(F\ AND\ N)$$

▶

Worked example 12.9 continued

These are conditional probabilities which we can write as:

$$P(F) = P(F / O) \times P(O) + P(F / N) \times P(N)$$

We know all of these, and:

$$P(F) = 0.15 \times 0.4 + 0.08 \times 0.6$$
$$= 0.108$$

Then:

$$P(O / F) = \frac{P(O / F) \times P(O)}{P(F)} = \frac{0.15 \times 0.4}{0.108}$$

$$= \frac{0.06}{0.108}$$

$$= 0.556$$

To check this result, we can also calculate the probability that the unit came from the new machine given that it is faulty:

$$P(N/F) = \frac{P(F / N) \times P(N)}{P(F)}$$

$$= \frac{0.08 \times 0.6}{0.108}$$

$$= 0.444$$

As the faulty unit must have come from either the older or the newer machine, the fact that P(O / F) + P(N / F) = 1 confirms the result.

Calculations for Bayes' theorem

The arithmetic for Bayes' theorem is straightforward, but it is messy for larger problems – so it makes sense to use a computer. There are two options for this. The first uses specialised statistical software that automatically does Bayesian analysis. Figure 12.4 shows a printout from a simple program for doing the calculations for Worked example 12.9. In this you can see the figures that we calculated (together with some others that we explain below).

The other option is to use a spreadsheet. Your spreadsheet may not have a standard function for this, but there are special add-ins – or you can do the calculations yourself. For this last option, there is a simple way of organising the calculations. Using the data from Worked example 12.9, this starts by putting the available values in a table.

	Conditional probabilities		Prior probabilities
	Faulty	Good	
Older machine	0.15	0.85	0.4
Newer machine	0.08	0.92	0.6

This box includes the 'conditional probabilities', which are the probabilities that units are good or faulty given that they come from each machine. So the conditional probabilities are P(F / O) = 0.15, P(F / N) = 0.08 etc. The entries to the right give the values of P(O) and P(N), which are called the 'prior probabilities'.

Now we form a third box by multiplying each conditional probability in the left-hand box by the prior probability on the same line. So 0.15 × 0.4 = 0.060, 0.08 × 0.6 = 0.048 etc. These results are called 'joint probabilities'.

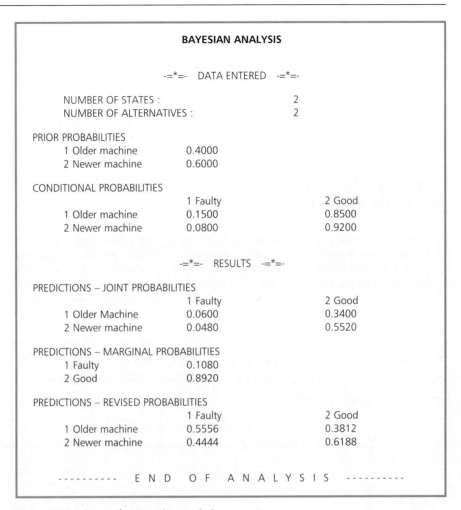

Figure 12.4 Printout for Bayesian analysis

	Conditional probabilities		Prior probabilities	Joint probabilities	
	Faulty	Good		Faulty	Good
Older machine	0.15	0.85	0.4	0.060	0.340
Newer machine	0.08	0.92	0.6	0.048	0.552
			Marginal probabilities	0.108	0.892
	Revised probabilities		Older machine	0.556	0.381
			Newer machine	0.444	0.619

Adding each column of joint probabilities gives a 'marginal probability'. Then 0.060 + 0.048 = 0.108, which is the probability that a unit is faulty; 0.340 + 0.552 = 0.892, which is the probability that a unit is good.

Finally, dividing each joint probability by the marginal probability in the same column gives a revised probability shown in a bottom box. Then 0.060 / 0.108 = 0.556, 0.340 / 0.892 = 0.381 etc. These revised probabilities are the results that we want, giving P(O/F), P(N/G) and so on.

At first this procedure seems strange, but if you look at the equation for Bayes' theorem you can see that we are simply repeating the calculations automatically. The joint probabilities are the top lines of Bayes' theorem, the marginal probabilities are the bottom line and dividing one by the other gives the final calculation.

WORKED EXAMPLE 12.10

The probabilities of two events X and Y are 0.3 and 0.7 respectively. Three events A, B and C can follow X and Y, with conditional probabilities given in the following table. What results do you get from using Bayes' theorem on these figures?

	A	B	C
X	0.1	0.5	0.4
Y	0.7	0.2	0.1

Solution

The table gives the conditional probabilities of P(A/X), P(B/X) etc. You know the prior probabilities of P(X) = 0.3 and P(Y) = 0.7. Figure 12.5 shows a spreadsheet of the results from the mechanical procedure for Bayes' theorem.

The marginal probabilities show P(A) = 0.52, P(B) = 0.29 and P(C) = 0.19. The predictions in the bottom boxes show the probability of P(X/A) = 0.058, P(X/B) = 0.517, P(Y/A) = 0.942 and so on.

	A	B	C	D	E	F	G	H
1	**Bayes' theorem**							
2								
3		Conditional probabilities			Priors		Joint probabilities	
4		A	B	C		A	B	C
5	X	0.1	0.5	0.4	0.3	0.03	0.15	0.12
6	Y	0.7	0.2	0.1	0.7	0.49	0.14	0.07
7						0.52	0.29	0.19
8					X	0.058	0.517	0.632
9					Y	0.942	0.483	0.368

Figure 12.5 Calculations for Bayes' theorem in Worked example 12.10

Probability trees

Venn diagrams give one way of visualising probabilities, and of indicating the calculations needed. A probability tree gives another format for picturing a series of calculations. Figure 12.6 shows a probability tree for Worked example 12.9, about faulty parts produced by two machines.

Probability trees consist of circles – called nodes – which represent points at which alternative events might occur. Branches emerge from the nodes to represent alternative events. Each branch has an associated probability.

You move through the diagram from left to right, starting at a single node. In Figure 12.6, node 1 is the starting point. From here there are two alternatives – either the part comes from the older machine (with a probability of 0.4) or it comes from the newer machine (with a probability of 0.6). Then at both nodes 2 and 3 there are two possibilities because a part is either faulty or good. Each branch is labelled with its probability – and because we

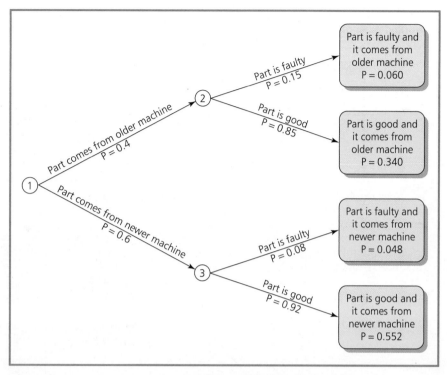

Figure 12.6 A probability tree of faulty parts for Worked example 12.9

include all possible events, the sum of probabilities on branches leaving any node must be 1. At the right of the tree are the terminal values that show the overall probability of reaching the points. To find a terminal probability, you simply multiply together all the probabilities along the path taken to reach that point. So, the first terminal node shows the probability that a part is faulty and comes from the older machine, which is $0.4 \times 0.15 = 0.060$. The second terminal node shows the probability that a part is good and comes from the older machine, which is $0.4 \times 0.85 = 0.340$ and so on. Again, the sum of all the terminal values should be 1.

WORKED EXAMPLE 12.11

60% of second-hand cars can be classified as good buys, and the remainder are bad buys. Among good buys, 70% have low oil consumption and 20% have medium oil consumption. Among bad buys 50% have high oil consumption and 30% have medium oil consumption. A test was done on a second-hand car and showed low oil consumption. What is the probability that this car is a good buy?

Solution

We start by defining the values that we know, using the abbreviations GB and BB for good buy

and bad buy, and HOC, MOC and LOC for high, medium and low oil consumption. We know figures for $P(LOC/GB)$, etc., and we are looking for $P(GB/LOC)$ – and we find these by substituting into Bayes' theorem. Figure 12.7 shows these results in a spreadsheet, and you can see that the probability that a car is a good buy, given that it has a low oil consumption, is 0.84. You can also see that the probability of a low oil consumption is 0.5. Figure 12.8 shows these results in a probability tree.

Worked example 12.11 continued

	A	B	C	D	E	F	G	H
1	**Bayes' theorem**							
2								
3		Conditional probabilities			Priors	Joint probabilities		
4		HOC	MOC	LOC		HOC	MOC	LOC
5	GB	0.1	0.2	0.7	0.6	0.06	0.12	0.42
6	BB	0.5	0.3	0.2	0.4	0.20	0.12	0.08
7						0.26	0.24	0.50
8					GB	0.23	0.50	0.84
9					BB	0.77	0.50	0.16

Figure 12.7 Calculations for Bayes' theorem in Worked example 12.11

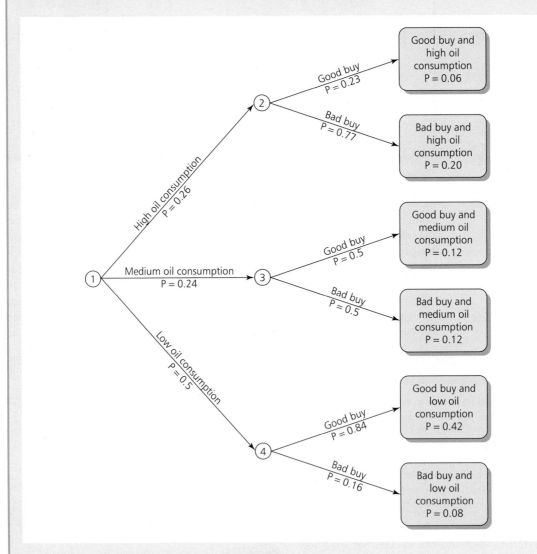

Figure 12.8 Probability tree for Worked example 12.11

Review questions

12.11 What are dependent events?

12.12 What are conditional probabilities?

12.13 What is Bayes' theorem and when is it used?

12.14 What is the benefit of a probability tree?

IDEAS IN PRACTICE US Coast Guard

The US Coast Guard monitors and protects America's 20,000 km of coastline.[3] They use many measures of performance – one of these considers the probability that they will intercept a target vessel. The probability that a target vessel is intercepted depends on the probability that it is detected. So a basic model has:

$$P(I) = P(I / D) \times P(D)$$

where: $P(I)$ = probability that a vessel is intercepted

$P(I / D)$ = probability that a vessel is intercepted, given that it is detected, which can beestimated from historical records.

A fuller model has:

$$P(I) = P(I / D) \times P(D / O) \times P(O / A) \times P(A)$$

where: $P(D / O)$ = probability that a target vessel is detected, given that a Coast Guard vessel is on patrol

$P(O / A)$ = probability that a Coast Guard vessel is on patrol, given that it is in the right area

$P(A)$ = probability that the Coast Guard vessel is in the right area.

This model helps in testing different methods of organising patrol vessels, and helps to increase the efficiency of the service.

Source: Kimbrough S.O., Oliver J.R. and Pritchett C.W., On post-evaluation analysis, *Interfaces*, Vol. 23(3), 1993.

CHAPTER REVIEW

This chapter introduced the idea of probability as a way of measuring uncertainty.

- Some problems are deterministic, where features are known with certainty. However, most real problems met by managers are stochastic or probabilistic. This means that there is some level of uncertainty.

- Probabilities give a way of measuring uncertainty. They define the likelihood that an event will occur, or its relative frequency.

- Probabilities can either be calculated *a priori* or observed empirically. Less reliable estimates might emerge as subjective probabilities.

- A probability gives a measure of relative frequency, so it is defined on a scale of 0 (meaning there is no chance of an event happening) to 1 (meaning that it is certain to happen). Probabilities outside this range have no meaning.

- Two basic rules for probabilities are:
  - for independent events, $P(a \text{ AND } b) = P(a) \times P(b)$
  - for mutually exclusive events, $P(a \text{ OR } b) = P(a) + P(b)$

- Conditional probabilities occur when two events are dependent – so that:

$$P(a) \neq P(a \mathbin{/} b) \neq P(a \mathbin{/} \not{b})$$

- The most important result for conditional probabilities is Bayes' theorem:

$$P(a \mathbin{/} b) = \frac{P(b \mathbin{/} a) \times P(a)}{P(b)} = \frac{P(a \text{ AND } b)}{P(b)}$$

- A probability tree shows the relationships between events as branches coming from nodes.

CASE STUDY The *Gamblers' Press*

The *Gamblers' Press* is a weekly paper that publishes large amounts of information that is used by gamblers. Its main contents are detailed sections on horse racing, greyhound racing, football and other major sporting activities. It also runs regular features on card games, casino games and other areas that gamblers find interesting.

The *Gamblers' Press* was founded in 1897 and now has a regular circulation of 50,000 copies. It is considered a highly respectable paper and has a strict policy of giving only factual information. It never gives tips or advice. Last year it decided to run a special feature on misleading or dishonest practices. This idea was suggested when four unconnected reports were passed to the editors.

The first report concerned an 'infallible' way of winning at roulette. Customers were charged $500 for the details of the scheme, which was based on a record of all the numbers that won on the roulette wheel during one evening. Then the customers were advised to bet on two sets of numbers:

- those that had come up more often, because the wheel might be biased in their favour
- those that had come up least often, because the laws of probability say that numbers that appear less frequently on one night must appear more frequently on another night.

The second report showed that a number of illegal chain letters were circulating in Germany. These letters contained a list of eight names. Individuals were asked to send €10 to the name at the top of the list. Then they should delete the name at the top, insert their own name at the bottom and send a copy of the letter to eight of their friends. As each name moved to the top

of the list they would receive payments from people who joined the chain later. The advertising accompanying these letters guaranteed to make respondents millionaires, claiming 'You cannot lose!!!' It also said that people who did not respond would be letting down their friends and would inevitably be plagued by bad luck.

The third report was about 'a horse racing consultant', who sent people a letter saying which horse would win a race the following week. A week later he sent a second letter saying how the selected horse had won, and giving another tip for the following week. This was repeated for a third week. Then after three wins the 'consultant' said he would send the name of another horse which was guaranteed to win next week – but this time there would be a cost of $5,000. This seemed a reasonable price because the horse was certain to win and gamblers could place bets of any size. Unfortunately this scheme had a drawback. Investigators thought that the 'consultant' sent out about 10,000 of the original letters, and randomly tipped each horse in a five-horse race. The second letter was sent only to those people who had been given the winning horse. The next two letters followed the same pattern, with follow-up letters sent only to those who had been given the winning horse.

The fourth report concerned a European lottery, where people entered by paying €1 and choosing six numbers in the range 00 to 99. At the end of a week a computer generated a set of six random numbers, and anyone with the same six numbers would win the major prize (typically several million euros), and people with four or five matching numbers would win smaller prizes. A magazine reported a way of dramatically increasing the chances of winning. This suggested taking your eight favourite numbers and then betting on all combinations of six numbers from these eight. The advertisement explained the benefit of this, 'Suppose there is a chance of one in a million of winning the first prize. If one of your lucky numbers is chosen by the computer, you will have this number in over a hundred entries, so your chances of winning are raised by 100 to only 1 in 10,000.'

Question

■ The *Gamblers' Press* finds schemes like these four almost every day, and often publishes articles on them. What do such schemes have in common? If you were asked to write an article about these four schemes, what would you say? You might start by explaining why the four schemes mentioned do not work, and then expand the study to include other examples of such schemes.

PROBLEMS

12.1 An office has the following types of employees.

	Female	Male
Administrative	20	21
Managerial	12	10
Operational	42	38

If one person from the office is chosen at random, what is the probability that the person is: (a) a male administrator, (b) a female manager, (c) male, (d) an operator, (e) either a manager or an administrator, (f) either a female administrator or a female manager?

12.2 A quality control test has five equally likely outcomes – A, B, C, D and E.

(a) What is the probability of C occurring?
(b) What is the probability of A or B or C occurring?
(c) What is the probability that neither A nor B occur?

12.3 Four mutually exclusive events A, B, C and D have probabilities of 0.1, 0.2, 0.3 and 0.4 respectively. What are the probabilities of the following occurring: (a) A and B, (b) A or B, (c) neither A nor B, (d) A and B and C, (e) A or B or C, (f) none of A, B or C?

12.4 If you choose a card at random from a complete pack, what is the probability that it is: (a) an ace, (b) a heart, (c) an ace and a heart, (d) an ace or a heart, (e) neither an ace nor a heart?

12.5 Bert Klassen schedules three calls for a particular day, and each call has a probability of 0.5 of making a sale. What are his probabilities of making (a) three sales, (b) two or more sales, (c) no sales?

12.6 There are 20 people in a room. What is the probability that they all have different birthdays?

12.7 If $P(a) = 0.4$ and $P(b/a) = 0.3$, what is $P(a$ AND $b)$? If $P(b) = 0.6$, what is $P(a/b)$?

12.8 The probabilities of two events X and Y are 0.4 and 0.6 respectively. The conditional probabilities of three other events A, B and C occurring, given that X or Y has already occurred, are:

	A	B	C
X	0.2	0.5	0.3
Y	0.6	0.1	0.3

What are the conditional probabilities of X and Y occurring, given that A, B or C has already occurred?

12.9 Kenny Lam works in a purchasing department that buys materials from three main suppliers, with X supplying 35% of the department's needs, Y supplying 25% and Z the rest. The quality of the materials is described as good, acceptable or poor with the following proportions from each supplier:

	Good	Acceptable	Poor
X	0.2	0.7	0.1
Y	0.3	0.65	0.05
X	0.1	0.8	0.1

What information can you find using Bayes' theorem on these figures? How would you show these results on a probability tree?

12.10 Data collected from Cape Town shows that 60% of drivers are above 30 years old. 5% of all the drivers over 30 will be prosecuted for a driving offence during a year, compared with 10% of drivers aged 30 or younger. If a driver has been prosecuted, what is the probability they are 30 or younger?

RESEARCH PROJECTS

12.1 Spreadsheets include a lot of statistical analyses, but these are often rather difficult to use and understand. Have a look at the statistics available on a typical spreadsheet and see what functions they include. If you want to do some large-scale statistical analysis, it is better to use specialised programs such as Minitab, SAS, S-plus, SPSS or STATISTICA. Do a small survey of statistical packages and see what extra features they have.

12.2 The *Gamblers' Press* case study showed some misleading uses of statistics. Unfortunately this is fairly common. Find some other example where statistics are used to give the wrong impression – either intentionally or unintentionally.

12.3 Marius Gensumara found that during a typical period the following numbers of people did not turn up to work at his company in consecutive days:

13, 16, 24, 21, 15, 23, 15, 26, 25, 11, 10, 24, 27, 30, 15, 31, 25, 19, 15, 27

He wanted to improve this and introduced a new scheme of incentives and payments in general. He did not discuss this with the workforce or anyone else, and when he rechecked the numbers of absentees he found these numbers:

31, 29, 27, 30, 26, 28, 38, 34, 40, 25, 29, 34, 33, 30, 28, 26, 41, 45, 30, 28

Marius felt that there was some unhappiness with his new scheme and the way that it had been introduced. So he had various negotiations and agreed another incentive scheme. Now, rechecking the absentees, he found the following numbers each day:

9, 12, 16, 8, 24, 9, 15, 16, 20, 21, 9, 11, 10, 10, 25, 17, 16, 18, 9, 8

What do these figures suggest? Find some examples of statistics that have been used in negotiations and say how they have been interpreted.

12.4 A lot of websites give tutorials on topics of statistics that are useful for managers. These sites are produced by universities, institutions, publishers, training companies, software providers, tutoring services, consultants and so on. Do some searches on the Web to find sites that are useful for this course.

Sources of information

References

1 RBC Asset Management, Inc., *Investment Update*, Royal Bank of Canada, Toronto, 2002.

2 CIS, promotional material, Co-operative Insurance Society, Manchester, 2006.

3 CIA, *World Factbook*, Brassey's Inc., Dulles, VA, 2000.

Further reading

There are many books on probability and statistics, ranging from the trivial through to the highly mathematical. You might look at the following as a starting point. These all include material that you can use for other chapters.

Aczel A.D. and Sounderpandian J., *Complete Business Statistics* (7th edition), McGraw Hill, New York, 2008.

Anderson D., Sweeney D., Williams T., Freeman J. and Shoesmith E., *Essentials of Statistics for Business and Economics*, Thomson Learning, London, 2007.

Berenson M.L., Levin D. and Krehbiel T.C., *Basic Business Statistics* (11th edition), Pearson Education, New York, 2008.

Campbell M.J., *Statistics at Square One*, Wiley-Blackwell, Hoboken, NJ, 2009.

Doane D. and Seward L., *Applied Statistics in Business and Economics* (3rd edition), McGraw Hill, New York, 2010.

Graham A., *Teach Yourself Statistics* (5th edition), Teach Yourself Books, London, 2008.

Groebner D.F., *Business Statistics* (7th edition), Pearson Education, New York, 2007.

Kazmier L., *Schaum's Outline of Business Statistics*, McGraw Hill, New York, 2009.

Kvanli A.H., *Concise Managerial Statistics*, South Western College Publishing, Cincinnati, OH, 2005.

McClave J., Benson P. and Sincich T., *Statisics for Business and Economics* (11th edition), Pearson Education, New York, 2010.

McGrane A. and Smailes J., *Essential Business Statistics*, FT/Prentice Hall, Harlow, 2000.

Moore D.S., McCabe G.P., Duckworth W. and Sclove S., *Practice of Business Statistics* (3rd edition), W.H. Freeman, New York, 2010.

Moore J.H. and Weatherford L.R., *Decision Modelling with Microsoft Excel* (6th edition), Prentice Hall, Upper Saddle River, NJ, 2001.

Newbold P., Carlson W.L. and Thorne B., *Statistics for Business and Economics* (6th edition), Prentice Hall, Englewood Cliffs, NJ, 2007.

Ragsdale C., *Spreadsheet Modelling and Decision Analysis* (5th edition), South-Western College Publishing, Cincinnati, OH, 2008.

Rowntree D., *Statistics Without Tears: a Primer for Non-mathematicians*, Allyn and Bacon, London, 2003.

Rumsey D., *Statistics for Dummies*, John Wiley, New York, 2003.

Taylor S., *Business Statistics* (2nd edition), Palgrave Macmillan, Basingstoke, 2007.

Upton G. and Cook I., *Dictionary of Statistics*, Oxford University Press, Oxford, 2008.

Weiers R., *Introduction to Business Statistics* (International edition), South Western College Publishing, Cincinnati, OH, 2007.

Winston W.L. and Albright S., *Spreadsheet Modelling and Applications*, Brooks Cole, Florence, KY, 2004.

Probability distributions

Chapter outline

Probability distributions are essentially the same as percentage frequency distributions; they show the relative frequencies – or probabilities – of related events. You can draw an empirical distribution for any set of data – but there are standard distributions that describe many real problems. This chapter describes three important distributions. The binomial distribution calculates the probable number of successes in a series of trials, the Poisson distribution describes random events, and the Normal distribution is the most widely used distribution, describing continuous data in many different circumstances.

After finishing this chapter you should be able to:

- understand the role of probability distributions
- draw an empirical probability distribution
- describe the difficulties of sequencing and scheduling
- calculate numbers of combinations and permutations
- know how to use a binomial distribution and calculate probabilities
- know how to use a Poisson distribution and calculate probabilities
- work with a Normal distribution and do related calculations
- ease calculations by approximating one distribution by another.

Frequency distributions

In Chapter 5 we described a percentage frequency distribution, which shows the proportion of observations in different classes. Chapter 12 described probabilities as measures of relative frequency. Combining these two ideas gives **probability distributions** – which describe the probabilities of observations being in different classes.

WORKED EXAMPLE 13.1

Every night the Luxor Hotel has a number of people who book rooms by telephone, but do not actually turn up. Managers recorded the numbers of no-shows over a typical period:

2 4 6 7 1 3 3 5 4 1 2 3 4 3 5 6 2 4 3 2 5 5

0 3 3 2 1 4 4 4 3 1 3 6 3 4 2 5 3 2 4 2 5 3 4

Draw a frequency table for the data. How can you use this to draw a probability distribution? What is the probability that there are more than four no-shows?

Solution

A frequency table shows the number of nights with various numbers of no-shows, given in this table:

No-shows	0	1	2	3	4	5	6	7
Frequency	1	4	8	12	10	6	3	1
Relative frequency or probability	0.02	0.09	0.18	0.27	0.22	0.13	0.07	0.02

Dividing each of the frequencies by the total number of observations (45) gives the relative frequency – or probability. For instance, there were 7 no-shows on one night, so the probability of 7 no-shows is 7 / 45 = 0.02. Repeating this calculation for each class gives the relative frequencies, or probability distribution. This is drawn as a bar chart in Figure 13.1.

The probability of more than four no-shows is:

$$P(5) + P(6) + P(7) = 0.13 + 0.07 + 0.02$$
$$= 0.22$$

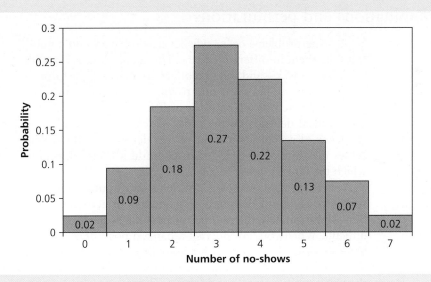

Figure 13.1 A probability distribution for Worked example 13.1

The probability distribution in Worked example 13.1 is empirical, which means that it came from actual observations. You can use this approach for any problem where you have enough observations. The result is useful for summarising data – but with the weakness that the resulting distribution is specific to a particular problem and it cannot be used for any other problem. The probability distribution in Figure 13.1 describes the number of no-shows in the Luxor Hotel, but you cannot assume that the same distribution works for other hotels, let alone other problems.

However, if you look at a lot of empirical distributions you often see common patterns. For instance, if you look at the probability distribution for the size of purchases from a website, it looks very similar to the distribution of the annual production from a fruit farm. This suggests that some probability distributions do not just refer to a specific problem, but are more widely applicable. Three common distributions of this type are:

- binomial distribution
- Poisson distribution
- Normal (or Gaussian) distribution.

We discuss the features of these three in the rest of the chapter. We start with the binomial distribution, but this uses some ideas from sequencing. So before we can look at the distribution itself, we have to review some of the related calculations.

Review questions	13.1	What is the purpose of a probability distribution?
	13.2	Is a probability distribution the same as a relative frequency distribution?
	13.3	What are empirical probability distributions?

Combinations and permutations

Sequencing problems occur whenever you have to do a number of tasks, and can take them in different orders. The sequence describes the order in which you do the tasks – and this can affect your overall performance. For example, a bus travelling between one town and another can visit stops in different orders, each of which gives a different travel time; the time it takes to cook a meal depends on the order in which you do all the related tasks; the efficiency of a communication system depends on the order in which it processes messages; the time taken to build a house depends on the order in which the builder does the jobs.

At first sight, sequencing problems seem quite easy – to solve them you simply consider all the possible sequences of activities, and then choose the best. Unfortunately the number of possible sequences makes this notoriously difficult. When you have to visit a bank, a post office and a supermarket, you have six possible sequences for your three visits. But suppose that you have to complete n activities and want to find the best sequence. You can choose the first activity as any one of the n. Then you can choose the second activity as any one of the remaining $(n - 1)$, so there are $n(n - 1)$ possible sequences for the first two activities. You can choose the third activity as any one of the remaining $(n - 2)$, giving you $n(n - 1)(n - 2)$ possible sequences for the first three activities. Then the fourth is any of the remaining $(n - 3)$ and so on. By the time you have chosen the final activity, the total number of possible sequences for n activities is:

$$\text{number of sequences} = n(n-1)(n-2)(n-3)\ldots\times 3\times 2\times 1 = n!$$

(Remember that $n!$ – pronounced 'n factorial' – is an abbreviation for $n(n-1)$ $(n-2)\ldots\times 3\times 2\times 1$. Also note that $1! = 0! = 1$)

If you have five activities, there are $5\times 4\times 3\times 2\times 1 = 120$ possible sequences. So with visits to a bank, post office, supermarket, petrol station and café there are 120 ways in which you can organise your trip. When you have 10 activities you have more than 3.6 million possible sequences, and with 15 activities this has risen to 1.3×10^{12}.

Instead of finding the best sequence of all n activities, suppose that you only want to find the best sequence of r of them. There are two calculations for this, which are called combinations and permutations.

When you want to select r things from n, and you are not interested in the order in which the r things are selected, only whether they are selected or not, then you are concerned with the **combination** of r things from n.

> The **combination** of r things from n is the number of ways of selecting r things when the order of selection does not matter. This is described as $^{n}C_{r}$ – pronounced 'n c r' – and is calculated from:
>
> $$^{n}C_{r} = \frac{n!}{r!\,(n-r)!}$$

When you enter a lottery you are interested only in the numbers that are chosen, not the order in which they are chosen – so you are interested in combinations. If there is a pool of 10 cars and 3 customers arrive to use them, it does not matter in which order the customers arrive, so there are $^{10}C_{3}$ ways of allocating cars:

$$^{10}C_{3} = \frac{10!}{3!\times(10-3)!}$$
$$= 120$$

If you have n things and want to select r of these, but this time you are concerned with the order of selection, then you are interested in the **permutation** of r things from n.

> The **permutation** of r things from n is the number of ways of selecting r things when the order of selection is important. This is described as $^{n}P_{r}$ – pronounced 'n p r' – and is calculated from:
>
> $$^{n}P_{r} = \frac{n!}{(n-r)!}$$

Suppose there are 10 applicants for a social club committee consisting of a chairman, deputy chairman, secretary and treasurer. You want to select four from 10, and the order in which you select them is important because it corresponds to the different jobs. Then the number of ways of choosing the committee of four is:

$$^nP_r = \frac{n!}{(n-r)!} = \frac{10!}{(10-4)!}$$

$$= 5,040$$

If you want to select four ordinary committee members – so they all do the same job and the order in which you choose them is not important – then you are interested in the combinations of four from 10:

$$^nC_r = \frac{n!}{r!(n-r)!} = \frac{10!}{4!(10-4)!}$$

$$= 210$$

Permutations depend on order of selection and combinations do not, so there are always a lot more permutations than combinations. The number of combinations of four letters of the alphabet is $n! / r!(n-r)! = 26! / (4! \times 22!) = 14,950$. One combination has the four letters A, B, C and D, and it does not matter in which order these are taken. The number of permutations of four letters from the alphabet is $n! / (n-r)! = 26! / 22! = 358,800$, and this time it matters in which order the letters are taken, so now we start listing the permutations as ABCD, ABDC, ACBD, ACDB, ADBC, ADCB . . . and so on.

WORKED EXAMPLE 13.2

(a) In their annual recruiting, ALM Holdings has eight applicants to fill eight different jobs. In how many different ways can it assign applicants to jobs?

(b) There is a sudden reorganisation in ALM and the number of jobs falls to six. In how many different ways can the jobs be filled with the eight applicants?

(c) Suppose the reorganisation leads to a reclassification of jobs and the six jobs are now identical. In how many different ways can they be filled?

Solution

(a) This essentially asks, 'How many different sequences of 8 candidates are there?'. The answer is 8! The applicants can be assigned to jobs in 8! = 40,320 different ways.

(b) This asks the number of ways in which 6 candidates can be selected from 8. As the jobs are different, we are interested in the order of selection, and hence the permutations. The number of permutations of 6 different jobs from 8 applicants is:

$$^nP_r = \frac{n!}{(n-r)!} = \frac{8!}{(8-6)!}$$

$$= 20,160$$

(c) This again asks the number of ways in which 6 candidates can be selected from 8, but now the jobs are identical so the order of selection is not important. The number of combinations of 6 identical jobs from 8 applicants is:

$$^nC_r = \frac{n!}{r!(n-r)!} = \frac{8!}{6!(8-6)!}$$

$$= 28$$

You can look at this the other way around and ask the number of ways of rejecting 2 applicants from 8. Not surprisingly, with $r = 2$ we again have:

$$^nC_r = \frac{n!}{r!(n-r)!} = \frac{8!}{2!(8-2)!}$$

$$= 28$$

WORKED EXAMPLE 13.3

Twelve areas off the Californian coast become available for oil exploration and the US government is encouraging competition by limiting the allocation of these to at most one area for any company.

(a) If 12 exploration companies bid for the areas, in how many ways can the areas be allocated?
(b) Initial surveys suggest that these areas are equally likely to produce oil, so they are equally attractive. If 20 exploration companies put in bids, how many ways are there of selecting winning companies?

Solution
(a) Twelve companies each receive one area, so the companies can be sequenced in 12! possible ways, or 4.79×10^8.
(b) Now there are 20 companies, only 12 of which will be selected. As each area is equally attractive, the order of choosing companies does not matter, so we want the number of combinations:

$$^nC_r = \frac{n!}{r!(n-r)!} = \frac{20!}{12!(20-12)!}$$

$$= 125{,}970$$

Review questions

13.4 In how many ways can n different activities be sequenced?

13.5 What is the difference between a permutation and a combination?

13.6 When selecting r things from n, are there more combinations or permutations?

Binomial distribution

We can use the ideas of sequencing in the first standard probability distribution, which is the **binomial distribution**. This is used whenever there is a series of trials that have these characteristics:

- each trial has two possible outcomes – conventionally called success and failure
- the two outcomes are mutually exclusive
- there is a constant probability of success, p, and of failure, $q = 1 - p$
- the outcomes of successive trials are independent.

Tossing a coin is an example of a binomial process. Each toss is a trial – each head, say, is a success with a constant probability of 0.5; each tail is a failure with a constant probability of 0.5; and each trial is independent. Quality control inspections give another example of a binomial process – each inspection of a unit is a trial, each fault is a success and each good unit is a failure.

The binomial distribution gives the probabilities of different numbers of successes in a series of trials. Specifically, it shows the probability of r successes in n trials. We can calculate this using the following reasoning. In each trial the probability of a success is constant at p. Then for independent trials the probability that the first r are successes is p^r. Similarly, the probability that the next $n - r$ trials are failures is q^{n-r}. So the probability that the first r trials are successes and then the next $n - r$ trials are failures is $p^r q^{n-r}$.

But the sequence of r successes followed by $n - r$ failures is only one way of getting r successes in n trials. We also need to look at the other possible sequences. In particular, we want to know the number of ways of selecting r successes in n trials when the order of selection is not important. In the last section we found that this to be $^{n}C_r = n! / r!(n - r)!$. So there are $^{n}C_r$ possible sequences of r successes and $n - r$ failures, each with probability $p^r q^{n-r}$. Then we find the overall probability of r successes by multiplying the number of sequences by the probability of each sequence. This gives the binomial probability distribution:

$$P(r \text{ successes in } n \text{ trials}) = {}^{n}C_r\, p^r q^{n-r} = \frac{n! p^r q^{n-r}}{r!(n - r)!}$$

WORKED EXAMPLE 13.4

The probability of success in a binomial trial is 0.3. What is the probability of two successes in five trials? What is the probability of four successes?

Solution
Here $p = 0.3$, $q = 1 - p = 0.7$, $n = 5$ and we want $P(2)$. Substituting in the equation for the binomial distribution gives:

$$P(r) = \frac{n! p^r q^{n-r}}{r!(n - r)!}$$

so

$$P(2) = \frac{5! \times 0.3^2 \times 0.7^2}{2! \times 3!} = 0.309$$

Similarly:

$$P(4) = \frac{5! \times 0.3^4 \times 0.7^1}{4! \times 1!} = 0.028$$

WORKED EXAMPLE 13.5

Jenny Albright knows that in the long term she has a 50% chance of making a sale when calling on a customer. One morning she arranges six calls.

(a) What is her probability of making exactly three sales?

(b) What are her probabilities of making other numbers of sales?

(c) What is her probability of making fewer than three sales?

Solution
The problem is a binomial process in which the probability of success (that is, making a sale) is $p = 0.5$, the probability of failure (not making a sale) is $q = 1 - p = 0.5$, and the number of trials, n, is 6.

(a) Her probability of making exactly 3 sales (so $r = 3$) is:

$$P(r \text{ successes in } n \text{ trials}) = {}^{n}C_r\, p^r q^{n-r}$$

so

$$P(3 \text{ sales in 6 calls}) = {}^{6}C_3 \times 0.5^3 \times 0.5^{6-3}$$

$$= \frac{6!}{3!3!} \times 0.125 \times 0.125$$

$$= 0.3125$$

(b) We can substitute other values for r into the equation and get corresponding values for the probabilities. However, we can take a short cut, and in Figure 13.2 we have used Excel's standard BINOMDIST function to automatically calculate the probabilities.

(c) The probability of making fewer than 3 sales is the sum of the probabilities of making 0, 1 and 2 sales:

P(fewer than 3 sales)
$= P(0 \text{ sales}) + P(1 \text{ sale}) + P(2 \text{ sales})$
$= 0.0156 + 0.0938 + 0.2344$
$= 0.3438$

Worked example 13.5 continued

	A	B	C	D	E	F	G	H
1	**Binomial distribution**							
2								
3	**Trials**	6	*r*	P(*r*)				
4	**P(success)**	0.5	0	0.0156				
5			1	0.0938				
6			2	0.2344				
7			3	0.3125				
8			4	0.2344				
9			5	0.0938				
10			6	0.0156				
11								
12								
13								
14								
15								
16								
17								
18								
19								
20								
21								
22								
23								
24								
25								
26								
27								

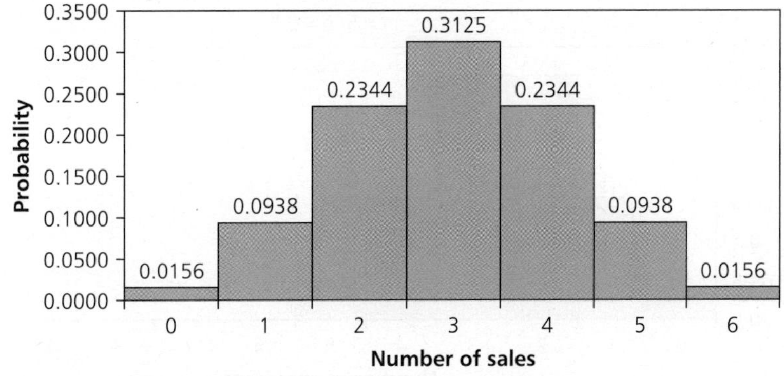

Figure 13.2 Binomial probability distribution for Jenny Albright

The shape of the binomial distribution actually varies with p and n. For small values of p the distribution is asymmetrical and the peak is to the left of centre. As p increases the peak moves to the centre of the distribution, and with $p = 0.5$ the distribution is symmetrical. As p increases further the distribution again becomes asymmetrical, but this time the peak is to the right of centre. For larger values of n the distribution is flatter and broader. Figure 13.3 shows these effects for a sample of values.

The mean, variance and standard deviation of a binomial distribution are calculated from these formulae:

For a binomial distribution:

- mean $= \mu = np$
- variance $= \sigma^2 = npq$
- standard deviation $= \sigma = \sqrt{(npq)}$

Notice that in these definitions we use the Greek letter μ (mu) for the mean rather than $\bar{x}$, and the Greek letter σ (sigma) for the standard deviation rather than s. This follows a common practice where:

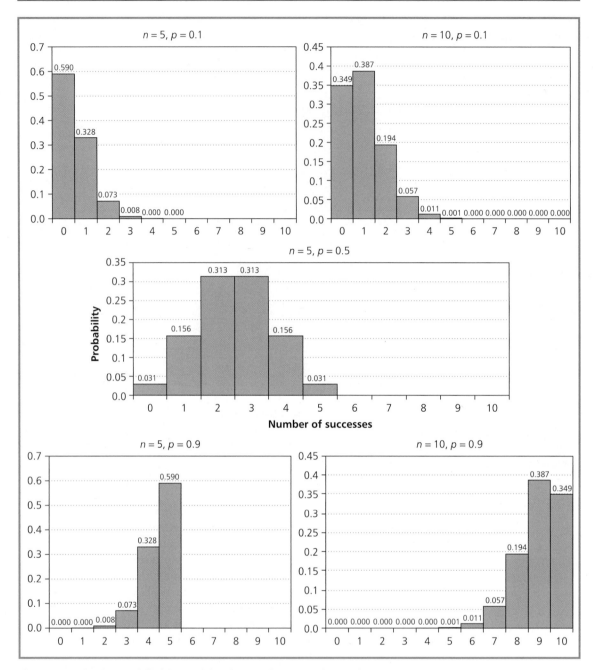

Figure 13.3 The shape of the binomial distribution changes with n and p

- the mean and standard deviation of a sample are called $\bar{x}$ and s respectively
- the mean and standard deviation of a population are called μ and σ respectively

This distinction is important in some analyses, and we shall meet it again in later chapters.

WORKED EXAMPLE 13.6

A company makes a particularly sensitive electronic component, and 10% of the output is defective. If the components are sold in boxes of 12, describe the distribution of defects in each box. What is the probability that a box has no defects? What is the probability that a box has one defect?

Solution

This is a binomial process, with success being a faulty unit. In each box $n = 12$ and $p = 0.1$. So:

- mean number of faulty units in a box: $np = 12 \times 0.1 = 1.2$
- variance: $npq = 12 \times 0.1 \times 0.9 = 1.08$
- standard deviation: $\sqrt{npq} = \sqrt{1.08} = 1.039$

The probability of 0 defects in a box is:

$P(0) = 0.9^{12} = 0.2824$

The probability of 1 defect comes from the binomial distribution calculation:

$P(r) = {}^nC_r p^r q^{n-r}$

so

$P(1) = {}^{12}C_1 \times 0.1^1 \times 0.9^{12-1}$

$= \dfrac{12! \times 0.1 \times 0.3138}{11! \times 1!}$

$= 0.3766$

We have already mentioned that Excel's BINOMDIST function automatically does these calculations, but there is another option – using standard tables. Appendix B contains tables for various combinations of n and p. If you look up the table for $n = 12$ and move across to the column where $p = 0.1$, you see a set of 12 numbers. These are the probabilities for each number of successes. The first number is 0.2824, which confirms our calculations for the probability of no defects in a box; the second number is 0.3766, which confirms our calculation for the probability of one defect in a box.

WORKED EXAMPLE 13.7

Boris Schwartz is a market researcher who has to visit 10 houses between 7.30 and 9.30 one evening. Previous calls suggest that there will be someone at home in 85% of houses. Describe the probability distribution of the number of houses with people at home. What is the probability of finding someone at home in 8 houses?

Solution

This is a binomial process with visiting a house as a trial and finding someone at home a success. Then we have $n = 10$, $p = 0.85$ and $q = 0.15$. Substituting in the standard equations gives:

- mean number of houses with someone at home $= np = 10 \times 0.85 = 8.5$
- variance $= npq = 10 \times 0.85 \times 0.15 = 1.275$
- standard deviation $= \sqrt{npq} = \sqrt{1.275} = 1.129$

You have three options to find these values. Firstly, you can do the calculation to find the probability that there is someone at home in 8 houses from:

$P(8) = {}^{10}C_8 \times 0.85^8 \times 0.15^2$
$= 45 \times 0.2725 \times 0.0225$
$= 0.2759$

Secondly, you can use a spreadsheet – or other standard software. Figure 13.4 shows the probability distribution in a spreadsheet, where the value of $P(8) = 0.2759$ confirms our calculation. It also shows the cumulative probabilities, so that the probability of finding up to 8 houses with people in is 0.4557. Similarly, the probability of finding at least 8 houses with someone in is:

$P(\geq 8) = 1 - P(\leq 7) = 1 - 0.1798$
$= 0.8202$

Thirdly, you can look up the figures in the standard tables in Appendix B. Values are given only for p up to 0.5, so to use the tables you must redefine 'success' as finding a house with no one at home – and then $p = 0.15$. Looking up the entry for $n = 10$, $p = 0.15$ and $r = 2$ (finding 8 houses with someone at home being the same as finding 2 houses with no one at home) confirms the value as 0.2759.

You could also use these tables to find cumulative probabilities, by saying:

$P(\geq 8) = P(8) + P(9) + P(10)$
$= 0.2759 + 0.3474 + 0.1969$
$= 0.8202$

Worked example 13.7 continued

	A	B	C	D	E	F	G	H
1	Binomial distribution							
2								
3	Trials / P(success)	10 / 0.85	r	P(r)	Cumulative probability			
4			0	0.0000	0.0000			
5			1	0.0000	0.0000			
6			2	0.0000	0.0000			
7			3	0.0001	0.0001			
8			4	0.0012	0.0014			
9			5	0.0085	0.0099			
10			6	0.0401	0.0500			
11			7	0.1298	0.1798			
12			8	0.2759	0.4557			
13			9	0.3474	0.8031			
14			10	0.1969	1.0000			

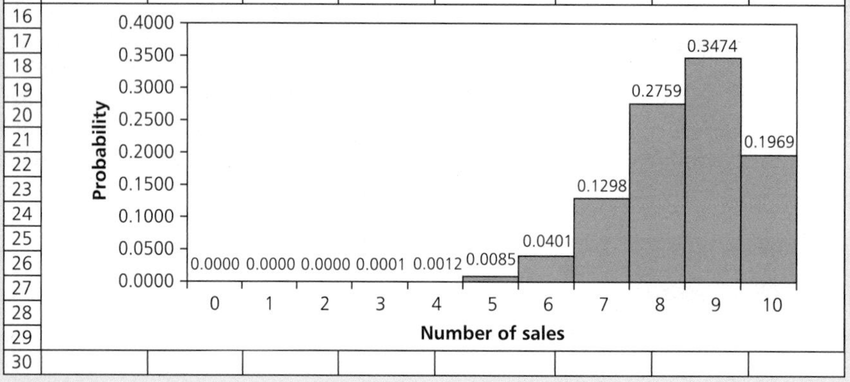

Figure 13.4 Probability distribution for Boris Schwartz

With the choice of calculation, standard tables and statistical software, you might think that the arithmetic for binomial probabilities is always straightforward. But sometimes it becomes difficult, and Worked example 13.8 illustrates the problem when n is very large and p is very small.

WORKED EXAMPLE 13.8

The accounts department of a company sends out 10,000 invoices a month, and has an average of five returned with an error. What is the probability that exactly four invoices are returned in a month?

$$P(r \text{ returns}) = \frac{n! \times p^r q^{n-r}}{r!(n-r)!}$$

$$= \frac{10,000!}{4! \times 9,996!} \times (0.0005)^4 \times (0.9995)^{9,996}$$

Solution

This is a typical binomial process, where a trial is sending out an invoice, and a success is having an error. Unfortunately when you start doing the arithmetic you see the problem. The values we have are $n = 10,000$, $r = 4$, $p = 5 / 10,000 = 0.0005$, $q = 9,995 / 10,000 = 0.9995$. Substituting these into the binomial distribution:

Although we can do this calculation – and find the result that P(4 returns) = 0.1755, it seems rather daunting to raise figures to the power of 9,996 or to contemplate 10,000 factorial, and it is also easy for errors to appear. Fortunately, there is an alternative. When n, the number of trials, is large and p, the probability of success, is small, we can approximate the binomial distribution by a Poisson distribution.

13.7   When would you use a binomial distribution?

13.8   Define all the terms in the equation $P(r) = {}^nC_r p^r q^{n-r}$

13.9   How can you calculate the mean and variance of a binomial distribution?

13.10 From the tables in Appendix B, find the probability of two successes from seven trials, when the probability of success is 0.2.

IDEAS IN PRACTICE   **University parking**

At a certain university an annual parking permit for the car park costs €850. A part-time academic visited the university an average of 100 times a year, and felt that this fee was too high. The fine for being found parking without a ticket was €35, but a brief survey led the academic to believe that checks were made only twice a week. This meant that the probability of being caught was 2 / 5 = 0.4.

The academic realised that this was a standard binomial process in which parking without a permit was an event, and being fined a success. The number of trials is 100 and the mean

number of successes a year is $100 \times 0.4 = 40$, each with a fine of €35, giving a total of €1,400. The standard deviation of the number of fines is $\sqrt{npq} = \sqrt{(100 \times 0.4 \times 0.6)} = 4.9$. Even allowing an error of 1 standard deviation from the mean would give $40 - 4.9 = 35.1$ penalties, at a total annual cost of $35.1 \times 35 = €1,228.50$. This is far more than the annual parking cost, so it is not worth taking the risks (even ignoring the inconvenience and embarrassment of all the fines).

Many people have done similar calculations for their own circumstances – as have car park operators.

Poisson distribution

The **Poisson distribution** is a close relative of the binomial distribution and can be used to approximate it when:

- the number of trials, n, is large (say greater than 20)
- the probability of success, p, is small (so that np is less than 5).

As n gets larger and p gets smaller the approximation becomes better.

The Poisson distribution is also useful in its own right for solving problems in which events occur at random. So you could use a Poisson distribution to describe the number of accidents each month in a company, the number of defects in a metre of cloth, the number of phone calls received each hour in a call centre and the number of customers entering a shop each hour.

The binomial distribution uses the probabilities of both success and failure – but the Poisson uses only the probability of success. It assumes that this is very small, and it looks for the few successes in a continuous background of failures. For instance, when it describes the random interruptions to a power supply it focuses on the very few times when there were disruptions, but not the large number of times when there were no disruptions. Similarly, when you consider the number of spelling mistakes in a long report, the number of faults in a pipeline or the number of accidents in a factory, you are interested only in the small number of successes – you are not concerned with the large number of failures.

A Poisson distribution is described by the equation:

$$P(r \text{ successes}) = \frac{e^{-\mu}\mu^r}{r!}$$

where: e = the exponential constant = 2.7183 (we met this in Chapter 2, as a rather strange but very useful number)

μ = mean number of successes

WORKED EXAMPLE 13.9

On a North Sea oil rig there have been 40 accidents that were serious enough to report in the past 50 weeks. In what proportion of weeks would you expect none, one, two, three and more than three accidents?

Solution

A small number of accidents occur, presumably at random, over time. We are not interested in the number of accidents that did *not* occur, so we have a Poisson process, with:

$$P(r \text{ successes}) = \frac{e^{-\mu}\mu^r}{r!}$$

The mean number of accidents in a week is 40 / 50 = 0.8, so substituting $\mu = 0.8$ and $r = 0$ gives:

$$P(0) = \frac{e^{-0.8} \times 0.8^0}{0!} = 0.4493$$

Similarly:

$$P(1) = \frac{e^{-0.8} \times 0.8^1}{1!} = 0.3595$$

$$P(2) = \frac{e^{-0.8} \times 0.8^2}{2!} = 0.1438$$

$$P(3) = \frac{e^{-0.8} \times 0.8^3}{3!} = 0.0383$$

and

$$
\begin{aligned}
P(>3) &= 1 - P(\leq 3) \\
&= 1 - P(0) - P(1) - P(2) - P(3) \\
&= 1 - 0.4493 - 0.3595 - 0.1438 - 0.0383 \\
&= 0.0091
\end{aligned}
$$

WORKED EXAMPLE 13.10

How does the Poisson distribution deal with the situation in Worked example 13.8, where an accounts department sends out 10,000 invoices a month and has an average of five returned with an error? What is the probability that exactly four invoices will be returned in a given month?

Solution

Here n is large and $np = 5$ (fairly high but the result should still be reasonable), so we can use a Poisson distribution to approximate the binomial distribution. The variables are $r = 4$ and $\mu = 5$.

$$P(r \text{ successes}) = \frac{e^{-\mu}\mu^r}{r!}$$

so

$$P(4 \text{ successes}) = \frac{e^{-5}5^4}{4!} = (0.0067 \times 625) / 24$$

$$= 0.1755$$

This confirms the result from the rather messy calculation in Worked example 13.8.

When events occur at random you can usually use a Poisson distribution, but strictly speaking there are a number of other requirements. In particular, a Poisson process requires that:

- the events are independent
- the probability that an event happens in an interval is proportional to the length of the interval
- in theory, an infinite number of events should be possible in an interval.

Then related calculations give:

For a Poisson distribution:

- mean, $\mu = np$
- variance, $\sigma^2 = np$
- standard deviation, $\sigma = \sqrt{(np)}$

WORKED EXAMPLE 13.11

A Poisson process has a mean of five events a day. Describe the probability distribution of events.

Solution

The mean number of events, μ, is 5. This is also the variance, and the standard deviation is $\sqrt{5} = 2.236$.

The probability of r events is:

$$P(r) = \frac{e^{-\mu}\mu^r}{r!}$$

For example,

$$P(2) = \frac{e^{-5} \times 5^2}{2!}$$

$$= 0.0842$$

We could do the calculations for other numbers of successes but, as with the binomial distribution, there are alternatives. Again there are standard tables, as given in Appendix C. If you look up the value for $\mu = 5$ and $r = 2$, you can confirm the probability as 0.0842. And you can also use statistical packages or spreadsheets. Figure 13.5 shows the results from Excel's standard POISSON function.

	A	B	C	D	E	F	G	H
1	**Poisson distribution**							
2								
3	**Mean**	5	*r*	P(r)	Cumulative probability			
4			0	0.0067	0.0067			
5			1	0.0337	0.0404			
6			2	0.0842	0.1247			
7			3	0.1404	0.2650			
8			4	0.1755	0.4405			
9			5	0.1755	0.6160			
10			6	0.1462	0.7622			
11			7	0.1044	0.8666			
12			8	0.0653	0.9319			
13			9	0.0363	0.9682			
14			10	0.0181	0.9863			
15			11	0.0082	0.9945			
16			12	0.0034	0.9980			
17								

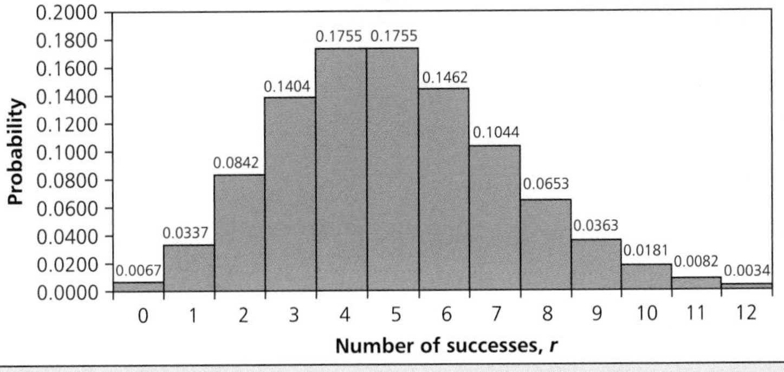

Figure 13.5 Spreadsheet of Poisson probabilities

Figure 13.5 also shows the shape of a Poisson distribution, which is similar to a binomial distribution. The shape and position of the Poisson distribution are determined by the single parameter, μ. For small μ the distribution is asymmetrical with a peak to the left of centre; then as μ increases the distribution becomes more symmetrical, as you can see from Figure 13.6.

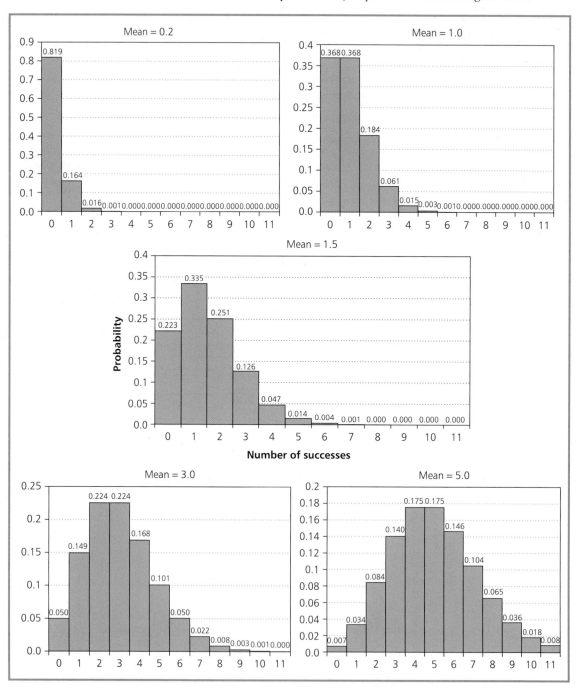

Figure 13.6 The shape of a Poisson distribution varies with μ

WORKED EXAMPLE 13.12

Hellier council ran a test to see whether a road junction should be improved. During this test they found that cars arrive randomly at the junction at an average rate of four cars every 5 minutes. What is the probability that more than eight cars will arrive in a 5-minute period?

Solution

Random arrivals mean that we have a Poisson process. The mean number of successes (that is, cars arriving at the junction in 5 minutes) is $\mu = 4$. Then the probability of exactly, say, 3 cars arriving is:

$$P(r) = \frac{e^{-\mu}\mu^r}{r!}$$

so

$$P(3) = \frac{e^{-4} \times 4^3}{3!}$$

$$= 0.1954$$

You can check this by looking at the tables in Appendix C, and Figure 13.7 confirms the result using Excel's POISSON function. You can find the probability that more than eight cars arrive at the junction in a 5-minute period, $P(\geq 8)$, from the cumulative probability shown in Figure 13.7.

$$P(\geq 8) = 1 - P(\leq 7) = 1 - 0.9489$$

$$= 0.0511$$

	A	B	C	D	E	F	G	H
1	Poisson distribution							
2								
3	Mean	4	r	$P(r)$	Cumulative probability			
4			0	0.0183	0.0183			
5			1	0.0733	0.0916			
6			2	0.1465	0.2381			
7			3	0.1954	0.4335			
8			4	0.1954	0.6288			
9			5	0.1563	0.7851			
10			6	0.1042	0.8893			
11			7	0.0595	0.9489			
12			8	0.0298	0.9786			
13			9	0.0132	0.9919			
14			10	0.0053	0.9972			
15			11	0.0019	0.9991			
16			12	0.0006	0.9997			
17								

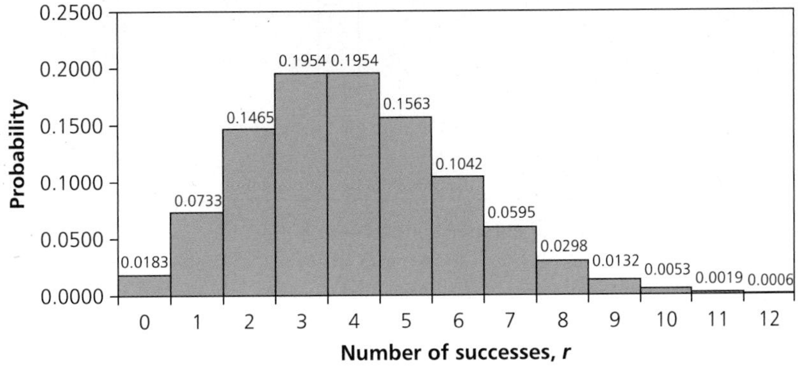

Figure 13.7 Spreadsheet of Poisson probabilities for Hellier council

Shingatsu Industries

In 2006 Shingatsu Industries bought a network of oil pipelines in Eastern Russia. Shingatsu knew the network was not in good condition, and they found that 40% of the oil pumping stations had faults, and there was an average of one fault in the pipeline every 20 km. In a key 100 km stretch of pipeline there are 20 pumping stations and Shingatsu wanted an idea of the likely number of problems.

They looked at the problem in two parts – faults in pumping stations and faults along the pipeline. Faults in the pumping station follow a binomial distribution because they are either faulty or not faulty. The number of trials is the number of stations (20), and the probability of success (a faulty station) $p = 0.4$. The mean number of faults in the pumping stations $= np = 20 \times 0.4 = 8$, and Figure 13.8 shows the probabilities of different numbers of faulty stations.

Assuming that faults along the pipeline are random, they follow a Poisson distribution. The average number of faults in a kilometre of pipeline is $1 / 20 = 0.05$, so in 100 km of pipeline the mean number of faults $\mu = 100 \times 0.05 = 5$. Figure 13.8 also shows the probabilities of different numbers of faults in the pipeline.

	A	B	C	D	E	F	G
1	**Pipeline faults**						
2							
3	**Pumping stations**				**Pipeline**		
4							
5	**Mean faults =**	8			**Mean faults =**	5	
6	**Standard deviation =**	2.19			**Standard deviation =**	2.24	
7							
8	**Faults**	**Probability**	**Cumulative**		**Faults**	**Probability**	**Cumulative**
9	0	0.0000	0.0000		0	0.0067	0.0067
10	1	0.0005	0.0005		1	0.0337	0.0404
11	2	0.0031	0.0036		2	0.0842	0.1246
12	3	0.0123	0.0159		3	0.1404	0.2650
13	4	0.0350	0.0509		4	0.1755	0.4405
14	5	0.0746	0.1256		5	0.1755	0.6159
15	6	0.1244	0.2500		6	0.1462	0.7621
16	7	0.1659	0.4159		7	0.1044	0.8666
17	8	0.1797	0.5956		8	0.0653	0.9319
18	9	0.1597	0.7553		9	0.0363	0.9681
19	10	0.1171	0.8724		10	0.0181	0.9863
20	11	0.0710	0.9434		11	0.0082	0.9945
21	12	0.0355	0.9789		12	0.0034	0.9979
22	13	0.0146	0.9935		13	0.0013	0.9993
23	14	0.0049	0.9984		14	0.0005	0.9997
24	15	0.0013	0.9996		15	0.0002	0.9999
25	16	0.0003	0.9999		16	0.0000	0.9999

Figure 13.8 Probability distributions for Shingatsu Industries oil pipeline

The arithmetic for calculating Poisson probabilities is straightforward but it can become tedious for large numbers, as you can see in Worked example 13.13.

WORKED EXAMPLE 13.13

A motor insurance policy is available only to drivers with a low risk of accidents. 100 drivers holding the policy in a certain area would expect an average of 0.2 accidents each a year. What is the probability that fewer than 15 drivers will have accidents in one year?

Solution

This is a binomial process with success as having an accident in the year. The mean number of accidents a year is $np = 100 \times 0.2 = 20$. So the probability that exactly r drivers have accidents in the year is:

$$^{20}C_r \times 0.2^r \times 0.8^{100-r}$$

To find the probability that fewer than 15 drivers have accidents in a year, we add this calculation for all values of r from 0 to 14:

$$P(< 15) = \sum_{r=0}^{14} {}^{20}C_r \times 0.2^r \times 0.8^{100-r}$$

Although we can do this calculation (finding that the probability is 0.1056), it is rather messy and we should look for a Poisson approximation. Unfortunately $np = 20$, which does not meet the requirement that np be less than 5. So we need to look for another approach, and this time we can use the most common probability distribution of all. When n is large and np is greater than 5 we can approximate the binomial distribution by the Normal distribution.

Review questions

13.11 In what circumstances can you use a Poisson distribution?

13.12 What are the mean and variance of a Poisson distribution?

13.13 The average number of defects per square metre of material is 0.8. Use the tables in Appendix C to find the probability that a square metre has exactly two defects.

13.14 In what circumstances can you use a Poisson distribution to approximate a binomial distribution?

Normal distribution

Both the binomial and Poisson distributions describe discrete data – showing the number of successes. But we often want a probability distribution to describe continuous data – such as the weight of a product. Although these two are similar in principle, there is a key difference – with discrete probabilities you want the probability of, say, exactly 3 successes, but with continuous data you cannot find the probability that a person weighs exactly 80.456456456 kg. If you make the measurement precise enough, the probability of this happening is always very close to zero. It would be far more useful to know the probability that a person weighs between 80.4 kg and 80.5 kg. This is the approach of continuous probability distributions, which find the probability that a value is within a specified range.

There are several continuous probability distributions, but the most widely used is the Gaussian or Normal distribution. This is a bell-shaped curve (illustrated in Figure 13.9) that describes many natural features such as the heights of trees, harvest from a hectare of land, weight of horses, flows in rivers, daily temperature, etc. It also describes many business activities, such as daily receipts, sales volumes, number of customers a week, production in a

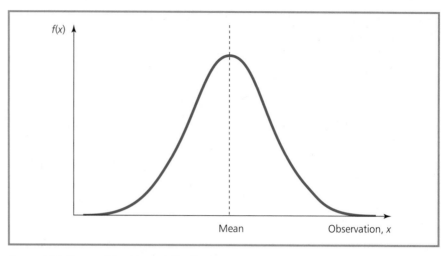

Figure 13.9 Shape of the Normal distribution

factory, and so on. The distribution is so common that a rule of thumb suggests that 'when you have a lot of observations, use the Normal distribution'.

The Normal distribution has the properties of:

■ being continuous
■ being symmetrical about the mean, μ
■ having mean, median and mode all equal
■ having the total area under the curve equal to 1
■ in theory, extending to plus and minus infinity on the x-axis.

In Chapter 5 we looked at histograms for describing continuous data, and emphasised that the areas of the bars are important, and not just their length. Similarly with continuous data, it is the area under the curve that gives the probabilities. The height of a continuous probability distribution – such as the Normal distribution – does not have much meaning.

Suppose a factory makes boxes of chocolates with a mean weight of 1,000 grams. There are always small variations in the weight of each box, and if the factory makes a large number of boxes the weights will follow a Normal distribution. Managers in the factory are not interested in the number of boxes that weigh, say, exactly 1,005.0000 g but they may be interested in the number of boxes that weigh more than 1,005 g. This is represented by the area under the right-hand tail of the distribution, as shown in Figure 13.10.

Unfortunately, there is no simple calculation for the area in the tail of the distribution. But there are two other ways of finding the probabilities – either using standard software (such as Excel's NORMDIST and NORMINV functions), or looking up the values in tables. We will start by looking at the tables (given in Appendix D).

Normal distribution tables are based on a value, Z, which is the number of standard deviations a point is away from the mean. Standard Normal tables show the probability of a value being greater than this – which is the area in the tail of the distribution. For example, with the boxes of chocolates

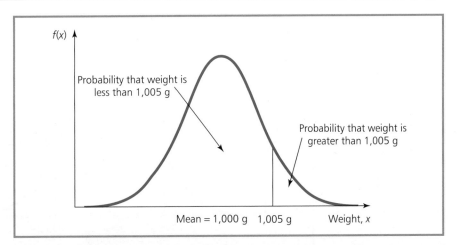

Figure 13.10 Continuous distribution shows the probability by the area under the curve

above the mean weight is 1,000 g and suppose the standard deviation is 3 g. The point of interest is 1,005 g so Z is given by:

Z = number of standard deviations from the mean

$$= \frac{\text{value} - \text{mean}}{\text{standard deviation}} = \frac{x - \mu}{\sigma} = \frac{1,005 - 1,000}{3}$$

$$= 1.67$$

If you look up 1.67 in the table in Appendix D (which means finding '1.6' in the left-hand column and then moving across to read the number in the column headed '.07') you see the figure 0.0475. This is the probability that a box weighs more than 1,005 g. (Tables for the Normal distribution can show these probabilities in slightly different ways, so you should always be careful when using them.)

Because the Normal distribution is symmetrical about its mean, we can do some other calculations. For example, the probability that a box of chocolates weighs less than 995 g is the same as the probability that it weighs more than 1,005 g and we have calculated this as 0.0475 (shown in Figure 13.11). Furthermore,

P(box is between 995 and 1,005 g) = 1 – P(<995g) – P(>1,005 g)
$$= 1 - 0.0475 - 0.0475$$
$$= 0.905$$

In general, a Normal distribution has the property that about 68% of observations are always within 1 standard deviation of the mean, 95% are within 2 standard deviations, and 99.7% are within 3 standard deviations (shown in Figure 13.12).

This is true regardless of the actual values of the mean and standard deviation. These determine the height and position of the curve (a larger standard deviation means there is more spread, and the mean gives the position of the distribution on the x-axis, as shown Figure 13.13), but they do not affect its basic shape.

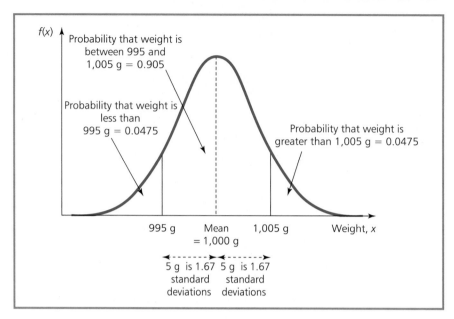

Figure 13.11 The Normal distribution is symmetrical about its mean

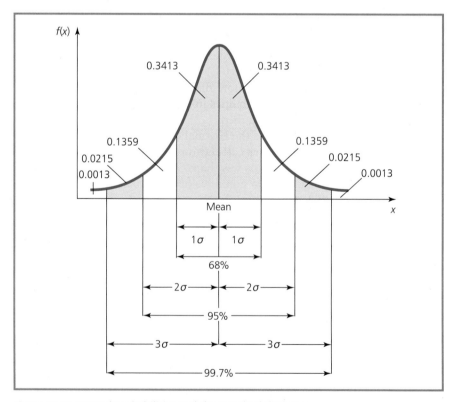

Figure 13.12 Normal probabilities and the standard deviation

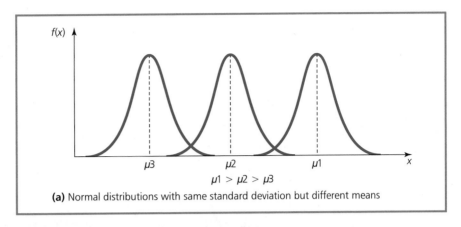

(a) Normal distributions with same standard deviation but different means

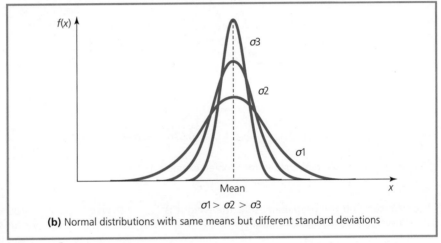

(b) Normal distributions with same means but different standard deviations

Figure 13.13 The mean and standard deviation affect the shape of the distribution

WORKED EXAMPLE 13.14

Figures kept by McClure and Hanover Auctioneers for the past 5 years show that the weight of cattle brought to market has a mean of 950 kg and a standard deviation of 150 kg. What proportion of the cattle have weights:

(a) more than 1,250 kg
(b) less than 850 kg
(c) between 1,100 kg and 1,250 kg
(d) between 800 kg and 1,300 kg?

Solution

We can assume that a large number of cattle are brought to market, so their weights are Normally distributed with $\mu = 950$ and $\sigma = 150$. For each of the probabilities we have to find Z, the number of standard deviations the point of interest is away from the mean, and use this to look up the associated probability in standard tables.

(a) For a weight greater than 1,250 kg we have:

Z = number of standard deviations from the mean
$= (1,250 - 950) / 150$
$= 2.0$

Looking this up in the Normal tables in Appendix D gives a value of 0.0228, which is the probability we want (shown in Figure 13.14).

Worked example 13.14 continued

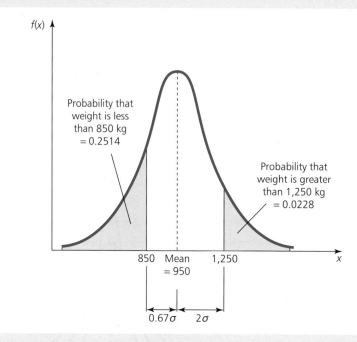

Figure 13.14 Normal probabilities for Worked example 13.14

(b) We can find the probability that the weight is less than 850 kg in the same way:

$$Z = (850 - 950) / 150$$
$$= -0.67$$

The table shows only positive values, but the distribution is symmetrical so we can use the value for +0.67, which is 0.2514.

(c) Because the tables show only probabilities under the tail of the distribution, we often have to do some juggling to get the values we want. There is usually more than one way of doing the calculations, but they should all give the same result. Here we want the probability that the weight is between 1,100 kg and 1,250 kg (as shown in Figure 13.15). For this we can say that:

P(between 1,100 kg and 1,250 kg)
= P(> 1,100 kg) − P(> 1,250 kg)

For weight above 1,100 kg: $Z = (1,100 - 950) / 150 = 1$, probability = 0.1587
For weight above 1,250 kg: $Z = (1,250 - 950) / 150 = 2$, probability = 0.0228
So the probability that the weight is between these two is 0.1587 − 0.0228 = 0.1359.

(d) To find the probability that the weight is between 800 kg and 1,300 kg (as shown in Figure 13.16) we can say:

P(between 800 kg and 1,300 kg)
= 1 − P(< 800 kg) − P(> 1,300 kg)

For weight below 800 kg: $Z = (800 - 950) / 150 = -1$, probability = 0.1587
For weight above 1,300 kg: $Z = (1,300 - 950) / 150 = 2.33$, probability = 0.0099
So the probability that the weight is between these two is 1 − 0.1587 − 0.0099 = 0.8314.

Worked example 13.14 continued

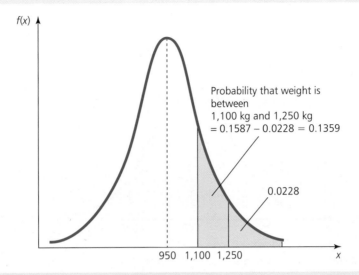

Figure 13.15 Probabilities for part (c) of Worked example 13.14

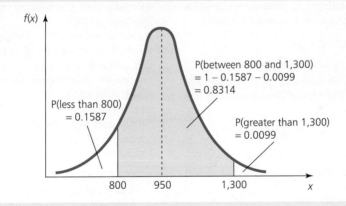

Figure 13.16 Probabilities for part (d) of Worked example 13.14

WORKED EXAMPLE 13.15

On average a supermarket sells 500 litres of milk a day with a standard deviation of 50 litres.

(a) If the supermarket has 600 litres in stock at the beginning of a day, what is the probability that it will run out of milk?

(b) What is the probability that demand is between 450 and 600 litres in a day?

(c) How many litres should the supermarket stock if it wants the probability of running out to be 0.05?

(d) How many should it stock if it wants the probability of running out to be 0.01?

Worked example 13.15 continued

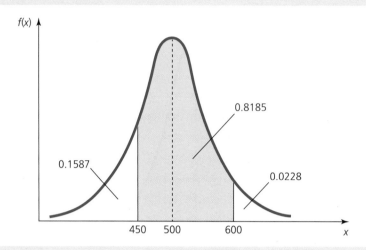

Figure 13.17 Probability that the supermarket runs out of milk

Solution

(a) We find the probability of running out of stock with 600 litres (shown in Figure 13.17) from:

$$Z = (600 - 500) / 50 = 2.0$$

which gives probability = 0.0228.

(b) The probability of demand greater than 600 litres is 0.0228. The probability of demand less than 450 litres is:

$$Z = (450 - 500) / 50 = -1.0$$

which gives probability = 0.1587. Then the probability of demand between 450 and 600 litres is:

$$1 - 0.0228 - 0.1587 = 0.8185$$

(c) Here we know the probability and can use this to find the corresponding value of Z, and hence the value that we want. We have a required probability of 0.05, and you look this up in the body of the Normal tables in Appendix D. This is midway between values of $Z = 1.64$ and $Z = 1.65$, so we set $Z = 1.645$. Now 1.645 standard deviations is $1.645 \times 50 = 82.25$ litres from the mean. So Figure 13.18 shows that the supermarket needs $500 + 83 = 583$

litres at the beginning of the day (rounding up to make sure the maximum probability of a shortage is 0.05).

(d) A probability of 0.01 corresponds to a value of $Z = 2.33$. So the point of interest is 2.33 standard deviations, or $2.33 \times 50 = 116.5$ litres from the mean. This means that the supermarket needs $500 + 117 = 617$ litres at the beginning of the day.

We can also do these calculations on a spreadsheet, with Figure 13.19 showing the results from Excel's two key functions:

■ NORMSDIST, where you enter the value of Z and it returns the cumulative probability. Alternatively, you can use NORMDIST where you enter the mean, standard deviation and point of interest, and it returns the probability of values less than the point of interest.

■ 'NORMSINV', where you enter the probability and it returns the corresponding value of Z. Alternatively, you can use 'NORMINV' where you also enter the mean and standard deviation, and it returns the point below which there is the given probability of falling.

Worked example 13.15 continued

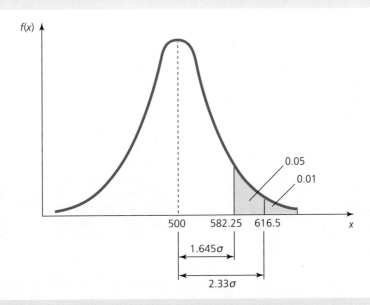

Figure 13.18 Setting the stock level to achieve target probabilities of running out of milk

	A	B	C	D	E	F	G	H	I
1	**Normal probabilities**								
2									
3	**Dairy example**								
4									
5	**Mean**	**500**	**Standard deviation**		**50**				
6									
7					**Calculation**				
8	(a) Probability demand >600 litres								
9		0.0228			1-NORMDIST(600,B5,E5,1)				
10									
11	(b) Probability demand between 450 and 600								
12		0.8186			NORMDIST(600,B5,E5,1)-NORMDIST(450,B5,E5,1)				
13									
14	(c) Number to give probability <0.05								
15		582.24			NORMINV(0.95,B5,E5)				
16									
17	(c) Number to give probability <0.01								
18		616.32			NORMINV(0.99,B5,E5)				

Figure 13.19 Using standard functions to calculate probabilities for a Normal distribution

WORKED EXAMPLE 13.16

Van Meerson are wholesalers who supply an average of 100,000 litres of white paint a day to retailers, with a standard deviation of 10,000 litres.

(a) If they have 110,000 litres in stock at the start of the day, what is the probability that they will run out?
(b) What is the probability that demand is between 110,000 and 90,000 litres?
(c) What amount of paint are they 90% sure that the daily demand is below?
(d) Within what range are they 90% sure that the demand will fall?

Solution

Figure 13.20 shows these calculations in a spreadsheet, using the standard functions NORMDIST and NORMINV.

(a) NORMDIST finds the probability that demand is greater than 110,000 litres – and subtracting this from 1 gives the probability that demand is less than 110,000 litres, which is 0.1587.
(b) NORMDIST calculates the probability that demand is greater than 90,000 litres, and you subtract from this the probability that demand is greater than 110,000 litres.
(c) Now we know the probability and want to see where this occurs. NORMINV finds the point where demand has the given probability of falling below – and there is a probability of 0.9 that demand is less than 112,815.52 litres.
(d) Here NORMINV shows that there is a probability of 0.05 that demand is above 116,448.54 litres, and there is a corresponding probability that demand is below 83,551.46 litres. It follows that there is a 90% chance that demand is between these two limits.

	A	B	C	D	E	F	G	H
1	**Normal probabilities**							
2								
3	**van Meerson example**							
4								
5	**Mean**	**100,000**	**Standard deviation**		**10,000**			
6								
7					**Calculation**			
8	(a) Probability demand >110,000 litres							
9		0.1587			1-NORMDIST(110,000,B5,E5,1)			
10								
11	(b) Probability demand between 110,000 and 90,000 litres				NORMDIST(110,000,B5,E5,1)			
12		0.6827			-NORMDIST(90,000,B5,E5,1)			
13								
14	(c) Number to give probability < 0.1							
15		112,815.52			NORMINV(0.9,B5,E5)			
16								
17	(d) Range that includes 90% of demands							
18	5% greater than	116,448.54			NORMINV(0.95,B5,E5)			
19	5% less than	83,551.46			NORMINV(0.05,B5,E5)			

Figure 13.20 Probabilities for demand at Van Meerson

Normal approximation to other distributions

Earlier we found that we could sometimes simplify arithmetic by using a Poisson distribution to approximate a binomial one. This is generally possible when there is a large number of trials (say more than 20) and the probability of success is small (so that $np < 5$). But when we tried to use this result in Worked example 13.13, where motor insurance is sold only to drivers with a low risk of accidents, we found that these conditions were not met. Specifically, we looked at 100 drivers (so that $n = 100$) who expect an average of 0.2 accidents each a year (so that $p = 0.2$ and $np = 100 \times 0.2 = 20$). Because np is greater than 5 we cannot use a Poisson distribution to approximate the binomial.

However, there is another option. When n is more than about 20, and p is near to 0.5, the binomial distribution can be approximated by a Normal one. You can see how this works in Worked example 13.17.

WORKED EXAMPLE 13.17

For the insurance policy described in Worked example 13.13, what is the probability that fewer than 15 drivers will have accidents in a year?

Solution
We know that $n = 100$ and $p = 0.2$. Ideally, p would be closer to 0.5, but the high value of n should still give a good approximation. Then for a binomial process, the mean = $np = 100 \times 0.2 = 20$, and the standard deviation is $\sqrt{npq} = \sqrt{100 \times 0.2 \times 0.8} = \sqrt{16} = 4$. To find the probability of fewer than 15 drivers having an accident we use:

$Z = (15 - 20) / 4$
$\quad = -1.25$

And Normal tables show that this corresponds to a probability of 0.1056.

There is one other issue here – the number of accidents is discrete, while the Normal distribution assumes that data is continuous. Provided the numbers are reasonably large, the effect of this is small, but to be safe we can add a 'continuity correction'. Here we are looking for the probability of fewer than 15 accidents, but it is clearly impossible to have *between* 14 and 15 accidents. So we can interpret 'less than 15' as 'less than 14.5'. Then

$Z = (14.5 - 20) / 4$
$\quad = -1.375$
$\quad$ probability = 0.0846

If the question had asked for '15 or less' accidents, we could have interpreted this as 'less than 15.5', with:

$Z = (15.5 - 20) / 4$
$\quad = -1.125$
$\quad$ probability = 0.1303

We have found that in certain circumstances it is possible to approximate a binomial distribution to a Poisson distribution, and in other circumstances it is possible to approximate it to a Normal distribution. You probably will not be surprised to find that in certain circumstances it is also possible to approximate a Poisson distribution to a Normal distribution. Specifically, when the mean of a Poisson distribution is greater than about 30 (meaning that it becomes symmetrical) we can approximate it to a Normal distribution. You can see how this works in Worked example 13.18, while Figure 13.21 shows the relationships between distributions.

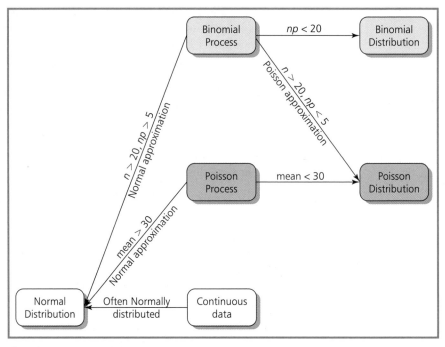

Figure 13.21 Approximations with probability distributions

WORKED EXAMPLE 13.18

The O'Hare Electric Cable Company finds an average of 30 faults in a week's production. What is the probability of more than 40 faults in a week?

so:
$$\mu = 30 = variance$$
$$\sigma = \sqrt{30} = 5.477$$

Solution

As there are random faults in cable, we can assume a Poisson process, with:

Figure 13.22 shows the results from a spreadsheet using the standard function POISSON to find the probability of more than 40 faults – this probability is 0.9677.

	A	B	C	D	E	F	G	H
1	**O'Hare Electric Cable Company**							
2								
3	**Mean**	30	**Variance**	30	**Standard deviation**		5.477	
4								
5	**Poisson calculation**							
6	*r*	**Cumulative probability**						
7	40	0.9677			cell B7 contains POISSON(A8,B3,TRUE)			
8								
9	**Normal calculation**							
10	*r*	*z*	**Probability**					
11	40	1.826	0.9661		cell C11 contains NORMSDIST(B13)			

Figure 13.22 Probabilities for O'Hare Electric Cable Company

Worked example 13.18 continued

When the mean is large, you can reasonably use a Normal distribution to approximate the Poisson process. With the NORMSDIST function in a spreadsheet you specify the value of Z and the function returns the cumulative probability. Figure 13.22 also shows the probability of more than 40 faults as:

$Z = (40 - 30) / 5.477$
$\quad = 1.826$
probability $= 0.9661$

As you can see the two results are close, confirming that the Normal distribution gives a good approximation to the Poisson.

Review questions

13.15 When would you use a Normal distribution?

13.16 What is the most obvious difference between a Normal distribution and a binomial or Poisson distribution?

13.17 What are the two most important measures of a Normal distribution?

13.18 When can you use a Normal distribution as an approximation to a binomial distribution?

13.19 If the mean of a set of observations is 100 and the standard deviation is 10, what proportion of observations will be between 90 and 110?

13.20 What is a 'continuity correction' for discrete data?

IDEAS IN PRACTICE   **Decisions involving uncertainty**

Most management problems involve uncertainty. However, probabilistic models get complicated, so managers often use simpler deterministic models as approximations. These give results that are reasonably good, but with far less effort.

Consider the break-even analysis described in Chapter 8, where the break-even point is the number of sales at which revenue covers all costs and a product begins to make a profit:

break-even point = fixed costs / (price charged
– variable cost)

In principle, managers should introduce a new product when forecast sales are above the break-even point, but they should not introduce a product when forecast demand is less than this. The problem is that sales forecasts are never entirely accurate. Typically a forecast will give an expected mean demand and a measure of possible spread about this. And, to be accurate, managers also have to include uncertainty in future costs (both fixed and variable) and prices.

A break-even analysis should, therefore, combine uncertainty in demands, costs and revenues, with the results giving managers not just a point estimate but a likely range of expected returns and corresponding probabilities. Then they can include elements of risk in their decisions. For instance, they may look more kindly on a product that is likely to make a small loss, but in certain conditions has a reasonable probability of giving a very high profit. Of course, risky decisions – by definition – can go wrong, and the actual outcomes may still come as a surprise. Uncertainty makes managers' jobs very difficult. Sometimes actual events work in their favour with unexpectedly good results; sometimes they do not – which is the reason why Napoleon liked to be surrounded by lucky generals.

This chapter introduced the ideas of probability distributions and described three of the most useful.

- A probability distribution is a frequency distribution for the probabilities of events. You can draw empirical distributions to describe specific situations, but each problem has its own unique distribution.

- In practice, some standard probability distributions can be used for a range of different problems. The three most widely used distributions are the binomial, Poisson and Normal.

- The binomial distribution depends on some results for sequencing problems, particularly the number of ways of ordering r items from n. These are given by combinations (when the order of selection is not important) and permutations (when the order of selection is important).

- The binomial distribution is used when a trial has two independent, mutually exclusive outcomes. Specifically, it calculates the probability of r successes in n trials as:

$$P(r \text{ successes in } n \text{ trials}) = {}^nC_r p^r q^{n-r}$$

- The Poisson distribution can be used as an approximation to the binomial distribution when the probability of success is small. It is more generally used to describe infrequent, random events:

$$P(r \text{ successes}) = \frac{e^{-\mu}\mu^r}{r!}$$

- Large numbers of observations usually follow a Normal probability distribution. This is the most common continuous distribution and is bell-shaped. The area under the curve shows the probability of observations being within a certain range. These probabilities are not easy to calculate, so they are always found from standard tables or software.

- Sometimes we can ease the calculations by approximating one distribution by another.

CASE STUDY   Machined components

The operations manager was speaking calmly to the marketing manager – 'I said it usually takes 70 days to make a batch of these components. We have to buy parts and materials, make subassemblies, set up machines, schedule operations, make sure everything is ready to start production – then actually make the components, check them and shift them to the finished goods stores. Actually making the components involves 187 distinct steps taking a total of 20 days. The whole process usually takes 70 days, but there's a lot of variability.

This batch you're shouting about is going to take about 95 days because we were busy working on other jobs and couldn't start immediately – and a major production machine broke down and we had to wait for parts to be flown in from Tokyo and that took another 5 days. It's your fault that you heard my estimate and then assumed that I was exaggerating and could promise the customer delivery in 65 days.'

The marketing manager looked worried. 'Why didn't you rush through this important job?

Case study continued

Why is there such variation in time? Why did the breakdown of one machine disrupt production by so much? What am I going to say to our customer?'

The operations manager's reply was, 'To answer your questions in order. Because I was rushing through other important jobs. The variation isn't really that much; our estimates are usually within 10 days. It is a central machine that affects the capacity of the whole plant. I can only suggest you apologise and say you will listen to the operations manager more carefully in the future.'

Despite his apparent calmness, the operations manager was concerned about the variability in production times. He could see why there was some variability, but the total amount for the component they were considering did seem a lot. As an experiment, he had once tried to match capacity exactly with expected throughput. Then he found that operations near the beginning of the process performed reasonably well, but towards the end of the process the variability was magnified and the throughput times went out of control. At one point he had eight machines in a line, each of which processed a part for 10 minutes before passing it to the next machine. Although this arrangement seemed perfectly balanced, he found that stocks of work in progress built up dramatically. Some people suggested that this was because the actual processing time could vary between 5 and 15 minutes. Whatever the reason, the experiment was stopped.

Question

■ Operations really need a study to see why there is variability, how much is acceptable, what its effects are, how it can be reduced, what benefits this will bring and so on. Such a study needs funding – and your job is to write an initial proposal for this funding, including a detailed proposal for a larger study.

PROBLEMS

13.1 Find the probability distribution of this set of observations:

10 14 13 15 16 12 14 15 11 13 17 15 16 14 12
13 11 15 15 14 12 16 14 13 13 14 13 12 14 15
16 14 11 14 12 15 14 16 13 14

13.2 Paul la Sauvage forecasts likely profit next year with the following probabilities:

Profit	−€100,000	−€50,000	€0	€50,000	€100,000	€150,000
Probability	0.05	0.15	0.3	0.3	0.15	0.05

What is the probability that the company will make a profit next year? What is the probability that the profit will be at least €100,000?

13.3 Find the values of ^nC_r and ^nP_r when (a) $r = 5$ and $n = 15$, (b) $r = 2$ and $n = 10$, (c) $r = 8$ and $n = 10$.

13.4 An open-plan office has ten desks. If ten people work in the area, how many different seating arrangements are there? If two people leave, how many arrangements are there?

13.5 A salesman has 12 customers to visit each day. In how many different ways can he visit the customers? One day he has time to visit only eight customers. In how many different ways can he select the eight? As the salesman has to travel between customers, the order in which his visits are scheduled is important. How many different schedules are there for eight customers?

13.6 A binomial process has a probability of success of 0.15. If eight trials are run, what are the mean number of successes and the standard deviation? What is the probability distribution for the number of successes?

13.7 In a town, 60% of families are known to drive European cars. In a sample of 10 families, what is the probability that at least 8 drive European cars? In a sample of 1,000 families, what is the probability that at least 800 drive European cars?

13.8 Norfisk Oil is drilling some exploratory wells on the mainland of Norway. The results are described as either a 'dry well' or a 'producer well'. Past experience suggests that 10% of exploratory wells are producer wells. If the company drills 12 wells, what is the probability that all 12 are producer wells? What is the probability that all 12 are dry wells? What is the probability distribution for the number of dry wells?

13.9 100 trials are run for a Poisson process. If the probability of a success is 0.02, what are the mean number of successes and the standard deviation? What is the probability distribution for the number of successes? What is the probability of at least six successes?

13.10 During a typical hour an office receives 13 phone calls. What is the distribution of phone calls in a 5-minute period?

13.11 During a busy period at an airport, planes arrive at an average rate of 10 an hour. What is the probability distribution for the number of planes arriving in an hour?

13.12 A machine makes a product, with 5% of units having faults. In a sample of 20 units, what is the probability that at least 1 is defective? In a sample of 200 units, what is the probability that at least 10 are defective?

13.13 A set of observations follow a Normal distribution with mean 40 and standard deviation 4. What proportions of observations have values: (a) greater than 46, (b) less than 34, (c) between 34 and 46, (d) between 30 and 44, (e) between 43 and 47?

13.14 A large number of observations have a mean of 120 and variance of 100. What proportion of observations is: (a) below 100, (b) above 130, (c) between 100 and 130, (d) between 130 and 140, (e) between 115 and 135?

13.15 The number of meals served in a week at Cath's Café is Normally distributed with a mean of 6,000 and a standard deviation of 600. What is the probability that in a given week the number of meals served is less than 5,000? What is the probability that more than 7,500 meals are served? What is the probability that between 5,500 and 6,500 are served? There is a 90% chance that the number of meals served in a week exceeds what value? There is a 90% chance that the number of meals served will fall within what range?

13.16 A service consists of two parts. The first part takes an average of 10 minutes with a standard deviation of 2 minutes; the second part takes an average of 5 minutes with a standard deviation of 1 minute. Describe how long it takes to complete the service. What is the probability that a customer can be served in less than 12 minutes? What is the probability that service to a customer will take more than 20 minutes?

RESEARCH PROJECTS

13.1 Why are scheduling problems so difficult? Plane, bus and train timetables show expected schedules – so how do you think these are designed? Choose a convenient service and collect data to show how actual arrival times compare with expected times. What can you say about these results?

13.2 The number of people visiting a shop each working hour for the past week has been recorded as follows:

12 23 45 09 16 74 58 21 31 07 26 22 14 24 50
23 30 35 68 47 17 08 54 11 24 33 55 16 57 27
02 97 54 23 61 82 15 34 46 44 37 26 28 21 07
64 38 71 79 18 24 16 10 60 50 55 34 44 42 47

What do these results show? Are they typical of the distribution of customer numbers at other shops? How would you set about collecting and analysing data to get more information about the distribution of customers?

13.3   Sometimes a binomial distribution seems close to a Normal distribution; sometimes a Poisson distribution seems close to a Normal distribution. Examine these three distributions and see how similar they really are.

13.4   The probability distributions described in this chapter are not the only ones available. What other distributions can you find, and when are they used?

Sources of information

Further reading

The statistics books mentioned in Chapter 12 contain descriptions of probability distributions. A few books specifically describe probability distributions, often at a technical level.

Balakrishnan N. and Nevzorov V., *A Primer of Statistical Distributions*, John Wiley, Chichester, 2003.

Forbes C., Evans M., Hastings N. and Peacock B., *Statistical Distributions*, Cambridge University Press, Cambridge, 2010.

Krishnamurty K., *Handbook of Statistical Distributions with Applications*, Chapman and Hall/CRC, Boca Raton, FL, 2006.

Using samples

Contents

Chapter outline

The previous two chapters have developed ideas of probabilities and probability distributions. This chapter applies these ideas to sampling. We have already met sampling in Chapter 4, where we looked at ways of collecting data. Essentially, sampling chooses a representative sample from a population, analyses the sample and uses the results to estimate properties of the population. This is the basis of statistical inference. This chapter discusses the reliability of statistical inference and considers the effects of sample size.

After finishing this chapter you should be able to:

- understand how and why to use sampling
- appreciate the aims of statistical inference
- use sampling distributions to find point estimates for population means
- calculate confidence intervals for means and proportions
- use one-sided distributions
- use t-distributions for small samples.

Purpose of sampling

In Chapter 4 we described different ways of collecting data, which almost invariably involves samples. Here we are going to look at sampling again and discuss the sample size and consequent reliability of results.

Statistical inference

The aim of sampling is to get reliable data about an entire population by looking at a relatively small number of observations. Remember that a 'population' is all the things or people that could provide data (rather than its more general use for populations of people) and a 'sample' is the smaller number of things or people from which we actually collect data.

Suppose that an election is approaching, and the various parties are concerned about the number of votes each might expect. There are two ways of finding this out:

- ask every person eligible to vote what their intentions are (giving a census)
- take a smaller sample of eligible people, ask their intentions and use these results to estimate the voting intentions of the population as a whole.

Often it is impossible to test all of a population. For example, it makes no sense for a food processing company to test every can of beans to make sure that they all taste good. Even when a census is possible, it is unlikely to be completely accurate. In the political opinion poll it is unlikely that everyone will answer the questions, tell the truth, not make a mistake and not change their mind before polling day. So a census has the disadvantages of being difficult – and sometimes impossible – time-consuming, expensive and still not entirely reliable. At the same time, a smaller, well-organised sample is easier, faster, cheaper and gives equally reliable results.

Not surprisingly, managers usually are happy to work with samples. However, they must recognise that alongside the advantages of working with a sample are the inherent risks. Despite our best endeavours, the results from a sample might not give an accurate representation of the population – and there is inevitably some variation between samples. If your breakfast cereal says that it contains 20% fruit, you do not expect every spoonful to contain exactly 20%. Sometime you get a spoonful with lots of fruit, and sometimes you get no fruit at all. And with sampling in general, you should usually get reasonable results, but sometimes the sample just does not reflect the whole population.

Realistically the more effort you put into sampling, the more accurate the results – which means that bigger samples are usually more reliable. This raises an obvious question about the best size for a sample. It should be big enough to give a fair representation of the population, but small enough to be practical and cost effective. Managers must consider this balance carefully when choosing an appropriate sample size. To help, they can do some related calculations, all of which are based on random samples, which means that every member of the population has the same probability of being chosen. This is an important condition for statistical analyses, and if it is not true the subsequent results are not valid.

In Chapter 4 we discussed the actual collection of data. Here we focus on the reliability of the samples collected for the process of statistical inference:

Statistical inference is a process that:

- considers data collected from a random sample of the population
- uses this data to estimate properties of the whole population.

Review questions 14.1 What is the purpose of sampling?

14.2 What is statistical inference?

IDEAS IN PRACTICE **Renewable energy statistics**

Most governments are encouraging the development of new and reusable sources of energy – illustrated by the UK government's target of generating 15% of electricity from renewable sources by 2020. This programme is led by the Department of Energy and Climate Change, but there are so many diverse initiatives and such a broad range of organisations involved that it is difficult to see exactly what is happening. To clarify the picture, the government collects and analyses information to monitor progress, check the effects of different policies and to compare the UK's performance with European and world standards.

The government contracts Future Energy Solutions (part of AEA Technology Environment) to collect data on renewable energy. They have run various surveys since 1989, with the results published in a database called RESTATS (Renewable Energy STATisticS database). This contains records of all the known renewable energy projects in the UK, including solar energy (both active and passive), onshore and offshore wind power, wave power, large- and small-scale hydroelectricity, geothermal aquifers and a range of biofuels.

Information for the database is collected from a number of sources:

- Large projects – annual surveys through questionnaires sent to project managers
- Small projects – estimates based on data collected from a sample of projects through:
  - renewable projects surveys
  - waste-to-energy questionnaires
- Mail shots to interested organisations
- Telephone follow-up of non-respondents
- Online survey forms
- Estimation where data is not available
- Expert review to identify any gaps in the data and to improve collection.

Results from the survey are used by various bodies, including UK Energy Statistics, Eurostat, the International Energy Agency and the World Energy Council.[1,2,3,4,5]

Sources: Websites at www.decc.gov.uk; www.restats.org.uk and www.future-energy-solutions.com.

Sampling distribution of the mean

Probably the most common use of statistical inference is to estimate the mean of some variable in a population by looking at the values in a sample. For example, you might want to estimate the mean weight of boxes of cauliflowers sent to market by weighing a sample of boxes, or estimate the average time taken to solve customers' problems by timing a sample of calls to a call centre, or estimate the average cost of a service by looking at a sample of invoices, or estimate the average delay in train journeys by asking some customers to record their experiences.

Whenever you take a series of samples from a population, you would expect to find some variation between samples. Suppose that boxes of apples with a nominal weight of 10 kg are delivered to a wholesaler; if you take a sample of 10 boxes you would expect the mean weight to be about 10 kg, but would not be surprised by small variations about this. For instance, samples of 10 boxes taken over consecutive days might have mean weights of 10.2 kg, 9.8 kg, 10.3 kg, 10.1 kg, 9.6 kg and so on. If you continue taking samples over some period, you can build a distribution of the sample means.

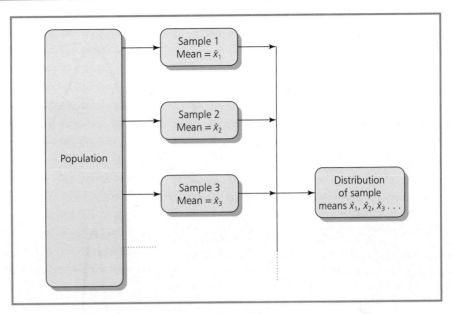

Figure 14.1 Creating the sampling distribution of the mean

Any distribution that is found from samples is called a sampling distribution. When we build a distribution of sample means it is a sampling distribution of the mean (illustrated in Figure 14.1).

We want to relate the properties of a sampling distribution of the mean back to the original population. For this we have to remember the standard notation that we mentioned in Chapter 13, with:

- a population of size N, mean μ (the Greek letter mu) and standard deviation σ (the Greek letter sigma);
- a sample of size n, mean $\bar{x}$ and standard deviation s.

Now we can use a standard result that is called the **central limit theorem**. This says that when you take large random samples from a population, the sample means are Normally distributed. This is true regardless of the distribution of the original population. To be more accurate the central limit theorem says:

- If a population is Normally distributed, the sampling distribution of the mean is also Normally distributed.
- If the sample size is large (say more than 30), the sampling distribution of the mean is Normally distributed regardless of the population distribution.
- The sampling distribution of the mean has a mean μ and standard deviation $\sigma / \sqrt{n}$.

To put it simply, the sampling distribution of the mean is Normally distributed (provided the sample size is more than 30 or the population is Normally distributed), with the same mean as the population and with a smaller standard deviation (as shown in Figure 14.2). And as the sample size increases, the standard deviation gets smaller, confirming the intuitive result that larger samples have smaller variation and give more reliable results.

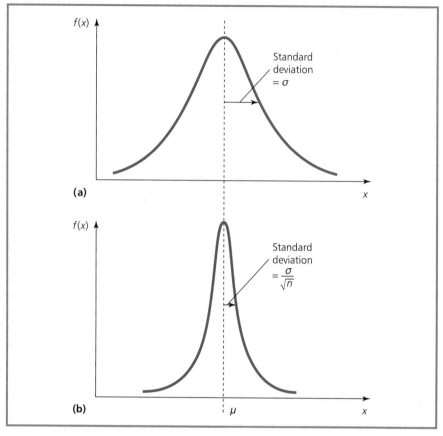

Figure 14.2 Comparisons of the distribution of (a) a population, and (b) a sampling distribution of the mean

WORKED EXAMPLE 14.1

A process makes units with a mean length of 60 cm and standard deviation of 1 cm. What is the probability that a sample of 36 units has a mean length of less than 59.7 cm?

Solution

Imagine what happens when you take a large number of samples of 36 units. You find the mean length of each sample, and the distribution of these means – the sampling distribution of the mean – is:

- Normally distributed
- with a mean length $= \mu = 60$ cm
- and with a standard deviation $= \sigma / \sqrt{n} = 1 / \sqrt{36}$
$$= 0.167 \text{ cm.}$$

You can find the probability that one sample has a mean length less than 59.7 cm from the area in the tail of this sampling distribution of the mean. To find this area you need Z, the number of standard deviations the point of interest (59.7) is away from the mean (have another look at Chapter 13 if you are unsure about this):

$$Z = (59.7 - 60) / 0.167$$
$$= -1.80$$

Looking up 1.80 in the Normal tables in Appendix D, or using a computer, shows that this corresponds to a probability of 0.0359. So we expect 3.59% of samples to have a mean length of less than 59.7 cm (as shown in Figure 14.3).

Worked example 14.1 continued

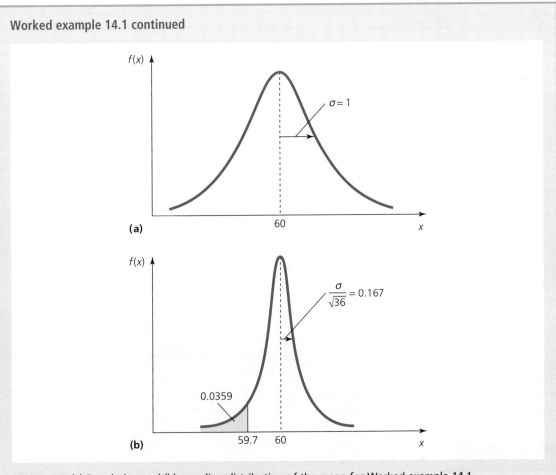

Figure 14.3 (a) Population and (b) sampling distribution of the mean for Worked example 14.1

You have probably noticed one drawback with statistical inference – the clumsy statements needed to describe, for example, 'the mean of the sampling distribution of the mean'. To make things a bit easier, the standard deviation of the sampling distribution of the mean is usually called the standard error. The ideas behind these phrases are fairly straightforward – but you have to be clear about what they describe. Remember that we have a population with a certain mean. We take samples from this and each sample has its own mean. The distribution of these sample means is the sampling distribution of the mean – and this in turn has its own mean and standard deviation.

WORKED EXAMPLE 14.2

Soft drinks are put into bottles that hold a nominal 200 ml, but the filling machine introduces a standard deviation of 10 ml. These bottles are packed into cartons of 25 and exported to a market which insists that the mean weight of a carton is at least the quantity specified by the manufacturer. To make sure this happens, the bottler sets the machine to fill bottles to 205 ml. What is the

Worked example 14.2 continued

probability that a carton chosen at random fails the quantity test?

Solution

The mean volume per bottle is 205 ml with a standard deviation of 10 ml. Taking a random sample of 25 cans gives a sampling distribution of the mean with mean 205 ml and standard deviation of 10 /

$\sqrt{25}$ = 2 ml. A case fails the quantity test if the average quantity per can is less than 200 ml. That is:

$$Z = (200 - 205) / 2$$
$$= -2.5$$

This corresponds to a probability of 0.0062, meaning that 62 cases in 10,000 will still fail the test (as shown in Figure 14.4).

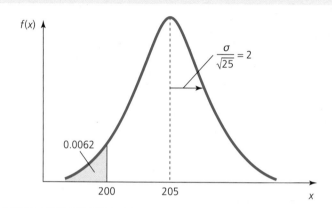

Figure 14.4 Sampling distribution of the mean for bottles (Worked example 14.2)

Review questions

14.3   What is the sampling distribution of the mean?

14.4   Describe the shape of the sampling distribution of the mean.

IDEAS IN PRACTICE   Bird Flu

In 2005 there were warnings that the world could be facing a pandemic of Influenza A/H5N1, commonly described as bird flu or avian flu. A series of related facts were reported:

- a flu pandemic in 1918 had killed more than 20 million people
- A/H5N1 had become common among birds in Asia, and spread quickly between bird populations
- in 1997 during an outbreak of avian flu in Hong Kong, 18 people caught bird flu and 6 of these died, suggesting a high fatality in humans
- it was feared that migrating birds could spread the disease widely, and more humans would be infected

- it was feared that the virus would mutate into a form that could pass between people, with reports of this happening in Thailand in 2004
- there was no vaccine or effective treatment for A/H5N1.

These facts were widely reported, often sensationally, and caused a level of panic, typically based on the *New Scientist's*[6] estimate that 'Bird flu outbreak could kill 1.5 billion'. Millions of domestic birds were slaughtered throughout Asia, travel restrictions were placed on people living near infections, a vaccine was developed and millions of people were injected, health services were organised to deal with peaks in demand, governments formulated emergency plans to deal with a pandemic and so on.

Ideas in practice continued

In the event, little actually happened. The World Health Organisation[7,8] reported the following figures for bird flu, which had no impact on the normal, underlying incidence of influenza.

Year	2003	2004	2005	2006	2007	2008	2009	2010
Number of infections	4	46	98	115	88	44	73	31
Number of deaths	4	32	43	79	59	33	32	13

One of the problems with the reports was the lack of reliable data. Even basic figures like infection rate were largely unknown because most people who caught flu accepted it as a seasonal illness and did not look for treatment. Similarly, figures for the death rate were collected by hospitals – but they saw only the few most severe cases with a high death rate, and not the great majority of milder cases where patients recovered normally. Other estimates of the death rate were far lower, at less than 1%, and were comparable with normal seasonal flu.

Sources: www.bbc.co.uk; www.balysis.blogspot.com

Confidence intervals

The last two worked examples found the features expected in a sample from the known features of the population. Usually, we work the other way around and estimate the features of a population from a sample.

Suppose we take a sample of 100 units of a product and find that the mean weight is 30 g. How can we estimate the mean weight of the whole population? Assuming that we have chosen the sample carefully and it represents the population fairly, the obvious answer is to suggest that the population mean is also 30 g. This single value is a point estimate.

A point estimate is our best estimate for the population mean, but we know that it comes from a sample and is unlikely to be exactly right. It should be close to the population mean – especially with a big sample – but there is still likely to be some error. A better approach is to define a range that the population mean is likely to be within. This gives an interval estimate, and for this we need two measures:

- the limits of the interval
- our confidence that the mean is within the interval.

If we set the interval very wide, we should be very confident that the population mean is within the range – but as the interval gets narrower our confidence that the mean is still within its limits declines. In our sample of 100 units with mean weight 30 g we might be 99% confident that the population mean is in the interval 20 to 40 g; we might be 95% confident that the mean is between 25 and 35 g; and we might be 90% confident that the mean is between 27 and 33 g. This kind of range is called a confidence interval.

> ■ A 95% (for instance) confidence interval defines the range within which we are 95% confident that the population mean lies.

We can calculate the 95% confidence interval using the following argument. The sample mean, $\bar{x}$, is the best point estimate for the population mean, μ.

But this point estimate is one observation from the sampling distribution of the mean. This sampling distribution of the mean is Normal, with mean μ and standard deviation $\sigma / \sqrt{n}$. As it is Normal, 95% of observations lie within 1.96 standard deviations of the mean, which is within the range:

$$\mu - 1.96\sigma / \sqrt{n} \quad \text{to} \quad \mu + 1.96\sigma / \sqrt{n}$$

We can phrase this as:

the probability $\bar{x}$ is between $\mu - 1.96\sigma / \sqrt{n}$ and $\mu + 1.96\sigma / \sqrt{n} = 0.95$
$$P(\mu - 1.96\sigma / \sqrt{n} \leq \bar{x} \leq \mu + 1.96\sigma / \sqrt{n}) = 0.95$$

And we can rearrange this to give the confidence interval for the population:

$$P(\bar{x} - 1.96\sigma / \sqrt{n} \leq \mu \leq \bar{x} + 1.96\sigma / \sqrt{n}) = 0.95$$

Repeating this calculation for different confidence intervals for the population mean gives:

- 90% confidence interval: $\bar{x} - 1.645\sigma / \sqrt{n}$ to $\bar{x} + 1.645\sigma / \sqrt{n}$
- 95% confidence interval: $\bar{x} - 1.96\sigma / \sqrt{n}$ to $\bar{x} + 1.96\sigma / \sqrt{n}$
- 99% confidence interval: $\bar{x} - 2.58\sigma / \sqrt{n}$ to $\bar{x} + 2.58\sigma / \sqrt{n}$

WORKED EXAMPLE 14.3

A machine produces parts that have a standard deviation in length of 1.4 cm. A random sample of 100 parts has a mean length of 80 cm. What is the 95% confidence interval for the mean length of all parts?

Solution

The sample of 100 parts has a mean length of 80 cm, so the point estimate for the population mean is 80 cm.

The sampling distribution of the mean has a mean of 80 cm and standard deviation of $\sigma / \sqrt{n} = 1.4 / \sqrt{100} = 0.14$ cm. 95% of observations are within 1.96 standard deviations of the mean, so the 95% confidence interval (as shown in Figure 14.5) is:

$$\bar{x} - 1.96\sigma / \sqrt{n} \quad \text{to} \quad \bar{x} + 1.96\sigma / \sqrt{n}$$
$$80 - 1.96 \times 0.14 \quad \text{to} \quad 80 + 1.96 \times 0.14$$
$$79.73 \text{ cm} \quad \text{to} \quad 80.27 \text{ cm}$$

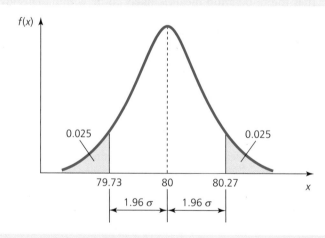

Figure 14.5 Confidence interval for Worked example 14.3

In this last example we estimated the population mean from a sample mean – but assumed that we knew the standard deviation of the population. It is unlikely that we would know the standard deviation of a population, but not its mean. So it is much more likely that the only information we have is from a sample, and then we use this to estimate both the population mean and standard deviation.

The obvious estimate of the population standard deviation is the sample standard deviation, s. Then the 95% confidence interval becomes:

$$\bar{x} - 1.96s / \sqrt{n} \quad \text{to} \quad \bar{x} + 1.96s / \sqrt{n}$$

WORKED EXAMPLE 14.4

Homelock Security employs night watchmen to patrol warehouses and they want to find the average time needed to patrol warehouses of a certain size. On a typical night they recorded the times to patrol 40 similar warehouses. These showed a mean time of 76.4 minutes, with a standard deviation of 17.2 minutes. What are the 95% and 99% confidence intervals for the population mean?

Solution

The point estimate for the population mean is 76.4 minutes. The standard deviation of the sample is 17.2 minutes, and using this as an approximation for the standard deviation of the population gives:

■ **95% confidence interval:**

$$\bar{x} - 1.96s / \sqrt{n} \quad \text{to} \quad \bar{x} + 1.96s / \sqrt{n}$$
$$76.4 - 1.96 \times 17.2 / \sqrt{40} \quad \text{to}$$
$$76.4 + 1.96 \times 17.2 / \sqrt{40}$$
$$71.07 \quad \text{to} \quad 81.73$$

meaning that we are 95% confident that the population mean is between 71.07 minutes and 81.73 minutes.

■ **99% confidence interval:**

$$\bar{x} - 2.58s / \sqrt{n} \quad \text{to} \quad \bar{x} + 2.58s / \sqrt{n}$$
$$76.4 - 2.58 \times 17.2 / \sqrt{40} \quad \text{to}$$
$$76.4 + 2.58 \times 17.2 / \sqrt{40}$$
$$69.38 \quad \text{to} \quad 83.42$$

meaning that we are 99% confident that the population mean is between 69.38 minutes and 83.42 minutes.

WORKED EXAMPLE 14.5

A company wants to find the average value of its customer accounts. An initial sample suggests that the standard deviation of the value is £60. What sample size would give a 95% confidence interval for the population mean that is (a) £25 wide, (b) £20 wide, (c) £15 wide?

Solution

The standard deviation of the initial sample is £60, so we can use this as an approximation for the standard deviation of the population, giving a standard error of $60 / \sqrt{n}$.

(a) A 95% confidence interval is:

$$\text{mean} - 1.96 \times 60 / \sqrt{n} \quad \text{to}$$
$$\text{mean} + 1.96 \times 60 / \sqrt{n}$$

giving a range of $2 \times 1.96 \times 60 / \sqrt{n}$. We want this range to be £25 wide, so:

$$2 \times 1.96 \times 60 / \sqrt{n} = 25$$
$$\sqrt{n} = 9.41$$
$$n = 88.5$$

In other words, a sample size of 88.5 (rounded to 89) gives a confidence interval for the population mean that is £25 wide.

Worked example 14.5 continued

(b) Repeating this calculation with a confidence interval of £20 has:

$$2 \times 1.96 \times 60 / \sqrt{n} = 20$$
$$\sqrt{n} = 11.76$$
$$n = 138.3$$

(c) Again repeating the calculation with a confidence interval of £15 has:

$$2 \times 1.96 \times 60 / \sqrt{n} = 15$$
$$\sqrt{n} = 15.68$$
$$n = 245.9$$

As expected, larger samples give narrower confidence intervals. But notice that decreasing the range from £25 to £20 increased the sample size by 138.3 – 88.5 = 49.8, while decreasing the range from £20 to £15 increased the sample size by 245.9 – 138.3 = 107.6. There are clearly diminishing returns with increasing sample size. As the standard deviation of the sampling distribution is proportional to $1/\sqrt{n}$, reducing the range to a half would need a sample four times as large; reducing the range to a third would need a sample nine times as large, and so on.

Correcting the standard deviation

It is safe to use a sample standard deviation as an approximation to the population standard deviation when the sample size is large – say more than about 30. But with smaller samples this tends to underestimate the population standard deviation. We can compensate for this bias with a small adjustment. Instead of the approximation $\sigma = s / \sqrt{n}$, we can use $\sigma = s / \sqrt{(n-1)}$. This is Bessel's correction and, although it seems rather arbitrary, there is a sound theoretical reason for using it.

WORKED EXAMPLE 14.6

MLP Mail-order collects a random sample of 40 customer orders, as shown in the table. What is the 95% confidence interval for the population mean?

Size of order	Number of customers
€0–€100	4
€100–€200	8
€200–€300	14
€300–€400	8
€400–€500	4
€500–€600	2

Solution

Remember (from Chapter 6) that for grouped data the mean and standard deviation are:

$$\bar{x} = \frac{\Sigma fx}{\Sigma f}; \quad s = \sqrt{\frac{\Sigma f(x - \bar{x})^2}{\Sigma f}}$$

where x is the midpoint of each range and f is the number of observations in each range. Doing these calculations, you find that:

$$\bar{x} = 265 \quad \text{and} \quad s = 127.57$$

These are the best point estimates for the population mean and standard deviation. Then the 95% confidence interval is 1.96 standard deviations from the mean, and using Bessel's correction, we get the range:

$$\bar{x} - 1.96s / \sqrt{(n-1)} \quad \text{to} \quad \bar{x} + 1.96s / \sqrt{(n-1)}$$
$$265 - 1.96 \times 127.57 / \sqrt{39} \quad \text{to}$$
$$265 + 1.96 \times 127 / 57 / \sqrt{39}$$
$$224.96 \quad \text{to} \quad 305.04$$

This range is wide because of the large variance of the data and the relatively small sample size.

In this example, Bessel's correction increased the estimated population standard deviation by about 1%, making very little difference to the calculation.

This is usually true and the adjustment makes a difference only with very small sample sizes.

Estimating population proportions

Sometimes instead of estimating the value of some variable in a population, we want to estimate the proportion of the population that share some characteristic. This is typical of a survey, that might show that that '25% of respondents believe this', or quality control that finds the proportion of output that is faulty, or financial analysts who find the proportion of invoices smaller than some amount, or personal records that show the proportion of people who work overtime. Then statistical inference takes a sample, finds the proportion of the sample with the required property and then estimates the proportion of the population with that property.

Suppose the proportion of a population with a certain property is π (the Greek letter pi). Another result of the central limit theorem is that when we take large sample (say more than 30) the sample proportions are:

- Normally distributed
- with mean π
- and standard deviation $\sqrt{(\pi(1 - \pi) / n)}$.

Then 95% of samples are within the range:

$$\pi - 1.96 \times \sqrt{(\pi(1 - \pi) / n)} \quad \text{to} \quad \pi + 1.96 \times \sqrt{(\pi(1 - \pi) / n)}$$

Now suppose that you take a sample which contains a proportion p with the property. This value of p gives the best estimate for the population proportion, π. But the point estimate is one observation from a sampling distribution. Using exactly the same reasoning as before, we can approximate π by p and define a confidence interval within which we are, say, 95% confident that the true proportion lies:

The 95% confidence interval for a population proportion is:
$$p - 1.96 \times \sqrt{(p(1-p) / n)} \quad \text{to} \quad p + 1.96 \times \sqrt{(p(1-p) / n)}$$

WORKED EXAMPLE 14.7

Queen Charlotte's Hospital gives a random sample of 50 patients a new treatment for an illness. 60% of these are cured. Find the 95% confidence interval for the proportion of all patients who will be cured by the treatment.

Solution

The proportion of patients in the sample who are cured, p, is 0.6. This is the point estimate for the proportion who will be cured in the population, π.

The 95% confidence interval for the proportion in the population is:

$$p - 1.96 \times \sqrt{(p(1 - p) / n)} \quad \text{to} \quad p + 1.96 \times \sqrt{(p(1 - p) / n)}$$
$$0.6 - 1.96 \times \sqrt{(0.6 \times 0.4 / 50)} \quad \text{to}$$
$$0.6 + 1.96 \times \sqrt{(0.6 \times 0.4 / 50)}$$
$$0.6 - 0.136 \quad \text{to} \quad 0.6 + 0.136$$
$$0.464 \quad \text{to} \quad 0.736$$

We are 95% confident that between 46.4% and 73.6% of patients given the new treatment will be cured. This seems a wide range, but we are dealing with small samples – and real medical trials are conducted on thousands of patients.

WORKED EXAMPLE 14.8

Last month an opinion poll in Helmsburg suggested that 30% of people would vote for the Green Party. This month the poll is being rerun. How many people must be interviewed for the poll to be within 2% of actual voting intentions with a 95% level of confidence?

Solution

The best point estimate for the proportion of people who will vote for the Green Party is $p = 0.3$, found in last month's poll. With the next poll of size n, the 95% confidence interval for the proportion of people voting for the Green Party is:

$p - 1.96 \times \sqrt{(p(1-p)/n)}$ to
$p + 1.96 \times \sqrt{(p(1-p)/n)}$
$0.3 - 1.96 \times \sqrt{(0.3 \times 0.7/n)}$ to
$0.3 + 1.96 \times \sqrt{(0.3 \times 0.7/n)}$

But we want the result to be within 2% of the mean, so that:

$0.02 = 1.96 \times \sqrt{(0.3 \times 0.7/n)}$

or $n = 2,017$
The poll needs a sample of 2,017 people to get the desired accuracy.

Review questions

14.5 Why is a point estimate for the population mean unlikely to be exactly right?

14.6 What is the 95% confidence interval for a value?

14.7 Is a 95% confidence interval wider or narrower than a 90% interval?

14.8 If a sample of size n produces a confidence interval that is w wide, how large a sample would you need to give a confidence interval that is $w/5$ wide?

14.9 When would you use Bessel's correction?

IDEAS IN PRACTICE Opinion polls

Many organisations – such as Gallup, Ipsos MORI, ComRes, GfK NOP and YouGov – routinely collect large amounts of information in opinion polls. You often see their results just before an election – but then you normally see only the headline result, which is the point estimate for the population. If you look carefully you will see a warning along the lines of 'this result is within 2% nineteen times out of twenty'.

One opinion poll of 2,127 people in 2010 suggested the following support for political parties.

Labour	35%	Green Party	3%
Conservatives	31%	BNP	2%
Liberal Democrats	22%	UKIP	0%
Scottish Nationalists	6%	Others	1%

If you look at, say, the Liberal Democrat result, the sample gives a point estimate for the proportion of people supporting them as 22%. But you can also calculate some confidence intervals. As $p = 0.22$, $(1 - p) = 0.78$ and $n = 2,127$, we can substitute these values to find the 95% confidence interval of:

$p - 1.96 \times \sqrt{(p(1-p)/n)}$ to
$p + 1.96 \times \sqrt{(p(1-p)/n)}$
$0.22 - 1.96 \times \sqrt{(0.22 \times 0.78/2,179)}$ to
$0.22 + 1.96 \times \sqrt{(0.22 \times 0.78/2,179)}$
0.2026 to 0.2374

In other words, the Liberal Democrats can be 95% confident that their support is between 20.26% and 23.74% of the electorate. This range might have considerable impact on the final election result.

One-sided confidence intervals

So far we have used a confidence interval that is symmetrical about the mean, and assumed that we use both sides of the sampling distribution. Then we are

95% confident that the true value is within a certain range, and there is a 2.5% chance that the true value is above the top of this range and a 2.5% chance that the true value is below the bottom of it. Often we are interested in only one side of the sampling distribution. For example, we might want to be 95% confident that the mean number of defects is below some maximum, or the weight of goods is above some minimum, or the cost is below some maximum. Then we are interested in only one tail of the distribution (illustrated in Figure 14.6).

To find a one-sided confidence interval we use the same general approach as for the two-sided interval. But while a two-sided 95% confidence interval has 2.5% of the distribution in each tail (a distance of 1.96 standard deviations away from the mean), a one-sided 95% confidence interval has 5% of the distribution in one tail (a distance of 1.645 standard deviations from the mean). Then we use the following rules for finding the one-sided 95% confidence interval:

- To find the value that we are 95% confident the population mean is above, use:

    $\bar{x} - 1.645$ standard errors

- To find the value that we are 95% confident the population mean is below, use:

    $\bar{x} + 1.645$ standard errors

Of course, we can use other levels of confidence, but 95% is convenient and generally the most common.

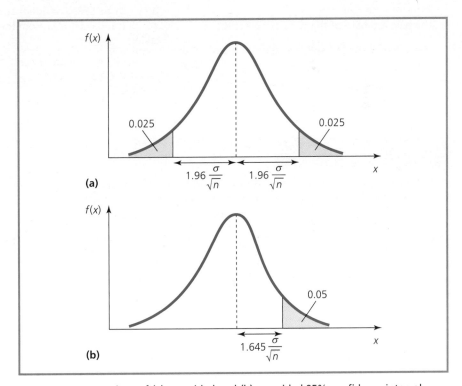

Figure 14.6 Comparison of (a) two-sided and (b) one-sided 95% confidence interval

WORKED EXAMPLE 14.9

Yamatsumo Electric use an automated process that introduces some variability into the weight of each unit. One day a sample of 60 units has a mean weight of 45 kg and standard deviation of 5 kg. What weight are Yamatsumo 95% confident the population mean is below? What weight are they 95% confident the population mean is above?

Solution

The best estimate of the population mean is 45 kg, and the best estimate of the standard error is

$s/\sqrt{(n-1)} = 5/\sqrt{59} = 0.65$. So Yamatsumo are 95% confident that the population mean is less than:

$\bar{x} + 1.645 \times$ standard error
$= 45 + 1.645 \times 0.65$
$= 46.07$ kg

And they are 95% confident that the population mean is more than:

$\bar{x} - 1.645 \times$ standard error
$= 45 - 1.645 \times 0.65$
$= 43.93$ kg

WORKED EXAMPLE 14.10

A sample of 40 accounts at PrixMin shows that customers owe an average of €842 with a standard deviation of €137. PrixMin can be 95% confident that customers owe an average of less than what amount? What amount can they be 99% confident that customers owe less than?

Solution

The best estimate of the standard error is:

$s/\sqrt{(n-1)} = 137/\sqrt{39} = 21.94$

The point estimate for customer debt is €842. PrixMin can be 95% confident that the average debt is below:

$\bar{x} + 1.645 \times$ standard error
$= 842 + 1.645 \times 21.94$
$= €878$

They can be 99% confident that the average debt is 2.33 standard errors from the mean (found from tables):

$\bar{x} + 2.33 \times$ standard error
$= 842 + 2.33 \times 21.94$
$= €893$

WORKED EXAMPLE 14.11

A quality assurance programme takes a random sample of 40 invoices and finds that 8 have mistakes. What proportion of mistakes is the company 95% sure that the population is below? What proportion of mistakes is the company 95% confident the population is above? What is the 95% two-sided confidence interval?

Solution

The proportion of defects in the sample, p, is 8 / 40 = 0.2. And we know that the best estimate for the standard error of a proportion is $\sqrt{(p(1-p)/n)}$ $= \sqrt{(0.2 \times 0.8/40)} = 0.063$. So the company is 95% confident that the proportion of mistakes in the population is less than:

$\bar{x} + 1.645 \times$ standard error
$= 0.2 + 1.645 \times 0.063$
$= 0.304$

Similarly, the company is 95% confident that the population mean is more than:

$\bar{x} - 1.645 \times$ standard error
$= 0.2 - 1.645 \times 0.063$
$= 0.096$

The two-sided 95% confidence limits are 1.96 standard errors from the mean, giving an interval of:

$\bar{x} - 1.96 \times 0.063$ to $\bar{x} + 1.96 \times 0.063$
$0.2 - 1.96 \times 0.063$ to $0.2 + 1.96 \times 0.063$
0.077 to 0.323

14.10 When would you use a one-sided confidence interval?

14.11 Put the following in order of nearest the mean: a one-sided 95% confidence interval, a one-sided 99% confidence interval, a two-sided 95% confidence interval.

Using small samples

Much of statistical inference is based on the central limit theorem – but this works only when a population is Normally distributed, or with a large sample. But suppose that you do not know the population distribution, or you can take only a small sample (where 'small' is below about 30). Then you cannot simply assume that the sampling distribution is Normal.

The problem is that small samples are always less representative of the population than large samples – and in particular, small samples include fewer outlying results and show less variation than the population. Once we recognise this pattern, we can make allowances. And this means using a slightly different probability distribution – the *t*-distribution, which is often called the **Student-*t*** distribution.

A *t*-distribution looks very similar to the Normal, but its shape depends on the degrees of freedom. For our purposes, when we take a sample of size *n*, the degrees of freedom are simply defined as $n - 1$. To be more rigorous, the degrees of freedom are the number of independent pieces of information used. You might ask why a sample of size *n* has $n - 1$ pieces of information rather than *n*. The answer is that we fix a value for the mean, so only $n - 1$ values can vary. Suppose you have four numbers whose mean is 5; the first three numbers can take any value (3, 5 and 7 perhaps) but then the fourth number is fixed (at 5) to get the correct mean.

When the sample size is close to 30, the *t*-distribution is virtually the same as a Normal distribution. But as the degrees of freedom get smaller – meaning the sample size gets smaller – the distribution gets wider and lower, as shown in Figure 14.7.

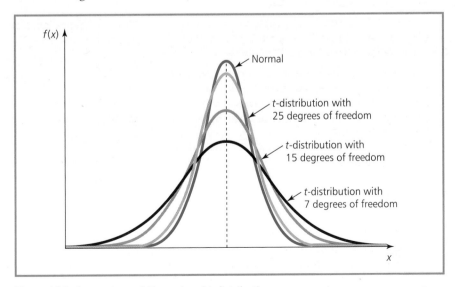

Figure 14.7 Comparison of Normal and *t*-distributions

You use t-distributions in the same way as Normal distributions, and can find values from either tables (shown in Appendix E) or statistical packages. With the Excel function TINV you enter the probability in the tails of the distribution and the degrees of freedom, and it returns the number of standard deviations the point of interest is away from the mean (that is, the equivalent of Z). There are slight differences in the tables, so you have to be careful. In Appendix E the figures show the probability in each tail. A two-sided 95% confidence interval means that the probability of being in each tail is 0.025, so you look at this column and see that with 1 degree of freedom this is 12.706 standard deviations away from the mean; with 2 degrees of freedom it is 4.303, with 3 degrees of freedom it is 3.182 and so on. As the number of degrees of freedom gets higher, the t-distribution gets closer to the Normal, and the number of standard deviations gets closer to the Normal result of 1.96.

WORKED EXAMPLE 14.12

A survey of 10 entries in a sales ledger has a mean value of £60 and a standard deviation of £8. What is the 95% confidence interval for the population of entries?

Solution

The point estimate for the population mean is £60. The sample size is only 10, so we cannot assume a Normal distribution and must use a t-distribution with $10 - 1 = 9$ degrees of freedom.

A 95% confidence interval has a probability of 0.025 in each tail, and looking this up in Appendix E shows that with 9 degrees of freedom this corresponds to 2.262 standard deviations. So the confidence limits are 2.262 standard deviations from the mean at:

$$\bar{x} - 2.262 \times s / \sqrt{(n-1)} \quad \text{to} \quad \bar{x} + 2.262 \times s / \sqrt{(n-1)}$$
$$60 - 2.262 \times 8 / \sqrt{9} \quad \text{to} \quad 60 + 2.262 \times 8 / \sqrt{9}$$
$$53.97 \quad \text{to} \quad 66.03$$

We have used Bessel's correction for the standard error of a small sample, and are now 95% confident that the population mean is within the range £54 to £66.

WORKED EXAMPLE 14.13

The time taken for eight people working in an office to travel to work has a mean of 37 minutes and a standard deviation of 12 minutes.

(a) What is the 90% confidence interval for the mean travel time of everyone in the office?
(b) What is the 95% confidence interval?
(c) What is the 95% confidence interval with a sample size of 20?
(d) What would the result of part (c) be using a Normal distribution?

Solution

(a) The sample size is 8, so there are 7 degrees of freedom. A 90% confidence interval has a probability of 0.05 in each tail, and looking up this value in Appendix E shows that it corresponds to 1.895 standard deviations. So the

90% confidence limits are 1.895 standard deviations from the mean at:

$$\bar{x} - 1.895 \times s / \sqrt{(n-1)} \quad \text{to} \quad \bar{x} + 1.895 \times s / \sqrt{(n-1)}$$
$$37 - 1.895 \times 12 / \sqrt{7} \quad \text{to} \quad 37 + 1.895 \times 12 / \sqrt{7}$$
$$28.40 \quad \text{to} \quad 45.60$$

(b) For the 95% confidence interval we look up a probability of 0.025 with 7 degrees of freedom and get a value of 2.365. Then the 95% confidence interval is:

$$37 - 2.365 \times 12 / \sqrt{7} \quad \text{to} \quad 37 + 2.365 \times 12 / \sqrt{7}$$
$$26.27 \quad \text{to} \quad 47.73$$

(c) With a sample of 20 the standard error becomes $12 / \sqrt{19}$ and there are 19 degrees of freedom. Then the 95% confidence interval is within 2.093 standard deviations of the mean:

Worked example 14.13 continued

$37 - 2.093 \times 12 / \sqrt{19}$ to $37 + 2.093 \times 12 / \sqrt{19}$

31.24   to   42.76

(d) 95% confidence limits with a Normal distribution are 1.96 standard errors from the mean, so the interval is:

$37 - 1.96 \times 12 / \sqrt{19}$ to $37 + 1.96 \times 12 / \sqrt{19}$

31.61   to   42.39

The small sample has not allowed for the full variability of the data, so the Normal distribution has assumed that the data is less spread out than it actually is. The confidence interval tends to be too narrow, but you can see that the differences are often small. Figure 14.8 shows all these calculations in a spreadsheet.

	A	B	C	D	E	F	G
1	**Student-t distribution**						
2							
3	**Sample size**			8			
4	**Mean**			37			
5	**Standard deviation**			12			
6							
7	**Part (a)**						
8	Degrees of freedom			7	D3 – 1		
9	Standard error			4.536	D5/SQRT(D3-1)		
10							
11	Confidence interval			90			
12	Number of standard deviations			1.895	TINV((100-D11/100,D8)		
13	Confidence interval	From		28.407	D4 – (D12*D9)		
14		To		45.593001	D4 + (D12*D9)		
15							
16	**Part (b)**						
17	Confidence interval			95			
18	Number of standard deviations			2.365	TINV((100-D17/100,D8)		
19	Confidence interval	From		26.275	D4 – (D18*D9)		
20		To		47.725	D4 + (D18*D9)		
21							
22	**Part (c)**						
23	Sample size			20			
24	Degrees of freedom			19			
25	Standard error			2.753	D5/SQRT(D23-1)		
26	Confidence interval			95			
27	Number of standard deviations			2.093	TINV((100-D26/100,D24)		
28	Confidence interval	From		31.238	D4 – (D27*D25)		
29		To		42.762	D4 + (D27*D25)		
30							
31	**Part (d)**						
32	Normal distribution						
33	Sample size			20			
34	Standard error			2.753	D5/SQRT(D33-1)		
35	Confidence interval			95			
36	Number of standard deviations			1.960	NORMSINV((100-D35/200)		
37	Confidence interval	From		31.604	D4 – (D36*D34)		
38		To		42.396	D4 + (D36*D34)		

Figure 14.8 Spreadsheet of calculations for Worked example 14.13

Review questions

14.12 Why are sampling distributions not Normal when samples are small?

14.13 What are the 'degrees of freedom'?

CHAPTER REVIEW

This chapter discussed sampling and the reliability of samples.

- Data collection usually needs sampling, which is easier, cheaper, faster and often as reliable as a census. Sampling collects data from a representative sample of the population and uses this to estimate features for the population as a whole. This is the basis of statistical inference.

- When you take samples from a population, values of the sample means, say, follow a sampling distribution of the mean. When the sample size is large, or the population is Normally distributed, the sampling distribution of the mean is Normally distributed, with mean μ and standard deviation $\sigma / \sqrt{n}$.

- For small samples it is better to use Bessel's correction to calculate the standard error as $\sigma / \sqrt{(n-1)}$.

- A sample mean gives a point estimate for the population mean, and a sample standard deviation gives a point estimate for the population standard deviation.

- Confidence intervals can be more useful because they define the range within which you have a specified level of confidence that the population value lies. The confidence interval for population means is:

$$\bar{x} - Zs / \sqrt{(n-1)} \quad \text{to} \quad \bar{x} + Zs / \sqrt{(n-1)}$$

- You can adjust this approach to find the confidence interval for the proportion of the population sharing some feature.

- Sometimes you are interested in only one tail of a distribution, and you can again adjust the standard approach to find a one-sided confidence interval.

- Small samples tend to underestimate the variability in a population. You can allow for this by using a t-distribution. This is similar to the Normal distribution, but its shape is affected by the degrees of freedom, and hence the sample size.

CASE STUDY Kings Fruit Farm

In the 1920s Edward Filbert became the tenant of Kings Farm in Cambridgeshire. In 1978 his grandson James Filbert became the latest manager. In the intervening years the farm has changed considerably. It has grown from 195 acres to over 3,000 acres and is owned by an agricultural company that owns several other farms in the area. Kings Farm grows a variety of vegetables, cereals and fruit, with Kings Fruit Farm as a subsidiary that focuses on their apple, pear, plum, damson and cherry orchards.

Recently James has been looking at the sales of plums. These are graded and sold as fruit to local shops and markets, for canning to a local cannery or for jam to a more distant processor. The plums sold for canning earn about half as much income as those sold for fruit, but twice as much as those sold for jam.

Case study continued

James is trying to estimate the weight of plums sold each year. He does not know this because the plums are sold by the basket rather than by weight, with each basket holding about 25 kg of plums. For a pilot study, James set up some scales to see if he could weigh the amount of fruit in a sample of baskets. On the first day he weighed 10 baskets, 6 of which were sold as fruit, 3 for canning and 1 for jam. The weights of fruit, in kilograms, were as follows:

25.6, 20.8, 29.4, 28.0, 22.2, 23.1, 25.3, 26.5, 20.7, 21.9

This trial seemed to work, so James then weighed a sample of 50 baskets on three consecutive days. The weights of fruit, in kg, were as follows:

- Day 1 24.6 23.8 25.1 26.7 22.9 23.6 26.6 25.0
  24.6 25.2 25.7 28.1 23.0 25.9 24.2 21.7
  24.9 27.7 24.0 25.6 26.1 26.0 22.9 21.6
  28.2 20.5 25.8 22.6 30.3 28.0 23.6 25.7
  27.1 26.9 24.5 23.9 27.0 26.8 24.3 19.5
  31.2 22.6 29.4 25.3 26.7 25.8 23.5 20.5
  18.6 21.5

- Day 2 26.5 27.4 23.8 24.8 30.2 28.9 23.6 27.5
  19.5 23.6 25.0 24.3 25.3 23.3 24.0 25.1
  22.2 20.1 23.6 25.8 24.9 23.7 25.0 24.9
  27.2 28.3 29.1 22.1 25.0 23.8 18.8 19.9
  27.3 25.6 26.4 28.4 20.8 24.9 25.4 25.6
  24.9 25.0 24.1 25.5 25.2 26.8 27.7 20.6
  31.3 29.5

- Day 3 27.2 21.9 30.1 26.9 23.5 20.7 26.4 25.1
  25.7 26.3 18.0 21.0 21.9 25.7 28.0 26.3
  25.9 24.7 24.9 24.3 23.9 23.0 24.1 23.6
  21.0 24.6 25.7 24.7 23.3 22.7 22.9 24.8
  22.5 26.8 27.4 28.3 31.0 29.4 25.5 23.9
  29.5 23.3 18.6 20.6 25.0 25.3 26.0 22.2
  23.9 25.7

He also recorded the numbers of each sample sent to each destination:

	Fruit	Cans	Jam
Day 1	29	14	7
Day 2	25	15	10
Day 3	19	15	16

Pickers are paid by the basket, and the payments book showed the number of baskets picked on the three days as 820, 750 and 700 respectively. During a good harvest, a total of around 6,000 baskets are picked.

Questions

- **What information can James find from these figures? How can he use this information?**

- **How should he set about a complete survey of the fruit crop?**

PROBLEMS

14.1 A production line makes units with a mean weight of 80 g and standard deviation of 5 g. What is the probability that a sample of 100 units has a mean weight of less than 79 g?

14.2 A machine makes parts with a variance of 14.5 cm in length. A random sample of 50 parts has a mean length of 106.5 cm. What are the 95% and 99% confidence intervals for the length of parts?

14.3 A frozen-food packer specifies the mean weight of a product as 200 g. The output is Normally distributed with a standard deviation of 15 g. A random sample of 20 has a mean of 195 g. Does this suggest that the mean weight is too low?

14.4 Hamil Sopa took a random sample of 60 invoices from his year's records. The mean value of invoices in this sample was £125.50 and the standard deviation was £10.20. What are the 90% and 95% confidence intervals for the mean value of all invoices?

14.5 Sheila Brown times 60 people doing a job. The mean time is 6.4 minutes, with a standard deviation of 0.5 minutes. How long would it take the population to do this job?

14.6 Wade (Retail) looked at a random sample of 100 invoices from a large population. Eight of these contained an error. What are the 90% and 95% confidence intervals for the proportion of invoices with errors?

14.7 A company wants to find the average weight of its products. A large initial sample shows the standard deviation of the weight is 20 g. What sample size would give a 95% confidence interval for the population that is (a) 10 g wide, (b) 8 g wide, (c) 5 g wide?

14.8 Last year a trial survey found that 65% of houses in Morrisey township had a computer. A follow-up survey wants to find the actual number of houses with a computer to within 3% with a 95% confidence interval. How many houses should it survey?

14.9 Henry Lom feels that the quantity of chocolates in a particular type of packet has decreased. To test this feeling he takes a sample of 40 packets and finds that the mean

weight is 228 g with a standard deviation of 11 g. What is the weight Henry can be 95% confident the mean falls below? What are the two-sided confidence limits on this weight?

14.10 BC's quality assurance programme chooses a random sample of 50 units and finds that 12 are defective. What is the number of defectives they can be 95% confident that the population mean is below? What is the number of defectives they can be 95% confident that the population mean is above? How do these compare with the two-sided 90% confidence interval?

14.11 A survey of 20 items in a sales ledger has a mean value of €100 and standard deviation of €20. What is the 95% confidence interval for the population of items? What is the 99% confidence interval?

14.12 The time taken for a sample of eight pieces of equipment to do a task has a mean of 52 minutes and a standard deviation of 18 minutes. What is the 90% confidence interval for the mean time of all the equipment to do the task? What is the 95% confidence interval? If the same results had been found from a sample of 20 pieces of equipment, what would be the 95% confidence interval? What would be the result if a Normal distribution had been used?

RESEARCH PROJECTS

14.1 The central limit theorem gives a fundamental result for sampling – that large samples, or any samples from a Normally distributed population, are Normally distributed. Test this result to see that it really works. For this you can:

- use a spreadsheet to generate a population of random numbers
- draw a frequency distribution of the numbers and confirm that they follow a uniform distribution (where each number has the same probability)
- take large samples from this population of numbers and calculate the mean of each sample

- draw a frequency distribution of these means (i.e. the sampling distribution of the mean)
- confirm that the result is Normally distributed.

Now repeat this process for different sample sizes and initial distributions of values to see what effect this has.

14.2 For small samples we have to use the *t*-distribution instead of the Normal distribution. How would you describe – and measure – the differences between these two distributions?

Sources of information

References

1 DTI, *Renewable Energy Statistics Database*, Department of Trade and Industry, London, 2006.

2 DTI, *Digest of UK Energy Statistics*, Department of Trade and Industry, London, 2005.

3 Statistical Office of the European Communities at www.eurostat.ec.europa.eu

4 International Energy Agency at www.iea.org

5 World Energy Council at www.worldenergy.com

6. Editorial, Bird flu outbreak could kill 1.5 billion, *New Scientist*, 5 February 2005 and www.newscientist.com

7. WHO, *Cumulative number of confirmed human cases of avian influenza A/H5N1*, World Health organisation, Geneva, 2010.

8. www.who.int

Further reading

Most of the statistics books listed in Chapter 12 contain material on sampling. More material is covered in books on quality control sampling and market research sampling. The following list gives some more specialised books on sampling.

Chandra M.J., *Statistical Quality Control*, CRC Press, Boca Raton, FL, 2001.

Chaudhuri A. and Stenger H., *Survey Sampling* (2nd edition), Chapman and Hall/CRC Boca Raton, FL, 2005.

Francis A., *Working with Data*, Thomson Learning, London, 2003.

Levy P.S. and Lemeshow S., *Sampling of Populations* (4th edition), John Wiley, Chichester, 2009.

Lohr S., *Sampling* (2nd edition), Duxbury Press, Cincinnati, OH, 2009.

Montgomery D., *Introduction to Statistical Quality Control* (6th edition), John Wiley, Chichester, 2008.

Ragsdale C., *Spreadsheet Modelling and Decision Analysis* (5th edition), South-Western College Publishing, Cincinnati, OH, 2008.

Rao S.R.S., *Sampling Methodologies with Applications*, CRC Press, Boca Raton, FL, 2000.

Schilling E.G. and Neubauer D., *Acceptance Sampling in Quality Control*, Chapman and Hall, Boca Raton, FL, 2009.

Thompson S., *Sampling* (2nd edition), John Wiley, Chichester, 2002.

Winston W.L. and Albright S., *Spreadsheet Modelling and Applications*, Brooks Cole, Florence, KY, 2004.

CHAPTER 15

Testing hypotheses

Chapter outline

Hypothesis testing starts with a statement describing some aspect of a population – giving the hypothesis to be tested. Then it examines a sample from the population and sees if there is evidence to support the hypothesis. Either the evidence supports the hypothesis or it does not support it and, by implication, supports some alternative hypothesis. You can use this general approach to hypothesis testing in many circumstances.

After finishing this chapter you should be able to:

- understand the purpose of hypothesis testing
- list the steps involved in hypothesis testing
- understand the errors involved and the use of significance levels
- test hypotheses about population means
- use one- and two-tail tests
- extend these tests to deal with small samples
- use the tests for a variety of problems
- consider non-parametric tests, particularly the chi-squared test.

Aim of hypothesis testing

In Chapter 14 we saw how statistical inference uses data from a sample to estimate values for a population. In this chapter we extend this idea by testing if a belief about a population is supported by the evidence from a sample. This is the basis of **hypothesis testing**.

Suppose you have some preconceived idea about the value taken by a population variable. For instance, you might believe that domestic telephone bills have fallen by 10% in the past year. This is a hypothesis that you want to test. So you take a sample from the population and see whether or not the results support your hypothesis. The formal procedure for this is:

- Define a simple, precise statement about a population (the hypothesis).
- Take a sample from the population.
- Test this sample to see whether it supports the hypothesis, or makes the hypothesis highly improbable.
- If the hypothesis is highly improbable reject it, otherwise accept it.

This seems a reasonable approach – but it needs a small adjustment. Statisticians are more cautious than this, and they do not talk about 'accepting' a hypothesis. Instead, they say that they 'can reject the hypothesis' if it is highly unlikely, or they 'cannot reject the hypothesis' if it is more likely.

WORKED EXAMPLE 15.1

Aceituna GmbH fills bottles with a nominal 400 ml of olive oil. There are small variations around this nominal amount and the actual contents are Normally distributed with a standard deviation of 20 ml. The company takes periodic samples to make sure that they are filling the bottles properly. If it is found that a sample bottle contains 446 ml, are the bottles being overfilled?

Solution

We start with an initial hypothesis that the bottles still contain 400 ml. We have a limited amount of data from a single sample but can use this to test the hypothesis. If the hypothesis is correct then we can find the probability of finding a bottle containing 446 ml by calculating the number of standard deviations this point is from the mean:

$$Z = (446 - 400) / 20 = 2.3$$

which corresponds to a probability of 0.01. If our hypothesis that the bottles contain 400 ml is correct, finding a bottle with 446 ml is highly improbable, occurring on only 1% of occasions. So we can reasonably reject the initial hypothesis that the bottles contain 400 ml.

The original statement is called the **null hypothesis** – usually called H_0. The name 'null' implies there has been no change in the value being tested since the hypothesis was formulated. If we reject the null hypothesis then we implicitly accept an alternative. In Worked example 15.1 we reject the null hypothesis that the bottles contain 400 ml, so we accept the **alternative hypothesis** that they do not contain 400 ml. For each null hypothesis there is always an alternative hypothesis – usually called H_1. If the null hypothesis, H_0, is that domestic telephone bills have fallen by 10% in the last year, the alternative hypothesis, H_1, is that they have not fallen by 10%.

The null hypothesis must be a simple, specific statement – while the alternative hypothesis is less precise and suggests only that some statement other than the null hypothesis is true. In practice, the null hypothesis is usually phrased in terms of one thing equalling another, while the alternative hypothesis is that the equality is not true. So a null hypothesis, H_0, says that the average salary in an office is €50,000 and the alternative hypothesis, H_1, is that the average salary is not €50,000.

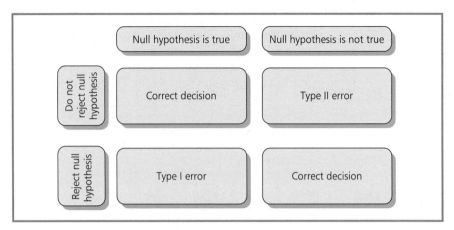

Figure 15.1 Errors in hypothesis testing

Errors in hypothesis testing

Sampling always contains uncertainty, so we can never be certain of the results from a hypothesis test. In Worked example 15.1, the result was said to be unlikely – occurring only 1 time in 100 – so we rejected the null hypothesis. But if the null hypothesis is actually true, we would still get this result in 1% of samples, and we would be rejecting a true hypothesis. Conversely, a sample might give evidence to support a null hypothesis, even when it is not true. So there are two ways of getting the wrong answer (shown in Figure 15.1):

■ Type I error – when we reject a null hypothesis that is actually true
■ Type II error – when we do not reject a null hypothesis that is actually false.

We want the probabilities of both Type I and Type II errors to be as close to zero as possible – and the only way of ensuring this is to use large samples. Otherwise, any adjustments to reduce the probability of Type I errors inevitably increase the probability of Type II errors, and vice versa. With a limited sample size, we have to accept a compromise between the two errors.

WORKED EXAMPLE 15.2

The city of Halifax, Nova Scotia, takes a survey of monthly costs of food and housing for a particular type of family. They think that the mean cost is $1,600 with a standard deviation of $489. A sample of 100 families has an average expenditure of $1,712.50. Does this support their initial views?

Solution

We start by defining the null hypothesis, H_0, that the monthly cost of food and housing is $1,600; while the alternative hypothesis, H_1, is that it does not equal $1,600.

Hypothesis tests assume that the null hypothesis is true for the test, so we assume that the population has a mean of $1,600 and a standard deviation of $489. Then we find the probability that a sample with a mean of $1,712.50 comes from this population. With a large sample of 100 the sampling distribution of the mean is Normal, with standard error $\sigma / \sqrt{n} = 489 / \sqrt{100} = 48.9$. Then:

$$Z = (1,712.5 - 1,600) / 48.9$$
$$= 2.3$$

Worked example 15.2 continued

This corresponds to a probability of 0.0107. If the null hypothesis is true, there is a probability of 0.0107 that the monthly cost of a sample is $1,712.50. This is very unlikely, so the evidence does not support the null hypothesis. We can reject this and accept the alternative hypothesis. But remember that in about 1% of cases we are making a Type I error and rejecting a hypothesis that is actually true.

WORKED EXAMPLE 15.3

Marcia Lopez says that the mean wage of her employees is €300 a week with a standard deviation of €60. She checks a random sample of 36 wages and decides to revise her views if the mean of the sample is outside the range €270 to €330. What is the probability she makes a Type I error?

Solution

The null hypothesis, H_0, is that the mean wage is €300, and the alternative hypothesis, H_1, is that the mean wage is not €300.

Assuming that the population has a mean of €300 and standard deviation of €60, with a sample of 36 the sampling distribution of the mean is Normal with standard error $\sigma / \sqrt{n} = 60 / \sqrt{36} = 10$. Then:

$$Z = (330 - 300) / 10$$
$$= 3$$

which corresponds to a probability of 0.0013. By symmetry, the probability of a sample mean being less than €270 is also 0.0013. So when the null hypothesis is true, there is a probability of $0.0013 + 0.0013 = 0.0026$ that the sample mean will be outside the acceptable range. This is the probability that Marcia rejects the null hypothesis when it is actually true.

Review questions

15.1 What is the purpose of hypothesis testing?

15.2 Which is a more precise statement, H_0 or H_1?

15.3 What are Type I and Type II errors?

IDEAS IN PRACTICE Politics and hypotheses

Most – but not all – legal systems work with the belief that someone accused of a crime is innocent until proven guilty. In other words, they start with a null hypothesis that someone is innocent, and if this is extremely unlikely the system rejects this hypothesis and accepts the alternative hypothesis that they are guilty.

No justice system is infallible, and a Type I error occurs when an innocent person is punished; a Type II error occurs when a guilty person is not punished. There is always a balance between these errors, and reducing the chance of one inevitably increases the chance of the other. People have different views about achieving a reasonable balance. Some emphasise the importance of punishing the guilty; others emphasise the injustice of condemning the innocent.

This effect can be broadened into other areas, such as public welfare payments – where a Type I error gives welfare payments to someone who does not deserve it and a Type II error fails to give payments to someone who really needs it.

In the USA, Hooke has suggested that liberals and conservatives have fundamentally different views of these errors. For example, with justice, liberals avoid Type I errors, while conservatives avoid Type II errors. With welfare payments it is the other way around – conservatives avoid Type I errors, while liberals avoid Type II errors. As it is impossible to eliminate one type of error without increasing the other type of error, the two political philosophies will never reach agreement.

Significance levels

So far we have rejected a null hypothesis if we consider the result from the sample to be unlikely. However, our judgement of what is 'unlikely' has been purely subjective. We can formalise this judgement in a significance level.

- A significance level is the minimum acceptable probability that a value actually comes from the hypothesised population.
- When the probability is less than this, we reject the null hypothesis; when the probability is more than this we do not reject it.

With a 5% significance level, we reject the null hypothesis when there is a probability of less than 0.05 that a sample value comes from the population – but we do not reject a null hypothesis if there is a probability greater than 0.05 that a sample value comes from the population. Of course, this still gives 5% of tests where values fall outside the acceptance range when the null hypothesis is actually true, and we reject a null hypothesis that is true. As this is a Type I error, you can see that the significance level is the maximum acceptable probability of making a Type I error.

You can use any value for a significance level, but the most common is 5%, followed by 1% and occasionally 0.1%. With a large sample, the sampling distribution is Normal, and 95% of observations are within 1.96 standard deviations of the mean – so this defines the acceptance level (shown in Figure 15.2). With a 1% significance level, you cannot reject the null hypothesis if the observation is within 2.58 standard deviations of the mean. This is clearly a less stringent test – and it shows that lower significance levels need stronger evidence to reject the null hypothesis.

Of course, a particular test might have you rejecting a hypothesis at a 5% level, but not rejecting it at a 1% level – or even a 4% level. So this might seem like a rather arbitrary border between reject and cannot reject decisions. It might be better to simply calculate the exact probability that a hypothesis is

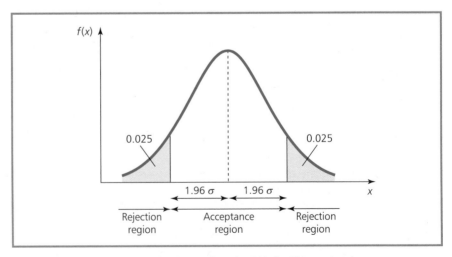

Figure 15.2 Acceptance and rejection regions for 5% significance level

true, and you could say, 'there is a probability of 0.002 that this sample comes from the hypothesised population'. In principle this would be better – but the standard format has been used for many years and is unlikely to change.

WORKED EXAMPLE 15.4

John Lo thinks that the mean value of orders received by his firm is €260. He checks a sample of 36 accounts and finds a mean of €240 and standard deviation of €45. Does this evidence support his belief?

Solution

The null hypothesis is that the mean value of accounts is €260, and the alternative hypothesis is that the mean is not €260. Then:

$$H_0 : \mu = 260 \quad H_1 : \mu \neq 260$$

We do not know the population standard deviation, but can estimate it from the sample standard deviation using $\sigma = s / \sqrt{n}$. Then with a sample of

36, the sampling distribution of the mean is Normal with mean 260 and standard error 45 / $\sqrt{36} = 7.5$. With a significance level of 5% we do not reject values that are within 1.96 standard deviations of the mean. So the acceptance range is:

$$260 - 1.96 \times 7.5 \quad \text{to} \quad 260 + 1.96 \times 7.5$$

or

$$245.3 \quad \text{to} \quad 274.4$$

The actual observation of €240 is outside this range, so we reject the null hypothesis, and accept the alternative hypothesis that the mean value of orders is not equal to €260.

Worked example 15.4 illustrates the steps in the formal procedure for hypothesis testing.

---

1 State the null and alternative hypotheses.
2 Specify the significance level.
3 Calculate the acceptance range for the variable tested.
4 Find the actual value for the variable tested.
5 Decide whether or not to reject the null hypothesis.
6 State the conclusion.

WORKED EXAMPLE 15.5

The Central Tax Office says that the average income in Port Elizabeth is $15,000. A sample of 45 people found their mean income to be $14,300 with a standard deviation of $2,000. Use a 5% significance level to check the claim. What is the effect of using a 1% significance level?

Solution

For this, you use the standard six-step procedure.

1 *State the null and alternative hypotheses:*

$$H_0 : \mu = 15,000 \quad H_1 : \mu \neq 15,000$$

2 *Specify the level of significance.* This is given as 5%.

3 *Calculate the acceptance range for the variable tested.* With a sample of 45, the sampling distribution of the mean is Normal with mean 15,000 and standard error approximated by $s / \sqrt{n} = 2,000 / \sqrt{45} = 298.14$. For a 5% significance level you cannot reject points that are within 1.96 standard deviations of the mean. So the acceptance range is:

$$15,000 - 1.96 \times 298.14 \quad \text{to}$$
$$15,000 + 1.96 \times 298.14$$

or   14,415.65   to   15,584.35

4 *Find the actual value for the variable tested.* This is $14,300.

Worked example 15.5 continued

5 *Decide whether or not to reject the null hypo-thesis.* The actual value is outside the acceptance range, so you reject the null hypothesis.
6 *State the conclusion.* At a 5% significance level, the evidence from the sample does not support the claim that the average income per capita in Port Elizabeth is $15,000. Instead, it supports the alternative hypothesis that the average income is not $15,000.

With a 1% significance level, the acceptance range is within 2.58 standard deviations of the mean, or:

$15,000 - 2.58 \times 298.14$ to $15,000 = 2.58 \times 298.14$

or $\qquad$ 14230.79 to 15,769.21

The actual observation of $14,300 is within this range, so you cannot reject the null hypothesis (as shown in Figure 15.3).

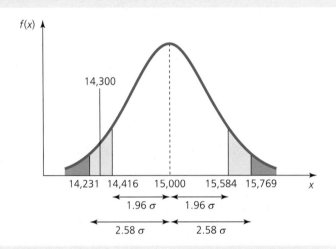

Figure 15.3 Acceptance range for incomes in Port Elizabeth (Worked example 15.3)

One-sided tests

In the problems we have looked at so far, we have stated a null hypothesis of the form:

$$H_0 : \mu = 10$$

and an alternative hypothesis in the form:

$$H_1 : \mu \neq 10$$

In practice, we often want to test whether a value is above or below some claimed value. If we buy a bottle of whisky, we want to be sure that the volume is not below the specified value; and if we are delivering parcels, we want to know that their weight is not above the claimed weight. We can tackle problems of this type by using the standard procedure, but with an adjustment to the phrasing of the alternative hypothesis.

If you are buying boxes of chocolates with a specified weight of 500 g, you want to be sure that the actual weight is not below this and use:

Null hypothesis, H_0 : $\qquad$ $\mu = 500$ g
Alternative hypothesis, H_1 : $\quad \mu < 500$ g

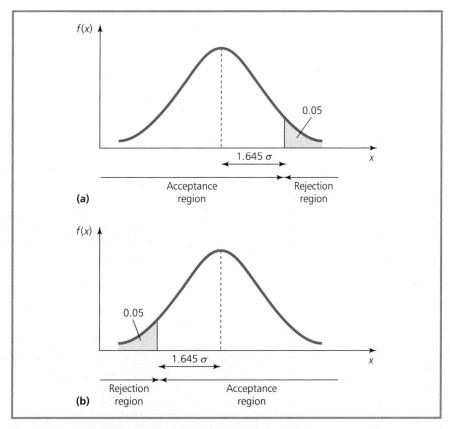

Figure 15.4 One-sided test for 5% significance level: (a) when concerned with a maximum value; (b) when concerned with a minimum value

If you are delivering parcels with a claimed weight of 25 kg, you want to be sure the actual weight is not above this and use:

Null hypothesis, H_0 : $\mu = 25$ kg
Alternative hypothesis, H_1 : $\mu > 25$ kg

In both examples you are interested in only one tail of the sampling distribution, so the acceptance range is altered. In particular, a 5% significance level has the 5% area of rejection in one tail of the distribution. In a Normal distribution this point is 1.645 standard deviations from the mean, as shown in Figure 15.4.

WORKED EXAMPLE 15.6

BookCheck Mail-Order charge customers a flat rate for delivery based on a mean weight for packages of 1.75 kg with a standard deviation of 0.5 kg. Postage costs have risen and it seems likely that the mean weight is greater than 1.75 kg. The company checked a random sample of 100 packages and found a mean weight of 1.86 kg. Does this support the view that the mean weight is more than 1.75 kg?

▶

Worked example 15.6 continued

Solution
We use the standard procedure.

1 *State the null and alternative hypotheses.* We want to test that the mean weight is not above 1.75 kg, so we have:

$$H_0 : \mu = 1.75 \text{ kg} \quad H_1 : \mu > 1.75 \text{ kg}$$

2 *Specify the level of significance.* This is not given, so we assume 5%.

3 *Calculate the acceptance range for the variable tested.* With a sample of 100, the sampling distribution of the mean is Normal with mean of 1.75 kg and standard deviation $\sigma / \sqrt{n} = 0.5 / \sqrt{100} = 0.050$ kg. For a 5% significance level and

a one-sided test, we reject points that are more than 1.645 standard deviations above the mean. The acceptance range is below $1.75 + 1.645 \times 0.05 = 1.83$ kg.

4 *Find the actual value for the variable tested.* The observed weight of parcels is 1.86 kg.

5 *Decide whether or not to reject the null hypothesis.* The actual value is outside the acceptance range, so we reject the null hypothesis.

6 *State the conclusion.* The evidence from the sample does not support the view that the mean weight of packages is 1.75 kg. The evidence supports the alternative hypothesis, that the mean weight is more 1.75 kg. This is illustrated in Figure 15.5.

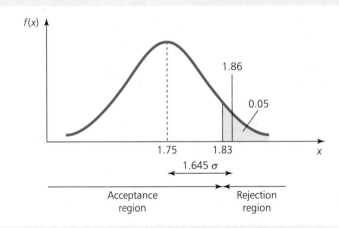

Figure 15.5 Acceptance region for BookCheck Mail-Order (Worked example 15.6)

WORKED EXAMPLE 15.7

Elisabeta Horst is a management consultant who has recently introduced new procedures to a reception office. The receptionist should do at least 10 minutes of paperwork in each hour. Elisabeta made a check on 40 random hours of work and found that the mean time spent on paperwork is 8.95 minutes with a standard deviation of 3 minutes. Can she reject the hypothesis that the new procedures meet specifications at a 1% level of significance?

Solution

1 *State the null and alternative hypotheses.* Elisabeta wants to check that the time spent on paperwork is at least 10 minutes in an hour. So:

$$H_0: \mu = 10 \text{ minutes} \quad H_1: \mu < 10 \text{ minutes}$$

2 *Specify the level of significance.* This is given as 1%.

3 *Calculate the acceptance range for the variable tested.* With a sample of 40, the sampling

Worked example 15.7 continued

distribution of the mean is Normal with a mean of 10 minutes and standard deviation $s / \sqrt{n} = 3 / \sqrt{40} = 0.474$ minutes. For a 1% significance level and a one-sided test, Elisabeta should reject values that are below 2.33 standard deviations below the mean. Then the acceptance range is above $10 - 2.33 \times 0.474 = 8.89$ minutes.

4 *Find the actual value for the variable tested.* The observed number of minutes spent on paperwork in each hour is 8.95.

5 *Decide whether or not to reject the null hypothesis.* The actual value is inside the acceptance range and Elisabeta cannot reject the null hypothesis.

6 *State the conclusion.* The evidence from the sample supports the view that the mean time spent on paperwork is at least 10 minutes an hour.

Review questions

15.4 What is a significance level?

15.5 Is the probability of a Type II error lower with a 5% significance level or a 1% significance level?

15.6 If a value is in the acceptance range, does this prove that the null hypothesis is true?

15.7 When would you use a one-sided hypothesis test?

Tests with small samples

In Chapter 14 we noted that sampling distributions are Normal only when the population is Normal or the sample size is more than 30. When this is not true, the sampling distribution follows a t-distribution. Remember that the shape of a t-distribution depends on the degrees of freedom, which is the sample size minus one.

WORKED EXAMPLE 15.8

A coffee machine is set to fill cups with 200 ml of coffee. A sample of 10 cups contained 210 ml with a standard deviation of 10 ml. Is the machine working properly?

Solution

We can use the standard approach for hypothesis testing, with a two-tail test, but because the sample size is small we have to use a t-distribution.

1 *State the null and alternative hypotheses.* The null hypothesis is that the dispenser is filling cups with 200 ml, while the alternative hypothesis is that it is not filling cups with 200 ml.

$H_0 : \mu = 200$ ml $H_1 : \mu \neq 200$ ml

2 *Specify the level of significance.* We can use the standard 5%.

3 *Calculate the acceptance range for the variable tested.* With a sample of size 10, the sampling distribution of the mean follows a t-distribution with $n - 1 = 10 - 1 = 9$ degrees of freedom, a mean of 200 ml and standard deviation $s / \sqrt{(n - 1)} = 10 / \sqrt{9} = 3.33$ ml. With the small sample we have again used Bessel's correction for small samples, dividing the sample standard deviation by $n - 1$ rather than n. For a 5% significance level and a two-sided test, we look up

➤

Worked example 15.8 continued

(either in tables or using the TINV function in a spreadsheet) a probability of 0.025 in each tail, and with 9 degrees of freedom the value is 2.262. Then the acceptance range is:

$$200 - 2.262 \times 3.33 \quad \text{to} \quad 200 + 2.262 \times 3.33$$
$$192.47 \qquad\qquad \text{to} \quad 207.53$$

4 *Find the actual value for the variable tested.* The actual mean of the sample was 210 ml.

5 *Decide whether or not to reject the null hypothesis.* The actual value is outside the acceptance range, so we reject the null hypothesis.

6 *State the conclusion.* The evidence from the sample does not support the view that the machine is filling cups with 200 ml of coffee.

WORKED EXAMPLE 15.9

A supermarket is getting complaints that its tins of strawberries contain a lot of juice, but few strawberries. A team from the supermarket make a surprise visit to the supplier who is about to deliver another batch. Each tin in this batch is claimed to have a minimum of 300 g of fruit, but a random sample of 15 tins found only 287 g with a standard deviation of 18 g. What conclusion can the supermarket make?

Solution

1 *State the null and alternative hypotheses.* The null hypothesis is that the mean weight of the fruit is 300 g, while the alternative hypothesis is that the weight is less than this.

$$H_0 : \mu = 300 \text{ g} \quad H_1 : \mu < 300 \text{ g}$$

2 *Specify the level of significance.* We can use the standard 5%.

3 *Calculate the acceptance range for the variable tested.* With a sample of size 15, the sampling distribution of the mean follows a t-distribution with $n - 1 = 15 - 1 = 14$ degrees of freedom and a mean of 300 g. The estimated standard error is $s / \sqrt{(n - 1)} = 18 / \sqrt{14} = 4.81$ g. For a 5% significance level and a one-sided test, we look up (either in tables or using the TINV function in a spreadsheet) a probability of 0.05. With 14 degrees of freedom the value is 1.761. Then the acceptance range is above $300 - 1.761 \times 4.81 = 291.53$ g.

4 *Find the actual value for the variable tested.* The actual mean of the sample was 287 g.

5 *Decide whether or not to reject the null hypothesis.* The actual value is outside the acceptance range, so we reject the null hypothesis.

6 *State the conclusion.* The evidence from the sample does not support the view that the mean weight is 300 g. It supports the alternative hypothesis that the mean weight of fruit is less than 300 g.

Review questions

15.8   Why do we not use the Normal distribution for small samples?

15.9   What shape is the t-distribution for large samples?

15.10 When would you use the approximation $s / \sqrt{(n - 1)}$ for $\sigma / \sqrt{n}$?

Testing other hypotheses

So far we have focused on hypothesis tests for population means, but we can use the same approach for a variety of other problems.

Population proportions

In Chapter 14 we mentioned that sampling could test the proportion of a population that shared some common feature. In particular, we used the standard result that when the proportion in the population is π, the sampling distribution of the proportion has a mean of π and standard deviation of $\sqrt{(\pi(1 - \pi) / n)}$. Now we can use this result to test hypotheses about proportions.

WORKED EXAMPLE 15.10

High street banks claim that they lend the money for 20% of all house purchases. To test this, a sample of 100 people with mortgages was interviewed, 15 of whom arranged their loan through a bank. Does this support the original claim?

Solution

Hypothesis tests always use the same procedure, and the only difference with this problem is that we are interested in a proportion, π, rather than a mean.

1 *State the null and alternative hypotheses.* The null hypothesis is that banks lend 20% of funds for mortgages, so using proportions we have:

$$H_0 : \pi = 0.2 \quad H_1 : \pi \neq 0.2$$

2 *Specify the level of significance.* This is not given, so we assume 5%.

3 *Calculate the acceptance range for the variable tested.* With a sample of 100, the sampling distribution is Normal with mean 0.2 and standard deviation $\sqrt{(\pi(1 - \pi) / n)} = \sqrt{(0.2 \times 0.8) / 100}$ = 0.04. For a 5% significance level we want points that are within 1.96 standard deviations of the mean. Then the acceptance range is:

$$0.2 - 1.96 \times 0.04 \quad \text{to} \quad 0.2 + 1.96 \times 0.04$$

or

$$0.122 \quad \text{to} \quad 0.278$$

4 *Find the actual value for the variable tested.* The sample had a proportion of 15 / 100 = 0.15.

5 *Decide whether or not to reject the null hypothesis.* The actual value is within the acceptance range, so we cannot reject the null hypothesis.

6 *State the conclusion.* We cannot reject the claim that banks lend money for 20% of mortgages.

Testing for differences in means

Managers often want to compare two populations, to see if there are significant differences. For example, they might have two shops and want to know whether each has the same profitability or not, or they might want to check sales before and after an advertising campaign.

We can use hypothesis testing to see if the means of two populations are the same. For this we take a sample from each population, and if the sample means are fairly close we can assume that the population means are the same, but if there is a large difference in the sample means we have to assume that the population means are different. So the procedure is to take the means of two samples, $\bar{x}_1$ and $\bar{x}_2$, and find the difference, $\bar{x}_1 - \bar{x}_2$. Then we use a standard result that for large samples the sampling distribution of $\bar{x}_1 - \bar{x}_2$ is Normal with:

$$\text{mean} = 0 \quad \text{and} \quad \text{standard error} = \sqrt{\frac{s_1^2}{n_1} + \frac{s_2^2}{n_2}}$$

where: n_1 = sample size from population 1
n_2 = sample size from population 2
s_1 = standard deviation of sample 1
s_2 = standard deviation of sample 2.

WORKED EXAMPLE 15.11

Krinkle Kut Krisps uses two machines to fill packets of crisps. A sample of 30 packets from the first machine has a mean weight of 180 g and a standard deviation of 40 g. A sample of 40 packets from the second machine has a mean weight of 170 g and a standard deviation of 10 g. Are the two machines putting the same amount in packets?

Solution

1 *State the null and alternative hypotheses.* We want to check that the two machines are putting the same amounts in packets, so the null hypothesis is that the means from each machine are the same. The alternative hypothesis is that the means are not the same.

$$H_0 : \mu_1 = \mu_2 \quad H_1 : \mu_1 \neq \mu_2$$

2 *Specify the level of significance.* We can use the standard 5%.

3 *Calculate the acceptance range for the variable tested.* We are looking at the sampling distribution of $\bar{x}_1 - \bar{x}_2$, with sample sizes $n_1 = 30$ and $n_2 = 40$, and standard deviations $s_1 = 14$ and $s_2 = 10$. This sampling distribution is Normal with:

mean = 0   and

$$\text{standard error} = \sqrt{\frac{s_1^2}{n_1} + \frac{s_2^2}{n_2}}$$

$$= \sqrt{\frac{14^2}{30} + \frac{10^2}{40}}$$

$$= 3.01$$

For a 5% significance level and a two-sided test, the acceptance range is within 1.96 standard deviations of the mean. This defines the range:

$$0 - 1.96 \times 3.01 \quad \text{to} \quad 0 + 1.96 \times 3.01$$

or

$$-5.90 \qquad \text{to} \quad +5.90$$

4 *Find the actual value for the variable tested.* The observed difference in samples is $\bar{x}_1 - \bar{x}_2 = 180 - 170 = 10$.

5 *Decide whether or not to reject the null hypothesis.* The actual value is outside the acceptance range, so we reject the null hypothesis.

6 *State the conclusion.* The evidence from the samples does not support the view that the mean weight put into packets is the same from each machine.

Paired tests

If you want to see whether a diet works or not, then you will weigh a set of people before the diet, and weigh them again after the diet. This gives a set of paired data – two weights for each person in your test – and you want to see if there is a difference between the two. This is the kind of problem that managers meet when, for example, they interview people before and after an advertising campaign, or to see if two people interviewing candidates for a job give different opinions.

To test for differences between paired observations, we find the difference between each pair. If the two sets of observations are similar, the mean difference should be around zero – but if there is a real distinction between the observations the mean difference becomes bigger. So we use hypothesis testing to see whether or not the differences between samples are small enough to suggest that the two samples are the same, or are big enough to suggest that they are different.

WORKED EXAMPLE 15.12

Amethyst Interviews counted the number of interviews that a sample of eight of their staff did in a day. Then they adjusted the way the questions were presented, and again counted the number of interviews the eight staff did. From the following results, can you say whether or not the adjustments had any effect?

Interviewer	1	2	3	4	5	6	7	8
Original interviews	10	11	9	6	8	10	7	8
Later interviews	10	9	11	10	9	12	9	11

Solution

Here we subtract the number of original interviews from the number of later interviews to get:

Interviewer	1	2	3	4	5	6	7	8
Difference	0	-2	2	4	1	2	2	3

Now we can use the standard approach on the sample differences.

1 *State the null and alternative hypotheses.* We want to test the null hypothesis that the mean difference is zero, and the alternative hypothesis that the mean difference is not zero.

$$H_0 : \mu = 0 \quad H_1 : \mu \neq 0$$

2 *Specify the level of significance.* We use the standard 5%.

3 *Calculate the acceptance range for the variable tested.* Using the basic definitions, the mean of the differences is $(0 - 2 + 2 + 4 + 1 + 2 + 2 + 3) / 8 = 1.5$, the variance is $(1.5^2 + 3.5^2 + 0.5^2 + 2.5^2 + 0.5^2 + 0.5^2 + 0.5^2 + 1.5^2) / 8 = 3.0$, and the standard deviation is $\sqrt{3.0} = 1.732$. With a small sample of eight pairs of observations, the sampling distribution is a t-distribution with $8 - 1 = 7$ degrees of freedom and standard error $s / \sqrt{(n-1)} = 1.732 / \sqrt{7} = 0.655$. For a two-tail 5% significance level, the t-distribution with 7 degrees of freedom is 2.365. So the acceptance range is:

$$0 - 2.365 \times 0.655 \quad \text{to} \quad 0 + 2.365 \times 0.655$$

or

$$-1.548 \quad \text{to} \quad 1.548$$

4 *Find the actual value for the tested variable.* The mean of the differences is 1.5.

5 *Decide whether or not to reject the null hypothesis.* The actual value is within the acceptable range, so we cannot reject the null hypothesis.

6 *State the conclusion.* The evidence says that we cannot reject the view that there is no difference between the number of interviews before and after the adjustment. This is an interesting result, as it seems fairly clear that the adjustments have made a difference – but the explanation is that the sample size is very small.

We have done the calculations for hypothesis testing by hand but, as always, we could have used a computer. Figure 15.6 shows results from putting data from Worked example 15.12 into Excel's data analysis option which does calculations for paired samples. Here the data is on the left, and the analysis is on the right. You can see that the computer presents the results in a slightly different way. We have calculated the limits within which we accept the null hypothesis, and then we see if the actual value lies within these limits. An alternative is to state the number of standard errors the acceptable range is from the mean, and then find how many standard errors the actual value is away from the mean. In this example, the 5% significance level sets the acceptable range for a two-tail test as within 2.3646 standard errors of the mean (called the critical t value), while the actual value is $1.5 / 0.655 = 2.29$ standard errors from the mean. As the actual value is within the acceptable range, we cannot reject the null hypothesis. However, you can see

	A	B	C	D	E	F
1	**Paired tests**					
2						
3	**Amethyst Interviews**					
4						
5	Data			*t*-test: paired two sample for means		
6	Original interviews	Later interviews			Original interviews	Later interviews
7	10	10		Mean	8.625	10.125
8	11	9		Variance	2.8393	1.2679
9	9	11		Observations	8	8
10	6	10		Hypothesised mean difference	0	
11	8	9		Degrees of freedom	7	
12	10	12		*t* Statistic	2.291	
13	7	9		$P(T<=t)$ one-tail	0.0279	
14	8	11		*t* Critical one-tail	1.8946	
15				$P(T<=t)$ two-tail	0.0557	
16				*t* Critical two-tail	2.3646	

Figure 15.6 Spreadsheet of paired test for Amethyst Interviews (Worked example 15.12)

that the probability that the value is within the acceptable range is only 0.0557, so it only just passes at this significance level.

Review questions

15.11 In what circumstances would you use hypothesis tests?

15.12 Is the significance level the same as a confidence interval?

IDEAS IN PRACTICE **Automatic testing systems**

Many automatic systems are programmed to make decisions under conditions of uncertainty. Then they check a response and follow prescribed rules to reach a decision. Because there is uncertainty, there is always the chance that they make a Type I or Type II error.

You can imagine this with an airport security system that is designed to detect passengers carrying weapons. When you walk through an airport metal detector, the detector has a null hypothesis that you are carrying a weapon, and it takes electromagnetic measurements to test this hypothesis. When it does not have enough evidence to support the null hypothesis it lets you through; when the evidence supports the null hypothesis it stops you. But there is uncertainty in its readings, caused by other things that you might be carrying,

and it makes two kinds of error. Either it stops people who are not carrying a weapon, or it does not stop people who are.

Another example is e-mail spam filters, which block junk messages or those that are somehow objectionable. The filter has a null hypothesis that a message is spam, and then examines the contents to test this hypothesis. If it finds evidence to support the hypothesis that the message is spam (the presence of key words, patterns in senders' address, multiple copies transmitted, types of content etc.), the filter blocks the message.

You can find many other examples of such systems, including Internet search engines, automatic recorders of earthquakes, burglar alarms, roadside speed cameras and so on.

Chi-squared test for goodness of fit

Variables that take a specific value during an investigation are called parameters, and hypothesis tests that concern the value of a parameter are parametric tests. Often we want to test a hypothesis, but there is no appropriate variable – or parameter – to measure. You can imagine this with nominal data like the type of industry, value, quality, colour and so on. For instance, you might suggest a hypothesis that one type of product offers better value than another – but there is no convincing parameter you can use to measure value. When you cannot use parametric hypothesis tests, you have to use the alternative non-parametric, or distribution-free, tests. These have the major benefit of making no assumptions about the distribution of the population – and the weakness of being somewhat less specific.

The most important non-parametric test is the chi-squared or χ^2 test (χ is the Greek letter chi – pronounced 'kie', rhyming with 'lie'). This is still a hypothesis test, so its general approach is the same as that of parametric tests. The difference is that it looks at the *frequencies* of observations and sees whether or not these match the expected frequencies.

Suppose you form a hypothesis about the distribution of values for some variable. Then you may expect a distribution with frequencies $E_1, E_2, E_3, \ldots, E_n$, but when you actually check the values you get a series of observations $O_1, O_2, O_3, \ldots, O_n$. The difference between these shows how closely the actual observations match your expectations. Squaring the difference between observed and expected frequencies removes negative values, and then dividing by the expected frequencies gives a distribution with a standard shape. In other words, we define χ^2 as:

$$\chi^2 = \frac{(O_1 - E_1)^2}{E_1} + \frac{(O_2 - E_2)^2}{E_2} + \frac{(O_3 - E_3)^2}{E_3} + \ldots + \frac{(O_n - E_n)^2}{E_n}$$

chi-squared = $\chi^2 = \sum \dfrac{(O - E)^2}{E}$

When observed frequencies are close to the expected frequencies, χ^2 is close to zero; but when there are bigger differences between observed and expected frequencies, χ^2 has a larger value. So for this type of test, we define a critical value for χ^2 – when the actual value is above this we say that observations do match our expectations, and reject the hypothesis; when the actual value is below the critical value we cannot reject the hypothesis. There are standard tables of critical values (shown in Appendix F) or you can use standard software, such as Excel's CHIINV function.

Like the *t*-distribution described in Chapter 14, the shape of the χ^2 distribution depends on the degrees of freedom. As we have seen, these measure the number of pieces of information that are free to take any value. Without going into the detailed reasoning, we will simply say that the number of degrees of freedom for a χ^2 distribution is:

degrees of freedom = number of classes – number of estimated
variables – 1

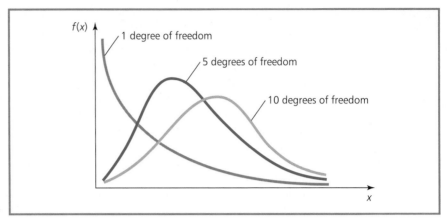

Figure 15.7 Chi-squared distribution with varying degrees of freedom

The following examples show how to use this, and Figure 15.7 compares the shapes of a χ^2 distribution with different degrees of freedom.

WORKED EXAMPLE 15.13

Over the past three years, five supermarkets have recorded the following numbers of minor accidents:

Supermarket	1	2	3	4	5
Number of accidents	31	42	29	35	38

Does this suggest that some supermarkets have more accidents than others?

Solution

We use the standard procedure for hypothesis testing.

1 *State the null and alternative hypotheses.* The null hypothesis, H_0, is that each supermarket has the same number of accidents. The alternative hypothesis, H_1, is that each supermarket does not have the same number of accidents.
2 *Specify the level of significance.* We can take this as 5%.
3 *Calculate the critical value of χ^2.* In this problem there are five classes, and no variables have been estimated, so the degrees of freedom are $5 - 0 - 1 = 4$. With a 5% significance level, we look in the '0.05' column of χ^2 tables and with 4 degrees of freedom we find a critical value of

9.49 (or we could get the same value using the CHIINV function in Excel).

4 Find the actual value of χ^2, where:

$$\chi^2 = \sum \frac{(O - E)^2}{E}$$

There are a total of 175 accidents. If each supermarket expects the same number of accidents, each expects $175 / 5 = 35$. Then we do the following calculations, which show that the actual value of χ^2 is 3.143.

Supermarket	O	E	$O - E$	$(O - E)^2$	$(O - E)^2/E$
1	31	35	−4	16	0.457
2	42	35	7	49	1.400
3	29	35	−6	36	1.029
4	35	35	0	0	0.000
5	38	35	3	9	0.257
Total	175	175			3.143

5 *Decide whether or not to reject the null hypothesis.* The actual value (3.143) is less than the critical value (9.4877), so we cannot reject the null hypothesis.
6 *State the conclusion.* The evidence supports the view that each supermarket has the same number of accidents, with any variation due to chance.

Worked example 15.13 effectively tested whether or not there was a uniform distribution of accidents across supermarkets. In other words, we hypothesised that the accident rate was uniformly distributed and checked if the data fitted this. We can use the same approach for other distributions, to see whether or not a set of data follows a specific distribution.

WORKED EXAMPLE 15.14

MailFast asked 10 people in each of 100 postcode areas if they would be prepared to pay more for a faster delivery service. They collected the following results. Do these follow a binomial distribution?

Number in sample willing to pay higher charges	0	1	2	3	4
Number of postcodes	26	42	18	9	5

Solution

If we define success as being willing to pay more and failure as being unwilling to pay, we have a binomial process. Then the number of successes in 10 trials should follow a binomial distribution, and we can test this using the standard procedure.

1 *State the null and alternative hypotheses.* The null hypothesis, H_0, is that the distribution of successes is binomial. The alternative hypothesis, H_1, is that the distribution is not binomial.
2 *Specify the level of significance.* We take this as 5%.
3 *Calculate the critical value of χ^2.* There are 5 classes – but we also need to find one parameter for the binomial distribution, which is the probability of success. So the number of degrees of freedom is:

   number of classes – number of estimated parameters – 1 = 5 – 1 – 1 = 3

Looking up the critical value for a significance level of 5% and 3 degrees of freedom gives a critical value of 7.81.

4 *Find the actual value of χ^2.* We have 10 results from each of 100 postcodes, giving 1,000 opinions, and of these the total number willing to pay more is:

   $(26 \times 0) + (42 \times 1) + (18 \times 2) + (9 \times 3) + (5 \times 4)$
   $= 125$

So the probability that someone is willing to pay more is 125 / 1,000 = 0.125. Now we can find the probabilities of 0, 1, 2, 3, 4 etc. successes out of 10 when the probability of success is 0.125, using the binomial calculations described in Chapter 13 (or the tables in Appendix B or statistical software). The probability of no successes is 0.263, the probability of one success is 0.376, the probability of two successes is 0.242 and so on. Multiplying these probabilities by the number of postcodes, 100, gives the expected number of postcodes with each number willing to pay higher charges. For convenience, we have taken the last class as '4 or more'.

Number willing to pay more	0	1	2	3	4 or more
Probability	0.263	0.376	0.242	0.092	0.027
Expected number of postcodes	26.3	37.6	24.2	9.2	2.7

Now we have both the expected and observed distributions of postcodes, and can calculate the value of χ^2.

Frequency	O	E	O − E	(O − E)²	(O − E)²/E
0	26	26.3	−0.3	0.09	0.003
1	42	37.6	4.4	19.36	0.515
2	18	24.2	−6.2	38.44	1.588
3	9	9.2	−0.2	0.04	0.004
4 or more	5	2.7	2.3	5.29	1.959
Total	100	100			4.069

5 *Decide whether or not to reject the null hypothesis.* The actual value of χ^2 (4.069) is less than the critical value (7.81), so we cannot reject the null hypothesis.
6 *State the conclusion.* The evidence supports the view that the observations follow a binomial distribution.

WORKED EXAMPLE 15.15

Performance Cables record the following numbers of faults per kilometre in a cable. Does this data follow a Poisson distribution?

Number of faults	0	1	2	3	4	5	6
Number of kilometres	37	51	23	7	4	2	1

Solution

1 *State the null and alternative hypotheses.* The null hypothesis, H_0, is that the distribution is Poisson. The alternative hypothesis, H_1, is that the distribution is not Poisson.
2 *Specify the level of significance.* We take this as 5%.
3 *Calculate the critical value of χ^2.* A small problem here is that the χ^2 distribution does not work well with expected frequencies of less than 5. We should really combine small adjacent classes so that the expected number of observations becomes greater than 5. Because of this adjustment, we will return to the critical value of χ^2 a little later.
4 *Find the actual value of χ^2.* We have 125 kilometres' worth of data, and the total number of defects is:

$$(37 \times 0) + (51 \times 1) + (23 \times 2) + (7 \times 3) + (4 \times 4) + (2 \times 5) + (1 \times 6) = 150$$

The mean number of defects is 150 / 125 = 1.2 per kilometre. Using this as the mean of a Poisson distribution, we can find the expected number of defects per kilometre in the usual ways. Then multiplying these probabilities by the number of observations, 125, gives the expected frequency distribution of defects. Figure 15.8 shows a spreadsheet with these results in columns A to C.

Now we should really combine adjacent classes so that each class has more than 5 observations. Adding the last four classes gives the revised table of expected values in column D, with subsequent calculations in columns F and G. Now you can see why we delayed the calculation of the critical value; there are now only four classes, so the number of degrees of freedom is:

number of classes – number of estimated parameters – 1 = 4 – 1 – 1 = 2

Here the parameter estimated is the mean of the distribution. Looking up the critical value for a significance level of 5% and 2 degrees of freedom gives a value of 5.99.

5 *Decide whether or not to reject the null hypothesis.* The actual value (1.459) is less than the critical value (5.99), so we cannot reject the null hypothesis.
6 *State the conclusion.* The evidence supports the view that the observations follow a Poisson distribution.

	A	B	C	D	E	F	G
1	**Chi-squared test**						
2							
3	**Number of defects**	**Probability**	**Expected frequency**	**Revised frequency (E)**	**Actual frequency (O)**	**(O – E)**	**(O – E)²/E**
4	0	0.301	37.649	37.649	37	−0.649	0.011
5	1	0.361	45.179	45.179	51	5.821	0.750
6	2	0.217	27.107	27.107	23	−4.107	0.622
7	3	0.087	10.843	15.064	14	−1.064	0.075
8	4	0.026	3.253				
9	5	0.006	0.781				
10	>=6	0.002	0.188				
11	**Totals**	**1.000**	**125.000**	**125.000**	**125.000**		**1.459**

Figure 15.8 Spreadsheet calculations for the chi-squared test in Worked example 15.15

15.13 What is the main difference between a parametric test and a non-parametric test?

15.14 When would you use a non-parametric test?

15.15 'When you cannot use a parametric test, you can always use a non-parametric test instead.' Do you think this is true?

15.16 Why does a χ^2 test have only a critical value rather than an acceptance range?

15.17 What is χ (the square root of χ^2) used for?

IDEAS IN PRACTICE   **Humbolt Farm Products**

Humbolt Farm Products routinely analyse the weights of materials received from suppliers. One type of delivery is known to have a mean weight of 45 g and a standard deviation of 15 g, but a sample of 500 units had this distribution:

Weight (in grams)	Number of observations	Weight (in grams)	Number of observations
less than 10	9	40 to 49.99	115
10 to 19.99	31	50 to 59.99	94
20 to 29.99	65	60 to 69.99	49
30 to 39.99	97	70 to 79.99	24
		80 to 89.99	16

Many types of statistical analyses are valid only if the data are Normally distributed, so Humbolt test this using χ^2 tests. For this example, they use the standard procedure as follows.

1 The null hypothesis, H_0, is that the distribution is Normal; the alternative hypothesis, H_1, is that the distribution is not Normal.
2 The significance level is 5%.
3 The number of degrees of freedom is $9 - 0 - 1 = 8$, giving a critical value of $\chi^2 = 15.5$.

4 The probability that an observation is in the range, say, 10 to 19.99 is:

$$P(\text{between 10 and 19.99}) = P(\text{less than 20})$$
$$- P(\text{less than 10})$$

Now 20 is $(20 - 45) / 15 = -1.67$ standard deviations from the mean, which corresponds to a probability of 0.048, and 10 is $(10 - 45) / 15 = -2.33$ standard deviations from the mean, which corresponds to a probability of 0.010, so:

$$P(\text{between 10 and 19.99}) = 0.048 - 0.010$$
$$= 0.038$$

The expected number of observations in this range is $0.038 \times 500 = 19$. Figure 15.9 shows a spreadsheet with these calculations, leading to a calculated value of χ^2 as 43.56.

5 The actual value of χ^2 (43.56) is greater than the critical value (15.5), so they reject the hypothesis that the sample is Normally distributed.
6 The evidence does not support the view that observations follow a Normal distribution, so Humbolt have to be careful with the analyses they do on this sample.

➤

Ideas in practice continued

	A	B	C	D	E	F
1	**Chi-squared test – Humbolt Farm Products**					
2						
3	**Weight from**	**to**	**Probability**	**Expected frequency**	**Observed frequency**	$(O - E)^2/E$
4	0	10.00	0.010	4.9	9	3.41
5	10	20.00	0.038	19.0	31	7.61
6	20	30.00	0.111	55.4	65	1.65
7	30	40.00	0.211	105.4	97	0.67
8	40	50.00	0.261	130.5	115	1.85
9	50	60.00	0.211	105.4	94	1.23
10	60	70.00	0.111	55.4	49	0.75
11	70	80.00	0.038	19.0	24	1.32
12	80	90.00	0.010	4.9	16	25.07
13			1.000	500.0	500	**43.56**

Figure 15.9 Calculations for Humbolt Farm Products (Worked example 15.16)

Tests of association

Suppose that you have a set of data that can be classified in two ways, such as a mortgage that can be classified according to both the amount borrowed and the type of lender. Then you can use a frequency table – called a contingency table – to show the number of observations that fall into each category. And a χ^2 test checks for associations between the two classifications. For example, if you build the following contingency table to show the number of mortgages with particular sizes and sources, you might ask whether or not there is any association between the size of a loan and the source.

		Size of loan			Total
		Less than £80,000	£80,000 to £150,000	More than £150,000	
Source of mortgage	Building society	30	55	40	**125**
	Bank	23	29	3	**55**
	Elsewhere	12	6	2	**20**
Total		**65**	**90**	**45**	**200**

WORKED EXAMPLE 15.16

Is there any association between the size of loan and its source in the contingency table above?

Solution

This is a hypothesis test, so we can use the standard procedure.

1 *State the null and alternative hypotheses.* When testing for association you normally use a null hypothesis that there is no association. Then the null hypothesis, H_0, is that there is no association between the size of mortgage and its source – in other words, the two are independent. The alternative hypothesis, H_1, is that there is an association.

2 *Specify the level of significance.* We take this as 5%.

3 *Calculate the critical value of χ^2.* For a contingency table the number of degrees of freedom is:

degrees of freedom = (number of rows − 1) × (number of columns − 1)

Here there are three rows and three columns (ignoring the totals), so there are

$(3 − 1) \times (3 − 1) = 4$ degrees of freedom

Looking up χ^2 tables for a 5% significance level and 4 degrees of freedom gives a critical value of 9.49.

4 *Find the actual value of χ^2.* For this we have to calculate the expected number of replies in each cell of the matrix. Starting at the top left-hand cell, we have the number of people who have a loan of less than £80,000 from a building society. A total of 125 loans come from a building society, so the probability that a particular loan comes from a building society is 125 / 200 = 0.625. A total of 65 loans are less than £80,000, so the probability that a particular loan is less than £80,000 is 65 / 200 = 0.325. Then the probability that a loan comes from a building society and is less than £80,000 is 0.625 × 0.325 = 0.203. Since there are 200 loans, the expected number of this type is 0.203 × 200 = 40.625. Repeating this calculation for every cell in the matrix gives these results:

		Size of loan		Total
		Less than £80,000	£80,000 to £150,000	More than £150,000	
Source of mortgage	Building society	40.625	56.250	28.125	**125**
	Bank	17.875	24.750	12.375	**55**
	Elsewhere	6.500	9.000	4.500	**20**
Total		**65**	**90**	**45**	**200**

Now we have a set of 9 observed frequencies, and a corresponding set of 9 expected frequencies. When we calculated the expected frequencies we assumed that there is no connection between the loan size and its source. Any significant differences between expected and observed values are caused by an association between the loan size and its source. The closer the association, the larger is the difference, and the larger the calculated value of χ^2. So now we have to find the actual value of χ^2, which you can see from the following table is 24.165.

O	E	O − E	(O − E)²	(O − E)²/E
30	40.625	− 10.625	112.891	2.779
55	56.250	−1.25	1.563	0.028
40	28.125	11.875	141.016	5.014
23	17.875	5.125	26.266	1.469
29	24.750	4.25	18.063	0.730
3	12.375	−9.375	87.891	7.102
12	6.500	5.500	30.250	4.654
6	9.000	−3.000	9.000	1.000
2	4.500	−2.500	6.250	1.389
200	200			24.165

5 *Decide whether or not to reject the null hypothesis.* The actual value (24.165) is greater than the critical value (9.49), so we reject the null hypothesis and accept the alternative hypothesis.

6 *State the conclusion.* The evidence supports the view that there is an association, and the size of a mortgage is related to its source.

Statistical packages can be quite difficult to use, confusing and give results that are difficult to

Worked example 15.16 continued

interpret. Figure 15.10 shows the printout from a simple package for this problem. This follows the steps that we have used, but notice that it gives a warning that one cell has fewer than 5 expected observations. We should be careful about this because it means that a chi-squared test may not work well, and we should really combine this cell with others to raise the number of expected observations. Alternatively, we could simply collect more observations.

```
001 > read data columns c1–c3
002 > 30 55 40
003 > 23 29 3
004 > 12 6 2
005 > column titles <80, 80–150, >150
006 > row titles building society, bank, elsewhere
007 > end data
008 > chisquare calculate c1–c3
```

Expected counts are printed below observed counts

	<80	80–150	>150	Total
building society	30	55	40	125
	40.62	56.25	28.12	
bank	23	29	3	55
	7.88	24.75	12.37	
elsewhere	12	6	2	20
	6.50	9.00	4.50	
Total	65	90	45	200

$$ChiSq = 2.779 + 0.028 + 5.014 +$$
$$1.469 + 0.730 + 7.102 +$$
$$4.654 + 1.000 + 1.389 = 24.165$$
$$df = 4$$

```
* WARNING *
1 cell with expected counts less than 5.0
   Merge rows or columns?
09 > no

010 > significance = 0.05
011 > chisquare test c1–c3
Critical value of ChiSq = 9.488
Calculated value of ChiSq = 24.165

Conclusion = reject null hypothesis
```

Figure 15.10 Printout from statistics package for chi-squared test

Review questions

15.18 What is a test of association?

15.19 Why would you use a statistical package for χ^2 tests?

IDEAS IN PRACTICE   Reports of findings

Newspapers find it difficult to report statistical information – they realise that most people will not fully understand it. Rather than confusing or boring their readers, they give heavily summarised results. You can see this effect in most reports, including the results from hypotheses tests. For example, one study found evidence that women who smoke during pregnancy have children who subsequently perform less well in school exams. The newspapers reported the headline results, 'Children born to women who smoke during pregnancy score an average of 9.2% lower marks in exams'. But it omitted the associated analysis, assumptions, significance levels and so on.

One survey of weight loss found that 47 people who only followed diets for six months lost 5.9 kg, while 43 people who only exercised lost 4.0 kg. The difference seems relatively large, but several magazines interpreted the results to mean that both methods are equally successful. However, the full study included a hypothesis test, using the standard deviations of weight loss (4.0 kg for diets and 3.9 kg for exercise). With a null hypothesis that the difference in mean weight loss between the two samples is zero, and an alternative hypothesis that the difference in mean weight loss is not zero, this result would occur in only 3% of tests. A fairer conclusion is that there is a statistically significant difference between the average weight loss for the two methods.

Abbreviated reports commonly do not give the full story about, for example, the effectiveness of alternative medicines, the effects of drinking alcohol, public opinions about government policies, customer reaction to new products, success rates of treatments for illnesses and so on.

CHAPTER REVIEW

This chapter described the approach of hypothesis testing, which reveals whether or not a statement about a population is supported by the evidence in a sample.

- Hypothesis testing starts with a null hypothesis, which is a precise statement about a population. Then it tests a sample from the population to see if there is evidence to support the null hypothesis. If the evidence does not support the null hypothesis it is rejected, otherwise it cannot be rejected.

- Samples always involve uncertainty and in hypothesis testing there are two types of error: Type I errors reject a null hypothesis that is true; and Type II errors do not reject a null hypothesis that is false.

- A significance level is the minimum acceptable probability that a value is a random sample from the hypothesised population. It is equivalent to the probability of making a Type I error.

- A common use of hypothesis testing checks whether or not the mean of a population has a specified value. A two-sided test checks the range within which a population mean is likely to lie; a one-sided test checks whether the population mean is likely to be above or below a specified value.

- The standard analysis can be extended to deal with small samples using a *t*-distribution, proportions of a population sharing some feature, differences between means and paired observations.

- When there is no parameter to test, typically with nominal data, we have to use a distribution-free, or non-parametric, test. The most common approach uses chi-squared tests, which check whether or not data follows a specified distribution. Chi-squared distribution can also be used to test the association between two parameters in a contingency table.

CASE STUDY **Willingham Consumer Protection Department**

Willingham Consumer Protection Department (WCPD) is responsible for administering all weights and measures laws in its area of North Carolina. A part of its service makes sure that packages of food and drink contain the quantities stated. One week, WCPD decided to test containers of milk. Most of these tests were done at dairies, where procedures and historical data were also examined, with other random samples taken from local shops and milk delivery services.

On two consecutive days WCPD bought 50 containers with a nominal content of 4 pints or 2.27 litres. The actual contents of these, in litres, are as follows.

- Day 1: 2.274 2.275 2.276 2.270 2.269 2.271
2.265 2.275 2.263 2.278 2.260 2.278
2.280 2.275 2.261 2.280 2.279 2.270
2.275 2.263 2.275 2.281 2.266 2.277
2.271 2.273 2.283 2.260 2.259 2.276
2.286 2.275 2.271 2.273 2.291 2.271
2.269 2.265 2.258 2.283 2.274 2.278
2.276 2.281 2.269 2.259 2.291 2.289
2.276 2.283

- Day 2: 2.270 2.276 2.258 2.259 2.281 2.265
2.278 2.270 2.294 2.255 2.271 2.284
2.276 2.293 2.261 2.270 2.271 2.276
2.269 2.268 2.272 2.272 2.273 2.280

2.281 2.276 2.263 2.260 2.295 2.257
2.248 2.276 2.284 2.276 2.270 2.271

When they were collecting these figures, WCPD inspectors were convinced that there were no problems with the main dairies, but some small operations were not so reliable. This was because large dairies invariably used modern, well-designed equipment, and they employed special quality assurance staff. Smaller operators tended to use older, less reliable equipment and could not afford to run a quality assurance department. Two companies, in particular, were identified as needing further checks. WCPD took random samples of 15 containers from each of these dairies, with these results:

- Company 1: 2.261 2.273 2.250 2.268 2.268
2.262 2.272 2.269 2.268 2.257
2.260 2.270 2.254 2.249 2.267

- Company 2: 2.291 2.265 2.283 2.275 2.248
2.286 2.268 2.271 2.284 2.256
2.284 2.255 2.283 2.275 2.276

Question

- What could the milk inspectors report about their findings? What follow-up action could they recommend? Are there any improvements they could make to their data collection and analysis?

PROBLEMS

15.1 The mean wage of people living in Alto Canillas is said to be £400 a week with a standard deviation of £100. A random sample of 36 people was examined. What is the acceptance range for a 5% significance level? What is the acceptance range for a 1% significance level?

15.2 The weight of packets of biscuits is claimed to be 500 g. A random sample of 50 packets has a mean weight of 495 g and a standard deviation of 10 g. Use a significance level of 5% to see whether or not the data from the sample supports the original claim.

15.3 Hamil Coaches Ltd say that their long-distance coaches take 5 hours for a particular journey. Last week a consumer group tested these figures by timing a sample of 30 journeys. These had a mean time of 5 hours 10 minutes with a standard deviation of 20 minutes. What report can the consumer group make?

15.4 A food processor specifies the mean weight of a product as 200 g. A random sample of 20 has a mean of 195 g and a standard deviation of 15 g. Does this evidence suggest that the mean weight is too low?

15.5 An emergency breakdown service suggests that 50% of all drivers are registered with their service. A random sample of 100 people had 45 who were registered. Does this sample support the original claim?

15.6 Quality Managers at CentralGen say that 12% of the letters they post contain errors. A sample of 200 letters was checked and 31 of them contained errors. What do these results suggest?

15.7 Health service managers say that doctors should not spend more than 2 hours a day doing paperwork. A sample of 40 doctors spends an average of 2 hours 25 minutes a day doing paperwork, with a standard deviation of 55 minutes. What does this show?

15.8 A mobile phone has an advertised life of 30,000 hours. A sample of 50 phones had a life of 28,500 hours with a standard deviation of 1,000 hours. What can you say about the advertisements?

15.9 Dorphmund Industries have two similar factories. There is some disagreement, because people working in each factory think those in the other factory are getting higher wages. A sample of wages was taken from each factory with the following results:

■ Sample 1: size = 45, mean = $250, standard deviation = $45
■ Sample 2: size = 35, mean = $230, standard deviation = $40

What can you say about the wages?

15.10 A car manufacturer says that its cars cost €500 a year less to maintain than those of its competitors. To test this, a consumer group found the cost of maintaining 10 cars for a year, and the mean saving was €79 with a standard deviation of €20. What does this say about the manufacturer's claim?

15.11 Five factories reported the following numbers of minor accidents in a year:

Factory	1	2	3	4	5
Number of accidents	23	45	18	34	28

Does this suggest that some factories have more accidents than others?

15.12 The following figures show the number of defective components supplied each day by a factory. Does this data follow a binomial distribution?

Number of defects	0	1	2	3	4	5
Number of days	8	22	33	29	15	3

15.13 The number of road accident victims reporting to a hospital emergency ward is shown in the following table. Do these figures follow a Poisson distribution?

Number of accidents	0	1	2	3	4	5	6
Number of days	17	43	52	37	20	8	4

15.14 Do the following figures follow a Normal distribution?

Weight (in grams)	Number of observations	Weight (in grams)	Number of observations
less than 5	5	65 to 79.99	97
5 to 19.99	43	80 to 94.99	43
20 to 34.99	74	95 to 109.99	21
35 to 49.99	103	110 and more	8
50 to 64.99	121		

15.15 Figure 15.11 shows a spreadsheet doing the calculations for a t-test on the mean of two samples. Explain the results and check the calculations. How could you improve the format?

	A	B	C	D	E	F	G
1	Two samples – *t*-test						
2							
3	Data			*t*-Test: Two-Sample assuming equal variances			
4	Variable 1	Variable 2					
5	10	8			*Variable 1*		*Variable 2*
6	16	10		Mean	10.6		7.786
7	13	9		Variance	12.489		4.335
8	6	6		Observations	10		14
9	8	4		Pooled variance	7.671		
10	9	10		Hypothesised mean difference	0		
11	16	9		df	22		
12	9	9		*t* Stat	2.454		
13	12	7		*P*(*T*<=*t*) one-tail	0.011		
14	7	4		*t* Critical one-tail	1.717		
15		10		*P*(*T*<=*t*) two-tail	0.023		
16		9		*t* Critical two-tail	2.074		
17		6					
18		8					

Figure 15.11 Calculations for Problem 15.15

RESEARCH PROJECTS

15.1 This chapter mentioned several examples of automatic systems that implicitly include hypothesis tests – including airport security systems, e-mail spam filters, Internet search results, automatic recorders of earthquakes, burglar alarms and roadside speed cameras. What other examples can you find? How do such systems actually incorporate hypothesis testing?

15.2 Hypothesis testing comes in many different forms, and it always seems to involve judgement. This makes it difficult to design a package that automatically takes data and does an appropriate hypothesis test. Do a small survey to see what facilities statistical packages have for hypothesis testing. How do they get around the practical problems?

15.3 Supermarkets and other retailers often claim that they offer the lowest prices in their area. How can you check their claims? Collect some data from competing stores and analyse the results. What conclusions can you reach?

15.4 Often a hypothesis may seem 'obvious', but on closer examination there is no evidence to support it. Find some real examples of this effect. What are the consequences?

Sources of information

Reference

1 Hooke R., *How to Tell the Liars from the Statisticians*, Marcel Dekker, New York, 1983.

Further reading

There are very few books specifically about hypothesis testing – and the odd ones are very technical. Three possible ones are given, but it may be better to look in general statistics books, like those listed in Chapter 12.

Lehmann E. and Romano J.P., *Testing Statistical Hypotheses* (3rd edition), Springer, New York, 2010.

Wellek S., *Testing Statistical Hypotheses of Equivalence*, Chapman and Hall / CRC, Boca Raton, FL, 2003.

Wilcox R.R., *Introduction to Robust Estimation and Hypothesis Testing* (2nd edition), Elsevier, Amsterdam, 2005.

PART FIVE

Management problems involving uncertainty

This book is divided into five parts, each of which covers a different aspect of quantitative methods. The first part gave the background and context for the rest of the book. The second part showed how to collect, summarise and present data. The third part used this data to tackle some common management problems. These were deterministic problems, where we knew conditions with certainty.

In reality, management problems are characterised by a great deal of uncertainty, where we do not know how circumstances will change or even the effect of particular actions. When a company decides to reduce the price of an item it does not really know how customers will react, the effects on sales and revenue, what competitors will do, the effect of general economic conditions, changing government regulations and so on. The fourth part of the book showed how such uncertainty can be measured and analysed using probabilities. This fifth part shows how to tackle a range of problems that include uncertainty, using these ideas of probabilities and statistical analyses.

There are five chapters in this part. Chapter 16 describes an approach to decision-making, where managers can give structure to problems and make decisions in conditions of uncertainty. Chapter 17 looks at the use of statistics in quality control and broader quality management. Chapter 18 describes some models for inventory management, and Chapter 19 shows how to use network analysis for planning and scheduling projects. Chapter 20 looks at the management of queues, and broader uses of simulation.

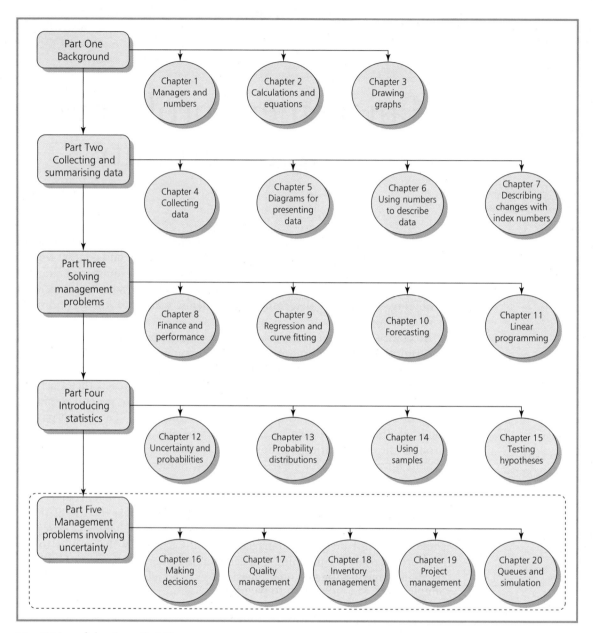

Map 5 Map of chapters – Part Five

Making decisions

Chapter outline

Managers work in complex and uncertain conditions, making the decisions that keep their organisations running effectively. They face many types of problem, but these often have a common structure. So a useful approach to decision-making considers the problems, identifies the features and puts them into standard formats. Then managers can use a structured approach to find solutions. We discuss several formats for describing problems, starting with simple maps and moving on to payoff matrices and decision trees. These help managers to tackle problems in a variety of circumstances, including certainty, uncertainty and risk.

After finishing this chapter you should be able to:

- appreciate the need to structure decisions
- draw maps of problems
- list the main elements of a decision and construct a payoff matrix
- tackle decisions under certainty
- describe situations of uncertainty and use decision criteria to suggest decisions
- describe situations of risk and use expected values to suggest decisions
- use Bayes' theorem to update conditional probabilities
- understand the use of utilities
- use decision trees to solve problems with sequential decisions.

Giving structure to decisions

Everybody has to make decisions – choosing the best car to buy, whether to invest in a personal pension, where to eat, which software to use, where to go on holiday, which phone to buy and whether to have tea or coffee. These decisions come in a steady stream. Most of them are fairly minor and we can make them using a combination of experience, intuition, judgement and common sense. But when decisions are more important, we have to use a more rigorous approach. For instance, imagine that you work for a company that is not making enough profit. This is a serious problem and two obvious remedies are to reduce costs or to increase prices. But if the company increases prices, demand may fall – while reducing the costs might allow a lower price and demand may rise. If demand changes, revenues and cost structures change and the company may have to reschedule operations, change capacity and adjust marketing strategies. But changing the operations schedules can affect the flows of materials in supply chains, stocks, employment prospects and so on. And then changing the flows of materials can affect relations with suppliers.

We could continue with these more or less random thoughts, showing how one adjustment triggers a series of related changes. But you already get the idea that interactions in business are complex and it is easy to get bogged down in the detail and lose track of the broader arguments. Managers have to balance many factors and for this they have to keep a clear picture of a problem. A useful starting point for this is to describe the interactions in a diagram called a problem map (sometimes called a relationship diagram or mind map). Figure 16.1 shows the first steps in a problem map for the discussion above.

As you can see, this map gives an informal way of presenting a stream of connected ideas, showing the interactions and giving some structure to a problem. You can extend these basic diagrams to add different kinds of interactions and related features, perhaps using different symbols for different kinds of interactions. A lot of software is available for producing these diagrams automatically, such as Amode, ConceptDraw's MindMap, FreeMind, iMindMap, MindManager and NovaMind.

Problem maps give a more formal structure – with the benefit that 'a problem well-defined is a problem half-solved'. But they only give a description and do not suggest a solution. To move to the next step of getting help with the actual decisions we have to do some more analysis. And for this we must consider the characteristics of a decision, which can be summarised as:

- *a decision-maker* – the manager – who is responsible for making the decision
- *a number of alternatives* available to the decision-maker
- *an aim* of choosing the best alternative
- after the decision has been made, *events occurring* over which the decision-maker has no control
- each combination of an alternative chosen followed by an event happening leading to *an outcome* that has some measurable value.

For example, imagine someone owning a house valued at €200,000 and deciding whether to take out fire insurance at an annual cost of €600. The

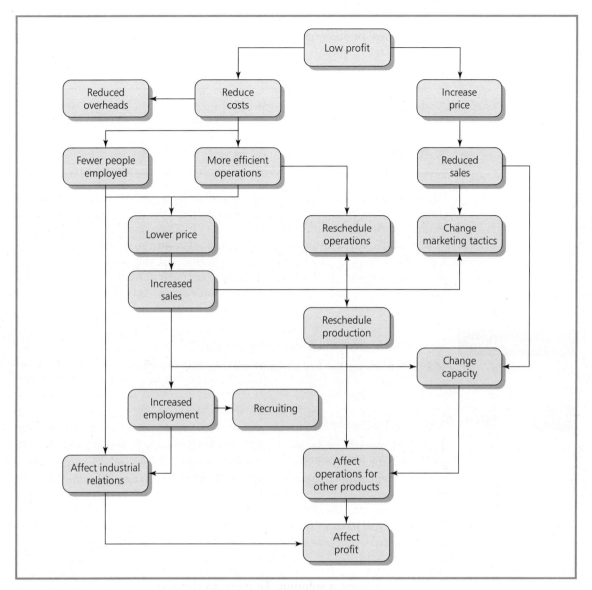

Figure 16.1 Start of a problem map for increasing profit

decision-maker is the person who owns the house and they have the alternatives of:

1 insure the house
2 do not insure the house.

Their aim is to minimise costs. After they make their decision an event happens, but the decision-maker cannot control whether it is:

1 the house burns down
2 the house does not burn down.

Each combination of choice (insure or not insure) and event (burns down or does not) has an outcome that we can show in the following table. This is a **payoff matrix** or **payoff table** and it shows the cost to the house owner of every combination of alternative and event.

	Event	
	House burns down	House does not burn down
Alternative		
Insure house	€600	€600
Do not insure house	€200,000	€0

Obviously, we have simplified the problem here and in reality there is a choice of many insurance companies and policies, the house may be damaged but not destroyed by fire, there may be costs of inconvenience and so on.

A payoff matrix shows the underlying structure of a problem but, like a problem map, it does not offer a solution. In the rest of this chapter we show how the structure can help managers to actually make decisions. We consider decisions in different circumstances, starting with decisions involving certainty.

Review questions

16.1 Why are maps and payoff matrices useful?

16.2 What are the five key elements in a decision?

Decision making with certainty

The characteristic of decision making with certainty is that we know, with certainty, which event will occur. So we have to consider only the single event we know will happen, and the payoff matrix has only one column. Then the method of solution is obvious – we list the outcomes for each alternative and simply choose the alternative that gives the best outcome.

Suppose you have $1,000 to invest for a year. With certainty, you can list all the alternatives that you want to consider and might get this payoff matrix:

		Event
		Earns interest
Alternative investments	Bank	$1,065
	Building society	$1,075
	Government stock	$1,085
	Stock market	$1,100
	Others	$1,060

Notice that this time the outcomes are benefits rather than costs. Again, this is clearly a simplified view, because we have used forecast returns for investments, and have included a wide range of alternatives in 'others'. There is only one event – 'earns interest' – and by looking down the list of outcomes you can identify the best alternative. The highest value at the end of the year comes from investing in the stock market.

In reality, even decisions under certainty can be difficult. For instance, would it be better for a health service to invest money in providing more kidney dialysis machines, giving nurses higher wages, doing open-heart surgery, funding research into cancer or providing more parking spaces at hospitals? Most decisions contain elements of subjectivity and even when managers know all the circumstances (which is rarely possible) they are still unlikely to agree on the best decision. Politicians can agree on an aim of economic growth, and they can be overwhelmed with information about alternative policies and events – but they rarely agree on the means of achieving this growth.

WORKED EXAMPLE 16.1

The manager of La Pigalle Restaurant has a booking for a large wedding banquet. She has a number of ways of providing staff, each with different costs. Her most convenient alternatives are to pay full-time staff to work overtime (costing £600), hire current part-time staff for the day (£400), hire new temporary staff (£500) or to use an agency (£750). What is her best alternative?

Solution
The payoff matrix for this decision under certainty is shown below. The entries are costs, so we want to identify the lowest. This is £400 for hiring current part-time staff for the day.

		Event
		Pay staff
Alternative	Pay full-time staff for overtime	£600
	Hire current part-time staff	£400
	Hire new temporary staff	£500
	Use an agency	£750

Review questions

16.3 What is meant by 'decision making with certainty'?

16.4 In reality, are you ever likely to meet decisions involving certainty?

16.5 Are decisions involving certainty always trivial?

Decision making with strict uncertainty

Most decisions do not have a single event that will definitely occur, but there are several possible events. 'Uncertainty' means that we can list the events that might occur, but do not know in advance which one actually will happen. And we also know the outcome for each combination of alternative and events. Because we know the alternatives, events and outcomes, we are not making decisions in ignorance, but only with uncertainty about the event that will actually occur.

Sometimes we can attach probabilities to events, and will discuss the ways of tackling such problems in the next section. But often we cannot even give realistic probabilities. For example, when you decide to accept a job offer a number of events can happen – you may not like the new job and quickly start looking for another; you may get the sack; you may like the job and stay; you may be moved by the company. One event will occur, but they are largely outside your control and it is impossible even to give reliable probabilities.

When we cannot give probabilities to events, we are dealing with **strict uncertainty** (which is often abbreviated to **uncertainty**). The most common way of solving problems involving uncertainty is to use simple rules – called **decision criteria** – to recommend a solution. There are many different criteria and we can illustrate with three common ones.

Laplace decision criterion

As we cannot give probabilities to the events, the Laplace criterion says that we should treat them as equally likely and choose the alternative with the best average outcome. The procedure for this is:

1 For each alternative, find the mean value of the outcomes – that is, the average of each row in the payoff matrix.
2 Choose the alternative with the best average outcome – the lowest average cost or the highest average gain.

WORKED EXAMPLE 16.2

A restaurateur is going to set up a cream tea stall at a local gala. On the morning of the gala she visits the wholesale market and has to decide whether to buy large, medium or small quantities of strawberries, scones, cream and other materials. Her profit depends on the number of people attending the gala, and this in turn depends on the weather. If her matrix of gains (in thousands of pounds) for different weather conditions is given below, what quantity of materials should she buy?

| | Event – weather is | | |
Alternative – buy	good	average	poor
large quantity	10	4	−2
medium quantity	7	6	2
small quantity	4	1	4

Solution

Following the procedure described:

1 Take the average value of outcomes for each alternative:
   - Large quantity: $(10 + 4 − 2) / 3 = 4$
   - Medium quantity: $(7 + 6 + 2) / 3 = 5$ (best)
   - Small quantity: $(4 + 1 + 4) / 3 = 3$
2 Choose the best average outcome. These figures are profits, so the best is the highest, which is to buy a medium quantity.

Wald decision criterion

Most organisations have limited resources and cannot afford to risk a big loss. This is the basis of the Wald decision criterion, which assumes that decision-makers are cautious – or even pessimistic – and want to avoid big potential losses. The steps are:

1 For each alternative find the worst outcome.
2 Choose the alternative from the best of these worst outcomes.

With a payoff matrix showing costs, this is sometimes known as the 'mini-max cost' criterion, as it looks for the maximum cost of each alternative and then chooses the alternative with the minimum of these – expressed as the minimum[maximum cost].

WORKED EXAMPLE 16.3

Use the Wald decision criterion on the example of the cream tea stall described in Worked example 16.2.

Solution

Following the procedure described:

1 Find the worst outcome for each alternative, and as the entries are gains the worst is the lowest:

- ■ Large quantity: minimum of [10, 4, –2] = –2
- ■ Medium quantity: minimum of [7, 6, 2] = 2
- ■ Small quantity: minimum of [4, 1, 4] = 1

Alternative – buy	Event – weather is			
	good	average	poor	Worst
large quantity	10	4	–2	–2
medium quantity	7	6	2	**2** (best)
small quantity	4	1	4	1

2 Choose the best of these worst outcomes. The figures are profits, so the best is the highest (in this case, 2), which comes from buying a medium quantity.

Savage decision criterion

Sometimes we are judged not by how well we actually did, but by how well we could possibly have done. Students who get 70% in an exam might be judged by the fact that they did not get 100%; investment brokers who advised a client to invest in platinum may be judged not by the fact that platinum rose 15% in value, but by the fact that gold rose 25%. This happens particularly when performance is judged by someone other than the decision-maker.

At such times there is a *regret*, which is the difference between an actual outcome and best possible outcome. A student who gets 70% in an exam has a regret of 100 – 70 = 30%; an investor who gains 15% when they could have gained 25% has a regret of 25 – 15 = 10%. If you choose the best option, there is clearly no regret. The Savage criterion is based on these regrets. It is essentially pessimistic and minimises the maximum regret, with these steps:

1 For each event find the best possible outcome – the best entry in each column of the payoff matrix.
2 Find the regret for every entry in the column – the difference between the entry itself and the best entry in the column.
3 Put the regrets found in Step 2 into a 'regret matrix' – there should be at least one zero in each column (for the best outcome) and regrets are always positive.
4 For each alternative find the highest regret – the highest number in each row.
5 Choose the alternative with the best – the lowest of these highest regrets.

As you can see, steps 1 to 3 build a regret matrix, and then steps 4 and 5 apply the Wald criterion to the regret matrix.

WORKED EXAMPLE 16.4

Use the Savage decision criterion on the example of the cream tea stall described in worked Example 16.2.

Solution

1 The best outcome for each event is underlined (that is, with good weather a large quantity, with average weather a medium quantity and with poor weather a small quantity).

	Event – weather is		
Alternative – buy	good	average	poor
large quantity	<u>10</u>	4	−2
medium quantity	7	<u>6</u>	2
small quantity	4	1	<u>4</u>

2 The regret for every other entry in the column is the difference between this underlined value and the actual entry. So when the weather is good and the caterer bought a medium quantity, the regret is 10 − 7 = 3; when the weather is good and the caterer bought a small quantity the regret is 10 − 4 = 6; when the weather is good and the caterer bought a large quantity, the regret is zero. Repeat this calculation for every column.

3 Put the regrets into a matrix, replacing the original profit figures.

	Event – weather is			
Alternative – buy	good	average	poor	Worst
large quantity	0	2	6	6
medium quantity	3	0	2	**3** (best)
small quantity	6	5	0	6

4 For each alternative find the highest regret:
- Large quantity: maximum of [0, 2, 6] = 6
- Medium quantity: maximum of [3, 0, 2] = **3** (best)
- Small quantity: maximum of [6, 5, 0] = 6

5 Choose the alternative with the lowest of these maximum regrets. This is the medium quantity.

Choosing the criterion to use

Different criteria often suggest the same alternative (as you can see in the worked examples above) and this can reduce the importance of finding the 'right' one for a particular problem. But there is no guarantee of this – and when they recommend different alternatives you should choose the most relevant. For example, if you are working as a consultant and other people judge the quality of your decisions, you might use the Savage criterion; if the decision is made for a small company that cannot afford high losses, then Wald may be best; if there really is nothing to choose between different events, Laplace may be useful.

Although it is difficult to go beyond such general guidelines, you should notice one other factor. Both the Wald and Savage criteria effectively recommend their decision based on one outcome – the worst for Wald and the one that leads to the highest regret for Savage. So the choice might be dominated by a few atypical results. The Laplace criterion is the only one that uses all the values to make its recommendation.

Of course, you might have a problem that does not suit any of the criteria we have described – but remember that we have only given three illustrations and there are many other options. For example, an ambitious organisation might aim for the highest profit and use a criterion that looks for the highest return (a 'maximax profit' criterion). Or it may try to balance the best and worst outcomes for each event and use a criterion based on the value of:

$$\alpha \times \text{best outcome} + (1 - \alpha) \times \text{worst outcome}$$

where α is a parameter between 0 and 1.

Remember that decision criteria are useful tools – and their strength is not necessarily in identifying the best alternative, but to give structure to a problem, show relationships and allow an informed debate of options.

WORKED EXAMPLE 16.5

Lawrence Pang has a problem with the following payoff matrix of costs. Use the Laplace, Wald and Savage decision criteria to show the best alternatives.

Alternative	Event		
	1	2	3
A	14	22	6
B	19	18	12
C	12	17	15

Solution

As the entries are costs, Laplace recommends the alternative with the lowest average costs – which is alternative A.

	1	2	3	Mean
A	14	22	6	14.0 (best)
B	19	18	12	16.3
C	12	17	15	14.7

Wald assumes that the highest cost will occur for each alternative, and then chooses the lowest of these – which is alternative C.

	1	2	3	Highest
A	14	22	6	22
B	19	18	12	19
C	12	17	15	17 (best)

Savage forms the regret matrix, finds the highest regret for each alternative, and chooses the alternative with the lowest of these – which is alternative A.

	1	2	3	Highest
A	2	5	0	5 (best)
B	7	1	6	7
C	0	0	9	9

Review questions

16.6   What is meant by decision making under strict uncertainty?

16.7   List three useful decision criteria.

16.8   How many of these criteria take into account all the outcomes for the alternatives?

16.9   Are the criteria described the only ones available? If not, can you suggest others that might be useful?

Paco Menendes

Paco Menendes ran a plumbing wholesale business based in the Mexican city of Guadalajara. He had an inventive flair and developed a simple valve mechanism for controlling the flow of water in domestic solar heating systems. He had to decide how to market his idea, and in the short term his options could be summarised as selling the valve locally, selling nationally through a website, entering a partnership with an existing company or selling the patent. His returns depended on demand, which he described as high, medium or low. Using this simple model, he developed the matrix of potential annual gains shown in Figure 16.2.

He considered a decision criterion that balanced the best and worst outcomes comparing alternatives by:

$$\alpha \times \text{best outcome} + (1 - \alpha) \times \text{worst outcome}$$

This is the Hurwicz criterion, where α is chosen to show how optimistic the decision-maker is. An optimistic decision-maker chooses a value of α close to one – a pessimistic decision-maker chooses a value close to zero. Paco Menendes used a value of 0.4, showing that he was slightly pessimistic. Then the criterion suggested that his best option (with the highest calculated value) was to sell through a website. However, when he explored his options more carefully, he decided to go into partnership with a national distributor.

	A	B	C	D	E	F	G
1	Annual gains for Paco Menendes						
2							
3				Demand		Alpha	
4			High	Medium	Low	0.4	
5	Options	Market locally	50	25	–20	8	
6		Use website	85	55	–10	28	Best
7		Partnership	40	25	10	22	
8		Sell patent	25	25	25	25	

Figure 16.2 Calculations for Paco Menendes

Decision making with risk

With strict uncertainty we know that there are a number of possible events, one of which will occur – but we have no idea of the likelihood of each event. With decision making under risk, we can give a probability to each event. We should include every relevant event, so these probabilities add to 1. A simple example of decision making under risk is spinning a coin. Possible events are the coin coming down heads or tails; the probability of each of these is 0.5, and these add to 1.

Expected values

The usual way of solving problems involving risk is to calculate the expected value of each alternative, which is defined as the sum of the probabilities multiplied by the value of the outcomes.

expected value = Σ (probability of event × value of outcome)

If you spin a coin and win €20 if it comes down heads and lose €40 if it comes down tails:

$$\text{expected value} = 0.5 \times 20 - 0.5 \times 40$$
$$= -10$$

The expected value of an alternative is the average gain (or cost) when a decision is repeated a large number of times. It is not the value of every decision. When spinning the coin above you will either win €20 or lose €40 on each spin, but in the long term you would expect to lose an average of €10 on every spin.

Having calculated the expected value for each alternative, you choose the one with the best expected value. So decision making with risk has two steps:

1 Calculate the expected value for each alternative.
2 Choose the alternative with the best expected value – the highest value for gains, and the lowest value for costs.

WORKED EXAMPLE 16.6

What is the best alternative for this matrix of gains?

Alternative	Event			
	1	2	3	4
	P = 0.1	P = 0.2	P = 0.6	P = 0.1
A	10	7	5	9
B	3	20	2	10
C	3	4	11	1
D	8	4	2	16

Solution
The expected value for each alternative is the sum of the probability times the value of the outcome:

- Alternative A:

  $0.1 \times 10 + 0.2 \times 7 + 0.6 \times 5 + 0.1 \times 9 = 6.3$

- Alternative B:

  $0.1 \times 3 + 0.2 \times 20 + 0.6 \times 2 + 0.1 \times 10 = 6.5$

- Alternative C:

  $0.1 \times 3 + 0.2 \times 4 + 0.6 \times 11 + 0.1 \times 1 = \mathbf{7.8}$
  (best)

- Alternative D:

  $0.1 \times 8 + 0.2 \times 4 + 0.6 \times 2 + 0.1 \times 16 = 4.4$

As these are gains, the best alternative is C with an expected value of 7.8. If this decision is made repeatedly, the average return in the long run will be 7.8; if the decision is made only once, the gain could be any of the four values 3, 4, 11 or 1.

IDEAS IN PRACTICE   H.J. Symonds Logistics

H.J. Symonds Logistics provides third-party transport and storage services. It usually signs long-term contracts to develop close working relationships with its customers. Recently it bid for a contract to move newspapers and magazines from a printing works to wholesalers. This distribution market is dominated by two major companies, and it might be a useful area for expansion.

The whole decision was complicated, but a part of one analysis showed that Symonds could submit one of three tenders – a low one that assumes newspaper sales will increase and unit transport costs will go down; a medium one that gives a reasonable return if newspaper sales stay the same; or a high one that assumes newspaper sales will decrease and unit transport costs will go up. The

➤

Ideas in practice continued

probabilities of newspaper sales and profits (in thousands of pounds) are summarised in the table.

	Newspaper sales		
Alternative	decrease	stay the same	increase
	P = 0.4	P = 0.3	P = 0.3
low tender	10	15	16
medium tender	5	20	10
high tender	18	10	−5

The expected value for each alternative is:

- Low tender:

    $0.4 \times 10 + 0.3 \times 15 + 0.3 \times 16 = \mathbf{13.3}$ (best)

- Medium tender:

    $0.4 \times 5 + 0.3 \times 20 + 0.3 \times 10 = 11.0$

- High tender:

    $0.4 \times 18 + 0.3 \times 10 - 0.3 \times 5 = 8.7$

The best alternative is the one with highest expected profit, which is the low tender. Based on a full analysis of costs, Symonds actually decided to submit a medium tender, but lost the contract to a cheaper competitor.

Using Bayes' theorem to update probabilities

In Chapter 12 we showed how Bayes' theorem updates conditional probabilities:

$$P(a/b) = \frac{P(b/a) \times P(a)}{P(b)}$$

where: $P(a/b)$ = probability of a happening given that b has already happened
$P(b/a)$ = probability of b happening given that a has already happened
$P(a)$, $P(b)$ = probabilities of a and b happening respectively.

The following examples show how Bayes' theorem can help with decisions under uncertainty. Each of the calculations is straightforward, but you have to keep a clear idea of what is happening.

WORKED EXAMPLE 16.7

The crowd for a sports event might be small (with a probability of 0.4) or large. The organisers can pay a consultant to collect and analyse advance ticket sales one week before the event takes place. Then advance sales can be classified as high, average or low, with the probability of advanced sales conditional on crowd size given by this table:

	Advance sales		
Crowd size	high	average	low
large	0.7	0.3	0.0
small	0.2	0.2	0.6

The organisers must choose one of two plans in running the event, and the table below gives the net profit in thousands of euros for each combination of plan and crowd size.

Crowd size	Plan 1	Plan 2
large	20	28
small	18	10

If the organisers use information about advance sales, what decisions would maximise their expected profits? How much should they pay for the information on advance sales?

Worked example 16.7 continued

Solution

To make things easier, we will start by defining the abbreviations:

- CL and CS for crowd size large and crowd size small
- ASH, ASA and ASL for advance sales high, average and small.

If the organisers do not use the information about advance sales, the best they can do is use the probabilities of large and small crowds (0.6 and 0.4 respectively) to calculate expected values for the two plans.

- Plan 1: $0.6 \times 20 + 0.4 \times 18 = 19.2$
- Plan 2: $0.6 \times 28 + 0.4 \times 10 = $ **20.8** (better plan)

Then they should use plan 2 with an expected profit of €20,800.

The information on advance ticket sales gives the conditional probabilities P(ASH/CL), P(ASH/CS) etc. The organisers would like these the other way around, P(CL/ASH), P(CS/ASH) etc. – and for this they use Bayes' theorem. The calculations for Bayes' theorem are shown in the following table (if you have forgotten the details of these calculations, refer back to Chapter 12).

	ASH	ASA	ASL		ASH	ASA	ASL
CL	0.7	0.3	0.00	0.6	0.42	0.18	0.00
CS	0.2	0.2	0.6	0.4	0.08	0.08	0.24
					0.50	0.26	0.24
				CL	0.84	0.69	0.00
				CS	0.16	0.31	1.00

The probability that advance sales are high is 0.5. If this happens, the probability of a large crowd is 0.84 and the probability of a small crowd is 0.16. Then, if the organisers choose plan 1, the expected value is $0.84 \times 20 + 0.16 \times 18 = 19.68$; if the organisers choose plan 2, the expected value is $0.84 \times 28 + 0.16 \times 10 = 25.12$. So with high advance sales the organisers should choose plan 2 with an expected profit of €25,120.

Extending this reasoning to the other results gives the expected values and best choices:

- ASH: Plan 1: $0.84 \times 20 + 0.16 \times 18 = 19.68$
  Plan 2: $0.84 \times 28 + 0.16 \times 10 = $ **25.12** (better plan)
- ASA: Plan 1: $0.69 \times 20 + 0.31 \times 18 = 19.38$
  Plan 2: $0.69 \times 28 + 0.31 \times 10 = $ **22.42** (better plan)
- ASL: Plan 1: $0.00 \times 20 + 1.00 \times 18 = $ **18.00** (better plan)
  Plan 2: $0.00 \times 28 + 1.00 \times 10 = 10.00$

The decisions that maximise the organiser's profit are: when advance sales are high or average, choose plan 2; when advance sales are low, choose plan 1.

We can go one step further with this analysis because we know that the probabilities of high, average and low advance sales are respectively 0.5, 0.26 and 0.24. So we can calculate the overall expected value of following the recommended decisions as:

$0.5 \times 25.12 + 0.26 \times 22.42 + 0.24 \times 18.00 = 22.71$

So the expected profit of using the advance sales information is €22,710. This compares with €20,800 when the advance sales information is not used, and the benefit of using the additional information is $22,710 - 20,800 = $ €1,910, or over 9%.

WORKED EXAMPLE 16.8

Humbolt Oil drills an exploratory well in deep water off the Irish coast. The company is uncertain about the amount of recoverable oil it will find, but experience suggests that it might be minor (with a probability of 0.3), significant (with probability 0.5) or major. The company has to decide how to develop the find and has a choice of either moving quickly to minimise its long-term debt, or moving slowly to guarantee continuing income. The profits for every combination of size and development speed are given in this table, where entries are in millions of dollars.

Worked example 16.8 continued

Development	Size of find		
	minor	significant	major
Quickly	100	130	180
Slowly	80	150	210

	A	B	C		A	B	C
MIN	0.3	0.4	0.3	0.3	0.09	0.12	0.09
SIG	0.5	0.0	0.5	0.5	0.25	0.00	0.25
MAJ	0.25	0.25	0.5	0.2	0.05	0.05	0.10
					0.39	0.17	0.44
				MIN	0.23	0.71	0.20
				SIG	0.64	0.00	0.57
				MAJ	0.13	0.29	0.23

Further geological tests can give a more accurate picture of the size of the find, but these cost $2.5 million and are not entirely accurate. The tests give three results – A, B and C – with the following conditional probabilities of results given the size of find.

Find size	Test result		
	A	B	C
minor	0.3	0.4	0.3
significant	0.5	0.0	0.5
major	0.25	0.25	0.5

What should Humbolt do to maximise its expected profits?

Solution

We can start by defining some abbreviations:

- MIN, SIG and MAJ for minor, significant and major finds
- QUICK and SLOW for the quick and slow development.

Without using further geological testing, the probabilities of minor, significant and major finds are 0.3, 0.5 and 0.2 respectively, so the expected profits for each speed of development are:

- QUICK: $0.3 \times 100 + 0.5 \times 130 + 0.2 \times 180 = 131$
- SLOW: $0.3 \times 80 + 0.5 \times 150 + 0.2 \times 210 = \mathbf{141}$ (better)

The company should develop the find slowly with an expected value of $141 million.

The information from further geological tests is in the form P(A/MIN), P(B/SIG) etc., but Humbolt want it in the form P(MIN/A), P(SIG/B) etc. It finds these using Bayes' theorem.

If the test result is A, the probabilities of minor, significant and major finds are 0.23, 0.64 and 0.13 respectively. Then developing the well quickly gives an expected profit of $0.23 \times 100 + 0.64 \times 130 + 0.13 \times 180 = 129.6$. Repeating this calculation for the other results gives these expected values and best choices:

- Result A: QUICK: $0.23 \times 100 + 0.64 \times 130 + 0.13 \times 180 = 129.6$
  SLOW: $0.23 \times 80 + 0.64 \times 150 + 0.13 \times 210 = \mathbf{141.7}$ (better)
- Result B: QUICK: $0.71 \times 100 + 0.00 \times 130 + 0.29 \times 180 = \mathbf{123.2}$ (better)
  SLOW: $0.71 \times 80 + 0.00 \times 150 + 0.29 \times 210 = 117.7$
- Result C: QUICK: $0.20 \times 100 + 0.57 \times 130 + 0.23 \times 180 = 135.5$
  SLOW: $0.20 \times 80 + 0.57 \times 150 + 0.23 \times 210 = \mathbf{149.8}$ (better)

The best policy is to develop the field slowly with test result A or C, and develop it quickly with test result B. As the probabilities of test results A, B and C are 0.39, 0.17 and 0.44 respectively, the overall expected profit is:

$$0.39 \times 141.7 + 0.17 \times 123.2 + 0.44 \times 149.8 = 142.12$$

The profit without doing further tests is $141 million, while doing the tests raises it to $142.12 minus the cost of $2.5 million, leaving $139.62. Clearly it is not worth doing the tests, and would not be worth doing them unless their cost is less than $1.12 million.

Utilities

Although they give useful results, expected values do have some drawbacks. In particular, they do not always reflect real preferences, as you can see in this payoff matrix:

Alternative	Event	
	gain	lose
	P = 0.1	P = 0.9
invest	£500,000	−£50,000
do not invest	£0	£0

The expected values are:

- Invest: $0.1 \times 500,000 - 0.9 \times 50,000 = £5,000$
- Do not invest: $0.1 \times 0 + 0.9 \times 0 = £0$

Expected values suggest investing – but there is a 90% chance of losing money. The expected value shows the average return when a decision is repeated many times, but it does not show the value for a single decision, so its advice can be misleading. In this example, if you repeat the decision many times you will, on average, gain £5,000 – but if you make only one decision you are likely to lose £50,000. With a single decision most people would choose not to invest.

Another weakness with expected values is that they assume a linear relationship between the amount of money and the value that managers place on it. So €1,000 is assumed to have a value 1,000 times as great as €1, and €1,000,000 has a value 1,000 times as great as €1,000. In practice, people do not see such a rigid linear relationship. For instance, many people are happy to spend £5 a week on lottery tickets, but would consider a bill of £20 a month too expensive. You hear the same effect with advertisements that say, 'It only costs 30 pence a day' because this seems much cheaper than £110 a year. And when someone is negotiating to buy a house they may increase their offer by £5,000 and consider it a relatively small amount. The same person might walk to another shop to save €3 when buying a DVD, but would not walk to another shop to save €3 when buying a television to view it.

The relationship between an amount of money and its perceived value is more complex that it initially seems. Utilities try to give a more accurate view of this relationship. For example, Figure 16.3 shows a utility function with three distinct regions. At the top, near point A, the utility is rising slowly with the amount of money. A decision-maker in this region already has a lot of money and would not put a high value on even more. However, the decision-maker would certainly not like to lose money and move nearer to point B where the utility falls rapidly. Gaining more money is not very attractive, but losing it is very unattractive – so this suggests a conservative decision-maker who does not take risks.

Region B on the graph has the utility of money almost linear, which is the assumption of expected values. A decision-maker here is likely to look for a balance of risk and benefit. Finally, a decision-maker at point C has little

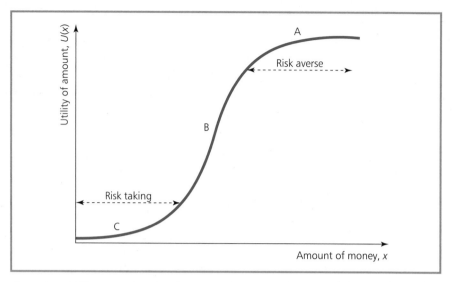

Figure 16.3 Utility curve showing the value of money

money, so losing some would not appreciably affect their utility. On the other hand, any gain in money would move nearer to B and have a high value. A decision-maker here is keen to make a gain and does not unduly mind a loss – which suggests a risk-taker.

Utilities are useful in principle, but the obvious problem is defining a reasonable function that describes the shape of the curve. Each individual and organisation has a different view of the value of money and works with a different utility function. And these curves change quickly over time – so you might feel confident and risk-taking in the morning and conservative and risk-averse in the afternoon. In principle, though, when we can establish a reasonable utility function, the process of choosing the best alternative is the same as with expected values, but replacing the expected values by expected utilities.

WORKED EXAMPLE 16.9

Mahendra Musingh's utility curve is a reasonable approximation to $\sqrt{x}$. What is his best decision with this gains matrix?

	Event		
	X	Y	Z
Alternative	P = 0.7	P = 0.2	P = 0.1
A	14	24	12
B	6	40	90
C	1	70	30
D	12	12	6

Solution

The calculations are similar to those for expected values, except that the amount of money, x, is replaced by its utility, which in this case is $\sqrt{x}$.

- Alternative A: $0.7 \times \sqrt{14} + 0.2 \times \sqrt{24} + 0.1 \times \sqrt{12} = 3.95$ (best)
- Alternative B: $0.7 \times \sqrt{6} + 0.2 \times \sqrt{40} + 0.1 \times \sqrt{90} = 3.93$
- Alternative C: $0.7 \times \sqrt{1} + 0.2 \times \sqrt{70} + 0.1 \times \sqrt{30} = 2.92$
- Alternative D: $0.7 \times \sqrt{12} + 0.2 \times \sqrt{12} + 0.1 \times \sqrt{6} = 3.36$

Although the difference is small, the best alternative is A. You can compare this with the expected values, which are 15.8, 21.2, 17.7 and 11.4 respectively, suggesting that alternative B is the best.

16.10 What is 'decision making with risk'?

16.11 What is the expected value of a course of action?

16.12 Could you use subjective probabilities for events under risk?

16.13 When can you use Bayes' theorem to calculate expected values?

16.14 Why might expected utilities be better than expected values?

Sequential decisions

Often managers are not concerned with a single decision, but they have to consider a series of related decisions. For example, when you buy a car your initial decision might be to choose a new one or a second-hand one. If you choose a new car this opens the choice of Japanese, French, German, Italian etc. If you choose a Japanese car you then have a choice of Toyota, Nissan, Mitsubishi, Honda and so on. If you choose a Toyota you then have a choice of models and then a choice of options. At each stage, choosing one alternative opens up a series of other choices – or sometimes it opens up a series of events that might occur. We can describe such problems in a decision tree, where the branches of a horizontal tree represent alternatives and events.

WORKED EXAMPLE 16.10

Patrick O'Doyle asked his bank for a loan to expand his company. The bank managers have to decide whether or not to grant the loan. If they grant the loan, Patrick's expansion may be successful or it may be unsuccessful. If the bank managers do not grant the loan, Patrick may continue banking as before, or he may move his account to another bank. Draw a decision tree of this situation.

Solution

A decision tree shows the sequence of alternatives and events. There is a notional time scale going from left to right with early decisions, or events on the left followed by later ones towards the right. There is only one decision in this example followed by events over which the bank managers have no control, so the sequence is:

1 The managers make a decision either to grant Patrick's loan or not.
2 If they grant the loan, the expansion may be successful or unsuccessful.
3 If they do not grant the loan, Patrick may continue or he may move his account.

Figure 16.4 shows these in a basic decision tree.

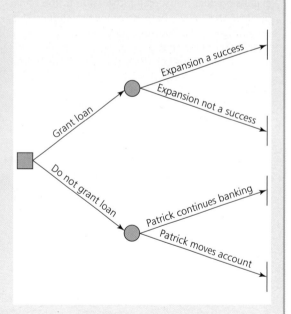

Figure 16.4 Decision tree for Patrick O'Doyle (Worked example 16.10)

In Worked example 16.10, we drew the alternatives and events as the branches of a tree with each branch opening a different path that may be followed through the tree. There are three types of nodes, which are the points between or at the ends of branches.

| Terminal nodes are at the right-hand side of the tree, and are the ends of all sequences of decisions and events.
○ Random nodes represent points at which things happen, so that branches leaving a random node are events with known probabilities.
□ Decision nodes represent points at which decisions are made, so that branches leaving a decision node are alternatives.

We now have the basic structure of a tree, and the next stage is to add the probabilities and outcomes.

WORKED EXAMPLE 16.11

Continuing the problem in Worked example 16.10, and suppose that Patrick O'Doyle's bank currently values his business at €20,000 a year. If the manager grants the loan and the expansion succeeds, the value to the bank of increased business and interest charges is €30,000 a year. If the expansion does not succeed, the value to the bank declines to €10,000, because of lower volumes and an allowance writing-off bad debt. There is a probability of 0.7 that the expansion plan will succeed. If the manager does not grant the loan, there is a probability of 0.6 that Patrick will transfer his account to another bank.

Solution

We can add this extra information to our decision tree. Figure 16.5 shows the probabilities added to event branches, making sure that all events are included and the sum of the probabilities from each random node is 1. It also has values on the terminal nodes, giving the total value (in this case the annual business expected by the bank) of moving through the tree and reaching the terminal node. This completes the drawing of the tree.

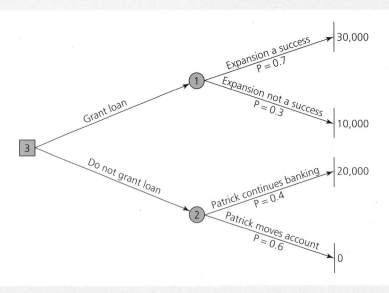

Figure 16.5 Decision tree with added probabilities and terminal values (Worked example 16.11)

Having drawn a decision tree, the next step is to analyse it, moving from right to left and putting a value on each node in turn. We do this by identifying the best decision at each decision node and calculating the expected value at each random node.

- *At each decision node* – alternative branches leaving are connected to following nodes. We compare the values on these following nodes, and identify the best – which shows the branch we should choose to move along. Then we transfer the value from the best following node to this decision node.
- *At each random node* – we find the expected value of following events. So for each branch we find the probability of leaving down the branch, and multiply this by the value of the following node. Adding these together for all branches from the random node gives its expected value.

Following this procedure from right to left through a tree, we eventually get back to the originating node, and the value on this is the overall expected value of making the best decisions.

WORKED EXAMPLE 16.12

Analyse the problem tree for Patrick O'Doyle's bank loan in Worked example 16.11.

Solution
Figure 16.6 shows the node values added to the tree. The calculations for this are:

- At random node 1, calculate the expected value:

  $0.7 \times 30,000 + 0.3 \times 10,000 = 24,000$

- At random node 2, calculate the expected value:

  $0.4 \times 20,000 + 0.6 \times 0 = 8,000$

- At decision node 3, select the best alternative:

  $\max[24,000, 8,000] = 24,000$

The best decision for the bank is to grant Patrick a loan, and this gives them an expected value of €24,000.

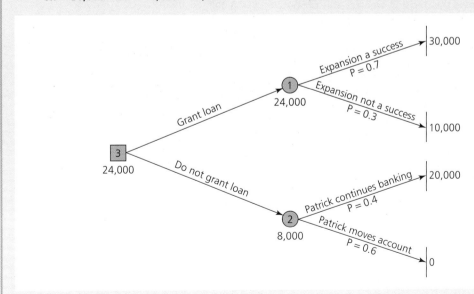

Figure 16.6 Analysing the decision tree – Worked example 16.12

WORKED EXAMPLE 16.13

Lars Van Hoek is about to install a new machine for making parts for domestic appliances. Three suppliers have made bids to supply the machine. The first supplier offers the Basicor machine, which automatically produces parts of acceptable, but not outstanding, quality. The output from the machine varies (depending on the materials used and a variety of settings) and might be 1,000 a week (with probability 0.1), 2,000 a week (with probability 0.7) or 3,000 a week. The notional profit for this machine is €4 a unit. The second supplier offers a Superstamp machine, which makes higher quality parts. The output from this might be 700 a week (with probability 0.4) or 1,000 a week, with a notional profit of €10 a unit. The third supplier offers the Switchover machine, which managers can set to produce either 1,300 high-quality parts a week at a profit of €6 a unit, or 1,600 medium-quality parts a week with a profit of €5 a unit.

If the chosen machine produces 2,000 or more units a week, Lars can export all production as a single bulk order. Then there is a 60% chance of selling this order for 50% more profit, and a 40% chance of selling for 50% less profit.

What should Lars do to maximise the expected profit?

Solution

Figure 16.7 shows the decision tree for this problem. Here the terminal node shows the weekly profit, found by multiplying the number of units produced by the profit per unit. If 1,000 are produced on the Basicor machine the profit is €4 a unit, giving a node value of €4,000 and so on. When the output from Basicor is exported profit may be increased by 50% (that is to €6 a unit) or reduced by 50% (to €2 a unit). Then the calculations at nodes are:

- Node 1: expected value at random node

  = 0.6 × 12,000 + 0.4 × 4,000
  = 8,800

- Node 2: expected value at random node

  = 0.6 × 18,000 + 0.4 × 6,000
  = 13,200

- Node 3: best alternative at decision node

  = maximum of 8,800 and 8,000
  = 8,800

- Node 4: best alternative at decision node

  = maximum of 13,200 and 12,000
  = 13,200

- Node 5: expected value at random node

  = 0.1 × 4,000 + 0.7 × 8,800 + 0.2 × 13,200
  = 9,200

- Node 6: expected value at random node

  = 0.4 × 7,000 + 0.6 × 10,000
  = 8,800

- Node 7: best alternative at decision node

  = maximum of 7,800 and 8,000
  = 8,000

- Node 8: best alternative at decision node

  = maximum of 9,200, 8,800 and 8,000
  = 9,200

The best decisions are to buy the Basicor machine and, if it produces more than 2,000 units, to export all production. The expected profit from this policy is €9,200 a week.

Worked example 16.13 continued

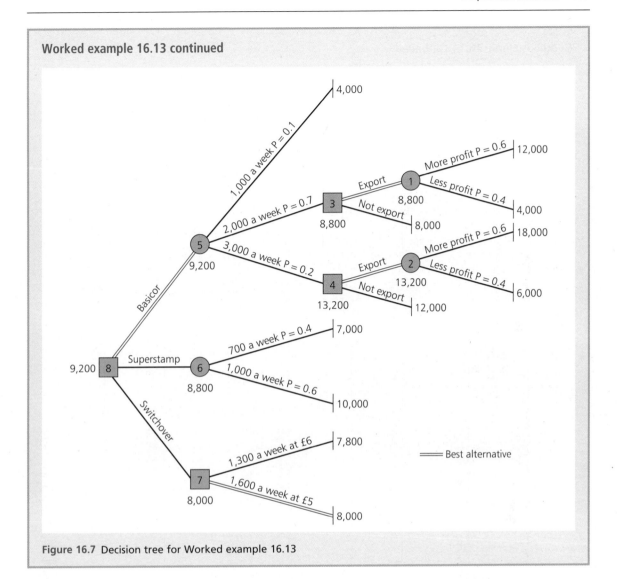

Figure 16.7 Decision tree for Worked example 16.13

WORKED EXAMPLE 16.14

Draw a decision tree for the problem of planning a sports event described in Worked example 16.7.

Solution
You can get specialised software for drawing decision trees that ranges from simple tools to do the calculations, through spreadsheet add-ins to sophisticated analysis packages. Figure 16.8 shows the results from one package as a sketch of the decision tree. Figure 16.9 shows the results from a package that simply organises the calculations in a spreadsheet. Both of these confirm our expected value of £22,710 advanced sales information.

Worked example 16.14 continued

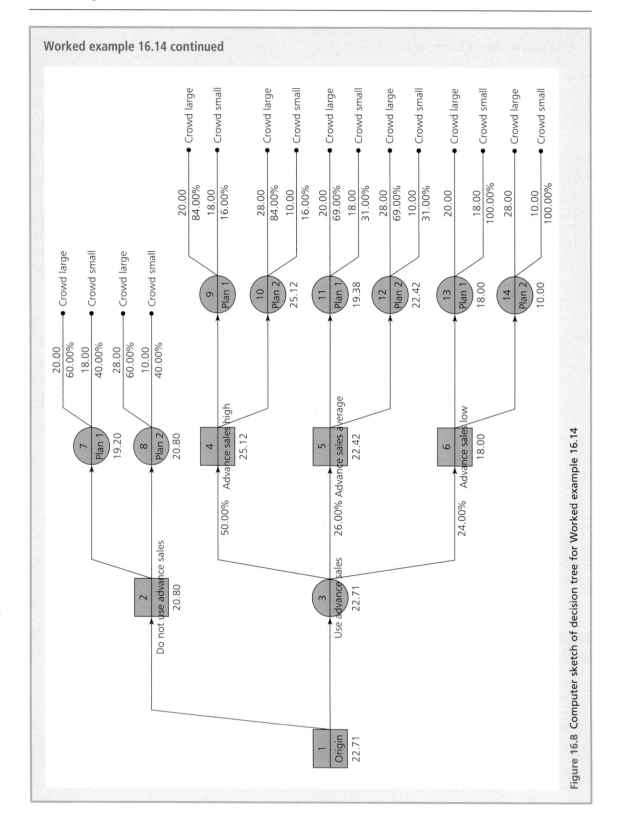

Figure 16.8 Computer sketch of decision tree for Worked example 16.14

Worked example 16.14 continued

	A	B	C	D	E	F	G
1	**Decision tree for organising a sports event**						
2							
3	Node #	**Node name**	**Type**	**Following**	**Probability**	**Expected value**	**Decision**
4	1	Origin	Decision	2,3		22.71	Use advance sales
5	2	Do not use advance sales	Decision	7,8		20.80	Plan 2
6	3	Use advance sales	Chance	4,5,6		22.71	
7	4	Advance sales high	Decision	9,10	0.50	25.12	Plan 2
8	5	Advance sales average	Decision	11,12	0.26	22.42	Plan 2
9	6	Advance sales low	Decision	13,14	0.24	18.00	Plan 1
10	7	Plan 1	Chance	15,16		19.20	
11	8	Plan 2	Chance	17,18		20.80	
12	9	Plan 1	Chance	19,20		19.68	
13	10	Plan 2	Chance	21,22		25.12	
14	11	Plan 1	Chance	23,24		19.38	
15	12	Plan 2	Chance	25,26		22.42	
16	13	Plan 1	Chance	27,28		18.00	
17	14	Plan 2	Chance	29,30		10.00	
18	15	Crowd large			0.60	20.00	
19	16	Crowd small			0.40	18.00	
20	17	Crowd large			0.60	28.00	
21	18	Crowd small			0.40	10.00	
22	19	Crowd large			0.84	20.00	
23	20	Crowd small			0.16	18.00	
24	21	Crowd large			0.84	28.00	
25	22	Crowd small			0.16	10.00	
26	23	Crowd large			0.69	20.00	
27	24	Crowd small			0.31	18.00	
28	25	Crowd large			0.69	28.00	
29	26	Crowd small			0.31	10.00	
30	27	Crowd large			0.00	20.00	
31	28	Crowd small			1.00	18.00	
32	29	Crowd large			0.00	28.00	
33	30	Crowd small			1.00	10.00	
34	31	Overall				22.71	

Figure 16.9 Calculations for the decision tree

Review questions

16.15 How do you calculate the node value at a terminal node, a decision node and a random node?

16.16 How do you find the expected value of following the best options in a decision tree?

Yield management in airlines

Yield management includes different types of analysis for allocating scarce resources to different types of customers. It is most common in airlines and hotels, where it is said to have brought significant benefits – for example, early work by American Airlines in the 1990s increased revenue by $500 million a year,[1] Delta Airlines generated an additional $300 million[2] and Marriott Hotels generated an extra $100 million.

For airlines, there are two key issues in yield management. The first is overbooking, where airlines forecast the number of people who book seats but then cancel or do not turn up for the flight – and then they overbook this number of seats. In effect, they sell more seats than are available on a flight, in the belief that some passengers will not turn up. This increases revenue but airlines have to juggle numbers carefully so that they do not have more people turn up than the aircraft will hold – or at least, they do not do this too often.

The second issue is the allocation of seats to different types of passengers. You can imagine this with the decision to sell a seat at a discount. Suppose the airline has a scheduled flight in several months' time and it receives a request for a discount seat. The airline has to balance the certainty of getting some cash now, with the expected value of waiting and seeing if they can sell the seat later at a higher price. Then the airline sells a seat at a discount only when the discounted price is greater than the expected value from selling the seat later. There are many types of passengers and fare offers, so this is not such a straightforward decision. And the probability of selling a seat changes right up to the point of filling the aircraft, so the calculations are continually updated. Sometimes when you leave buying a ticket until the last minute you get a bargain (suggesting that the airline is unlikely to sell the seat for a higher price) – and sometimes you have to pay a supplement (when many people are still wanting to buy tickets).

CHAPTER REVIEW

This chapter showed how managers can approach decisions, describing the foundations of decision analysis.

- Managers make decisions in complex situations. These decisions are easier when the problems are well-structured and presented in standard formats.
- Problem maps give a useful way of adding structure for decisions. Alternatives are given by payoff matrices and decision trees.
- The main elements of a decision are a decision-maker, their aims, alternatives they can choose, events that happen and outcomes for each combination of chosen alternative and uncontrolled events.
- With decision making under certainty there is only one event. In principle these are easy because managers compare outcomes and choose the alternative that gives the best result. In practice, they are considerably more difficult.
- With decision making under uncertainty there are several possible events, but we do not know which will occur and cannot even give them probabilities. The usual way of tackling these problems is to use decision criteria. We illustrated these with Laplace, Wald and Savage criteria, but there are many others for different circumstances.
- With decision making under risk there are several possible events, and we can give each a probability. The usual analysis finds an expected value for the combination of alternatives, which is:

$$\Sigma(\text{probability of event occurring} \times \text{outcome})$$

- Expected values may not reflect real preferences, and in principle it is better to use expected utilities.

- One decision often leads to a series of others. You can draw sequential decisions on a decision tree, where branches show the events and alternatives that follow each node. To analyse the tree you choose the best alternative at a decision node and calculate the expected value at a random node.

CASE STUDY   The Newisham Reservoir

Newisham has a population of about 30,000. It traditionally got its water supply from the nearby River Feltham but increasing quantities of water were being extracted from the river by industry upstream. When the flow reaching the Newisham water treatment works became too small to supply the town's needs, the council decided to build a reservoir by damming the Feltham and diverting tributaries. This work was finished in 2002 and gave a guaranteed supply of water to the town.

Unfortunately, the dam reduced the amount of water available to farmers downstream, and two of them recently found the water supply to their cattle had effectively dried up. The farmers now face the option of either connecting to the local mains water supply at a cost of £44,000 or drilling a new well. The drilling company cannot give an exact cost for the work but suggest guidelines of £32,000 (with a probability of 0.3), £44,000 (with a probability of 0.3) or £56,000, depending on the underground rock structure and depth of water.

A local water survey company can do some more onsite tests. For a cost of £600 they will give either a favourable or an unfavourable report on the chances of easily finding water. The reliability of this report (phrased in terms of the probability of a favourable report, given that the drilling cost will be low etc.) is given in this table:

	Drilling well cost		
	£32,000	£44,000	£56,000
Favourable report	0.8	0.6	0.2
Unfavourable report	0.2	0.4	0.8

Questions

- What would a decision tree of the farmers' problem look like?

- What are their best choices and expected costs?

PROBLEMS

16.1 O'Brian's pub on the seafront at Blackpool notices that its profits are falling. The landlord has a number of alternatives for increasing his profits (attracting more customers, increasing prices, getting customers to spend more etc.) but each of these leads to a string of other effects. Draw a map showing the interactions for this situation.

16.2 Choose the best alternative in the following matrix of gains.

Event	Gain
A	100
B	950
C	−250
D	0
E	950
F	500

```
                    -=*=-  INFORMATION ENTERED   -=*=-
NUMBER OF STATES:                    5
NUMBER OF ALTERNATIVES:              5
NUMBER OF CRITERIA CHOSEN:           5
HURWICZ COEFFICIENT:                 0.3

                        PAYOFF TABLE

                VALUE OF EACH ALTERNATIVE
                1        2        3        4        5
     1        1.00     5.00     9.00     2.00     6.00
     2        3.00     7.00     3.00     5.00     1.00
     3        6.00     4.00     4.00     6.00     8.00
     4        8.00     2.00     7.00     5.00     6.00
     5        6.00     9.00     4.00     1.00     2.00

                    -=*=-  RESULTS  -=*=-

CRITERION                 ALTERNATIVE        PAYOFF
1. MAXIMAX                    A2              9.00
2. MINIMIN                    A3              3.00
3. LIKELIHOOD                 A2              5.40
4. MINIMAX REGRET             A3              5.00
5. HURWICZ RULE              A3              4.80

--------------------------------  END  OF  ANALYSIS  ------------------------------
```

Figure 16.10 Computer printout for decision criteria in Problem 16.4

16.3 Use the Laplace, Wald and Savage decision criteria to select alternatives in the following matrices. What results would you get for other decision criteria?

(a) Cost matrix

Alternative	Event				
	1	2	3	4	5
A	100	70	115	95	60
B	95	120	120	90	150
C	180	130	60	160	120
D	80	75	50	100	95
E	60	140	100	170	160

(b) Gains matrix

Alternative	Event			
	1	2	3	4
A	1	6	3	7
B	2	5	1	4
C	8	1	4	2
D	5	2	7	8

16.4 Figure 16.10 shows a printout from a program which does the calculations for decision criteria. Describe the criteria that it uses and design your own spreadsheet to check the results. What results would other criteria give?

16.5 Which is the best alternative in the following gains matrix? Would this decision change using a utility function $U(x) = \sqrt{x}$?

Alternative	Event		
	1	2	3
	P = 0.4	P = 0.3	P = 0.3
A	100	90	120
B	80	102	110

16.6 GKR WebSpace can launch one of three versions of a new product, X, Y or Z. The profit depends on market reaction and there is a 30% chance that this will be good, a 40% chance it will be medium and a 30% chance it will be poor. Which version should the company launch with the profits given in the following table?

	Market reaction		
Version	good	medium	poor
X	100	110	80
Y	70	90	120
Z	130	100	70

The company can do another survey to give more information about market reaction. Experience suggests that these surveys give results A, B or C with probabilities P(A/Good), P(A/Medium) etc., shown in the following table.

	Result		
Market reaction	A	B	C
good	0.2	0.2	0.6
medium	0.2	0.5	0.3
poor	0.4	0.3	0.3

How much should the company pay for this survey?

16.7 Schwartz Transport owns a lorry with a one-year-old engine. It has to decide whether or not to replace the engine at a cost of €2,000. If it does not replace the engine, there is an increased chance that it will break down during the year and the cost of an emergency replacement is €3,200. Then at the end of next year, the company again has to decide whether to replace the engine or not. When an engine is replaced any time during the year, it is assumed to be one year old at the end of the year. The probabilities that an engine breaks down during the next year are as follows:

	Age of engine		
	0	1	2
Probability of breakdown	0.0	0.2	0.7

Draw a decision tree for this problem, and find the decisions that minimise the total cost over the next two years. If a three-year-old engine is virtually certain to break down sometime in the

next year, what is the minimum expected cost over three years?

16.8 Wilshaw Associates is considering launching an entirely new service. If the market reaction to this service is good (which has a probability of 0.2) they will make $30,000 a month; if market reaction is medium (with probability 0.5) they will make $10,000; and if reaction is poor (with probability 0.3) they will lose $15,000 a month. Wilshaw can run a survey to test market reaction with results A, B or C. Experience suggests that the reliability of such surveys is described by the following matrix of P(A/good), P(A/medium), etc. Use a decision tree to find the most that Wilshaw should pay for this survey.

	Results		
Market reaction	A	B	C
good	0.7	0.2	0.1
medium	0.2	0.6	0.2
poor	0.1	0.4	0.5

16.9 A television company has an option on a new six-part series. They could sell the rights to this series to the network for £100,000 or they could make the series themselves. If they make the series themselves, advertising profit from each episode is not known exactly but could be £15,000 (with a probability of 0.25), £24,000 (with a probability of 0.45) or £29,000, depending on the success of the series.

A local production company can make a pilot for the series. For a cost of £30,000 they will give either a favourable or an unfavourable report on the chances of the series being a success. The reliability of their report (phrased in terms of the probability of a favourable report, given the likely advertising profit etc.) is given in the following table. What should the television company do?

	Advertising profit		
	£15,000	£24,000	£29,000
Unfavourable report	0.85	0.65	0.3
Favourable report	0.15	0.35	0.7

RESEARCH PROJECTS

16.1 We have described several formats for presenting decisions – problem maps, payoff matrices and decision trees. But these are not the only options. What other formats are available? Find some examples where different formats have been used in practice.

16.2 Some software packages – or special add-ins for spreadsheets – draw decision trees automatically. Do a small survey to see what features these contain.

You can also draw a decision tree on a standard spreadsheet, as illustrated in Figure 16.11. This uses the DRAW options for

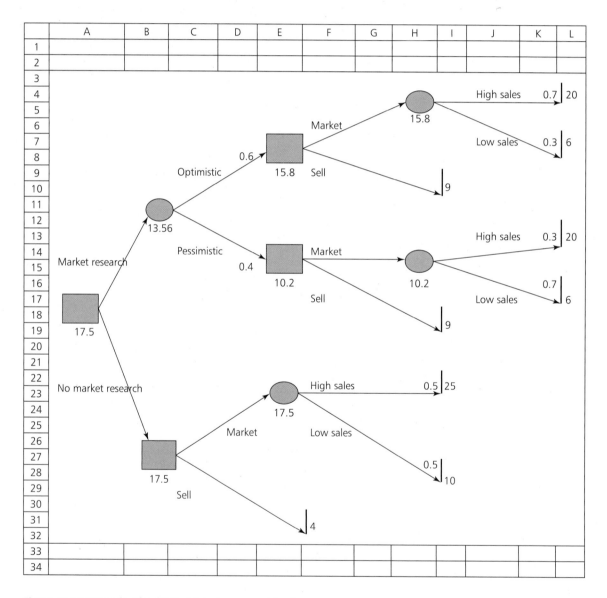

Figure 16.11 Example of a decision tree in a spreadsheet

drawing the skeleton of the tree, with calculations described in appropriate cells using normal spreadsheet functions. In particular, the MAX function identifies the best alternatives at a decision node and expected values are calculated as usual at random nodes. A useful tool here is the GOAL SEEK function, which you can use to find the probabilities needed to achieve a specific return. See how this works and explore the possibilities it offers.

Sources of information

References

1 Smith B.C., Leimkuhler J.F. and Darrow R.M., Yield management at American Airlines, *Interfaces*, Vol. 22(1), 1992.

2 Boyd A., Airline alliance revenue management, *OR/MS Today*, Vol. 25, 1998.

Further reading

Material in this section is covered in books on management science, operational research and operations management. The following list includes more specialised books on decision analysis.

Clemen R.T. and Reilly T., *Making Hard Decisions*, Cengage Learning, Florence, KY, 2005.

Daellenbach H.G. and McNickle D., *Decision Making through Systems Thinking*, Palgrave Macmillan, Basingstoke, 200.

Edwards W., Miles R.F. and Winterfeldt D., *Advances in Decision Analysis*, Cambridge University Press, Cambridge, 2007.

Golub A.L., *Decision Analysis*, John Wiley, New York, 1997.

Goodwin P. and Wright G., *Decision Analysis for Management Judgement* (4th edition), John Wiley, Chichester, 2009.

Keeney R.L. and Raiffa H., *Decisions with Multiple Objectives*, Cambridge University Press, Cambridge, 1993.

Moore J.H. and Weatherford L.R., *Decision Modelling with Microsoft Excel* (6th edition), Prentice Hall, Upper Saddle River, NJ, 2001.

Ragsdale C., *Managerial Decision Modelling* (6th edition), South-Western College Publishing, Cincinnati, OH, 2011.

Steinhouse R., *Brilliant Decision Making*, Prentice Hall., New York, 2010.

Winston W.L. and Albright S., *Spreadsheet Modelling and Applications*, Brooks Cole, Florence, KY, 2004.

CHAPTER 17

Quality management

Chapter outline

'Quality' describes how good a product is. A high-quality product meets, and preferably exceeds, the requirements of both customers and producers, while a low-quality product is in some way deficient. The broad function that is responsible for all aspects of quality is generally described as *quality management*. The fundamental problem for quality management is that some variation is inevitable in a product. Then managers have to use a range of tools to reduce the variation and make products that are of consistently high quality.

After finishing this chapter you should be able to:

- discuss the meaning of quality and appreciate its importance
- describe the costs of quality management
- review the principles of Total Quality Management (TQM)
- see how quality control forms part of the broader quality management function
- discuss the variation in a process and the need to control it
- describe some key tools of quality control
- design sampling plans for acceptance sampling
- draw process control charts.

Measuring quality

The first problem when talking about quality management is defining exactly what we mean by 'quality'. You might start with your own experiences and say that you are happy with the quality of, say, a pen when it writes easily and clearly; you think an airline gives a high-quality service when you get to your destination on time and without too much hassle; an electricity supplier gives high quality if you never have to worry about supplies or costs. So we can suggest a fairly obvious statement that customers view products as having high quality if they do the jobs they were designed for.

> In its broadest sense, **quality** is the ability of a product to meet – and preferably exceed – customer expectations.

But this definition is still vague because it offers no direct measures of quality and cannot give a clear view when different customers have different expectations. With any product, each customer might judge quality by a number of different criteria, putting different emphases on innate excellence, fitness for intended use, performance, reliability, durability, features, level of technology, conformance to design specifications, uniformity, status, convenience of use, attractive appearance, value, after-sales service, on-time delivery and so on. When you look at a television you might judge its quality by how expensive it is, how big it is, how easy it is to use, how clear the picture is, the technology it uses, how often it needs repairing, how long it will last, how many channels it can pick up, how good the sound is and the additional features it has. But someone else will judge it by a different set of criteria.

Even a basic definition of quality is difficult but we avoid this by bundling criteria together and talking about a general concept of 'customer satisfaction'. A high-quality product gives general customer satisfaction; a low-quality product does not. What this really means is that most – or at least enough – customers are satisfied with the product because it meets their specific requirements.

One important observation about customers' requirements is that they rarely demand products with the highest possible technical quality. Instead they look for some balance of features that gives an acceptable overall picture. For instance, a Rolls-Royce car has the highest possible quality of engineering, but most people include price in their judgement and buy a cheaper make; champagne may be the highest quality wine, but most of us normally buy other types.

You also have to remember that as well as satisfying customers, products have to help in achieving the aims of the producers. No company would supply products that gave high customers satisfaction if they made a loss on every unit sold. So quality also has an internal aspect, where a product has to meet the requirements of the producer. We can use this distinction to suggest two views of quality:

■ Designed quality is the quality that a product is designed to have. This takes an external view, sees what features customers want, designs a product to supply these features and judges quality by how well the product actually satisfies customers. So for example, a bar of chocolate is high quality if it has a taste that customers want, satisfies their hunger etc.
■ Achieved quality takes an internal view and sees how closely the product actually made conforms to its design specifications. So a bar of chocolate is high quality if it is close to the specified weight, contains the right amount of cocoa and so on.

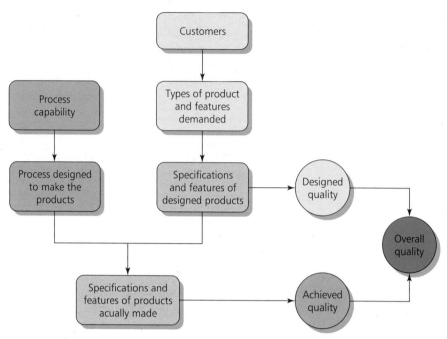

Figure 17.1 Designed, achieved and overall quality

An airline that aims at having 98% of its flights arrive on time has a high designed quality; if only 30% of flights are actually on time then its achieved quality is much lower. A satisfactory product needs both high designed and high achieved quality, as shown in Figure 17.1.

Quality management

All decisions about quality in an organisation are brought together under the general heading of quality management.

> **Quality management** is the broad function responsible for all aspects of a product's quality.

It is easy to see why organisations have to make high-quality products. If they make poor products customers do not buy them and simply move to a competitor who is better at meeting their expectations. If you buy a pair of shoes that get a hole the first time you wear them, you will not buy another pair from that source, no matter how cheap they are. So making high-quality products is the only way that an organisation can survive in the long term. And while high-quality products may not guarantee a firm's success, low-quality ones will certainly guarantee its failure.

The question, of course, is how to achieve high quality. We can begin answering this by looking at what happens when you go into a clothes shop to buy a suit. You will be satisfied only if the suit is well-designed, if it is well-made, if there are no faults in the material, if the price is reasonable, if the salesperson is helpful, if the shop is pleasant and so on. In other words, everyone involved with supplying the suit – from the person who designs it to the person who sells it, and from the person who owns the organisation to the person who keeps it clean – is directly involved in the quality of their product. If even a single person does something that the customers do not like, it is enough to make customers look for other suppliers. This is the view taken by Total Quality Management (TQM).

> ■ **Total Quality Management** has the whole organisation working together to guarantee – and systematically improve – quality.
> ■ The aim of TQM is to satisfy customers by making products with no defects.
> ■ A defect is any aspect of the product that reduces customer satisfaction.

In recent years there have been so many developments in quality management that some people refer to a 'quality revolution'. This happened for four main reasons:

■ Improved operations can make products with guaranteed high quality.
■ Producers use high quality to get a competitive advantage.
■ Consumers have become used to high-quality products and will not accept anything less.
■ High quality reduces costs.

The first three of these are fairly obvious, and move firms towards higher quality. But the view that high quality reduces costs seems to go against the commonsense view that you can only buy higher-quality products at a higher price. But if you look at the costs more carefully you see that some really do go down with higher quality.

Costs of quality

Imagine that you buy a washing machine and when it is delivered you find that it is faulty. You complain and the manufacturer arranges for the machine to be repaired. The manufacturer could have saved money by finding the fault before the machine left the factory – and it could have saved even more by making a machine that did not have a fault in the first place. If, say, 5% of machines are faulty then the manufacturer has to increase production by 5% just to cover the defects, and it has to maintain systems for dealing with customer complaints, collecting defective machines, inspecting, repairing or replacing them and returning them to customers. By eliminating the defects the manufacturer increases productivity, reduces costs, eliminates customer complaints and removes all the systems needed to correct faults.

Of course, some costs must rise with increasing quality, and to consider these we separate the total cost of quality into four components.

■ **Prevention costs** are the costs of preventing defects happening. These include direct costs spent on the product, such the use of better materials, adding extra features and extra time to make the product. They also include indirect costs of employee training, pilot runs, testing prototypes, designing and maintaining control systems, improvement projects etc. All things being equal, prevention costs rise with the quality of the product.

- Appraisal costs are the costs of making sure the designed quality is actually achieved. These costs include sampling, inspecting, testing, checking and all the other elements of quality control. Generally, the more effort that is put into quality control, the higher is the final quality of the product – and the higher the costs of achieving this.
- Internal failure costs are the costs of making defective products that are detected somewhere within the production process. This includes allowances for units that are scrapped, returned to an earlier point in the process or repaired. Part of the internal failure costs come directly from the loss of material, wasted labour, wasted machine time in making the defective item, extra testing, duplicated effort and so on. Another part comes from the indirect costs of higher stock levels, longer lead times, extra capacity needed to allow for scrap and rejections, loss of confidence etc. Internal failure costs generally decline with increasing quality.
- External failure costs are the costs of having a unit go through the entire production process and being delivered to a customer, who then finds a fault. External failure faults are usually the highest costs of quality management and are the ones that you should avoid. Again, external failure costs generally decline with higher quality.

Adding together these four components gives the total cost of quality – the result is often surprisingly high. Failure costs are particularly high and as they fall with increasing quality we get the pattern shown in Figure 17.2. This suggests that the lowest total cost comes with products of perfect quality. So a firm can minimise its costs by ensuring that every unit it makes it guaranteed to be fault-free.

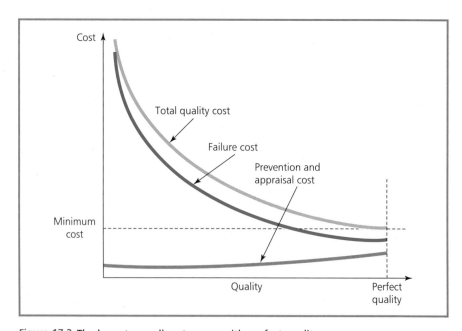

Figure 17.2 The lowest overall cost comes with perfect quality

WORKED EXAMPLE 17.1

Ying Shu Tang recorded her company's costs (in thousands of dollars a year) during a period when they introduced a new quality management programme. How effective do you think the new programme has been?

Year		−3	−2	−1	0	1	2	3
Sales value		1,225	1,247	1,186	1,150	1,456	1,775	1,865
Costs	Prevention	7.3	8.1	9.1	26.8	30.6	32.9	35.2
	Appraisal	27.6	16.9	20.1	47.4	59.7	59.6	65.5
	Internal failure	72.8	71.9	75.0	40.3	24.0	20.0	19.4
	External failure	66.5	59.9	65.8	27.3	18.8	15.6	12.5

Solution

The best way of judging the quality management programme is to calculate the total cost of quality as a percentage of sales. The results for this are shown in the spreadsheet in Figure 17.3.

The quality management programme was introduced in year zero. This put more emphasis on prevention and appraisal, where costs have risen. Product quality has clearly risen, giving lower failure costs. Customers have apparently noticed the improvement, with sales no longer falling but rising sharply. Overall, quality costs have fallen and sales have risen, so we must judge the programme a success.

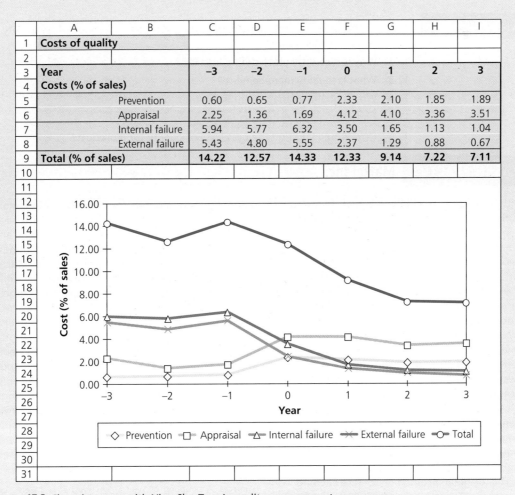

	A	B	C	D	E	F	G	H	I
1	**Costs of quality**								
2									
3	**Year**		**−3**	**−2**	**−1**	**0**	**1**	**2**	**3**
4	**Costs (% of sales)**								
5		Prevention	0.60	0.65	0.77	2.33	2.10	1.85	1.89
6		Appraisal	2.25	1.36	1.69	4.12	4.10	3.36	3.51
7		Internal failure	5.94	5.77	6.32	3.50	1.65	1.13	1.04
8		External failure	5.43	4.80	5.55	2.37	1.29	0.88	0.67
9	**Total (% of sales)**		**14.22**	**12.57**	**14.33**	**12.33**	**9.14**	**7.22**	**7.11**
10									

Figure 17.3 Changing costs with Ying Shu Tang's quality management programme

'Quality gurus'

Many people have contributed to the growth of quality management, and a group of them have become known as the 'quality gurus'. Different people claim to be in this group, but the main members are:

- *Edwards Deming*[1] – emphasised the role of management in setting quality and the importance of reducing variability in the process.
- *Armand Fiegenbaum*[2] – looked at failure costs and developed the idea of 'total quality' involving everyone in the organisation.
- *Joseph Juran*[3] – emphasised the role of senior management and the definition of good quality as satisfying customer demand.
- *Philip Crosby*[4] – analysed the total costs of quality and described straightforward methods for implementing quality management.
- *Genichi Taguchi*[5] – showed the importance of product designs that allow high quality with suitable control of the process.
- *Kaoru Ishikawa*[6] – emphasised the contribution of 'workers' to quality and introduced the idea of quality circles.

Review questions	
	17.1 'If the price is right, people will buy a product regardless of its quality.' Do you think this is true?
	17.2 Why is it so difficult to define 'quality'?
	17.3 What is 'quality management'?
	17.4 Why is quality management important to an organisation?
	17.5 Higher quality inevitably comes at a higher cost. Is this true?
	17.6 How would you find the best level of quality for a product?

IDEAS IN PRACTICE   Mattel Inc.

With a turnover of $5 billion a year, Mattel is one of the world's leading makers of toys, including many household names. In 2007 the company had a major problem when some toys purchased from Chinese manufacturers were found to be decorated with paint that contained high levels of lead. This is widely banned because of its harmful effects, potentially causing learning and behavioural problems in children. Some of the suspect Mattel toys had paint with lead content of more than 180 times the legal limits in international markets. Within a short period, Mattel identified 20 million toys at risk worldwide, and had three separate recalls (including 600,000 Barbie dolls).

Mattel's problems started when it outsourced manufacturing to low-cost areas. They had a long-term supplier based in Hong Kong, but this company then subcontracted work to another company that did not use Mattel-approved paint.

The original problem had far-reaching consequences. There was a public outcry when the problems emerged; many companies looked more carefully at their outsourced manufacturing; more frequent tests found other products with high levels of lead paint (such as ceramic dishes and various PVC products); the owner of one Chinese manufacturer's plant committed suicide; Mattel founded a new corporate responsibility unit; national governments encouraged the Chinese government to strengthen its regulations and enforcement (recognising that local governments within China have a history of avoiding national policies that affect their local economies negatively); enterprising companies started to market home lead-test kits for worried parents; companies outsourcing manufacturing to China increasingly monitored operations and moved their own employees to local factories; countless lawsuits were taken out against Mattel, which won a 'bad product' award in 2007. Needless to say, Mattel's sales, profits and share price all suffered.

Sources: A sampling of *Wall Street Journal* and *New York Times* from August and September 2007; www.mattel.com; www.bbc.com.

Quality control

Traditionally, quality management developed as a separate function to check the output of production departments. But TQM says that everyone within an organisation is involved with quality. In particular, quality management should move back to the people actually doing the work, so that it is no longer a separate function but is an integral part of the process. This move has brought changes to the timing and role of inspections. Traditionally, most effort was put into inspections in the later stages of the process, often just before finished products were delivered to customers. At first, this seems a sensible approach because all faults can be found in one big inspection. However, the longer a unit is in a process the more time and money is spent on it. A more sensible approach would be to find faults as early as possible, before any more money is wasted on a unit that is already defective. For instance, it is cheaper for a baker to find bad eggs when they arrive, rather than using the eggs in cakes and then scrapping these when they fail a later inspection.

WORKED EXAMPLE 17.2

Svenson Electrics make light fittings on an assembly line. When the electric wiring is fitted, faults are introduced to 4% of units. An inspection at this point would find 95% of faults, with costs of €2 for the inspection and €3 to correct a fault. Any fault not found continues down the line and is detected and corrected later at a cost of €20.

Without the inspection after wiring, later tests cost an extra €1.20 a unit and each fault corrected costs €40. Is it worth inspecting light fittings after the wiring?

Solution

We can answer this by comparing the expected cost per unit of doing the inspection and not doing it.

- With an inspection after wiring, the expected costs per unit are:
  - cost of inspection = €2.00
  - cost of faults detected and corrected after wiring

    = proportion of faults detected × cost of repairing each
    = 0.04 × 0.95 × 3
    = €0.114

- cost of faults not found until later

    = proportion not detected × cost of later repair
    = 0.04 × (1 − 0.95) × 20
    = €0.04

This gives a total of 2.00 + 0.114 + 0.04 = €2.154 a unit.

- Without an inspection after wiring, the expected costs per unit are:
  - additional cost of later inspection = €1.20
  - cost of faults detected and corrected after wiring

    = proportion with faults × cost of repair
    = 0.04 × 40
    = €1.60

This gives a total of 1.20 + 1.60 = €2.80 a unit.

It is clearly cheaper to do an inspection when the wiring is fitted and to correct faults as soon as they are found.

Product variability

Of course, you may ask why inspections are needed if everyone is following TQM advice and doing everything possible to make sure that no faults are introduced and products are always perfect. The answer is that no matter how good a process there is always some variation in the products. Differences in materials, weather, tools, employees, moods, time, stress and a whole range of other factors combine to give some level of variation. The variations are largely unexplained, apparently random and hopefully small – but they are always present. This is why a marathon runner never finishes a series of races in exactly the same times, and products never finish their process with exactly the same performance.

The design of products and operations must be robust enough to allow for these variations and still give perfect quality. The traditional way of arranging this is to give a tolerance in the specifications. Provided a unit's performance is within a specified range, it is considered acceptable. A 250 g bar of chocolate might weigh between 249.9 g and 250.1 g and still be considered the right weight. A unit is considered faulty only if its performance is outside this tolerance, as shown in Figure 17.4.

Taguchi[5] pointed out that this approach has an inherent weakness. Suppose a bank sets an acceptable time to open a new account at between 20 and 30 minutes. If the time taken is 20, 25 or 30 minutes, the traditional view says that these are equally acceptable – the process is achieving its target, so there is no need for improvement. But customers would probably not agree that taking 30 minutes is as good as taking 20 minutes. On the other hand, there might be little real difference between taking 30 minutes (which is acceptable) and 31 minutes (which is unacceptable). The answer, of course, is that there are not such clear cut-offs. If you are aiming for a target, then the further you are away from the target the worse your performance. This effect is described by a **loss function**, which gives a notional cost of missing the target (see Figure 17.5).

To minimise costs, managers have to get actual performance as close to the target as possible, and this means reducing the variability in a process. To test whether or not this is actually happening they have to monitor performance over time. So firms routinely inspect units, test them and make sure that everything is working properly and that the variation between units is small. This is the purpose of **quality control**.

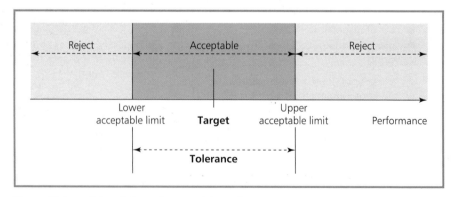

Figure 17.4 Traditional view of acceptable performance

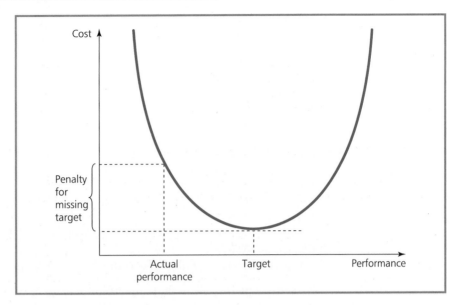

Figure 17.5 Loss function showing the cost of missing a specified target

Quality control uses a series of independent inspections and tests to make sure that designed quality is actually being achieved.

TQM has everybody in the organisation working to make sure that no defects are introduced, so the purpose of quality control is not to find faults, but to give independent evidence that the process is working properly and that there really are no defects. If it finds a defective unit then it means that something has gone wrong with the process, and managers should find the cause of the problem and correct it before any more defectives are made. Typical causes of faults are:

- human error
- faults in equipment
- poor materials
- faults in operations – such as speed or temperature changes
- changes in the environment – such as humidity, dust or temperature
- errors in monitoring equipment – such as errors in measuring tools.

Review questions

17.7   What is the difference between quality control and quality management?

17.8   What is a loss function?

17.9   'With proper quality control, production departments can eliminate all variability.' Is this true?

Tools for quality control

When something goes wrong with a process – perhaps a sudden increase in customer complaints – it is often surprisingly difficult to find the cause. To help with this – and subsequent analyses – several tools have been developed for quality control. The simplest tool continues to ask a series of questions until the cause becomes clearer. You can imagine a session of this kind starting as follows.

Question: What is the problem?
Answer: A customer complained because we couldn't serve her.
Question: Why?
Answer: Because we had run out of stock.
Question: Why?
Answer: Because our suppliers were late in delivering.
Question: Why?
Answer: Because our order was sent in late.
Question: Why?
Answer: Because the purchasing department got behind with its orders.
Question: Why?
Answer: Because it used new staff who were not properly trained.

By this point it is clear that something has gone wrong in the purchasing department, and with more questions you could pinpoint the cause of the problem more accurately. For obvious reasons, this is called the '5 whys' method.

Another simple way of finding the cause of a problem is to record the number of times a specific problem occurs. For instance, when customers repeatedly mention the time taken to deliver a service or the reliability of a product, this pinpoints an area where something has clearly gone wrong. A checksheet lists possible problems and records the number of times each is mentioned. A more formal version of this is a Pareto chart, which uses the 'rule of 80/20' to suggest that 80% of problems come from 20% of causes, while the remaining 20% of problems come from 80% of causes. Then managers can draw a bar chart of problems, identify the few areas that give most problems and give these special attention.

IDEAS IN PRACTICE   Pengelly's Restaurant

Pengelly's Restaurant is a well-established business near the centre of Cape Town. It serves business lunches and there is a healthy demand for its high-quality, expensive dinners. Jonas Subello is the owner of Pengelly's and looks after all the administration personally. There are few complaints from customers, but Jonas always keeps a record of them. Over the past three years he has collected the figures shown in Figure 17.6, where a bar chart highlights the areas for concern.

There were almost no complaints about the food, so customers were clearly pleased with what they were eating. Over half of the complaints came from faults in the bill. Jonas reduced these by installing new computerised cash registers. Sometimes the service was slow, particularly at busy times or when one of the staff was away. Jonas contacted an agency that could provide waiters at very short notice. These two measures alone dealt with almost three-quarters of complaints. When the restaurant needs refurbishing, Jonas can get some more comfortable chairs and increase the size of the non-smoking area. This would deal with another 19% of complaints. By these simple procedures, Jonas had dealt with 90% of complaints.

Ideas in practice continued

	A	B	C	D	E
1	**Complaints at Pengelly's Restaurant**				
2					
3	**Cause**	**Number of complaints**	**Percentage of complaints**		
4	Faults in the bill	80	51		
5	Slow service	31	20		
6	Smokers too near non-smokers	19	12		
7	Comfort of the chairs	11	7		
8	Wine	5	3		
9	Temperature of the restaurant	5	3		
10	Wait for a table	2	1		
11	Too limited menu	2	1		
12	Food: ingredients	2	1		
13	Food: cooking	1	1		
14					

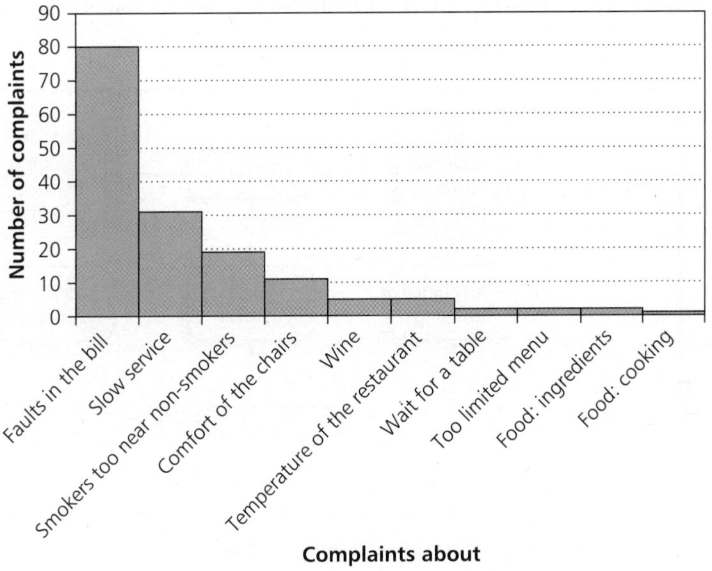

Figure 17.6 Pareto chart for complaints at Pengelly's Restaurant

Cause-and-effect diagrams – also called Ishikawa and fishbone diagrams – give a different view of the sources of problems. Suppose a customer complains at a hamburger restaurant. The problem may be caused by the raw materials, the cooking, the staff or the facilities. Problems with the raw materials may, in turn, be caused by suppliers, storage or costs. Then we could go into more details about the problems with, say, suppliers. A cause-and-effect diagram draws these relationships as coming from spines, like a fish bone, as shown in Figure 17.7.

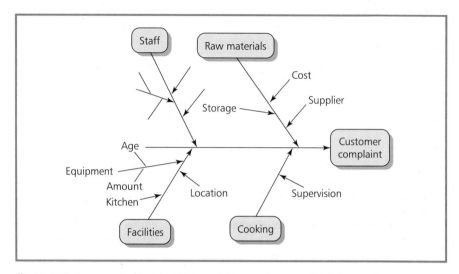

Figure 17.7 Cause-and-effect (or fishbone) diagram for complaints in a restaurant

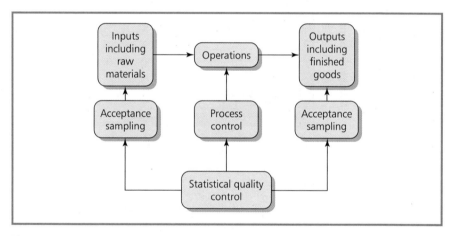

Figure 17.8 Aspects of statistical quality control

Probably the best known tool for quality control is routine sampling. There are really two types of sampling used for quality control:

■ **Acceptance sampling** checks the quality of a batch of products. It takes a sample of units from a batch and tests if the whole batch is likely to reach an acceptable level of quality, or whether or not it should be rejected. These checks focus on materials entering a process and on products leaving the process (as shown in Figure 17.8).

■ **Process control** checks the performance of the process. It takes a sample of units to test if the process is working within acceptable limits, or whether or not it needs adjusting.

Together these two types of sampling form the core of statistical quality control.

17.10 'The best way to get high-quality products is to have a lot of inspections to find faults.' Is this true?

17.11 'Many diagrams can help in identifying the main causes of problems with quality.' Do you agree?

17.12 Who is responsible for the quality of a product?

IDEAS IN PRACTICE New York Containers

New York Containers make a range of scented products in spray cans. These include hair sprays, deodorants and room fresheners. In 2005 they appointed George Steinway as Director of Quality Assurance with clear instructions to improve the quality of the company's products.

George spent the first few weeks talking to people and trying to find the real problems with quality. He quickly found one problem with the production department's ambition of meeting output quotas – almost regardless of price. So when a quality inspector rejected some aerosols as being overfilled and asked an operator to set

them aside until she could find the cause of the problem, the production supervisor was concerned about his schedule and told the operator not to bother with the faults but to release a little pressure from the cans and ship them out as usual. Later the quality inspector found that the pressure gauge on the filling machine was not working properly, the spray can nozzles delivered by a regular supplier were not up to standard, the production supervisor was judged by the number of cans produced with no concern for quality and the machine operator was new and not fully trained.

Acceptance sampling

Acceptance sampling checks the quality of products – in particular, it considers a batch of products, takes a sample from this batch and uses this to test whether the whole batch reaches designed levels of quality and should be accepted, or is defective and should be rejected. We can show the approach of acceptance sampling by considering some continuous property of a product, such as its weight, length, time or strength. This is called sampling by variable. We have already discussed this type of sampling in Chapter 14 (and if you are unsure of the details it would be useful to review them before continuing).

WORKED EXAMPLE 17.3

A batch of materials arrives at a service bay, where a sample of 40 units is found to have a mean weight of 25 kg and a standard deviation of 1 kg. Within what range is the bay 95% certain that the mean weight of units in the batch lies?

Solution

The best estimate for the mean weight of units in the batch is 20 kg, with a standard deviation of 1 kg. Then the sampling distribution of the mean is Normally distributed with mean 20 kg and unbiased

standard deviation of $1 / \sqrt{(n-1)} = 1 / \sqrt{39} = 0.16$ kg. The 95% confidence interval for the mean weight in the batch is within 1.96 standard deviations of the mean, giving a range of:

$$25 + 1.96 \times 0.16 \quad \text{to} \quad 25 - 1.96 \times 0.16$$

or

$$25.31 \text{ kg} \quad \text{to} \quad 24.69 \text{ kg}$$

So the service bay is 95% certain that the mean weight of units in the batch is within this range.

The alternative to sampling by variables is **sampling by attribute**, which needs some criterion that describes a unit as either 'acceptable' or 'defective'. Sometimes this criterion is obvious – a light bulb either works or does not; boxes either contain at least 1 kg of soap powder or do not; a train either arrives on time or does not. Sometimes the criterion relies less on measurement and more on judgement. For instance, a piece of furniture may be rejected because its polished finish does not look good enough to an experienced inspector, or a service person might be considered rude.

Sampling by attribute uses another result that we saw in Chapter 14, which says that when the proportion of defective units in a population is π, the proportion of defects in samples of size n is Normally distributed with

$$\text{mean} = \pi \text{ and standard deviation} = \sqrt{\frac{\pi(1-\pi)}{n}}.$$

WORKED EXAMPLE 17.4

SemiShan Communications use outside agents to check details of their contracts with customers. They insist that the agents make errors in fewer than 4% of contracts. One day they receive a large shipment of contracts from the agents. They take a sample of 200 contracts and check them. What criterion should SemiShan use to reject a batch if it wants to be 97.5% sure of not making a mistake?

Solution

If the proportion of errors is 4%, $\pi = 0.04$. Samples of size n have a Normally distributed proportion of defective units with:

- mean $= \pi = 0.04$
- standard deviation $= \sqrt{\pi(1-\pi)/n}$
  $= \sqrt{0.04 \times 0.96 / 200}$
  $= 0.014$.

When SemiShan reject a batch of contracts, they want to be 97.5% sure that the mean is above 0.04. With a Normal distribution, the point with 2.5% of the population in the tail is 1.96 standard deviations from the mean (as shown in Figure 17.9). So they should reject a batch when the number of errors is more than:

$0.04 + 1.96 \times 0.014 = 0.067$

With a sample of 200 units this means $0.067 \times 200 = 13.4$ defects.

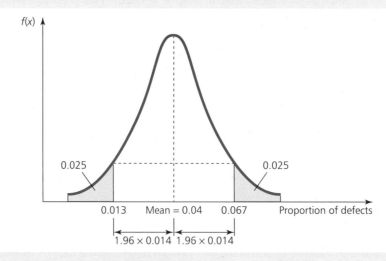

Figure 17.9 Sampling for SemiShan Communications

Worked example 17.4 illustrates the overall approach of acceptance sampling:

- Specify a sample size, n.
- Take a random sample of this size from a batch.
- Specify a maximum allowed number of defects in the sample, c.
- Test the sample to find the number that are actually defective.
- If the number of defects is greater than the allowed maximum number, reject the batch.
- If the number of defects is less than the allowed maximum number, accept the batch.

The maximum allowed number of defects in a sample is largely a matter of management policy because it relies on their judgement about acceptable levels of quality. But remember that this idea of 'defects' can be misleading – it suggests that products are not working properly. In practice, variability should be very small and a product can be described as defective even when it works properly and satisfies customers. Being defective simply means that a unit does not meet the supplier's internal targets – which might be considerably more demanding than those of the customers. You can imagine this with a call centre where most customers are happy to wait 3 seconds before their call is answered, but operators describe a response as defective if it is not answered before the second ring.

Suppose that managers are prepared to accept a batch of products when fewer than 2% are defective. (This is just to illustrate the principles because managers are increasingly demanding far better levels of quality than this.) In principle, they will take a sample and reject the whole batch if more than 2% of the sample is defective. But you know that sampling is not this reliable and even the best sample is unlikely to be a perfect reflection of the population. So using this approach managers will reject some batches that are good (Type I errors) and accept some batches that are defective (Type II errors). The best they can do is to give batches with few defects a high probability of acceptance, and batches with more defects a high probability of rejection. The way to achieve this is with big samples – but more generally we have to consider four related measures. The first two are:

- acceptable quality level (AQL) is the poorest level of quality that we will accept – in other words, the maximum proportion of defects that still allows us to describe a batch as 'good'. We want to accept any batch with fewer defects than AQL, perhaps using a figure for AQL around 1%.
- lot tolerance percent defective (LTPD) is the quality that is unacceptable – and we want to reject any batch with a higher proportion of defects than LTPD. We might use a value of LTPD around 2%.

These two values determine the overall response to a sample – they require a high probability of accepting a batch with fewer defects than AQL and a low probability of accepting one with more than LTPD. Between the two is an indeterminate region, illustrated in Figure 17.10.

However, we know that there is inherent uncertainty in sampling, and have to accept mistakes. This gives rise to the other two measures:

- producer's risk (α) – the highest acceptable probability of rejecting a good batch, with fewer defects than the AQL. This is typically set around 5%.

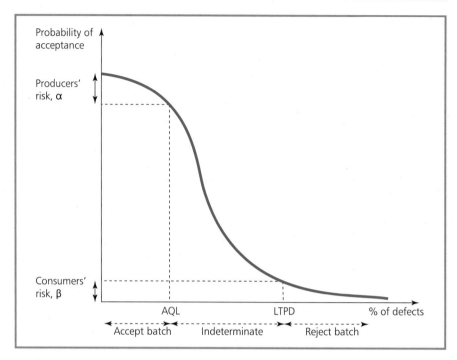

Figure 17.10 Operating characteristic curve for sampling plan

- consumer's risk (β) – the highest acceptable probability of accepting a bad batch, with more defects than LTPD. This is typically set around 10%.

We can use these four measures to define a sampling plan to specify values for n, the sample size, and c, the maximum number of allowed defects. Each sampling plan has its own operating characteristic curve (OC curve) of the form illustrated in Figure 17.10, which shows the probability of accepting batches with different proportions of defects. The OC curve effectively shows how well the sampling plan actually separates good and bad batches. Ideally, it should make a clear distinction between good and bad batches, so the OC curve should be as steep as possible. A perfect OC curve would have a vertical central part differentiating perfectly between a good batch (with a probability of acceptance of 1) and a bad batch (with a probability of acceptance of 0). The only realistic way of getting close to this is to take large samples.

A huge amount of work has been done on quality-control statistics and we do not have to duplicate this, but can use previously established results. The easiest way of doing this is to use a standard quality-control package, many of which are available.

WORKED EXAMPLE 17.5

Juliet Ndalla buys components in batches from a supplier. The supplier uses an acceptance quality level of 2% defective, while Juliet accepts batches with a maximum of 6% defective. What are appropriate values of n and c?

Solution

We are given two figures, which specify:

AQL = 0.02

LTPD = 0.06

Worked example 17.5 continued

Now we can find values for n and c from standard sampling plans. Traditionally, managers would calculate the ratio of LTPD / AQL and find the corresponding entry in standard sampling tables. Here LTPD / AQL = 0.06 / 0.02 = 3 and Figure 17.11 shows an extract from sampling tables, where we look up the value that is equal to, or slightly greater than 3. The best result is 3.21, which corresponds to $c = 6$. Then we use the third column of the table to find an implied sample size. The corresponding value of $n \times$ AQL is 3.29. We know that AQL = 0.02, so $n \times 0.02 = 3.29$, or $n = 164.5$. This gives the sampling plan:

- Take samples of 165 units.
- If 6 or fewer units are defective, accept the batch.
- If more than 6 units are defective, reject the batch.

Managers do not generally use sampling tables because all the work is done by standard programs.

Figure 17.12 shows a simple printout, where four alternative plans are suggested based on different values of α and β.

LTPD/AQL	c	$n \times$ AQL
44.89	0	0.05
10.95	1	0.36
6.51	2	0.82
4.89	3	1.37
4.06	4	1.97
3.55	5	2.61
3.21	6	3.29
2.96	7	3.98
2.77	8	4.70
2.62	9	5.43
2.50	10	6.17

Figure 17.11 Extract from a table of sampling statistics

****** **QUALITY CONTROL STATISTICS** ******

Title:	Design of quality control sampling plan
For:	Attribute sampling

DATA ENTERED
- Acceptance quality level   AQL   =   0.02
- Lot tolerance percent defective   LTPD   =   0.06
- Producer's risk α =   0.05
- Consumer's risk β =   0.10

CRITICAL VALUES

LTPD/AQL	=	3.00	
Inferred n	=	6	maximum number of defects
$n \times$ AQL	=	3.29	
Inferred n	=	165	sample size

SUGGESTED PLANS
Take a sample of 165 units from a batch
If 6 or less units are defective accept the batch
If more than 6 units are defective reject the batch

SENSITIVITY AND ALTERNATIVE PLANS

Plan Number	Sample size (n)	Number of failures (c)	Actual alpha	Actual beta
1	165	6	0.051	0.137
2	176	6	0.067	0.099
3	200	7	0.051	0.090
4	197	7	0.048	0.098

Figure 17.12 Example of a printout giving alternative sampling plans

17.13 What is the difference between acceptance sampling and process control?

17.14 What is the difference between sampling by variable and sampling by attribute?

17.15 Why does an ideal operating characteristic curve have a vertical central section?

Process control

Acceptance sampling checks the quality of products, while process control checks that the process making the products is working as planned. In other words, it makes sure that the random variation in products stays within acceptable limits. More specifically, it takes a series of samples over time to check for trends or noticeable problems. For instance, if the number of units being rejected is steadily rising, it is probably a sign that the process needs some kind of adjustment.

Process control charts give a straightforward format for monitoring performance. A basic chart looks at a series of samples over time and plots a graph of the proportion of defects in each. The result is called a *p*-chart. The proportion of defects in the samples should remain close to the proportion of defects in the population. Provided it does not vary far from this, we can say that the process is working as planned and that everything is under control. But when one or more samples are some distance away from the expected value, it is a sign that something is wrong.

The usual format for a *p*-chart draws a mean, expected proportion of defects in a sample. Then it adds two control limits – an upper control limit (UCL) above the mean level, and a lower control limit (LCL) below the mean level. Provided the output stays between these two limits we say that the process is in control – but if it moves outside the limits there is something wrong (as shown in Figure 17.13).

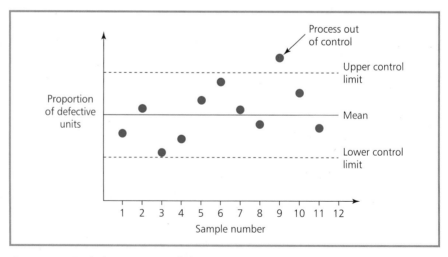

Figure 17.13 Typical process control chart

We can calculate control limits from the results we already know. If the proportion of defects in a population is π, the proportion of defects in a sample of size n is Normally distributed, with mean π and standard deviation $\sqrt{(\pi(1 - \pi) / n)}$. Then we can calculate the control limits from:

- upper control limit = UCL = $\mu + Z \times$ standard deviation
- lower control limit = LCL = $\mu - Z \times$ standard deviation

where Z is the number of standard deviations of the specified confidence limit.

WORKED EXAMPLE 17.6

Joan McKenzie collected a sample of 500 units of the output from a process for each of 30 working days when it was known to be working normally. She tested these samples and recorded the number of defects as follows.

Day	Number of defects	Day	Number of defects	Day	Number of defects
1	70	11	45	21	61
2	48	12	40	22	57
3	66	13	53	23	65
4	55	14	51	24	48
5	50	15	60	25	42
6	42	16	57	26	40
7	64	17	55	27	67
8	47	18	62	28	70
9	51	19	45	29	63
10	68	20	48	30	60

What are the process control limits with 95% confidence?

Solution

The mean proportion of defects is:

$$\pi = \frac{\text{total number of defects}}{\text{number of observations}}$$

$$= \frac{1{,}650}{30 \times 500}$$

$$= 0.11$$

$$\text{standard deviation} = \sqrt{\pi(1 - \pi)/n)}$$
$$= \sqrt{(0.11 \times 0.89 / 500)}$$
$$= 0.014$$

The 95% confidence limit shows the range within which 95% of samples lie when the process is working normally, and this has $Z = 1.96$, so:

- UCL = $p + Z \times$ standard deviation
  = $0.11 + 1.96 \times 0.014$
  = 0.137
- LCL = $p - Z \times$ standard deviation
  = $0.11 - 1.96 \times 0.014$
  = 0.083

With samples of 500, the number of defects should stay close to the mean of $0.11 \times 500 = 55$. Joan can assume that the process is under control when the number of defects is between $0.083 \times 500 = 42$ and $0.137 \times 500 = 69$. If the proportion of defects moves outside this range, the process is out of control.

Notice that the data for drawing the control charts was collected when the process was known to be working normally. Obviously, if the process was already out of control when the data were collected, the results would be meaningless.

Some observations will be outside the control limits purely by chance – and with a 95% confidence interval, random variations leave 5% of samples outside. So managers should not assume that every observation outside the limits is a real problem, but they should check whether the process is really out of control or it is actually working normally.

As well as checking the proportion of defects, we can use control charts to monitor the value of some variable, such as weight or cost. The usual approach is to plot two charts – one showing the mean values of the samples, and a second showing the ranges (where the range is the difference between the largest and smallest observation in the sample). For example, a mobile telephone company might take samples to monitor the duration of calls. It can plot two control charts – one showing the mean length of calls in each sample, and a second showing the range. Provided samples keep within control limits for both charts, the process is in control. If a sample moves outside the control limits on either chart then the process may be out of control.

WORKED EXAMPLE 17.7

A company has taken samples of 10 units from a process in each of the past 20 days. Each unit in the sample was weighed, and the mean weight and range were recorded (shown in Figure 17.14). Draw process control charts for the sample means and ranges.

Solution

We could calculate the ranges, but these analyses are done so often that the easiest way of finding control limits is to use standard software. Figure 17.14 shows the results from one package. This has estimated the sample mean and standard deviation, and has used these to set control limits that are 3 standard deviations away from the mean.

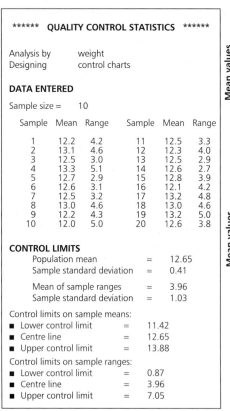

```
******  QUALITY CONTROL STATISTICS  ******

Analysis by        weight
Designing          control charts

DATA ENTERED

Sample size =      10

  Sample  Mean  Range    Sample  Mean  Range

    1     12.2   4.2       11    12.5   3.3
    2     13.1   4.6       12    12.3   4.0
    3     12.5   3.0       13    12.5   2.9
    4     13.3   5.1       14    12.6   2.7
    5     12.7   2.9       15    12.8   3.9
    6     12.6   3.1       16    12.1   4.2
    7     12.5   3.2       17    13.2   4.8
    8     13.0   4.6       18    13.0   4.6
    9     12.2   4.3       19    13.2   5.0
   10     12.0   5.0       20    12.6   3.8


CONTROL LIMITS
    Population mean               =    12.65
    Sample standard deviation     =    0.41

    Mean of sample ranges         =    3.96
    Sample standard deviation     =    1.03

Control limits on sample means:
  ■ Lower control limit    =    11.42
  ■ Centre line            =    12.65
  ■ Upper control limit    =    13.88
Control limits on sample ranges:
  ■ Lower control limit    =    0.87
  ■ Centre line            =    3.96
  ■ Upper control limit    =    7.05
```

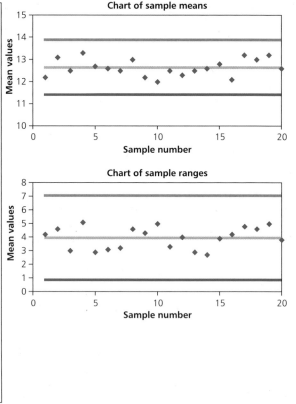

Figure 17.14 Sample of a printout for process control charts

17.16 What does it mean if an observation is outside the limits in a process control chart?

17.17 What patterns should you investigate in a control chart?

IDEAS IN PRACTICE   **Stroh Brewery Company**

Until 1999, when they sold their brands, the Stroh Brewery Company was the third-largest producer of beer in the USA. One of their plants was the WinstonSalem brewery, which occupied over 100,000 square metres and made 200 million gallons of beer a year.

Quality control of beer was rigorous, with the brewery checking everything from taste to the quantity in each can. For this they employed 38 people in three separate laboratories for microbiology, brewing and packaging. These people did 1,100 separate tests on each batch of beer. If they found problems, the quality control department stopped production and investigated.

A typical test in the brewing laboratory took a small sample during fermentation, diluted it and counted the yeast cells. Beer must have a standard 16 million yeast cells (± 2 million) per millilitre of beer.

A typical test in the packaging laboratory checked the amount of air in a beer can. Because air might affect the taste, the company allowed a maximum of 1 cm^3 of air in a can. This was checked by testing 3 cans from the production line, 5 times a shift. If a sample was found with more than 1 cm^3 of air, the entire batch was put into 'quarantine' and systematically tested to find the point where the canning went wrong. As each line fills 1,600 cans a minute, this could mean a lot of testing.

CHAPTER REVIEW

This chapter introduced the broad area of quality management, which is the function responsible for all aspects of quality.

- It is difficult to give a general definition of 'quality'. A common view describes it as the ability to meet – and preferably exceed – customer expectations.

- In reality, products have to satisfy both internal and external requirements. Design quality has an external focus and means that product designs will meet the requirements of customers. Achieved quality has an internal focus and makes sure that products actually made meet the designed specifications.

- The four components of quality cost are prevention, appraisal, internal failure and external failure costs. Failure costs can be particularly high, but fall with increasing quality. This means that overall cost is minimised by making products with perfect quality.

- Making products with perfect quality requires the focused effort of everyone in the organisation. This is the essence of Total Quality Management.

- Even the best processes have some variation. High quality comes by reducing the amount of variation and keeping actual performance close to targets. Quality control monitors performance using a number of standard tools including '5-whys', Pareto analyses and cause-and-effect diagrams.

However, the main work of quality control is statistical sampling. This considers either acceptance sampling or process control.

- Acceptance sampling checks that a batch of products reaches the design quality. It takes a random sample from a batch and checks that the number of defects is below a maximum permitted number.
- Sampling is also used for process control to check that a process continues to work normally. The usual tests are based on process charts that monitor performance over time.

CASE STUDY   Bremen Engineering

Jurgen Hansmann is the Quality Control Manager of Bremen Engineering. On Tuesday morning he got to work at 7.30 and was immediately summoned by the General Manager. As Jurgen approached, the General Manager threw him a letter that had obviously come in the morning mail. Jurgen saw that the General Manager had circled two sections of the letter in red ink.

'We have looked at recent figures for the quality of one of the components you supply, AM74021-74222. As you will recall, we have an agreement that requires 99.5% of delivered units of this product to be within 5% of target output ratings. While your supplies have been achieving this, we are concerned that there has been no apparent improvement in performance over time.'

'We put considerable emphasis on the quality of our materials, and would like to discuss a joint initiative to raise the quality of your components. By working together we can share ideas and get mutual benefits.'

The General Manager waited for a few minutes and said, 'I find it incredible that we are sending poor quality goods to one of our biggest customers. We have a major complaint about our quality. Complete strangers think that we can't do our job properly, so they'll come and show us how to do it. This is your problem. I suggest you start solving it immediately.'

The General Manager's tone made Jurgen rather defensive and his reply was less constructive than normal, 'There is nothing wrong with our products. We agreed measures for quality and are consistently achieving them. We haven't improved quality because we didn't agree to improve it, and any improvement would increase our costs. We are making 995 units in 1,000 at higher quality than they requested, and the remaining 0.5% are only just below it. To me, this seems a level of quality that almost anyone would be proud of.'

The process for making AM74021-74222 has five stages, each of which is followed by an inspection. The units then have a final inspection before being sent to customers. Jurgen now considered more 100% inspections, but each manual inspection costs about €0.60 and the selling price of the unit is only €24.75. There is also the problem that manual inspections are only 80% accurate. Automatic inspections cost €0.30 and are almost completely reliable, but they cannot cover all aspects of quality and at least three inspections have to remain manual.

Jurgen produced a weekly summary of figures to show that things were really going well.

Case study continued

	Inspection											
	A		B		C		D		E		F	
Week	Inspect	Reject	Inspect	Reject	Inspect	Reject	Inspect	Reject	Inspect	Reject	Inspect	Reject
1	4,125	125	350	56	287	0	101	53	3,910	46	286	0
2	4,086	136	361	0	309	0	180	0	3,854	26	258	0
3	4,833	92	459	60	320	0	194	0	4,651	33	264	0
4	3,297	43	208	0	186	0	201	0	3,243	59	246	0
5	4,501	83	378	0	359	64	224	65	4,321	56	291	0
6	4,772	157	455	124	401	0	250	72	4,410	42	289	0
7	4,309	152	420	87	422	0	266	123	3,998	27	287	64
8	4,654	101	461	0	432	0	278	45	4,505	57	310	0
9	4,901	92	486	0	457	0	287	0	4,822	73	294	0
10	5,122	80	512	0	488	0	301	0	5,019	85	332	0
11	5,143	167	524	132	465	48	290	61	4,659	65	287	0
12	5,119	191	518	0	435	0	256	54	4,879	54	329	0
13	4,990	203	522	83	450	0	264	112	4,610	55	297	0
14	5,231	164	535	63	475	0	276	0	5,002	32	267	0
15	3,900	90	425	56	288	0	198	0	3,820	37	290	58
16	4,277	86	485	109	320	0	229	0	4,109	38	328	0
17	4,433	113	435	0	331	0	265	67	4,259	29	313	0
18	5,009	112	496	0	387	0	198	62	4,821	52	269	0
19	5,266	135	501	65	410	0	299	58	5,007	51	275	64
20	5,197	142	488	0	420	72	301	73	4,912	48	267	0
21	4,932	95	461	0	413	0	266	0	4,856	45	286	0
22	5,557	94	510	0	456	0	160	64	5,400	39	298	61
23	5,106	101	488	74	488	0	204	131	4,795	36	326	0
24	5,220	122	472	0	532	0	277	125	4,989	29	340	56
25	5,191	111	465	0	420	0	245	185	4,927	42	321	0
26	5,620	87	512	45	375	0	223	134	5,357	48	332	0

Notes on inspections

For sampling inspections, all production is considered in notional batches of 1 hour's output. Random samples are taken from each batch and if the quality is too low the whole batch is rejected, checked and reworked as necessary.

- A – automatic inspection of all units: rejects all defects
- B – manual inspection of 10% of output: rejects batch if more than 1% of batch is defective
- C – manual inspection of 10% of output: rejects batch if more than 1% of batch is defective
- D – manual inspection of 5% of output: rejects batch if more than 2% of batch is defective
- E – automatic inspection of all units: rejects all defects
- F – manual inspection of 5% of output: rejects batch if more than 1% of batch is defective

Questions

- Do you think the General Manager's view is reasonable? What about Jurgen Hansmann's reaction?
- How effective is quality control at Bremen Engineering?
- Do you think the product quality needs to be improved? How would you set about this?

PROBLEMS

17.1 Amwal Corporation had the following costs (in thousands of pounds) over the past six years. Describe what has been happening.

Year	1	2	3	4	5	6
Sales value	623	625	626	635	677	810
Costs:						
Design	6	8	18	24	37	43
Appraisal	15	17	22	37	45	64
Internal failure	91	77	32	36	17	10
External failure	105	101	83	51	27	16

17.2 Hung Gho Chan make a part on an assembly line. At one point they find that 2% of units are defective. It costs $1 to inspect each unit at this point, but the inspection would find only 70% of faults. If the faults are left, all parts will be found and corrected further down the line at a cost of $8. Is it worth inspecting all units at this point?

17.3 Sentinal Phoneback answers customer enquiries with telephone calls. When they timed a sample of 40 calls, they found a mean duration of 14.9 minutes and a standard deviation in duration of 2 minutes. What are the 95% and 99% confidence intervals for the true length of calls?

17.4 Eriksonn Catering says that its suppliers should send at most 2% of units that do not meet its 'outstanding' standard of quality. It receives a large shipment and takes a sample of 100 units. The company wants to be 95% sure that a rejected batch is really unsatisfactory. What criteria should it use to reject a batch?

17.5 Carn Bay Components make batches of a basic product in Toronto and transfer it to their main manufacturing plant in Chicago. When the product is made, an acceptance quality level of 1% defective is used, but transferred batches are allowed a maximum of 4% defective. The company accept a 5% risk of rejecting good batches, and a 10% risk of accepting bad batches. What would be a reasonable sampling plan for the component?

17.6 A service provider checks 24 samples of 200 clients to see whether or not they are giving an acceptable level of service. The numbers of unsatisfactory results were as follows.

Day	Number of defects	Day	Number of defects	Day	Number of defects
1	21	9	15	17	20
2	32	10	13	18	19
3	22	11	16	19	25
4	17	12	17	20	16
5	16	13	20	21	15
6	14	14	19	22	13
7	21	15	17	23	24
8	17	16	22	24	25

Draw control charts with 95% and 99% confidence limits on the process.

17.7 Gunta Hans took 30 samples of 15 units from a process. The average sample range for the 30 samples is 1.025 kg and the average mean is 19.872 kg. Draw control charts for the process.

17.8 Pioneer Remedial found that a particular repair takes a mean time of 75.42 minutes with a standard deviation of 2.01 minutes. If samples of eight are taken, find the control limits that include 99% of sample means if the process is working normally.

RESEARCH PROJECTS

17.1 Find a product that you have been particularly pleased with. Describe the aspects of its quality that you like. How many of these aspects can you measure? How many people – from initial designers through to the person who delivered it – were involved in supplying this high-quality product? How could you make the product even better?

17.2 Quality management has undergone a revolution in recent years, with customers no longer willing to accept defective products. A key element of this has been the changing role of quality control. Describe, giving suitable examples, how this role has changed in practice.

17.3 A lot of software is available for quality control. Figure 17.15 shows a printout from a simple package that takes data, suggests a sampling plan and shows the operating curve for this plan and the average outgoing quality. How does this compare with other software? What features do you think there should be?

17.4 Despite the attention paid to quality management, many products still do not meet acceptable standards. Give some examples of products that you think are unsatisfactory. Why is this? What can be done to improve these products?

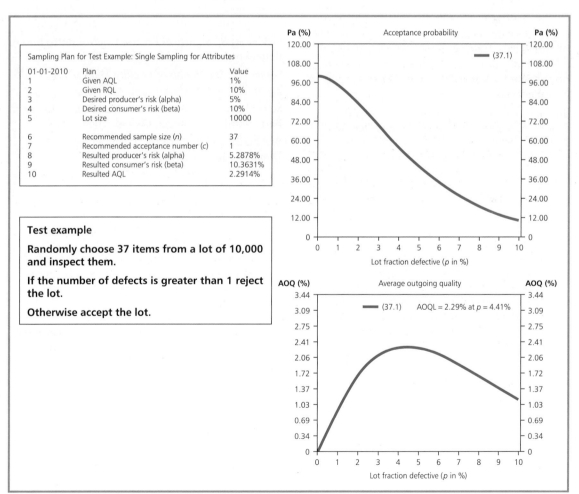

Figure 17.15 Printout from a quality control package

Sources of information

References

1 Deming W.E., *Out of the Crisis*, MIT Press, Cambridge, MA, 1986.

2 Fiegenbaum A., *Total Quality Control*, McGraw-Hill, New York, 1983.

3 Juran J.M., *Juran on Planning for Quality*, Free Press, New York, 1988.

4 Crosby P.B., *Quality is Free*, McGraw-Hill, New York, 1979.

5 Taguchi G., *Introduction to Quality Engineering*, Asian Productivity Association, Tokyo, 1986.

6 Ishikawa K., *What is Total Quality Control?* Prentice-Hall, Englewood Cliffs, NJ, 1985.

Further reading

Quality management has been such a popular topic in recent years that there is no shortage of books. The following list gives some ideas, but you can find many others.

Brussee W., *Six Sigma Made Easy*, McGraw-Hill, New York, 2004.

Burr J.T. (ed.), *Elementary Statistical Quality Control* (2nd edition), Marcel Dekker, New York, 2005.

Chandra M.J., *Statistical Quality Control*, CRC Press, Boca Raton, FL, 2001.

Dale B.G., van der Wiele T. and van Iwaarden J., *Managing Quality* (5th edition), Blackwell, Oxford, 2007.

Evans J.R. and Lindsay W.M., *The Management and Control of Quality* (8th edition), South Western College, Cincinnati, OH, 2010.

Gitlow H.S., Oppenheim A.J. and Oppenheim R., *Quality Management* (3rd edition), McGraw-Hill, New York, 2004.

Hoyle D., *Quality Management Essentials*, Butterworth-Heinemann, Oxford, 2006.

Kemp S., *Quality Management Demystified*, McGraw-Hill, New York, 2006.

Montgomery D.C., *Introduction to Statistical Quality Control* (6th edition), John Wiley, New York, 2009.

Oakland J.S., *Statistical Process Control* (6th edition), Butterworth-Heinemann, Oxford, 2007.

Seaver M., *Handbook of Quality Management* (3rd edition), Gower Press, Aldershot, 2003.

Stapenhurst T., *Mastering Statistical Process Control*, Butterworth-Heinemann, Oxford, 2005.

Webber L. and Wallace M., *Quality Control for Dummies*, John Wiley, Chichester, 2007.

Inventory management

Chapter outline

Stocks are the stores of materials that are held in every organisation. These stocks are surprisingly expensive, so managers look for ways of minimising their costs. This chapter describes some models for inventory management, starting with the classic economic order quantity. There are many extensions to this basic model. In practice, organisations increasingly attempt to minimise their stock by organising efficient flows of materials through supply chains. These often involve just-in-time or lean operations.

After finishing this chapter you should be able to:

- appreciate the need for stocks and the associated costs
- discuss different approaches to inventory management
- calculate an economic order quantity and reorder level
- calculate the effects of fixed production rates
- appreciate the need for safety stock and define a service level
- calculate safety stock when lead time demand is Normally distributed
- describe periodic review models and calculate target stock levels
- do ABC analyses of inventories.

Background to stock control

If you look around any organisation you will find stocks. These are the stores of materials that an organisation holds until it needs them. The problem is that stocks always incur costs for tied-up capital, storage, warehousing, deterioration, loss, insurance, movement and so on. So you might ask the obvious question, 'Why do organisations hold stock?' There are several answers to this, but the main one is that stocks give a buffer between supply and demand.

Imagine a supermarket that keeps a stock of goods on its shelves and in its stockroom. It holds the stock because lorries make large deliveries at relatively infrequent intervals, while customers make small demands that are almost continuous. So there is a mismatch between supply and demand, and the supermarket overcomes this by holding stock.

> - **Stocks** are the stores of materials that an organisation holds until it needs them.
> - The main purpose of stocks is to act as a buffer between supply and demand.

The short-term mismatch between supply and demand is only one reason for holding stock – others include:

- to act as a buffer between different production operations – 'decoupling' consecutive operations
- to allow for demands that are larger than expected or come at unexpected times
- to allow for deliveries that are delayed or too small
- to take advantage of price discounts on large orders
- to buy items when the price is low but is expected to rise
- to buy items that are going out of production or are difficult to find
- to make up full loads and reduce transport costs
- to give cover for emergencies.

Types of stock

Just about everything is held as stock somewhere, whether it is raw materials in a factory, finished goods in a shop or tins of baked beans in your pantry. We can classify these stocks as:

- Raw materials – the materials, parts and components that have been delivered to an organisation, but are not yet being used.
- Work-in-progress – materials that have started but not yet finished their journey through operations.
- Finished goods – goods that have finished their operations and are waiting to be delivered to customers.

This is a fairly arbitrary classification because one company's finished goods are another company's raw materials. Some organisations (notably retailers and wholesalers) have stocks of finished goods only, while others (like manufacturers) have all three types in different proportions. Some items are not

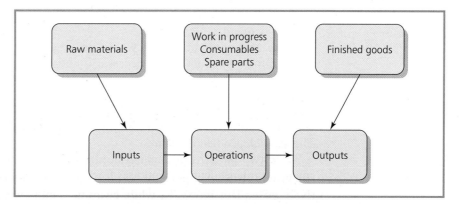

Figure 18.1 Classification of stocks

used in the final product but support related activities, and we can define two additional types (illustrated in Figure 18.1):

- spare parts for machinery, equipment etc.
- consumables such as oil, fuel, paper etc.

Approaches to inventory management

Managers have dramatically changed their views on stock in recent years. Historically, they saw it as a benefit, with high stocks allowing operations to continue normally when there were problems with deliveries from suppliers. Stocks were even seen as a measure of wealth, giving a clear display of the owner's possessions. This thinking encouraged organisations to maximise their stock – and it is still the main reason why countries keep reserves of gold and individuals keep more food than they need in their freezer. But in the twentieth century it became clear that these stocks had costs that were surprisingly high. Then managers began to view stocks not as an unreserved benefit, but as a resource that needed careful control. In particular, they looked for ways of balancing the costs of holding stocks against the costs of shortages to find optimal policies that minimised the overall costs.

More recently organisations have gone further in reducing stocks, and they now aim at working with very low levels. Lean operations move materials quickly and efficiently through supply chains, matching supply to demand so that stocks do not accumulate. Specifically, just-in-time operations organise the delivery of materials so that they always arrive just as they are needed. When such methods can be used they give considerable savings, but they are not realistic options for all types of operation. Most organisations cannot work properly without stock, and then they have to consider its management.

The conventional approach to inventory management assumes that overall demand for a product is made up of individual demands from many separate customers. These demands are independent of each other, so that the demand from one customer is not related to the demand from another. If you are selling Nike shoes, the overall demand comes from hundreds of separate customers, all independently asking for a pair of shoes. This gives an independent demand.

There are many situations where demands are not independent. One demand for a product is not necessarily independent of a second demand for the product; demand for one product is not independent of demand for a second product. For instance, when a manufacturer uses a number of components to make a product, clearly the demands for all components are related because they all depend on the production plan for the final product. This gives dependent demand.

These two patterns of demand need different methods of inventory management. Independent demand uses forecasts of future demand, usually based on past patterns (which we discussed with projective forecasting in Chapter 10). Dependent demand typically uses the methods of materials requirement planning to expand a production schedule and design timetables for the delivery of materials. You can see the differences between independent and dependent demand approaches in the way that a restaurant chef plans the ingredients for a week's meals. An independent demand system sees what ingredients were used in previous weeks, uses these past demands to forecast future demands and then buys enough to make sure that there is enough in the pantry to cover these forecast demands. The alternative dependent demand approach looks at the meals the chef plans to cook each day, analyses these to see what ingredients are needed and then orders the specific ingredients to arrive when they are needed.

Here we describe some models for independent demand. These look for ways of minimising overall costs, so we should start by taking a closer look at the costs involved.

Costs of holding stock

The cost of holding stock is typically around 25% of its value over a year. This is made up of four components – unit, reorder, holding and shortage costs.

- Unit cost (U) – this is the price of an item charged by the supplier, or the cost to an organisation of acquiring one unit of an item. It may be fairly easy to find this by looking at quotations or recent invoices from suppliers. But sometimes it is more difficult when several suppliers offer alternative products or give different purchase conditions. If a company makes an item itself then it can be difficult to set a production cost or to calculate a reasonable transfer price.
- Reorder cost (R) – this is the cost of placing a repeat order for an item and includes all the cost of administration, correspondence, delivery, insurance, receiving, checking, follow-up, expediting and so on. Sometimes, costs such as quality control, transport, finding suppliers, negotiation and a whole range of other things are included in the reorder cost. These can be difficult to find, and in practice you often get a good estimate for the reorder cost by dividing the total annual budget of a purchasing department by the number of orders it sends out.
- Holding cost (H) – this is the cost of holding one unit of an item in stock for a period of time (typically a year). The obvious cost is tied-up money, which is either borrowed (with interest payable) or could be put to other

use (in which case there are opportunity costs). Other holding costs are for storage space, damage, deterioration, obsolescence, handling, special packaging, administration and insurance.

■ Shortage cost (S) – if an item is needed but cannot be supplied from stock, there is usually a cost associated with this shortage. In the simplest case a retailer may lose profit from a sale, but the effects of shortages are usually much more widespread. There may also be some loss of customer goodwill and future sales, as well as lost reputation. When there is a shortage of raw materials for production there can be severe disruption to operations, rescheduled production, retiming of maintenance, laying-off of employees, late deliveries to customers and so on. There can also be allowances for positive action to overcome the shortage, perhaps sending out emergency orders, paying for special deliveries, storing partly finished goods or using other, more expensive, suppliers.

Shortage costs are always difficult to find – but there is general agreement that they can be very high. This allows us to look at the purpose of stocks again and rephrase our earlier statement by saying, 'the cost of shortages can be very high and, to avoid these costs, organisations are willing to incur the relatively lower costs of carrying stock'.

Review questions

18.1   What is the main reason for holding stock?

18.2   What is 'independent demand'?

18.3   List four types of cost associated with stock.

IDEAS IN PRACTICE   Stock holdings at Schultz-Heimleich

Schultz-Heimleich make veterinary pharmaceuticals in their Swiss laboratories, and they use stocks of finished goods to give a buffer between production and sales. This gives two important benefits. Firstly, the company can smooth its operations so that production does not have to follow the seasonal pattern of demand. The result is more efficient operations, easier planning, regular schedules, routine workflow, fewer changes and so on. Secondly, the company does not have to install enough capacity to match peak sales, when this would be underutilised during quieter periods. It installs enough capacity to meet the average demand – when production is higher than sales, stock builds up; when sales are higher than production, stock declines.

Managers at Schultz-Heimleich collected figures over eight quarters to illustrate this effect. The following table (where values are in millions of Swiss francs) shows that production remained stable, with two small adjustments during a period

when sales varied by up to 57%. In quarter 3, the company met a record high demand without increasing production, and their costs fell as they reduced investment in stock. If the company had installed enough capacity to meet this peak demand, its utilisation would have been only 52% in quarter 1.

Quarter	1	2	3	4	5	6	7	8
Sales	14	22	27	21	14	16	15	22
Percentage change	–	+57	+23	–22	–33	+14	–6	+47
Production	20	21	21	19	19	19	19	19
Percentage change	–	+5	0	–10	0	0	0	0
Change in stock	+6	–1	–6	–2	+5	+3	+4	–3
Average stock level	10	9	3	1	6	9	13	10

The economic order quantity

There are two basic policies for dealing with independent demand.

- Fixed order quantity – where an order of fixed size is placed whenever stock falls to a certain level. For example, a central heating plant orders 25,000 litres of oil whenever the amount in its tank falls to 5,000 litres. Such systems need continuous monitoring of stock levels and are better suited to low, irregular demand for relatively expensive items.
- Periodic review – where orders of varying size are placed at regular intervals. For example, displays of clothes in a shop might be refilled every evening to replace whatever was sold during the day. The operating cost of this system is generally lower, so it is better suited to high, regular demand for low-value items.

We start by looking at fixed order quantities. The basic analysis here calculates an economic order quantity, which is the order size that minimises costs for a simple inventory system. The analysis considers a single item whose demand is known to be continuous and constant at D per unit time. It assumes that we know the unit cost (U), reorder cost (R) and holding cost (H), while the shortage cost (S) is so high that all demand must be met and no shortages are allowed.

With fixed order quantities the stock level alternately rises with deliveries and falls more slowly as units are removed to meet demand, giving the saw-tooth pattern shown in Figure 18.2.

Consider one cycle of this pattern, shown in Figure 18.3. At some point, a delivery of an amount Q arrives and this is sold to customers at a constant rate D until no stock remains, and we arrange for another delivery to arrive at this point. The stock cycle has length T and we know that:

amount entering stock in the cycle = amount leaving stock in the cycle

$$Q = D \times T$$

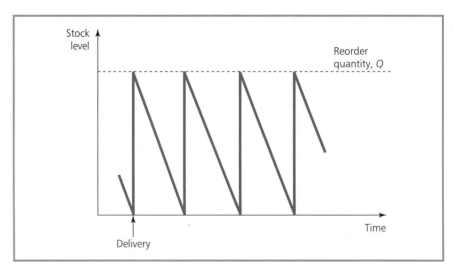

Figure 18.2 Stock level over time with fixed order quantities

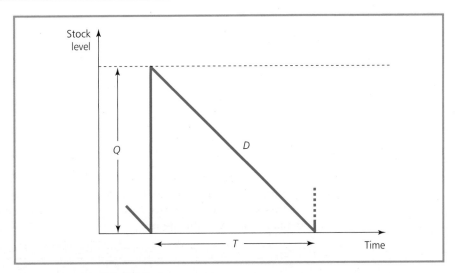

Figure 18.3 A single stock cycle

We also know that the stock level varies between Q and 0, so the average level is $(Q + 0) / 2 = Q / 2$.

We can find the total cost for the cycle by adding the four components of cost – unit, reorder, holding and shortage. No shortages are allowed so they incur no costs, so we can ignore these. At the same time, the cost of buying materials is constant (at $D \times U$ per unit time) regardless of the timing of orders, so we can also leave this out of the calculations and focus on the other two costs. The variable cost for the cycle is:

■ total reorder cost = number of orders (1) × reorder cost (R) = R
■ total holding cost = average stock level $(Q / 2)$ × time held (T) × holding cost (H) = $HQT / 2$

Adding these two components gives the variable cost for the cycle, and if we divide this by the cycle length, T, we get the variable cost per unit time, VC, as:

$$\text{VC} = (R + HQT / 2) / T$$
$$= R / T + HQ / 2$$

But we know that $Q = DT$, or $T = Q / D$, and substituting this gives:

$$\text{VC} = RD / Q + HQ / 2$$

If we plot the two components on the right-hand side of this equation separately against Q, we get the result shown in Figure 18.4. The reorder cost component falls with increasing order size, while the holding cost component rises, giving a total cost with a distinct minimum. This minimum identifies the optimal order size, or economic order quantity. You can see that the economic order quantity is at the point where the holding cost component equals the reorder cost component. In other words:

$$RD / Q = HQ / 2$$

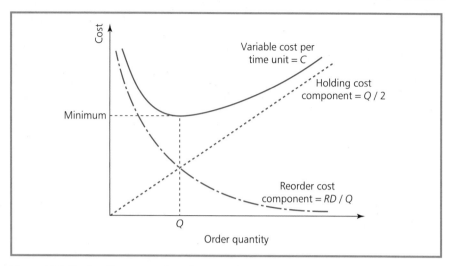

Figure 18.4 Finding the economic order quantity

or $\quad 2RD = HQ^2$

$\quad\quad Q^2 = 2RD / H$

Giving the result:

$$\text{economic order quantity} = Q_0 = \sqrt{\frac{2RD}{H}}$$

If you order less than this then you place small, frequent orders giving a high reorder cost component; if you order more than this then you place large, infrequent orders giving high stock levels and holding costs.

If you substitute this value for the economic order quantity back into the equation for the variable cost, VC, and do a bit of manipulation, you get the equation for the optimal variable cost. Then adding in the fixed cost of purchasing materials, UD, gives the optimal total cost as:

- optimal variable cost $= VC_0 = \sqrt{2RHD}$
- optimal total cost $= TC_0 = UD + VC_0$

WORKED EXAMPLE 18.1

The demand for an item is constant at 20 units a month. Unit cost is £50, the cost of processing an order and arranging delivery is £60, and the holding cost is £18 per unit per year. What are the economic order quantity, corresponding cycle length and costs?

Solution

Listing the values we know in consistent units:

$D = 20 \times 12 = 240$ units per year

$U = £50$ per unit

$R = £60$ per order

$H = £18$ per unit per year.

Worked example 18.1 continued

Substituting in the standard equations gives:

$Q_0 = \sqrt{(2RD/H)}$
$= \sqrt{(2 \times 60 \times 240 / 18)}$
$= 40$ units

$VC_0 = \sqrt{(2RHD)}$
$= \sqrt{(2 \times 60 \times 18 \times 240)}$
$= £720$ a year

$TC_0 = U \times D + VC_0$
$= 50 \times 240 + 720$
$= £12{,}720$ a year

We can find the cycle length, T_0, from $Q = DT$, so $40 = 240T$, or $T = 1/6$ year or 2 months.

The optimal policy (with total costs of £12,720 a year) is to order 40 units every 2 months.

Reorder level

The economic order quantity shows how much to order, but it does not say when to place an order. To make this decision we have to know the lead time, L, between placing an order and having it arrive in stock. For simplicity, we will assume that this is fixed, so we get the pattern shown in Figure 18.5. To make sure that a delivery arrives just as stock runs out, we must place an order a time L before stock actually falls to zero. The easiest way to identify this point is to look at the current stock and place an order when there is just enough left to last the lead time. With constant demand of D, this means that we place an order when the stock level falls to lead time × demand, and this point is the reorder level.

reorder level = ROL = lead time × demand = LD

In practice, a 'two-bin system' gives a useful way of timing orders. This has stock kept in two bins – one bin holds the reorder level, and the second holds all remaining stock. Demand is met from the second bin until this is empty.

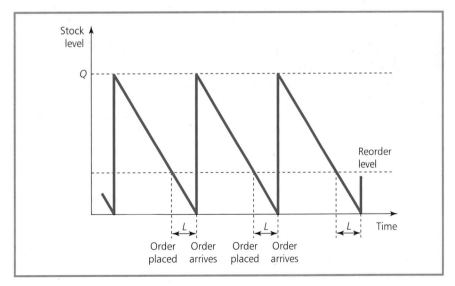

Figure 18.5 Stock level with a fixed lead time, L

At this point you know that stock has declined to the reorder level and it is time to place an order.

WORKED EXAMPLE 18.2

Demand for an item is constant at 20 units a week, the reorder cost is £125 an order and the holding cost is £2 per unit per week. If suppliers guarantee delivery within 2 weeks, what is the best ordering policy?

Solution

Listing the variables in consistent units:

$D = 20$ units per week

$R = £125$ per order

$H = £2$ per unit per week

$L = 2$ weeks

Substituting these gives:

- economic order quantity: $Q_0 = \sqrt{(2RD/H)}$

$= \sqrt{(2 \times 125 \times 20/2)}$

$= 50$ units

- reorder level: ROL $= LD = 2 \times 20$

$= 40$ units

The best policy is to place an order for 50 units whenever stock falls to 40 units. We can find the cycle length from:

$Q_0 = DT_0$ so $T_0 = 50/20 = 2.5$ weeks

The variable cost is:

$VC_0 = \sqrt{(2RHD)}$

$= \sqrt{2 \times 125 \times 2 \times 20}$

$= £100$ a week

The total cost is £100 + purchase costs (UD) a week.

Review questions

18.4 What is the economic order quantity?

18.5 If small orders are placed frequently (rather than placing large orders infrequently) does this:
(A) reduce total costs
(B) increase total costs
(C) either increase or decrease total costs?

18.6 What is the reorder level?

18.7 How would you calculate a reorder level?

IDEAS IN PRACTICE El Asiento Rojolo

El Asiento Rojolo makes parts for speedboats, most of which it sells to a major manufacturer whose factory is in the same area of San Diego. They made products in small batches to give some flexibility but still control costs. The Operations Manager used a system based loosely on economic order quantities to plan production. A typical product had demand of 150 units a month from a major customer, with notional batch setup and holding costs of $2,000 and $10 respectively. This gave an optimal batch size of 245 units, which was rounded to 300 units. The supply was organised as one production run and delivery every two months to the customer.

However, El Asiento had to change its operations completely when its largest customer moved to just-in-time operations and said that they would accept deliveries in batches of no more than 20 units. El Asiento did not want to keep stocks themselves because this would increase their costs considerably. Their only option was to dramatically reduce the batch setup cost. To get an economic order quantity of 29, the company had to reduce the notional batch setup cost from $2,000 to $13. To get anywhere close to this they had to completely redesign their operations, renegotiating terms with their own suppliers and introducing continuous, flexible automation.

Stock control for production

The economic order quantity makes a series of assumptions, but we can remove these to give models that are more realistic and useful in many different circumstances. We can illustrate this with one extension to the basic model, where replenishment occurs at a fixed rate rather than having all units delivered at the same time.

If a company manufactures a product at a rate of 10 units an hour, the stock of finished goods will increase at this rate. In other words, there is not a single large delivery, but the stock level slowly rises over a period of time. We can allow for this by a simple adjustment to the economic order quantity. When the rate of production, P, is less than the rate of demand, D, there is no problem with stock holding – supply is not keeping up with demand and as soon as a unit is made it is passed straight out to customers. There are stock problems only when the rate of production is higher than the demand (which means that $P > D$). Then stock builds up at a rate $(P - D)$ for as long as production continues. At some point managers must stop production and transfer operations to make other items. So after some time, T_P, production stops – demand from customers continues at a rate D and this is met from the accumulated stock. After some further time, T_D, the stock is exhausted and production must restart. Figure 18.6 shows the resulting stock level.

We want to find an optimal value for the batch size. This is equivalent to finding the economic order quantity, so we use the same approach – finding the total cost for a single stock cycle, dividing this by the cycle length to give a cost per unit time, and then minimising this cost.

If we make batches of size Q, this would be the highest stock level with instantaneous replenishment. But as units are actually fed into stock at a fixed rate and are continuously removed to meet demand, the maximum stock level is lower than Q, and occurs at the point where production stops.

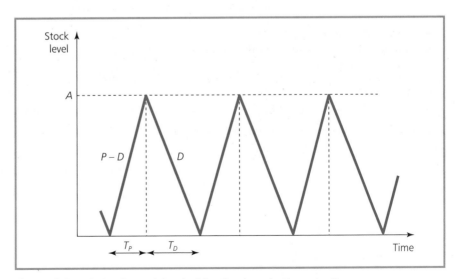

Figure 18.6 Variation in stock level with a fixed production rate, P

We can find the value for A, the highest actual stock level, from the following argument. During the productive part of the cycle, T_P, we have:

$$A = (P - D) \times T_P$$

We also know that total production during the period is:

$$Q = P \times T_P \quad \text{or} \quad T_P = Q / P$$

Substituting this value for T_P into the equation for A gives:

$$A = Q(P - D) / P$$

So the stock level is lower than it would be by the factor $(P - D) / P$.

We could continue the analysis – remembering that R is now a production setup cost rather than a reorder cost – and would again find that the results differ from the economic order quantity only by the factor $(P - D) / P$. (You can see these calculations in the companion website **www.pearsoned.co.uk/waters**).

- optimal order quantity $= Q_0 = \sqrt{\dfrac{2RD}{H}} \times \sqrt{\dfrac{P}{P - D}}$
- total cost $= TC_0 = UD + VC_0$
- variable cost $= VC_0 = \sqrt{2RHD} \times \sqrt{\dfrac{P - D}{D}} = \sqrt{2RHD} \; \sqrt{P / (P - D)}$

WORKED EXAMPLE 18.3

Joanna Lum notices that demand for an item is 600 units a month with relevant costs of:

- production setup $640 per order
- administration $500 per order
- scheduling $110 per order
- insurance at 1% of unit cost per year
- obsolescence, deterioration and depreciation of 2% of unit cost per year
- capital at 20% of unit cost per year
- storage space at $50 a unit per annum
- handling of $60 a unit per annum
- shortage costs are so large that no shortages are allowed.

Each unit costs the company $200 and the rate of production is 1,200 units per month. What are the optimal batch quantity and the minimum variable cost per year?

Solution

Every cost must be classified as unit, reorder or holding (with no shortage costs). Then:

$D = 600 \times 12 = 7{,}200$ units a year

$P = 1{,}200 \times 12 = 14{,}400$ units a year

$U = \$200$ a unit

Collecting together all costs for an order:

$R = 640 + 500 + 110 = \$1{,}250$ an order

There are two parts to the holding cost – a percentage (1%, 2% and 20%) of unit costs, and a fixed amount ($50 + $60) per unit per year. So:

$H = (50 + 60) + (0.01 + 0.02 + 0.2) \times 200$
$\quad = \$156$ per unit per year

Substituting these values gives:

$Q_0 = \sqrt{(2RD / H)} \times \sqrt{(P / (P - D))}$
$\quad = \sqrt{(2 \times 1{,}250 \times 7{,}200 / 156)}$
$\qquad \times \sqrt{(14{,}400 / (14{,}400 - 7{,}200))}$
$\quad = 339.68 \times 1.414$
$\quad = 480$ units

The best policy is to make a batch of 480 units every ($T = Q / D = 480 / 600 =$) 0.8 months, with variable costs of:

$VC_0 = \sqrt{(2RHD)} / \sqrt{(P / (P - D))}$
$\quad = \dfrac{\sqrt{(2 \times 1{,}250 \times (156 \times 7{,}200))}}{\sqrt{(14{,}400 / (14{,}400 - 7{,}200))}}$
$\quad = 52{,}991 / 1.414 = \$37{,}476$ a year

18.8   Are fixed production rates important for stock control when the production rate is greater than demand, equal to demand, or less than demand?

18.9   Does a fixed production rate give larger or smaller batches than instantaneous replenishment?

18.10 Is a fixed production rate the only possible extension to the basic economic order calculation?

Variable demand

The economic order quantity assumes that demand is constant and is known exactly. In practice this is rarely true and the demand for almost any item is uncertain and varies over time. Fortunately these effects are generally small and the economic order quantity still gives useful guidelines. Sometimes, though, the variations are too large and we have to use another approach. The most common is based on the assumption that shortage costs are much higher than holding costs, so organisations are willing to hold additional stocks – above their perceived needs – to add a margin of safety and avoid the risk of shortages. These safety stocks are available if the normal working stock runs out (as shown in Figure 18.7).

In principle we should be able to find the cost of shortages and balance this with the cost of holding stock. Unfortunately shortage costs are notoriously difficult to find and are generally little more than informed guesses. Analyses based on these estimated shortage costs are notoriously unreliable and most managers prefer an alternative approach that relies more directly on their opinions. This defines a service level, which is the probability that a demand can be met from stock. Then managers make a positive decision to specify a desired level. A 90% service level means that on average 90% of demands are met from stock – or, conversely, managers are willing to accept

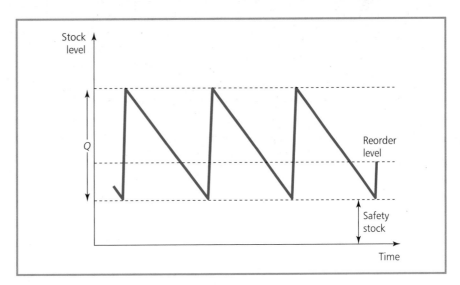

Figure 18.7 Stock level with an added safety stock

that 10% of demands will not be met from stock. Service level varies widely but is commonly around 95%, implying a probability of 0.05 that a demand cannot be met.

There are really several ways of defining the service level, including percentage of orders fully met from stock, percentage of units met from stock, percentage of periods without shortages, percentage of stock cycles without shortages, percentage of time there is stock available and so on. Here we use the probability of not running out of stock in a stock cycle, which is the cycle-service level. We can show how this works in practice by looking at a problem where the demand in a period is not known with certainty, but is known to follow a Normal distribution.

Normally distributed demand

Consider an item whose demand is Normally distributed with a mean of D per unit time and standard deviation of σ. We can add variances in demand, but not standard deviations. So:

- demand in a single period has mean D and variance σ^2
- demand in two periods has mean $2D$ and variance $2\sigma^2$
- demand in three periods has mean $3D$ and variance $3\sigma^2$ etc.

and when the lead time is constant at L:

- demand in L periods has mean LD and variance $L\sigma^2$.

When demand is constant we can use the lead time demand, LD, as a reorder level. But when the lead time demand is Normally distributed about a mean of LD, the demand is actually greater than this mean in half of stock cycles – and by symmetry it is less than the mean in the other half of cycles. If we simply used LD as the reorder level there would be shortages in the 50% of cycles when the lead time demand is greater than the mean – and spare stock in the 50% of cycles when the lead time demand is less than the mean. This effect is summarised in Figure 18.8.

To give a cycle service level above 50% we have to add a safety stock that is used when demand is greater than the mean – and then the reorder level becomes:

---

reorder level = mean lead time demand + safety stock

The size of the safety stock depends on the service level specified by managers – if they specify a high service level, the safety stock must also be high. Specifically, the service level is defined as the probability that the lead time demand is less than the reorder level. And with a Normally distributed demand we can find this from the area under the tail of the distribution, as shown in Figure 18.9. This is set by the value of Z, the number of standard deviations the safety stock is away from the mean, as we discussed in Chapter 13. The appropriate safety stock is calculated from:

---

safety stock = $Z \times$ standard deviation of lead time demand = $Z\sigma\sqrt{L}$

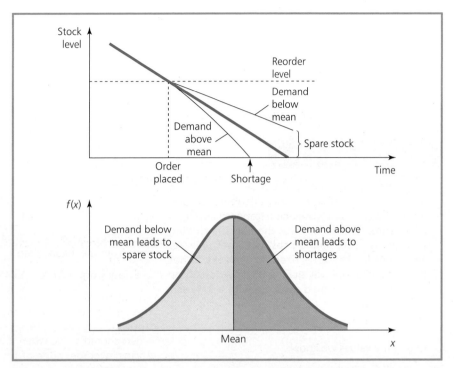

Figure 18.8 Service level with Normally distributed demand

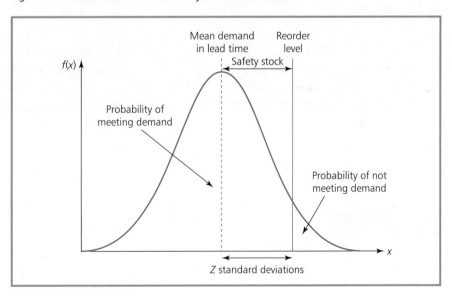

Figure 18.9 Calculating the safety stock with Normal demand

You can use the usual Normal tables or statistics packages to find the following typical values for Z and the corresponding service level.

Service level	90%	95%	97%	98%	99%
Corresponding Z	1.28	1.645	1.88	2.05	2.33

When demand varies widely, the standard deviation of lead time demand is high, and we would need very high safety stocks to give a service level anywhere close to 100%. This may be too expensive so organisations usually set a lower level, typically around 95%. Sometimes it is convenient to give items different service levels depending on their importance. Very important items may have levels close to 100%, while less important ones are set around 85%.

WORKED EXAMPLE 18.4

Rawcliffe Commercial send out service packs to meet demand that is Normally distributed with a mean of 200 units a week and a standard deviation of 40 units. Reorder cost for the packs, including delivery, is €200, holding cost is €6 per unit per year, and lead time is fixed at 3 weeks. What ordering pattern will give a 95% cycle-service level? How much would costs rise with a 97% service level?

Solution

Listing the values we know:

D = 200 units per week

σ = 40 units

R = €200 per order

H = €6 per unit per year

L = 3 weeks

Substituting these into the equation for the economic order quantity and reorder level gives:

order quantity, $Q_0 = \sqrt{(2RD / H)}$

$$= \sqrt{(2 \times 200 \times 200 \times 52 / 6)}$$

$$= 832.67$$

reorder level, ROL = LD + safety stock

$$= 3 \times 200 + \text{safety stock}$$

$$= 600 + \text{safety stock}$$

For a 95% service level, Z = 1.645 standard deviations from the mean. Then:

safety stock = $Z\sigma\sqrt{L}$ = 1.645 × 40 × $\sqrt{3}$

$$= 113.97$$

The best policy is to order 833 packs whenever stock falls to 600 + 114 = 714 units. On average, orders should arrive when there are 114 units left. And on average, none of the safety stock is used, so its cost is:

$Z\sigma\sqrt{L} \times H$ = 114 × 6

$$= €684 \text{ a year}$$

Raising the service level to 97% gives Z = 1.88 and:

safety stock = $Z\sigma\sqrt{L}$ = 1.88 × 40 × $\sqrt{3}$

$$= 130$$

The cost of holding this is 130 × 6 = €780 a year, giving a rise of €96 or 14%.

18.11 What is a service level and why is it used?

18.12 What is the purpose of safety stock?

18.13 How can you increase the service level?

Periodic review

Earlier we said that there are two different ordering policies:

- *fixed order quantity* – which we have been discussing, where an order of fixed size is placed whenever stock falls to a certain level
- *periodic review* – where orders of varying size are placed at regular intervals.

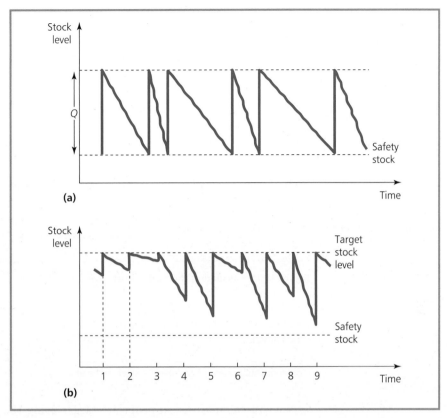

Figure 18.10 Two ways of dealing with varying demand: (a) fixed order quantity; (b) periodic review

When demand is constant these two systems are identical, so differences appear only when the demand varies (shown in Figure 18.10).

Suppose that we want to design a periodic review system when the demand is Normally distributed. The usual approach defines a target stock level, and managers order enough to raise the stock to this level. For example, if a car showroom has a target stock level of 20 cars and at the end of the week it has 16 cars in stock, it orders 4 more to raise its stock to the target. Clearly such systems have to answer two basic questions:

- How long should the interval between orders be?
- What should the target stock level be?

The order interval can be any convenient period. For example, it might be easiest to place an order at the end of every week, or every morning, or at the end of a month. If there is no obvious cycle we might aim for a certain number of orders a year or some average order size. We might calculate an economic order quantity and then find the period that gives orders of about this size. The final decision is largely a matter for management judgement.

Whatever interval is chosen, we need to find a suitable target stock level – and the system works by finding the amount of stock on hand when it is time

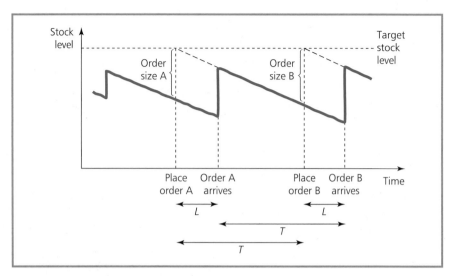

Figure 18.11 Calculating the target stock level

to place an order, and ordering the amount that brings this up to the target stock level.

> order quantity = target stock level − stock on hand

We can calculate an appropriate target using the following reasoning. Suppose the lead time is constant at L and orders are placed every period, T. When an order is placed, the stock on hand plus this order must be enough to last until the next order arrives, which is $T + L$ away (as shown in Figure 18.11).

The target stock level, TSL, should be high enough to cover mean demand over this period, so it must be at least $D(T + L)$. However, as with the fixed order quantity model, if we only ordered this amount there would be shortages in the halves of cycles when demand is above the mean. And again, the way to raise the service level above 50% is to add some safety stock. We can calculate the amount of safety stock using the same arguments that we used for a fixed order quantity.

If we assume that the both the cycle length and lead time are constant, the demand over $T + L$ is Normally distributed with mean of $D(T + L)$, variance of $\sigma^2(T + L)$ and standard deviation of $\sigma\sqrt{(T + L)}$. Then we can define a safety stock as:

$$\text{safety stock} = Z \times \text{standard deviation of demand over } (T + L)$$
$$= Z\sigma\sqrt{(T + L)}$$

and:

> target stock level = mean demand over $(T + L)$ + safety stock
> $$= D(T + L) + Z\sigma\sqrt{(T + L)}$$

WORKED EXAMPLE 18.5

Paola Ricardo manages an item with mean demand of 200 units a week and standard deviation of 40 units. She places an order every four weeks, with a constant lead time of two weeks. How can she get a 95% service level? If the holding cost is €20 per unit per week, how much would a 98% service level cost?

Solution
The variables are:

D = 200 units

σ = 40 units

H = €20 per unit per week

T = 4 weeks

L = 2 weeks

For a 95% safety stock, Z is 1.645. Then:

- safety stock = $Z\sigma\sqrt{(T + L)}$ = 1.645 × 40 × $\sqrt{6}$
  = 161
- target stock level = $D(T + L)$ + safety stock
  = 200 × (4 + 2) + 161
  = 1,361

When it is time to place an order, Paola's policy is to count the stock on hand and place an order for:

order size = 1,361 – stock on hand

For instance, if she found 200 units in stock, she would order 1,361 – 200 = 1,161 units.

If there were no safety stock, the working stock would, on average, vary between DT (being the target stock level minus the lead time demand) and none. The cost of holding this is fixed, so the variable element comes from the safety stock. On average the safety stock is always held, so each unit costs H per period. Here the safety stock for a 95% service level costs 161 × 20 = €3,220 per week. If the service level is increased to 98%, Z = 2.05, and:

safety stock = 2.05 × 40 × $\sqrt{6}$
  = 201

The target stock level is then 1,200 + 201 = 1,401 units and the cost of the safety stock is 201 × 20 = €4,020 per week.

Review questions

18.14 How is the order size calculated for a periodic review system?

18.15 How would you calculate a target stock level?

18.16 Is the safety stock higher for a fixed order quantity system or a periodic review system?

IDEAS IN PRACTICE   Vancouver Electrical Factors

In 2005 Edwin Choi worked for Vancouver Electrical Factors, who make and supply around 10,000 products for their range of electric motors. He demonstrated the use of the economic order quantity for one of their core products. The annual demand for this product was constant at around 1,000 units, each unit cost the company $400 to make and each batch had setup costs of $1,000. The annual holding costs for the product were 18% of unit cost for interest charges, 1% for insurance, 2% allowance for obsolescence, $20 for building overheads, $15 for damage and loss, and $40 miscellaneous costs.

Edwin calculated the economic order quantity from these figures:

Demand, D = 1,000 units a year

Unit cost, UC = $400 a unit

Reorder cost, RC = $1,000 an order

Holding cost, HC = (0.18 + 0.01 + 0.02) × 400
  + 20 + 15 + 40

  = $159 a unit a year

Then he suggested ordering 120 units, with an order about every six weeks and annual costs of $18,000. But operations managers felt that this

▶

Ideas in practice continued

schedule made too many assumptions, and they suggested an adjustment of ordering 85 units at the end of each month, with annual costs around $18,500. They argued that their batch size was 35% below Edwin Choi's optimal, but variable costs increased by only 5% – and they thought that this was a reasonable cost for the improved schedules. In practice, costs usually rise slowly near to the economic order quantity, so provided actual orders are somewhere close to this the inventory costs should be close to a minimum.

ABC analysis of stock

Stock control systems are usually computerised, often with automated purchasing from suppliers. But some items are very expensive and need special care above the routine calculations. An **ABC analysis** is a way of putting items into categories that reflect the amount of effort worth spending on stock control. This is really a Pareto analysis – or 'rule of 80/20' – which we saw with quality defects in Chapter 17. Here, it suggests that 80% of stock items need 20% of the attention, while the remaining 20% of items need 80% of the attention. To be specific, ABC analyses define:

- **A** items as expensive and needing special care
- **B** items as ordinary ones needing standard care
- **C** items as cheap and needing little care.

Typically an organisation would use automated procedures for all C items – or it might leave them out of the system and use simple *ad hoc* procedures. B items are automated with regular monitoring to make sure that everything is working normally. Most effort is given to A items, with managers making final decisions.

An ABC analysis starts by calculating the total annual use of each item in terms of value, by multiplying the number of units used in a year by the unit cost. Usually a few expensive items account for a lot of use, while many cheap ones account for little use. If we list the items in order of decreasing annual use by value, A items are at the top of the list, B items are in the middle and C items are at the bottom. We might typically find:

Category	Percentage of items	Cumulative percentage of items	Percentage of use by value	Cumulative percentage of use by value
A	10	10	70	70
B	30	40	20	90
C	60	100	10	100

Plotting the cumulative percentage of annual use against the cumulative percentage of items gives the graph shown in Figure 18.12.

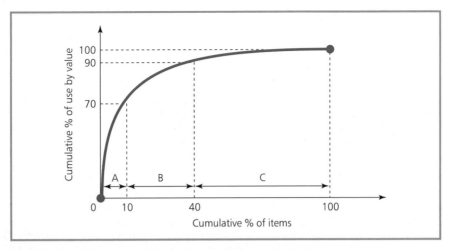

Figure 18.12 ABC analysis of stocks for Worked example 18.6

WORKED EXAMPLE 18.6

A small store has 10 categories of product with these costs and annual demands:

Product	P1	P2	P3	P4	P5	P6	P7	P8	P9	P10
Unit cost (£)	20	10	20	50	10	50	5	20	100	1
Annual demand	250	5,000	2,000	6,600	1,500	600	1,000	500	100	5,000

Do an ABC analysis of these items. If resources for stock control are limited, which items should be given least attention?

Solution

The annual use of P1 in terms of value is 20 × 250 = £5,000; annual use of P2 in terms of value is 10 × 5000 = £50,000. Repeating this calculation for the other items and sorting them into order of decreasing annual use gives the results shown in Figure 18.13. The boundaries between categories of items are sometimes unclear, but in this case P4 is clearly an A item, P2, P3 and P6 are B items, and the rest are C items. The C items account for only 10% of annual use by value, and these should be given least attention when resources are limited.

	A	B	C	D	E	F	G	H	I
1	**ABC analysis of stock**								
2									
3	**Category**	**Product**	**Percentage of items**	**Cumulative percentage of items**	**Unit cost**	**Annual demand**	**Annual use (£s)**	**Cumulative annual use (£s)**	**Cumulative percentage of annual use**
4	A	P4	10	10	50	6,600	330,000	330,000	66
5	B	P2	10	20	10	5,000	50,000	380,000	76
6	B	P3	10	30	20	2,000	40,000	420,000	84
7	B	P6	10	40	50	600	30,000	450,000	90
8	C	P5	10	50	10	1,500	15,000	465,000	93
9	C	P8	10	60	20	500	10,000	475,000	95
10	C	P9	10	70	100	100	10,000	485,000	97
11	C	P1	10	80	20	250	5,000	490,000	98
12	C	P7	10	90	5	1,000	5,000	495,000	99
13	C	P10	10	100	1	5,000	5,000	500,000	100

Figure 18.13 ABC analysis for Worked example 18.6

18.17 What is the purpose of an ABC analysis of inventories?

18.18 Which items can best be dealt with by routine, automated control procedures?

CHAPTER REVIEW

This chapter introduced the idea of quantitative models for stock control.

- Stocks are the stores of materials that organisations hold until they are needed. Virtually every organisation holds stocks of some kind. These inevitably incur costs, which are often surprisingly high.

- There are several reasons for holding stock, but the main one is to give a buffer between supply and demand. Then, depending on circumstances, there are several ways of controlling the stocks. The two main options consider either dependent or independent demand.

- Dependent demand systems often relate demand back to a production plan, or try to eliminate stocks using lean operations.

- Independent demand models look for a balance of unit, reorder, holding and shortage costs that minimises the overall inventory costs. The basic model calculates an optimal order size – the economic order quantity – with related calculations giving the costs and optimal cycle length.

- The reorder level indicates when it is time to place an order. With constant lead time and demand, an order is placed when stock on hand falls to the lead time demand.

- The economic order quantity analysis can be extended in many ways. We illustrated this by adding a fixed production rate.

- When there are large variations in demand it is better to work with service level models. A cycle service level is the probability of meeting all demand in a cycle. When the lead time demand is Normally distributed, we can achieve a specified service level by adding extra safety stock.

- An alternative approach uses periodic reviews to place orders of variable size at regular intervals. Then the order quantity is the amount that raises current stock to a target level.

- ABC analyses categorise items according to their importance. Typically, 20% of items account for 80% of use by value (A items) while the bulk of items account for very little use by value (C items).

CASE STUDY Templar Manufacturing

James Templar founded his own manufacturing company when he was 21 years old. He has continued to run it for the past 35 years and through steady expansion it now employs over 200 people.

A management consultant recently suggested improving the stock control system, but Mr Templar is not sure that this is necessary. He was talking to a meeting of managers and said, 'I don't know how much the present stock control system costs, if it works as well as it could or if the proposals would save money. I do know that we have the things we need in stock and if we have a shortage then enough people complain to make sure that things get sorted out and we don't have problems again. What I want is someone to show me if the proposals are worth looking at.'

The management consultant asked what kind of demonstration Mr Templar would like and was told, 'I know you wanted to run a pilot scheme before starting work on a revised stock control system. I still need convincing that it is even worth going ahead with the pilot scheme. I don't want anything fancy. Let me give you an example of

one of the components we make and see what you can do.'

'This component is basically a flanged orbital hub which costs us about £15 to make. We use about 2,000 a year. At the moment we can make them at a rate of 70 a week, but plan only one batch every quarter. Each time we set up the production it costs £345 to change the production line and £85 for preparation and scheduling costs. Other stock holding costs are related to the unit costs including insurance (1% a year), deterioration and obsolescence (2%) and capital (13%). I think that we could make them a bit faster, say up to 90 a week, and the unit cost could even fall a few per cent. Of course, we could make them a bit slower, but this would raise the cost by a few per cent.'

Questions

■ If you were the management consultant, how would you demonstrate the benefit of a new stock control system to Mr Templar?

■ What information would you need for your demonstration?

PROBLEMS

18.1 The demand for an item is constant at 100 units a year. Unit cost is £50, the cost of processing an order is £20 and holding cost is £10 a unit a year. What are the economic order quantity, cycle length and costs?

18.2 Beograd Inc. works 50 weeks a year and has demand for a part that is constant at 100 units a week. The cost of each unit is $200 and the company aims for a return of 20% on capital invested. Annual warehouse costs are 5% of the value of goods stored. The purchasing department costs $450,000 a year and sends out an average of 2,000 orders. Find the optimal order quantity for the part, the time between orders and the minimum cost of stocking the part.

18.3 Demand for an item is steady at 20 units a week and the economic order quantity has been calculated at 50 units. What is the reorder level when the lead time is (a) 1 week, (b) 2 weeks?

18.4 How would the results for Problem 18.1 change if the part could be supplied only at a fixed rate of 10 units a week? Would there be any benefit in reducing production to 5 units a week?

18.5 H.R. Prewett Limited forecasts the demand for one component to average 18 a day over a 200-day working year. If there are any shortages, production will be disrupted with very high costs. The total cost of placing an order is £800 and holding costs are £400 a unit a year. What is the best inventory policy for the component? How does this compare with the option of making the component internally at a rate of 80 units a day?

18.6 A company advertises a 95% cycle-service level for all stock items. Stock is replenished from a single supplier who guarantees a lead time of four weeks. What reorder level should the company use for an item that has a Normally distributed demand with mean of 1,000 units a week and standard deviation of 100 units? What is the reorder level for a 98% cycle-service level?

18.7 An item of stock has a unit cost of £40, a reorder cost of £50 and a holding cost of £1 a unit a week. Demand for the item has a mean of 100 a week with a standard deviation of 10. Lead time is constant at three weeks. Design a stock policy that gives the item a service level of 95%. How would the costs change with a 90% service level?

18.8 Describe a periodic review system with an interval of two weeks for the company described in Problem 18.6.

18.9 A small store holds 10 categories of product with the following costs and annual demands:

Product	X1	X2	X3	Y1	Y2	Y3	Z1	Z2	Z3	Z4
Unit cost (€)	20	25	30	1	4	6	10	15	20	22
Annual demand	300	200	200	1,000	800	700	3,000	2,000	600	400

Do an ABC analysis of these items.

18.10 Annual demand for an item is 2,000 units, each order costs £10 to place and the annual holding cost is 40% of the unit cost. The unit cost depends on the quantity ordered as follows:

- for quantities less than 500, unit cost is £1
- for quantities between 500 and 1,000, unit cost is £0.80
- for quantities of 1,000 or more, unit cost is £0.60.

What is the best ordering policy for the item?

RESEARCH PROJECTS

18.1 Virtually all inventory control systems are automated. Not surprisingly, there is a lot of software for the routine calculations. Figure 18.14 shows the printout from a computer program that has done some basic calculations. How can managers use such information? What features would you expect to see in commercial inventory management software? Do a survey to compare available packages.

18.2 A small company wants to control the stocks of 30 items. It seems extravagant to buy an inventory control system for this number of items, and there is no one in the company to write their own software. It has been suggested that a spreadsheet can record weekly sales and do related calculations. Do you think this is a reasonable approach? If so, show how you would start designing a spreadsheet for the company to use.

18.3 Current thinking has managers trying to eliminate their stocks. This has been assisted by just-in-time operations, e-business, efficient customer response, point-of-sales equipment, electronic fund transfer, efficient transport and so on. Is this a sensible direction to move in? How do you think technology has affected views of inventory management? Give real examples to illustrate your points.

```
+++ === ECONOMIC ORDER QUANTITY === +++

EOQ Input Data:

    Demand per year (D)                                    =        400
    Order or setup cost per order (Co)                     =       £650
    Holding cost per unit per year (Ch)                    =        £20
    Shortage cost per unit per year (Cs)                   =     £1,000
    Shortage cost per unit, independent of time (π)        =       £100
    Replenishment or production rate per year (P)          =        500
    Lead time for a new order in year (LT)                 =       0.25
    Unit cost (C)                                          =        120

EOQ Output:

    EOQ                =    360.56
    Maximum inventory  =     72.11
    Maximum backorder  =      0.00
    Order interval     =      0.90 year
    Reorder point      =    100.00
        Ordering cost  =    721.11
        Holding cost   =    721.11
        Shortage cost  =      0.00

    Subtotal of inventory cost per year   =    £ 1,442.22
    Material cost per year                =    £48,000.00
    Total cost per year                   =    £49,442.22
```

Figure 18.14 Printout from an inventory control package

Sources of information

Further reading

Material about inventory management is generally included in books on operations management, management science and operational research. There are some books specifically on inventory management and the following list gives a useful starting point.

Arnold J.R., Chapman S.N. and Clive L.M., *Introduction to Materials Management* (6th edition), Pearson Education, Harlow, 2007.

Axsater S., *Inventory Control* (2nd edition), Springer, New York, 2006.

Brooks R., Robinson S. and Lewis C.D., *Simulation and Inventory Control*, Palgrave Macmillan, Basingstoke, 2001.

Cheaitou A., *Production Planning and Inventory Control*, Academic Press, Maryland Heights, MO, 2010.

Emmett S. and Granville D., *Excellence in Inventory Management*, Cambridge Academic, Cambridge, 2007.

Muller M., *Essentials of Inventory Management*, Jaico Publishing House, Mumbai, 2008.

Toomey J.W., *Inventory Management*, Kluwer Acedemic Publishers, Boston, MA, 2000.

Waters D., *Inventory Control and Management* (2nd edition), John Wiley, Chichester, 2003.

Wild T., *Best Practices in Inventory Management* (2nd edition), Butterworth-Heinemann, Oxford, 2002.

Zipkin P.H., *Foundations of Inventory Management*, McGraw-Hill, Boston, MA, 2000.

CHAPTER 19

Project management

Contents

Chapter outline

A 'project' consists of a set of related activities with a clear start and finish and the aim of making a distinct product. Each project is largely unique and needs careful planning to keep it on time and within budget. Network analysis is the most widely used tool for planning projects. This identifies the set of activities that make up a project, shows the relationships between them and presents these in a network. This allows detailed analyses of timing, costs and resources.

After finishing this chapter you should be able to:

- appreciate the need to plan complex projects
- divide a project into distinct activities and show the relationships between them
- draw a project as a network of connected activities
- calculate the timing of activities
- identify critical paths and the overall project duration
- reduce the duration of a project
- draw Gantt charts
- consider the resources needed during a project
- use PERT when there is uncertainty in activity durations.

Project planning

Most of the operations done within organisations are repetitive. For instance, a train operator runs a particular service at the same time every day, a manufacturer makes a stream of similar cars, surgeons do a series of identical operations and a shop serves a series of customers. But not all operations are repetitive. Some are distinct pieces of work that are largely self-contained and make a unique product. These are described as projects.

> - A **project** is a unique and self-contained piece of work that makes a one-off product.
> - It has a distinct start and finish, and all activities must be coordinated within this timeframe.

With this broad definition you can see that we all do small projects every day, such as preparing a meal, writing an essay, building a fence or organising a party. Each of these projects needs planning, and in particular we have to identify:

- the activities that form the project
- the order in which these activities are done
- the timing of each activity
- the resources needed at each stage
- the costs involved.

This is fairly easy for small projects and a little thought is enough to make sure that they run smoothly. But business projects can be very large and expensive – such as the installation of a new information system, building a power station, organising the Olympic Games, writing a major consultancy report, launching a new product or moving to new offices. Such large projects can run smoothly only if they are carefully planned and managed. In this chapter we look at project network analysis, which is the most widely used method of organising complex projects.

In recent years there has been a huge growth in interest in project management. There are several reasons for this, including:

- wider recognition of the distinct features of projects
- recognition that traditional management methods could not deliver acceptable results for projects
- development of new methods that were brought together in the discipline of project management
- the observed success of early projects using these methods
- a growing number of large or mega-projects that relied on formal management.

Perhaps the key point was the recognition that many apparently continuous processes were actually – or could best be organised as – projects. For instance, the surgeons we mentioned above doing a series of identical operations would be more effective if they divided their work into a series of distinct projects – in the same way that marketing teams work on a series of distinct campaigns, management consultants work on a series of projects for different clients, a manufacturing process can often be broken down into a series of distinct parts and so on.

19.1 What is a project?

19.2 What is project management?

19.3 Project management is concerned only with major capital projects. Is this true?

IDEAS IN PRACTICE   The Channel Tunnel

In December 1990 Transmanche Link, a consortium of 10 British and French companies, finished the first continuous tunnel under the English Channel. The main tunnels were opened in 1994 and handed over to Eurotunnel to start operations. This was a significant step in a huge project.[1]

The Channel Tunnel was the world's largest privately funded construction project, needing the largest banking syndicate ever assembled, with 200 participating banks and finance institutions. By 1994 the estimated cost of the tunnel was £9 billion, and by 1998 this had risen to £15 billion with rail companies investing another £3 billion in rolling stock and infrastructure. At its peak the project employed 14,500 people.

The idea of a tunnel under the Channel is not new. In 1802 Albert Mathieu, one of Napoleon's engineers, drew a crude plan and at various times several trial tunnels were dug. This project had clearly been developing for a very long time and it was executed by very successful and experienced companies. They dug a total of 150 km of tunnels,

with two main rail tunnels and a third service tunnel. By all accounts, the tunnel was a triumph of construction. Nonetheless, its costs were several times the original estimates of £4.5 billion, the consortium was continually looking for additional funding, the opening date was delayed so much that extra interest charges, bankers' and lawyers' fees amounted to £1 billion and participants were plagued by legal disputes. Sceptical reports suggest that the final cost of the project was £10 billion more than the benefits.[2]

It is common for major projects to overrun their budgets and schedules. In 1994 the British Library was half-built after 12 years, the cost had tripled to £450 million and a House of Commons Committee reported that 'no one – ministers, library staff, building contractors, anyone at all – has more than the faintest idea when the building will be completed, when it will be open for use or how much it will cost.'[3] In a study of 1,449 projects by the Association of Project Managers, only 12 came in on time and under budget.

Network analysis

A 'project network' is a diagram that shows the relationships between all the activities that make up the project. It consists of a series of alternating circles – or nodes – connected by arrows. There are two formats for this:

- *Activity on arrow* – each arrow represents an activity, and nodes represent the points when activities start and finish.
- *Activity on node* – each node represents an activity, and arrows show the relationships between them.

Suppose you have a project with three activities, A, B and C, which have to be done in that order. B has to wait until A finishes before it can start, and B must then finish before C can start. We can represent this using the two formats in Figure 19.1.

The choice between these is largely a matter of personal preference. Activity-on-arrow networks are better at showing some relationships and the calculations are easier; activity-on-node networks are easier to draw and put into project planning software. In practice, activity-on-node networks have probably become more common, so we will stick to this format.

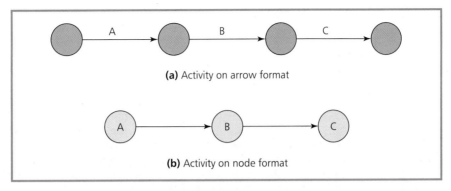

(a) Activity on arrow format

(b) Activity on node format

Figure 19.1 Alternative formats for project networks

WORKED EXAMPLE 19.1

A gardener is building a greenhouse from a kit. The instructions show that this is a project with four main activities:

- A – levelling the ground, which takes 2 days
- B – building the base, which takes 3 days
- C – building the frame, which takes 2 days
- D – fixing the glass, which takes 1 day.

Draw a network for the project.

Solution

The four activities must be done in a fixed order – levelling the ground must be done first, followed by building the base, building the frame and finally fixing the glass. We can describe this order by a dependence table. Here each activity is listed along with those activities that immediately precede it.

Activity	Duration (days)	Description	Immediate predecessor
A	2	level ground	–
B	3	build base	A
C	2	build frame	B
D	1	fix glass	C

Labelling the activities A, B, C and D is a convenient shorthand and allows us to say that activity B has activity A as its immediate predecessor – which is normally stated as 'B depends on A'. In this table we list only the immediate predecessors, so we do not need to say that C depends on A as well as B, since this follows from the other dependencies. Activity A has no immediate predecessors and can start whenever convenient.

Now we can draw a network from the dependence table, shown in Figure 19.2.

Figure 19.2 Network for building a greenhouse

The directions of the arrows show precedence – each preceding activity must finish before the following one starts – and following activities can start as soon as preceding ones finish. In Worked example 19.1, levelling the ground must be done first and as soon as this is finished the base can be built. The frame can be built as soon as the base is finished, and the glass can be fixed as soon as the frame is built.

Find the schedule for activities in Worked example 19.1. What happens if the base takes more than 3 days, or the glass is delayed, or erecting the frame takes less than 2 days?

Solution

The schedule gives the time when each activity is done. If we take a notional starting time of zero, we can finish levelling the ground by the end of day 2. Then we can start building the base, and as this takes 3 days we finish by the end of day 5. Then we can start building the frame, and as this takes 2 days we finish by the end of day 7. Finally, we can start fixing the glass, which takes 1 day so we finish by the end of day 8.

If the base takes more than 3 days to build, or the glass is not delivered by day 7, the project is delayed. If building the frame takes less than 2 days, the project finishes early.

Now we have a timetable for the project showing when each activity starts and finishes – and we can use this timetable to schedule resources. We know exactly when we need a concrete mixer, when equipment is needed to clear the ground, when woodworkers should be hired and so on. In other words, we have an outline of the way that the project will run and the overall approach of project planning. We will look at the details in the rest of the chapter. These involve the major steps of:

- defining the separate activities and their durations
- determining the dependence of activities
- drawing a network
- analysing the timing of the project
- scheduling resources
- reviewing costs.

Drawing larger networks

In principle, you can draw networks of any size, simply by starting at the left-hand side with activities that do not depend on any others. Then you add activities that depend only on these first activities; then add activities that depend only on the latest activities and so on. The network expands systematically, working from left to right, until you have added all the activities and the network is complete. The two main rules are:

- Before an activity can begin, all preceding activities must be finished.
- The arrows only show precedence and neither their length nor their direction has any significance.

There are several other rules to make sure the completed network is sensible:

- To make things clear, you add one 'start' and one 'finish' activity to a network to define the whole project.
- Every arrow must have a head and a tail connecting two different activities.
- Every activity (apart from the start and finish) must have at least one predecessor and at least one successor activity.
- There must be no loops in the network.

WORKED EXAMPLE 19.3

When Prahalad Commercial opened a new office, they defined the work as a project with these activities and dependencies:

Activity	Description	Depends on
A	Find office location	–
B	Recruit new staff	–
C	Make office alterations	A
D	Order equipment needed	A
E	Install new equipment	D
F	Train staff	B
G	Start operations	C, E, F

Draw a network of this project.

Solution

Activities A and B have no predecessors and can start as soon as convenient. As soon as activity A is finished, both C and D can start; E can start as soon as D is finished, and F can start as soon as B is finished. G can start only when C, E and F have all finished. Figure 19.3 shows the resulting network.

The network shows that the project starts with activities A and B, but this does not mean that these must start at the same time – only that they can both start as soon as convenient and must be finished before any following activity can start. On the other hand, activity G must wait until C, E and F are all finished. This does not mean that C, E and F must finish at the same time – only that they must all finish before G can start.

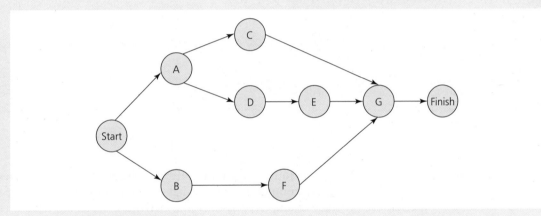

Figure 19.3 Network for Prahalad Commercial

WORKED EXAMPLE 19.4

This dependence table describes a software development project. Draw a network of the project.

Activity	Depends on	Activity	Depends on
A	J	I	J
B	C, G	J	–
C	A	K	B
D	F, K, N	L	I
E	J	M	I
F	B, H, L	N	M
G	A, E, I	O	M
H	G	P	O

Solution

This seems a difficult network, but the steps are fairly straightforward. Activity J is the only one that does not depend on anything else, so this starts the network. Then we can add activities A, E and I, which depend only on J. Then we can add activities that depend on A and E. Continuing this systematic addition of activities leads to the network shown in Figure 19.4.

Worked example 19.4 continued

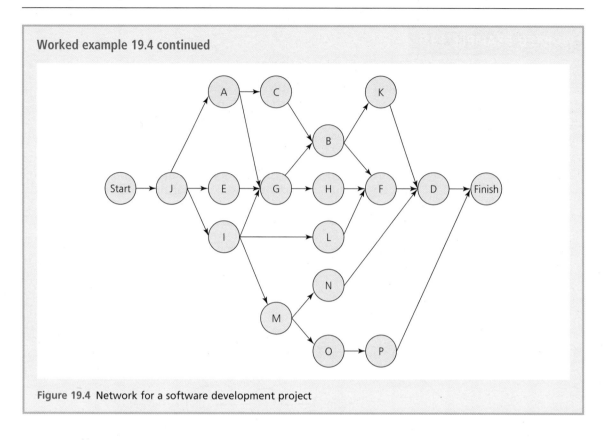

Figure 19.4 Network for a software development project

Bigger networks obviously take more effort to draw and analyse – even when this is done by computer. We divided our initial task of building a greenhouse (Worked example 19.1) into four activities. We could have used a lot more – perhaps clearing vegetation, laying hardcore, digging the foundations and so on. However, adding more activities gives a more complex network and the significance of each activity declines. So we have to choose the number of activities, balancing the usefulness of a network with its complexity. The best solution is often to use several layers of networks. An entire project may be divided into a number of major parts, represented by an overall network. Then each major part can be taken in turn and broken down into further activities, represented by a series of more detailed networks. If necessary, these more detailed networks can, in turn, be broken down into yet more detail – and so on until managers have the appropriate level of detail to work with.

Although it might sound easy, agreeing a reasonable set of activities is usually the most difficult part of project planning, particularly with large projects. There can be a lot of disagreement between managers about what activities should be included, what order they should be done in, how long they will take and what resources are needed. When this difficult area has been agreed, the later stages of analysing the project often reduce to mechanical procedures that are largely automated.

19.4   In the networks we have drawn, what do the nodes and arrows represent?

19.5   What basic information do you need to draw a project network?

19.6   What are the main rules of drawing a project network?

Timing of projects

After drawing a project network, we know what order the activities have to be done in and can design the detailed schedule. This means that we find the time when each activity must be done – in particular the four key times:

- earliest start time of an activity – the time at which all preceding activities are finished
- earliest finish time – the earliest start time plus the activity duration
- latest finish time of an activity – the time by which it must be finished to allow the whole project to be completed on schedule
- latest start time – the latest finish time minus the activity duration.

These four times define the time slot that is available for the activity (illustrated in Figure 19.5).

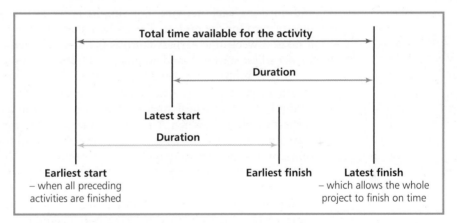

Figure 19.5 Timing of an activity

We can illustrate the calculations for these timings with an example. Suppose a project has the following dependence table, which includes the duration of each activity in weeks. Figure 19.6 shows the network for this project.

Activity	Duration	Depends on
A	3	–
B	2	–
C	2	A
D	4	A
E	1	C
F	3	D
G	3	B
H	4	G
I	5	E, F

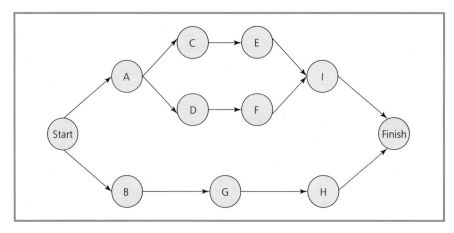

Figure 19.6 Network for timing example

Earliest times

The first part of the timing analysis finds the earliest possible time for starting and finishing each activity. For simplicity we will assume a notional start time of zero for the project. The earliest start of activity B is clearly 0, and as it takes 2 weeks the earliest finish is $0 + 2 = 2$. When B finishes G can start, so its earliest start is 2, and adding the duration of 3 gives an earliest finish of $2 + 3 = 5$. When G finishes H can start, so its earliest start is 5, and adding the duration of 4 gives an earliest finish of $5 + 4 = 9$.

Similarly, the earliest start of A is clearly 0, and as it takes 3 weeks the earliest finish is 3. When A finishes both C and D can start, so the earliest start time for both of these is 3. Adding the durations gives earliest finish times of 5 and 7 respectively. Then E follows C with an earliest start of 5 and earliest finish of 6; F follows D with an earliest start of 7 and earliest finish of 10.

Activity I must wait until both E and F finish. The earliest finishes for these are 6 and 10 respectively, so activity I cannot start until week 10. Then we add the duration of 5 to get the earliest finish of 15. The finish of the project comes when both H and I are finished. These have earliest finish times of 9 and 15 respectively, so the earliest finish of the whole project is week 15. We can show these times in the following table.

Activity	Duration	Earliest start	Earliest finish
A	3	0	3
B	2	0	2
C	2	3	5
D	4	3	7
E	1	5	6
F	3	7	10
G	3	2	5
H	4	5	9
I	5	10	15

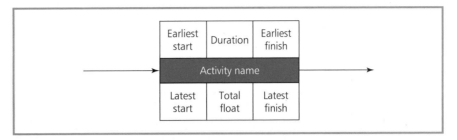

Figure 19.7 Format for the times added to activities

Alternatively we can add them directly to the network, with each node drawn as a box containing the times with the format shown in Figure 19.7. Here the earliest start, duration and earliest finish are written across the top of the box.

It is easiest to add these times to the network, using the form in Figure 19.7. The earliest times are shown in the top row of each activity. The next calculations, described below, find the latest times, with results for the whole project shown in Figure 19.8.

Latest times

The next part of the timing analysis finds the latest time for starting and finishing each activity. The procedure for this is almost the reverse of the procedure for finding the earliest times.

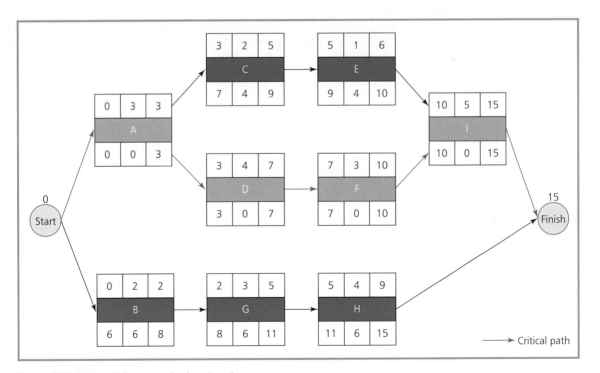

Figure 19.8 Network for example showing times

The earliest finish time for the whole project is week 15. If we want the project to finish then, we set this as the latest finish time. The latest finish time of activity H is clearly 15, so its latest start time is the duration 4 earlier than this at $15 - 4 = 11$. Activity G must finish before this so its latest finish is 11, and its latest start is the duration of 3 earlier at $11 - 3 = 8$. Activity B must be finished before this so its latest finish is 8, and the latest start is the duration 2 earlier at $8 - 2 = 6$.

Now activity I must also finish by week 15, so its latest start is its duration of 5 earlier than this, at 10. But for I to start at 10 both E and F must finish by 10, so this gives both of their latest finish times. They must start their durations earlier at time $10 - 1 = 9$ for E and $10 - 3 = 7$ for F. Activity C must finish by time 9, so its latest start is $9 - 2 = 7$, and activity D must finish by time 7, so its latest start is $7 - 4 = 3$.

Activity A must finish in time for both C and D to start. Activity C has a latest start of 7 and activity D has a latest start of 3, so A must be finished for both of these giving a latest finish of 3 and a latest start of 0. Similarly the latest time to start the project must allow both A to start at 0 and B to start at 6, so it must start at time 0. This gives the timings in the following table, and you can also see these at the ends of the bottom rows of figures for each activity in Figure 19.8.

Activity	Duration	Earliest start	Earliest finish	Latest start	Latest finish
A	3	0	3	0	3
B	2	0	2	6	8
C	2	3	5	7	9
D	4	3	7	3	7
E	1	5	6	9	10
F	3	7	10	7	10
G	3	2	5	8	11
H	4	5	9	11	15
I	5	10	15	10	15

Critical activities

You can see that some activities have flexibility in their timing – activity G can start as early as week 2 or as late as week 8, while activity C can start as early as week 3 or as late as week 7. On the other hand, some activities have no flexibility at all – activities A, D, F and I have no flexibility because their latest start time is the same as their earliest start time. The activities that have to be done at fixed times are the critical activities.

> - Each of the critical activities has to be done at a fixed time.
> - They form a continuous path through the network, called the critical path.

The length of the critical path sets the overall project duration. If one of the critical activities is extended by a certain amount, the overall project duration is extended by this amount; if one of the critical activities is delayed by some time, the overall project duration is extended by this delay. On the other hand, if one of the critical activities is made shorter then the overall project duration may be reduced.

The activities that have some flexibility in timing are the non-critical activities and these may be delayed or extended without necessarily affecting the overall project duration. However, there is a limit to the amount by which a non-critical activity can be extended without affecting the project duration, and this is measured by the total float. The total float – sometimes called slack – is the difference between the amount of time available for an activity and the time it actually needs. If an activity takes three weeks and there is a five-week slot during which it can be done, the total float is 5 – 3 = 2 weeks. It is the difference between the earliest and latest start times – which is clearly the same as the difference between the earliest and latest finish times.

$$\text{total float} = \text{latest start time} - \text{earliest start time}$$

or

$$\text{total float} = \text{latest finish time} - \text{earliest finish time}$$

The total float is zero for critical activities and has some positive value for non-critical activities. In the example above, the earliest and latest starts of activity D are both 3, so the total float is 3 – 3 = 0, showing that this is one of the critical activities. The earliest and latest starts of activity G are 2 and 8, so the total float is 8 – 2 = 6, showing that this is a non-critical activity. These values are also shown – in the middle of the bottom line – on the activities in the network in Figure 19.8.

The total float shows the time that an activity can expand or be delayed without affecting the overall project duration. For instance, the duration of G can expand by up to 6 weeks without affecting the duration of the project, but if it takes more than this the project will be delayed. A negative total float means that an activity is already late and the project cannot be finished within the proposed time. The following table shows the complete calculations for the example.

Activity	Duration	Earliest time		Latest time		Total float
		Start	Finish	Start	Finish	
A	3	0	3	0	3	0
B	2	0	2	6	8	6
C	2	3	5	7	9	4
D	4	3	7	3	7	0
E	1	5	6	9	10	4
F	3	7	10	7	10	0
G	3	2	5	8	11	6
H	4	5	9	11	15	6
I	5	10	15	10	15	0

WORKED EXAMPLE 19.5

ArcticCom build communication satellite receiving stations for isolated communities in Northern Europe. The table shows the activities for building a small station, the expected durations (in days) and dependences. Draw the network for this project, find its duration and calculate the total float of each activity.

Activity	Description	Duration	Depends on
A	Design internal equipment	10	–
B	Design building	5	A
C	Order parts for equipment	3	A
D	Order material for building	2	B
E	Wait for equipment parts	15	C
F	Wait for building material	10	D
G	Employ equipment assemblers	5	A
H	Employ building workers	4	B
I	Install equipment	20	E, G, J
J	Complete building	30	F, H

Solution

Figure 19.9 shows the network for this problem. Repeating the calculations described above gives this table of results.

Activity	Duration	Earliest time Start	Earliest time Finish	Latest time Start	Latest time Finish	Total float
A	10	0	10	0	10	0 *
B	5	10	15	10	15	0 *
C	3	10	13	39	42	29
D	2	15	17	15	17	0 *
E	15	13	28	42	57	29
F	10	17	27	17	27	0 *
G	5	10	15	52	57	42
H	4	15	19	23	27	8
I	20	57	77	57	77	0 *
J	30	27	57	27	57	0 *

The duration of the project is 77 days, defined by the critical path* A, B, D, F, I and J.

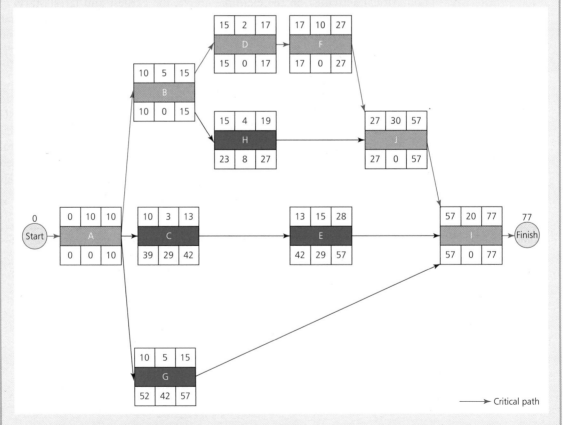

Figure 19.9 Network for building a communications station

Reducing a project duration

Suppose that you have drawn a network and analysed the timing, only to find that the project takes longer than you want. How can you reduce its length? The underlying idea is that you can put more resources into an activity – typically more people working on it – and finish it faster. This is often described as 'crashing' an activity. Obviously more resources come at higher cost, so there is always a balance. Putting in more resources makes the project shorter – but this comes at a higher cost. When there are penalty costs for late completion and bonuses for early completion – as well as the usual costs and other work competing for scarce resources – the allocation of resources becomes a difficult problem.

Then there is the question of which activities to reduce in length. For this you have to remember that the overall duration is set by the critical path, so you can reduce the overall duration only by reducing the durations of critical activities. Reducing the duration of non-critical activities has no effect on the project duration. But you have to be careful here. Small reductions are generally alright, but if you keep reducing the length of the critical path there must come a point when some other path through the network becomes critical. You can find this point from the total float on paths parallel to the critical path. Each activity on a parallel path has the same total float, and when you reduce the critical path by more than this then the parallel path itself becomes critical.

WORKED EXAMPLE 19.6

The project network in Figure 19.10 has a duration of 14 with A, B and C as the critical path. If each activity can be reduced by up to 50% of the original duration, how would you reduce the overall duration to: (a) 13 weeks, (b) 11 weeks, (c) 9 weeks? If reductions cost an average of $1,000 per week, what is the cost of finishing the project by week 9?

Solution
The analysis of activity times is as follows.

Activity	Duration	Earliest		Latest		Total float
		Start	Finish	Start	Finish	
A	8	0	8	0	8	0 *
B	4	8	12	8	12	0 *
C	2	12	14	12	14	0 *
D	3	0	3	2	5	2
E	6	3	9	5	11	2
F	3	9	12	11	14	2
G	2	0	2	4	6	4
H	4	2	6	6	10	4
I	4	6	10	10	14	4

There are three parallel paths, A–B–C, D–E–F and G–H–I. The critical path is A–B–C and these critical activities have zero total float. The total float of activities on the other two paths are 2 and 4 respectively. This means that we can reduce the critical path A–B–C by up to 2, but if we reduce it any more then the path D–E–F becomes critical. If we reduce the critical path by more than 4, the path G–H–I also becomes critical.

(a) To finish in 13 weeks we need to reduce the critical path by one week. It is usually easiest to find savings in longer activities, so we can suggest reducing the duration of A to seven weeks.

(b) To finish in 11 weeks needs a further reduction of two weeks in the critical path. We can also remove this from A, but the path D–E–F has now become critical with a duration of 12 weeks. We have to reduce this by one week, and can remove this from E – again chosen as the longest activity in the critical path.

▶

Worked example 19.6 continued

(c) To finish in 9 weeks needs five weeks removed from the path A–B–C (say four from A and one from B), three weeks removed from the path D–E–F (say from E), and one week removed from the path G–H–I (say from H).

To get a five-week reduction in the project duration, we have reduced the durations of individual activities by a total of 5 + 3 + 1 = 9 weeks. This gives a total cost of 9 × 1,000 = $9,000.

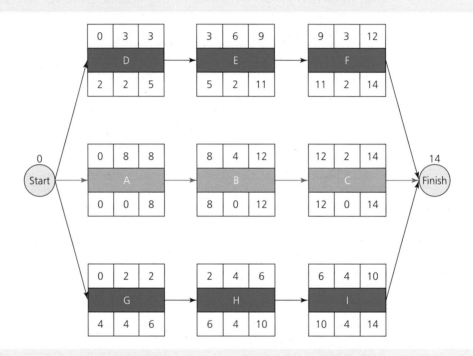

Figure 19.10 Network for Worked example 19.6

Resource levelling

When a project has been properly planned and is actually being executed, managers have to monitor progress to make sure that everything is done at the scheduled times. But these times are not really clear from a network. It is much easier to see the times in a Gantt chart. This is a form of bar chart that consists of a time scale across the bottom, with activities listed down the left-hand side and times when activities should be done blocked off in the body of the chart.

WORKED EXAMPLE 19.7

Draw a Gantt chart for the original data in Worked example 19.6, assuming that each activity starts as early as possible.

Solution

We have already done the timing analysis for this project. If each activity starts as early as possible, we can show the times needed by the blocked-off areas in Figure 19.11. The total float of each activity is added afterwards as a broken line. The total float is the maximum expansion that still allows the project to finish on time – so provided an activity is completed before the end of the broken line, there should be no problem in keeping to the planned duration.

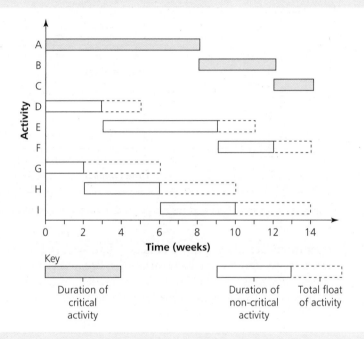

Figure 19.11 Gantt chart for Worked example 19.7

The main benefit of Gantt charts is that they show clearly the state of each activity at any point in the project. They show which activities should be in hand, as well as those that should be finished and those about to start. Gantt charts are also useful for planning the allocation of resources. For simplicity, suppose that each activity in the Gantt chart in Figure 19.11 uses one unit of a particular resource – perhaps one team of workers. If all activities start as soon as possible, we can draw a vertical bar chart to show the resources in use at any time. The project starts with activities A, D and G, so these need three teams. At the end of week 2 one team can move from G to H, but three teams will still be needed. Continuing these allocations gives the graph of resources shown in Figure 19.12.

In this example, the use of resources is steady for most of the project and begins to fall only near the end. It is rare to get such a smooth pattern of resource use and usually there is a series of peaks and troughs. Smooth

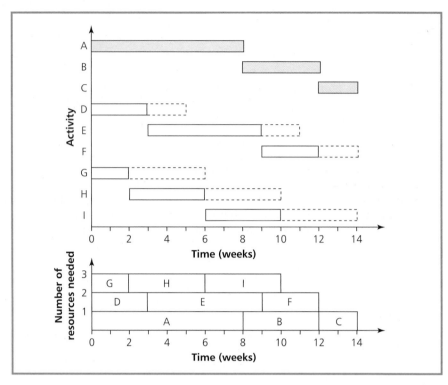

Figure 19.12 Gantt chart and resources used during a project (Worked example 19.7)

operations are always more efficient than widely fluctuating ones, so managers try to smooth out such variations. Because critical activities are at fixed times, they must do this levelling by rescheduling non-critical activities, and in particular by delaying activities with relatively large total floats. This kind of adjustment can become rather messy so it is usually best to use standard software. This can also be used for the routine calculations for workloads, times and costs – along with all the information processing needed to monitor actual operations. A lot of software is available for project management – as usual ranging from the basic to the very sophisticated. A few widely used packages are ConceptDraw Project, Fast Track Schedule, Microsoft Project, Oracle Projects, Primavera Project Planner, SuperProject and TurboProject.

Review questions

19.7 How do you calculate the earliest and latest start times for an activity?

19.8 What is the total float of an activity?

19.9 How big is the total float of a critical activity?

19.10 What is the significance of the critical path?

19.11 Which activities must be shortened to reduce the overall duration of a project?

19.12 By how much can a critical path usefully be shortened?

19.13 What are the main benefits of Gantt charts?

19.14 How can resource use be smoothed during a project?

Bechtel Corporation

Bechtel Corporation is one of the world's leading engineering, construction and project management companies. Its headquarters are in San Francisco, from which it runs 40 offices around the world, and employs 50,000 people. With annual revenues of more than $30 billion, it is regularly ranked as America's leading contracting company.

Bechtel has more than a century of experience in complex projects, and has been involved in 25,000 projects in most countries of the world – including construction of pipelines, power stations, airports, roads, nuclear power plants, railways, chemical and petrochemical plants and mining. Among these projects are a number of 'signature projects'. These are typically mega-projects that cost over a billion dollars – they are commercially, technically and organisationally complex, take a long time, involve high risk, are difficult to evaluate, are politically sensitive and include environmental concerns. Historically, these included construction of the Hoover Dam, with a selection of other signature projects including:

1985 – James Bay Hydro Complex harnessing the power of three rivers in Quebec to generate 10,300 megawatts of electricity at a cost of $13.8 billion
1994 – the 32-mile undersea leg of the Channel Tunnel between England and France
1998 – the new Hong Kong Airport at a total cost of US$20 billion
2000 – one of the world's largest aluminium smelters in Alma, Quebec for Alcan with a capacity of more than 400,000 tons a year
2004 – Athens metro for the summer Olympic games
2004 – 600-kilometre Salah natural gas pipelines in the desert of Algeria
2005 – Jubail Industrial City, Saudi Arabia, recognised as the largest single industrial development project in history with a cost of $20 billion
2005 – CSPC Petrochemicals project in Nanhai, China covering 1,055 acres and costing $4.3 billion
2006 – Boston Central Artery, the most complex urban transport project ever undertaken in the USA, taking 30 years of planning and 12 years in construction.

Source: Website at www.bechtel.com.

Project evaluation and review technique

The approach we have described so far is the critical path method (CPM) where each activity is given a single, fixed duration. But, as you know from experience, the time needed for any job can vary quite widely. Project evaluation and review technique (PERT) is a useful extension to CPM that allows for uncertainty in duration. In particular, it uses the observation that activity durations often follow a beta distribution. This looks like a skewed Normal distribution and has the useful property that the mean and variance can be found from three estimates of duration:

- An *optimistic duration* (O) – the shortest time an activity takes if everything goes smoothly and without any difficulties.
- A *most likely duration* (M) – the duration of the activity under normal conditions.
- A *pessimistic duration* (P) – the time needed if there are significant problems and delays.

Then we can find the expected activity duration and variance from the rule of sixths:

$$\text{expected duration} = \frac{O + 4M + P}{6}$$

$$\text{variance} = \frac{(P - O)^2}{36}$$

If an activity has an optimistic duration of 4 days, a most likely duration of 5 days and a pessimistic duration of 12 days, then:

$$\begin{aligned}
\text{expected duration} &= (O + 4M + P) / 6 \\
&= (4 + 4 \times 5 + 12) / 6 \\
&= 6
\end{aligned}$$

$$\begin{aligned}
\text{variance} &= (P - O)^2 / 36 \\
&= (12 - 4)^2 / 36 \\
&= 1.78
\end{aligned}$$

We can use the expected values in the same way as the single estimate of CPM – but the variance allows us to do some more calculations with the timings.

WORKED EXAMPLE 19.8

The table shows the dependences and estimated durations of nine activities in a project. What is the project's expected duration?

Activity	Depends on	Duration		
		Optimistic	Most likely	Pessimistic
A	–	2	3	10
B	–	4	5	12
C	–	8	10	12
D	A, G	4	4	4
E	B	3	6	15
F	B	2	5	8
G	B	6	6	6
H	C, F	5	7	15
I	D, E	6	8	10

Solution

We can find the expected duration and variance of each activity from the rule of sixths.

For activity A:

$$\begin{aligned}
\text{expected duration} &= (O + 4M + P) / 6 \\
&= (2 + 4 \times 3 + 10) / 6 \\
&= 4
\end{aligned}$$

$$\begin{aligned}
\text{variance} &= (P - O)^2 / 36 \\
&= (10 - 2)^2 / 36 \\
&= 1.78
\end{aligned}$$

Repeating these calculations for other activities gives the results shown in Figure 19.13. We can use these to draw the network in Figure 19.14.

	A	B	C	D	E	F	G	H	I	J	K
1	**PERT Analysis**										
2											
3		**Duration**						**Earliest**		**Latest**	
4	**Activity**	**Optimistic**	**Most likely**	**Pessimistic**	**Expected**	**Variance**	**Start**	**Finish**	**Start**	**Finish**	**Total float**
5	A	2	3	10	4	1.78	0	4	8	12	8
6	B	4	5	12	6	1.78	0	6	0	6	0
7	C	8	10	12	10	0.44	0	10	6	16	6
8	D	4	4	4	4	0.00	12	16	12	16	0
9	E	3	6	15	7	4.00	6	13	9	16	3
10	F	2	5	8	5	1.00	6	11	11	16	5
11	G	6	6	6	6	0.00	6	12	6	12	0
12	H	5	7	15	8	2.78	11	19	16	24	5
13	I	6	8	10	8	0.44	16	24	16	24	0

Figure 19.13 Activity timing analysis for Worked example 19.8

Worked example 19.8 continued

From this you can see that the critical path for the project is B, G, D and I. The expected duration of the project is 24. The network shows the earliest and latest times for each activity, along with the floats, and we have added these timings to the spreadsheet in Figure 19.13.

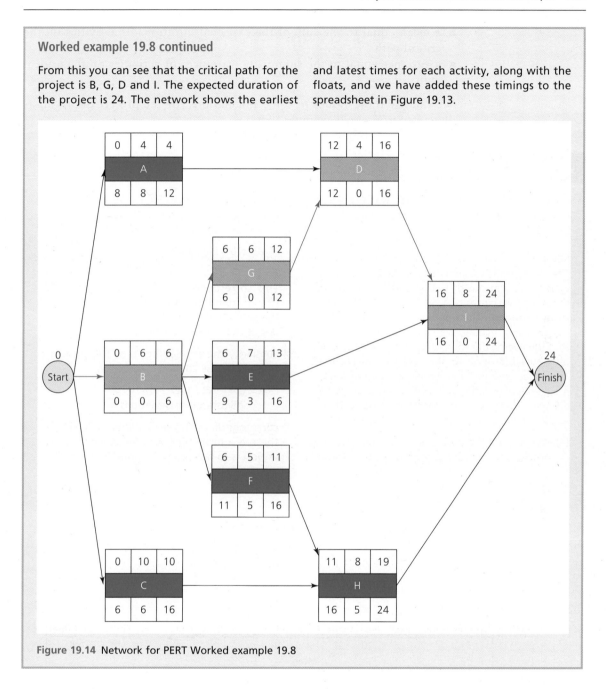

Figure 19.14 Network for PERT Worked example 19.8

The duration of the critical path is the sum of the durations of activities making up that path – and when the duration of each activity is variable, the overall duration of the project is also variable. The central limit theorem tells us that when there is a large number of activities on the critical path, and assuming that the duration of each activity is independent of the others, the overall duration of the project is Normally distributed. This distribution has:

- a mean equal to the sum of the expected durations of activities on the critical path
- a variance equal to the sum of the variances of activities on the critical path.

We can use these values in some calculations for the project duration, as illustrated in Worked example 19.9.

WORKED EXAMPLE 19.9

What are the probabilities that the project in Worked example 19.8 is finished before (a) day 26, (b) day 20?

Solution

The critical path is activities B, G, D and I with expected durations of 6, 6, 4 and 8 days respectively, and variances of 1.78, 0, 0 and 0.44 respectively. Although the number of activities on the critical path is small, we can reasonably assume that the overall duration of the project is Normally distributed (at least to illustrate the calculation). The expected duration then has a mean of $6 + 6 + 4 + 8 = 24$. The variance in project duration is $1.78 + 0 + 0 + 0.44 = 2.22$, so the standard deviation is $\sqrt{2.22} = 1.49$.

(a) We can find the probability that the project is not finished before day 26 from the Normal distribution shown in Figure 19.15. As usual Z is the number of standard deviations the point of interest is away from the mean:

$$Z = (26 - 24) / 1.49$$
$$= 1.34 \text{ standard deviations}$$

This corresponds to a probability of 0.0901 (found from tables or a statistical package). So the probability that the project is finished by day 26 is $1 - 0.0901 = 0.9099$.

(b) Similarly, the probability that the project is finished by day 20 has:

$$Z = (24 - 20) / 1.49$$
$$= 2.68 \text{ standard deviations}$$

corresponding to a probability of 0.0037. So there is a probability of only 0.0037 that the project is completed before day 20.

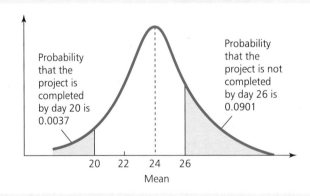

Figure 19.15 Normal distribution for project duration

Review questions

19.15 What is the difference between CPM and PERT?

19.16 What is the 'rule of sixths' and when is it used?

19.17 How can you calculate the expected duration of a project and its variance?

Loch Moraigh Distillery

The managers of Loch Moraigh whisky distillery examined the inventory control system to find the best stock levels to meet forecast demand. They concluded that an expanded computer system was needed. This would extrapolate past-demand patterns and use these to set appropriate stock levels. These stock levels would then be passed to a production control module that varies the quantities bottled.

The first part of this proposed system was called DFS (Demand Forecasting System) while the second part was ICS (Inventory Control System). The introduction of these systems took about 12 months, including linking to the production control module that was already working. The introduction of DFS and ICS was a self-contained project with these activities:

Activity	Description
A	Examine existing system and environment of ICS
B	Collect costs and other data relevant to ICS
C	Construct and test models for ICS
D	Write and test computer programs for ICS models
E	Design and print data input forms for ICS data
F	Document ICS programs and monitoring procedures
G	Examine sources of demand data and its collection
H	Construct and test models for DFS
I	Organise past demand data
J	Write and test computer programs for DFS models
K	Design and print data input forms for DFS data
L	Document DFS programs and monitoring procedures
M	Train staff in the use of DFS and ICS
N	Initialise data for ICS programs (ICS staff)
P	Initialise data for DFS programs (DFS staff)
Q	Create base files for DFS
R	Run system for trial period
S	Implement final system

An initial run of a project management package gave the results shown in Figure 19.16

Original network data

No.	Code	Name	Expected completion time	Immediately preceding activities 1	2	3	4	5	6	7
1	A	Examine system	2.00							
2	B	Collect ICS data	1.00	A						
3	C	Test ICS models	2.00	A						
4	D	Program ICS	4.00	C						
5	E	Design ICS forms	1.00	C						
6	F	Document ICS	2.00	D	E					
7	G	Examine demand	2.00							
8	H	Test DFS models	4.00	A	G					
9	I	Organise data	2.00	G						
10	J	Program DFS	6.00	H	K					
11	K	Design DFS forms	2.00	A	G					
12	L	Document DFS	3.00	J						
13	M	Train staff	2.00	F	L					
14	N	Initialise ICS	1.00	B	M					
15	P	Initialise DFS	1.00	I	M					
16	Q	Create DFS files	1.00	P						
17	R	Trial period	4.00	N	Q					
18	S	Implement	2.00	R						

Figure 19.16 Initial printout for the project at Loch Moraigh Distillery

Ideas in practice continued

Activity report

Activity			Planning times					
No	Code	Name	Exp.t	ES	LS	EF	LF	Slack
1	A	Examine system	2.0	0.0	0.0	2.0	2.0	0.0
2	B	Collect ICS	1.0	2.0	17.0	3.0	18.0	15.0
3	C	Test ICS models	2.0	2.0	7.0	4.0	9.0	5.0
4	D	Program ICS	4.0	4.0	9.0	8.0	13.0	5.0
5	E	Design ICS forms	1.0	4.0	12.0	5.0	13.0	8.0
6	F	Document ICS	2.0	8.0	13.0	10.0	15.0	5.0
7	G	Examine demand	2.0	0.0	0.0	2.0	2.0	0.0
8	H	Test DFS models	4.0	2.0	2.0	6.0	6.0	0.0
9	I	Organise data	2.0	2.0	15.0	4.0	17.0	13.0
10	J	Program DFS	6.0	6.0	6.0	12.0	12.0	0.0
11	K	Design DFS forms	2.0	2.0	4.0	4.0	6.0	2.0
12	L	Document DFS	3.0	12.0	12.0	15.0	15.0	0.0
13	M	Train staff	2.0	15.0	15.0	17.0	17.0	0.0
14	N	Initialise ICS	1.0	17.0	18.0	18.0	19.0	1.0
15	P	Initialise DFS	1.0	17.0	17.0	18.0	18.0	0.0
16	Q	Create DFS files	1.0	18.0	18.0	19.0	19.0	0.0
17	R	Trial period	4.0	19.0	19.0	23.0	23.0	0.0
18	S	Implement	2.0	23.0	23.0	25.0	25.0	0.0

Expected project duration = 25

The following path(s) are critical:

$A \rightarrow H \rightarrow J \rightarrow L \rightarrow M \rightarrow P \rightarrow Q \rightarrow R \rightarrow S$
$G \rightarrow H \rightarrow J \rightarrow L \rightarrow M \rightarrow P \rightarrow Q \rightarrow R \rightarrow S$

Figure 19.16 continued

CHAPTER REVIEW

This chapter introduced the topic of project management, which is an increasingly important area for managers.

- A project is defined as a self-contained piece of work that has a clear start and finish. It consists of the activities needed to make a distinct product.

- Projects are often large and need detailed planning. Project network analysis is the most widely used tool for planning projects. This starts by dividing the project into separate activities, with a dependence table showing the relationships between activities.

- The dependence table can be used to draw a network of nodes and connecting arrows to represent the project.

- After drawing a network, you can analyse the timing. This means finding the earliest and latest start and finish times for each activity. The total float measures the amount of flexibility in timing.

- Some activities have no total float and are at fixed times. These form the critical path that sets the project duration. Other activities have flexibility in timing and are non-critical.

- When managers want to reduce the duration of a project, they have to reduce the length of the critical path. They can reduce the critical path only by a certain amount before another parallel path becomes critical. This limit is set by the total float of activities on parallel paths.

- Gantt charts give another view of projects, emphasising the timing. They give useful formats for monitoring progress during project execution and for planning resources.

- The use of resources is an important part of project planning, with managers generally aiming for a steady work level. They achieve this by moving activities within their time slots, usually using specialised software.

- PERT assumes that there is uncertainty in activity durations, and the rule of sixths gives an expected duration and variance. The overall project duration is Normally distributed with mean and variance given by adding values for activities on the critical path.

CASE STUDY   Westin Contractors

William Purvis looked across his desk at the company's latest management recruit and said, 'Welcome to Westin Contractors. This is a good company to work for and I hope you settle in and will be very happy here. Everyone working for Westin has to be familiar with our basic tools, so you should start by looking at network analysis. Here is a small project we have just costed – I have to give the customer some details about schedules, workloads and budgets by the end of the week. I would like a couple of alternative views with your recommendation of the best. Everything you need is available in the office so don't be afraid to ask for help and advice.'

William Purvis supplied the following data and said that there is a penalty cost of £3,500 for every week the project finished after week 28.

Activity	Depends on	Normal		Crashed		Number of teams
		Time	Cost	Time	Cost	
A	–	3	13	2	15	3
B	A	7	25	4	28	4
C	B, E	5	16	4	19	4
D	C	5	12	3	24	2
E	–	8	32	5	38	6
F	E	6	20	4	30	1
G	F	8	30	6	35	5
H	–	12	41	7	45	6
I	H	6	25	3	30	4
J	E	4	18	3	26	6
K	I, J	12	52	10	60	4
L	I, J	6	20	3	30	1
M	D, G, I	2	7	1	14	1
	B, E	6	18	5	24	5

Question

- If you were the recruit, how would you set about this job and what would you say in your report?

PROBLEMS

19.1 A project has the activities shown in the following dependence table. Draw the network for this project.

Activity	Depends on	Activity	Depends on
A	–	G	B
B	–	H	G
C	A	I	E, F
D	A	J	H, I
E	C	K	E, F
F	B, D	L	K

19.2 (a) BiilsMoore Amateur Dramatic Society is planning its annual production and wants to use a network to coordinate the various activities. What activities do you think should be included in the network?
(b) If discussions lead to the following activities, what would the network look like?
■ assess resources and select play
■ prepare scripts
■ select actors and cast parts
■ rehearse
■ design and organise advertisements
■ prepare stage, lights and sound
■ build scenery
■ sell tickets
■ final arrangements for opening.

19.3 Draw a network for the following dependence table.

Activity	Depends on	Activity	Depends on
A	H	I	F
B	H	J	I
C	K	K	L
D	I, M, N	L	F
E	F	M	O
F	–	N	H
G	E, L	O	A, B
H	E	P	N

19.4 If each activity in Problem 19.3 has a duration of one week, find the earliest and latest start and finish times for each activity and the corresponding total floats.

19.5 Sven Sengler has divided a project into the following activities. What does the network for the project look like?
(a) If each activity can be reduced by up to two weeks, what is the shortest duration of the project and which activities should he reduce?

Activity	Duration (weeks)	Depends on
A	5	–
B	3	–
C	3	B
D	7	A
E	10	B
F	14	A, C
G	7	D, E
H	4	E
I	5	D

(b) Draw a Gantt chart for this project.
(c) If each activity uses one team of people, draw a graph of the manpower needed. How can the manpower be smoothed?

19.6 A project consists of ten activities with estimated durations (in weeks) and dependences shown in the following table.

Activity	Depends on	Duration	Activity	Depends on	Duration
A	–	8	F	C, D	10
B	A	6	G	B, E, F	5
C	–	10	H	F	8
D	–	6	I	G, H, J	6
E	C	2	J	A	4

(a) What are the estimated duration of the project and the earliest and latest times for activities?
(b) If activity B needs special equipment, when should this be hired?
(c) A check on the project at week 12 shows that activity F is running two weeks late, that activity J will now take six weeks and that the equipment for B will not arrive until week 18. How does this affect the overall project duration?

19.7 (a) Analyse the timing and resource use of the project described by the following values.

Activity	Depends on	Duration	Resources
A	–	4	1
B	A	4	2
C	A	3	4
D	B	5	4
E	C	2	2
F	D, E	6	3
G	–	3	3
H	G	7	1
I	G	6	5
J	H	2	3
K	I	4	4
L	J, K	8	2

(b) It costs €1,000 to reduce the duration of an activity by 1. If there is €12,000 available to reduce the duration, what is the shortest time the project can be completed within? What are the minimum resources needed by the revised schedule?

19.8 A project is shown in the following dependence table.

(a) What is the probability that the project will be completed before week 17?
(b) By what time is there a probability of 0.95 that the project will be finished?

Activity	Depends on	Duration (weeks)		
		Optimistic	Most likely	Pessimistic
A	–	1	2	3
B	A	1	3	6
C	B	4	6	10
D	A	1	1	1
E	D	1	2	2
F	E	3	4	8
G	F	2	3	5
H	D	7	9	11
I	A	0	1	4
J	I	2	3	4
K	H, J	3	4	7
L	C, G, K	1	2	7

RESEARCH PROJECTS

19.1 Most projects seem to finish late and over budget. But why should this happen, when there are many tools to help and a lot of experience and knowledge in the area? Find some examples of particularly bad projects and say what went wrong.

19.2 Project managers often say that their jobs consist of processing huge amounts of information, from supplier contacts through to customer delivery. What information is needed for successful project management?

19.3 Find a project with which you are familiar and break it into about 50 activities. Draw the network for the project and do the relevant analyses. Do a small survey of software to help with this analysis. Which package did you use and how useful was it?

19.4 Two project managers were given the following data for eight activities. They calculated a normal completion time of 53 days and a cost of £29,300 – or a crashed completion time of 40 days and a cost of £33,350. See how they got these results, and find how the cost of the project is related to its duration.

Activity number	Activity name	Start event	End event	Normal duration (days)	Crashed duration (days)	Normal cost (£)	Crashed cost (£)
1	Start 1	1	2	15	12	4,500	5,500
2	Start 2	1	3	10	8	3,000	4,500
3	Check	2	3	7	5	1,500	1,800
4	Build	2	4	8	6	800	1,200
5	Employ	3	4	15	10	4,000	5,000
6	Purchase	3	5	12	10	3,500	4,000
7	Install	4	6	16	12	6,000	8,000
8	Operate	5	6	12	8	6,000	8,000

Sources of information

References

1 Fetherston D., *The Chunnel*, Random House, New York, 1997.

2 O'Connell D., Channel tunnel project has made Britain £10 billion poorer, *The Sunday Times*, 8 January 2006.

3 Caulkin S., Noah man who can? *The Observer*, 31 July 1994.

Further reading

Project management is a popular topic and you can find many useful books. These include light reading as well as more serious texts. The following list gives a range that you might try.

Badiru A., *Industrial Project Management*, CRC Press, New York, 2007.

Baker S. and Baker K., *The Complete Idiot's Guide to Project Management*, Alpha Books, Indianapolis, IN, 2000.

Barker S. and Cole R., *Brilliant Project Management*, Prentice Hall, Englewood Cliffs, NJ, 2009.

Berkun S., *The Art of Project Management*, O'Reilly, Sebastopol, CA, 2008.

Burke R., *Fundamentals of Project Management* (2nd edition), Burke Publishing, London, 2010.

Cleland D.I. and Ireland L.R., *Project Management* (5th edition), McGraw-Hill, New York, 2006.

Gido J. and Clements J.P., *Successful Project Management* (4th edition), South-Western College Publishing, Cincinnati, OH, 2008.

Kerzner H., *Project Management* (10th edition), John Wiley, New York, 2009.

Lock D., *The Essentials of Project Management* (9th edition), Gower, Aldershot, 2007.

Lockyer K. and Gordon J., *Project Management and Project Planning* (7th edition), FT Prentice Hall, London, 2005.

Maylor H., *Project Management* (4th edition), FT Prentice Hall, Harlow, 2010.

Meredith J.R. and Mantel S.J., *Project Management: a Managerial Approach* (7th edition), John Wiley, Hoboken, NJ, 2009.

Moore J.H. and Weatherford L.R., *Decision Modelling with Microsoft Excel* (6th edition), Prentice Hall, Upper Saddle River, NJ, 2001.

Portny S., *Project Management for Dummies* (2nd edition), Wiley Publishing, Indianapolis, IN, 2007.

Project Management Institute, *A Guide to the Project Management Body of Knowledge* (4th edition), PMI Publications, Drexel Hill, PA, 2009 (an online version is available from www.pmi.org).

Shtub A., Bard J. and Globerson S., *Project Management* (2nd edition), Prentice Hall, Englewood Cliffs, NJ, 2004.

Verzuh E., *The Fast Forward MBA in Project Management* (3rd edition), John Wiley, Chichester, 2008.

Winston W.L. and Albright S., *Spreadsheet Modelling and Applications*, Brooks Cole, Florence, KY, 2004.

Young T., *Successful Project Management* (3rd edition), Kogan Page, London, 2010.

Queues and simulation

Chapter outline

We are all familiar with queues – but few of us enjoy them. Managers can shorten queues but only by using more servers, and this means higher costs. Models of queues look for ways to reduce the time for which customers wait and still give acceptable costs. In practice, not all queues involve people and there are many queues of inanimate – and even intangible – objects. Queuing problems are notoriously difficult, so analytical solutions are available only for relatively small problems. Simulation gives a more robust method of tackling bigger and more complex problems by imitating the operations of a system over a typical period.

After finishing this chapter you should be able to:

■ appreciate the scope of queuing problems and describe the features of queues
■ calculate the characteristics of a single-server queue
■ describe the characteristic approach of simulation
■ do manual simulations of queuing systems
■ use computers for bigger simulations.

Features of queues

Queues form when customers want some kind of service, but find that the server is already busy. Then they have the choice of either joining a queue

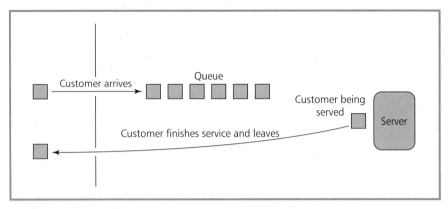

Figure 20.1 A single-server queuing system

and waiting to be served, or leaving and possibly going to a competitor with a server who is not busy. Here we consider the situation where they decide to join the queue. As you know, you are likely to meet a queue whenever you buy a train ticket, get money from a bank, go to a supermarket, wait for traffic lights to change and in many other circumstances.

However, not all queues involve people – for example, there are queues of programs waiting to be processed on a computer, telephone calls waiting to use a satellite, items moving along an assembly line, faulty equipment waiting to be repaired, ships queuing for a berth, aeroplanes queuing to land and so on. By convention a 'customer' is anyone or anything wanting a service, and a 'server' is the person or thing providing that service. Whatever parties are involved, all queues have common features – Figure 20.1 shows a basic queuing system.

> ■ A **queue** is the line of people or things waiting to be served.
> ■ A queue is formed whenever a customer arrives at a service, finds the server is already busy, and waits to be served.

There are many different configurations of queues, with variations including:

- the number of servers may vary from one to a very large number
- customers may arrive singly or in batches – for example, when a bus-load of people arrive at a restaurant
- arrivals may be at random, following some probability distribution, or organised through an appointment system
- customers may form a single queue or a separate queue for each server
- customers may be served individually or in batches – for example, at an airport customers are served a plane-load at a time
- servers may be in parallel – where each does the same job – or in series – where each gives part of the service and then passes the customer on to the next stage
- service time may be constant or variable
- customers may be served in order of arrival or in some other order – for example, hospitals admit patients in order of urgency.

The quality of a service is judged – at least in part – by the time that customers have to wait. You might assume any process in which customers have to wait a long time is inherently inefficient – more efficient operations would have smoother flows of work and move customers and servers quickly on to other tasks. Specifically, you know from experience that to stand in a long queue of people is irritating (at best) and encourages customers to move to other services and organisations. So an initial aim might be to have short waiting times. However, there can be genuine reasons for having long queues – particularly when demand is variable, service is restricted or organisations are trying to reduce the cost of servers. For instance, you probably have to queue in morning rush-hour traffic (because of variable demand on the road network), to wait for specialised medical treatment (because there is a limited supply of servers) and at a supermarket checkout (because it is too expensive to provide enough check-outs to eliminate queues).

The length of a queue depends on three factors:

- the rate at which customers arrive
- the time taken to serve each customer
- the number of servers available.

Call centres, for example, try to reduce the time that callers wait by reducing the time servers spend talking to each one. Usually, though, the easiest thing that managers can adjust is the number of servers, and in any particular circumstances having a lot of servers gives the shortest queues. Unfortunately, servers cost money and these short queues come with high costs. So managers look for a balance that seems to satisfy all parties – combining reasonable queue length with acceptable costs. The point of balance differs according to circumstances. When you visit a doctor's surgery you often have a long wait. This is because the doctor's time is considered expensive while patients' time is cheap. To make sure that doctors do not waste their valuable time waiting for patients, they make appointments close together and patients are expected to wait. On the other hand, in petrol stations the cost of servers (petrol pumps) is low and customers can nearly always drive to a competitor when there is a queue. Then it is better to have a large number of servers with low utilisation, ensuring that customers only have a short wait in any queue.

Review questions

20.1 What causes a queue?

20.2 'Customers do not like to wait, so there should always be enough servers to eliminate queues.' Do you think this is true?

Single-server queues

The simplest type of queue has:

- a single server dealing with a queue of customers
- random arrival of customers joining a queue
- all customers waiting to be served in first-come-first-served order
- random service time.

Chapter 13 showed that a Poisson distribution describes random occurrences, so we can use this to describe customer arrivals. When the average number of customers arriving in unit time is λ, the probability of r arrivals in unit time is given by the Poisson distribution:

$$P(r) = \frac{e^{-\lambda} \times \lambda^r}{r!}$$

where: r = number of arrivals
λ = mean number of arrivals
e = exponential constant $(2.71828 \ldots)$.

Service time is also random – but now the data is continuous so we cannot use a discrete Poisson distribution. Instead, we use a closely related continuous distribution called a negative exponential distribution. You need not worry about its exact form (illustrated in Figure 20.2), except that it has the useful feature that the probability of service being completed within some specified time, T, is:

$$P(t \leq T) = 1 - e^{-\mu T}$$

where: μ = mean service rate
= the average number of customers served in a unit of time.

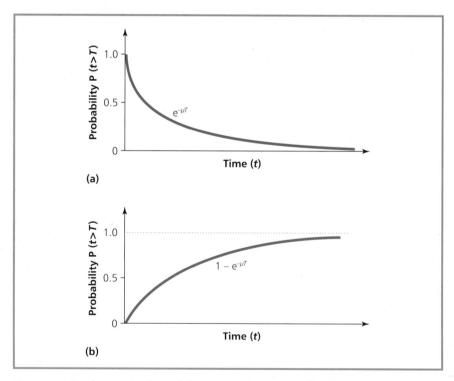

Figure 20.2 Random service times follow a negative exponential distribution:
(a) probability that service is not completed within a time T; (b) probability that service is completed within a time T

And the probability that service is not completed by time T is 1 minus this, or:

$$P(t > T) = 1 - P(t \le T)$$
$$= e^{-\mu T}$$

When an average of 10 customers are served an hour the probability that service takes less than 5 minutes is:

$$P(t \le 5 / 60) = 1 - e^{-10 \times 5/60}$$
$$= 1 - 0.435$$
$$= 0.565$$

The probability that it takes more than 10 minutes is:

$$P(t > 10 / 60) = e^{-10 \times 10/60}$$
$$= 0.189$$

Now we have descriptions of the random arrival of customers in terms of λ (the mean arrival rate) and of random service times in terms of μ (the mean service rate). If the mean arrival rate is greater than the mean service rate, the queue will never settle down to a steady state but will continue to grow indefinitely. So any analysis of queues must assume a steady state where μ is greater than λ.

We can derive some standard results for a single-server queue – which are called the operating characteristics. Unfortunately the formal derivations are rather messy, so we will develop the results intuitively. Some of these are not obvious, so we will simply state them as standard results.

Imagine a queue where the mean arrival rate is 2 customers an hour and the mean service rate is 4 customers an hour. On average a customer arrives every 30 minutes, and takes 15 minutes to serve, so the server is busy for half the time. Extending this reasoning, we can suggest that a server is generally busy for a proportion of time λ / μ, and this is described as the utilisation factor. This is also the proportion of time that a customer is either being served or waiting – technically described as being 'in the system'. Looking at it in other ways, it is also the probability that an arriving customer has to wait, and is the average number of customers being served at any time.

$$\text{utilisation factor} = \lambda / \mu$$

The probability that there is no customer in the system is:

$$P_0 = 1 - \text{the probability there is a customer in the system}$$
$$= 1 - \lambda / \mu$$

This is the probability that a new customer is served without any wait.

The probability that there are n customers in the system is:

$$P_n = P_0(\lambda / \mu)^n$$

We can use this result – which is not intuitively obvious – to calculate some other characteristics of the queue. To start with, the average number of customers in the system is:

$$L = \sum_{n=0}^{\infty} nP_n = \frac{\lambda}{\mu - \lambda}$$

where the symbol ∞ ('infinity') shows that the summation continues indefinitely.

The average number of customers in the queue is the average number in the system minus the average number being served:

$$L_q = L - \frac{\lambda}{\mu}$$

$$= \frac{\lambda}{\mu - \lambda} - \frac{\lambda}{\mu}$$

$$= \frac{\lambda^2}{\mu(\mu - \lambda)}$$

The average time a customer has to spend in the system is:

$$W = \frac{L}{\lambda}$$

$$= \frac{1}{\mu - \lambda}$$

The average time spent in the queue is the average time in the system minus the average service time:

$$W_q = W - \frac{1}{\mu}$$

$$= \frac{\lambda}{\mu(\mu - \lambda)}$$

You can see from these calculations, and the following worked examples, that analysing even the simplest queue is rather messy.

WORKED EXAMPLE 20.1

People arrive randomly at a bank teller at an average rate of 30 an hour. If the teller takes an average of 0.5 minutes to serve each customer, what is the average number of customers in the queue and how long do they wait to be served? What happens if average service time increases to 1 or 2 minutes?

Solution

The average arrival rate is $\lambda = 30$. If the teller takes an average of 0.5 minutes to serve each customer,

this is equivalent to a service rate of 120 an hour. Then the average number of customers in the queue (excluding anyone being served) is:

$$L_q = \frac{\lambda}{\mu(\mu - \lambda)}$$

$$= \frac{30^2}{120 \times (120 - 30)}$$

$$= 0.083$$

Worked example 20.1 continued

The average time in the queue is:

$$W_q = \frac{\lambda}{\mu(\mu - \lambda)}$$

$$= \frac{30}{120 \times (120 - 30)}$$

$$= 0.003 \text{ hours} = 0.167 \text{ minutes}$$

The average number of people in the system is:

$$L = L_q + \lambda / \mu$$
$$= 0.083 + 30 / 120$$
$$= 0.333$$

and the average time in the system is:

$$W = W_q + 1 / \mu$$
$$= 0.003 + 1 / 120$$
$$= 0.011 \text{ hours} = 0.667 \text{ minutes}$$

With an average service time of one minute, $\mu = 60$ and:

$$L_q = \frac{\lambda^2}{\mu(\mu - \lambda)} = \frac{30^2}{60 \times (60 - 30)} = 0.5$$

$$L = L_q + \lambda / \mu = 0.5 + 30 / 60 = 1.0$$

$$W_q = \frac{\lambda}{\mu(\mu - \lambda)} = \frac{30}{60 \times (60 - 30)} = 0.017 \text{ hours}$$

$$= 1.0 \text{ minutes}$$

$$W = W_q + 1 / \mu = 1.0 + 1 / 60 = 1.017 \text{ minutes}$$

If the average service time increases to 2 minutes, the service rate is $\mu = 30$. This does not satisfy the condition that $\mu > \lambda$, so the system will not settle down to a steady state and the queue will continue to grow indefinitely.

WORKED EXAMPLE 20.2

Customers arrive randomly at a railway information desk at a mean rate of 20 an hour. There is one person at the desk who takes an average of 2 minutes with each customer, and incurs total employment costs of £30 an hour. If customers' waiting time is valued at £10 an hour, what is the cost of the system?

Solution

The mean arrival rate, λ, is 20 an hour and the mean service rate, μ, is 30 an hour. The probability that there is no one in the system is:

$$P_0 = 1 - \lambda / \mu = 1 - 20 / 30$$
$$= 0.33$$

So there is a probability of $1 - 0.33 = 0.67$ that a customer has to wait to be served. The probability of n people in the system is $P_0 (\lambda / \mu)^n$. For example, $P_1 = 0.33 \times 20 / 30 = 0.22$; $P_2 = 0.33 \times (20 / 30)^2 = 0.15$; $P_3 = 0.33 \times (20 / 30)^3 = 0.10$; $P_4 = 0.33 \times (20 / 30)^4 = 0.07$ and so on.

The average time a customer spends in the system is:

$$W = 1(\mu - \lambda) = 1 / (30 - 20)$$
$$= 0.1 \text{ hours} = 6 \text{ minutes}$$

If customers' costs are assigned to the time they are both waiting and being served, the cost per hour is:

> number arriving × average time in the system
> × hourly cost = $20 \times 6 / 60 \times 10$
> $= £20$

Adding the server's cost of £30 gives a total cost of £50 an hour.

The average time a customer spends in the queue is:

$$W_q = \frac{\lambda}{\mu(\mu - \lambda)}$$

$$= \frac{20}{30 \times 10}$$

$$= 0.0667 \text{ hours}$$
$$= 4 \text{ minutes}$$

If customers' costs are assigned to only the time they are waiting, the cost per hour is

$(20 \times 4 / 60 \times 10) = £13.33$, giving a total cost of $(13.33 + 30) = £43.33$ an hour.

```
QUEUE ANALYSIS
-----------------------------------------------------------------------------
PROBLEM NAME: Example
-----------------------------------------------------------------------------

MODEL: Multiple Channels

Arrival Rate (lambda)   = 100
Service Rate (mu)       =  30
Number of Channels      =   4

Average Number of Units in Waiting Line = 3.2886
Average Number of Units in System       = 6.6219
Average Waiting Time in Line            = 0.0329
Average Time in System                  = 0.0662

Probability of Idle System              = 0.0213

Probability of 1 units in the system    = 0.0710
Probability of 2 units in the system    = 0.1184
Probability of 3 units in the system    = 0.1315
Probability of 4 units in the system    = 0.1096
Probability of 5 units in the system    = 0.0914
Probability of 6 units in the system    = 0.0761
Probability of 7 units in the system    = 0.0634
Probability of 8 units in the system    = 0.0529
Probability of 9 units in the system    = 0.0441
Probability of 10 units in the system   = 0.0367
Probability of 11 units in the system   = 0.0306
Probability of 12 units in the system   = 0.0255
Probability of 13 units in the system   = 0.0212
Probability of 14 units in the system   = 0.0177
Probability of 15 units in the system   = 0.0148
Probability of 16 units in the system   = 0.0123
Probability of 17 units in the system   = 0.0102


COSTS

Average cost of units in the system     = £20 per time period
Average cost per server                 = £35 per time period
Total cost per time period              = £272.44
```

Figure 20.3 Example of a printout for a multi-server queue

We have described the operating characteristics of a single-server queue, and could now go on to describe multi-server and other types of queue. However, you can probably guess that the arithmetic becomes even messier, and we would normally use a computer. Figure 20.3 shows the printout from a simple package analysing a queue with four servers. Another option is to look for another method of solving these problems, and this is where we move on to simulation.

Review questions

20.3 What are the variables λ and μ in a queuing system?

20.4 What happens in a queue if $\lambda \geq \mu$?

20.5 What are the assumptions of the single-server queue model?

20.6 'It is impossible to solve queuing problems with several servers.' Is this true?

IDEAS IN PRACTICE Meecham Financial Services

Fred McMurray runs an independent financial service from a shop in the centre of Meecham. He has developed a good local reputation, and with the global economic problems of 2008 he has a steady stream of customers looking for advice. At a practical level he has to balance the costs of running his business with the service given to customers. As part of this, he has designed a spreadsheet to do some basic calculations on queues.

Figure 20.4 shows the results when he works alone and has an average of two customers an hour spending 20 minutes with each. Then the average time a customer spends in the queue is 40 minutes, followed by their 20 minutes of service. When Fred assigns a notional waiting cost of £20 an hour for a customer waiting and £40 an hour for his service, the total cost per hour is:

number of customers × average wait
× hourly cost + server cost
$= 2 \times 2 / 3 \times 20 + 40 = £26.67 + £40$
$= £66.67$ an hour or £533 a day.

Fred considered reducing the customer queues by hiring an assistant at a cost of £25 an hour. The spreadsheet showed that this reduced the time customers wait in the queue to 0.042 hours. Then the total costs are:

$2 \times 0.042 \times 20 + 40 + 25 = £1.68 + 65$
$= £66.68$ an hour

The overall cost is almost exactly the same, but Fred actually has to pay more while the customers pay less. In reality, all Fred's costs are ultimately paid by his customers. So with an extra assistant they pay more for the service but less for waiting – meaning that they have shorter queues with the same overall cost. This seems an attractive move, but the customers have to be convinced that it is worth paying Fred more to get the better service. Fred considered this question, along with other effects of different types of operations before reaching his decision.

	A	B	C
1	**Meecham Financial Services**		
2			
3	**Queueing models**		
4			
5	**Arrival rate**	**2**	
6	**Service rate**	**3**	
7	**Number of servers**	**1**	**2**
8			
9			
10	Average server utilisation	0.6667	0.3333
11	Average number of customers in the queue	1.3333	0.0833
12	Average number of customers in the system	2.0000	0.7500
13	Average waiting time in the queue	0.6667	0.0417
14	Average waiting time in the system	1.0000	0.3750
15	Probability there is no one in the system	0.3333	0.5000
16			
17	Probability of number in system		
18	0	0.3333	0.5000
19	1	0.2222	0.3333
20	2	0.1482	0.1111
21	3	0.0988	0.0370
22	4	0.0659	0.0123
23	5	0.0439	0.0041
24	6	0.0293	0.0014
25	7	0.0195	0.0005

Figure 20.4 Spreadsheet for Meecham Financial Services

Simulation models

Simulation gives a way of tackling big queuing problems – or any other complex problem. It does not solve a set of equations, but simulates the operations to see how they behave over a typical period. Simulation effectively imitates the working of a real situation, giving a dynamic view of a system over an extended time. An ordinary model looks at the system, collects data for some fixed point in time and draws conclusions – simulation follows the operations of the system and sees exactly what happens over time. A simple analogy has an ordinary model giving a snapshot of the system at some fixed point, while a simulation model takes a movie of the system.

We can show the general approach of simulation with a simple example, illustrated in Figure 20.5. Here an item is made on a production line at a rate of one unit every two minutes. At some point there is an inspection, which takes virtually no time. At this inspection, 50% of units are rejected and the remaining 50% continue along the line to the next operations, which take three minutes a unit.

Managers want to answer a series of questions about this system:

- How much space should they leave for the queue between the inspection and the next operations?
- How long will each unit stay in the system?
- What is the utilisation of equipment?
- Are there any bottlenecks?

This system is essentially a single-server queue, so we could use a queuing model. An alternative is to stand and watch the system actually working over a typical period and see what happens. We could follow a few units through the system and record information, perhaps using a table like that shown in Figure 20.6.

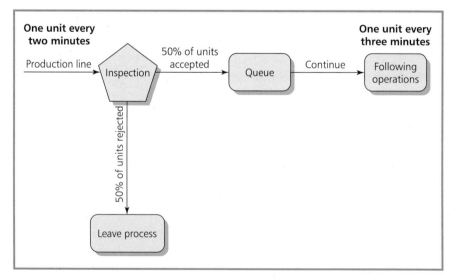

Figure 20.5 Example of a simulation

	A	B	C	D	E	F	G	H	I
1	Collecting data by observation								
2									
3	Unit number	Arrival time	Accept or reject	Time joins queue	Number in queue	Time operations start	Time operations finish	Time in queue	Time in system
4	1	0	A	0	0	0	3	0	3
5	2	2	A	2	1	3	6	1	4
6	3	4	A	4	1	6	9	2	5
7	4	6	R	0					
8	5	8	R	0					
9	6	10	A	10	0	10	13	0	3
10	7	12	A	12	1	13	16	1	4
11	8	14	R	0					

Figure 20.6 Information collected by watching a process

Here the first unit arrived for inspection at some time which we arbitrarily set to 0. The unit was accepted and moved straight through to operations that took 3 minutes. The unit was in the system – consisting of inspection, queue and operations – for 3 minutes.

The second unit arrived at time 2 from the arbitrary start time, was accepted and joined the queue (column E shows the number in the queue after this unit joins it). Operations could not start on unit 2 until unit 1 was finished at time 3, and then unit 2 left the system 3 minutes later at time 6.

We could stand and watch the operation for as long as we needed to get a reliable view of its working. Then we could analyse the figures to get all the information we want. But this approach clearly has a number of disadvantages – it is time-consuming, difficult to organise, needs many reliable observations, considers only one way of working (so it cannot compare different methods) and needs someone observing operations (which is unpopular with the people doing them). However, there is an alternative approach. We could collect enough data to show how the system actually works – and then we could make up other sets of figures that have exactly the same patterns. In other words, we generate observations with the same characteristics as those in Figure 20.6, without actually standing and watching the operations.

In our example, there is only one element of uncertainty, which is whether a unit is accepted or rejected. To simulate the actual acceptance or rejection decision we need some method of randomly assigning each unit a 50% chance of being accepted and a 50% chance of being rejected. An obvious way of doing this is to spin a coin – when it comes down heads we reject the unit, and when it comes down tails we accept it (or vice versa). A more formal method uses random numbers, which we described in Chapter 4. If we have this string of random digits:

5284778016941356756454793017714943179046825

we could use even digits (including 0) for acceptance, and odd digits for rejection. Then we reject the first unit (based on 5), accept the second (based on 2), accept the third (based on 8) and so on. Now we can develop a typical set of results for the process without actually watching it, like those in Figure 20.7.

	A	B	C	D	E	F	G	H	I	J
1	**Simulation of process**									
2										
3	Unit number	Arrival time	Random number	Accept or reject	Time joins queue	Number in queue	Time operations start	Time operations finish	Time in queue	Time in system
4	1	0	5	R		0				
5	2	2	2	A	2	0	2	5	0	3
6	3	4	8	A	4	1	5	8	1	4
7	4	6	4	A	6	1	8	11	2	5
8	5	8	7	R		0				
9	6	10	7	R		0				
10	7	12	8	A	12	0	12	15	0	3
11	8	14	0	A	14	1	15	18	1	4
12	9	16	1	R		0				
13	10	18	6	A	18	0	18	21	0	3
14	**Mean**					0.30			0.67	3.67
15	**Maximum**					1.00			2.00	5.00

Figure 20.7 Simulating the process

We know that one unit arrives for inspection every 2 minutes, so we can complete column B. Column C shows the sequence of random numbers, with the corresponding decision in column D. Units that are rejected leave the system, while those that are accepted join the queue at their arrival time, shown in column E. Column F shows the number in the queue after a unit arrives. Column G shows the time when operations start, which is the later of the arrival time and the time the previous unit finishes (from column H). Column H shows that operations finish 3 minutes after they start. Column I shows the time in the queue (the difference between the arrival time in column B and the time operations start in column G). Column J shows the total time in the system (the difference between the arrival time in column B and the time operations finish in column H).

So the rules for generating entries in each column are as follows:

- Column A – the number increases by 1 for each unit entering.
- Column B – arrival time increases by 2 for each unit entering.
- Column C – form a string of random numbers, using the RAND function in a spreadsheet.
- Column D – a unit is accepted if the corresponding random number is even and rejected if it is odd.
- Column E – the accepted units join the queue straight away at their arrival time; rejected ones leave the system.
- Column F – the number already in the queue is one more than it was for the last arrival minus the number that left since the last arrival.
- Column G – operations start at the arrival time when they are idle, or when they finish work on the previous unit (the previous entry in column H).
- Column H – the finishing time for operations, which is column G plus 3.
- Column I – the time in the queue is the difference between the arrival time in the queue and the time operations start (column G minus column E).
- Column J – the time in the system is the difference between the arrival time and the finish of operations (column H minus column B).

The simulation has been run for 10 units arriving and we can use the figures to give a number of results. For example, we can note that there was at most 1 unit in the queue for the processor. We can also find:

- number accepted = 6 (in the long run this would be 50% of units)
- number rejected = 4 (again this would be 50% in the long run)
- maximum time in queue = 2 minutes
- average time in queue = 4 / 6 minutes = 40 seconds
- maximum time in system = 5 minutes
- average time in system = 22 / 6 = 3.67 minutes
- average time in system including rejects = 22 / 10 = 2.2 minutes
- operations were busy for 18 minutes
- utilisation of operations = 18 / 21 = 86%.

It is important to ask how reliable these figures are. The simulation certainly gives a picture of the system working through a typical period of 21 minutes, but this is a very small number of observations and the results are not likely to be very accurate. So the next step is to extend the simulation for a much larger number of observations. Once we have built the simulation model and defined all the logic, it is easy to extend it to give more repetitions. And when we have information for several hundred arrivals we can be more confident that the results are reliable. As the model includes a random element, we can never be certain that the results are absolutely accurate, but with large numbers of repetitions we can be confident that they give a reasonable picture. This amount of repetition clearly needs a lot of arithmetic, so simulations are always done by computer.

Review questions

20.7   What does it mean when people describe simulation as a 'dynamic' representation?

20.8   'Simulation can be used to model complex situations.' Do you think this is true?

20.9   'Simulation uses artificial data, so it cannot guarantee accurate results.' Is this true?

IDEAS IN PRACTICE   Taco Bell

Taco Bell – part of Yum! Brands Inc. – is a fast-food restaurant chain that specialises in Mexican cuisine. Its restaurants aim at serving customers quickly – normally within three to five minutes. A major part of their costs is employing staff for their restaurants, and managers have to balance the level of customer service with the cost of providing it. Taco Bell wants all staff to be fully utilised, but – in common with all fast-food restaurants – they have major problems with variable demand. Typically there are major peaks in demand at lunchtime and in the early evening, with very quiet periods in the afternoon and early morning.

To tackle this problem Taco Bell developed its SMART (Scheduling Management And Restaurant Tool) system. This has three modules:

- A forecasting module, which predicts the number of customers arriving at a store in 30-minute – or even 15-minute – time slots. This gives a detailed picture of the number of customers and what they will buy throughout every day. Managers can add special events, holidays and other features to adjust the underlying forecasts.
- A simulation module, which takes the forecast demands, adds the features of the restaurant

such as size, opening hours, drive-through service, menu options etc. and shows how many employees of different types are needed throughout each day.

■ An employee scheduling module, which takes the pattern of employees needed and the staff available in the store and uses linear programming to produce schedules for staff members.

The resulting schedules are available four weeks in advance and they allow for specific staff requirements, non-critical tasks scheduled during slack periods, performance monitoring, a broad history of data that gives forecasts for new products and stores, and identification of special risks.

Sources: www.tacobell.com; Bistritz M., Taco Bell finds recipe for success, *OR/MS Today*, October 1997.

Monte Carlo simulation

Simulation models that include a lot of uncertainty are described as Monte Carlo simulation. In the last example, the only uncertainty was whether a unit was accepted or rejected, and we used random numbers for this decision. Most real problems have much more variability, but we can still use random numbers to describe them. For example, suppose we want the probability of acceptance at an inspection to be 0.6. One way of arranging this is to use random digits 0 to 5 to represent acceptance and 6 to 9 to represent rejection. Then the string:

52847780169413567564547930177149431790465825

represents accept, accept, reject, accept, reject and so on. We can extend this approach to sampling from more complex patterns. If 50% of units are accepted, 15% sent for reworking, 20% for reinspection and 15% rejected, we can split the stream of random digits into pairs:

52 84 77 80 16 94 13 56 75 64 54 79 30 17 71 etc.

Then:

■ 00 to 49 (that is 50% of pairs) represent acceptance
■ 50 to 64 (that is 15% of pairs) represent reworking
■ 65 to 84 (that is 20% of pairs) represent reinspection, and
■ 85 to 99 (that is 15% of pairs) represent rejection.

The stream of random digits then represents rework, reinspect, reinspect, reinspect, accept and so on. In the long term the proportion of outcomes will match the requirements, but in the short term there will obviously be some variation. Here three of the first four units need reinspecting and if you are tempted to 'adjust' such a figure you should not. Remember that simulation needs many repetitions to give typical figures and these occasionally include unlikely occurrences. Removing these takes away the purely random element and ultimately makes the analyses less reliable.

WORKED EXAMPLE 20.3

Conal Fitzgerald checks the stock of an item at the beginning of each month and places an order so that:

order size = 100 − opening stock

The order is equally likely to arrive at the end of the month in which it is placed, or one month later. Demand follows the pattern:

Monthly demand	10	20	30	40	50	60	70
Probability	0.1	0.15	0.25	0.25	0.15	0.05	0.05

There are currently 40 units in stock, and Conal wants to simulate the system for the next 10 months. What information can he get from the results?

Solution

There is uncertainty in delivery time and demand, and Conal can create typical patterns for these using random numbers in the following ways:

- For *delivery time*, using single-digit random numbers –
  - an even random number means the delivery arrives in the current month
  - an odd random number means the delivery arrives in the next month.
- For *demand*, using a two-digit random number:

Demand	10	20	30	40	50	60	70
Probability	0.1	0.15	0.25	0.25	0.15	0.05	0.05
Random number	00–09	10–24	25–49	50–74	75–89	90–94	95–99

These schemes need two streams of random digits, which Conal can generate using a spreadsheet's RANDBETWEEN function. Then Figure 20.8 shows a set of results from following the system through 10 months.

The main calculation here is the stock at the end of a month, which is the initial stock plus arrivals minus demand. Then in month 1 the initial stock is 40, so Conal orders 100 − 40 = 60 units. The arrival random number determines that this arrives in the same month. The demand random number determines a demand of 50 in the month, so the closing stock is:

closing stock = opening stock + arrivals − demand
= 40 + 60 − 50
= 50

There are no shortages and the closing stock is transferred to the opening stock for month 2. These calculations are repeated for the following 10 months.

The conclusions from this very limited simulation are not at all reliable. But if Conal continued the simulation for a much longer period – hundreds or thousands of months – he could find reliable figures for the distribution of opening and closing stocks, the distribution of orders, mean demand, shortages and mean lead time. Adding costs to the model would allow a range of other calculations.

	A	B	C	D	E	F	G	H	I	J	K
1	Simulation of stocks										
2											
3	Month	1	2	3	4	5	6	7	8	9	10
4											
5	Opening stock	40	50	10	20	80	150	130	80	60	20
6	Order	60	50	90	80	20	−50	−30	20	40	80
7	Arrival RN	2	5	9	1	0	7	3	8	7	6
8	Arrival month	1	3	4	5	5	7	8	8	10	10
9											
10	Demand RN	83	50	56	49	37	15	84	2	66	41
11	Demand size	50	40	40	30	30	20	50	40	40	30
12	Arrival	60	0	50	90	100	0	0	20	0	120
13	Closing stock	50	10	20	80	150	130	80	60	20	110
14	Shortages	0	0	0	0	0	0	0	0	0	0

Figure 20.8 Simulation of stock for Worked example 20.3 (RN = random number)

	A	B	C	D	E	F	G	H	I	J
1										
2	5-minute time block	Random number	Number of customers arriving	Number of customers in queue	Number of customers served	Number of customers delayed		Probability	Cumulative probability	Number of arriving customers
3	0		0	0	0	0		0.7	0	0
4	1	0.29299	0	0	0	0		0.12	0.7	1
5	2	0.89180	2	2	2	0		0.16	0.82	2
6	3	0.75413	1	1	1	0		0.02	0.98	3
7	4	0.70409	1	1	1	0				
8	5	0.15254	0	0	0	0				
9	6	0.59668	0	0	0	0				
10	7	0.23973	0	0	0	0				
11	8	0.32246	0	0	0	0				
12	9	0.95431	2	2	2	0				
13	....	....	....	....	....	....				
14	....	....	....	....	....	....				
15	1997	0.37057	0	0	0	0				
16	1998	0.18580	0	0	0	0				
17	1999	0.98664	3	3	3	0				
18	2000	0.56001	0	0	0	0				
19	Maximum		3	3	3	0				
20	Total		926	926	926	0				
21	Average		0.463	0.463	0.463	0				

Figure 20.9 Simulation in a spreadsheet

The problem with simulation is that it needs a considerable effort. Each problem needs its own specific model and these can be both large and complex – which means that they can be expensive and time-consuming. The large number of calculations and repetitions mean that computers are always used to get solutions for simulation and the models have to be programmed and tested. For simple problems this work can be done on a spreadsheet, but this soon becomes complicated. Figure 20.9 shows the start of a simulation in a spreadsheet, where a variable number of customers arrives at a service in each 5-minute time block. To get a reasonable run of observations takes 2,000 rows of the spreadsheet – but this is still only one simulation run, and for the final problem this should be repeated a large number of times to get an accurate view.

In practice, it is far easier to use specialised programs. Some of these are fairly basic and analyse simple problems; others are complex simulation languages. Most real simulation is done by comprehensive languages such as Renque, SimEvents, SimPy, SIMSCRIPT and Simul8,

WORKED EXAMPLE 20.4

An office organises appointments for its customers so that one should arrive at a reception desk every eight minutes. After answering some standard questions, which takes an average of two minutes, customers are passed on to one of two offices. 30% of customers (chosen at random) go to office A, where they are served for an average of five minutes; the remaining customers go to office B where they are served for an average of seven minutes. Then all customers go to office D where they fill in forms for an average of six minutes before leaving. How would you set about simulating this system?

Solution

Figure 20.10 shows the elements of this system, and Figure 20.11 shows the analysis given by a simple simulation package.

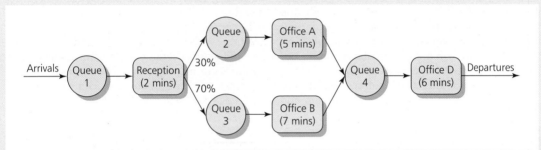

Figure 20.10 System for Worked example 20.4

Customer analysis for queuing system

Data entered
Arrival   Queue 1 to Queue 2 and Queue 3   Queue 2 and Queue 3 to Queue 4   Departure

Arrivals Poisson mean = 8

Queue 1
Reception   Normal   mean = 2   standard deviation = 0.5
Queue 2   Probability = 0.3
Office A   Normal   mean = 5   standard deviation = 1.0
Queue 3   Probability = 0.7
Office B   Normal   mean = 7   standard deviation = 2.0
Queue 4
Office D   Normal   mean = 6   standard deviation = 1.0

Results

1	Total number of arrivals	128
2	Total number of baulking	0
3	Average number in the system (L)	1.97
4	Maximum number in the system	5
5	Current number in the system	3
6	Number finished	125
7	Average process time	13.74
8	Std. dev. of process time	2.10
9	Average waiting time (Wq)	1.69
10	Std. dev. of waiting time	2.85
11	Average transfer time	0
12	Std. dev. of transfer time	0
13	Average flow time (W)	15.61
14.	Std. dev. of flow time	4.06
15	Maximum flow time	31.13

Date Collection: 0 to 1000 minutes
CPU Seconds = 0.1420

Figure 20.11 Sample printout for simulating queues in the office

20.10 Why are random numbers used in simulation?

20.11 How many repetitions would you need to guarantee accurate results from simulation?

IDEAS IN PRACTICE **SenGen Instrumental**

SenGen Instrumental has a warehouse outside Geneva, from which it supplies materials to Central and Southern Europe. They use an inventory management system that was installed by a local IT specialist and it has worked well for several years. Before adjusting the system, the company wanted to check the effects of their proposed changes and ran a series of simulations. These trials are too big to describe in detail, but we can illustrate their general approach.

The first requirement was a description of the sequence of activities in the current system and

for this SenGen used a comprehensive flow diagram. Figure 20.12 shows the sequence of activities – starting by analysing the known data, including costs and demand pattern, and then calculating various factors including economic order quantity and timing of deliveries. Then it follows the operations through a typical series of months. Starting with the first month, it checks the demand and deliveries due, sets the opening stock (which is last month's closing stock), finds the closing stock (which is opening stock plus deliveries minus demand) and calculates all the costs. Then it

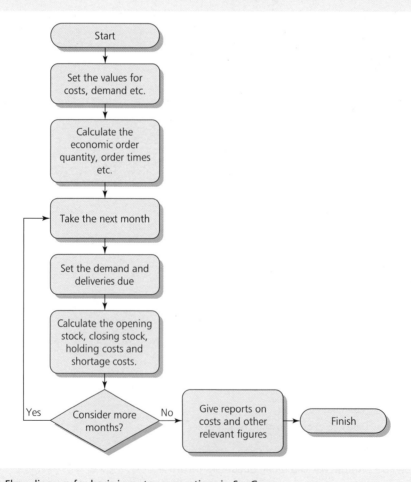

Figure 20.12 Flow diagram for basic inventory operations in SenGen

Ideas in practice continued

goes to the second month and repeats the analysis. The model repeats the calculations for as many months as are needed to get a reliable view of the operations and then prepares summaries and analyses for all the figures. (In reality, the model looked at demand every hour and used a combination of ordering policies.)

Having described the logic in a flow diagram, SenGen moved to the detailed simulation. They

designed the basic calculations on a spreadsheet, illustrated in Figure 20.13. Here the economic order quantity is calculated as 200, corresponding to one delivery a month. The simulation follows the operations for 12 months and in this run you can see that there is a build-up of stock in the first half of the year followed by shortages in the second half. This gives high costs and suggests that the company might look for a different order pattern.

	A	B	C	D	E	F	G
1	**Simulation of stocks at SenGen**						
2							
3	**Notes:**	Effects of variable demand on costs					
4							
5	**Inputs**	Annual demand		2400			
6		Unit cost	SFr	10.00			
7		Holding cost amount	SFr	6.00			
8		Holding cost percentage		0%			
9		Reorder cost	SFr	50.00			
10		Shortage cost	SFr	100.00			
11							
12	**Results**	Annual holding cost	SFr	6.00			
13		Order size		200.00			
14		Time between orders		1.00			
15		Number of orders a year		12.00			
16		Fixed unit costs	SFr	24,000.00			
17		Variable cost	SFr	1,200.00			
18		Total annual cost	SFr	25,200.00			
19							
20	Month	Opening stock	Demand	Delivery	Closing stock	Holding cost	Shortage cost
21	1	0	140	200	60	SFr 30.00	SFr –
22	2	60	120	220	160	SFr 80.00	SFr –
23	3	160	145	190	205	SFr 102.50	SFr –
24	4	205	165	180	220	SFr 110.00	SFr –
25	5	220	295	225	150	SFr 75.00	SFr –
26	6	150	245	215	120	SFr 60.00	SFr –
27	7	120	315	200	5	SFr 2.50	SFr –
28	8	5	225	200	–20	SFr –	SFr 166.67
29	9	–20	245	220	–45	SFr –	SFr 375.00
30	10	–45	250	225	–70	SFr –	SFr 583.33
31	11	–70	205	210	–65	SFr –	SFr 541.67
32	12	–65	110	200	25	SFr 12.50	SFr –
33							
34					**Summary costs**		
35					Holding cost	SFr	472.50
36					Reorder cost	SFr	600.00
37					Shortage cost	SFr	1,666.67
38					Unit cost	SFr	24,000.00
39					**Total cost**	SFr	26,739.17

Figure 20.13 Basic simulation of stock at SenGen

Ideas in practice continued

Now SenGen had the basic steps of a simulation, and they added details to give a better picture of the real system. For example, they added more variability to all aspects of demand, lead time, amount delivered, costs and so on. Then they transferred the ideas to specialised software for the actual runs (with a single run illustrated in Figure 20.14).

SIMULATION SYSTEMS

SYSTEM: Inventory management   Originator: SenGen 43/df
Created on 01.01.11   **Modified on 01.01.11**   **This run at 0000 on 01.01.11**

DATA REVIEW

Order quantity	Automatic
Reorder level	Automatic
Forecasting method	Exponential smoothing
Forecasting parameters	Optimised
Number of stock items	1

Stock item 1

Name	Component		
Unit cost	SFr 20	Demand history	Defined
Reorder cost	SFr 75	Demand distribution	Normal
Holding cost	SFr 1	Lowest demand	100
Fixed holding cost	SFr 0	Highest demand	500
Shortage cost	SFr 50	Lead time distribution	Uniform
Fixed shortage cost	SFr 0	Shortest lead time	3
Backorders	0	Longest lead time	5
Urgent orders	No	Service level	93%
Emergency orders	No		

Period	Week		
Number of periods	13	Number of runs	100
Random number seed	Random	Analysis	None
Reports	Transaction (#1,1), Summary (1)		

INITIAL VALUES

Opening stock	1500	Mean lead time	4
Mean demand	300	Lead time demand	1200
Reorder quantity	212	Safety stock	83
Outstanding orders	Defined	Reorder level	1283

SIMULATION RESULTS

TRANSACTION REPORT(1) – first run

Week	Opening	Demand	Closing	Shortage	Order	Arrival
1	1500	331	1169			
2	1169	372	797		210 #1	
3	797	229	568		210 #2	
4	568	205	363		210 #3	
5	363	397	0	34	250 #4	
6	0	227	0	227	260 #5	
7	215	0	0	215	270 #6	210 #1
8	210	326	0	116	280 #7	210 #2
9	210	329	0	119	290 #8	210 #3
10	210	336	0	126	300 #9	250 #4
11	250	295	45		310 #10	260 #5
12	305	280	25		310 #11	270 #6
13	295	263	32		310 #12	280 #7

SUMMARY RESULTS(1)

Number of periods	13			
Number of runs	100			
Demand	296.7			
Lead time	5.13 weeks			
Stock level	396.2 units	Holding cost	SFr	396.20
Shortages	812.3 units	Shortage cost	SFr	40615.00
		Reorder cost	SFr	787.50
		Variable cost	SFr	41798.70
Deliveries	1681 units	Fixed cost	SFr	33620.00
		Total cost	**SFr**	**75418.70**

Figure 20.14 Example of more detailed simulation for SenGen

CHAPTER REVIEW

This chapter discussed the concept of queuing theory, and used this to introduce simulation as a way of tackling complex problems.

- A queue forms whenever a customer arrives at a server and finds that the server is already busy. In practice queues occur in many situations, not all of which involve people.

- For any given situation the queue length depends on the number of servers. More servers reduce waiting time and increase customer service – but incur higher costs. Managers look for a balance between service level and costs.

- The simplest queue has a single server with random arrivals and service times. We can calculate the operating characteristics of such systems in terms of mean queue length, time in the system, probability of having to queue etc.

- We could move on to more complex queuing systems but the calculations become very messy.

- Simulation gives an alternative way of tackling complex problems. Rather than solve a series of equations, it duplicates the operations over some period, producing a typical – but artificial – set of results.

- Monte Carlo simulation includes variability and uncertainty, which it achieves by using random numbers.

- Simulation involves a lot of repetitive calculations so it is always done on a computer. The easiest way to organise this in practice is usually with a specialised simulation package.

CASE STUDY The Palmer Centre for Alternative Therapy

Jane and Andrew Palmer run a business in Florida that they describe as an 'alternative therapy centre'. Their treatments range from fairly traditional ones, such as osteopathy, to more experimental ones that work with the body's 'energy pathways'. Their clients have a range of problems of different severity and symptoms, but in practice their main concern is people who suffer from long-term back problems.

The Palmer Centre employs a receptionist who deals with around 20 customers an hour. 70% of these only ask for information and the receptionist can deal with them in a couple of minutes. The remainder are actual patients.

Each patient takes about three minutes to give the receptionist information before moving on to consultations with either Jane or Andrew. Roughly two-thirds of patients see Andrew, who spends around 15 minutes with each; the rest see Jane, who spends around 20 minutes with each. After they have finished treatment, the patients return to the receptionist, who takes two minutes to collect information, prepare bills and arrange follow-up appointments.

This arrangement seems to work well, but some patients complain of having to wait. This is particularly important because the Palmers are thinking of expanding and employing another therapist. They will have to do some marketing to attract new clients, but realise that alternative treatments are becoming more popular and finding new business should not be difficult.

For the expansion they will have to make some changes to the centre, and build another office

➤

Case study continued

and waiting area for the new therapist. If the expansion is a success, they might be tempted to expand even more in the future. This raises the questions of how many offices the centre will need for varying levels of demand and how big the waiting areas should be.

Questions

- How can you judge the current performance of the centre?

- Can you find the resources that the centre will need to maintain – or improve – the current level of service with increasing numbers of patients?

PROBLEMS

20.1 Describe the operating characteristics of a single-server queue with random arrivals at an average rate of 100 an hour and random service times at an average rate of 120 an hour.

20.2 A single-server queue has random arrivals at a rate of 30 an hour and random service times at a rate of 40 an hour. If it costs £20 for each hour a customer spends in the system and £40 for each hour of service time, how much does the queue cost?

20.3 Piotr Banasiewicz is a self-employed plumber who offers a 24-hour emergency service. For most of the year, calls arrive randomly at a rate of six a day. The time he takes to travel to a call and do the repair is randomly distributed with a mean of 90 minutes. Forecasts for February suggest cold weather and last time this happened Piotr received emergency calls at a rate of 18 a day. Because of repeat business, Piotr is anxious not to lose a customer and wants the average waiting time to be no longer in February than during a normal month. How many assistants should he employ to achieve this?

20.4 Figure 20.15 shows the printout from a program that analyses queues. The title 'M/M/3' is an abbreviation to show that the queue has random arrivals, random service time and three servers. What do the results show? How can you check them?

20.5 Customers arrive for a service at a rate of 100 an hour and each server can deal with 15 customers an hour. If customer time is valued at $20 an hour and server time costs $50 an hour, how can you identify the best number of servers?

20.6 A supermarket has an average of 240 customers an hour arriving at peak times. During these periods all 10 checkouts could be used with each serving an average of 35 customers an hour. Simulate this process to show the effects of actually opening different numbers of checkouts.

Input data of queuing example

M/M/3

Customer arrival rate (lambda)	=	20.000
Distribution	:	Poisson
Number of servers	=	3
Service rate per server	=	8.000
Distribution	:	Poisson
Mean service time	=	0.125 hour
Standard deviation	=	0.125 hour
Queue limit	=	Infinity
Customer population	=	Infinity

Solution for queuing example

M/M/3

With lambda = 20 customers per hour and μ = 8 customers per hour

Utilisation factor (p) = 0.833
Average number of customers in the system (L) = 6.011
Average number of customers in the queue (L_q) = 3.511
Average time a customer in the system (W) = 0.301
Average time a customer in the queue (W_q) = 0.176
The probability that all servers are idle (P_o) = 0.004
The probability an arriving customer waits (P_w) = 0.702

P(1) = 0.11236 P(2) = 0.14045 P(3) = 0.11704 P(4) = 0.09753
P(5) = 0.08128 P(6) = 0.06773 P(7) = 0.05644 P(8) = 0.04704
P(9) = 0.03920 P(10) = 0.03266

$$\sum_{i=1}^{10} P(i) = 0.791736$$

Figure 20.15 Printout from a queuing analysis program

RESEARCH PROJECTS

20.1 There are many specialised programs for simulation. Some of these are sophisticated simulation languages that include animation and many other features. If you were looking for a simulation program what features would you expect to see in a major package? Illustrate your answer with references to real packages.

20.2 Spreadsheets can be used for some types of simulation. Look at a specific queuing problem and build a simple model on a spreadsheet. What results can you find? How would you expand your model to deal with more complex situations?

20.3 Find a real queuing problem and show how you would begin to analyse it. How can simulation help with your problem? How does your problem compare with the queuing problems that managers have solved in other circumstances?

20.4 Simulations of various kinds are widely used in practice. Find some examples where they have been particularly useful.

Sources of information

Further reading

Books on queuing – like the subject – soon become very mathematical. The following books give a useful starting point for queuing and simulation.

Banks J., Carson J.S., Nelson B. and Nicol D., *Discrete-event Simulation* (5th edition), Pearson Education, Englewood Cliffs, NJ, 2010.

Brooks R., Robinson S. and Lewis C.D., *Simulation and Inventory Control*, Palgrave Macmillan, Basingstoke, 2001.

Fishman G.S., *Discrete Event Simulation*, Springer, New York, 2001.

Gross D., Shortle J.F., Thomson J.M. and Harris C.M., *Fundamentals of Queuing Theory* (4th edition), John Wiley and Sons, Hoboken, NJ, 2008.

Haghighi A.M. and Mishey D.P., *Queuing Models in Industry and Business*, Nova Science Publishers, Hauppauge, New York, 2008.

Law A., *Simulation Modelling and Analysis* (4th edition), McGraw-Hill, New York, 2006.

Leemis L.H. and Park S.K., *Discrete Event Simulation*, Prentice Hall, Upper Saddle River, NJ, 2005.

Moore J.H. and Weatherford L.R., *Decision Modelling with Microsoft Excel* (6th edition), Prentice Hall, Upper Saddle River, NJ, 2001.

Oakshott L., *Business Modelling and Simulation*, Pitman, London, 1996.

Pidd M., *Computer Simulation in Management Science* (5th edition), John Wiley, Chichester, 2004.

Ragsdale C., *Spreadsheet Modelling and Decision Analysis* (5th edition), South-Western College Publishing, Cincinnati, OH, 2008.

Ross S.M., *Simulation* (4th edition), Elsevier, Amsterdam, 2006.

Sokolowski J.A. and Banks C.M., *Modelling and Simulation Fundamentals*, John Wiley and Sons, Hoboken, NJ, 2010.

Winston W.L. and Albright S., *Spreadsheet Modelling and Applications*, Brooks Cole, Florence, KY, 2004.

GLOSSARY

[Figures in brackets show the chapter where the topic is discussed]

5-whys method [17] – repeatedly asking questions to find the cause of faults

ABC analysis [18] – Pareto analysis for inventory items

acceptable quality level (AQL) [17] – the poorest level of quality, or the most defects, that is acceptable in a batch

acceptance sampling [17] – tests a sample from a batch to see whether or not the whole batch reaches an acceptable level of quality

achieved quality [17] – shows how closely a product conforms to its designed specifications

aggregate index [7] – monitors the way that several variables change over time

algebra [2] – use of symbols to represent variables and to describe relationships between them

alternative hypothesis [15] – hypothesis that is true when the null hypothesis is rejected

annual equivalent rate or annual percentage rate [8] – true interest rate for borrowing or lending money

annuity [8] – amount invested to give a fixed income over some period

a-priori [12] – probability calculated by analysing circumstances

arithmetic [2] – any kind of calculation with numbers

arithmetic mean [6] – the 'average' of a set of numbers

autocorrelation [9] – relationship between the errors in multiple regression

average [6] – typical value for a set of data, often the arithmetic mean

axes [3] – rectangular scales for drawing graphs

bar chart [5] – diagram that represents the frequency of observations in a class by the length of a bar

base [2] – value of b when a number is represented in the logarithmic format of $n = b^p$

base period [7] – fixed point of reference for an index

base-weighted index [7] – aggregate index which assumes that quantities purchased do not change from the base period

base value [7] – value of a variable in the base period

Bayes' theorem [12] – equation for calculating conditional probabilities bias [4] – systematic error in a sample

binomial distribution [13] – distribution that shows the probabilities of different numbers of successes in a number of trials

break-even point [8] – sales volume at which an organisation covers its costs and begins to make a profit

calculations [1] – arithmetic manipulation of numbers

capacity [8] – maximum output that is possible in a specified time

cardinal data [4] – data that can be measured

causal forecasting [9] – using a relationship to forecast the value of a dependent variable that corresponds to a known value of an independent variable

causal methods [10] – quantitative methods of forecasting that analyse the effects of outside influences and use these to produce forecasts

cause-and-effect diagram, Ishikawa diagram or fishbone diagram [17] – diagram that shows the causes of problems with quality

census [4] – sample of the entire population

central limit theorem [14] – theorem that describes the distribution of observations about the mean

chi-squared (or χ^2) test [15] – non-parametric hypothesis test

class [5] – range or entry in a frequency distribution

cluster sample [4] – result of choosing a sample in clusters rather than individually

coefficient of correlation or Pearson's coefficient [9] – measure of the strength of a linear relationship

coefficient of determination [9] – proportion of the total sum of squared errors from the mean that is explained by a regression

coefficient of skewness [6] – measure of the symmetry or skewness of a set of data

coefficient of variation [6] – ratio of standard deviation over mean

combination [13] – number of ways of selecting r things from n when the order of selection does not matter

common fraction or fraction [2] – part of a whole expressed as the ratio of a numerator over a denominator, such as 1/5

common logarithm [2] – logarithm to the base 10

compound interest [8] – interest paid on both the principal and the interest previously earned

conditional probabilities [12] – probabilities for dependent events with the form P(a/b)

confidence interval [14] – interval that we are, for instance, 95% confident that a value lies within

constant [2] – number or quantity that always has the same fixed value, such as π, e or 2 constrained optimisation [11] – problems with an aim of optimising some objective subject to constraints

consumer's risk [17] – highest acceptable probability of accepting a bad batch with more defects than LTPD

contingency table [15] – table showing the relationship between two parameters

continuous data [4] – data that can take any value (rather than just discrete values)

coordinates [3] – values of x and y that define a point on Cartesian axes

critical activities [19] – activities at fixed times in a project

critical path [19] – series of critical activities in a project

critical path method (CPM) [19] – method of project planning that assumes each activity has a fixed duration

critical value [15] – test value for a chi-squared test

cumulative frequency distribution [5] – diagram showing the sum of frequencies in lower classes

cumulative percentage frequency distribution [5] – diagram showing the sum of percentage frequencies in lower classes

current-weighted index [7] – aggregate index which assumes that the current amounts bought were also bought in the base period

curve fitting [9] – finding the function that best fits a set of data

cycle-service level [18] – probability that all demand can be met in a stock cycle

data [4] – raw facts that are processed to give information

data collection [4] – gathering of facts that are needed for making decisions

data presentation [5] – format for showing the characteristics of data and emphasising the underlying patterns

data reduction [5] – reducing the amount of detail in data to emphasise the underlying patterns

decimal fraction [2] – part of a whole described by a number following a decimal point, such as 0.5

decimal places [2] – number of digits following a decimal point

decision criteria [16] – simple rules that recommend an alternative for decisions involving uncertainty

decision nodes [16] – points in a decision tree where decisions are made

decision tree [16] – diagram that represents a series of alternatives and events by the branches of a tree

decision variables [11] – variables whose values we can choose

degrees of freedom [14] – measure of the number of independent pieces of information used in probability distributions

denominator [2] – bottom line of a common fraction

dependence table [19] – table showing the relationships between activities in a project

dependent demand [18] – situation in which demands for materials are somehow related to each other

dependent events [12] – events in which the occurrence of one event directly affects the probability of another

dependent variable [3] – variable whose value is set by the value of the independent variable (usually the y value on a graph)

depreciation [8] – amount by which an organisation reduces the value of its assets

designed quality [17] – quality that a product is designed to have

deterministic [12] – describing a situation of certainty

deviation [6] – distance an observation is away from the mean

discount factor [8] – value of $(1 + i)^{-n}$ when discounting to present value

discount rate [8] – value of i when discounting to present value

discounting to present value [8] – calculating the present value of an amount available at some point in the future

discrete data [4] – data that is limited to integer values

diseconomies of scale [8] – effect where the average cost per unit rises as the number of units produced increases

distribution-free tests (or non-parametric test) [15] – hypothesis tests that make no assumptions about the distribution of the population

e or exponential constant [2] – constant calculated from $(1 + 1/n)^n$, where n is an indefinitely large number; it equals approximately 2.7182818

economic order quantity [18] – order size that minimises costs for a simple inventory system

economies of scale [8] – effect where the average cost per unit declines as the number of units produced increases

empirical probability [12] – probability found by observation or experiment

equation [2] – algebraic formula that shows the relationship between variables, saying that the value of one expression equals the value of a second expression

error [9] – difference between an expected value and the actual observation, often described as noise

expected value [16] – sum of the probability multiplied by the value of the outcome

exponential constant or e [2] – constant calculated from $(1 + 1/n)^n$, where n is an indefinitely large number; it equals 2.7162816. . .

exponential smoothing [10] – weighting based on the idea that older data is less relevant and therefore should be given less weight

extrapolation [9] – causal forecasting with values of the independent variable outside the range used to define the regression

extreme point [11] – corner of the feasible region in linear programming feasible region [11] – area of a graph in which all feasible solutions lie for a linear programme

feedback [1] – return of information to managers so that they can compare actual performance with plans

forecast [10] – some form of prediction of future conditions

float, total float (or sometimes slack) [19] – difference between the amount of time available for an activity in a project and the time actually used

formulation [11] – getting a problem in an appropriate form, particularly with linear programming

fraction [2] – usual name for a common fraction

frequency distribution [5] – diagram showing the number of observations in each class

frequency table [5] – table showing the number of observations in each class

Gantt chart [19] – diagram for showing the schedule of a project

gradient [3] – measure of how steeply a graph is rising or falling

graph [3] – pictorial view of the relationship between two (usually) variables, often drawn on Cartesian coordinates

grouped data [6] – raw data already divided into classes

histogram [5] – frequency distribution for continuous data

hypothesis testing [15] – seeing whether or not a belief about a population is supported by the evidence from a sample

independent demand [18] – demand where there is no link between different demands for items

independent equations [2] – equations that are not related, and are not different versions of the same equation

independent events [12] – events for which the occurrence of one event does not affect the probability of a second

independent variable [2] – variable that can take any value, and sets the value of a dependent variable (usually the x value on a graph)

index or index number [7] – number that compares the value of a variable at any point in time with its value in a base period

inequality [2] – relationship that is less precise than an equation, typically with a form like $a \leq b$

information [4] – data that has been processed into a useful form

integer [2] – whole number without any fractional parts

intercept [3] – point where the graph of a line crosses the y-axis

interest [8] – amount paid to lenders as reward for using their money

internal rate of return [8] – discount rate that gives a net present value of zero interquartile range [6] – distance between the first and third quartiles

interval estimate [14] – estimated range within which the value for a population is likely to lie

judgemental forecasts [10] – forecasts that rely on subjective assessments and opinions

Laspeyres index [7] – base-weighted index

line graph [3] – graph that shows the relationship between two variables, usually on Cartesian axes

line of best fit [9] – line that minimises some measure of the error (usually the mean squared error) in a set of data

linear programming (LP) [11] – method of solving some problems of constrained optimisation

linear regression [9] – process that finds the straight line that best fits a set of data

linear relationship [3] – relationship between two variables of the form $y = ax + b$, giving a straight-line graph

logarithm [2] – value of p when a number is represented in the logarithmic format of $n = b^p$

Lorenz curve [5] – a graph of cumulative percentage wealth (income or some other measure of wealth) against cumulative percentage of the population

loss function [17] – function that shows the notional cost of missing a performance target

lot tolerance percent defective (LTPD) [17] – level of quality that is unacceptable, or the highest number of defects that customers are willing to accept

marginal benefit [4] – benefit from the last unit made, collected etc.

marginal cost [4] – cost of one extra unit made, collected etc.

marginal revenue [8] – revenue generated by selling one extra unit of a product

mean [6] – 'average' of a set of numbers

mean absolute deviation [6] – average distance of observations from the mean

mean absolute error [9] – average error, typically in a forecast

mean price relative index [7] – composite index found from the mean value of indices for separate items

mean squared deviation or variance [6] – average of the squared distance of observations from the mean

mean squared error [9] – average value of squared errors, typically in a forecast

measure [1] – numerical description of some attribute

measure of location [6] – showing the 'centre' or typical value for a set of data measure of spread [6] – showing how widely data is dispersed about its centre

median [6] – middle value of a set of numbers

mind map, problem map or relationship diagram [16] – diagram that shows interactions and relationships in a problem

mode [6] – most frequent value in a set of numbers

model [1] – simplified representation of reality

Monte Carlo simulation [20] – type of simulation model that includes a lot of uncertainty

mortgage [8] – amount borrowed for buying a house or other capital facilities

moving average [10] – average of the most recent periods of data

multicollinearity [9] – relationship between the independent variables in multiple regression

multiple (linear) regression [9] – process that finds the line of best fit through a set of dependent variables

multi-stage sample [4] – sample that successively breaks a population into smaller parts, confining it to a small geographical area

mutually exclusive events [12] – events where only one can happen but not both

natural logarithm [2] – logarithm to the base e

negative exponential distribution [20] – probability distribution used for continuous random values

negative number [2] – number less than zero

net present value [8] – result of subtracting the present value of all costs from the present value of all revenues

nodes [12] – representation of decisions or events in networks

noise [9] – random errors in observations (often described as errors)

nominal data [4] – data for which there is no convincing quantitative measure

non-critical activities [19] – activities in a project that have some flexibility in their timing

non-linear regression [9] – procedure to find the function that best fits a set of data

non-linear relationship [3] – any relationship between variables that is not linear

non-negativity constraint [11] – constraint that sets all variables to be positive, especially in linear programmes

non-parametric tests or distribution-free tests [15] – hypothesis tests that make no assumptions about the distribution of the population

Normal distribution [13] – most widely used, bell-shaped probability distribution for continuous data

null hypothesis [15] – original hypothesis that is being tested

numerator [2] – top line of a common fraction

objective function [11] – function to be optimised, especially in linear programming

ogive [5] – graph of the cumulative frequency against class for continuous data

operating characteristics [20] – features and calculations for a queuing system

operating characteristic curve [17] – curve that shows how well a sampling plan separates good batches from bad ones

ordinal data [4] – data that cannot be precisely measured but that can be ordered or ranked

origin [3] – point where x and y Cartesian axes cross

Paasche index [7] – current-weighted index

parametric test [15] – hypothesis test that concerns the value of a parameter

Pareto chart [17] – 'rule of 80/18' method to identify the small number of causes for most problems

partial productivity [8] – output achieved for each unit of a specified resource

payoff matrix or payoff table [16] – table that shows the outcomes for each combination of alternatives and events in a decision

Pearson's coefficient [9] – measure of the strength of a linear relationship (known as the coefficient of correlation)

percentage [2] – fraction expressed as a part of 100

percentage frequency distribution [5] – diagram showing the percentage of observations in each class

percentage point change [7] – change in an index between two periods

performance ratio [8] – some measure of actual performance divided by a standard reference value

permutation [13] – number of ways of selecting r things from n, when the order of selection is important

pictogram [5] – bar chart where the plain bar is replaced by some kind of picture

pie chart [5] – diagram that represents the frequency of observations in a class by the area of a sector of a circle

point estimate [14] – single estimate of a population value from a sample

Poisson distribution [13] – probability distribution largely used for describing random events

polynomial [3] – equation containing a variable raised to some power

population [4] – every source of data for a particular application

positive number [2] – number greater than zero

positive quadrant [3] – top right-hand quarter of a graph on Cartesian co-ordinates, where both x and y are positive

power [2] – value of b when a number is represented as a^b (i.e. the number of times a is multiplied by itself) present value [8] – discounted value of a future amount

price index [7] – index for monitoring the price of an item

primary data [4] – new data that is collected for a particular purpose

principal [8] – amount originally borrowed for a loan

probabilistic or stochastic [12] – containing uncertainty that is measured by probabilities

probability [12] – likelihood or relative frequency of an event

probability distribution [13] – description of the relative frequency of observations

probability tree [12] – diagram showing a series of related probabilities

problem map, relationship diagram or mind map [16] – diagram that shows interactions and relationships in a problem

process control [17] – taking a sample of products to check that a process is working within acceptable limits

process control chart [17] – diagram for monitoring a process over time

producer's risk [17] – highest acceptable probability of rejecting a good batch, with fewer defects than the AQL

productivity [8] – amount of output for each unit of resource used

profit [8] – residue when all costs are subtracted from all revenues

project [19] – distinct and unique set of activities that make a one-off product

project (or programme) evaluation and review technique (PERT) [19] – method of project planning that assumes each activity has an uncertain duration

project network analysis [19] – most widely used method of organising complex projects

projective methods [10] – quantitative methods of forecasting that extend the pattern of past demand into the future

quadratic equation [3] – equation with the general form $y = ax^2 + bx + c$

qualitative [1] – not using numbers, but based on opinions and judgement

quality [17] – ability of a product to meet, and preferably exceed, customer expectations

quality control [17] – using a series of independent inspections and tests to make sure that designed quality is actually being achieved

quality management [17] – all aspects of management related to product quality

quantitative [1] – using numbers

quantitative methods [1] – broad range of numerical approaches to solving problems

quartile deviation [6] – half the interquartile range

quartiles [6] – points that are a quarter of the way through data when it is sorted by size

questionnaire [4] – set of questions used to collect data

queue [20] – line of customers waiting to be served

quota sample [4] – sample structured in such a way that it has the same characteristics as the population

random nodes [16] – points in a decision tree where events happen

random numbers [4] – string of digits that follow no patterns

random sample [4] – sample in which every member of the population has the same chance of being selected

range [6] – difference between the largest and smallest values in a set of data

regression [9] – method of finding the best equation to describe the relationship between variables

regret [16] – difference between the best possible outcome and the actual outcome in a decision

relationship diagram, problem map or mind map [16] – diagram that shows interactions and relationships in a problem

reorder level [18] – stock level when it is time to place an order

roots of a quadratic equation [3] – points where the curve crosses the x-axis

round [2] – to state a number to a specified number of decimal places or significant figures

rule of sixths [19] – rule to find the expected duration of an activity for PERT

safety stock [18] – additional stock that is used to cover unexpectedly high demand

sample [4] – members of the population chosen as sources of data

sampling by attribute [17] – taking a quality control sample where units are described as either acceptable or defective

sampling by variable [17] – taking a quality control sample where units have a measurable feature

sampling distribution of the mean [14] – distribution of the mean of samples from the population

sampling frame [4] – list of every member of a population

scatter diagram [5] – unconnected graph of a set of points (x, y)

scientific notation [2] – representation of a number in the form $a \times 10^b$

seasonal index [10] – amount by which a deseasonalised value is multiplied to get a seasonal value

secondary data [4] – data that already exists and can be used for a problem

semi-interquartile range [6] – half the interquartile range

sensitivity [10] – speed at which a forecast responds to changing conditions

sensitivity analysis [11] – seeing what happens when a problem (particularly a linear programme) is changed slightly

sequencing [13] – putting activities into an order for processing service level [18] – probability that demand can be met from stock

shadow price [11] – marginal value of resources in a linear programme

significance level [15] – minimum acceptable probability that a value actually comes from the hypothesised population

significant figures [2] – main digits to the left of a number

simple aggregate index [7] – composite index that adds all prices (say) together and calculates an index based on the total price

simple interest [8] – has interest paid on only the initial deposit, but not on interest already earned

simulation [20] – process that analyses problems by imitating real operations, giving a set of typical, but artificial, results

simultaneous equations [2] – independent equations that show the relationship between a set of variables

sinking fund [8] – fund that receives regular payments so that a specified sum is available at a specified point in the future

slack [19] – sometimes used to mean float or total float, being the difference between the amount of time available for an activity in a project and the time actually used

smoothing constant [10] – parameter used to adjust the sensitivity of exponential smoothing forecasts

solution [11] – finding an optimal solution to a problem (particularly a linear programme)

solving an equation [2] – using the known constants and variables in an equation to find the value of a previously unknown constant or variable

Spearman's coefficient (of rank correlation) [9] – a measure of the correlation of ranked data

spreadsheet [1] – general program that stores values in the cells of a grid, and does calculations based on defined relationships between cells

square root [2] – square root of n, $\sqrt{n}$, is the number that is multiplied by itself to give n

standard deviation [6] – measure of the data spread, equal to the square root of the variance

standard error [14] – standard deviation of the sampling distribution of the mean

statistical inference [14] – process of collecting data from a random sample of a population and using it to estimate features of the whole population

stochastic or probabilistic [12] – containing uncertainty that is measured by probabilities

stocks [18] – stores of materials that organisations keep until needed

stratified sample [4] – sample taken from each distinct group in a population

strict uncertainty or uncertainty [16] – situation in which we can list possible events for a decision, but cannot given them probabilities

Student-t distribution [14] – see t-distribution

symbolic model [1] – model where real properties are represented by symbols, usually algebraic variables

systematic sample [4] – sample in which data is collected at regular intervals

t-distribution or Student-*t* distribution [14] – distribution used instead of the Normal distribution for small samples

target stock level [18] – stock level that determines the order size with periodic review

terminal nodes [16] – points in a decision tree at the end of each path

time series [10] – series of observations taken at regular intervals of time

total float [19] – difference between the amount of time available for an activity in a project and the time actually used

Total Quality Management (TQM) [17] – system of having the whole organisation working together to guarantee, and systematically improve, quality

tracking signal [10] – measure to monitor the performance of a forecast

turning points [3] – maxima and minima on a graph

uncertainty or strict uncertainty [16] – situation in which we can list possible events for a decision, but cannot given them probabilities

utilisation [8] – proportion of available capacity that is actually used

utilisation factor [20] – proportion of time a queuing system is busy (= λ/μ for a single server)

utility [16] – measure that shows the real value of money to a decision-maker

variable [2] – quantity that can take different values, such as x, a or P

variance [6] – measure of the spread of data using the mean squared deviation

Venn diagram [12] – diagram that represents probabilities as circles that may or may not overlap

weighted index [7] – aggregate price index (say) that takes into account both prices and the importance of items

weighted mean [6] – mean that uses a different weight for each observation

Solutions to review questions

Chapter 1 – Managers and numbers

1.1 They give clear, precise and objective measures of features, and allow calculations and rational analysis of problems.

1.2 No – managers make decisions.

1.3 No – but they must be aware of the types of analysis available, understand the underlying principles, recognise the assumptions and limitations, do some analyses themselves, have intelligent discussions with experts and interpret the results.

1.4 There are several reasons for this including availability of computers, improving software, fiercer competition forcing better decisions, new quantitative methods, good experiences with earlier analyses, better education of managers and so on.

1.5 To develop solutions for problems, allow experimentation without risk to actual operations, allow experiments that would not be possible in reality, check the consequences of decisions, see how sensitive operations are to change and so on.

1.6 We describe four stages – identifying a problem, analysing it, making decisions and implementing the results.

1.7 Generally in the analysis stage.

1.8 No – we can use any approach that is efficient and gets a good answer.

1.9 No – you can get a feel for the numbers without doing the detailed calculations.

1.10 Because spreadsheets are widely available, they use standard formats that are familiar and easy to use and you do not have to learn how to use a new program for each problem.

Chapter 2 – Calculations and equations

2.1 You might want to check the figures, do some easy calculations by hand, do initial calculations to get rough estimates, get a feel for the numbers involved or a host of other reasons.

2.2 (a) 4, (b) 56 / 5 or 11.2, (c) 3.

2.3 There is no difference – the choice of best depends on circumstances.

2.4 1,745,800.362 and 1,750,000.

2.5 Because it gives a precise way of describing and solving quantitative problems.

2.6 Yes.

2.7 A constant always has the same fixed value; a variable can take any one of a range of values.

2.8 There is no best format for all occasions – you should use the format that best suits your needs.

2.9 Using an equation to find a previously unknown value from related known values.

2.10 No – to find two unknowns you need two equations.

2.11 By rearranging them to (a) $x = 11 - 8pr / 3q$ and (b) $x = q / 4 - 7pq / 2r$.

2.12 A relationship that is not a precise equation but takes some other form, such as $a \leq b$.

2.13 Independent equations that show the relationships between a set of variables.

2.14 Six.

2.15 No – the equations contradict each other.

2.16 In ascending order, $(\frac{1}{2})^4 = 0.0625$; $4^{-1} = 0.25$; $1^4 = 1$; $4^{1/2} = 2$; $4^1 = 4$; $(\frac{1}{2})^{-4} = 16$.

2.17 $9^{1.5} / 4^{2.5} = (\sqrt{9})^3 / (\sqrt{4})^5 = 3^3 / 2^5 = 27 / 32 = 0.84$.

2.18 1 – anything raised to the power zero equals 1.

2.19 1.23×10^9 and 2.53×10^{-7}.

2.20 Logarithms are defined by the relationship that $n = b^p$ meaning that $p = \log_b n$. They are used mainly to solve equations that contain powers.

Chapter 3 – Drawing graphs

3.1 A variable whose value is set by the value taken by the independent variable.

3.2 No – graphs show relationships, but do not suggest cause and effect.

3.3 (0, 0).

3.4 Yes – the distance between the two points is 10.

3.5 It is a straight line with a gradient of –2 that crosses the y-axis at –4.

3.6 (a) 0, (b) 1, (c) –6.

3.7 They correspond to the points where $y > 3x + 5$.

3.8 No – they are the same general shape, but differ in detail.

3.9 The points where the curve crosses the x-axis.

3.10 They are imaginary.

3.11 Because graphs are difficult to draw exactly and calculations give more accurate results.

3.12 A function containing x raised to some power.

3.13 A peak or trough, corresponding to a point where the gradient changes from positive to negative, or vice versa.

3.14 Using the usual procedure to draw a graph of the general form $y = ne^{mx}$, where n and m are positive constants.

3.15 You cannot draw this on a two-dimensional graph. You can draw it on a three-dimensional graph, but the results are generally complicated and difficult to interpret.

3.16 The equations for both graphs are true, so this point identifies the solution to the simultaneous equations.

3.17 Because they are more accurate and you can use more than two variables.

Chapter 4 – Collecting data

4.1 Data are the raw numbers, measurements, opinions etc. that are processed to give useful information.

4.2 Because managers need reliable information to make decisions, and the first step for this is data collection.

4.3 No – there is an almost limitless amount of data that can be collected, but only some of it is useful and cost effective.

4.4 Because different types of data are collected, analysed and presented in different ways.

4.5 There are several possible classifications, including quantitative/qualitative, nominal/cardinal/ordinal, discrete/continuous and primary/secondary.

4.6 Discrete data can take only integer values; continuous data can take any values.

4.7 There are many possible examples.

4.8 In principle it is better, but in practice we have to balance its benefits with the cost and effort of collection.

4.9 Because it is too expensive, time-consuming or impractical to collect data from whole populations.

4.10 Yes (at least almost always).

4.11 Because using the wrong population would make the whole data collection and analysis pointless.

4.12 One classification has census, random, systematic, stratified, quota, multi-stage and cluster samples.

4.13 Every member of the population has the same chance of being selected.

4.14 Suggestions are: (a) telephone survey, (b) personal interview, (c) longitudinal survey, (d) observation.

4.15 (a) leading question, (b) too vague, (c) several questions in one, (d) speculative.

4.16 You can try contacting non-respondents and encourage them to reply. Realistically, this will have little success so you should search for common features to ensure that no bias is introduced.

4.17 Because interviewers keep asking people until they fill the required quotas.

4.18 No – all data collection must be carefully planned before it is started.

Chapter 5 – Diagrams for presenting data

5.1 Data are the raw numbers, measurements, opinions etc. that are processed to give useful information.

5.2 To simplify raw data, remove the detail and show underlying patterns.

5.3 Unfortunately not – though this is the aim.

5.4 Using diagrams and numbers.

5.5 They can display lots of information, show varying attributes and highlight patterns.

5.6 A description of the number of observations in a set of data falling into each class.

5.7 This depends on the nature of the data and the purpose of the table. A guideline suggests between 4 and 10 classes.

5.8 Because they are a very efficient way of presenting a lot of detail. No other format can fit so much information into such a small space.

5.9 To a large extent yes – but the choice often depends on personal preference, and a diagram of any kind may not be appropriate.

5.10 To show that they are scaled properly, accurately drawn and give a true picture.

5.11 No – there are many possible variations and the best is often a matter of opinion.

5.12 Any diagram can give an impact – but possibly some kind of pictogram may be best.

5.13 They are not very accurate, show a small amount of data and can be misleading.

5.14 Unfortunately, you can find many of these.

5.15 No – it is true for bar charts, but in histograms the area shows the number of observations.

5.16 The average height of the two separate bars.

5.17 Often there is no benefit from histograms and it makes sense to stick with bar charts. Sometimes histograms help with further statistical analyses.

5.18 To show the cumulative frequency against class for continuous data.

5.19 Perhaps – the diagonal line shows equally distributed wealth, but we do not know whether this is fair or desirable.

Chapter 6 – Using numbers to describe data

6.1 Diagrams give an overall impression, but they do not consider objective measures.

6.2 A measure of the centre of the data – some kind of typical or average value.

6.3 No – these only partially describe a set of data.

6.4 A measure for the centre of the data or a typical value.

6.5 No.

6.6 The most common measures are: arithmetic mean = $\Sigma x / n$; median = middle observation; mode = most frequent observation.

6.7 $(10 \times 34 + 5 \times 37) / 15 = 35$.

6.8 In Excel useful functions are AVERAGE, MEDIAN and MODE.

6.9 We concentrated on range, mean absolute deviation, variance and standard deviation. Yes.

6.10 Because positive and negative deviations cancel and the mean deviation is always zero.

6.11 Metres^2 and metres respectively.

6.12 Because it gives standard results that we can interpret and use in other analyses.

6.13 210 is nine standard deviations away from 120, and the chances of this are very small. The result is possible, but it is more likely that there has been a mistake – perhaps writing 210 instead of 120.

6.14 Useful ones include MAX, MIN, VARP, STDEVP and QUARTILE.

6.15 To give a relative view of spread that can be used to compare different sets of data.

6.16 The general shape of a distribution.

6.17 The coefficients of variation are 0.203 and 0.128 respectively (remembering to take the square root of the variance), which shows that the first set of data is more widely dispersed than the second set.

Chapter 7 – Describing changes with index numbers

7.1 To measure the changes in a variable over time.

7.2 The base index is not always 100. It is often used, but only for convenience.

7.3 A percentage rise of 10% increases the value by 10% of the value; a percentage point rise of 10 increases the value by 10% of the base value.

7.4 When circumstances change significantly or when the old index gets too high.

7.5 $132 \times 345 / 125 = 364.32$.

7.6 The mean price relative index is the average of the separate price indices; the simple aggregate index is based on the total price paid.

7.7 They depend on the units used and do not take into account the relative importance of each item.

7.8 Base-period weighting assumes that the basket of items used in the base period is always used; current-period weighting considers price changes based on the current basket of items.

7.9 Because the basket of items bought is actually affected by prices, with items whose prices rise rapidly replaced by ones with lower price rises.

7.10 Yes.

7.11 Not really – the RPI monitors the changing prices paid for some items by a 'typical' family – but people question its reliability.

Chapter 8 – Finance and performance

8.1 Because they give some context for the measures.

8.2 No.

8.3 Yes.

8.4 No.

8.5 The number of units processed (made, sold, served etc.).

8.6 The number of units that must be sold before covering all costs and making a profit.

8.7 No – there may also be diseconomies of scale.

8.8 The optimal production quantity is the point where the marginal cost equals the marginal revenue.

8.9 £1,000 now.

8.10 Because you also earn interest on the interest that has been paid earlier, so your returns increase over time.

8.11 No.

8.12 By reducing all costs and revenues to present values, and calculating either the net present value or the internal rate of return for each project.

8.13 An estimate of the proportional increase or decrease in the value of money in each time period.

8.14 NPV uses a fixed discount rate to get different present values; IRR uses different discount rates to get a fixed present value.

8.15 Straight-line depreciation reduces the value by a fixed amount each year; the reducing-balance method reduces the value by a fixed percentage each year.

8.16 A fund that receives regular payments so that a specified sum is available at some point in the future.

8.17 By using the equation $A_n = A_0 \times (1 + i)^n + [F \times (1 + i)^n - F] / i$, to find A_0 when $A_n = 0$ and F is the regular payment received.

8.18 No – other factors should be included.

Chapter 9 – Regression and curve fitting

9.1 The errors, or deviations from expected values.

9.2 Real relationships are almost never perfect and errors are introduced by noise, incorrectly identifying the underlying pattern, changes in the system being modelled etc.

9.3 The mean error is $\Sigma E_i / n$. Positive and negative errors cancel each other, so the mean error should be around zero unless there is bias.

9.4 Mean absolute error and mean squared error.

9.5 By calculating the errors – mean errors, mean absolute deviations and mean squared errors – for each equation. All things being equal, the stronger relationship is the one with smaller error.

9.6 To find the line of best fit relating a dependent variable to an independent one.

9.7 x_i and y_i are the ith values of independent and dependent variables respectively; a is the intercept of the line of best fit, and b is its gradient; E_i is the error from random noise.

9.8 The time period.

9.9 No – there is no implied cause and effect.

9.10 Interpolation considers values for the independent variable within the range used to define the regression; extrapolation considers values outside this range.

9.11 The proportion of the total sum of squared error that is explained by the regression.

9.12 Values from –1 to +1.

9.13 The coefficient of correlation is the square root of the coefficient of determination.

9.14 They are essentially the same, but Pearson's coefficient is used for cardinal data and Spearman's is used for ordinal data.

9.15 No – it shows that 90% of the variation in the dependent variable is explained by, but not necessarily caused by, the relationship with the independent variable.

9.16 Multiple (linear) regression and non-linear regression.

9.17 No – there are several independent variables and one dependent one.

9.18 By comparing the coefficients of determination.

9.19 There is no difference.

9.20 Yes.

Chapter 10 – Forecasting

10.1   All decisions become effective at some point in the future, so they must take into account future circumstances – and these must be forecast.

10.2   No.

10.3   Judgemental, projective and causal forecasting.

10.4   Relevant factors include what is to be forecast, why this is being forecast, availability of quantitative data, how the forecast affects other parts of the organisation, how far into the future forecasts are needed, reliability of available data, what external factors are relevant, how much the forecast will cost, how much errors will cost, how much detail is required, how much time is available and so on.

10.5   Forecasts based on subjective views, opinions and intuition rather than quantitative analysis.

10.6   Personal insight, panel consensus, market surveys, historical analogy and the Delphi method.

10.7   The drawbacks are that the method is unreliable, experts may give conflicting views, cost of data collection is high, there may be no available expertise and so on. On the other hand they can be the only methods available, are flexible, can give good results, include subjective data etc.

10.8   Because observations contain random noise which cannot be forecast.

10.9   By using both forecasts over a typical period and comparing the errors.

10.10   Because older data tends to swamp more recent – and more relevant – data.

10.11   By using a lower value of n.

10.12   It can be influenced by random fluctuations.

10.13   By using a moving average with n equal to the length of the season.

10.14   Because the weight given to the data declines exponentially with age, and the method smoothes the effects of noise.

10.15   By using a higher value for the smoothing constant, α.

10.16   Deseasonalise the data, find seasonal adjustments, project the underlying trend and use the seasonal adjustments to get seasonal forecasts.

10.17   An additive model adds a seasonal adjustment; a multiplicative model multiplies by a seasonal index.

10.18   Regression is generally preferred.

Chapter 11 – Linear programming

11.1   A problem where managers want an optimal solution, but there are constraints that limit the options available.

11.2   A method of tackling some problems of constrained optimisation.

11.3   The problem is constrained optimisation, both constraints and objective function are linear with respect to decision variables, proportionality and additivity assumptions are valid, problem variables are non-negative and reliable data is available.

11.4   You put a problem into a standard form.

11.5   Decision variables, an objective function, problem constraints and a non-negativity constraint.

11.6   The area representing feasible solutions that satisfy all constraints, including the non-negativity conditions.

11.7   To give the measure by which solutions are judged, and hence allow an optimal solution to be identified.

11.8   The corners of the feasible region (which is always a polygon); optimal solutions are always at extreme points.

11.9   By moving the objective function line as far away from the origin as possible (for a maximum), or moving it as close to the origin as possible (for a minimum), and identifying the last point it passes through in the feasible region.

11.10   The analyses that look at changes in the optimal solution with small changes to the constraints and objective function.

11.11   Its marginal value, or the amount the objective function changes with one more – or less – unit of the resource.

11.12   Until so many resources become available that the constraint is no longer limiting (or resources are reduced until a new constraint becomes limiting).

11.13   Because the procedures to find a solution need a lot of simple arithmetic.

11.14   The usual information includes a review of the problem tackled, details of the optimal solution, limiting constraints and unused resources, shadow prices and ranges over which these are valid, and variations in the objective function that will not change the position of the optimal solution.

11.15   Not usually.

Chapter 12 – Uncertainty and probabilities

12.1   To a large extent yes.

12.2   A measure of its likelihood or relative frequency.

12.3   No – you can know a lot about a situation without knowing everything with certainty.

12.4   Yes.

12.5 $10,000 \times 0.01 = 100$

12.6   Events where the probability of one occurring is not affected by whether or not the other occurs.

12.7   Events that cannot both occur.

12.8   By adding the separate probabilities of each event.

12.9   By multiplying the separate probabilities of each event.

12.10 $P(X) + P(Y) - P(X \text{ AND } Y)$

12.11   Two (or more) events are dependent if they are not independent – meaning that $P(a) \neq P(a / b) \neq P(a / \not b)$.

12.12   Probabilities of the form $P(a / b)$, giving the probability of event a occurring, given that event b has already occurred.

12.13   Bayes' theorem states that $P(a / b) = P(b / a) \times P(a) / P(b)$; it is used for calculating conditional probabilities.

12.14   It shows a diagrammatic view of a problem and a way of organising calculations.

Chapter 13 – Probability distributions

13.1   To describe the probabilities or relative frequencies of events or classes of observations.

13.2   Yes – essentially.

13.3   Probability distributions found from observation of events that actually occurred.

13.4 $n!$

13.5   The order of selection is not important for a combination, but it is important for a permutation.

13.6   Permutations.

13.7   When there is a series of trials, each trial has two possible outcomes, the two outcomes are mutually exclusive, there is a constant probability of success, p, and failure, $q = 1 - p$ and the outcomes of successive trials are independent.

13.8 $P(r)$ is the probability of r successes, n is the number of trials, p is the probability of success in each trial, q is the probability of failure in each trial, $^{n}C_{r}$ is the number of ways of combining r items from n.

13.9   Mean $= np$; variance $= npq$

13.10 0.2753.

13.11 When independent events occur infrequently and at random, the probability of an event in an interval is proportional to the length of the interval and an infinite number of events should be possible in an interval.

13.12 Mean $=$ variance $= np$.

13.13 0.1438.

13.14 When the number of events, n, in the binomial process is large and the probability of success is small, so np is less than 5.

13.15 In many – arguably most – situations where there is a large number of observations.

13.16 Binomial and Poisson distributions describe discrete data; the Normal distribution describes continuous data.

13.17 The mean and standard deviation.

13.18 When the number of events, n, is large and the probability of success is relatively large (with np greater than 5).

13.19 About 68% of observations are within one standard deviation of the mean.

13.20 The Normal distribution describes continuous data, so a small continuity correction should be used for discrete data (perhaps replacing 'between 3 and 6 people' by 'between 2.5 and 6.5 people').

Chapter 14 – Using samples

14.1   To take a sample of observations that fairly represents the whole population.

14.2   A process where some property (quality, weight, length etc.) in a representative sample is used to estimate the property in the population.

14.3   When a series of samples are taken from a population and a mean value of some variable is found for each sample, these means form the sampling distribution of the mean.

14.4 If the sample size is more than about 30, or the population is Normally distributed, the sampling distribution of the mean is Normally distributed with mean μ and standard deviation $\sigma / \sqrt{n}$.

14.5 Because it comes from a sample that is unlikely to be perfectly representative of the population.

14.6 The range within which we are 95% confident the actual value lies.

14.7 Wider.

14.8 $25n$.

14.9 With small samples.

14.10 When you want to be confident that a value is either above or below a certain point.

14.11 One-sided 95%, two-sided 95%, one-sided 99%.

14.12 Because the samples are not representative of the population and tend to underestimate variability.

14.13 The number of independent pieces of data.

Chapter 15 – Testing hypotheses

15.1 To test whether or not a statement about a population is supported by the evidence in a sample.

15.2 The null hypothesis, H_0.

15.3 A Type I error rejects a null hypothesis that is true; a Type II error does not reject a null hypothesis that is false.

15.4 The minimum acceptable probability that an observation is a random sample from the hypothesised population.

15.5 5% significance.

15.6 We cannot be this confident – but the evidence does support the null hypothesis and means it cannot be rejected.

15.7 When you want to make sure that a variable is above or below a specified value.

15.8 Because a small sample underestimates the variability in the population.

15.9 Very close to a Normal distribution.

15.10 When you want an unbiased estimator for small samples.

15.11 There are many circumstances – but generally whenever you want to check a hypothesis about a population.

15.12 No – the confidence interval is a range that we are confident a value is within; a significance level is the maximum acceptable probability of making a Type I error.

15.13 A parametric test makes assumptions about the distribution of variables, and works only with cardinal data; a non-parametric test does not assume any distribution and can be used for all types of data.

15.14 When the conditions needed for a parametric test are not met.

15.15 No – there may be no appropriate test.

15.16 Because the distribution takes only positive values, so the acceptance range is from 0 to the critical value.

15.17 Nothing.

15.18 A test to see whether or not there is a relationship between two parameters, or if they are independent.

15.19 As usual, it is easier and more reliable than doing the calculations by hand – and spreadsheets are not really suited for this kind of analysis.

Chapter 16 – Making decisions

16.1 Because they give structure to a problem, defining relationships and clearly presenting alternatives, events and consequences.

16.2 A decision-maker, a number of alternatives, a number of events, a set of measurable outcomes and an objective of selecting the best alternative.

16.3 There is only one event, so in principle we can list the outcomes and identify the alternative that gives the best outcome.

16.4 Probably not – but remember that models are simplifications to help with decisions and they do not replicate reality.

16.5 No – decision-makers interpret aims, alternatives, events and outcomes differently, and may not agree about the best decision.

16.6 One of several events may occur, but there is no way of telling which events are more likely.

16.7 The three criteria described are due to Laplace, Wald and Savage.

16.8 Only the Laplace criterion.

16.9 No – many other criteria could be devised to fit particular circumstances.

16.10 There are several possible events and we can give probabilities to each of them.

16.11 The sum of the probabilities multiplied by the values of the outcomes – expected value = $\Sigma(P \times V)$.

16.12 Yes – but the results may be unreliable.

16.13 When the conditional probabilities are available in situations of risk.

16.14 Expected values do not reflect real preferences, and a utility function describes a more realistic relationship.

16.15 The value of a terminal node is the total cost or gain of reaching that node; the value of a decision node is the best value of nodes reached by leaving alternative branches; the value of a random node is the expected value of the leaving branches.

16.16 By doing the analysis back to the left-hand, originating node – the value at this node is the overall expected value of following the best policy.

Chapter 17 – Quality management

17.1 No.

17.2 Because there are so many opinions, viewpoints and possible measures.

17.3 The function that is responsible for all aspects of quality.

17.4 Because it has implications for survival, reputation, marketing effort needed, market share, prices charged, profits, costs, liability for defects and almost every other aspect of an organisation's operations.

17.5   No.

17.6   By minimising the total quality cost – and this usually means perfect quality.

17.7   Quality control inspects products to make sure they conform to designed quality; quality management is a wider function that is responsible for all aspects of quality.

17.8   A measure of the cost of missing target performance.

17.9   Unfortunately not – there are always random variations.

17.10 No.

17.11 Yes.

17.12 Everyone involved with its supply.

17.13 Acceptance sampling checks that products are conforming to design quality; process control checks that the process is working properly.

17.14 Sampling by attribute classifies units as either acceptable or defective; sampling by variable measures some continuous value.

17.15 Because it gives perfect differentiation between good batches (where the probability of acceptance is 1) and bad batches (where the probability of acceptance is 0).

17.16 The process needs adjusting – but check for random fluctuations before doing this.

17.17 A single reading outside the control limits – or an unexpected pattern such as a clear trend, several consecutive readings near to a control limit, several consecutive readings on the same side of the mean, very erratic observations etc.

Chapter 18 – Inventory management

18.1   To act as a buffer between supply and demand.

18.2   Demands that are distinct from each other, so that there is no kind of relationship between separate demands.

18.3   Unit cost, reorder cost, holding cost and shortage cost.

18.4   The fixed order quantity that minimises costs (when a number of assumptions are made).

18.5   C – depending on the economic order quantity.

18.6   The stock level when it is time to place an order.

18.7   From the lead time demand.

18.8   Greater than demand.

18.9   Larger batches (all things being equal).

18.10 No – many extensions are possible.

18.11 The probability that a demand can be satisfied (we used cycle-service level, which is the probability that an item remains in stock during a cycle). It is used because alternative analyses need shortage costs, which are very difficult to find.

18.12 It reduces the probability of shortages and increases service levels.

18.13 By increasing the amount of safety stock.

18.14 It is the difference between target stock level and the current stock when an order is placed.

18.15 Target stock level = expected demand over $T + L$ plus safety stock, and $= D(T + L) + Z\sigma\sqrt{(T + L)}$.

18.16 A periodic review system (all things being equal).

18.17 To see where most (and least) effort should be spent in inventory management.

18.18 B items and probably C items, depending on circumstances.

Chapter 19 – Project management

19.1 A coherent piece of work with a clear start and finish, consisting of the set of activities that make a distinct product.

19.2 The function responsible for the planning, scheduling and controlling of activities in a project and hence the management of resources.

19.3 No.

19.4 Nodes represent activities; arrows show the relationships between activities.

19.5 A list of all activities in the project and the immediate predecessors of each one. Durations, resources needed and other factors can be added, but these are not essential for drawing the network.

19.6 The two main rules are:
   - Before an activity can begin, all preceding activities must be finished.
   - The arrows representing activities imply precedence only and neither their length nor their orientation is significant.

19.7 The earliest time an activity can start is the latest time by which all preceding activities can finish. The latest time an activity can finish is the earliest time that allows all following activities to be started on time.

19.8 The difference between the maximum amount of time available for an activity and the time it actually needs.

19.9 Zero.

19.10 It is the chain of activities that determines the project duration. If any critical activity is extended or delayed then the whole project is delayed.

19.11 The critical activities – usually starting with the longest.

19.12 By the amount of total float of activities on a parallel path. Reductions beyond this make a parallel path critical.

19.13 They give a clear picture of the stage that each activity in a project should have reached at any time.

19.14 By delaying non-critical activities until times when less resources are needed.

19.15 CPM assumes fixed activity durations; PERT assumes that activity durations follow a known distribution.

19.16 It assumes that the duration of an activity follows a beta distribution, in which expected duration $= (O + 4M + P) / 6$ and variance $= (P - O)^2 / 36$.

19.17 The project duration is Normally distributed with mean equal to the sum of the expected durations of activities on the critical path, and variance equal to the sum of the variances of activities on the critical path.

Chapter 20 – Queues and simulation

20.1 Customers want a service but find the server is busy, so they have to wait.

20.2 No – a balance is needed between the costs of providing a large number of servers and losing potential customers.

20.3 λ is the average arrival rate and μ is the average service rate.

20.4 Customers arrive faster than they are served and the queue continues to grow.

20.5 Assumptions include a single server, random arrivals, random service time, first-come-first-served discipline, the system has reached its steady state, there is no limit to the number of customers allowed in the queue, there is no limit on the number of customers who use the service and all customers wait until they are served.

20.6 No – multi-server queuing problems can be solved, but they are rather complicated.

20.7 Ordinary quantitative analyses describe a problem at a fixed point of time, while simulation models follow the operation of a process over an extended time.

20.8 Yes.

20.9 No – with proper care, artificial data can still have the same features as real data.

20.10 To give typical – but random – values to variables.

20.11 This depends on circumstances, but a usual guideline suggests several hundred.

Probabilities for the binomial distribution

n	r	.05	.10	.15	.20	p .25	.30	.35	.40	.45	.50
1	0	.9500	.9000	.8500	.8000	.7500	.7000	.6500	.6000	.5500	.5000
	1	.0500	.1000	.1500	.2000	.2500	.3000	.3500	.4000	.4500	.5000
2	0	.9025	.8100	.7225	.6400	.5625	.4900	.4225	.3600	.3025	.2500
	1	.0950	.1800	.2550	.3200	.3750	.4200	.4550	.4800	.4950	.5000
	2	.0025	.0100	.0225	.0400	.0625	.0900	.1225	.1600	.2025	.2500
3	0	.8574	.7290	.6141	.5120	.4219	.3430	.2746	.2160	.1664	.1250
	1	.1354	.2430	.3251	.3840	.4219	.4410	.4436	.4320	.4084	.3750
	2	.0071	.0270	.0574	.0960	.1406	.1890	.2389	.2880	.3341	.3750
	3	.0001	.0010	.0034	.0080	.0156	.0270	.0429	.0640	.0911	.1250
4	0	.8145	.6561	.5220	.4096	.3164	.2401	.1785	.1296	.0915	.0625
	1	.1715	.2916	.3685	.4096	.4219	.4116	.3845	.3456	.2995	.2500
	2	.0135	.0486	.0975	.1536	.2109	.2646	.3105	.3456	.3675	.3750
	3	.0005	.0036	.0115	.0256	.0469	.0756	.1115	.1536	.2005	.2500
	4	.0000	.0001	.0005	.0016	.0039	.0081	.0150	.0256	.0410	.0625
5	0	.7738	.5905	.4437	.3277	.2373	.1681	.1160	.0778	.0503	.0312
	1	.2036	.3280	.3915	.4096	.3955	.3602	.3124	.2592	.2059	.1562
	2	.0214	.0729	.1382	.2048	.2637	.3087	.3364	.3456	.3369	.3125
	3	.0011	.0081	.0244	.0512	.0879	.1323	.1811	.2304	.2757	.3125
	4	.0000	.0004	.0022	.0064	.0146	.0284	.0488	.0768	.1128	.1562
	5	.0000	.0000	.0001	.0003	.0010	.0024	.0053	.0102	.0185	.0312
6	0	.7351	.5314	.3771	.2621	.1780	.1176	.0754	.0467	.0277	.0156
	1	.2321	.3543	.3993	.3932	.3560	.3025	.2437	.1866	.1359	.0938
	2	.0305	.0984	.1762	.2458	.2966	.3241	.3280	.3110	.2780	.2344
	3	.0021	.0146	.0415	.0819	.1318	.1852	.2355	.2765	.3032	.3125
	4	.0001	.0012	.0055	.0154	.0330	.0595	.0951	.1382	.1861	.2344
	5	.0000	.0001	.0004	.0015	.0044	.0102	.0205	.0369	.0609	.0938
	6	.0000	.0000	.0000	.0001	.0002	.0007	.0018	.0041	.0083	.0516

							p				
n	r	.05	.10	.15	.20	.25	.30	.35	.40	.45	.50
7	0	.6983	.4783	.3206	.2097	.1335	.0824	.0490	.0280	.0152	.0078
	1	.2573	.3720	.3960	.3670	.3115	.2471	.1848	.1306	.0872	.0547
	2	.0406	.1240	.2097	.2753	.3115	.3177	.2985	.2613	.2140	.1641
	3	.0036	.0230	.0617	.1147	.1730	.2269	.2679	.2903	.2918	.2734
	4	.0002	.0026	.0109	.0287	.0577	.0972	.1442	.1935	.2388	.2734
	5	.0009	.0002	.0012	.0043	.0115	.0250	.0466	.0774	.1172	.1641
	6	.0000	.0000	.0001	.0004	.0013	.0036	.0084	.0172	.0320	.0547
	7	.0000	.0000	.0000	.0000	.0001	.0002	.0006	.0016	.0037	.0078
8	0	.6634	.4305	.2725	.1678	.1001	.0576	.0319	.0168	.0084	.0039
	1	.2793	.3826	.3847	.3355	.2670	.1977	.1373	.0896	.0548	.0312
	2	.0515	.1488	.2376	.2936	.3115	.2965	.2587	.2090	.1569	.1094
	3	.0054	.0331	.0839	.1468	.2076	.2541	.2786	.2787	.2568	.2188
	4	.0004	.0046	.0185	.0459	.0865	.1361	.1875	.2322	.2627	.2734
	5	.0000	.0004	.0026	.0092	.0231	.0467	.0808	.1239	.1719	.2188
	6	.0000	.0000	.0002	.0011	.0038	.0100	.0217	.0413	.0703	.1094
	7	.0000	.0000	.0000	.0001	.0004	.0012	.0033	.0079	.0164	.0312
	8	.0000	.0000	.0000	.0000	.0000	.0001	.0002	.0007	.0017	.0039
9	0	.6302	.3874	.2316	.1342	.0751	.0404	.0207	.0101	.0046	.0020
	1	.2985	.3874	.3679	.3020	.2253	.1556	.1004	.0605	.0339	.0176
	2	.0629	.1722	.2597	.3020	.3003	.2668	.2162	.1612	.1110	.0703
	3	.0077	.0446	.1069	.1762	.2336	.2668	.2716	.2508	.2119	.1641
	4	.0006	.0074	.0283	.0661	.1168	.1715	.2194	.2508	.2600	.2461
	5	.0000	.0008	.0050	.0165	.0389	.0735	.1181	.1672	.2128	.2461
	6	.0000	.0001	.0006	.0028	.0087	.0210	.0424	.0743	.1160	.1641
	7	.0000	.0000	.0000	.0003	.0012	.0039	.0098	.0212	.0407	.0703
	8	.0000	.0000	.0000	.0000	.0001	.0004	.0013	.0035	.0083	.0716
	9	.0000	.0000	.0000	.0000	.0000	.0000	.0001	.0003	.0008	.0020
10	0	.5987	.3487	.1969	.1074	.0563	.0282	.0135	.0060	.0025	.0010
	1	.3151	.3874	.3474	.2684	.1877	.1211	.0725	.0403	.0207	.0098
	2	.0746	.1937	.2759	.3020	.2816	.2335	.1757	.1209	.0763	.0439
	3	.0105	.0574	.1298	.2013	.2503	.2668	.2522	.2150	.1665	.1172
	4	.0010	.0112	.0401	.0881	.1460	.2001	.2377	.2508	.2384	.2051
	5	.0001	.0015	.0085	.0264	.0584	.1029	.1563	.2007	.2340	.2461
	6	.0000	.0001	.0012	.0055	.0162	.0368	.0689	.1115	.1596	.2051
	7	.0000	.0000	.0001	.0008	.0031	.0090	.0212	.0425	.0746	.1172
	8	.0000	.0000	.0000	.0001	.0004	.0014	.0043	.0106	.0229	.0439
	9	.0000	.0000	.0000	.0000	.0000	.0001	.0005	.0016	.0042	.0098
	10	.0000	.0000	.0000	.0000	.0000	.0000	.0000	.0001	.0003	.0010

							p				
n	r	.05	.10	.15	.20	.25	.30	.35	.40	.45	.50
11	0	.5688	.3138	.1673	.0859	.0422	.0198	.0088	.0036	.0014	.0005
	1	.3293	.3835	.3248	.2362	.1549	.0932	.0518	.0266	.0125	.0054
	2	.0867	.2131	.2866	.2953	.2581	.1998	.1395	.0887	.0513	.0269
	3	.0137	.0710	.1517	.2215	.2581	.2568	.2254	.1774	.1259	.0806
	4	.0014	.0158	.0536	.1107	.1721	.2201	.2428	.2365	.2060	.1611
	5	.0001	.0025	.0132	.0388	.0803	.1321	.1830	.2207	.2360	.2256
	6	.0000	.0003	.0023	.0097	.0268	.0566	.0985	.1471	.1931	.2256
	7	.0000	.0000	.0003	.0017	.0064	.0173	.0379	.0701	.1128	.1611
	8	.0000	.0000	.0000	.0002	.0011	.0037	.0102	.0234	.0462	.0806
	9	.0000	.0000	.0000	.0000	.0001	.0005	.0018	.0052	.0126	.0269
	10	.0000	.0000	.0000	.0000	.0000	.0000	.0002	.0007	.0021	.0054
	11	.0000	.0000	.0000	.0000	.0000	.0000	.0000	.0000	.0002	.0005
12	0	.5404	.2824	.1422	.0687	.0317	.0138	.0057	.0022	.0008	.0002
	1	.3413	.3766	.3012	.2062	.1267	.0712	.0368	.0174	.0075	.0029
	2	.0988	.2301	.2924	.2835	.2323	.1678	.1088	.0639	.0339	.0161
	3	.0173	.0852	.1720	.2362	.2581	.2397	.1954	.1419	.0923	.0537
	4	.0021	.0213	.0683	.1329	.1936	.2311	.2367	.2128	.1700	.1208
	5	.0002	.0038	.0193	.0532	.1032	.1585	.2039	.2270	.2225	.1934
	6	.0000	.0005	.0040	.0155	.0401	.0792	.1281	.1766	.2124	.2256
	7	.0000	.0000	.0006	.0033	.0115	.0291	.0591	.1009	.1489	.1934
	8	.0000	.0000	.0001	.0005	.0024	.0078	.0199	.0420	.0762	.1208
	9	.0000	.0000	.0000	.0001	.0004	.0015	.0048	.0125	.0277	.0537
	10	.0000	.0000	.0000	.0000	.0000	.0002	.0008	.0025	.0068	.0161
	11	.0000	.0000	.0000	.0000	.0000	.0000	.0001	.0003	.0010	.0029
	12	.0000	.0000	.0000	.0000	.0000	.0000	.0000	.0000	.0001	.0002
13	0	.5133	.2542	.1209	.0550	.0238	.0097	.0037	.0013	.0004	.0001
	1	.3512	.3672	.2774	.1787	.1029	.0540	.0259	.0113	.0045	.0016
	2	.1109	.2448	.2937	.2680	.2059	.1388	.0836	.0453	.0220	.0095
	3	.0214	.0997	.1900	.2457	.2517	.2181	.1651	.1107	.0660	.0349
	4	.0028	.0277	.0838	.1535	.2097	.2337	.2222	.1845	.1350	.0873
	5	.0003	.0055	.0266	.0691	.1258	.1803	.2154	.2214	.1989	.1571
	6	.0000	.0008	.0063	.0230	.0559	.1030	.1546	.1968	.2169	.2095
	7	.0000	.0001	.0011	.0058	.0186	.0442	.0833	.1312	.1775	.2095
	8	.0000	.0000	.0001	.0011	.0047	.0142	.0336	.0656	.1089	.1571
	9	.0000	.0000	.0000	.0001	.0009	.0034	.0101	.0243	.0495	.0873
	10	.0000	.0000	.0000	.0000	.0001	.0006	.0022	.0065	.0162	.0349
	11	.0000	.0000	.0000	.0000	.0000	.0001	.0003	.0012	.0036	.0095
	12	.0000	.0000	.0000	.0000	.0000	.0000	.0000	.0001	.0005	.0016
	13	.0000	.0000	.0000	.0000	.0000	.0000	.0000	.0000	.0000	.0001

						p					
n	*r*	.05	.10	.15	.20	.25	.30	.35	.40	.45	.50
14	0	.4877	.2288	.1028	.0440	.0178	.0068	.0024	.0008	.0002	.0001
	1	.3593	.3559	.2539	.1539	.0832	.0407	.0181	.0073	.0027	.0009
	2	.1229	.2570	.2912	.2501	.1802	.1134	.0634	.0317	.0141	.0056
	3	.0259	.1142	.2056	.2501	.2402	.1943	.1366	.0845	.0462	.0222
	4	.0037	.0348	.0998	.1720	.2202	.2290	.2022	.1549	.1040	.0611
	5	.0004	.0078	.0352	.0860	.1468	.1963	.2178	.2066	.1701	.1222
	6	.0000	.0013	.0093	.0322	.0734	.1262	.1759	.2066	.2088	.1833
	7	.0000	.0002	.0019	.0092	.0280	.0618	.1082	.1574	.1952	.2095
	8	.0000	.0000	.0003	.0020	.0082	.0232	.0510	.0918	.1398	.1833
	9	.0000	.0000	.0000	.0003	.0018	.0066	.0183	.0408	.0762	.1222
	10	.0000	.0000	.0000	.0000	.0003	.0014	.0049	.0136	.0312	.0611
	11	.0000	.0000	.0000	.0000	.0000	.0002	.0010	.0033	.0093	.0222
	12	.0000	.0000	.0000	.0000	.0000	.0000	.0001	.0005	.0019	.0056
	13	.0000	.0000	.0000	.0000	.0000	.0000	.0000	.0001	.0002	.0009
	14	.0000	.0000	.0000	.0000	.0000	.0000	.0000	.0000	.0000	.0001
15	0	.4633	.2059	.0874	.0352	.0134	.0047	.0016	.0005	.0001	.0000
	1	.3658	.3432	.2312	.1319	.0668	.0305	.0126	.0047	.0016	.0005
	2	.1348	.2669	.2856	.2309	.1559	.0916	.0476	.0219	.0090	.0032
	3	.0307	.1285	.2184	.2501	.2252	.1700	.1110	.0634	.0318	.0139
	4	.0049	.0428	.1156	.1876	.2252	.2186	.1792	.1268	.0780	.0417
	5	.0006	.0105	.0449	.1032	.1651	.2061	.2123	.1859	.1404	.0916
	6	.0000	.0019	.0132	.0430	.0917	.1472	.1906	.2066	.1914	.1527
	7	.0000	.0003	.0030	.0138	.0393	.0811	.1319	.1771	.2013	.1964
	8	.0000	.0000	.0005	.0035	.0131	.0348	.0710	.1181	.1647	.1964
	9	.0000	.0000	.0001	.0007	.0034	.0116	.0298	.0612	.1048	.1527
	10	.0000	.0000	.0000	.0001	.0007	.0030	.0096	.0245	.0515	.0916
	11	.0000	.0000	.0000	.0000	.0001	.0006	.0024	.0074	.0191	.0417
	12	.0000	.0000	.0000	.0000	.0000	.0001	.0004	.0016	.0052	.0139
	13	.0000	.0000	.0000	.0000	.0000	.0000	.0001	.0003	.0010	.0032
	14	.0000	.0000	.0000	.0000	.0000	.0000	.0000	.0000	.0001	.0005
	15	.0000	.0000	.0000	.0000	.0000	.0000	.0000	.0000	.0000	.0000

		p									
n	r	.05	.10	.15	.20	.25	.30	.35	.40	.45	.50
16	0	.4401	.1853	.0743	.0281	.0100	.0033	.0010	.0003	.0001	.0000
	1	.3706	.3294	.2097	.1126	.0535	.0228	.0087	.0030	.0009	.0002
	2	.1463	.2745	.2775	.2111	.1336	.0732	.0353	.0150	.0056	.0018
	3	.0359	.1423	.2285	.2463	.2079	.1465	.0888	.0468	.0215	.0085
	4	.0061	.0514	.1311	.2001	.2252	.2040	.1553	.1014	.0572	.0278
	5	.0008	.0137	.0555	.1201	.1802	.2099	.2008	.1623	.1123	.0667
	6	.0001	.0028	.0180	.0550	.1101	.1649	.1982	.1983	.1684	.1222
	7	.0000	.0004	.0045	.0197	.0524	.1010	.1524	.1889	.1969	.1746
	8	.0000	.0001	.0009	.0055	.0197	.0487	.0923	.1417	.1812	.1964
	9	.0000	.0000	.0001	.0012	.0058	.0185	.0442	.0840	.1318	.1746
	10	.0000	.0000	.0000	.0002	.0014	.0056	.0167	.0392	.0755	.1222
	11	.0000	.0000	.0000	.0000	.0002	.0013	.0049	.0142	.0337	.0667
	12	.0000	.0000	.0000	.0000	.0000	.0002	.0011	.0040	.0115	.0278
	13	.0000	.0000	.0000	.0000	.0000	.0000	.0002	.0008	.0029	.0085
	14	.0000	.0000	.0000	.0000	.0000	.0000	.0000	.0001	.0005	.0018
	15	.0000	.0000	.0000	.0000	.0000	.0000	.0000	.0000	.0001	.0002
	16	.0000	.0000	.0000	.0000	.0000	.0000	.0000	.0000	.0000	.0000
17	0	.4181	.1668	.0631	.0225	.0075	.0023	.0007	.0002	.0000	.0000
	1	.3741	.3150	.1893	.0957	.0426	.0169	.0060	.0019	.0005	.0001
	2	.1575	.2800	.2673	.1914	.1136	.0581	.0260	.0102	.0035	.0010
	3	.0415	.1556	.2359	.2393	.1893	.1245	.0701	.0341	.0144	.0052
	4	.0076	.0605	.1457	.2093	.2209	.1868	.1320	.0796	.0411	.0182
	5	.0010	.0175	.0668	.1361	.1914	.2081	.1849	.1379	.0875	.0472
	6	.0001	.0039	.0236	.0680	.1276	.1784	.1991	.1839	.1432	.0944
	7	.0000	.0007	.0065	.0267	.0668	.1201	.1685	.1927	.1841	.1484
	8	.0000	.0001	.0014	.0084	.0279	.0644	.1134	.1606	.1883	.1855
	9	.0000	.0000	.0003	.0021	.0093	.0276	.0611	.1070	.1540	.1855
	10	.0000	.0000	.0000	.0004	.0025	.0095	.0263	.0571	.1008	.1484
	11	.0000	.0000	.0000	.0001	.0005	.0026	.0090	.0242	.0525	.0944
	12	.0000	.0000	.0000	.0000	.0001	.0006	.0024	.0081	.0215	.0472
	13	.0000	.0000	.0000	.0000	.0000	.0001	.0005	.0021	.0068	.0182
	14	.0000	.0000	.0000	.0000	.0000	.0000	.0001	.0004	.0016	.0052
	15	.0000	.0000	.0000	.0000	.0000	.0000	.0000	.0001	.0003	.0010
	16	.0000	.0000	.0000	.0000	.0000	.0000	.0000	.0000	.0000	.0001
	17	.0000	.0000	.0000	.0000	.0000	.0000	.0000	.0000	.0000	.0000

Probabilities for the Poisson distribution

| | | | | | μ | | | | |
r	.005	.01	.02	.03	.04	.05	.06	.07	.08	.09
0	.9950	.9900	.9802	.9704	.9608	.9512	.9418	.9324	.9231	.9139
1	.0050	.0099	.0192	.0291	.0384	.0476	.0565	.0653	.0738	.0823
2	.0000	.0000	.0002	.0004	.0008	.0012	.0017	.0023	.0030	.0037
3	.0000	.0000	.0000	.0000	.0000	.0000	.0000	.0001	.0001	.0001

| | | | | | μ | | | | |
r	0.1	0.2	0.3	0.4	0.5	0.6	0.7	0.8	0.9	1.0
0	.9048	.8187	.7408	.6703	.6065	.5488	.4966	.4493	.4066	.3679
1	.0905	.1637	.2222	.2681	.3033	.3293	.3476	.3595	.3659	.3679
2	.0045	.0164	.0333	.0536	.0758	.0988	.1217	.1438	.1647	.1839
3	.0002	.0011	.0033	.0072	.0126	.0198	.0284	.0383	.0494	.0613
4	.0000	.0001	.0002	.0007	.0016	.0030	.0050	.0077	.0111	.0153
5	.0000	.0000	.0000	.0001	.0002	.0004	.0007	.0012	.0020	.0031
6	.0000	.0000	.0000	.0000	.0000	.0000	.0001	.0002	.0003	.0005
7	.0000	.0000	.0000	.0000	.0000	.0000	.0000	.0000	.0000	.0001

| | | | | | μ | | | | |
r	1.1	1.2	1.3	1.4	1.5	1.6	1.7	1.8	1.9	2.0
0	.3329	.3012	.2725	.2466	.2231	.2019	.1827	.1653	.1496	.1353
1	.3662	.3614	.3543	.3452	.3347	.3230	.3106	.2975	.2842	.2707
2	.2014	.2169	.2303	.2417	.2510	.2584	.2640	.2678	.2700	.2707
3	.0738	.0867	.0998	.1128	.1255	.1378	.1496	.1607	.1710	.1804
4	.0203	.0260	.0324	.0395	.0471	.0551	.0636	.0723	.0812	.0902
5	.0045	.0062	.0084	.0111	.0141	.0176	.0216	.0260	.0309	.0361
6	.0008	.0012	.0018	.0026	.0035	.0047	.0061	.0078	.0098	.0120
7	.0001	.0002	.0003	.0005	.0008	.0011	.0015	.0020	.0027	.0034
8	.0000	.0000	.0001	.0001	.0001	.0002	.0003	.0005	.0006	.0009
9	.0000	.0000	.0000	.0000	.0000	.0000	.0001	.0001	.0001	.0002

					μ					
r	2.1	2.2	2.3	2.4	2.5	2.6	2.7	2.8	2.9	3.0
0	.1225	.1108	.1003	.0907	.0821	.0743	.0672	.0608	.0550	.0498
1	.2527	.2438	.2306	.2177	.2052	.1931	.1815	.1703	.1596	.1494
2	.2700	.2681	.2652	.2613	.2565	.2510	.2450	.2384	.2314	.2240
3	.1890	.1966	.2033	.2090	.2138	.2176	.2205	.2225	.2237	.2240
4	.0992	.1082	.1196	.1254	.1336	.1414	.1488	.1557	.1662	.1680
5	.0417	.0476	.0538	.0602	.0668	.0735	.0804	.0872	.0940	.1008
6	.0146	.0174	.0206	.0241	.0278	.0319	.0362	.0407	.0455	.0504
7	.0044	.0055	.0068	.0083	.0099	.0118	.0139	.0163	.0188	.0216
8	.0011	.0015	.0019	.0025	.0031	.0038	.0047	.0057	.0068	.0081
9	.0003	.0004	.0005	.0007	.0009	.0011	.0014	.0018	.0022	.0027
10	.0001	.0001	.0001	.0002	.0002	.0003	.0004	.0005	.0006	.0008
11	.0000	.0000	.0000	.0000	.0000	.0001	.0001	.0001	.0002	.0002
12	.0000	.0000	.0000	.0000	.0000	.0000	.0000	.0000	.0000	.0001

					μ					
r	3.1	3.2	3.3	3.4	3.5	3.6	3.7	3.8	3.9	4.0
0	.0450	.0408	.0369	.0334	.0302	.0273	.0247	.0224	.0202	.0183
1	.1397	.1304	.1217	.1135	.1057	.0984	.0915	.0850	.0789	.0733
2	.2165	.2087	.2008	.1929	.1850	.1771	.1692	.1615	.1539	.1465
3	.2237	.2226	.2209	.2186	.2158	.2125	.2087	.2046	.2001	.1954
4	.1734	.1781	.1823	.1858	.1888	.1912	.1931	.1944	.1951	.1954
5	.1075	.1140	.1203	.1264	.1322	.1377	.1429	.1477	.1522	.1563
6	.0555	.0608	.0662	.0716	.0771	.0826	.0881	.0936	.0989	.1042
7	.0246	.0278	.0312	.0348	.0385	.0425	.0466	.0508	.0551	.0595
8	.0095	.0111	.0129	.0148	.0169	.0191	.0215	.0241	.0269	.0298
9	.0033	.0040	.0047	.0056	.0066	.0076	.0089	.0102	.0116	.0132
10	.0010	.0013	.0016	.0019	.0023	.0028	.0033	.0039	.0045	.0053
11	.0003	.0004	.0005	.0006	.0007	.0009	.0011	.0013	.0016	.0019
12	.0001	.0001	.0001	.0002	.0002	.0003	.0003	.0004	.0005	.0006
13	.0000	.0000	.0000	.0000	.0001	.0001	.0001	.0001	.0002	.0002
14	.0000	.0000	.0000	.0000	.0000	.0000	.0000	.0000	.0000	.0001

					μ					
r	4.1	4.2	4.3	4.4	4.5	4.6	4.7	4.8	4.9	5.0
0	.0166	.0150	.0136	.0123	.0111	.0101	.0091	.0082	.0074	.0067
1	.0679	.0630	.0583	.0540	.0500	.0462	.0427	.0395	.0365	.0337
2	.1393	.1323	.1254	.1188	.1125	.1063	.1005	.0948	.0894	.0842
3	.1904	.1852	.1798	.1743	.1687	.1631	.1574	.1517	.1460	.1404
4	.1951	.1944	.1933	.1917	.1898	.1875	.1849	.1820	.1789	.1755
5	.1600	.1633	.1662	.1687	.1708	.1725	.1738	.1747	.1753	.1755
6	.1093	.1143	.1191	.1237	.1281	.1323	.1362	.1398	.1432	.1462
7	.0640	.0686	.0732	.0778	.0824	.0869	.0914	.0959	.1002	.1044
8	.0328	.0360	.0393	.0428	.0463	.0500	.0537	.0575	.0614	.0653
9	.0150	.0168	.0188	.0209	.0232	.0255	.0280	.0307	.0334	.0363
10	.0061	.0071	.0081	.0092	.0104	.0118	.0132	.0147	.0164	.0181
11	.0023	.0027	.0032	.0037	.0043	.0049	.0056	.0064	.0073	.0082
12	.0008	.0009	.0011	.0014	.0016	.0019	.0022	.0026	.0030	.0034
13	.0002	.0003	.0004	.0005	.0006	.0007	.0008	.0009	.0011	.0013
14	.0001	.0001	.0001	.0001	.0002	.0002	.0003	.0004	.0004	.0005
15	.0000	.0000	.0000	.0000	.0001	.0001	.0001	.0001	.0001	.0002

					μ					
r	5.1	5.2	5.3	5.4	5.5	5.6	5.7	5.8	5.9	6.0
0	.0061	.0055	.0050	.0045	.0041	.0037	.0033	.0030	.0027	.0025
1	.0311	.0287	.0265	.0244	.0225	.0207	.0191	.0176	.0162	.0149
2	.0793	.0746	.0701	.0659	.0618	.0580	.0544	.0509	.0477	.0446
3	.1348	.1293	.1239	.1185	.1133	.1082	.1033	.0985	.0938	.0892
4	.1719	.1681	.1641	.1600	.1558	.1515	.1472	.1428	.1383	.1339
5	.1753	.1748	.1740	.1728	.1714	.1697	.1678	.1656	.1632	.1606
6	.1490	.1515	.1537	.1555	.1571	.1584	.1594	.1601	.1605	.1606
7	.1086	.1125	.1163	.1200	.1234	.1267	.1298	.1326	.1353	.1377
8	.0692	.0731	.0771	.0810	.0849	.0887	.0925	.0962	.0998	.1033
9	.0392	.0423	.0454	.0486	.0519	.0552	.0586	.0620	.0654	.0688
10	.0200	.0220	.0241	.0262	.0285	.0309	.0334	.0359	.0386	.0413
11	.0093	.0104	.0116	.0129	.0143	.0157	.0173	.0190	.0207	.0225
12	.0039	.0045	.0051	.0058	.0065	.0073	.0082	.0092	.0102	.0113
13	.0015	.0018	.0021	.0024	.0028	.0032	.0036	.0041	.0046	.0052
14	.0006	.0007	.0008	.0009	.0011	.0013	.0015	.0017	.0019	.0022
15	.0002	.0002	.0003	.0003	.0004	.0005	.0006	.0007	.0008	.0009
16	.0001	.0001	.0001	.0001	.0001	.0002	.0002	.0002	.0003	.0003
17	.0000	.0000	.0000	.0000	.0000	.0001	.0001	.0001	.0001	.0001

	μ									
r	6.1	6.2	6.3	6.4	6.5	6.6	6.7	6.8	6.9	7.0
0	.0022	.0020	.0018	.0017	.0015	.0014	.0012	.0011	.0010	.0009
1	.0137	.0126	.0116	.0106	.0098	.0090	.0082	.0076	.0070	.0064
2	.0417	.0390	.0364	.0340	.0318	.0296	.0276	.0258	.0240	.0223
3	.0848	.0806	.0765	.0726	.0688	.0652	.0617	.0584	.0552	.0521
4	.1294	.1249	.1205	.1162	.1118	.1076	.1034	.0992	.0952	.0912
5	.1579	.1549	.1519	.1487	.1454	.1420	.1385	.1349	.1314	.1277
6	.1605	.1601	.1595	.1586	.1575	.1562	.1546	.1529	.1511	.1490
7	.1399	.1418	.1435	.1450	.1462	.1472	.1480	.1486	.1489	.1490
8	.1066	.1099	.1130	.1160	.1188	.1215	.1240	.1263	.1284	.1304
9	.0723	.0757	.0791	.0825	.0858	.0891	.0923	.0954	.0985	.1014
10	.0441	.0469	.0498	.0528	.0558	.0588	.0618	.0649	.0679	.0710
11	.0245	.0265	.0285	.0307	.0330	.0353	.0377	.0401	.0426	.0452
12	.0124	.0137	.0150	.0164	.0179	.0194	.0210	.0227	.0245	.0264
13	.0058	.0065	.0073	.0081	.0089	.0098	.0108	.0119	.0130	.0142
14	.0025	.0029	.0033	.0037	.0041	.0046	.0052	.0058	.0064	.0071
15	.0010	.0012	.0014	.0016	.0018	.0020	.0023	.0026	.0029	.0033
16	.0004	.0005	.0005	.0006	.0007	.0008	.0010	.0011	.0013	.0014
17	.0001	.0002	.0002	.0002	.0003	.0003	.0004	.0004	.0005	.0006
18	.0000	.0001	.0001	.0001	.0001	.0001	.0001	.0002	.0002	.0002
19	.0000	.0000	.0000	.0000	.0000	.0000	.0000	.0001	.0001	.0001

APPENDIX D

Probabilities for the Normal distribution

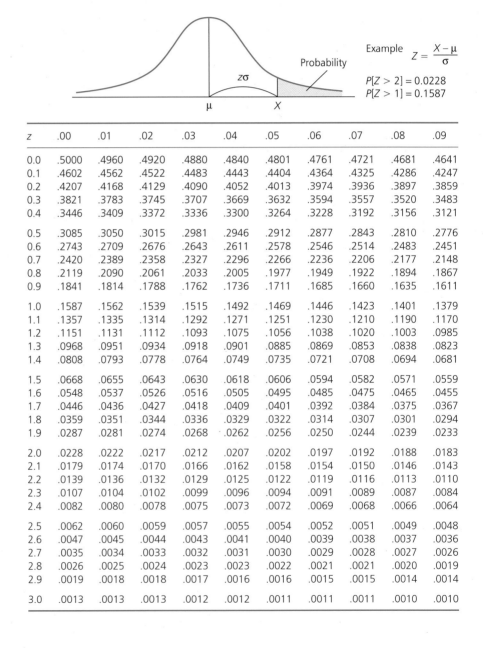

Example $Z = \dfrac{X - \mu}{\sigma}$

$P[Z > 2] = 0.0228$
$P[Z > 1] = 0.1587$

z	.00	.01	.02	.03	.04	.05	.06	.07	.08	.09
0.0	.5000	.4960	.4920	.4880	.4840	.4801	.4761	.4721	.4681	.4641
0.1	.4602	.4562	.4522	.4483	.4443	.4404	.4364	.4325	.4286	.4247
0.2	.4207	.4168	.4129	.4090	.4052	.4013	.3974	.3936	.3897	.3859
0.3	.3821	.3783	.3745	.3707	.3669	.3632	.3594	.3557	.3520	.3483
0.4	.3446	.3409	.3372	.3336	.3300	.3264	.3228	.3192	.3156	.3121
0.5	.3085	.3050	.3015	.2981	.2946	.2912	.2877	.2843	.2810	.2776
0.6	.2743	.2709	.2676	.2643	.2611	.2578	.2546	.2514	.2483	.2451
0.7	.2420	.2389	.2358	.2327	.2296	.2266	.2236	.2206	.2177	.2148
0.8	.2119	.2090	.2061	.2033	.2005	.1977	.1949	.1922	.1894	.1867
0.9	.1841	.1814	.1788	.1762	.1736	.1711	.1685	.1660	.1635	.1611
1.0	.1587	.1562	.1539	.1515	.1492	.1469	.1446	.1423	.1401	.1379
1.1	.1357	.1335	.1314	.1292	.1271	.1251	.1230	.1210	.1190	.1170
1.2	.1151	.1131	.1112	.1093	.1075	.1056	.1038	.1020	.1003	.0985
1.3	.0968	.0951	.0934	.0918	.0901	.0885	.0869	.0853	.0838	.0823
1.4	.0808	.0793	.0778	.0764	.0749	.0735	.0721	.0708	.0694	.0681
1.5	.0668	.0655	.0643	.0630	.0618	.0606	.0594	.0582	.0571	.0559
1.6	.0548	.0537	.0526	.0516	.0505	.0495	.0485	.0475	.0465	.0455
1.7	.0446	.0436	.0427	.0418	.0409	.0401	.0392	.0384	.0375	.0367
1.8	.0359	.0351	.0344	.0336	.0329	.0322	.0314	.0307	.0301	.0294
1.9	.0287	.0281	.0274	.0268	.0262	.0256	.0250	.0244	.0239	.0233
2.0	.0228	.0222	.0217	.0212	.0207	.0202	.0197	.0192	.0188	.0183
2.1	.0179	.0174	.0170	.0166	.0162	.0158	.0154	.0150	.0146	.0143
2.2	.0139	.0136	.0132	.0129	.0125	.0122	.0119	.0116	.0113	.0110
2.3	.0107	.0104	.0102	.0099	.0096	.0094	.0091	.0089	.0087	.0084
2.4	.0082	.0080	.0078	.0075	.0073	.0072	.0069	.0068	.0066	.0064
2.5	.0062	.0060	.0059	.0057	.0055	.0054	.0052	.0051	.0049	.0048
2.6	.0047	.0045	.0044	.0043	.0041	.0040	.0039	.0038	.0037	.0036
2.7	.0035	.0034	.0033	.0032	.0031	.0030	.0029	.0028	.0027	.0026
2.8	.0026	.0025	.0024	.0023	.0023	.0022	.0021	.0021	.0020	.0019
2.9	.0019	.0018	.0018	.0017	.0016	.0016	.0015	.0015	.0014	.0014
3.0	.0013	.0013	.0013	.0012	.0012	.0011	.0011	.0011	.0010	.0010

Probabilities for the *t*-distribution

Degrees of freedom	Significance level							
	0.25	0.20	0.15	0.10	0.05	0.025	0.01	0.005
1	1.000	1.376	1.963	3.078	6.314	12.706	31.821	63.657
2	.816	1.061	1.386	1.886	2.920	4.303	6.965	9.925
3	.765	.978	1.250	1.638	2.353	3.182	4.541	5.841
4	.741	.941	1.190	1.533	2.132	2.776	3.747	4.604
5	.727	.920	1.156	1.476	2.015	2.571	3.365	4.032
6	.718	.906	1.134	1.440	1.943	2.447	3.143	3.707
7	.711	.896	1.119	1.415	1.895	2.365	2.998	3.499
8	.706	.889	1.108	1.397	1.860	2.306	2.896	3.355
9	.703	.883	1.100	1.383	1.833	2.262	2.821	3.250
10	.700	.879	1.093	1.372	1.812	2.228	2.764	3.169
11	.697	.876	1.088	1.363	1.796	2.201	2.718	3.106
12	.695	.873	1.083	1.356	1.782	2.179	2.681	3.055
13	.694	.870	1.079	1.350	1.771	2.160	2.650	3.012
14	.692	.868	1.076	1.345	1.761	2.145	2.624	2.977
15	.691	.866	1.074	1.341	1.753	2.131	2.602	2.947
16	.690	.865	1.071	1.337	1.746	2.120	2.583	2.921
17	.689	.863	1.069	1.333	1.740	2.110	2.567	2.898
18	.688	.862	1.067	1.330	1.734	2.101	2.552	2.878
19	.688	.861	1.066	1.328	1.729	2.093	2.539	2.861
20	.687	.860	1.064	1.325	1.725	2.086	2.528	2.845
21	.686	.859	1.063	1.323	1.721	2.080	2.518	2.831
22	.686	.858	1.061	1.321	1.717	2.074	2.508	2.819
23	.685	.858	1.060	1.319	1.714	2.069	2.500	2.807
24	.685	.857	1.059	1.318	1.711	2.064	2.492	2.797
25	.684	.856	1.058	1.316	1.708	2.060	2.485	2.787
26	.684	.856	1.058	1.315	1.706	2.056	2.479	2.779
27	.684	.855	1.057	1.314	1.703	2.052	2.473	2.771
28	.683	.855	1.056	1.313	1.701	2.048	2.467	2.763
29	.683	.854	1.055	1.311	1.699	2.045	2.462	2.756
30	.683	.854	1.055	1.310	1.697	2.042	2.457	2.750
40	.681	.851	1.050	1.303	1.684	2.021	2.423	2.704
60	.679	.848	1.046	1.296	1.671	2.000	2.390	2.660
120	.677	.845	1.041	1.289	1.658	1.980	2.358	2.617
∞	.674	.842	1.036	1.282	1.645	1.960	2.326	2.576

Critical values for the χ^2 distribution

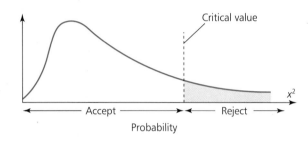

	Significance level						
Degrees of freedom	0.250	0.100	0.050	0.025	0.010	0.005	0.001
1	1.32	2.71	3.84	5.02	6.63	7.88	10.8
2	2.77	4.61	5.99	7.38	9.21	10.6	13.8
3	4.11	6.25	7.81	9.35	11.3	12.8	16.3
4	5.39	7.78	9.49	11.1	13.3	14.9	18.5
5	6.63	9.24	11.1	12.8	15.1	16.7	20.5
6	7.84	10.6	12.6	14.4	16.8	18.5	22.5
7	9.04	12.0	14.1	16.0	18.5	20.3	24.3
8	10.2	13.4	15.5	17.5	20.3	22.0	26.1
9	11.4	14.7	16.9	19.0	21.7	23.6	27.9
10	12.5	16.0	18.3	20.5	23.2	25.2	29.6
11	13.7	17.3	19.7	21.9	24.7	26.8	31.3
12	14.8	18.5	21.0	23.3	26.2	28.3	32.9
13	16.0	19.8	22.4	24.7	27.7	29.8	34.5
14	17.1	21.1	23.7	26.1	29.1	31.3	36.1
15	18.2	22.3	25.0	27.5	30.6	32.8	37.7
16	19.4	23.5	26.3	28.8	32.0	34.3	39.3
17	20.5	24.8	27.6	30.2	33.4	35.7	40.8
18	21.6	26.0	28.9	31.5	34.8	37.2	42.3
19	22.7	27.2	30.1	32.9	36.2	38.6	43.8
20	23.8	28.4	31.4	34.2	37.6	40.0	45.3
21	24.9	29.6	32.7	35.5	38.9	41.4	46.8
22	26.0	30.8	33.9	36.8	40.3	42.8	48.3
23	27.1	32.0	35.2	38.1	41.6	44.2	49.7
24	28.2	33.2	36.4	39.4	43.0	45.6	51.2

Degrees of freedom	Significance level						
	0.250	0.100	0.050	0.025	0.010	0.005	0.001
25	29.3	34.4	37.7	40.6	44.3	46.9	52.6
26	30.4	35.6	38.9	41.9	45.6	48.3	54.1
27	31.5	36.7	40.1	43.2	47.0	49.6	55.5
28	32.6	37.9	41.3	44.5	48.3	51.0	56.9
29	33.7	39.1	42.6	45.7	49.6	52.3	58.3
30	34.8	40.3	43.8	47.0	50.9	53.7	59.7
40	45.6	51.8	55.8	59.3	63.7	66.8	73.4
50	56.3	63.2	67.5	71.4	76.2	79.5	86.7
60	67.0	74.4	79.1	83.3	88.4	92.0	99.6
70	77.6	85.5	90.5	95.0	100	104	112
80	88.1	96.6	102	107	112	116	125
90	98.6	108	113	118	123	128	137
100	109	118	124	130	136	140	149